MIDWEST

and

ITS CHILDREN

The Psychological Ecology
of an American Town

by ROGER G. BARKER

and HERBERT F. WRIGHT

ROW, PETERSON AND COMPANY

Evanston, Illinois: White Plains, New York

Made and printed in Great Britain by
William Clowes and Sons, Limited, London and Beccles

TO

KURT LEWIN

AND

THE PEOPLE OF MIDWEST

Preface

THIS book is about the children of the town of Midwest U.S.A. in the middle years of the twentieth century. It describes in plain language and in concrete detail the everyday behavior of Midwest children and the ordinary circumstances of their lives as these were seen by skilled observers. The volume includes, as well, description in terms of theories and concepts of the behavior and living conditions of these children. It also contains some comparative data upon the children of the Lawton School, a school for crippled children situated in neighboring Capitol City. Parts of the book present methods which, although they were developed to meet specific requirements of the research, are believed to have significance beyond the reported findings.

The investigation would not have been possible without the assistance of many people. Our intellectual debt to Kurt Lewin will be obvious to all. We are very much aware, too, of the influence on our thinking in connection with the investigation of Donald K. Adams, William McDougall, Calvin P. Stone, and Lewis M. Terman, who were our teachers, of Fritz Heider, our associate at the University of Kansas, and of Henry A. Murray and Edward C. Tolman whom we have known largely through their writings. To all of these we express our sincere thanks.

The people of Midwest have made an essential contribution to the success of the study by their willing participation in many of its burdensome phases. We appreciate especially the help of the teachers of the Midwest School and of the families of the children on whom detailed studies were made. We are similarly indebted to the staff of the Lawton School. It has been one of the impressive results of the study for the investigators to see the acuteness of the people of Midwest in assessing the goals and general procedures of the study. This is doubtless the basis of their effective coöperation and an important factor in their tolerant acceptance of the many exacting demands of the research. A very agreeable feature of the project for the investigators has been the personal associations which the field work in Midwest has made possible.

Our material obligations are easy to list, but it is difficult to describe the reassurance and encouragement we received from the expressions of confidence which this support signified. Here, we would like to mention especially steady encouragement from John C. Eberhart, John W. Gardner, Paul B. Lawson, Leonard W. Mayo, and John H. Nelson. The National Institute of Mental Health has borne the greatest part of the expense of the research (grant M H-6). The University of Kansas, the Association for the Aid of

Crippled Children, the Carnegie Corporation of New York, and Dr. Wilbur Bailey, have supplied necessary funds for crucial special problems.

The research was done under the administrative supervision and scientific direction of the senior authors with the active participation in planning and policy-making of the following persons who served as research associates: Louise S. Barker, William A. Koppe, Jack Nall, Phil Schoggen, and Lorene Wright. Research Assistants who worked with these staff members in making most of the observations and in carrying out most of the analytical operations were: Don Albert, Chris Argyris, Margery Baldwin, William A. Binns, Harold R. Dickman, William Dreese, Beverly Fox, Milton Horowitz, Lucille Johnson, Blaine Kincaid, John Lubach, Louise Mason, Irene Nall, Merle R. Newton, Howard V. Perlmutter, Robert Reiff, Mariana Remple, Maxine Schoggen, and James E. Simpson. Extensive secretarial work was done by Elizabeth Albert, Joan Bradford, Ruth Finley, Meredith Koppe, Olive Laing, Marguerite Reiff, Carolyn Shoemaker, Eleanor Simpson, Mary Townsend, and Elizabeth Walz.

We are greatly indebted to Lee Meyerson for assistance in making photographs, and to Ruth McKinnis, Director of the Lawton School, for welcoming us to the school and for assisting with the work there. To Alfred Baldwin and Anthony Smith we owe much for guidance on statistical problems. Robert B. MacLeod read the first manuscript of this book and made invaluable suggestions for increasing the clarity of the exposition.

We wish it were possible to name all of the individuals who have put a shoulder to our wheel and cleared our path. We wish especially that we could acknowledge every child who has served as a subject. But the list would be too long. We can only hope they will accept this general expression of our gratitude.

Parts of this investigation were done independently by particular persons to satisfy thesis requirements for advanced degrees. These contributions are indicated by footnotes in the proper places.

All names of persons and communities in the book are code names used to protect the privacy of the individuals concerned.

The organization and format of the book have been planned for the convenience of both the general reader and the specialist. The busiest reader will find a panorama of the problems, methods, and findings of the investigation in the first and last chapters. For the general reader who wishes to follow more closely the steps of our exploration without, however, concerning himself with details of the techniques, we have provided a consecutive narrative in the portions of the book set in the larger type. The more critical reader and the specialist will want to read the small print, the footnotes, and the appendices—and doubtless wish for still more of the details.

Lawrence, Kansas
June, 1954

ROGER G. BARKER
HERBERT F. WRIGHT

the duration, the scope, the complexity, and the magnitude of some conditions that it is important to investigate. In this, psychology has much in common with meteorology. Some of the principles of the whirlwind and the thunderbolt can be studied in the laboratory, but to extend the curves into the high values, and to include all complicating factors, it is necessary to go to the plains and to observe these events as they occur under natural conditions. In principle, the same is true in psychology for studies of conditions which are frequent in daily life, but which are difficult to create experimentally. This should not be discouraging. Experiments in nature are occurring every day. We need only the techniques and facilities to take advantage of them. Public health scientists have long used naturally occurring differences in sanitation, population characteristics, and nutrition to test hypotheses regarding the etiology of health and disease. Astronomers, agronomists, geologists, paleontologists, and anthropologists regularly test basic scientific theories in naturally occurring situations. When we consider the great theoretical advances made by these so-called descriptive sciences, it would appear reasonable to hope that similar advances can be made in psychology by field studies.

The Midwest Field Station was established with the hope that a station for making ecological studies of human behavior and its natural, psychological habitat would contribute similarly to the solution of practical and theoretical problems of psychology.[1]

The tasks set for this field station have much in common with time-honored problems of social anthropology and sociology. However, for good or ill, we chose to make a purely psychological approach to these problems in the present study—psychological in a narrow, intra-professional sense. This was done with full recognition that inter-disciplinary coöperative research has proven to be highly productive in many cases. It seemed apparent, however, that there are other avenues of cross-disciplinary invigoration. One of these might be called cross-disciplinary colonization. We noted that new productivity and vitality sometimes occurs in areas of psychology when representatives of other disciplines—engineers, artists, mathematicians, medical men, and zoölogists—engage in psychological research. We conjectured that one of the reasons for this might be a sharp break with old, traditional methods of investigating persistent problems and the introduction of new techniques and conceptions. At any rate, these observations and conjectures emboldened us to enter the territory of the sociologist and the anthropologist without a passport, or a guide, or even a guide book. A consequence of our calculated professional chauvinism, with

[1] The term ecology has been used in psychology with other meanings than the one we have assigned to it here. In this connection see, for example, the definitions of Brunswik (14) and of Lewin (35). It seems to us that flexibility in the use of this term is desirable in the present state of our understanding of problems in this general area, if its meaning is made explicit in each case.

its effort to devise new field techniques and to adapt to this purpose procedures which have been developed within the tradition of experimental psychology, has been the necessity of devoting a relatively great amount of attention in this report to the description of methods.

Ecological Units

Research in psychological ecology requires the identification of units which are suitable for use in the description and analysis of the naturally occurring behavior and psychological living conditions of a community. In approaching this problem, paucity of materials was not a difficulty; in fact, quite the contrary. The field workers were overwhelmed with promising possibilities. Children were playing, crying, learning, fighting, regressing, submitting, and identifying on every hand to the accompaniment of adults' efforts to teach, ignore, amuse, dominate, spoil, deprive, and love them. There were the social classes, the streets and back alleys, the school classes, the churches, the movies, the government agencies, the taverns, the basketball games, the jail, and the lake; there were Boy Scouts, public dances, Brownies, Halloween, Ladies Aid, and other parts of the town in endless array. From this miscellany it was necessary to select units which were suitable for the required descriptions and analyses.

Behavior Episodes

One such unit was obviously the behavior and situation of each individual child. At some point ecological research must deal with the individual. However, the individual's behavior and psychological habitat are not uniform. Although a biography is an unbroken sequence from before birth until death, it has a great variety of discriminable parts. They range from parts as short as a startle reflex to action sequences which may continue for years, such as "providing for my old age;" and they vary in degree of involvement of the total person from the pupillary reflex to activities requiring the mobilization of all physical and psychological resources, such as "fighting for my life." For ecological studies, a standard unit of an individual's life course was required. For this purpose we chose an easily discriminated part of the stream of behavior and situation which we have called a *behavior episode*. Here is an example :

MOVING CRATE ACROSS PIT

The record from which this episode is taken describes the behavior and psychological habitat of seven-year-old Raymond Birch. In this part of the observation, Raymond was playing with his friends Stewart and Clifford in a shallow pit in a vacant lot near his home. Raymond had lost interest in their play with miniature cars. The record continues:

Raymond absently scanned the landscape.

Noticing a large crate in another corner of the pit he proposed, "Let's go over and play with that crate."

Stewart said flatly, "No."

> The wobbly old crate was constructed of several loosely connected boards and measured about 5 feet by 30 inches by 30 inches. It was open completely at one end and the sides had openings which were large enough for the children to climb through. The crate was upright on its open end.

Raymond hopped down from the bank into the excavation and walked purposefully over to the crate.

Strenuously he pulled on the crate. He evidently intended to drag it to the place where the boys had been playing together.

The crate caught; he had to yank strenuously to move it at all.

. . . .

He absently chanted, "Dum, dum, dum," as he tugged energetically on the crate.

It stuck again on something in the weeds.

He jerked quickly, leaning all his weight backwards as he tried to pull the crate.

As the crate came loose suddenly, he stumbled back a few steps.

. . . .

Raymond grunted as he tugged with both hands.

When he got the crate almost over to the other boys, he pulled so hard that the crate tilted upright.

He seemed satisfied with the upright position although it was achieved accidentally (8, 344-45).[2]

After moving the crate, Raymond crawled inside and a new episode began.

The behavior in this and every other episode has three basic attributes: it has *constant direction*, it is within the *normal behavior perspective*, and it has approximately *equal potency* throughout its course.

Constant direction refers to the fact that all parts of the action in an episode appear to carry the person toward a particular behavioral end. An episode of behavior is seen by observers to be aimed at, directed toward, or converging upon a special behavioral resultant. In the example given above, this resultant is having the crate available for play. The directional characteristic of behavior has been noted by many writers; it is one of the attributes of so-called molar behavior. It will be shown later that a high degree of agreement can be attained by different observers in identifying directed units of behavior, even though the stimulus properties of this phenomenal aspect of behavior are complex and have not been well identified.

---

[2] This and other quotations from *One Boy's Day* (8) are made with the permission of Harper & Bros., New York. The points (. . .) indicate the omission of portions of the record which are not relevant to this discussion.

Behavior episodes are within the *normal behavior perspective*. This means that in the ordinary course of living, episodes are among the features of behavior which people see. Neither instruments nor inferences are needed to discern them. Behavior episodes are analogous to physical objects which can be seen with the "naked eye." They are the common "things" of behavior; they correspond to the stones, chairs, and buildings of the physical world. This criterion of an episode is equivalent to the practice of defining some features of a physical object by its perceptibility. We hear it said that atoms are so small they are far below the limen of visual acuity; that the largest protozoan can hardly be seen without a microscope; that stars of the sixth magnitude can be seen in peripheral vision; that a bluejay can easily be recognized at 100 meters; that Mount Everest is so high it can be seen from a distance of 400 miles; that the Pacific Ocean is so vast that only an infinitesimal part can be seen from one place; and that the whole can be comprehended only by complex and extended analytical and integrative intellectual processes. It is similar in the realm of behavior. Muscle contractions, body sway, and reaction time can be identified with precision only if they are magnified by instruments; whereas social mobility, inferiority feelings, and overweening ambition are so diffuse and extended that they, like the Pacific Ocean, can be seen only piecemeal and apprehended as behavior units only by complicated cognitive processes. On the other hand, an episode of behavior, such as *Moving Crate Across Pit* is perceived without instruments or elaborate analyzing and synthesizing behavior by both the behaving person, himself, and by those who view his behavior from the "outside." In both cases, behavior episodes are within the ordinary behavior perspective of normally sensitive persons.

A behavior episode has approximately *equal potency* throughout its course. In no segment of the episode is there evidence that the unidirectional flow of the stream of action toward its behavioral end has stopped or seriously faltered. The behavioral evidence of this is approximately equal "attention to," "preoccupation with," and "absorption in," all segments of the on-going action by the subject. Let us suppose that, in the episode given above, Raymond had become so absorbed in the process of freeing the crate from the weeds that the onward flow of the behavior toward the goal of moving the crate to a convenient place appeared to stop temporarily. In this event a new episode, *Freeing Crate From Weeds*, would have occurred, even though the direction had not changed.

Later in this chapter the situational side of behavior episodes will be introduced. The more precise characteristics of episodes, their theoretical aspects, and the techniques of identifying and describing them will be considered in detail in Chapters VII and VIII. Here we have wished only to define episodes in a general way and to point out that they are useful, natural units into which the unwieldy behavior-situation continuum can be divided for study.

Behavior Settings

The behavior episodes of individual persons are the smallest units which appear to be of value in ecological studies.   They can be considered the particles of ecological research.   Early in our study it became clear, however, that data regarding the particles were not enough, that there was something more in Midwest of significance to us than the behavior of its individual citizens, and that even this partial picture was beyond the scope of our scientific apparatus.   The truth is that we soon became overwhelmed with individual behavior.   We estimated that the 119 children of Midwest engaged in about 100 thousand episodes of behavior each day, over 36 million in a year.   In our efforts to sample this universe adequately, we found that our behavior sample was improved if, in addition to using the usual stratification guides—age, sex, social class, race, education, and occupation—we sampled behavior in such divergent places as the drug store, the Sunday-School classes, the 4-H Club meeting, and the football games.   Early, we made the not very startling discovery that if we collected behavior in a variety of behavior areas, the variability of our behavior sample was greatly increased. At this point we stopped focusing exclusively upon the ecological particles, and saw for the first time a thing that is obvious to native Midwesterners, namely, that behavior comes not only in particle form, but in extra-individual wave patterns that are as visible and invariant as the pools and rapids in Slough Creek west of town.   The Presbyterian worship services, the high-school basketball games, and the post office, for example, persist year after year with their unique configurations of behavior, despite constant changes in the persons involved.   These persisting, extra-individual behavior phenomena we have called the *standing behavior patterns* of Midwest.

With this new sensitivity we began to see that for the people of Midwest, particle behavior and pattern behavior were about equally visible and apparently about equally important.   Any issue of the *Midwest Weekly*, whose job it is to report the community's behavior to the citizens, confirmed this.   In the issue of August 6, 1953, for example, 393 instances of individual behavior were reported in such items as this:

> Mr. and Mrs. Vernon Main and their 11-year-old daughter, Sandra, escaped from their burning home last Friday morning with only the clothing they wore.

In the same issue, 395 occurrences of extra-individual, standing behavior patterns were recorded thus:

> Amateur contests again played an important part in the entertainment at the Old Settlers' Reunion at Midwest.

In the former item, the behavior of three particular individuals is described; in the latter item, three patterns of behavior which are independent of particular persons are identified, namely, amateur contests, entertainment, and the Old Settlers' Reunion.

Standing patterns of behavior such as contests, entertainments, picnics, 4-H Club meetings, choir practice, and first-grade reading are hard, empirical facts in Midwest. They are as real to Midwest citizens as the Mains' escape from their burning home. Anyone in Midwest on a Sunday at noon, can see the churches suddenly pour forth their congregations which hurry sedately away down streets and sidewalks. On any morning at 8:30 the behavior pattern is unmistakable in the post office: efficient business against a background of the relaxed conversation of loiterers.

Standing behavior patterns are in many cases very complex configurations with many discriminable subordinate figures. Thus the Old Settlers' Reunion contains the subordinate figure, Amateur Contest, and within this figure special acts are discriminated. The basis of the perceptual unity of these behavior patterns is not clear. The fact remains, however, that they are prominent perceptual features of the behaviorial scene.

The discovery of standing behavior patterns was the crucial step in our identification of a community unit suitable to our purposes. While important progress can be made toward describing general characteristics of the living conditions and behavior of a community by adding together the behavior characteristics and situations of representative individuals, it seems clear that these patterned features of behavior which can be seen directly should not be ignored.

When the standing behavior patterns of Midwest came into focus, a number of other relationships were simultaneously seen. First, it was obvious that most of the standing behavior patterns are attached to particular places, things, and times, i.e., to parts of the nonbehavioral context of the town. Shopping occurs in stores, bicycling is performed on streets and sidewalks, and dancing takes place at the American Legion Hall; sweeping is done with brooms, stirring with spoons, and cutting with knives. There is almost never a change in these attachments; bicycling never occurs in the American Legion Hall, dancing does not take place in the stores, nor is shopping done on the streets and sidewalks. Sweeping is not done with knives, nor stirring with brooms, nor cutting with spoons. We have called the place-thing-time constellation to which a standing pattern of behavior is attached the *nonpsychological milieu* or simply the *milieu*.

Second, there is often a perceived fittingness or *synomorphism* between the patterns of behavior and the attributes of the nonpsychological context to which they are anchored. It is seen as appropriate that writing should occur in connection with a pencil rather than a shovel, and that eating should occur in the cafe rather than in the library. A baseball game fits a baseball diamond, and walking and riding on streets and sidewalks conform to the directions of these routes. The total constellation of standing behavior pattern and synomorphic milieu we have called a *behavior-milieu synomorph*.

Third, there are often abrupt changes in the behavior of a person as he leaves one of these synomorphs and enters another. Margaret Reid's hyperactivity, aggressiveness, and verbalization, gave way like magic to passivity, submissiveness, and silence when she passed from the synomorph Home Outdoors to the synomorph Neighbor's Birthday Party. The second graders cease writing, reading, spelling, sitting, whispering, etc., with startling swiftness and unanimity when they cross the line from School Academic to the School Playground. On the basis of many observations of this kind we were driven to the hypothesis that, in addition to being conspicuous features of the behavioral landscape of Midwest, standing patterns of behavior involve forces which in some way coerce individual behavior.

Fourth, behavior-milieu synomorphs are ubiquitous; very little behavior in Midwest occurs outside their limits.

It is important to note that standing patterns of behavior are not qualities of behavior in general, like tempo, prevailing mood, or motivation. They are not of the same order as the ethos or eidos of a community. Neither do they refer to the content of behavior; to the customs, the habits, the institutions; to the ways of preparing food, or of exchanging goods. Rather they are differentiated parts of behavior which themselves have complex qualities; they, too, are behavioral "things" like episodes. They are perceived units of behavior phenomena but they are not units of individual behavior; they are units in the behavior of men en masse.

We are now in a position to define two extra-individual, ecological behavior units which we have used in this research. The *behavior setting* is one of these units. A behavior setting is a standing behavior pattern together with the context of this behavior, including the part of the milieu to which the behavior is attached and with which it has a synomorphic relationship. Examples are: Kane's Grocery, 4-H Club Picnic, Thanksgiving Day. An essential feature of a behavior setting is the circumjacence of the milieu to the standing pattern of behavior. A person is seen to enter, to be included in, to be surrounded by a store, a picnic, or Thanksgiving Day, and the standing pattern of behavior occurs on the stage which is thus provided.

The factors which led us to select behavior settings as a community unit for our studies in psychological ecology can be summarized as follows:

1. *Visibility.* Behavior settings are prominent units of extra-individual behavior identified with a high degree of agreement by independent observers. They are obvious empirical facts about behavior in Midwest.

2. *Phenomenal Character.* They are features of the phenomenal worlds of both laymen and scientists, and a description of the community in terms of behavior settings corresponds to common experience.

3. *Internal Dynamics.* Behavior settings involve persons, nonpsychological milieu, and behavior in an interacting field of forces. Behavior settings coerce behavior and vice versa.

4. *Comprehensiveness*. Behavior settings blanket the community. We estimate that in Midwest 95 per cent of all behavior occurs within the behavior settings we have identified.

5. *Variety of Attributes*. Behavior settings have many discriminable behavioral and nonbehavioral characteristics. They are rich material for analysis.

6. *External Dynamics*. Behavior settings are not independent community units, and in fact, the pattern of one setting is often radically changed by the behavior occurring in another behavior setting.

7. *Theoretical Position*. Behavior settings are at present empirical facts. They can be demonstrated to the hardest empiricist. However, they are theoretically promising. Their internal structure and dynamics and their external relations suggest that they can be profitably conceptualized and incorporated into productive theory.

Further consideration of behavior settings is presented in Chapters III and IV.

Behavior Objects

Behavior objects are the other community units that we have used in this research. They, like behavior settings, are standing patterns of behavior and the part of the nonpsychological milieu to which the behavior is anchored; they are behavior-milieu synomorphs. Examples are dolls, books, ladders, and tooth brushes. Behavior objects are differentiated from behavior settings on two grounds. First, the pattern of behavior associated with a behavior object is circumjacent to the milieu rather than the reverse, as with behavior settings. A person does not enter and behave within the boundaries of a doll or a book as he does in the case of a store and a picnic. The behavior pattern of a behavior object surrounds and incorporates the synomorphic milieu within it. Second, behavior objects are, themselves, located within behavior settings. They are the furniture of behavior settings. Behavior objects are related to behavior settings as stage properties are related to the scenes of a play. In other respects behavior objects and behavior settings are identical.

Behavior objects are described in detail in Chapter IX.

The Psychological Habitat

It must be emphasized that behavior episodes, behavior settings, and behavior objects all consist of discriminable patterns of behavior and the psychological context of this behavior. They are all behavior-situation units. Both the behavior and the psychological context of behavior can be directly seen in these cases, but not to the same degree. The context of behavior appears to have a more inferential basis; at least its apprehension involves less explicit stimulus conditions than the apprehension of behavior.

We shall, therefore, introduce here some of the problems met in observing, describing, and conceptualizing the psychological context of behavior.

Following biological usage, we shall call the naturally occurring psychological context of behavior the *psychological habitat*. The habitat lies at the intersection of the behaving person and the nonpsychological milieu; it is jointly determined by the person and the milieu. The habitat is a dynamic system within which the person and the environment are interconnected.

In the episode *Moving Crate Across Pit*, Raymond's habitat consisted of the pit and its contents as Raymond interacted with them. It appeared to contain on the phenomenal level the following:

> Crate-as-attractive-place-to-play
> Stewart-as-possible-playmate-in-crate
> Stewart-as-barrier-to-social-play-at-site-of-crate
> Crate-as-moveable-to-site-of-playmate
> Crate-as-moveable-with-great-effort

It undoubtedly involved other conditions of which Raymond and the observer were unaware.

The physical and social situation surrounding Raymond contained an almost endless list of other things such as: a square pit, 3 feet deep with irregularly sloping sides, covering 150 square feet; a rough dirt floor; approximately 30 tough weeds, 2 feet tall, randomly distributed over the floor and sides of the pit; toy cars; clods; bricks; a 10-year-old boy intent on play with toy cars; tin cans; a 3-year-old boy absorbed in play with toy cars; a wobbly old crate, 5 feet by 30 inches by 30 inches. These were some of the physical and social characteristics of Raymond's situation independent of his interaction with them. They constituted the nonpsychological milieu; they were the potential substructures of Raymond's psychological habitat. The actual psychological habitat, crate-as-attractive, Stewart-as-barrier, etc., arose from the Raymond-milieu interaction. Some features of the milieu remained psychologically neutral during this episode, e.g., the bricks, the tin cans, the clods, and possibly the weeds.

Being a dynamic system involving both the person and the milieu in an interdependent relationship, the psychological habitat overlaps the person and the milieu. We have found it unprofitable to attempt to separate the parts of the psychological habitat which fall within the person and those which fall within the environment, although this has been done on a theoretical level by Lewin (33) in his conception of the psychological person and the psychological environment. In this research it has proven to be more rewarding to conceive of the psychological habitat as being coextensive with the life space, in Lewin's sense.

Identification of the psychological habitat is based upon three kinds of data: data regarding the milieu, data regarding the person, and data regarding the behavior. Knowledge of the milieu immediately limits the habitat possibilities. Raymond in the pit could not enter the habitat "pleasant place to wade" because of the absence of water in the pit. Likewise, knowledge of the person limits habitat possibilities. We know from experience that the habitat "place to be tidied up" is less likely to occur for children than for adults. However, the habitat cannot be determined from knowledge of the milieu and the person alone; behavior data are crucial. The fact that it is possible to comprehend the setting of a dramatic monologue, or even a pantomime, without stage properties is evidence of the primary importance of behavior and the secondary significance of the milieu and the person in perceiving the psychological habitat. In the case of behavior episodes such as we shall deal with, where a familiar person is observed as he behaves in a well-known milieu, some features of the psychological habitat are immediately apprehended with a high degree of agreement between different observers. This is the part of the psychological habitat we have used in the present study and is the part we shall refer to when we use the term psychological habitat. The complete psychological habitat, i.e., the naturally occurring life space, includes many conditions which are accessible only by indirect, inferential cognitive processes to both the person himself and to an observer. These conditions have not been included in this study.

The psychological context of standing patterns of behavior is less clear both conceptually and operationally than it is with the behavior of individuals in episodes. What little we have been able to do with this will be considered later in connection with the detailed discussion of behavior settings and behavior objects.

Field Methods of Psychological Ecology

The essential method of research in psychological ecology is simple, namely, to describe the naturally occurring behavior and the psychological habitat within which it occurs. In practice, however, the difficulties are great.

Maintaining the Natural Habitat

Difficulties arise partly from the necessity of leaving the habitat undisturbed by the investigator's field study techniques. This creates a dilemma, because an essential feature of most methods of psychological diagnosis, testing, and measurement is the creation by the investigator of a special, standard psychological situation within which to observe behavior, thus destroying the natural habitat. Most tests, questionaires, interviews, and experiments attempt to create for the subject a psychological situation designed for the special purposes of the investigator. To use these methods, except for very limited purposes, would be methodologically parallel to a plant ecologist's importing soil, broadcasting seeds, and coming back later to study the "natural" vegetation. The task of an ecological field study is to determine the state of affairs that exists independently of the investigator's methods. The questions that exist in a subject's mind are as important as his answers to them. If the investigator asks the questions and poses the problems, he changes the subject's habitat and destroys the very thing he aims to study. Furthermore, free or nondirective interviews can cause profound changes in the subject's perception of himself and his world.

These difficulties are greatly magnified in a continuing field station which uses the same subjects over a period of time. Here, the second, third, and subsequent tests and interviews are certain to bring about changes in the psychological habitat. The basic methodology of a psychological field station must be, therefore, the direct observation of behavior and psychological habitat.

Observations can be made at first-hand by the investigator himself, or they can be supplied by informants. Informants, however, must be used with caution. It is obvious, for example, that a mother who reports at intervals about the conditions existing in her home will, in some degree, become a changed factor in the situation, if only because of her awareness of conditions of which she was previously unaware. Continuing field stations which aim to leave intact the conditions that are the object of their study cannot make much use of informants. This leaves direct observation of behavior and situation by the investigator as the primary method of psychological ecology.

Describing the Psychological Habitat

Psychologists have spent much time and energy, and have had considerable success, in devising observational techniques for describing and measuring behavior and personality. Little of a comparable nature has been done with the psychological situation. In consequence, investigators frequently resort to the use of such nonpsychological categories as the situation of "only children," "urban children," "children of divorced parents," "institutionalized children," and "upper-class children." It is hoped that in these ways such psychological complexes as emotional warmth, security, approval, pressure to high achievement, or their opposites will, in some degree, be captured. Actually, of course, such categories are concerned with the nonpsychological milieu. It has already been mentioned that these milieu categories are not entirely useless in the absence of psychological descriptions of the habitat. They do, at least, restrict in some degree the range of habitat possibilities. Unfortunately the range is not often well known.

If the psychological habitat is to be described with complete adequacy, two requirements must be met. First, it is necessary to include the environment in terms that will do justice to its great richness. The psychological environment has been included in theories for a long time. Freud's cathected objects and Lewin's regions, valences, barriers, and routes give the psychological environment a prominent place. However, Heider (**27**) has emphasized the richness of the psychological environment and has pointed out how meager such concepts as cathexis and valence are in dealing with it. It is clear that a major job of conceptualization has yet to be done.

Secondly, any useful method of dealing with the psychological environment in ecological studies must provide for quantification of environmental characteristics. It is essential to have quantified, normative data in order to judge how far psychological living conditions in particular communities, institutions, and families differ from living conditions in other communities, institutions, and families. We cannot study the influence of psychological conditions upon behavior and personality effectively without having knowledge of the existing range of these conditions.

Securing Theoretically Neutral Data

Another methodological problem of a field station arises from its aim to assemble data useful in the study of many problems, some of them not forseen by the person who collects the data. This means that the more theoretically neutral the data, the better they serve the long-time purposes of a field station. Some will say that theoretically neutral data do not exist, that data are good or bad only in relation to the questions asked by a particular investigator, and that without specific theoretical guides data collection becomes blind.

With this we do not entirely agree. Data have other values than their relevance to a single theory or problem. For one thing, the appearance of behavior, the phenotype, has practical importance in itself. The phenotype is the part of the child's behavior which gets to bed at a reasonable time, slaps its baby sister, eats a good meal. We have to live with it. For another thing, the directly perceived action is the starting place of much theory construction, and is the final testing ground of important phases of theoretical systems. While it may readily be granted that science should leave the surface of behavior and achieve a more basic and inclusive reality, this deeper understanding must, nevertheless, begin and end at the surface.

Despite the practical and theoretical importance of behavior as it is directly seen, one can not go to the scientific literature of child behavior to find what the behavior of children looks like. One must go to the novelists, the diarists, the news reporters. This is true because most data of psychology have been assembled in terms of particular problems or theories and this almost always requires the fractionation of behavior to such a degree that its appearance is destroyed. The psychological landscape is strewn with the debris of these dismantling operations. This is true, too, because others, notably psychoanalysts, believe that the surface of behavior is hardly ever univocally related to psychological realities and that the observer, himself, must become an instrument for perceiving the inner man directly. This results in highly selective, disconnected, cryptic reports of the appearance of behavior.

Nevertheless, to be scientifically useful, theoretically neutral data must be in a form which allows for the conceptualization and application of theories. Here is a fundamental problem of methodology which has scarcely been touched by psychologists. It is to some degree a matter of the richness and wholeness of the data, but undoubtedly more precise guides for collecting such data can be discovered. It has been one of the aims of the Midwest Field Station to explore the possibility of conceptualizing certain kinds of theoretically neutral behavior data. The results of these efforts are presented in detail in a later part of this report.

We are encouraged in the hope that a middle ground of relatively neutral data is possible by the observation that every other science with which we are familiar has been able to formulate principles of good phenotypic data collection with relative theoretical neutrality, and that they have found such data invaluable. Natural history museums, herberia, astronomical charts and photographs, and anthropological archives are examples of collections of such data. We hesitate to think that child psychology is so different from other natural sciences in this respect.

In the light of these requirements for ecological field methods in psychology, and after considering and exploring many possibilities, including moving pictures, sound recordings, and on-the-spot reporting via portable radio, we concluded that the best method available to us is that used regularly by the citizens of Midwest: looking, listening, and telling. We have developed these methods in three directions: the *Specimen Record*, the *Behavior Setting Survey*, and the *Behavior Object Inventory*. These will be described in detail later, but a brief introduction to them is in order here.

THE SPECIMEN RECORD

The specimen record is a detailed, sequential narrative of a long segment of a child's behavior and situation as seen by skilled observers. It describes in concrete detail the stream of the child's behavior and psychological habitat. In its most extensive form the specimen record covers a day's activities. Such a record is made by a team of seven to nine observers taking turns throughout the day. The report usually covers over 300 typed pages. One episode from a specimen record has already been given (pp. 4–5); other examples will be found in Chapters VII and XI.

In the early days of child psychology, records somewhat similar to specimen records were frequently used in research. Here are some examples:

Tiedmann (1770) "On the 30th (of November, 100 days old) he first heard piano music and gave evidence of inordinate delight and happiness" (**56**, 215).

Preyer (1882) "On the following (26th) day he started suddenly when a dish he could not see was noisily covered near him. He is frightened, then, already at unexpected loud noises, as adults are. On the thirtieth day this fright was still more strongly manifested. I was standing before the child as he lay quiet, and being called, I said aloud, 'Ja!' Directly the child threw both arms high up and made a convulsive start . . . " (**47**, 82).

Stern (1920) "One day Eva (2.5) at dinner gave the command, 'Father, pick up the spoon.' We asked 'What else should Eva say?' She understood perfectly she should say, 'please,' but she only made a wry face and wouldn't say it . . . she cried bitterly . . . but she remained obstinate" (**54**, 499).

So-called "diary records," "anecdotal records," or "running accounts" of this kind have been severely criticized for their biased selection of incidents, for their unreliable reporting, for their unwarranted interpretations, and for the difficult recording and analysis they entail. Consequently, they have almost completely disappeared in modern psychological research. Their place has been taken by time-sample records of various sorts, by check lists, and by ratings. The criticisms which led to the abandonment of diary records were undoubtedly fully justified in many cases. Nonetheless, the reading of anecdotal records, even early, inadequate records, reveals an advantage that has not often been pointed out: they provide a relatively intact specimen of behavior; they present a multi-variable picture of the molar aspects of behavior and situation with many of the simultaneous and successive interrelations preserved.

Records of this kind do not need to have the inadequacies of the earliest examples. Adequate sampling procedures can be used to guide the collection of such records; great skill in reporting can be attained by most people through practice and the use of modern note-taking and dictating equipment; interpretation can be kept to any minimum desired; and methods of analysis can be devised. Much of the basic data of this research are in the form of specimen records. Consequently, techniques of making and analyzing specimen records constitute an important part of the methodology sections of this report as given in Chapters VI and X.

THE BEHAVIOR SETTING SURVEY

The behavior setting survey is a catalogue and description of the behavior settings of the community. The town of Midwest has a vast number of physical and social parts. A crew of physical and social scientists could make a limitless list of its features, but to only a few of these is the synomorphic behavior pattern coordinated. Thus, the Courthouse Lawn is a behavior setting since a discriminable and fitting pattern of behavior occurs there. The abandoned railroad grade at the edge of town, however, is not a behavior setting since the behavior which takes place on the railroad grade has no constant patterned features. Similarly, July 4 is a behavior setting by reason of the associated behavior configuration, while May 14, an equally well discriminated time, is not a behavior setting since no discriminable pattern of behavior is attached to it. The behavior setting survey provides a psychological map of Midwest representing those areas of the town that have general behavioral significance to the citizens. The techniques for discriminating behavior settings and for describing their standing patterns of behavior constitute the other major methodology of this research. These are reported in Chapter III.

THE BEHAVIOR OBJECT INVENTORY

We have not had the time to develop the behavior object inventory beyond an initial stage. As we have used it, the inventory involves the identification and analysis of the behavior objects which entered the psychological habitat of a particular person in the course of a day. For this purpose, we have used the data of day-long specimen records. The inventory and analysis of three such specimen records are presented in Chapter IX.

Special Problems and Methods of a Psychological Field Station

A field station should provide easy access to good material for study. Its location is, therefore, of the utmost importance. In looking for a suitable community for the Midwest Field Station, we were guided by the following considerations:

1. The community should be small enough that all the people of the town could be included in particular studies, yet large enough that important population subgroups would have stability.

2. It should be geographically and socially segregated but not isolated from the currents of American culture.

3. It should be a community that is complete enough and vital enough that many of the functions of modern life are performed by its citizens within its borders.

4. It should have community unity and at the same time social differentiation and variety of institutions.

5. The town should have a relatively stable population, economy, and culture.

6. There should be no special conditions making the community clearly atypical.

7. It should be accessible.

8. The citizens should be interested in the establishment of the field station in their midst.

Data to be presented in Chapter II will show where Midwest stands with respect to these considerations. We can say here, however, that we have found Midwest to be in all respects the "intelligible field of study" which Bates (12) thinks is the basic requirement of a community for natural history studies, and which is, perhaps, the common factor in the requirements listed above which guided our selection of a community. Midwest encompasses most of the behavior of Midwest citizens and most of the conditions which are relevant to this behavior. It is to a surprising degree a self-contained dynamic system so far as the behavior of its citizens is concerned.

An important requirement of a social psychology field station, and one which is not usually of great consequence for biological field stations, is a favorable attitude toward the station and its activities by the people of the community. In this respect, Midwest has been most satisfactory. The people have been understanding and coöperative. It seems to be easy for them to see the importance of scientific studies of children. This may be due in part to the fact that Midwest County is a progressive agricultural county and its people have had more than a generation of experience with the methods and values of scientific studies of grain and livestock production. They have directly experienced the procedures and the benefits of science. When to this is added the fact that the people of Midwest value nothing more than the welfare of their own children, it creates a generally favorable climate for field studies of children.

The citizens of the community in which a continuing field station is established must be frankly and fully informed of the purposes of the station, of its methods of operation, and of the problems being studied. This policy is necessary, entirely aside from imperative ethical considerations, to insure continuity of functioning. A quick survey of a community, with the investigators withdrawing thereafter to sheltered anonymity within a university, may make use of indirect or even, in some cases, secret procedures. This is impossible, however, in the case of a continuously operating psychological field station dependent upon public good will and cooperation. This means that problems and methods which are inadmissable in terms of community mores cannot be included in the program of the station. From the beginning the citizens of Midwest were kept informed of the program of the field station by way of public meetings, by a moving picture showing the operations of the station, through the *Midwest Weekly*, and by exhibits of pictures and publications in store windows and in the library.

It is essential that some members of the staff of a psychological field station reside in the community. This is not only necessary in order to secure the needed information and observations, but also to demonstrate a respect for and a confidence in the community as a place to live. Resident staff members must, of course, be acceptable within the local culture. This appears, on the basis of our experience, to be more a matter of the tolerant attitudes of staff members than of cultural background.

Equally important is the role of the resident staff in the community. This is directly related to the technical necessity, in continuing ecological field studies, of leaving the native habitat undisturbed. During most of the time the Midwest Field Station has been in operation, resident staff members and their families have numbered 15 to 20 persons. It is clear that these people, in a total population of 750, might affect the town in important ways. To avoid this, the role of the resident staff member of Midwest was defined as one of normal participation in community activities in accordance with his own interests and talents, but without initiating or changing community enterprises. Both nonparticipation and missionary zeal can be almost equally disturbing to a community. The task of the resident staff member, therefore, was to achieve behavioral "protective coloration."

We involved Midwest citizens in the station's program to a limited degree by informing them clearly of the program, by stressing the essential coöperative nature of the research, and by giving them a free choice to participate if they desired. Stress was placed upon the fact that the function of the field station was to learn rather than to teach. We pointed out that we came to Midwest to find out how children should be raised, not to give advice. We emphasized that we were not interested in the children of Midwest as individuals, but as representatives of certain kinds of children, and that the firm policy of the station was to maintain the anonymity of particular individuals. This was accomplished by the use of code names in all records and all publications.

Two motives led us to obtain data upon physically disabled children of age and cultural background comparable to the children of Midwest: first, a desire to test the field methods we had developed upon persons whose psychological living conditions and behavior might be expected to differ appreciably from those of Midwest children; and second, an interest in contributing to an understanding of the psychological problems of the physically disabled. It seemed to us that if the methods of psychological ecology are to be effective, they must be able to describe essential differences in the circumstances of life and in the behavior of socially and culturally important classes of people. For testing this, physically disabled children seemed to be ideally suited. We believed that if ecological procedures were unable to define some of the ways the living conditions and behavior of physically disabled children differed from those of normal children, the effectiveness of the procedures would be limited. We saw this as a scientifically and a socially important problem upon which to test the methods of psychological ecology.

Disabled children were secured from two sources: from towns neighboring Midwest, and from the Lawton School for Crippled Children in Capitol City. Day-long specimen records were made of four disabled children, two at the Lawton School and two in neighboring towns, and a behavior setting survey of the Lawton School was completed.

These were the aims, the guiding principles, the problems, and the general methods of the investigation which is reported in this volume. Before turning to the detailed presentation of ecological data, general information about Midwest and its people will be presented in Chapter II.

Chapter II

Midwest and the U.S.A.

HERE are some facts about the town of Midwest which were recorded on November 1, 1950:

Location	Central United States
Date of founding	1856
Population	707
Children under 12 years	119
Area of townsite	400 acres
Terrain	Rolling
Elevation	1100 feet
Mean temperature	54 degrees F.
Annual temperature range	− 10 to 100 degrees F.
Annual rainfall	33 inches
Number of dwellings	269
Number of business buildings	54
Number of public buildings	6
Number of organized social groups exclusive of church groups	50
Number of businesses	85
Number of government agencies	26
Number of churches	3
Number of schools	2
Number of family owned automobiles	179
Number of families keeping chickens, pigs, horses, cows, sheep	90
Number of liquor stores	0
Number of railroads	0
Number of families	295
Family size	1–13; average 2.5
Per cent of families receiving daily newspaper	97
Per cent of families owning radio	99+
Per cent of families with pets	51
Per cent of families with telephone	70
Per cent of population with various church affiliation:	
Methodist	34

Presbyterian	37
African Methodist Episcopal	4
Church in other towns	7
None	15
Unknown	3
Per cent of adults literate	99+
Number of blind persons	4
Number of severely crippled persons	8
Births in preceeding year	9
Deaths in preceeding year	6
Number of Negro residents	27

A complete catalogue of facts about Midwest would be almost endless. Yet these multitudinous aspects of the town combine to make a unitary picture of Midwest in the minds of its residents and visitors. This picture varied from person to person. Here is Midwest as seen by a woman from University Place who visited Midwest two or three times a year:

My husband and I often say to each other, if Midwest were only 10 or 15 miles closer to University Place, we would like to live there.

Midwest is to us in no way beautiful, exciting, glamorous, atmospheric, or fascinating. Yet although many small towns of similar style and kind are somewhat depressing, Midwest has an indefinable quality of pleasantness and openness. Its streets are wide and shady. The unimaginative early-century houses are neat and homelike. Open country impinges everywhere, geographically and in feeling tone. Perhaps it is the relative height of land on which Midwest stands which gives it this pleasant "tone," a height from which the land rolls down and away, gently and unexcitingly, in keeping with the town.

There is an almost Spartan quality to Midwest, nothing lush or grandiose, no huge mansions or wealthy "gentleman" farms. One feels it is a simple town of people who have worked hard for what they have and who take a quiet, independent pride in their homes, their gardens, their lawns.

There is much about Midwest that suggests a "period piece," a Grant Wood painting, a Willa Cather novel. One would not be surprised to see, on a dusty summer day, a woman out strolling in a white dress of the Gibson-girl era, with a parasol over her head. Yet, it comes as no surprise to see the blue-jeaned teenager on a bicycle.

Midwest is a pleasant, restful kind of town, not too surprised by modern life.

A New Englander who visited Midwest occasionally, writes:

As a stranger drives into Midwest he is apt to be struck by the evidence of its mixed heritage. In the center of the town is the courthouse, not unlike those which one sees in New England. Like the New England courthouse it sits on its village green, dominating the life of the community. But here the resemblance ends. The streets around the Midwest courthouse continue at right angles into the squared highway system of the county, instead of following the winding paths made over the years by the cattle and citizens of the New England town. And this courthouse, instead of being in the midst of the homes and churches that grew up with it, is surrounded by the business houses of the county: bank, newspaper, restaurant, moving picture house, and stores. These stand square and stark against the sky and beyond them, on the outer rim of the town, are the Midwest homes and churches.

And, of course, one must mention the flatness of the landscape with its wide open skies and the feeling which it gives of going endlessly on into the plains beyond. Actually this impression is misleading, since the roads by which the visitor has approached the town are more hilly than many in the state of Midwest and often suggest that there might be higher land beyond.

A city visitor spent a week in Midwest caring for a friend's children. She writes:

If you don't watch for landmarks or signs you are likely to drive past Midwest without being aware that you have left it behind. You may vaguely recall that Midwest is like hundreds of other small American towns with a large central square around which small shops carry on their business, with surrounding unpaved streets bordered by white frame houses which look peaceful enough but colorless in their sameness. You may note the big, red brick building in the middle of the square and silently tag Midwest as a county seat.

If you have the occasion to stop, however, and look around and talk to the people, then Midwest emerges with its own individuality.

Here it was that the sow escaped her pen to career through the streets while first one neighbor and then another joined in the rescue. It was here that the five-year-old boy who was stricken with polio came home for Christmas Day after his mother appealed to the hospital for this special privilege. People told us how the members of the high-school basketball team put their whole hearts into the game even though they knew they weren't very good. We were told how a native Midwesterner achieved national political fame and how another married into a famous family.

Yes, Midwest is not devoid of interest when you stay awhile.

When the Midwest Rotary Club entertained some foreign students from the State University, the editor of the *Midwest Weekly* talked to the group on the history of the town. He closed his address with this description:

Please do not sell Midwest short because of its people. I have traced the careers of the graduates of Midwest High School from 1891 through 1924. Of the 116 men, 68 have engaged in skilled trades and business, 20 in farming, 7 in engineering, 6 in teaching, 5 in medicine, 2 in law, 2 in the ministry, 2 in chemistry, 3 in military service, and 1 in dentistry. Several of these Midwesterners have, by any standard of achievement, risen high in the nation in their chosen fields.

Please do not sell Midwest short because of its geographical location. It lies within the circle of Mid-America's greatest garden spot.

Please do not sell Midwest short because of its meager size. It is small enough that its citizens will greet you in the street, yet big enough that they won't meddle in your personal affairs. Our people are housed, not in crowded apartments, but largely in comfortable homes of their own; our merchants own and manage their own business establishments; we enjoy as genuine a freedom of enterprise as may be dreamed of anywhere. We are not harassed with problems of organized labor or of capitalist greed.

Please do not sell Midwest short on the theory of its isolation. Midwest is but a step removed from the noise and discomforts and distractions and vices of the major centers. Midwest offers unexcelled opportunities for quietude of mind and growth of soul, for time to listen to the morning song of the brown thrush in the berry patch, the gay note of the meadowlark, and the whippoorwill's mournful note in the valley at eventide. We are far enough removed from the faster currents of metropolitan life to see life in better perspective than city dwellers themselves, yet close enough to these centers to take frequent and selective advantage of the best they have to offer in the avenues of trade, of culture, and of amusement.

These are impressions which Midwest made upon people with widely varying backgrounds and relationships to the town. These sketches set the stage for our task of systematically describing the milieu, the psychological habitat, and the behavior of Midwest children.

However, before turning to these tasks, we would like to indicate where Midwest falls within the larger framework of American culture and to present some facts about the sociology and demography of the town. The remainder of this chapter was prepared in 1950 on the basis of data collected at that time. It provides a contemporary view of Midwest. The data came from both official government records and from special enumerations made by the Field Station staff. Most of these kinds of data were compiled yearly beginning in 1948; the year 1950 was chosen for presentation because of the availability of national census data for comparisons. Data for other years indicate that 1950 was not an atypical year in Midwest, and they indicate that confidence can be placed in the accuracy of the 1950 data.

Midwest and American Culture

Midwest represents in relatively pure form a single strand of the complex fabric of American life. This particular strand has been called by some the "core American culture." Without considering what the elements of American culture may be and which of them are central, we can, nevertheless, point out that the people who founded Midwest almost a century ago were, even then, old Americans with a way of life that had been formed under peculiarly American influences during the previous century. We can point out, too, that during the century of Midwest's history, the town has been relatively insulated from influences which during this time were seen as alien. Direct and indirect evidence of Midwest's cultural homogeneity and isolation from foreign influences are found in the following data.

MIDWEST IS ISOLATED FROM DIRECT ALIEN INFLUENCES

Midwest is equidistant from the borders of the country. Most "foreign" influences are filtered through many layers of American culture before they reach Midwest. Few foreigners visit the town. In a two year period from November, 1949 to October, 1951, eight foreign persons came to Midwest, all of them as guest speakers of the Rotary Club, the women's clubs, the church missionary societies, or the Parent-Teachers' Association. In all cases the visits were of only a few hours duration. During this same period eight Midwest residents visited foreign countries, all of them as members of the armed services. Meager direct contact with alien influences has characterized Midwest throughout its history.

In contrast to the small amount of direct social contact with foreign people, much foreign news reaches Midwest via newspapers and radio. Midwest residents are consistent listeners to radio news, much of which originates in Eastern seaboard cities. This means that much news does not, as in earlier days, pass through intermediate channels where foreign stories can be edited or eliminated. Moreover, the newspapers which circulate in Midwest carry a considerable amount of foreign news. The churches, too, provide a regular channel by which some kinds of information about foreign cultures reach Midwest. Church publications circulate 750 copies a month in the town and most of them have regular departments of foreign mission news. In addition, the missionary societies have continuous study courses; 25 per cent of the adult women of Midwest regularly attend missionary society meetings. Thus, although Midwest is geographically far removed from foreign shores, modern communication brings much information about foreign cultures to the town.

MIDWEST'S GROWTH HAS BEEN SHAPED BY UNIQUELY AMERICAN INFLUENCES

The people who founded the town in 1856 came from two strongholds of old American society: the Northeast and the South. The greater number of the founders came from New England via Ohio and Iowa, a minority of the white people came from the South, and a smaller number of Negroes arrived during and after the Civil War. The forces which led these people to settle in Midwest were peculiarly native. None came to escape intolerable economic, political, military, or religious conditions in Europe. No real estate or railroad promoters sold Midwest County land across the Atlantic. Midwest was settled by American farmers who were attracted by the newly opened Indian lands, and by proslavery and antislavery zealots who came to insure that the area would be safe for their causes.

MIDWEST RESIDENTS ARE NATIVE BORN AND LOCALLY REARED

In 1950, Midwest's citizens were largely locally born and reared as the following tabulation shows:

	Per Cent of Population
Born and reared in Midwest	24
Born and reared outside Midwest but in Midwest County	45

Per Cent of
Population

Born and reared outside Midwest County
but in Midwest State or nearest bordering
state 29
Born in other parts of U.S. 2
Foreign born (2 persons)

MIDWEST RESIDENTS EXHIBIT FEW CHARACTERISTICS OF ALIEN CULTURES

A series of items for rating persons with respect to their conformity to the "core American culture" has been developed by Ruesch, Jacobson, and Loeb (**49**). On each of 24 items, a person is rated on a 4-point scale for his conformity to this core culture as defined by the authors on the basis of anthropological and sociological investigations. Descriptive scale points are given for each item; scale point *1* indicates complete conformity with the American prototype, and scale point *4* indicates greatest deviation.

We rated 24 Midwest adults on these items.[1] These adults were the parents of 12 Midwest children selected for special study (see pp. 42–43) as representative of Midwest children; presumably, too, their parents were representative of Midwest adults. In the paragraphs below, these 24 Midwest adults are described in terms of the scale points which were modal in the distributions of their ratings. On 19 items, this modal scale point was *1*, indicating complete conformity to the core American culture, on 5 items the mode either fell between scale points *1* and *2* or included elements of both scale points. After each descriptive statement, the per cent of the cases falling at the modal point is given. These paragraphs constitute a description of representative Midwest adults in terms of their approximation to the American prototype as defined by Reusch, *et al.*

Modal Midwest adults are native born of native American parents (100), their most deviant grandparents having been born and educated in the United States (87.5), and their only contact having been with American culture (92). They speak the American language as their mother tongue with no accent (100). Both their given names and their surnames are Anglo-Saxon (100); they dress and gesture in American ways (100), and they enthusiastically celebrate the American holidays such as Thanksgiving and Fourth of July (100).

As parents, their role with their children is primarily that of friend and guide, with authority evenly divided between the parents (100).

The Midwesterners' religion is Protestant, or indistinct (100).

Their diet falls across points *1* and *2* of the scale, having both high protein elements, said to be characteristic of the core culture, and high carbohydrate features. Common foods are: cottage cheese; baked, French fried, and mashed potatoes; potato soup; peas; string beans; baked beans; corn on the cob; roast beef; hamburger steak; round steak; hot dogs; roast turkey; fried and fricasseed chicken; pork chops; ham; corn beef; cold cuts; white bread; ice cream; apple,

---

[1] We have not computed the reliability of these ratings. They represent the concensus of three staff members amongst whom there were very few disagreements.

berry, and cream pie; jello; cake; coffee; milk; vegetable and fruit juice; milk shake; tea; chocolate; lemonade (100). Likewise, the Midwest citizens' attitude toward food is a combination of scale points *1* and *2*. Food is seen as nourishment, with great emphasis on its hygienic and nutritional value, but it is also greatly enjoyed, and good cooking is a highly valued art (100).

Although many adults are abstemious, when Midwesterners drink alcoholic beverages they drink beer, whiskey, gin, or rum (100).

Recreation is a social affair for Midwest residents, with little separation of the sexes. Typically they go to the movies or ball games, play cards, listen to the radio, and watch television. The men go hunting and fishing with other men (100).

With respect to personality and character, the modal adult sees himself as having a good sense of humor, as being warm, casual, playful, fair, vivacious, healthy, a good sport, self-sufficient, tough (100); ideally he wants to be relaxed, democratic, successful, energetic, flexible, cheerful, enterprising, nonargumentative, and resourceful (100).

The meaning of success to a Midwesterner combines features placed under scale points *1* and *2*. While success is measured to some degree in terms of money and popularity (getting along in a group, being accepted, winning friends, and influencing people), the achievement of skill in a chosen vocation irrespective of its economic rewards, and the earning of one's fellows' honor and respect also are highly valued. In Midwest, success is less dependent upon money than upon reputation, and aggressive seeking of publicity is considered in bad taste (100).

Midwest residents subscribe to the view that women are the equal of men, and that they have the right to vote and to work outside the home (100).

Although there are no class stratified residential areas in Midwest, on moving to a city Midwesterners would seek a residence in harmony with their class status (100). Modal Midwesterners belong to two nonreligious clubs or organizations without any ethnic limitations (100).

Midwesterners like music. The taste of the modal residents falls across scale points *1* and *2*, including jazz, musical comedy, swing, Negro spirituals, semi-classical and classical opera, and religious music (100).

Few Midwesterners vary from this picture. Of the 1056 ratings made on this sample of 24 adults, less than 1 per cent fell outside of the modal classes which have been described above, and none of the ratings fell more than one scale point from the mode.

The mean rating of these 24 parents of Midwest children was 1.11. The distribution of ratings for the individual parents is as follows:

Average Rating per Item	Number of Cases
1.10	19
1.15	5

For purposes of comparison, some other ratings may be cited as follows:

Most culturally deviant resident of Midwest	1.75
Mean rating of 25 foreign-born, San Francisco subjects (Data presented by Reusch, Jacobson, and Loeb)	1.81
Hindu woman who lectured in Midwest	3.10

The data given in this section suggest that in Midwest one thread of the whole pattern of American culture is emphasized. This thread is the mid-twentieth century expression of one that has been in the American picture since the earliest days. In this sense it is old. It may be, too, that it is central to American society. At least in Midwest, it has been directly influenced by alien forces in only a small degree.

Midwest and the Currents of American Life

The currents of American life flow strongly through Midwest as the following data indicate.

MIDWEST HAS EASY ACCESS TO INDUSTRIAL, GOVERNMENTAL, AND EDUCATIONAL CENTERS

The position of Midwest with respect to neighboring towns and cities is shown on the map below. It is located within 20 to 55 miles of five cities, and is connected with them by all-weather roads, scheduled bus transportation, telephone, and radio.

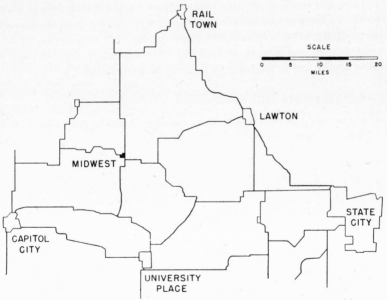

FIG. 2.1—Geographical position of Midwest in relation to neighboring cities.

The distance in minutes to these cities and the frequency of public transportation is as follows:

	Population	Minutes	Busses per Day
State City	700,000	70	3
Capitol City	100,000	55	4
Lawton	20,000	50	2
Rail Town	15,000	80	2
University Place	20,000	40	0

The *Midwest Weekly* reports many news items of this kind:

> Bill Marble and two daughters of Austin, Texas spent several days last week with his uncle, George Wall.

Fifteen randomly selected issues of the *Midwest Weekly* reported 160 visitors to Midwest, 103 from within the state and 57 from outside. Although the *Midwest Weekly* is an efficient paper, it can report only a portion of the visitors who come to town.

On 10 randomly chosen days, the automobiles parked on the streets of Midwest had the following places of origin, as revealed by their license plates:

Midwest County	83%
Out-of-county but within state	13%
Out-of-state	4%

On these 10 days, 1100 cars were inspected.

Twenty-five residents of other communities regularly commute to Midwest to work. This does not include persons who live on farms in the immediate vicinity of the town. Of these commuters, 10 work in government offices, 7 are teachers, and 8 work in business establishments. Six of these commuters would live in Midwest if housing were available.

MIDWEST RESIDENTS VISIT NEIGHBORING AND DISTANT PLACES

The issues of the *Midwest Weekly* mentioned above report 178 vacation or business trips by Midwest citizens, 99 within the state, and 79 outside the state. The destination of 64 of these trips was more than 500 miles from Midwest.

Residents of Midwest who regularly commute to other towns to work number 18; 20 work in the immediately surrounding rural region as farmers, road workers, or rural teachers; and 17 work in and out of Midwest as truck drivers, salesmen, and government officials. In all, 55 Midwest adults (10 per cent) are gainfully employed wholly or partly outside the limits of the town.

Twenty-three Midwest citizens served in foreign theaters during World War II and returned to live in Midwest. In addition, 12 postwar immigrants to Midwest had foreign military service. No Midwest resident has visited a foreign country in a civilian capacity in recent years.

NEW RESIDENTS IMMIGRATE TO MIDWEST AND MIDWEST RESIDENTS EMIGRATE TO OTHER COMMUNITIES

In the year November 1, 1949 to October 31, 1950, 102 new residents settled in Midwest; i.e., on October 31, 1950, 14 per cent of the residents of Midwest had migrated to the town during the preceding year.

In the same year, 103 Midwest residents moved away from the town; i.e., of the residents of Midwest on November 1, 1949, 14 per cent had moved away by October 31, 1950.

The rate of flow of residents through Midwest, approximately 14 per cent per year, would appear to be a vital factor in keeping Midwest in touch with American life.

REGULAR CHANNELS OF COMMUNICATION BRING MESSAGES TO MIDWEST

A daily newspaper is taken by 95 per cent of the families of Midwest, and 45 per cent receive a morning and an evening paper. Radios are owned by 99 per cent of the families. In November, 1950, there were 12 television sets; at this time, television had been available to the area for 9 months. By May, 1953, there were 54 television sets in the town. The Midwest Theater shows a film every night; 150 different pictures are exhibited during the year.

REGULAR CHANNELS OF COMMUNICATION CARRY MESSAGES FROM MIDWEST

The *Midwest Weekly* circulates to 275 subscribers outside of Midwest County each week. This news of Midwest goes to 24 states and 6 foreign countries. Midwest citizens make approximately 75 long distance telephone calls each day. The post office does about $11,000 worth of business annually in stamps and money order fees, approximately $10 per year per person in Midwest's trade area.

In view of the absence of any commercial establishments engaging in a great amount of business by mail, this indicates a considerable amount of correspondence by individuals with the outside world.

MIDWEST RECEIVES MANUFACTURED GOODS FROM THE OUTSIDE

Virtually no tools, machines, clothing, building materials, or processed foods are produced in Midwest. Its two manufacturing establishments—a window and door assembly plant and a print shop—usually employ 10 full-time persons. In addition, a blind resident weaves rag rugs by hand for commercial sale. For the physical equipment of modern life, Midwest is dependent upon other communities. If transportation of goods into the town were to be interrupted for more than a week, the behavior of Midwest residents would rapidly change to a more primitive pattern: walking would replace riding in automobiles; home processing of foods would replace opening cans and packages; word-of-mouth rumors would take the place of the *Midwest Weekly*; local herbs, hot packs, minor surgery, and diet would take the place of vaccination, antibiotics, major surgery, and vitamins in medical practice. Only with respect to garden products, meat animals, and grains from plots within the town and from the immediately bordering fields would Midwest be even partly self-sufficient.

MIDWEST'S MATERIAL AND INDUSTRIAL CONTRIBUTION TO AMERICA IS
    ALMOST NIL

Farm products are hauled directly to city markets; Midwest is not a substation in the route from farm to market.   Midwest's exports consist largely of men, ideas, and services.   It supplies governmental and legal service to Midwest County, and it provides educational, religious, social, recreational, distributive, and repair facilities for the surrounding rural area.   In the last two capacities Midwest serves as a depot from which the farmers secure the behavior objects of American culture, and as a repair shop for farm and household machinery.

MIDWEST EXPORTS PEOPLE

Midwest's greatest export is men.   Of 813 graduates of Midwest High School for the years 1889 through 1942, 100 or 12 per cent of them settled permanently in the area served by the school district.   The place of residence in 1953 of the 32 members of the class of 1928 was as follows:

Midwest school district	5
Midwest County	3
Midwest State or nearest bordering state	15
Other states	6
Foreign	1
Deceased	2

In other words, 25 per cent of this graduating class stayed at home; the remainder were exported to Midwest State, the U.S.A., and the world.

A summary of these data on the geographical position of Midwest, the visitors to and from the town, the channels of communication, the importing of goods, and the exporting of men indicate that Midwest is in vital connection with American life.   It is not an American backwater.   This connection is symptomized by traffic flow studies (70) on the four highways which radiate from the town.   These studies show that approximately 3700 vehicles pass control points on these highways in an average 24 hour period. In truth, the currents of American life flow strongly through Midwest.

Midwest's Independence of American Culture

Although Midwest has a vital connection with American life, it is also separated from American society.   It is to an important degree an independent, segregated social unit.   Modern life can be, and is, lived with a high degree of completeness within the borders of the town.   Midwest is the center of the life of its citizens.   Upon its stages are played most of the acts in the dramas of Midwest lives.   Midwest is not the satellite of any other community; it is not in the wings of a larger stage; it is not a specialized, subordinate department of a larger enterprise.

Evidence of this is found in the extent to which people of Midwest lead their lives within the borders of the town. The following tabulation shows how much of the various kinds of behavior in which Midwest citizens engage occurs within the town. These estimates refer to the per cent of the total time Midwesterners spend in these activities. The methods of making these estimates are discussed in Chapter III.

Kinds of Behavior	Per Cent of Different Kinds of Behavior of Midwest Residents Occurring Within the Town
Grade- and high-school attendance	100
Dental care	98
Club and lodge attendance	95
Church attendance	93
Vocational activities	90
Marriage of women	90
Funerals	90
Purchasing of processed and manufactured goods	85
Attendance at athletic contests	50
Medical care	40
Births	5
College attendance	0

One kind of behavior which frequently occurs outside the borders of Midwest is the securing of specialized medical care and hospitalization, including obstetrical care in childbirth. Midwest has no hospital and only nonspecialized medical service is available. A considerable amount of recreation also occurs outside of the town; this is largely made up of scheduled out-of-town football, basketball, and baseball games by school and amateur club teams. However, it includes trips to the cities to theaters, restaurants, skating rinks, etc. Aside from these activities, most of the behavior of Midwest citizens takes place within the town.

Data on the per cent of time Midwest residents spend within the limits of the town are given below for age and sex groups:

Population Group	Per Cent of Total Time Spent in Town
Infant	98.0
Preschool	98.0
Younger school	98.5
Older school	97.5
Adolescent	96.0
Adult:	
Males	91.8
Females	97.5
Aged	97.5

The index of community living or average per cent of time spent in town by Midwest residents stands at 95.

MIDWEST HAS THE FACILITIES FOR MANY KINDS OF BEHAVIOR

We have compared the kinds of behavior facilities available in Midwest with those listed in the classified telephone directory of a city one thousand times as large. If manufacturing and wholesale facilities are omitted, Midwest provides about 80 per cent of the kinds of behavior facilities available in a metropolis. Our sample covered 14 per cent of the nonmanufacturing, nonwholesale establishments listed in the city directory. In this sample, the following behavior facilities, available in the city, were absent from Midwest: airport; elevator, sales and service; fur dealer, sales and repair; liquor store; bath and massage; portrait photographer; pawn broker; furniture storage; telephone message bureau; employment agency. Some behavior settings which were lacking in Midwest are, in fact, not appropriate to a small town. The telephone operators regularly carry out some of the functions of a telephone message service and, for example, keep the town informed on the whereabouts of the doctor. The employment opportunities within the town can be canvassed by anyone in a few hours.

It appears that American cities differ from towns like Midwest by providing many duplications of the behavior facilities which are found in the small places, and by providing more complete and more specialized services within each kind of facility. It was possible in 1950 to live a relatively "modern" life within the borders of the town. A city dweller could maintain himself in Midwest, if he wished, according to most metropolitan standards of living. The fact that the behavior supports required for modern living can be provided in a small, segregated community is an impressive example of twentieth century technology; it makes it possible for community autonomy to be maintained without marked cultural differentiation.

The People of Midwest

Data describing the people of Midwest are presented in the following paragraphs.

POPULATION

In November, 1950, 707 persons lived in Midwest. This number does not include 26 individuals who maintained official residence in the town but who actually lived elsewhere, such as college students and members of the armed forces, and it does not include the Field Station staff and their families who totaled 17 persons. The number of residents in the town differed from day to day; on seven bi-annual enumerations beginning in November, 1949, the population varied from 707 to 750. Assessor's and census reports showed that for a period of 40 years the size of Midwest had fluctuated between 600 and 800.

The age distribution of Midwest citizens in terms of the age subgroups used in this study are given in the tabulation below. The adolescent subgroup in this tabulation includes persons between 18 and 21 who were financially dependent upon their parents, in addition to those in the age range cited; in 1950 this numbered 1 individual. This person was not included in the adult category. In the subsequent discussion, the term *child* will refer to persons under 12 years; *adolescent* will refer to those 12 to 18 years, with the limitation noted above; *adult* will refer to persons 18 to 65, with the exception noted; and *aged* will refer to individuals 65 and older.

| | *Number of Persons* | |
	Males	*Females*
Infants (birth to 1 year, 11 months)	15	10
Preschool (2 years to 5 years, 11 months)	18	12
Younger School (6 years to 8 years, 11 months)	14	15
Older School (9 years to 11 years, 11 months)	14	21
Adolescents (12 years to 17 years, 11 months)	25	25
Adults (18 years to 64 years, 11 months)	172	204
Aged (65 years and over)	82	80
Total	340	367

A larger proportion of Midwesterners are in the older ages than is true for the country as a whole; residents 45 years old or older are 20 per cent more numerous in Midwest than the 1950 national census reports for the United States. Males constitute 48 per cent of the population. The excess of males over females in the aged group is due in some degree to the fact that there is in Midwest a boarding home for old men, but no similar institution for women.

STABILITY OF RESIDENCE

Although Midwest's total population is relatively stable, the stability of particular citizens is not so constant. This is illustrated by data for the year November 1, 1949 to October 31, 1950. During this time 596 persons resided continuously in the town, 109 residents left through emigration or death, and 111 persons came to live in Midwest through birth or immigration. In other words, there was a flow of citizens through Midwest during this 12 month interval equivalent to approximately 16 per cent of its population; 826 different people resided in the town at some time during this period. Reports of city officials and inspection of the assessor's rolls indicated that this rate of population turnover had been relatively constant for a number of years.

Midwest, however, has a core of permanent citizens who participate to a very limited degree in the population exchange with the outside world. In an analysis of Midwest adults, in 1950, the length of time citizens had lived in town was: more than 17 years, 42 per cent; 7 to 17 years, 21 per cent;

less than 7 years, 37 per cent.   There is both stability and change in Midwest's population.

FAMILY RELATIONSHIPS

The people of Midwest live in 295 family units with the following structural characteristics (the head or heads of the family are the reference points in each case and are named first):

Family Structure	Per Cent of 295 Families
Male, single	10.8
Female, single	15.2
Husband and wife	29.5
Husband, wife, and child*	28.5
Husband, wife, child, and parent	1.7
Husband, wife, child, and grandchild	1.0
Husband, wife, child, and sibling	0.7
Husband, wife, and parent	0.7
Husband, wife, and grandchild	1.7
Husband, wife, and sibling	0.3
Father and child	1.0
Mother and child	3.7
Mother, child, and grandchild	0.3
Mother, child, and child's spouse	0.3
Mother, child, child's spouse, and grandchild	0.3
Daughter and mother	0.3
Sisters	1.0
Sister, brother, and mother	0.3
Brother and sister	1.4
Niece and aunt	0.3
Unrelated women	1.0

* In the tabulation, "child" signifies relationship to the head of the family, not age.

Single persons comprise 26 per cent of Midwest's family units; 30 per cent are made up of husband and wife without children; 28 per cent consist of husband, wife, and children; and 16 per cent are extended or atypical families.   The size of Midwest family units varies from 1 to 13, and averages 2.5.   Ninety family units (30 per cent) contain children and adolescents, the number varying from 1 to 10, and averaging 1.7.   Children are found in 77 families (26 per cent), the average number of children being 1.6.

Few Midwesterners are without family ties in the town; 80 per cent have one or more of the following relatives living within the town's borders: parent, grandparent, sibling, aunt, uncle, first cousin, child, grandchild, niece, nephew; 23 per cent have five or more such relatives.   When spouses are included, 96 per cent of the citizens have family members living within the 40 city blocks of the town.   The people are, in truth, at home in Midwest.

FINANCIAL STATE

Midwest families are supported financially by the following persons:

	Per Cent of Families
Male head only	42.4
Female head only	14.9
Male and female heads jointly	25.1
Male and/or female head and children jointly	10.2
Welfare and other*	7.8

* Other refers to family units where the members were financially independent of each other as "unrelated women."

The male head is the chief financial support of Midwest families, being the sole support of 42 per cent and a contributing supporter of 75 per cent of them. However, in 17 per cent of the families the female supports the family either alone or with the help of her children, and she makes a direct financial contribution by means of outside work to the support of 45 per cent of them. In 10 per cent of the family units, husband and wife jointly operate the family business. These data include family units consisting of single men and single women.

The chief sources of the incomes of Midwest adults are as follows:

	Per Cent of 538 Adults
Locally owned business (owners and employees)	41.4
Branch business in Midwest (employees)	2.8
Nearby farms (owners, renters, employees)	4.0
State government (employees)	0.7
City government (employees)	2.0
County government (employees)	7.4
Federal government (employees)	2.8
Business in other communities or over an area wider than Midwest County	3.0
Pensions (private, state, federal)	3.5
Welfare (county, state, federal)	6.0
Not gainfully employed	24.9

It is clear from these data that Midwest is a community where most of the enterprises are local. Of all employed adults, i.e., those covered in the first eight of the above categories, 74 per cent are connected with business or governmental units which are managed and financed within the town, and 85 per cent are employed in organizations which are managed and controlled within the county. In addition, an unknown proportion of the remainder, including those receiving pensions and those on welfare, receive their incomes from social units that are to some degree financed and controlled within the county.

Precise data are not available on the wealth of Midwest citizens. However, the town is known as only a fair business town by persons who have business contacts with similar communities in the central part of the United States. There is general agreement that less money is available in Midwest than in many towns of similar size. There are no wealthy families and no highly paid trades in the town. The economic position of the people is a reflection of the agriculture of Midwest County upon which their wealth depends almost completely. In this connection, then, a brief description of the agriculture of the county is relevant.

Midwest is situated almost in the center of Midwest County, a roughly square area of 351,560 acres. In 1950, 94 per cent of this land area was in 1,725 farms; the remainder comprised such areas as the townsites, roadways, and cemeteries of the county. The soil of the County is classified by the experts (**68**) of the Midwest County Soil Conservation District into the following classes:

Class	Description	Per Cent of Land Area
I	Very good farm land that can be cultivated safely with ordinary farm methods. It is nearly level and easily worked.	11
II	Good land that can be cultivated safely with contouring, protective cover crops, and simple water management.	5
III	Moderately good land that can be cultivated safely with such intensive treatments as terracing and strip cropping. Common requirements are crop rotation, cover crops, and fertilizer.	44
IV	Fairly good land that is best suited to pasture and hay but can be cultivated occasionally—usually not more than one year in six.	15
V	None.	
VI	Suited to grazing and foresting with minor limitations; needs protective measures.	5
VII	Suited for grazing or foresting with major limitations; needs extreme care to prevent erosion.	18

Midwest County farmers had 51 per cent of this land in crops, 30 per cent in grass, and 13 per cent in woodland in 1950. The main crops and the per cent of the land area in each were: corn, 16 per cent; wheat, 11 per cent; hay, 8 per cent; oats, 6 per cent.

Midwest County's reputation as a moderately good agricultural county agrees very closely with the experts' description of its soil. This is reflected in its 1950 crops which were a little better than average. In this year, the county produced per acre 34.6 bushels of corn, 18.5 bushels of wheat, and 27.1 bushels of oats. The county's agricultural produce was valued at $12,100,000. The contribution of crops to this total was $5,600,000; of meat animals, $4,200,000; of milk, $1,600,000; and of poultry, $700,000 (**67**).

In 1950, the per family income was $2,186 in rural nonfarm areas of the United States; for Midwest County the comparable figure was $1,490 (69). All the evidence is in accord with the judgment of informed laymen that Midwest in 1950 was below the average of rural county seat towns in wealth.

It is probable, however, that most individual residents of Midwest are better off economically than the town is as a whole. This is judged to be the case because Midwest's limited income is more evenly distributed among its citizens than is the case in some communities. The two or three most prosperous families in town live on scales indicative of incomes of $8,000–$10,000 a year. At the lower end of the distribution, one family consisting of husband, wife, and grandchild had a gross income of $1,100 in 1950. In this year, there were no able-bodied persons on the public assistance rolls; all welfare clients in the town were aged or physically disabled persons.

It is probable, too, that the real income of many Midwest families is greater than their cash income indicates because of the relatively low cost of some things in Midwest, the great amount of home growing and preserving of food, and the time, skill, and tools many Midwesterners have for home repairs and improvements that require a cash expenditure in many communities. In 1950 the low income family mentioned above was purchasing by installment payments a piano and an electric refrigerator.

Professor J. Murray Luck (39) has reported the cost of food for a week's liberal diet for an adult man engaged in moderate physical activity. In 1953 the cost of these foods in Palo Alto, California, was $6.65. In the stores of Midwest they cost $5.89 in 1953. However, many Midwest families achieved a diet similar to Professor Luck's liberal diet for less than the $5.89 cash outlay it cost in the stores of the town. One family of 5, fairly representative of the 60 per cent of Midwest families which raise a garden, had a year's cash income of approximately $3,600 in 1953. At the store, this amounted to 611 LDU's (Liberal Diet Units) per year. Actually, however, the cash cost of a LDU to this family was only $4.80 since practically all their canned vegetables were produced in the family garden with almost no cash investment, and canned products were substituted for about half of the fresh vegetables and fruit, e.g., canned tomatoes for fresh oranges. Thus, this family's income amounted to 750 LDU's. It is estimated that this occurred in the case of about half of the Midwest family units. We judge, too, that these same conditions operated for some of the other items which enter into the cost of living, notably housing and clothing.

This picture of a thrifty people who despite a lower than average cash income are able to live in most respects according to modern living standards is supported by some of the data which follow.

HOUSING

In 1950, 90 per cent of Midwest families lived in houses more than 25 years old and 96 per cent lived in houses more than 10 years old. In general,

Midwest houses are not well constructed, but they are, nonetheless, long lasting.   Perhaps this is because they are progressively remodeled, in many cases by the family members themselves.   Roofing, plastering, plumbing, flooring, painting, and papering, often one room at a time, are always in progress in some of the houses of the town.   Midwest gives the impression that reconstruction is continuously going on.   In consequence, the most modern construction, decoration, furniture, and appliances are frequently seen in company with their late nineteenth and early twentieth century counterparts in the same house or in the same room.

Wood construction is the basis for 95 per cent of Midwest dwellings; 90 per cent are painted white, and 8 per cent are light buff or gray.   This uniform material and color gives an impression of homogeneity to the town despite considerable variation in the size and design of the houses.

The 269 dwellings are distributed in a fairly even way over the approximately 40, 2.5 acre blocks of that part of the townsite which has been developed.   Dwellings have on the average about 0.25 acres of surrounding land, and the yards of 85 houses on the periphery of the town border upon farm fields.   Only 37 dwellings are on lots smaller than 75 by 150 feet. Sixty-seven per cent of the dwelling units have outbuildings.   The land area of Midwest has an important economic function; 60 per cent of the families raise vegetable gardens, and 30 per cent have livestock or poultry.   Fifty-one per cent of Midwest families have pets.

In 90 per cent of the dwellings a single family is housed, and 68.8 per cent of the dwellings are owned by the family which lives in them, as opposed to 55 per cent for the nation as a whole (71).

Except for electric lights and electric equipment, Midwest dwellings have modern conveniences less frequently than the nation's dwellings as reported in the national census for 1950 (71).   Specifically, a smaller per cent of Midwest's dwellings have central heat (28.1 per cent vs. 50.4 per cent), running water (73.4 per cent vs. 85.2 per cent), and inside toilets (62.7 per cent vs. 75.5 per cent).   On the other hand, Midwest dwelling units are less crowded than the national average, having 2.4 instead of 3.4 persons per unit.

The housing of Midwest is relatively uncongested and spacious both indoors and out.   Though little of it is new, modernization progresses continuously.

TRANSPORTATION FACILITIES

Although the greatest distance between residences within the borders of the town is 1.4 miles, it is customary for Midwest residents to ride in their automobiles on both pleasure and business even if the trip is only two or three blocks.   Passenger cars are owned by 60 per cent of the families in Midwest, and 63 per cent own a car or a truck; 13 per cent have 2 or more motor vehicles.   In addition, there are 36 cars and trucks owned by business concerns.   In all, there are 250 cars and trucks in Midwest, or one for every 2.8 persons.   Forty-two per cent of the passenger cars are not over five years old.   Other vehicles found are: horse and wagon, 5 families; bicycles, 45 families; motorcycles, 3 families.   Convenient transportation is highly prized by Midwesterners.

VOCATIONS

The vocational activities of Midwesterners will be considered in other contexts.   However, it should be said here that in line with the general occupational richness of the town already mentioned, the vocational activities of many Midwesterners are so varied that it is often impossible to identify a single one as predominant for a particular person.   Thus, Mr. Trench regularly carried out 14 of the occupational activities described in the Dictionary of Occupational Titles (**66**).   These included:

1. Plumber	8. Furnace installer and repairman
2. Electrician	9. Sheet metal maintenance
3. Electrical appliance serviceman	10. Sheet metal furnace repair
4. Sewage and waterworks foreman	11. Public address serviceman
5. Gas engine repairman	12. Fire marshal
6. Water meter installer	13. Sales person
7. Water meter repairman	14. Bookkeeper, general

As consequence of this fact it is impossible to present meaningful frequency data on the vocations of Midwest citizens.

RELIGION

There are three churches in Midwest: Methodist, Presbyterian, and African Methodist Episcopal.   These churches include 75 per cent of all Midwest citizens as members or as regular attendants; 7 per cent attend churches in other communities.   Among the latter are 6 Roman Catholics, 14 members of the Church of Jesus Christ of Latter-day Saints, and 31 Protestants of various denominations.

The church affiliations of Midwesterners have been given on pages 20–21. While the limited number of churches reflects a basic uniformity of religious belief, it also imposes the appearance of greater uniformity than exists.   If Midwesterners were transported to a community with a greater variety of churches, they would undoubtedly display much greater diversity of church affiliation.   Efforts are occasionally made by dissidents in the established churches to found new ones, but in recent years these efforts have not been successful.   It will be noted in Chapter IV, where data for the year 1951/52 are presented, that a fourth church functioned in Midwest for most of this year; it was soon abandoned, however.

The data on church affiliation provide little indication of church attendance.   Enumerations showed that the following per cents of Midwest citizens attended some religious services on alternate Sundays or more frequently: male adults, 25; female adults, 45; children, 60. On a normal Sunday, approximately 280 (40 per cent) of Midwest residents attended a religious service.

EDUCATION

Detailed data on the education of Midwesterners are not available. However, the general educational level is clearly indicated. For 25 years, most Midwest children have completed the four-year high-school course. This standard is general in Midwest state, and it means that most of the adult citizens under 45 years of age have at least a high-school education. Four years of college have been completed by 8.2 per cent of Midwest adults and 2.0 per cent have specialized training beyond the A.B. degree. The number of Midwesterners who have some college education or specialized training of college level in such fields as teaching, agriculture, pharmacy, and dentistry is not known precisely, but totals more than 12 per cent of the adult population. This means that at least 20 per cent of all Midwest adults have educational experiences beyond the secondary school level.

SOCIAL CLASS IN MIDWEST

Among the white residents of Midwest there are three social classes, as these have been defined by Warner (58) in terms of participation. We shall call these Social Group I, II, and III; they correspond fairly closely to Warner's Upper Middle, Lower Middle, and Upper Lower Classes. The identification of these population categories in Midwest is based upon the reconciled judgments of three resident staff members who used Warner's criteria. These judgments were checked independently with the Index of Status Characteristics (58) on a sample of 71 white families. The two methods agreed upon the placement of 87 per cent of the families. When the disagreements were carefully scrutinized, the class assignment on the basis of participation appeared to be justified in every case; hence the original staff judgments are used.

The number of persons in each group in Midwest is: Group I, 80; Group II, 246; Group III, 354. Members of a Group IV can sometimes be identified in Midwest. These are almost always people who establish residence in the town for only a brief time. In 1950 there were 11 questionable Group IV residents. However, they were clearly not equivalent to Warner's Lower Lower Class and they corresponded in many ways with Group III. We have considered these people a transitional category between Group III and a potential Group IV; in the analyses we have placed them in Group III.

Some features of social stratification in Midwest will be discussed in detail in connection with the analysis of the behavior data. Here it should be mentioned, however, that social class might be expected to have somewhat different significance in Midwest than in Yankee City or Jonesville because of the absence of the upper and the lowest classes, because the family origins of most residents are well known, and because the population is small in comparison with the town's relatively high level of technology and social organization.   Social class is a reality in Midwest, but it is a different reality than in some other communities where it has been studied.

CASTE IN MIDWEST

The 27 Negro residents of Midwest are a remnant of a much larger group which settled in the town during and after the Civil War.   In 1950, 56 per cent of the Negroes were over 65 years old; there were 1 infant, 1 younger school child, 2 older school children, 3 adolescents, and 5 adults. Class divisions are discernible among Midwest's Negroes, but the group is so small that caste influences overshadow those of class.   Data on the pattern of Negro participation in Midwest are given in Chapter IV.

The Children of Midwest

The focus of our attention has been upon the children of the town.   We have taken as our target group all residents of Midwest under 12 years of age.   In this section we shall present general information about this special subgroup of Midwest's population.

There were in 1950, 119 children in Midwest.   Their age, sex, class, and caste distributions are given in Table 2.1.

TABLE 2.1

THE AGE, SEX, GROUP, AND CASTE OF MIDWEST
CHILDREN UNDER 12 YEARS

AGE GROUP	MALE				FEMALE			
	Group and Caste				Group and Caste			
	I	II	III	NE.	I	II	III	NE.
Infant	1	4	10	0	1	2	6	1
Preschool	1	10	7	0	1	3	8	0
Younger school	1	3	10	0	2	6	6	1
Older School	3	5	6	0	3	12	4	2

Totals

Infant	25	Male	61	Group I	13
Preschool	30	Female	58	Group II	45
Younger School	29			Group III	57
Older School	35			White	115
				Negro	4

These 119 children lived in 77 different families.   In some cases older children were not living at home; these children are not included in the following data. "Only" children made up 30 per cent of the total, 27 per cent had 1 sibling living at home, 21 per cent had 2 siblings at home, 15 per cent had 3 siblings, 2 per cent had 4 siblings, and 5 per cent had 10 siblings living at home. "Natural" families, consisting of a father, mother, and child or children without other family members included 81 per cent of the Midwest children; 10 per cent lived in "broken" families where the father or both parents were not present; 12 per cent lived in families with grandparents; and 13 per cent lived in families with grandparents and/or adult family members other than parents. Ten per cent of these children lived in families where the parents were divorced. The total number of persons in all families with children varied from 2 to 13, and averaged 4.2.

The financial status of 6 per cent of the families was judged to be well above the average of Midwest families, 75 per cent were judged to be in the middle ranges, and 17 per cent were judged to be in the lower income groups. No families with children received public assistance in 1950. The income was provided by the male head exclusively in 52 per cent of the families, by the female head in 4 per cent (in all of these cases some assistance from the divorced father was received), by the male and female head jointly in 27 per cent, by the male and female heads and children in 6.5 per cent, by the male head and children in 8 per cent, and by the male or female head and son-in-law in 2.5 per cent of the families. The male head contributed to the family support of all but one of these families (in three cases via alimony), the female head made a financial contribution to 39 per cent, young adult children living at home contributed to 8 per cent, adolescent children contributed to 22 per cent, and children under 12 contributed to the finances of 8 per cent of these families.

The houses of 86 per cent of these children's families were single-family dwellings, and 61 per cent of the families owned their homes. All houses had electricity, 23 per cent had central heat, 80 per cent had running water, and 65 per cent had inside toilets. Vegetable gardens were regularly raised by 70 per cent of the families, 39 per cent raised chickens or livestock, and 78 per cent had pets.

Passenger cars were owned by 82 per cent of the children's families and 22 per cent had a second car or truck in addition. In 46 per cent of the families there were one or more bicycles.

Church was attended regularly by the male head of 31 per cent of the families, by the female head of 43 per cent of the families, and by the children of 64 per cent of the families.

Children Selected for Special Study

Day-long specimen records were secured upon 12 children. Data on the age, sex, and social group of these children are given in Table 2.2. It will be noted that these subjects represent all age, group, and sex categories of

Midwest children. Day-long specimen records were not secured upon Negro children.

In view of the extensive use that is made of these 12 subjects, a brief sketch of each child and his family situation is given in Appendix 1. In addition to defining more precisely the children selected for special study, the sketches will provide, too, a more concrete account of typical family situations than the general, statistical data have been able to provide.

TABLE 2.2

MIDWEST CHILDREN SELECTED FOR SPECIAL STUDY

	Sex	Age	Age Classification	Grade in School	Group
Mary Chaco	F	1-10	Infant	–	II
Jimmy Sexton	M	1-11	Infant	–	II
Lewis Hope	M	2-11	Preschool	–	II
Dutton Thurston	M	3-10	Preschool	–	III
Margaret Reid	F	4-6	Preschool	–	III
Maud Pintner	F	5-0	Preschool	–	I
Roy Eddy	M	6-2	Younger school	1	III
Ben Hutchings	M	7-4	Younger school	2	I
Raymond Birch	M	7-4	Younger school	2	II
Mary Ennis	F	8-7	Younger school	3	II
Douglas Crawford	M	9-2	Younger school	3	III
Claire Graves	F	10-9	Older school	5	III

Children with Physical Disabilities: A Comparative Group

The Lawton School is a privately endowed institution for crippled children. In 1950, 12 children were resident students and 12 were day students. A big old home housed the school. The downstairs area was used for classrooms, occupational therapy, physical therapy, dining and living rooms; the bedrooms, bathrooms, and sleeping rooms for the resident staff and children were upstairs. A spacious yard provided outdoor play space.

The children varied from 6 to 15 years in age. Their disabilities varied; the only criteria for admission were that the disability be too great for the child to attend public schools and that in the judgment of the staff, the child be teachable. Although the entire school entered into the settings survey, specimen records were made only on the 7 younger children who were six and seven years old. Of these children, 4 were cerebral palsied, 1 had a serious congenital heart defect, one suffered from amyotonia, and 1 from *spina bifida*.

The atmosphere of the Lawton School was informal and homelike. In addition to regular school work, specialized treatment was given in speech and in physical and occupational therapy.

Information about the disabled children upon whom day records were secured is provided in Table 2.3, and in the brief sketches presented in Appendix 2.

TABLE 2.3

PHYSICALLY DISABLED CHILDREN

Name	Sex	Age	Age Classification	Disability
Wally Wolfson	M	4-3	Preschool	Post polio
Sue Dewall	F	7-1	Younger School	Cerebral palsy
Bobby Bryant	M	7-4	Younger School	Congenital heart defect
Verne Trennell	M	7-5	Younger School	*Spina bifida*

In this chapter we have sought to provide the reader with a general impression of Midwest and its people, and of the Lawton School for Crippled Children. These are some of the geographic, demographic, and cultural aspects of the communities in which our studies in psychological ecology were made.

Chapter III

The Behavior Setting Survey: Methods

MIDWEST has a limitless number of parts. These include such varied features of the town as the weather vane on the Courthouse, the town constable, the upper social class, Delaware Street, the Methodist Church, the Old Settlers' Picnic, auctions, the Negro residents, the Culver family, the Stop-for-Pedestrians signs, weddings, the volunteer fire department, a school tax of 9 mills, May Day, the North precinct, Mrs. Arla Grainger, a bonded indebtedness of $8,500, the *Midwest Weekly*, and the prevailing southwest wind. Early in this investigation we were faced with the problem of selecting from this endless list of discriminable parts of the town those which were relevant to our efforts to describe the living conditions and behavior of Midwest children. This was, of course, an impossible task; indeed, the final and unmistakable identification of these relevant community units will be the end product of this and other investigations. Nevertheless, it was necessary at an early stage of the research to divide the town into manageable parts. Such an arbitrary selection of a working unit is an essential step in every exploratory investigation. It amounts to making a crude hypothesis regarding the fundamental nature of the material with which one is dealing, an hypothesis which is verified or disproved by the outcome of the research.

The influences which led us to select behavior settings[1] as one of the units of this investigation have been described in Chapter I. Here, we shall review and expand the definition of behavior settings before turning to a description of the methods of the behavior setting survey.

The Definition and General Characteristics of Behavior Settings

A behavior setting has been defined as a standing pattern of behavior and a part of the milieu which are synomorphic and in which the milieu is circumjacent to the behavior. The essential terms of this definition can be elaborated as follows.

STANDING PATTERN OF BEHAVIOR

Many units of behavior have been identified: reflex, actone, action, molar unit, group action are some of these. These terms identify discriminable parts of behavior phenomena. A standing pattern of behavior is another

---

[1] The extensive work of William A. Koppe in connection with his doctoral thesis (**30**) is one of the bases of Chapters III and IV.

45

such unit. It is a discriminable pattern in the behavior of men (or animals) en masse that is independent of the particular individuals involved, and that is apprehended without instruments or indirect analysis. Examples are the rush hour in a city, a flight of ducks, a basketball game.

Little can be said in a systematic way about either the appearance or the conceptual nature of these supra-individual behavior phenomena. About all we can do at the present time is to point them out. The data we have to work with are the reliable discriminations of scientists and laymen. One characteristic of these behavioral "things" is quite clear, however; they are bounded perceptual units. They are not characteristics of Midwesterners' behavior in general, as is Midwestern speech or the Midwestern economic system. The locus and the limits of a standing pattern of behavior are clear. A ball game, a church service, or a music lesson has a delimited position; it is a perceptually segregated unit of extra-individual behavior.

SYNOMORPHIC RELATION

The adjective synomorphic means, of similar structure (shape, form) and it describes an essential feature of a behavior setting. The structure of the behavior pattern and the structure of the milieu of a behavior setting are seen to be congruent, to fit, to be synomorphic. The criterion of this synomorphism is perceptual; it is directly seen. Synomorphism undoubtedly has multiple stimulus conditions; however, one frequent condition is congruence between the boundary of the behavior and the boundary of the milieu. Thus, the boundary of a football field is also the boundary of the game; the beginning and the end of the school music period marks the limits of the pattern of music behavior. Other factors bearing upon the synomorphy of behavior and milieu in behavior settings are discussed later in this chapter (see pp. 54–57).

MILIEU

The nonpsychological context or milieu side of a behavior setting can consist of any discriminable constellation of physical-temporal parts of the community. Both "natural" parts of the town, such as hills, storms, and July 4, and parts that are the products of behavior such as buildings, streets, and baseball diamonds can comprise the milieu. Often the milieu is an intricate complex of various temporal and physical discriminanda. Thus the milieu of Cub Scout Den Meeting is a constellation of a particular room in a particular residence at a particular time with particular behavior objects distributed in a particular pattern.

Sometimes an essential part of the milieu involved in a behavior setting is carried around by the person. There are a number of mobile behavior settings in Midwest. The behavior setting Grand Union Tea Company Route, for example, consists of a delivery truck containing teas, coffee, spices, etc., with a driver salesman. In this case one enters the setting

Grand Union Tea Company Route by going to the truck or having the salesman bring his basket of products into the house. In other cases, only a symbol of the milieu is carried about by the occupant of the setting in the form of a uniform, a badge, or other paraphernalia. In all cases the significance of these symbols is clear; they mean, "This is behavior setting X (Scoutmaster, Bakery Delivery Man, Gas Company Representative, Doctor, Preacher) in which you will find the appropriate pattern of behavior occurring." Almost all mobile settings have a home base with circumjacent milieu, e.g., Parsonage, Doctor's Office.

In all cases the nonpsychological milieu of a setting exists independently of the standing pattern of behavior associated with it. When the behavior setting 4-H Club Meeting is not in session, its paraphernalia, its constitution, its minute book, its roll of members are in independent existence. If the club should disband and the setting 4-H Club Meeting cease to occur, its milieu parts would continue to exist.

CIRCUMJACENCY OF MILIEU TO BEHAVIOR

The milieu aspect of a behavior setting is seen as circumjacent to the standing pattern of behavior. Two conditions under which this perception tends to occur are: (a) when the temporal or physical boundaries of the milieu actually surround the behavior pattern as in the case of a store or a holiday, and (b) when the behavior pattern is distributed among spatially separated parts of the milieu as in the case of a paper route or a game of hide-and-seek.

There are borderline cases where the phenomenal distinction between behavior settings (milieu circumjacent to behavior) and behavior objects (behavior circumjacent to milieu) is not clear. This is the case with a chair or an automobile, for example, and with some of the mobile settings and those that involve a symbolic milieu which have been mentioned above. In our research we have handled these few cases in an arbitrary way and have assigned each of them consistently to one or the other category. Furthermore, almost all behavior settings are on some occasions perceived as behavior objects, and many behavior objects are sometimes seen as behavior settings. An example of the former is a church when the building is painted, and of the latter is a packing box when used for a playhouse. These cases have been handled in accordance with their most common phenomenal appearance.

These are the basic, general characteristics of behavior settings. Some of their special features and limiting conditions are discussed in the sections which follow.

We should like to conclude this section by emphasizing again that at the present stage, behavior settings are empirical facts observed by both laymen and scientists. They are analogous to the distinctive shore-wave patterns of particular coasts, or to the channel-current configurations of different parts of a river. The fundamental nature and theoretical significance of behavior settings remain to be determined. In our research a beginning has been made in this direction, although most of our efforts have been devoted to operations for discriminating and describing behavior settings. Implications for their conceptualization are largely implicit in what has been accomplished.

The Nomenclature of Behavior Settings

The nomenclature of behavior settings presents difficulties. While a behavior setting is the total, supra-individual behavior pattern *and* the associated milieu, the common names often refer to only one of these aspects. For example, the behavior setting School Lunch Room, while its name specifies its physical locus, includes also the pattern of the behaving persons within it. The physical school lunch room, per se, without the behavior is not a behavior setting. On the other hand, the name of the setting Presbyterian Sunday-School Exercises stresses the behavior. Actually, this setting is comprised of the integrated action of the congregation, the superintendent, the song leader, and the church auditorium and equipment. Again, the name of the behavior setting County Superintendent of Schools implicates at any particular time a particular person. Actually, this setting is the behavior-milieu complex associated with a number of different individuals over a period of time and certain persisting parts of the community (a suite of offices labeled "County Superintendent of Schools," a certificate of election). The same comments apply to the settings Butcher in Kane's Grocery, Customer of Clifford's Drug Store, and Elder of Presbyterian Church. Each of these refers to an identifiable behavior-milieu complex which is independent of particular individuals. If Mr. Green, the Butcher in Garnett's Grocery, should resign and Mr. Garnett should hire a new man to wear the aprons and use the tools in the appropriate patterns of cutting, weighing, wrapping, and selling meat in the meat market area of Garnett's Grocery, the behavior setting Butcher in Garnett's Grocery would continue undisturbed.

Structural Characteristics of Behavior Settings

Behavior settings have many structural aspects which deserve study. We have been able to consider only a few of these in this investigation.

INCLUSIVENESS HIERARCHIES OF BEHAVIOR SETTINGS

Behavior settings occur in different hierarchical arrangements on the basis of inclusiveness. Thus, the behavior setting Presbyterian Church, includes within it the behavior setting Worship Service, which contains the behavior setting Offering, which includes the behavior setting Deacon. This is represented in Figure 3.1.

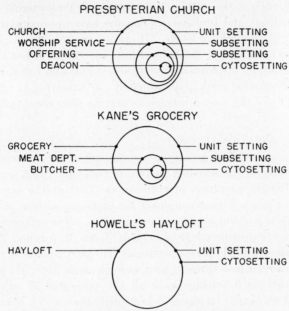

Fig. 3.1—Structural types of behavior settings.

A shorter hierarchical series of behavior settings is found in Kane's Grocery (Figure 3.1), namely, Kane's Grocery, Meat Department, Butcher. On the other hand, some Midwest behavior settings have no included settings; Howell's Hayloft is an example. We have used the following terms to designate the different kinds of behavior settings as they occur on the inclusiveness scale.

1. Unit Setting: A behavior setting which is not a part of another setting. *Examples*: Presbyterian Church, Thanksgiving Day, Kane's Grocery, Howell's Hayloft.

2. Subsetting: A behavior setting which is a part of another behavior setting. *Examples*: Presbyterian Church Worship Service, Thanksgiving Dinner, Meat Department of Kane's Grocery.

3. Cytosetting: A behavior setting which does not include any subsetting within its boundaries. *Examples*: Presbyterian Deacon, Thanksgiving Dinner Desert Course, Butcher in Kane's Grocery, Howell's Hayloft.

The general term, *behavior setting*, or sometimes the single word, *setting*, is used to designate any behavior setting whether unit setting, subsetting, or cytosetting.

DIFFERENTIATION OF BEHAVIOR SETTINGS

A further structural difference in behavior settings is found in the total number of included subsettings without reference to their hierarchical arrangement. Thus, the settings Midwest School, Presbyterian Church, and Midwest Hardware and Implement Company have approximately the same arrangement of hierarchical levels. However, the school is highly differentiated and includes almost 200 subsettings; the church is less highly differentiated, containing approximately 80 subsettings; and the hardware store is least differentiated with approximately 40 subsettings. A commonly accepted index of the size of a behavior setting is its total number of subsettings.

CAPACITY OF BEHAVIOR SETTINGS

Behavior settings differ greatly in the number of persons who simultaneously participate in the standing pattern of behavior. In a setting such as Halloween Parade, hundreds of persons take part at the same time. In others, only a single person can enact the standing pattern of behavior at one time; this is particularly true of cytosettings. The cytosettings Presbyterian Minister, Superintendent of Schools, Town Mayor, and Proprietor of the Pearl Cafe are single person settings. The participants in the standing pattern of behavior pass through, as it were, in single file. We have already mentioned that such settings have all the properties of other behavior settings, and we cannot emphasize too strongly that such a behavior setting as Town Mayor refers only to the behavior-milieu complex which exists when the "office" of mayor is in operation: when the City Council meets, when the mayor represents the city in court, etc. When the mayor mows his lawn, he is not in the behavior setting Town Mayor, but in the setting Home Outdoors. This does not mean that Mr. Dempster as the occupant, on occasion, of the setting Town Mayor does not mow his lawn differently from the way he otherwise would. The way a person is changed when he occupies a behavior setting is another problem. It may be that the concept of role enters here in terms of the person's changed perception of himself after occupying a behavior setting, e.g., after "joining" the Methodist Church, being elected Mayor, entering the first grade.

Dynamic Characteristics of Behavior Settings

Behavior settings have both internal and external dynamic processes. The former coerce behavior within the setting and the latter govern inter-setting relationships. The external dynamics of behavior settings provide a basis for identifying settings of equivalent degrees of unity.

THE EXTERNAL DYNAMICS OF BEHAVIOR SETTINGS: THE K-21 BEHAVIOR
    SETTING UNIT

It is well understood in Midwest that behavior settings are not independent of each other. The members of the Methodist Evening Guild are well aware that the behavior setting Methodist Evening Guild Food Sale should not be arranged for the same day or even for the day following the behavior setting 4-H Club Food Sale; they know that the standing pattern of behavior would be weak and the setting a "failure." It is well known, too, that the behavior setting Boy Scout Pop Stand thrives when it coincides in time with the behavior setting Old Settlers' Reunion. The merchants, preachers, teachers, and organization leaders of Midwest are astute judges of the interrelations of behavior settings. The interdependence of behavior settings is clear, but only a beginning has been made at precise theoretically oriented investigations of their interrelations.

The fact that the behavior settings of Midwest constitute a network of interconnected systems makes it possible to determine settings with the same degree of internal unity. This may be clarified by an analogy. The climate of a country can be described in terms of "climatic areas" and the economy in terms of "economic regions." There are two common ways of defining the extent of such areas and regions: (a) in terms of a defined amount of intra-area variability; e.g., an average annual rainfall differential of two inches might be established as the limit of the territory to be included in the same climatic area; (b) in terms of a defined degree of dynamic interdependence; e.g., a correlation between indices of economic change of .70 might be fixed as the limit of the domain included in the same economic region. We have used the first kind of criterion as a basis for identifying varieties of behavior settings (see pp. 57–58), and the second kind of criterion as a basis for defining behavior setting units for purposes of enumeration and comparative study.

The nature of the interdependence criterion of a unit may be indicated as follows: Lewin (35) has pointed out that in all interdependent systems, whether they involve behavior settings or physiological, physical, or economic systems, a unit can be defined in terms of any degree of interdependence desired. Thus, we might divide the population of Midwest into economic units on the basis of financial interdependence. Such an economic unit can be defined as follows: individuals A, B, C, . . . N make up an economic unit if a change in the economic state of A (or B, or C . . . or N) of x amount is accompanied by a change of Kx in the economic state of B, C . . . N. An interdependence index (K) of .9 would divide the town into many economic units, for only persons as highly interdependent as husband, wife, and minor children would fall into so close an economic unit. An interdependence index of .5 would undoubtedly combine some immediate family units into extended family units, and perhaps some business associates and their families would fall within the same unit; hence the town would have fewer economic units. If the degree of interdependence were placed very low, e.g., .01, the community might turn out to be a single economic unit.

This can be exemplified by the hypothetical case of Mr. Joe Lamprey, and what might happen if he were to inherit an annuity of $500 a month.

Detailed study of the monthly income of a number of people might reveal the following:

	Previous Monthly Income	Subsequent Monthly Income	Per Cent Change
1. Mr. Joe Lamprey	$500	$1000	100
2. Mrs. Joe Lamprey	300	575	92
3. George Lamprey, son	10	20	100
4. Mary Lamprey, daughter	5	15	200
5. Mrs. Ella Lamprey, mother	200	250	25
6. James Hill, business partner	400	424	6
7. Jack Rolf, insurance agent	300	312	4
8. Ten Midwesterners (average)	200	206	3
9. One hundred and fifteen Midwesterners (average)	1500	1500.50	0.3

In terms of an interdependency index (K) of .90, the economic unit with reference to Joe Lamprey contains the first 4 persons of the above list, since an increase of 100 per cent in Joe's income is accompanied by an increase of 90 per cent or more in theirs. If this relationship were mutual for all members of this group of 4, and if this were the average number of persons with an economic interdependency index of .90, there would be 187 such economic units in a total population of 750. An interdependency index of .25 would increase the unit centering about Joe to 5 persons; and again if this were general, it would reduce the number of economic units to 150. An interdependency index of .03 would, according to the data of the tabulation, include 17 in Joe's economic unit, making 44 such units in the town. With an index of .003 there would be only 6 economic units in the community.

The same principles of interdependence can be used to define such diverse community units as friendship groups, ground water or air pollution units, information units, and behavior setting units. In every case, the unit can be made larger or smaller by varying the degree of interdependence by which the unit is defined. The practical feasibility of determining these units depends upon the formulation of criteria of interdependence and upon the development of techniques for their measurement.

By means of indices of interdependence to be presented later, we have divided the town into behavior setting units with equivalent degrees of interdependence. This index incorporates into the same behavior setting unit all settings with a degree of interdependence greater than a precisely defined amount. We have called this unit the K-21 Behavior Setting after the K-value used. The unity of the K-21 Behavior Setting can be indicated by some examples:

K-21 Behavior Setting Unit	Behavior Settings Included
Kane's Grocery	Grocery Department, Meat Department, Feed Department, Proprietor, Butcher, Clerks.

K-21 Behavior Setting Unit	*Behavior Settings Included*
High-School Football Game	Ticket Sellers, Coach, Officials, Players, Audience, Game, Intermission, Band, Concession Hut.
Trafficways	Sidewalks, Streets.
Howell's Hayloft	Howell's Hayloft, only.

A complete catalogue of the K-21 behavior settings of Midwest will be found on pages 154–76.

INTERNAL DYNAMICS OF BEHAVIOR SETTINGS

Evidence of the influence of behavior settings upon the behavior of individuals is found in natural "experiments" which occur in Midwest. In these "experiments," behavior settings are the independent variable and the behavior of Midwest children the dependent variable. Some data of one such "experiment" are presented below. Here, some features of the behavior of the children of the second grade are summarized in Table 3.1 as they passed from one behavior setting to another during the school day. The same individuals exhibit these different patterns of behavior in the different settings day after day. Furthermore, the "experiment" is repeated each year with a new group of "subjects" with the same results. The conclusion would appear to be justified, therefore, that the changes observed in the behavior of children as they change from one setting to another can be ascribed to conditions in the behavior setting.

The identification of a behavior setting rests upon the direct perception of a synomorphic relation between a standing pattern of behavior and a part of the nonpsychological milieu. It can be easily demonstrated that both laymen and scientists commonly perceive this relation and that there is a high degree of agreement between different observers with regard to it (see pp. 58–66). However, it is true, also, that some features of the behavior of different persons who enter the same behavior setting often differ widely. One person may enter a drug store to buy medicine for a friend, another to buy poison for an enemy. One person may go to church for spiritual satisfaction, another for social advantage. One patient in the doctor's office may have his anxieties allayed, another may have his worst fears confirmed. One pupil in a class may experience great success, another profound failure. Yet all of these people will conform to the standing pattern which is characteristic of the behavior in the setting.

In other words, the content and structure of a person's own psychological world, his life space, is by no means determined by the behavior setting. It is only modified in some respects. The extent to which this modification occurs, the forces which cause it and their sources are poorly understood at the present time. Unfortunately our data do not bear directly upon these problems. However, in the course of our work, some suggestions relative to these matters have come to light.

TABLE 3.1

PATTERN OF BEHAVIOR OF THE SAME CHILDREN IN DIFFERENT BEHAVIOR SETTINGS

| | BEHAVIOR SETTING | | | |
	Classroom; Before School	Academic Activities	Playground	Music Class
Milieu	Second-Grade Classroom, 8:30–8:50 a.m., Monday through Friday.	Scheduled periods for school work; books, paper, pencils, etc.	School playground at recess; swings, teeter, balls, etc.	Scheduled period in music room; piano, music books, etc.
Behavior Pattern	Unorganized activity; free locomotion; medium tempo, noise, and energy; cheerful mood; large variety of behavior.	Organized activity; little change in positions; slow tempo, noise, and energy; serious mood; limited variety of behavior.	Unorganized or partly organized activities; fast tempo. loudness, and vitality; exuberant mood; large variety of behavior.	Organized activities; variation in tempo, noise, and energy; medium cheerfulness; little variety of behavior, singing predominant.

There appear to be eight possible sources of the synomorphy of standing patterns of behavior and the nonpsychological milieu, as follows:

1. *Physical Forces*. The physical arrangements of some behavior settings enforce rather precise patterns of behavior and prevent others, thereby limiting the range of variation of the behavior occurring within them. The behavior setting High-School Building, Halls, for example, allows locomotion in certain directions only, their narrowness prevents the playing of circle games, and the absence of chairs or ledges encourages standing and walking and discourages sitting or lying. The layout of streets and sidewalks, the size and arrangement of rooms, and the distribution of furniture and equipment are often important factors in coercing certain features of the standing patterns of behavior and in restricting others. The physical forces impelling and hindering behavior do not have to be absolute, like a wall which cannot be breached; they can be effective by making actions of some kinds easier than others. It is physically easier to walk on the streets and sidewalks of Midwest than across lots; even dogs follow the streets and sidewalks to a considerable degree. In all of these cases, physical forces from the milieu mold behavior to conform to its shape.

2. *Social Forces*. Social forces are strongly coercive in many behavior settings. The power attaching to the cytosettings Teacher, Organization President, and Store Manager to enforce a particular pattern of behavior is well known. In addition, social forces to conform to the standing pattern issue from the behavior pattern itself. Thus, a child who "holds back" as the third and fourth grades rush pell mell through the school halls to the playground for recess is pushed along by the tide of behavior, by physical forces in the form of crowding and shoving, by social force in the form of threats and promises.

3. *Physiological Processes*. Without question there are built-in behavior mechanisms in men which respond with mechanical compulsiveness to some features of the nonpyschological milieu. In Kerr's Locker, where the temperature is maintained near zero, behavior is brisk, and movements stiff and ungraceful.

4. *Physiognomic Perception*. An important factor in molding standing patterns of behavior in settings is the coercive influence upon perception of some configurations of stimuli originating in the nonpsychological milieu. The children of Midwest appear to see a smooth, level area which is free from obstructions, such as the football field, the Courthouse lawn, the school gymnasium, or the American Legion hall, as places for running and romping in unorganized, exuberant activity. The milieu features of such behavior settings appear via perception to demand this kind of behavior. Open spaces seduce children. The behavior settings of Midwest are loaded with these perceived, seductive characteristics. The displays and arrangements of the stores, the order of the church services, the ceremony at weddings, the guide lines painted on the streets, the furnishings of homes

are all calculated to coerce behavior to the pattern appropriate for the setting.

It is our impression that the social milieu is even more seductive. The force upon an individual to rise when the congregation rises, to sit when it sits, and to be silent when it is silent are strong indeed. The social pressures to be gay at a carnival, businesslike at the annual school meeting, and sad at a funeral are strong.

5. *Learning.* The learning of behavior suitable for particular behavior settings is an important source of the conformity of individuals to the standing patterns of behavior. The process of teaching children to conform; to be quiet in church, to eat at mealtime, to sit still in school proceeds continually.

6. *Selection of Behavior Settings by Persons with Suitable Behavior Repertoires.* There is an affinity between the standing pattern of a behavior setting and the behavior repertoires of the persons who enter it. This occurs partly via the discriminative and selective behavior of individuals. An adolescent boy who finds the behavior pattern of a Sunday-School class intolerable will refuse to attend. Those who remain will, therefore, be self-selected for their ability to conform to the standing pattern of behavior.

7. *Differential Selection of Behavior by Behavior Settings.* Some behavior settings have entrance requirements which exclude persons whose behavior does not readily conform to that of the standing pattern and to the requirements of the milieu. Boys younger than 11 years cannot join the Boy Scouts; candidates for membership in the Masonic Lodge are examined to make sure that they can abide by the behavioral requirements of the lodge. Furthermore, many settings eject persons who do not conform to the standing pattern of behavior; a member of a bridge club who insisted on playing poker would soon be dropped, "incorrigible" boys are expelled from school, "inactive" members are dropped from the church rolls.

8. *Influence of Behavior on the Milieu.* The channels so far mentioned by which the association and the synomorphy of behavior pattern and milieu arise have been via direct physical and social forces acting on behavior, via the native or learned reactions to the milieu through perception, or via selection of persons with appropriate behavior possibilities. Another source of the association and synomorphism of behavior and milieu is through the effect of behavior on the milieu. This can occur as an incidental resultant of the behavior. The path from the south entrance of the Midwest school house to the corner of the yard is a prominent behavior-milieu synomorph; a great part of the going to and coming from the school is associated with this path. In this case the milieu was created by the feet of many children taking the shortest way home. At the present time, it undoubtedly coerces travelers not to stray from its physically smooth and perceptually demanding course, but this is a secondary effect. In the beginning the path was created by behavior.

The synomorphy of milieu and behavior arises, too, from the explicit demand of behavior for a particular milieu. The boys of Midwest want to play basketball. This requires a particular milieu, including special behavior objects. Midwest boys have, therefore, created the necessary milieu and assembled the necessary behavior objects, and in consequence the behavior setting Howell's Hayloft, basketball court, is a behavior-milieu synomorph of Midwest. Similarly, when preparations are made for the Senior Class festivities, the school gymnasium is transformed into a banquet hall and the behavior-milieu synomorph Junior Class Banquet for Seniors occurs in Midwest. As a matter of fact, a great amount of behavior in Midwest is concerned with creating new milieu arrangements to support new standing patterns of behavior, or altering old milieu features to conform to changes in old patterns of behavior.

In conclusion, the evidence available suggests that the sources of behavior-milieu synomorphy of Midwest behavior settings includes direct physical and social forces acting on behavior, native and learned ways of perceiving the milieu, selection of persons with appropriate behavior characteristics, and incidental and explicit restructuring of the milieu by the behavior. The reciprocating causal relationship between behavior and milieu is by no means contradictory and, in fact, is an essential feature of all interdependent systems. Indeed, in any behavior-milieu synomorph, whether it be a whole national culture such as the French nation, Clifford's Drug Store, or the Culver Family Breakfast, the behavior pattern both creates and is maintained by the milieu.

One hardly need emphasize that the relationships between behavior settings and the behavior and personality of the individuals who enter them urgently require systematic investigation and theoretical consideration. Similarly crucial is the question of how to conceive of behavior settings: in terms of extra-individual concepts, or in terms of the summation of influences upon separate individuals.

Varieties of Behavior Settings

Behavior settings can be classified in many ways and into wide or narrow groupings. In investigating the variety of behavior settings in Midwest we are faced with a classification problem similar to that faced by taxonomists: How similar must Midwest behavior settings be to belong to the same class? Obviously this depends on one's purposes. The essential methodological requirement is that, whatever the criterion of the class, the basis for inclusion be precise and communicable. The criteria by which we have defined the different varieties of behavior settings are based upon the degree of similarity in the pattern and content of the behavior and on the similarity of the structure of the milieu.

We have identified all behavior settings with a defined degree of similarity in these respects as belonging to the same variety of setting. These are called the S-30 varieties after the degree of similarity arbitrarily established. Details are presented on pages 81–83.

Techniques of the Behavior Settings Survey

A behavior settings survey is an inventory and description of the behavior settings of a town. Five distinct operations are involved in making a behavior setting survey, namely: (*a*) identifying potential behavior settings; (*b*) organizing the initial inventory; (*c*) discarding items of the inventory which upon closer examination do not meet the criteria of behavior settings; (*d*) enumerating the behavior settings; (*e*) describing the behavior settings.

These steps all consist of perceptual discriminations, and it is important to be explicit about whose perceptions are involved. In the final analysis, all discriminations and identifications are those of the Field Station staff. However, the survey techniques assure that the view of Midwest which is provided is also a view that is familiar to the citizens of the town. This is true for the following reasons:

1. The first list of potential behavior settings (step *a*) was secured largely from the writings and conversations of Midwesterners. This list contained the parts of the town as seen by the residents.

2. These original parts remained intact throughout the survey. Although the original list of parts was sorted, sifted, and combined in various ways, the units obtained from lay citizens were not destroyed.

3. The staff members who worked on the behavior settings survey had all been residents of Midwest from three to five years; their perceptions were subject to the same influences as those of other residents.

4. Behavior settings are defined in terms of their directly apprehended characteristics. They are phenomenal features of the town. Although step *d* of the procedure involves an interdependence criterion that is not a directly perceived attribute of behavior settings, this is used only as a means of securing behavior settings of equivalent unity for purposes of enumeration. The unit chosen for enumeration was selected on the basis of its common visibility in Midwest.

At no point in the procedure was an explicit effort made to see the town through the eyes of Midwesterners, yet the aspects of the method mentioned above would appear to warrant that the description of Midwest in terms of behavior settings is essentially the picture of Midwest as seen by its residents, presented more comprehensively, more precisely, and more systematically than laymen ordinarily report it. Each step in making a behavior setting survey will be described in turn.

Identifying Potential Behavior Settings

The first step in making a behavior settings survey is a systematic exploration to discover every behavior setting of the community. In Midwest this was done by gathering the town's public literature for one year—the local newspaper, school programs and schedules, church bulletins, placards, hand-bills, and the like—and recording from these the names of all community parts which might possibly fit the definition of a behavior setting.   Doubtful settings were included in the initial inventory, as the stress at this stage was upon inclusiveness rather than upon precision.   Here is an example of an item from the *Midwest Weekly* of the sort which provided material for the initial collection of the settings:

Box Social

Wednesday, October 15, at 7:30 p.m. the Senior Class of M.H.S. will sponsor a Box Social in the high-school gym.   Come and play Bingo, walk for a cake, eat pie and ice cream.

Girls: Be sure to bring a box!
Boys: Be sure to bring plenty of money!

From this, the following potential settings were included in the preliminary list: Box Social, Senior Class, Midwest High School, High-School Gym, Bingo, Walk for a Cake.   The list secured from public documents was supplemented by settings mentioned by Midwest residents in casual conversation, and by settings observed by the members of the field staff.   Here is a sample from the original list.

1. Box Social by Senior Class
2. Senior Class of Midwest High School
3. Midwest High School
4. High-School Gym
5. Bingo Game at Box Social
6. Walk for a Cake at Box Social
7. Boy Scout Tenderfoot Test at Home
8. 4-H Club Skating Party
9. Trash Fire at Murray's Grocery
10. Soda Fountain at Clifford's Drug Store
11. J. Wiley, Attorney
12. Lent Barber Shop
13. Methodist Children's Day Service
14. High School, Girls' Locker Room
15. Practical Joke Played by Ed Combs
16. Paved Area in Front of High School
17. Beaver Patrol, Scout Troop 72
18. J. Wiley, Private Music Lesson
19. Friendly Conversation at Post Office
20. Methodist Adult Choir Practice
21. 4-H Club Election of Officers
22. New Hymnals for Presbyterian Church
23. 4-H Club Regular Meeting
24. 4-H Club Achievement Banquet
25. Payment of Taxes at County Treasurer's Office
26. Scout Troop 72

Organizing the Initial Inventory

The second step in making a behavior setting survey is to organize the initial, random collection into an efficient working list.   In the Midwest survey the items of the inventory were grouped by unit settings and subsettings, i.e., the list was unitized.   For example, in the sample list above, item 7, Boy Scout Tenderfoot Test at Home, and item 17, Beaver Patrol were listed under item 26, Scout Troop 72.   The field workers saw items 7 and 17 as parts of Scout Troop 72 and the latter was not seen to be a part of any other Midwest setting.   The disposition of the other items is given in the organized sample list in Table 3.2.

We cannot consider here the perceptual problems involved in unitizing a list of behavior settings.   We can only say at this point that unitizing was done with a high degree of agreement by independent workers and that it provided a meaningful structure for the behavior setting inventory.   The agreement of independent workers in unitizing the behavior settings was tested on a random sample of 100 items from the initial inventory.   These items were grouped into unit settings by four judges independently.   The instructions to judges are reproduced in Appendix 3.   Following these instructions, the four judges grouped the 100 items into exactly the same unit settings with two exceptions.   One judge placed the American Legion (and its subsettings) and the American Legion Auxiliary (and its subsettings) together in a single unit setting.   The other judges considered these to be separate unit settings.   Another judge called an event sponsored by the Chamber of Commerce a separate unit setting while the other judges made it a subsetting of that organization.   In summary, the 100 items of the initial list were unitized into the same 21 unit settings by two of the judges; one judge agreed to 19 of these but combined 2 of them into a single setting, ending with 20 unit settings; the other judge listed the same 21 unit settings, but added an extra one, ending with 22 unit settings.   The perceptual organization of Midwest's behavior settings by different persons is surprisingly similar.

After the items of the inventory were grouped by unit settings, these unit settings were classified into six broad kinds of setting—a classification widely used in Midwest: Business Settings, Church Settings, Government Settings, Social Organization Settings, School Settings, and Miscellaneous Settings. This classification had little theoretical importance; however, it served as a convenient way to locate items in the inventory.   After the second step the items in the sample list were arranged as in Table 3.2.

Discarding Nonsettings

In the initial steps of a behavior setting survey, the aim is to include all parts of the community which might possibly fit the definition of a behavior setting.   In this way, settings are discovered which might otherwise be missed.   The third step in the procedure is to eliminate items from the inventory which do not fit the definition of a setting.   To be included as a behavior setting, a community part must be:

1. a discriminable pattern in the behavior of men en masse which

TABLE 3.2

SAMPLE LIST OF POTENTIAL BEHAVIOR SETTINGS ARRANGED ACCORDING
TO KIND OF SETTING, UNIT SETTINGS, AND SUBSETTINGS

Kind of Setting	Unit Setting	Subsetting
Business Settings		
	Clifford's Drug Store	
		Soda Fountain
	J. Wiley, Attorney	
	Bank Barber Shop	
	J. Wiley, Private Music Lessons	
	Murray's Grocery Trash Fire	
Church Settings		
	Methodist Church	
		Children's Day Service
		Adult Choir Practice
	Presbyterian Church	
		New Hymnals
Government Settings		
	County Treasurer's Office	
	Payment of Taxes	
	Post Office, friendly conversation in	
Social Organization Settings		
	Boy Scout Troop 72	
		Tenderfoot Test at Home
		Beaver Patrol
	4-H Club	
		Skating Party
		Election of Officers
		Regular Meeting
		Achievement Banquet
School Settings		
	High School	
		Senior class
		Box Social
		Bingo Game
		Walk for Cake
		High-School Gym
		Girls' Locker Room
		Paved Area
Miscellaneous Settings		
	Practical joke played by Ed Combs	

occurs independently of the particular persons involved in it; i.e., a
standing pattern of behavior
2. which has a synomorphic relation with ·
3. a particular milieu complex
4. that exists independently of the standing pattern of behavior, and
5. is circumjacent to the standing pattern of behavior.

Directions for eliminating nonsetting units will be found in Appendix 4.

The agreement between two judges in eliminating nonsettings from the
initial list was investigated as follows. All potential settings mentioned in
one issue of the *Midwest Weekly* were listed; this amounted to 89 possible
settings. The judges agreed on identifying 74 of the items as settings and
11 as nonsettings; 4 items were eliminated as settings by one judge and were
not eliminated by the other. This means that the judges agreed on their
identification of settings and nonsettings in 95 per cent of the cases, an agreement significant at the .001 level of confidence.

By the criteria given above the following potential settings were eliminated
from the sample list:

New Hymnals in Presbyterian Church (criterion #5; milieu not circumjacent
to behavior pattern).

Payment of Taxes at County Treasurer's Office (criterion #1; no standing
pattern of behavior clearly discriminable from other behavior in County Treasurer's Office).

Friendly Conversation in Post Office (criteria #2 and #3; friendly conversation not synomorphic with Post Office, in fact it is not associated with any
particular milieu).

Paved Area in front of High School (criteria #2; no pattern of behavior
synomorphic with paved area).

Practical Joke Played by Ed Combs (criteria #1 and #3; no standing pattern
and no milieu; a behavior characteristic of Ed Combs).

Enumerating the Behavior Settings

Thus far we have considered only the directly apprehended characteristics
of behavior settings. The problem of enumerating behavior settings, however, requires a more precise identification. The problem can be illustrated
by an analogous one in geology, namely, the problem of counting and mapping
the hot springs in a volcanic region.

It is likely that a field geologist would proceed in this project essentially
as we have in enumerating the behavior settings of Midwest. First, via his
own and other's field notes he would identify all possible hot springs in an
area; second, he would make a tentative sketch of the region with the
location of probable hot springs; third, he would make a closer inspection

and eliminate everything that did not conform to the definition of a hot spring, such as geysers, fumaroles, cold springs, mud pots, etc. He would then be faced with the kind of problem which confronts us, namely the problem of defining a spring for purposes of enumeration. He would have to decide whether to count as a separate spring each seepage and current of hot water issuing from every orifice, fissure, and layer of porous material, or whether to consider a number of currents discharging into the same pool or stream as a single spring. He would have to decide whether to enumerate a small seepage as equivalent to one which flowed thousands of gallons an hour.

There are a number of solutions to this problem. One is to consider each separate orifice or area of porous material from which hot water issues as a separate spring. Another solution is to consider as belonging to the same spring each flow from the same underground source. The latter criterion of a spring requires the use of indirect evidence of subterranean origin such as locus in relation to topography and geological structure, rate of flow, water temperature, mineral content of water, etc.

In a rich spring area with thousands of seepages and flows, some of them inaccessible at the bottom of pools and streams, complete solution by either of these methods would be almost impossible. Probably the most practical solution would involve a combination of the two methods in which:

1. Flows and seepages which were widely separated geographically would be considered as separate springs or clusters of springs.

2. Flows and seepages which were small and close together, e.g., which all issued directly into the same small pool, and which were without differentiating characteristics, would be considered as the same spring.

3. Segregated surface flows which were, however, in the same physical area would be grouped according to indirect evidence of their sources.

A hypothetical map of a spring area is shown in Figure 3.2. Here spring A, spring B, and spring C would be identified and enumerated on the basis of geographical separation (criterion 1). Springs D and E would be discriminated on the basis of indirect evidence regarding source (criterion 3); the pools on spring E might be of the same temperature and exhibit the same fluctuation in flow while spring D might be much hotter and of constant flow. The multiple fissures in spring B would be grouped together as a single spring on the basis of physical proximity, size, and lack of differentiating characteristics (criterion 2).

However adequate or inadequate this analysis of springs may be from the geological point of view, it is a paradigm of the procedure used in the fourth step of the behavior settings survey to identify and enumerate the behavior settings.

In terms of Figure 3.2, unit settings are equivalent to the geographically separated springs *A*, *B*, and *C* and are all enumerated; examples: Brownies, Regular Meeting; State Journal Paper Route; Trafficways. Interdependence tests to be described later indicate that all unit settings are separate settings dynamically, by the criteria used.

Cytosettings and minor subsettings are equivalent to the fissures and seepage areas represented in *B*, and are not enumerated; examples: Brownie Leader and Brownie Member. Again, sample interdependency tests indicate that practically all cytosettings and minor subsettings are not dynamically separate settings.

Major subsettings are equivalent to the segregated, but geographically contiguous springs represented in *D* and *E* and are enumerated or not according to the indications of the interdependency tests. Those subsettings which are closely interconnected, i.e., have a K-value of 21 or less, are put

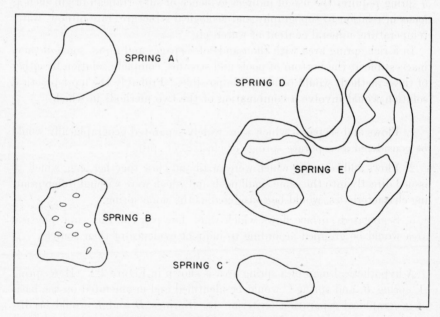

Fig. 3.2—A hypothetical map of a spring area.

together and enumerated as a single K-21 behavior setting. Halloween celebration becomes divided into four K-21 settings: Parade, Movies at High School for Young Children, Party at High School for Older Children, Dance at Legion Hall; the Old Settlers' Reunion and the Boy Scout Pop Stand merge as one K-21 setting. This means that the behavior settings which are identified and enumerated in Midwest are, in fact, essentially the settings which would have been discovered if the interdependency index could have been computed for all settings.

The general basis of an interdependency measure has been discussed (see pp. 50–53). It is necessary here to describe the particular method used to test the degree of independence of the major subsettings in this study. The K-test of interdependency of two behavior settings is based upon ratings of the degree to which:

1. the same people enter both settings;
2. the same power figure or leaders are active in both settings;
3. both settings use the same physical space or spaces that are near together;
4. both settings occur at the same time or at times that are near together;
5. both settings use the same or similar behavior objects;
6. the same molar action units span the two settings;
7. the same kinds of behavior mechanisms occur in the settings.

These criteria of interdependence assume that, in general, the greater the degree to which behavior settings involve the same people, the same place or contiguous places, the same time or contiguous times, the same or similar behavior objects, the same molar actions and similar behavior mechanisms, the greater their interdependence. To estimate the degree of interdependence of a pair of behavior settings, both were judged with respect to each of these criteria on a 7-point scale. A rating of 1 represented the greatest possible commonality or similarity between the settings on the criterion in question and a rating of 7, the greatest difference. The K-score for the pair of settings equalled the sum of the ratings on the 7 criteria. The total interdependence scale, then, ranged from a low score of 7, indicating minimal independence (maximal interdependence) to a high score of 49, indicating maximum independence (minimal interdependence). The interdependence scale is reproduced in Appendix 5.

A K-value of 21 (with qualifications mentioned below) was set as the cutting point for differentiating the behavior settings of Midwest. Pairs of unit settings with a K-value of less than 21 were considered as belonging to the same setting and those with a K-value of 21 or greater were numerated as separate settings.

Pairs of settings having K-values below and above this criterion are given below:

Pairs of Behavior settings with K-values below 21; each of these pairs of settings was combined into a single setting.

	K-value
First-Grade Music Class vs. Second-Grade Music Class	16
Clifford's Drug Fountain vs. Cigar and Candy Counter	19
February Meeting Women's Club I vs. March Meeting Women's Club I	19
Vacant Lot B vs. Vacant Lot C	20

Pairs of Behavior Settings with K-values greater than 21; each member of these pairs of settings was identified as a separate setting.

	K-value
First-Grade Academic Activities vs. Second-Grade Academic Activities	28
County Engineer's Office vs. County Register of Deeds, Office	28
Presbyterian Worship Service vs. Presbyterian Sunday-School Exercises	22
Rotary Club Regular Meeting vs. Rotary Club Farmers' Night	22

The reliability of the interdependence scale was investigated as follows. Three judges computed K-values for a stratified sample of 100 setting pairs; the sample was selected to represent every kind of comparison. All judges agreed that 79 per cent of these setting pairs had K-values above the criterion, *21*, and that 10 per cent had K-values below it—a total agreement of 89 per cent. This agreement was better than chance at the .001 level of confidence. Correlations between the ratings of pairs of judges were .93, .93, and .92.

Because these correlations were not perfect, the criterion score could not be accepted as absolute. In a few instances the judges rated the K-values of a particular pair of settings inconsistently with the K-values for similar pairs of settings. For example, the subsetting Service Station and the subsetting Garage of the unit setting Eastman Garage and Sales turned up with a K-value of 22, i.e., an interdependency index requiring that these subsettings be separated. However, ratings of similar businesses produced scores ranging from 16 to 19. The K-value of 22 was therefore judged to be in error and the service station and garage were placed together as the single setting Eastman Garage and Sales. Such adjustments were made only within a K-value range of 18 to 24.

Describing the Behavior Settings

The fifth and final step in making a behavior setting survey is to describe the behavior settings. Here there are limitless possibilities. For the purposes of the Midwest survey we selected six descriptive categories: *occupancy time, penetration, action patterns, mechanisms, richness,* and *centrality.* Each of these will be described.

OCCUPANCY TIME

The basic data upon the extent to which a behavior setting was entered and occupied was the occupancy time, i.e., the total number of hours Midwest residents spent in the setting during the survey year. Examples are listed below:

Behavior Setting	Occupancy Time (Hours)
Midwest Hardware and Implement Co.	13250
Third-Grade Academic Activities	7290
School Lunch Room	6246

Behavior Setting	Occupancy Time (Hours)
Broyer Beauty Shop	5000
Presbyterian Church Worship Service	3750
High-School Football Game in Town	3470
Arkwright Garage	3150
Dixon's Barber Shop	3050
Women's Club I Meeting	1107
Methodist Church Kindergarten Sunday-School Class	850
Presbyterian Church Funerals	357
Old Settlers' Reunion Dance	320
Baby Shower	308

Occupancy time was computed by multiplying the number of times a setting occurred during the survey year (its frequency f), by the number of Midwest citizens who entered the setting during each occurrence (its population p), by the time, in hours, these persons spent in the setting when they entered it (its duration, d). This product, fpd, is the person-hours-per-year, or the occupancy time of the behavior setting.

Separate estimates of occupancy time were computed for the 14 divisions of the population listed in Table 3.3, which illustrates the computation of occupancy time for the behavior setting Father-Son Banquet.

TABLE 3.3

OCCUPANCY TIME FOR THE BEHAVIOR SETTING FATHER-SON BANQUET

Population Subgroup	Frequency of Occurence f	Population p	Duration in Hours d	Occupancy Time
Infant	1	2	2.5	5
Preschool	1	5	2.5	15
Younger School	1	8	2.5	20
Older School	1	12	2.5	30
Adolescent	1	16	2.5	40
Adult	1	50	2.5	125
Aged	1	10	2.5	25
Male	1	96	2.5	240
Female	1	8	2.5	20
Group I	1	20	2.5	50
Group II	1	60	2.5	150
Group III	1	24	2.5	60
White	1	104	2.5	260
Negro	1	0	2.5	0
Total	1	104	2.5	260

The total occupancy time of individual Midwest settings varied from 78,000 person-hours-per-year for Trafficways to 3 person-hours-per-year for Cancer Control Committee Meeting. For purposes of manipulating the data, it was necessary to group these indexes into a smaller number of intervals. The grouping system or coded index used is given in Appendix 6.

Great effort was made to obtain accurate occupancy times. In the case of a considerable number of settings, very precise records of frequency, population, and duration were available. This was true of most school and Sunday-School settings and many social organization settings. With other settings, however, it was necessary to estimate one or more of the values involved. One staff member computed the occupancy times for all the settings. The reliability of his judgments was checked by correlating his coded indexes for a random sample of 46 settings with the coded indexes judged independently by another staff member. The correlation of .89 indicated a significant agreement. No significant difference was found in the absolute size of the estimated occupancy times of the two judges. In a conference of staff members, the disagreements found in this sample of judgments by two judges were reconciled, and the types of error discovered were corrected for the sample and for all other behavior settings.

As a further check on accuracy of estimated occupancy time, one of the staff members who had not been involved in this work, but who knew the town well, sorted business settings into five groups, placing together those settings which, according to her immediate, global judgment, were roughly equivalent as to "size," i.e., the amount of time Midwest citizens spent in them. The same was done for social organization settings. The rank order correlations, corrected for continuity and ties, between these groupings and the estimated occupancy time were .59 (N=118) for social organization settings and .87 (N=114) for business settings. Both of these correlations were significant. These two categories of settings were the most variable and difficult to estimate because of the absence of precise data on population, so the correlations obtained between our detailed judgments and the global impressions of a well informed resident gave us confidence in the accuracy of the judgments of occupancy time.

The various occupancy time ratios, population indices, and data on number of settings occupied are discussed in connection with the presentation of data.

PENETRATION OF BEHAVIOR SETTINGS

Midwesterners not only entered settings for different amounts of time, but they entered and participated in them in different capacities and with different degrees of involvement and responsibility. One index of the involvement and responsibility of a person in a behavior setting is the position of the cytosetting he enters. Cytosettings have been discussed earlier in this chapter. Each cytosetting can be characterized in terms of the centrality of its position within its behavior setting. Six zones of centrality are defined. The more central the zone, the deeper the penetration and the greater the involvement and responsibility of its occupants. These zones with their number designation and a descriptive title in each case are as follows:

Zone 1. Onlooker. This is the most peripheral zone of a cytosetting. Persons in this zone are within the behavior setting but take no active part in the standing pattern of behavior; at most they are onlookers. They are tolerated but not welcomed; they have no power. *Examples*: the infant who accompanies his mother to Kane's Grocery; loafers at the Post Office; a child waiting in the Dentist's Office while her friend has a tooth filled.

Zone 2. Audience or Invited Guest. The inhabitants of this zone have a definite place; they are welcome, but they have little power in the setting; at most they can applaud or express disapproval. *Examples*: spectators at a ball game; those in the church congregation who are not members of the church; the mothers invited to the setting Cub Scout Den Meeting when the Christmas party is scheduled.

Zone 3. Member or Customer. Occupants of Zone 3 have great potential power, but usually little immediate power. They are the voting members, the paying customers who ultimately make or break the leaders of the setting. *Examples*: member at Rotary Club Meeting; subscriber to *Midwest Weekly*; pupil in First-Grade Academic Activities.

Zone 4. Active Functionary. This zone includes the cytosettings which have a part in the operation of a setting but which do not lead it. Included here are store clerk, church deacon, organization secretary. The people in this zone have direct power over a limited part of the setting. *Examples*: cast of the Junior Class Play; clerks in Kane's Grocery.

Zone 5. Joint Leaders. Persons who enter the cytosettings of Zone 5 lead the setting jointly with others in this zone. Persons in Zone 5 have immediate authority over the whole setting but their power is shared with others. *Examples*: Mr. and Mrs. Cabell who jointly own and operate Cabell Department Store; the president of the High-School Drama Club and the teacher who sponsors it.

Zone 6. Single Leader. Zone 6 is the most central zone of cytosettings. Here are included the positions of all persons who serve as single leaders of behavior settings. These single leaders may have helpers or subordinate leaders in Zone 4. Persons in Zone 6 have immediate authority over the whole setting. *Examples*: the teacher in Second-Grade Academic Activities; the scout master at a Boy Scout Troop Meeting; the band leader at the summer Band Concert.

The zones of penetration into behavior settings are represented schematically in Figure 3.3.

The maximum depth of penetration into Midwest's behavior settings was rated for each Midwest resident and for each population subgroup. The maximum depth of penetration of a subgroup was defined as the most central position *any* member of a population subgroup had entered during the survey year. For example, one preschool child sang in the program of the setting

Parent-Teachers' Association Meeting during the year; since no preschool child penetrated further, preschool children were rated as having a maximum penetration rating of *4*, i.e., active functionary, for the behavior setting Parent-Teachers' Association Meeting.

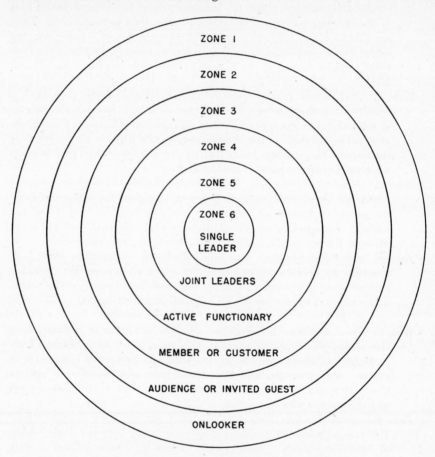

FIG. 3.3.—Zones of penetration into behavior settings.

Ratings were made on the basis of information secured from the field station staff, other informants, news items in the *Midwest Weekly*, programs of meetings, church bulletins, etc. Two independent judges agreed within one zone of centrality upon 93 per cent of 574 ratings. A chi-square test indicated that this was better than chance agreement beyond the .001 level of confidence.

BEHAVIOR SETTING ACTION PATTERNS

The standing behavior patterns of behavior settings have many discriminable features. We have rated them on 13 variables called *action patterns* which refer to their more molar features. The names of the action patterns are Aesthetics, Business, Earning a Living, Education, Government, Nutrition, Orientation, Personal Appearance, Philanthropy, Physical Health, Recreation, Religion, and Social Contact. They are described below, following the description of the scales for rating them.

The degree to which each action pattern occurs in a setting is rated on a scale made up of a number of subscales. Each of these subscales will be described and illustrated with the action pattern *Education*. Notes giving some conventions for rating particular action patterns are given in Appendix 7. In all cases ratings are made in accordance with local perceptions and values as these are seen by the observer.

1. *Participation Subscale*. Participation means actually behaving within the setting in ways which are described in the definition of the action pattern. The per cent of the total person-hours of behavior in the setting which involves the action pattern is judged and converted to a rating on the following scale:

Rating.
0   The action pattern does not occur in the setting.
1   The action pattern occurs in 1 to 20 per cent of the person-hours.
2   The action pattern occurs in 21 to 40 per cent of the person-hours.
3   The action pattern occurs in 41 to 60 per cent of the person-hours.
4   The action pattern occurs in 61 to 80 per cent of the occupancy time.
5   The action pattern occurs in 81 to 100 per cent of the occupancy time.

Example: It was judged that normally 81 to 100 per cent of all the occupancy time of the setting Mrs. Wiley, Music Lesson involved the action pattern Education, i.e., formal teaching by Mrs. Wiley and learning by the pupil. This setting was, therefore, rated *5* (maximum) for participation in the action pattern Education.

2. *Supply Subscale*: Supply refers specifically to providing materials for carrying out the action pattern in *another* setting. Buying and eating a milkshake at the drug store soda fountain is judged on the participation subscale, but buying ice cream to take home is judged on the supply scale.

Rating.   Rate as on participation subscale.

Example: The buying and selling of text books, paper, pencils, and other school supplies at Clifford's Drug Store was judged to constitute 1 to 20 per cent of its occupancy time. Clifford's Drug Store was therefore rated *1* on Supply for the action pattern Education.

3. *Evaluation and Appreciation Subscale*: Evaluation refers to behavior which explicitly recognizes the values of the action pattern, whether good or bad, or tests its effectiveness. Applauding at a play is an evaluation of the action patterns Aesthetics and Recreation; presenting attendance pins in Sunday School for a year's perfect attendance is a recognition of the action pattern Religion;

giving tests in school is evaluation of the action pattern Education. Rate on the following scale:

Rating.

0   No behavior in the setting explicitly evaluates or appreciates the action pattern.

1   Less than half of the occupancy time of the setting is devoted to evaluation or appreciation of the action pattern.

2   More than half of the occupancy time of the setting is devoted to evaluation or appreciation of the action pattern.

Example: Public recognition of educational achievement was judged to constitute less than half of the occupancy time of the setting Eighth-Grade Graduation; Education was, therefore, rated *1* on this subscale.

4. *Teaching and Learning Subscale*: This subscale refers only to explicit teaching and learning of the action pattern; it does not include incidental learning.

Rating.   Rate as on evaluation and appreciation subscale.

Example: Teacher's Institute in Midwest is a place where teachers not only participate in being educated but learn how to educate. This was rated *2* (maximum) for learning about the action pattern Education.

The rating of an action pattern in a setting is the sum of the ratings on the subscales for Participation, Supply, Appreciation, and Learning. The total rating varies from zero to 14. Sample ratings of a number of behavior settings on the action pattern Recreation are given in Table 3.4.

TABLE 3.4

SAMPLE RATINGS OF SELECTED SETTINGS ON THE ACTION
PATTERN, RECREATION

BEHAVIOR SETTING	RATING ON SUBSCALE				TOTAL
	Participation	Supply	Appreciation	Learning	
Red Cross Home Nursing Course	1	0	0	0	1
Trafficways	2	0	0	0	2
Midwest Theater	5	0	1	1	7
Lambert Lumber Yard	1	0	0	0	1
Men's Town Baseball Game	5	0	2	2	9

The names and brief definitions of the different action patterns follow, together with examples of behavior settings given higher ratings on each subscale. The settings can be identified in the Behavior Settings Catalogue by the number given in parentheses (see pp. 154–76).

Aesthetics.   Applies to any artistic activity, to any behavior aimed at making the environment more pleasing.

Participation: doing artistic things, decorating or removing the unsightly; e.g., Music Recital at Home (80), Spring Cleanup Drive (482).

Supply: supplying art, cleaning, landscaping materials; e.g., Sherwin Furniture Store (107), Clifford's Drug Store (46), Blanchard Hardware Store (109).

Evaluation and Appreciation: appreciating products of art or persons with aesthetic talents or accomplishments; e.g., Midwest Theater (49), City Library (513).

Learning: teaching art, learning art; e.g., School Band Practice (290).

Business. Applies to the exchange of goods, services, or privileges where payment is obligatory. Does not include gifts of money or service (see Philanthropy) or hiring out for wages (see Earning a Living).

Participation: exchanging merchandise, service, or privileges; transporting persons or goods for a fee, processing raw materials into saleable form; e.g., Garnett's Grocery (34), Lent's Barber Shop (158), County Treasurer's Office (96).

Supply: supplying objects and materials necessary for the execution of business in other settings; e.g., Bank of Midwest (179), Standard Oil Bulk Branch (308), Hopkin's Feed Store (32).

Evaluation and Appreciation: examining and appreciating the achievements or values of business, businessmen, or business institutions; e.g., Bank of Midwest (179), Chamber of Commerce Regular Meeting (407).

Learning: learning or teaching how to do business; e.g., High School, Bookkeeping I (15), serving as an apprentice where there is explicit instruction in business practices as in Clifford's Drug Store (46).

Earning a Living. Applies to any activity for which wages are received. Does not include the behavior of an entrepreneur whose rewards are from his profits or fees received on each transaction.

Participation: hiring out for wages; e.g., teacher in First-Grade Academic Activities (3), clerk in Cabell Department Store (45).

Supply: supplying materials, tools, and equipment for earning a living; e.g., Blanchard Hardware Store (109) sells tools to carpenters.

Evaluation and Appreciation: evaluating the worth of earning a living, examining or recognizing persons who serve in particular jobs; e.g., service awards by Telephone Company (156).

Learning: teaching or learning skills and values of earning a living; e.g., training of apprentices in the *Midwest Weekly* shop (274).

Education. Applies to formal education of any kind; does not include incidental learning or teaching.

Participation: teaching individuals or classes of students, learning in individual or group lessons; e.g., High School, Biology (14), Home Demonstration Unit Meeting (271).

Supply: supplying materials for teaching or learning in other settings; e.g., Parent-Teachers' Association Book Exchange (581), giving homework in High School, Algebra and Geometry (13).

Evaluation and Appreciation: approving of education or of persons who have completed a course of study, recognizing or evaluating educational achievements; e.g., High School, Senior Class Commencement (486), School Music Program (77).

Learning: teaching or learning procedures of education or stimulating people to increase education; e.g., Sunday-School Teachers' Meeting (430).

Government.   Applies to behavior which has to do with government at any level.

Participation: engaging in civic affairs or in behavior which is controlled in any degree by government regulations; e.g., County Clerk's Office (91), City Council Meeting (439), Polling Place, North Side (502).

Supply: supplying materials for governing activities; e.g., printing ballots at *Midwest Weekly* print shop (274).

Evaluation and Appreciation: recognition of patriotic people or events, evaluating laws; e.g., Fourth of July (401), saluting flag in Second-Grade Academic Activities (4).

Learning: teaching or learning about government or legal procedures; e.g., High School, Social Sciences (21).

Nutrition.   Applies to behavior which has to do with eating or drinking for nutritional purposes.

Participation: eating, drinking, preparing, or serving food; e.g., Pearl Cafe (85), Corner Tavern (87), Father-Son Banquet (365).

Supply: acquiring food, drink, eating utensils, or preparing food for use in another setting; e.g., Poole's Grocery (31), Everging Variety Store (48).

Evaluation and Appreciation: judging or appreciating the values of nutrition, of ways and means of serving food, or recognizing persons who excel in the preparation of meals; e.g., Mother-Daughter Banquet (360), 4-H Club Achievement Banquet (573).

Learning: teaching or learning ways and means of preparing and serving meals; e.g., Seventh- and Eighth-Grade Home Economics (12), Boy Scouts, Summer Camp (488).

Orientation.   Applies to behavior in settings which has to do with giving temporal, geographic, or social information.

Participation: giving information about geography, identifying persons, locations, and times of events; e.g., *Midwest Weekly* (274), Chaco Service Station (41).

Supply: supplying orientation materials, distributing bulletins, maps, telephone books; e.g., distributing bulletins at Presbyterian Church: Worship Service (188).

Evaluation and Appreciation: recognizing the values of orientation, evaluating communication media; e.g., official inspection of Post Office (234).

Learning: teaching and learning about one's geographical, temporal, and social locus; e.g., Fourth-Grade Academic Activities, geography (6), First-Grade Academic Activities, learning to tell time (3).

Personal Appearance.   Applies to improving, or appreciating personal appearance, to wearing uniforms or symbolic clothing.

Participation: dressing, getting well groomed, looking one's best, wearing uniforms; e.g., Burgess Beauty Shop (159), Methodist Church Worship Service (181), High-School Basketball Game (133).

Supply: supplying materials for personal adornment or grooming; e.g., Denton's Drug Store (47), Cabell Department Store (45).

Evaluation and Appreciation: recognizing well-groomed persons; appreciating clothing or equipment for grooming; e.g., County 4-H Fashion Show (61).
Learning: teaching or learning ways and means of proper grooming and personal appearance; e.g., High School, Home Economics (19).

Philanthropy. Applies to behavior which has to do with giving to good causes, being charitable.
Participation: donating gifts or services for a noncommercial cause; e.g., Red Cross Fund Drive (534).
Supply: providing material to promote philanthropic purposes in another setting; e.g., Infantile Paralysis Committee Meeting to prepare for fund drive (450).
Evaluation and Appreciation: public recognition of results of philanthropy, recognizing a philanthropist; e.g., Methodist Church Worship Service, Joash Sunday (181).
Learning: teaching or learning about philanthropic causes or values of philanthropy, or learning about specific philanthropic projects or needs; e.g., Presbyterian Church Women's Missionary Society Meeting (319).

Physical Health. Applies to behavior which promotes or maintains physical health, to recognizing the healthy. Applies specifically to physical, not mental health.
Participation: caring medically for people in any way, promoting physical health; e.g., Lewis Sterne, Dentist Office (296), High-School Boys' Basketball Practice (132).
Supply: supplying medicines and medical or athletic equipment; e.g., Clifford's Drug Store (46), Midwest Hardware (110).
Evaluation and Appreciation: recognizing healthy people, judging health; e.g., All-School Assemblies, athletic awards (64).
Learning: teaching or learning ways and means of being healthy, stimulating healthful ways of living, learning medical skills; e.g., High School, Home Economics Class (19), Red Cross Home Nursing Course (1).

Recreation. Applies to behavior which gives pleasure.
Participation: playing, having fun, reading for pleasure; e.g., Old Settlers' Reunion: Midway (347), Men's Town Baseball Game (167).
Supply: supplying materials and behavior objects for recreation; e.g., Everging Variety Store (48), City Library (513).
Evaluation and Appreciation: recognizing or appreciating entertainment or entertainers; e.g., Old Settlers' Reunion: Amateur Show (324), High-School Assemblies (66).
Learning: teaching or learning about ways and means of recreation, stimulating the use of facilities for entertainment; e.g., High-School Boys' Basketball Practice (132), Senior Class Play Practice (73).

Religion. Applies to behavior which has to do with worship.
Participation: engaging in religious exercises; e.g., Union Memorial Day Worship Service (183).
Supply: supplying religious artifacts or materials for purposes of worship; e.g., Clifford's Drug Store, sells Bibles, (46).

Evaluation and Appreciation: recognizing religious values or religious persons or leaders; e.g., examining candidates for church membership at Presbyterian Church, Session Meeting (433).

Learning: teaching or learning about religion or ways to practice religion; e.g., Methodist Church, Elementary Sunday-School Class (214).

Social Contact. Applies to visiting, being pleasant, having fellowship, having interpersonal contact.

Participation: being sociable, engaging in social interaction; e.g., Last Day of School Dinner (373).

Supply: supplying ways and means of being sociable; e.g., Telephone Company (156).

Evaluation and Appreciation: recognizing sociable persons or values of sociability; e.g., All-School Assemblies, introducing most popular boy or girl (64).

Learning: teaching and learning social techniques; e.g., Home Demonstration Unit Meetings (271).

Independent judges agreed in their rating of behavior setting action patterns on a random sample of 45 behavior settings to a degree indicated by product-moment correlation between pairs of judges from .68 to .97 with an average of .89. The reliability coefficients for the different action patterns are:

Action Patterns	Correlation	Action Patterns	Correlation
Aesthetics	.85	Orientation	.70
Business	.68	Personal Appearance	.84
Earning a Living	.97	Philanthropy	.92
Education	.91	Recreation	.93
Government	.94	Religion	.95
Health	.86	Social Contact	.85
Nutrition	.91		

BEHAVIOR SETTING MECHANISMS

Standing behavior patterns of behavior settings have also been rated on 7 variables called *behavior mechanisms* which refer to their more molecular features. These behavior mechanisms are: Affective Behavior, Gross Motor Activity, Listening, Looking, Manipulating, Talking, and Thinking. They are defined following presentation of the rating methods.

The extent to which these mechanisms, with the exception of Looking and Listening, occurred in each behavior setting was judged by a rating method similar to that used with the behavior setting action patterns. Three subscales were defined as follows:

1. Participation Subscale. Participation refers to the degree of occurrence of the mechanism in the standing behavior pattern of the setting; it is rated according to the following scale:

Rating.

0   The mechanism occurs in less than 10 per cent of the person-hours of the setting.

1   The mechanism occurs in 10 to 33 per cent of the person-hours of the setting.
2   The mechanism occurs in 34 to 66 per cent of the person-hours of the setting.
3   The mechanism occurs in 67 to 90 per cent of the person-hours of the setting.
4   The mechanism occurs in more than 90 per cent of the person-hours of the setting.

Example: Talking, including singing, was judged to be involved in 34 to 66 per cent of the total person-hours of the setting Primary-School Music Classes (285), hence it was rated *2* for the mechanism Talking.

2. Tempo Subscale. This subscale refers to the maximum speed with which the mechanism normally occurs in the setting; the unusual, abnormal burst of speed is not rated. The terms *slow, median, rapid*, and *top speed*, used in describing the scale points, refer to the *total* range of speed with which the mechanism in question occurs in a normal population in a wide variety of behavior settings.

Rating.
0   When the mechanism occurs, its maximal speed is normally slow; reaction times are long.
1   The maximal speed of the mechanism is normally in the median range, neither fast nor slow.
2   The maximal speed of the mechanism is normally above the median range.
3   The maximal speed of the mechanism regularly occurs at top speed, near the physiological limit.

Example: In the setting Milk Co. Route (334) the maximal speed of Gross Motor Activity is regularly more rapid than the median rate of gross motor movement, the milk man "hurries," rated *2*. High-School Boys' Basketball Practice (132) involves Gross Motor Activity at top speed, rated *3*.

3. Intensity Subscale. Intensity refers to the usual, maximal rate of energy expenditure via the mechanism.

Rating.
0   When the mechanism occurs, the maximal rate of energy expenditure is very low.
1   The maximal energy expenditure is normally in the median range.
2   The maximal energy expenditure is normally above the median range.
3   The maximal amount of energy exerted is near the physiological limit.

Example: The events in the High-School Track Meet (177) regularly involve a maximal energy expenditure via Gross Motor Activity, rated *3*.

A behavior setting mechanism rating is the sum of the ratings on these three subscales.   The range of ratings is from zero to 10.

The five mechanisms rated on these scales are defined below, together with examples of behavior settings given higher and lower ratings on each subscale.

Gross Motor Activity. Refers to the active movement of the large muscles of the body; gross motor activity is opposed to sedentary behavior.
Participation: extent to which movements involving the large muscles occur in the standing behavior pattern of the setting; e.g. Bellows, Painter (140) rated *4*. Presbyterian Men's Sunday-School Class Meeting (223) rated *0*.
Tempo: speed of large muscle movement in a setting; e.g., High-School Football Game (174) rated *3*, Bridge Club I Meeting (256) rated *1*.
Intensity: force used in gross motor activity when it occurs; e.g., Lambert Lumber Yard (139) rated *3*, Baby Shower (394) rated *1*.

Talking. Any form of verbalizing; includes singing and cheering.
Participation: extent to which talking occurs in the behavior pattern of a setting; e.g., a social gathering such as Presbyterian Church Women's Sunday-School Class Party (385) where almost everyone talks most of the time is rated *3*; a setting with an audience, where one or a few talk and many listen, such as Methodist Church Worship Service (181) is rated *2*.
Tempo: maximal speed of verbalizing; almost all settings rated *1*.
Intensity: maximal loudness of verbalizing; e.g., High-School Basketball Program (133) with organized cheering rated *3*, Presbyterian Church Funeral (496) rated *0*.

Manipulation. Refers to the use of the hands in prehension.
Participation: degree to which hands are used in the behavior pattern to grasp and manipulate; e.g., Hagedorn, Contractor (143) rated *3*, Midwest Theater (49) rated *0*.
Tempo: maximal speed of grasping and manipulating; e.g., Men's Town Baseball Game (167) rated *3*, District Court Sessions (300) rated *0*.
Intensity: maximal force of grasp when manipulating; e.g., Corliss, Blacksmith (44) rated *3*; High School, Social Sciences (21) rated *0*.

Thinking. Refers to decision making and problem solving; does not include routine behavior or emotional expression.
Participation: the degree to which the standing behavior pattern involves decision making or problem solving; e.g., High School, Algebra and Geometry (13) rated *3*, and Trafficways (26) rated *0*.
Tempo: maximal speed with which decisions are normally made and problems solved; e.g., Football Game (174) rated *3*, fishing at Lake (208) rated *0*.
Intensity: Refers to the maximal level of thinking which takes place in a setting; e.g., District Court Sessions (300) rated *3*, Baby Shower (394) rated *0*.

Affective Behavior. Refers to overtly expressed emotionality.
Participation: degree to which the standing behavior pattern of the setting involves emotional behavior; e.g., Senior Class Graduation (486) rated *3*, Post Office (234) rated *0*.
Tempo: speed with which emotionality normally changes in a setting; e.g., Junior Class Play (68), rated *3*. Funeral (496) rated *0*.
Intensity: the directly perceived intensity of the emotional behavior which occurs; e.g., Wedding (549) rated *3*, County Register of Deeds, Office (94) rated *0*.

Looking and Listening. Because of the ubiquity of the mechanisms Looking and Listening, it was discovered that a different method of rating was required.

To rate these mechanisms we assumed that they were normally involved in a setting to the degree that blindness or deafness would interfere with participation in the action patterns of the setting, and the amount of interference due to these handicaps was estimated. The scales for making these judgments are given in Appendix 8.

The reliability of the ratings of the behavior setting mechanisms was investigated on a sample of 59 settings. Independent judges did not differ significantly in rating the mechanisms, Gross Motor Activities, Talking, Affective Behavior, Looking, and Listening. They did differ significantly beyond the 1 per cent level of confidence on the mechanisms, Thinking and Manipulation. Systematic errors were corrected for the latter two mechanisms.

RICHNESS OF BEHAVIOR SETTINGS

In general, the richness of a behavior setting refers to the variety of behavior possibilities within it. Three special richness indexes and a general richness index have been computed, each based upon one or several of the previously described categories.

1. Population Richness Index. The number of different categories of persons responsibly participating in a behavior setting is one indication of the potential variety of social experiences in the setting. Settings in which people of widely ranging age, sex, social class, and race penetrate deeply are places where a diversity of interpersonal relations is possible and where the behavior pattern must accommodate wide individual differences. We have used as an index of the population richness of a setting the sum of its penetration ratings (see pp. 68–71) for the 14 population subgroups. The setting with the highest Population Richness Index was Clifford's Drugstore (46) with an index of *55*; Vacant Lot (209) had one of the lower indexes, *27*.

2. Action Pattern Richness Index. Settings with many action patterns, many of them with high ratings, provide a variety of rewarding behavior possibilities for their inhabitants. The Action Pattern Richness Index of a behavior setting is the sum of all ratings on the 13 action pattern variables (see pp. 70–76). A high index indicates that the behavior setting performs many "functions," that many goals and subgoals can be achieved within it. Clifford's Drug Store (46) had the highest Action Pattern Richness Index, *47*, and Primary School, Fire Drill (565) had one of the lowest, *12*.

3. Mechanism Richness Index. The Mechanism Richness Index was computed exactly as the Action Pattern Richness Index, i.e., the 7 separate mechanism ratings of each setting were summed. For Clifford's Drug Store (46), the Mechanism Richness Index was *31*; for Mr. Stanton, Rug Weaving (427) it was *14*.

4. General Richness Index. A General Richness Index was computed for each behavior setting by summing the separate richness indexes just described and weighting the total for the occupancy time of the setting. For the latter purpose,

the code number of occupancy time was used (see Appendix 6).   This index
can be defined as follows:

$$\text{GRI}_x = \frac{(\text{PRI}_x + \text{APRI}_x + \text{MRI}_x)\text{COT}_x}{100}$$

where GRI_x = General Richness Index of setting X.
        PRI_x = Population Richness Index of setting X.
        APRI_x = Action Pattern Richness Index of setting X.
        MRI_x = Mechanism Richness Index of setting X.
        COT_x = Code number of Occupancy Time of setting X.

General Richness Indexes of Midwest behavior settings varied from *51* for
Clifford's Drug Store (46) to *2* for Farm Bureau Regular Meeting (408).   A
behavior setting with a high General Richness Index is one in which a relatively
large number of people belonging to many different population subgroups
engaged responsibly in numerous action patterns via a variety of behavior
mechanisms.   They are the settings where the standing behavior pattern was
most extensive and most varied.

THE CENTRALITY OF BEHAVIOR SETTINGS

   We have defined the centrality of a behavior setting in terms of the degree
of its interdependence with all other behavior settings of the town, as
measured by K.   The most central setting is the one with the lowest average
K-value when this is computed for all pairs of behavior settings.   Because
the number of computations involved was so large, a shortened procedure
was adopted.   This involved two steps: (*a*) A core behavior setting was
identified; (*b*) K-values were computed between every behavior setting and
this core setting.   These K-values were therefore, measures of the "dynamic
distance" of each setting from the core setting.

   The core setting was selected as follows: The 10 behavior settings having the
highest General Richness Index were identified; they are listed in the tabulation
below.   The average intersetting K-value of these 10 settings was computed and
the setting with the smallest average K-value, i.e., the setting with the closest
dynamic relations with these rich settings, was chosen as the core behavior
setting of Midwest.

   The data are given below, where it will be seen that the core setting is Clifford's
Drug Store.

Behavior Setting	General Richness Score	Average Intersetting K-value
Clifford's Drug Store	51	31.67
Denton's Drug Store	46	31.89
Kane's Grocery and Feed Store	49	32.44
Garnett's Grocery	47	32.22
Midwest Hardware and Implement Co.	43	33.22
Trafficways	53	33.67
Midwest Theater	75	36.44
Telephone Co.	44	36.78
Midwest Weekly	42	37.11
High-School Basketball Program in town	42	38.22

This core setting can be defined as the Midwest behavior setting which is most closely related dynamically to the 10 richest settings of the community. The centrality of every community setting in Midwest was computed with reference to this core setting in terms of its K-value with this setting. This is presented graphically on the Behavior Settings Base Map, Figure 4.32.

Varieties of Behavior Settings

Two bases for defining a unit of any dispersed material have been suggested, namely, the degree of dynamic interdependence and the degree of the similarity of the parts of the material. The interdependence criterion has been used to define a K-21 behavior setting unit. This brings together settings which have a defined degree of mutual interdependence without reference to the similarity in the structure or the content of the behavior or milieu. The similarity criterion will now be used as a basis for defining different *varieties* of K-21 behavior settings. This classification is based upon the similarity between the action patterns, the mechanisms, the circumjacent milieu, and the behavior objects of a pair of settings. Settings which have a prescribed degree of similarity in these respects have been classified as belonging to the same variety of behavior setting.

The residents of Midwest agree with this procedure. They speak of the five grocery stores, the seven gasoline stations, and the two drug stores collectively as the groceries, the service stations, and the drug stores. In so doing, they imply that the settings within each of these varieties are, in important ways, equivalent to one another, that the separate stores, for example, are different representatives of the same kind of behavior setting.

The total number of these groups of similar settings is an indication of the variety of behavior settings in the town. This, of course, points to an important difference between communities. If two towns have the same number of behavior settings, but one has 100 different varieties and the other 25, they will undoubtedly be quite different places to live.

There are great difficulties in classifying behavior settings into generally similar varieties. For example, the Midwest Hardware and Implement Company is a setting where hardware and home appliances are sold and where farm machinery and their parts are sold and repaired. This setting can be grouped with other hardware stores under the variety, Hardware Stores, or it can be classed with the other farm implement dealers under the variety, Implement Dealers. The 4-H Food Sale has some things in common with grocery stores and some things in common with a 4-H Club Meeting. The fact of the matter is that behavior settings have overlapping affiliations.

Another practical problem concerns the level of similarity desired. One can form groups of settings in which the intravariety differences are small; in this case the number of varieties will be large. Or one can form broad varieties with relatively large intravariety differences and have a relatively few varieties.   This indefiniteness with respect to the varieties of behavior settings is a symptom of the lack of a firm theoretical structure for behavior settings.   This being the case, we have at the present time to be guided by empirical considerations.   We set the Similarity Index (S) at a level which systematically grouped the settings of Midwest into varieties which did not differ appreciably from the groupings commonly made by Midwest citizens.

The Similarity Index (S) of two settings is the sum of the four following similarity scores:

1. Action Pattern Similarity Score.   This score is the sum of the *differences* in the 13 action pattern ratings of two settings, disregarding their direction. When the sum of these differences is small the action patterns of the two settings are similar, and vice versa.   For the settings Sheriff's Office (303) and County Register of Deeds, Office (94) this score is *17*; for Sheriff's Office (303) and Women's Club II (260) it is *34*.

2. Mechanism Similarity Score.   This score is the sum of the *differences* in the behavior mechanism ratings of two settings, disregarding the direction of the differences.   When the sum of these differences is small, the behavior in the two settings is performed in the same way, and vice versa.   For Sheriff's Office (303) and County Register of Deeds, Office (94) this score is *10*; for Sheriff's Office (303) and Women's Club II (260) it is *16*.

3. Locus Similarity Score.   Similarity of the physical loci of two settings was measured by estimating the per cent of behavior that would normally not be possible in each setting if their physical loci were exchanged.   The highest of these two per cents was converted to the Locus Similarity Score by means of the following scale.

Per Cent of Behavior Made Impossible by Change of Locus	Locus Similarity Score
0–5	0
6–15	1
16–25	2
26–35	3
36–45	4
46–55	5
56–65	6
66–75	7
76–85	8
86–95	9
96–100	10

In the case of the Sheriff's Office (303) and the Register of Deeds, Office (94) cited above, it was judged that less than 5 per cent of the behavior in either setting would be interfered with by exchange of loci.   Therefore, the score was *0* on this scale.   For Sheriff's Office (303) *vs.* Women's Club II (260), this score was *9*.

4. Behavior Object Similarity Score. The same method and scale were used with behavior objects as with locus. In the examples, the kinds of things used in the Sheriff's Office (303) were judged to be roughly similar to those used in the Register of Deeds, Office (94). It was estimated that about 25 per cent of the behavior that normally occurs in the Register of Deeds, Office (94) would not be possible if the behavior objects were transferred. The similarity score, then, was *2.* For the Sheriff's Office (303) and Women's Club II (260) this score was *10.*

The sum of the four ratings described above was the Similarity Index. A low index meant that the two settings were similar while a high index meant they were dissimilar. For the settings in our example, Sheriff's Office (303) *vs.* Register of Deeds, Office (94), the Similarity Index is *29*; for Sheriff's Office (303) and Women's Club II (260) the Similarity Index is *69.*

On a stratified sample of 100 pairs of settings designed to include a wide range of differences in settings, the product-moment correlation for similarity scores judged by independent staff members was .98.

The similarity scale provided a relatively stable basis for judging the degree of similarity of settings with respect to behavior and milieu. Similarity scores of 30 or less were arbitrarily defined as placing settings pairs within the same variety of behavior settings. Listed below are examples of settings pairs having Similarity Indexes above and below 30.

> Similarity Scores above 30 (different varieties)
> > High-School English Period
> > High-School Boys Shop
>
> > Midwest Theater Free Show (Christmas)
> > Charavarie
>
> > Cabell Department Store
> > Kane's Grocery
>
> Similarity Scores below 30 (same variety)
> > County Teachers Institute
> > High-School Social Sciences
>
> > Grade-School Operetta
> > Midwest Theater
>
> > Hagedorn, Contractor
> > Mrs. Woodale, Wallpapering

Some technical problems of grouping behavior settings into varieties are presented in Appendix 9.

In this chapter we have attempted to present the conception and techniques of the behavior setting survey in such detail that the reader can evaluate their research products. Some features of the methods will be clarified in the next chapter where the results of the survey of Midwest are presented.

Chapter IV

The Behavior Setting Survey: Results

The Differentiation of Midwest

DURING the survey year, July 1, 1951 to June 30, 1952, there were 2030 K-21 behavior settings identified in Midwest of which 1445 were located within the homes of the town, and 585 were found in its more public behavior areas. The former are called *family behavior settings*, and the latter *community behavior settings*. Common varieties of family behavior settings are Home Meals, Home Indoors, Home Outdoors, Home Bathroom, and Home Festive Occasions. Common varieties of community settings have been mentioned in the preceding chapter. Here we shall be largely concerned with the community behavior settings of Midwest.

The community settings, arranged by varieties in order of occupancy time, are listed in the Behavior Settings Catalogue at the end of this chapter. These are the basic data of the behavior setting survey; they constitute a descriptive catalogue of the public behavior areas of Midwest. The settings are represented in the base maps, Figures 4.32 and 4.33. When, in the following discussion, a number appears in parentheses following the name of a behavior setting it refers to the number in the catalogue and on the map.

The total number of settings in a community is one index of its degree of differentiation, and it is undoubtedly a variable which has important psychological consequences. It has been possible to make preliminary investigations of some of the ways the differentiation of Midwest influenced the behavior of its citizens.

The Performance-Performer Ratio

Community behavior settings are the public stages upon which the people perform their parts in the life of a town. We have defined a *performance* on Midwest's stages as the behavior of one person in penetration Zones 4,5,6 of one behavior setting. A performance refers to all the behavior of a leader, a joint leader, or a responsible functionary in a particular setting. It corresponds to the parts played by the main characters of a play.

There were six performances in the setting Kane's Grocery, namely those of Mr. Kane, the proprietor; Mrs. Kane, clerk and bookkeeper; Walter Kane, stock boy, janitor, and clerk; Mr. Ropes, feed and produce salesman and warehouseman; Mrs. Buch, clerk; and Mrs. Dewdney, clerk. The setting Second-Grade Academic Activities had but one performance, that of Mrs.

Grinstead, the teacher. The behavior of the customers and visitors in Kane's Grocery and of the members of the Second-Grade Class are not included in the definition of a performance; it covers only the behavior of those who have leading positions in the standing behavior pattern.

This definition of a performance has a number of implications: (a) The same person engages in more than one performance if he enters penetration Zones 4, 5, or 6 of more than one setting. (b) Some performances occur daily for the entire survey year, e.g., Mr. Denton's performance as proprietor of Denton's Drug Store; others occur only infrequently, e.g., the toastmaster's performance at the annual Father-Son Banquet. (c) A performance may be a specialized action, as ushering at a church service, or it may be a varied series of actions such as Mr. Kane's performance which included clerking, bookkeeping, meat cutting, buying, stocking shelves, extending credit, and sweeping. (d) Persons who occupy the same position in Zones 4, 5, or 6 of a behavior setting, as, for example, the rotating program chairmen of the 4-H Club, each engage in a separate performance.

The total number of performances in a community is the sum of the performances in each behavior setting. Estimates of the performances in Midwest were made by the same methods as estimates of occupancy time and penetration. Inasmuch as more precise data on performances were available than on occupancy time or penetration, we judge the reliability of the performance data to be at least as great as those on occupancy time or penetration.

In 1951/52 approximately 5659 performances occurred in Midwest's 585 community behavior settings. Of these, 566 were performed by outsiders, leaving 5093 presidencies, chairmanships, captaincies, pastorates, clerkships, mechanics positions, superintendencies, editorships, etc., to be filled by Midwest residents. On the average, therefore, each of the 721[1] residents of Midwest had to take part in 7.0 performances during the year. We have called this the Performance/Performer ratio, Pa/Pe, where Pa is the number of performances in a community and Pe the maximum number of different performers, i.e., the population. A community's Performance/Performer ratio has a number of implications for the behavior of its inhabitants.

THE RICHNESS OF LIFE

The size of the Pa/Pe ratio of a community is an index of the average amount of participation, versatility, and responsibility of its citizens in community settings. Our systematic observations in Midwest, and more casual observations elsewhere, have led us to hypothesize that there is a general, inverse relationship between the size and behavioral variety of

[1] The population data for the survey year, 1951/52, are based on the population count of November 1, 1951 made by the staff of the Midwest Social Psychology Field Station.

communities of the same general technical and cultural level and the variety of life for the *individuals* who live in them.   It is quite obvious for example that a three-ring circus of 50 acts, 500 performers, and 750 performances provides less variety for the members of the cast than a one-ring circus of 15 acts, 20 performers, and 120 performances.   Although the former is a greater spectacle to the audience, the one-ring circus provides greater variety for the performers.   It has no bored sword swallowers; in the one-ring circus, the sword swallower must also play on the calliope and be shot from the cannon.   This is a behavioral manifestation of the fact that the Pa/Pe ratio is 6.0 for our hypothetical small circus and 1.5 for our large one.

The Pa/Pe ratio undoubtedly is higher in Midwest than in a metropolis. New York has 10 thousand times more performers than Midwest, but it is our impression that the number of performances is far fewer than the 50 million it would have if the Midwest Pa/Pe ratio held.   It is a triumph of modern technology that a town of 721 people can have a level of culture within the same general range of that of a city of 7 million.   It is a triumph which, for one thing, requires a high Pa/Pe ratio, and constrains the town dwellers to be more versatile and broadly competent than city dwellers.

Figure 4.1 represents the situation we have described.   The curve of performers presents the range of population of American towns from a few hundred to a few million, the curve of performances expresses our hypothesis that the number of performances increases more slowly than the number of performers, and the curve representing the Pa/Pe ratio expresses the conse-quence that this ratio, which we presume to be an index of the variety and richness of life for individuals, declines with community size.   These re-lationships undoubtedly do not hold for such atypical communities as one-industry towns, suburbs, primitive backwoods villages, or settlements which are so small they can implement only a fragment of the prevailing culture. We have not investigated the limits of the relations represented by the curves of Figure 4.1.

It was evident, however, that the Pa/Pe ratio occurred in Midwest as represented in the figure, and the meaning of Midwest's ratio of 7 is un-mistakable.   To keep the town functioning, thousands of performances requiring many special skills and complex actions were needed.   Yet there were only 721 people to accomplish this.   This limited number of people had to provide the behavior involved in a wide variety of actions: drawing legal contracts, operating X-ray equipment, repairing Diesel engines, teaching Latin, playing the church organs, conducting and playing band music, operating fire-fighting equipment, interpreting the Bible, chlorinating the public drinking water, fixing corn pickers, arranging for elections, marketing municipal bonds, preparing large banquets, testing soil for fertilizer require-ments, and conducting funerals.   To maintain Midwest's level of functioning, the average Midwesterner had to take part in a number of performances, some of which encompassed several of these actions.   The fact of the matter is that in 1951 Midwest was shorthanded, not because of the total amount of work to be done, but because of the variety of different actions required to keep the behavior settings functioning.   There was not enough work in Midwest to justify an X-ray specialist, but the community demanded X-ray service.   There were not enough fires in Midwest to support a professional fire-fighter; nevertheless Midwest, and the insurance companies, required

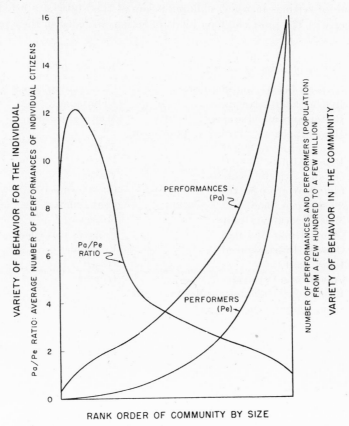

RANK ORDER OF COMMUNITY BY SIZE

FIG. 4.1.—Schematic representation of assumed relation between performers (Pe), performances (Pa), and Pa/Pe ratio in communities of different sizes.

efficient fire protection.   This meant that one person had to turn his single pair of hands to a number of these actions in the course of his performances in Midwest.

Other data which bear upon the question of the variety and richness of life in Midwest will be presented later.   Here we shall mention only the further point that the high level held for all age segments of Midwest's population, for children as well as for adults.   Because Midwest was shorthanded, everyone who could contribute to the actions which had to be performed was important.   In fact, the children of Midwest had a higher

Pa/Pe ratio than the population as a whole. In 1951/52, children under 12 years old took part in 1077 performances in 83 different behavior settings of 32 varieties. These performances involved real power and responsibility with respect to adults as well as children. The Pa/Pe ratio for children was 9.0, indicating that the average Midwest child entered positions of importance to the community at large in nine different behavior settings. The varieties of settings in which children achieved this status are listed below together with the most common kinds of actions included in their performances.

Variety of Behavior Setting	*Kind of Action*
Grocery, Locker, and Feed Stores	Clerk, janitor, stock boy
Indoor Entertainments	Entertainer
Restaurants and Taverns	Waitress, cashier
Home Appliance, Hardware, Implement, and Furniture Stores	Janitor
Indoor Athletic Contests	Player
Outdoor Athletic Contests	Player
Church Worship Services	Choir member
Shoe Repair Shop	Clerk, janitor
Music Education Groups	Musician
Church Group Meetings	Program participant
Outdoor Entertainments	Entertainer
Dairy Barn	Helper
Circuses and Carnivals	Laborer
Recreational Organization Meetings without Refreshments	Officer
Recreational Organization Meetings with Refreshments	Participant in program
Dinners and Banquets	Participant in program
Parties	Entertainer
Membership Business Meetings without Refreshments	Officer
Horse Show	Exhibitor
Paper Routes	Proprietor
School Classroom Recreation	Participant in program
Parades	Exhibitor
Outings	Leader
Recognition Program	Participant in program
Fund Membership Drives	Solicitor
Food Sales and Rummage Sales	Clerk
Weddings	Participant in ceremony
Utility Pay Station	Clerk
Extension Achievement Program	Participant in program
Ballet Classes	Performer
Child's Sales Stand	Proprietor
Qualifying Tests for Entrance	Performer

The pressure on Midwesterners to take part in a number of performances was especially clear in the high school. Outside forces came from the State to provide an accredited curriculum, from the interschool athletic association to participate in a full program of sports, from the State University to engage in cultural activities, from the Federal Government to offer a school lunch program, and from the citizens of Midwest for a school that would honor the town and provide for all of its children. Forces from within the school came from the teachers to offer a modern educational program, from the coach to turn out winning teams, from the principal to have a reputable school, from the college preparatory students to have an accredited course of study, from other students for practical courses, and from all the students for winning teams, marching bands, drama groups, and a beautiful Annual for a lifetime momento. This was quite an order for 85 students and 7 teachers.

The multiplicity of high-school activities was undertaken and the varied goals achieved by virtue of strong, intra-institutional demands upon all the students and staff members for participation in a number of performances. The median number of extracurricular activities of the graduating seniors of Midwest High School was 10.5; for the seniors of a neighboring city high school (enrollment 600) the comparable figure was 3.4. The most versatile Midwest senior's list of school activities included:

Junior Play	Girls Sextette (4 years)
Senior Play	Junior-Senior Banquet, functionary
Basketball (4 years)	Cheer Leader (1 year)
Chorus (4 years)	Majorette (1 year)
Cub Reporter Staff	Drama Club (4 years)
Annual Staff	President of Drama Club
Class Secretary	County Play Contest
Student Council (2 years)	Pep Club (4 years)

The least active class member participated in:

Football (1 year)	Senior Play
Annual Staff	Band (1 year)
Cub Reporter Staff	Junior-Senior Banquet, functionary
Junior Play	

The Midwest High School tended to develop not experts, but broadly competent persons; it valued and encouraged versatility in its pupils rather than high competence in special areas. In this respect, the high school was representative of the town as a whole.

Some meager comparative data on children's participation in another community are available. At the Lawton School, the Pa/Pe ratio for children under 12 years of age was 2.4.[2] In comparison with Midwest

[2] These data and others relating to the behavior settings of the Lawton School are from the Master of Arts Thesis of Merle R. Newton (44).

children, Lawton children entered fewer positions of responsibility and status. This was doubtless in part a function of the institutional situation and was in part due to the disabilities of the children. It is one of the sharpest differences discovered in the living conditions of Midwest and Lawton children.

THE REALITY OF LIFE

Life was not only busy and varied for the average Midwest citizen; it was close to basic realities of man and nature; it had depth as well as breadth. The high Pa/Pe ratio meant that Midwesterners met the hard, the sad, and the seamy sides of life as well as the easy, the pleasant, and the beautiful. The disagreeable features of the town could not be walled off from any substantial segment of the population. This was accentuated by a geographical fact. The different varieties of behavior settings were close together, and were not segregated in special areas. Grocery stores, flower shows, the doctor's office, machine shops, and taverns were randomly distributed about the square and into the side streets. There was no retail district, no medical building, no auto row, no slum area.

In their daily paths about the town children sampled behavior and living conditions ranging from the mean to the noble, from the comic to the tragic, from the hard to the easy. Births and deaths, good fortune and catastrophy were known at close range. About every two months, on the average, there were a birth and a death in Midwest. In most of these cases, the individuals involved were known personally to most of the children of the town. A boy of nine years, after living in the town for a year, asked why more people died in Midwest. During his eight years in a city he had not known one human death, but his first year in Midwest confronted him with a number of them. It was impossible to protect the children of the town from the realities of life.

In Midwest, man's weaknesses and his strengths were clear to everyone. The town was close to uncontrolled natural forces. The whole economy depended on the rains, winds, and frosts. Children were not likely to get a false idea of either the power or the weakness of men when almost every year they saw their parents and other adult acquaintances coping, sometimes successfully, sometimes unsuccessfully, with floods, drought, wind, heat, or cold. The fact that despite the buffetings of nature, Midwesterners were able, by and large, to live satisfying lives would appear to have presented the children with a lesson in man's basic competence. This is our impression; we have no data directly revealing the children's perceptions of this aspect of their world.

LEVELS OF PERFORMANCE

We have no systematic data, either, on the level of various performances in Midwest. However, it was clear to the field workers that behavioral versatility was gained at some sacrifice of general performance level. Midwesterners did not have time for perfection. A music critic would have found the annual School Music Program below the standards of schools where a small proportion of the students specialized in music, perhaps even in *a cappella* choir music. The teaching of biology by a teacher who also taught all the mathematics and coached the athletic teams was probably in some respects less effective than the teaching in a school with a biology department. The most complicated parts of television sets, air pumps, electric motors, and shotguns could not be repaired in town. Mr. Hagedorn, a carpenter, complained bitterly that the demands upon his time for rough work (roofs, floors, foundations) prevented him from turning out the perfect cabinet work he valued and was capable of doing. There was general recognition that the demands of versatility interfered with achieving the levels of performance of which Midwesterners were capable, and there was a general tolerance of less than maximal performance. Versatility, responsibility, and willingness "to try" were more valued than high achievement. This was especially evident in the Midwest adult's evaluation of children's performances. A five-year-old girl who haltingly played the piano piece "Sea Shells" at Ladies Aid was as genuinely applauded as the adult who performed on a professional level. In the child's case the applause was for the child's social skills, willingness "to do her part," and for her future promise.

RANGE OF BEHAVIOR

A consequence of Midwest's limited differentiation and population was restriction on the maximal range of behavior possibilities within the borders of the town. Midwest High School had no courses in photography, folk dancing, calculus, or even French or German; one could not have a lens ground in Midwest or ride on a roller coaster. Although life was varied and rich for the average individual, only a portion of the total range of American behavior occurred in the town. There were not enough people, behavior settings, or performances to exhibit the total spectrum of American culture. It is probable that the range of behavior possibilities within a community is closely related to the number of performances, and that a curve representing them would parallel the performance curve of Figure 4.1.

It seems evident from our observations in Midwest that the degree of differentiation of a community affects the behavior of its inhabitants by way of conditions associated with the Performance/Performer ratio. There is also evidence that a community's differentiation affects behavior via the relationship which exists between the individual citizen's psychological habitat and the total scope of habitat possibilities within the community. We shall turn to this relationship in the next section.

The Individual's Psychological Habitat in
The Community Behavior Settings

There were 585 community behavior settings in Midwest during the survey year. However, only 205 of these occurred on an average weekday. About 200 of the weekday settings recurred daily; the others recurred biweekly, weekly, or less frequently. These 205 concurrent behavior settings were far beyond the maximal span of apprehension of any individual citizen. Even with the aid of informants, a Midwesterner could apprehend in a single cognitive act only a part of Midwest. This was true, too, of the inhabitants of the town; no one of them could be simultaneously aware of the other 720 Midwest residents.

A further fact of importance in the present connection is that the 205 daily community settings were relatively independent behavior areas. The conceptual meaning of K and the operations by which its value is determined signify that the psychological conditions in one behavior setting have little dynamic interdependence with those in another setting. When, for example, Dutton Thurston went from the alley to the Pearl Cafe, his experiences and learning in the alley did little to prepare him for what would happen in the Pearl Cafe. Furthermore, the larger the value of K the greater the independence of behavior settings. K is an index of the insularity of behavior settings as loci of the psychological habitats of individuals.

These two conditions, the first relating to the scope of the individual's cognitive world within the community settings of the town and the second to the dynamic interdependence of the community settings meant that, from the citizen's viewpoint, Midwest was not a unitary place. At a particular time, some parts of the town were foreign to every Midwesterner; at any moment his psychological habitat was influenced by the conditions in a single or a few behavior settings.

When on an average weekday a Midwest school child left the behavior setting Home Meals (Breakfast) on his round of activities, he was confronted with about 205 different stages, each set for and playing a different act. On a usual day, he appeared on about 12 of these stages, being swept into first one and then another relatively independent, unrelated act, and confronted with first one and then another set of values and attitudes within the limits of those occurring in Midwest.

However, this lack of unity and integration in Midwest as a psychological habitat area was reduced by some other conditions. First, although the number of behavior settings in Midwest and the number of people who inhabited them were beyond an individual's span of apprehension, they were within the normal acquaintance or recognition span. Most behavior settings were familiar to most residents of the town, and most Midwesterners had a "speaking acquaintance" with almost every other regular resident. Second, few pairs of behavior settings had K-values of 49, indicating complete independence by the measures used; most Midwest community settings reflected in some degree occurrences in other settings. Third, as has been stated in the previous section and in Chapter II, the range of behavior in Midwest in comparison with total variety in American culture was limited to a relatively homogeneous segment.

As Midwesterners moved about the town, they were continually confronted by the new against a background of the familiar. We estimate that for most school children the scope of the daily habitat, the area of familiarity, and the totality of the day's behavior settings were related in approximately the proportion of 1:10:12.

FREEDOM, ALERTNESS, AND UNCERTAINTY

New situations create uncertainty, conflict, and tension for a person and require alertness if he is to cope with them (11). Familiar situations are experienced according to their known characteristics and, if they are of positive valence and without impassable barriers, they provide a place of freedom for a person to achieve according to his own needs. Both newness and familiarity, in proper degree and proportion, appear to be psychologically desirable: psychological newness by instigating alertness and tension, and familiarity by making planning and achievement possible. Midwest provided both newness and familiarity for its children.

That the children of Midwest were not overly inhibited by barriers of strangeness is indicated by the fact that six-year-olds freely entered 36 per cent of the settings in their entire territorial range (see pp. 99–102) unchaperoned by a special adult. They were regularly seen without older companions in such settings as Trafficways, Everging Variety Store, Midwest Theater, Gwynn Cafe, Dixon Barber Shop, and Men's Town Baseball Game. Responsible adults were, of course, present in all of these settings; this undoubtedly was why parents did not feel they had to arrange for older persons to accompany their young children about the town. The resulting feeling of freedom which children experienced was expressed by a four-year-old on a Halloween evening at about nine o'clock. He was alone. He knocked at a door for "tricks or treats" in a distant part of the town from his home— five blocks away. The adult, surprised at seeing so small a person, asked, "Aren't you a long way from home?" "Oh, no," quickly came the reply with gusto and confidence, "I go all over the whole world."

Evidence that Midwest community settings were not without elements of uncertainty however, is found in the converse data, namely, that six-year-olds were accompanied by older guardians in 64 per cent of the community settings. It is found, too, in the facts that children regularly entered zones of leadership and responsibility where uncertainty is the rule and that the area of freedom of children regularly increased with age (see pp. 102 and 118).

The situation was different at the Lawton School. Most Lawton residents were aware of the state of affairs in most of each day's settings. Furthermore, the value of K for the settings which Lawton children entered was smaller than the average for Midwest children. The average value of K was 24.5 for all pairs of community behavior settings between which the Lawton seven-year-olds Sue Dewall and Verne Trennell passed on the days the specimen records were made (based upon 135 K-values). The comparable figure for the seven-year-old Midwest children Ben Hutchings and Raymond Birch was 29.9 (based on 124 K-values). The probability that this difference in means is greater than chance is .001. This suggests that the life of children in Lawton was more familiar and predictable than the life of children in Midwest, engendering less tension and requiring less alertness.

On the other hand, it is doubtless true that the average K-values of the behavior settings of Midwest children were smaller than those of city children, with proportionately greater familiarity, security, and freedom to plan and to act in Midwest. We have data available for only one boy in a small city. The data for Bobby Bryant are far from representative, however, because of the disability which limited his locomotion. In spite of this the average K-value for the pairs of community settings between which Bobby traversed was 38.0 (based on 6 K-values).

COMMUNICATION AND INTERPERSONAL UNDERSTANDING

The balance of the familiar and the new had an important influence on interpersonal relations in Midwest. For one thing, it facilitated communication. Almost every pair of citizens entered some settings that were common to their everyday lives, and were therefore intimately known to both; they also entered some settings that were only generally familiar to one of both members of the pair. There was both divergence and convergence in lives of Midwesterners. No one in Midwest could say to a fellow citizen, "I have nothing in common with you." The state of affairs in Midwest is favorable to interpersonal communication. The settings which are common and those which are unique to the persons of a communicating group provide something old and something new, something similar and something different—conditions which favor communication. Midwesterners were great visitors, and this friendly conversation in turn increased the common background of vicariously gained knowledge of the town and its people.

Easy communication is a necessary condition for mutual understanding. Midwest's size provided yet another circumstance favorable to interpersonal understanding. Because of its size in terms of behavior settings, Midwest citizens were in an advantageous position to make well-balanced assessments of their associate's actions. This may be indicated by comparing the Lawton School, a city, and Midwest in this respect.

At Lawton, most residents were aware of the state of affairs in most of each day's settings, and they were aware of little else.　The psychological habitats of all Lawton residents were formed within a common context of behavior settings.　An important source of the variety in the psychological habitats and behavior of particular Lawton residents was, therefore, what they as individuals brought to this common context.　In the Lawton community, individual differences in action, values, and emotionality were necessarily seen to derive in an important degree from the personalities of the members.　The staff and the pupils of Lawton inevitably focused their attention upon the "inside" determinants of the behavior of their associates. Personality, intelligence, and motor skills—all properties of the individual— were in the forefront of interpersonal relations in Lawton.

In a metropolis, on the other hand, conditions undoubtedly favor a different focus.　Here, a person's associates must often be identified and "known" in terms of such impersonal characteristics as their ages, sex, places of residence, physical characteristics, social class identifications, and vocations.　In this situation a person has a meager basis for assessing the determinants of his associates' actions.　The consequence is likely to be a resort to stereotyped explanations based upon characteristics which are only remotely related to behavior, or to an acceptance of the impossibility of more than shallow understanding.

In Midwest, conditions were favorable to more adequate perception of the determiners of behavior.　Variations in the behavior of a Midwesterner's associates were not restricted, as in Lawton, to those occurring within a single context of behavior settings.　A Midwesterner associated with persons who had other experiences than he.　In order to understand them, he had to consider situational influences as well as personality influences.　However, his knowledge of the normal range of behavior in Midwest behavior settings, and of the forces within them, provided a basis for recognizing behavior peculiarities attributable to personality differences.　There was not the pressure to deal with associates personally, as in Lawton, or superficially, as in a city.　Midwest did, in fact, provide an unusually good "observation room" with a variety of contexts to elicit a variety of responses, but with sufficient commonness and familiarity that implicit norms and standards provided a basis for assessing behavior deviations due to personality determiners.　Many Midwest residents had an excellent understanding of the actions and personalities of their associates, and there was unusual tolerance of individual differences (see pp. 114–16).

SUCCESS AND FAILURE

The degree of differentiation of Midwest, and the freedom of children to range over the town's community settings appeared to be of relevance for their experience of success and failure.　The experimental and theoretical work on level of aspiration, success, and failure has demonstrated their importance for social behavior and for personal adjustment, and it has provided a basis for judging the degree to which conditions favorable to their occurrences exist in particular situations (**36**). Success as defined in the experimental work refers to the behavior of a person who achieves by his own efforts goals that are important to him, and which are near the top of his ability level. The experimental work shows quite clearly that the level of aspiration mechanism which assures success by lowering goals after failure and raising them after success is easily thrown out of gear. This commonly occurs when social pressure for achievement above a person's ability level is too great, when gratuities are provided which deprive a person of the possibility of achieving his own goals by his own efforts, or when restrictions or a meager situation prevent the development of hierarchical goal structures.

The level of aspiration mechanism functions optimally, and success is maximal, when there is freedom for persons to set their own goals in accordance with their own ability levels. The definition of the K-21 behavior setting implies that this will be fostered when a person has the opportunity of participating freely in a number of behavior settings, for, in this case, there is a high probability that he will meet varied action patterns, behavior mechanisms, performance levels, and social conditions. When to this is added some other characteristics of life in Midwest, namely, the approval of a wide range of levels of performance, the tolerance of individual differences, and the absence of segregation on the basis of ability, it is evident that Midwest residents on all ability levels had many opportunities for success, with the heightened self-esteem and social status which accompany success.

Roy Eddy, for example, entered 17 behavior settings on the day the specimen record was made; the average K-value of the settings between which he made transitions was 29.6. Prominent action patterns in these settings were Recreation, Government, Social Contact, Education, Aesthetics, Nutrition, Business, Earning a Living, Personal Appearance, and Health. All behavior mechanisms occurred. The social atmospheres for Roy in these settings were described as cool and distant, middling permissive, restrictive and overhelping, warm and coercive, warm and permissive, warm and restrictive, warm and attentive. There were appropriate levels of achievement for all ages from infants to aged. In some settings Roy was ignored, restricted, and coerced; but in others he was warmly welcomed, helped, and given great freedom. He had ample opportunity for satisfying his needs for social approval and self-esteem.

This was less true of Sue Dewall at the Lawton School on the day of the observation. Sue also entered 17 K-21 behavior settings. Their average K-value was 24.0; they contained 7 rather than 10 action patterns, 5 rather than 7 constellations of social weather, and the levels of achievement open to her were largely restricted to own age group. Sue's day was more of a piece than Roy's and was less likely to satisfy varied and fluctuating aspirations. Roy was not confined to a narrow range of behavior possibilities and evaluative atmospheres. If he was a failure and oppressed in one setting, he had opportunity to succeed and expand in others. This was not so true of Sue.

Of particular importance for the balance of success and failure in the lives of children was the relatively small amount of competition within peer groups in Midwest. Midwest children were not commonly placed in settings where age, sex, and social group differences were restricted. The problem of Midwest children was not how to cope with the strong competition which often arises in highly segregated peer groups, or how to handle the failure experiences which frequently occur in these groups. Their problem was how to weld persons of differing abilities and interests into functional groups where success was possible at a wide range of levels of achievement. This is discussed in a subsequent section of this chapter where it is suggested that lack of segregation is to an important degree a resultant of the Pa/Pe ratio.

Detailed analyses of the occurrence of success, failure, and related phenomena in the behavior of individual children in Midwest behavior settings are presented in Chapter VIII.

SUMMARY

We have conjectured that two of the mechanisms by which the size of a community affects the experiences and behavior of its inhabitants are connected with the Performance/Performer ratio and with the relationship between an individual's psychological habitat and the total scope of the community's habitat possibilities. Each of these mechanisms points to certain consequences which, so far as our data go, are true for Midwest. Although the data are insufficient to establish the generality of these mechanisms, it has seemed desirable to propose them in any case, for speculation on the basis of the available data appears to be essential in the present state of knowledge.

The size of communities of all kinds—of town, of schools, of businesses, of churches, of nations—is a crucial factor in some of the social-psychological problems which confront them. If the psychological significance of size, per se, can be determined, and if the mechanisms by which community size operates upon individuals can be discovered, it may be possible to reduce the ill effects of community size, or to establish optimal size limits for different kinds of communities.

The Occupancy of Community Behavior Settings

The inhabitants of Midwest divided their time between family behavior settings, community behavior settings, and foreign behavior settings (settings outside the borders of the town). During the survey year we estimate that Midwesterners spent 5,130,000 hours in family settings, 1,030,658 hours in community settings, and 330,620 hours in foreign settings. Data on the average number of hours per day each resident spent in these classes of settings are given in Figure 4.2. These data are averages for all days of the year, including weekdays, Sundays, and holidays. They are based on estimates of occupancy time as described in Chapter III. Inasmuch as the estimates were not made separately for each individual, variability data are not available. In spite of this, some conclusions are justified.

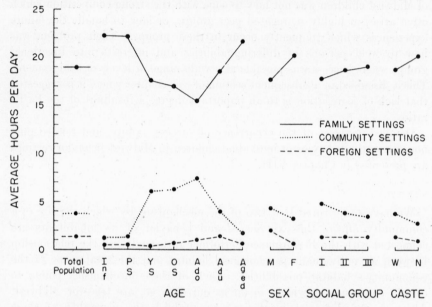

Fig. 4.2.—Average hours per day spent in family, community, and foreign behavior settings by the total population of Midwest and by various subgroups.

The data show that family settings were the primary focus of the behavior of Midwest citizens. The amount of time Midwesterners spent in family settings was 5 times as great as the time spent in community settings and 15 times as great as that spent in foreign settings. The data also indicate quite dramatically the regular decline from infancy to adolescence in the temporal dominance of the family, and the return to the family in adulthood and old age. In spite of the dominance of family settings, community behavior settings were by no means negligible. For the population as a whole, Midwesterners spent 16 per cent of all their time, and 25 per cent of their waking time in community settings. For school children these figures were 25 per cent and 43 per cent respectively, and for adolescents they were 31 per cent and 46 per cent. The family and community settings competed on almost equal terms for the waking time of the school children and adolescents of Midwest.

The data suggest that males, white citizens, and members of social

Group I, respectively, spent more time in community settings and less time in family settings than females, Negro citizens, and members of social Groups II and III.

Population subgroups differed also in the number of different community settings they inhabited, and in the amount of time they spent in particular settings or groups of settings. We call the former the *territorial range* of the subgroup, and the latter its *occupancy time* with respect to a particular setting or group of settings. The *territorial index* of a subgroup is the per cent of all community settings (585) which members of the subgroup inhabited, and the *occupancy index* is the per cent of the total occupancy time (1,030,658 hours) which the subgroup spent in the setting or group of settings. Territorial ranges and indexes can be computed for classes of settings as well as for population subgroups; thus, for example, we have determined the territorial range and the territorial index of educational settings, and of settings where aesthetic behavior was prominent. Territorial ranges and indexes can also be computed for varieties of settings, as well as for individual settings.

Territorial Ranges of Subgroups

Territorial range maps of different population subgroups are presented in Figures 4.3 to 4.9. The particular settings represented on the maps can be identified by means of the numbered Base Map, Figure 4.32 and the Behavior Settings Catalogue, pp. 154–76.

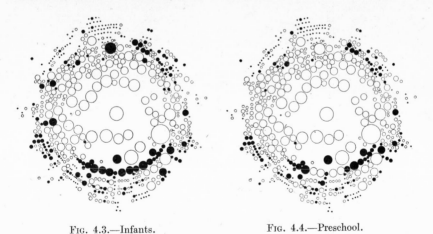

FIG. 4.3.—Infants.   FIG. 4.4.—Preschool.

The chief significance of these data so far as the children of Midwest are concerned is that the town was remarkably open to their coming and going at all ages. During the survey year, the territorial index of infants was 60, and that of adolescents was 79. This does not mean, of course, that all infants entered 60 per cent of Midwest's community settings or that all adolescents entered 79 per cent of them. It means that these proportions

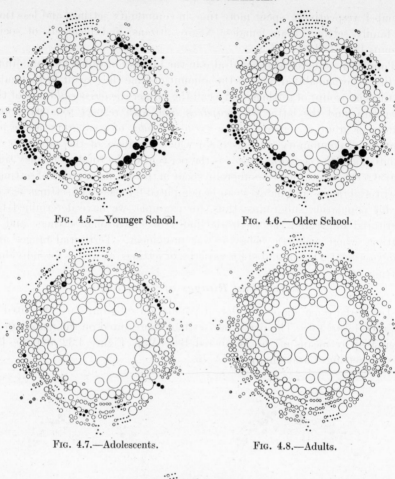

FIG. 4.5.—Younger School.   FIG. 4.6.—Older School.

FIG. 4.7.—Adolescents.   FIG. 4.8.—Adults.

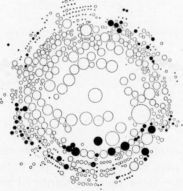

FIG. 4.9.—Aged.

Territorial range maps for population subgroups. The shaded circles are those settings not entered by members of the subgroups.

of the town's behavior areas were regularly inhabited by some members of these subgroups. We believe, however, that in Midwest the territorial index of a subgroup had a psychological significance for most of its members. It signified, for example, that the freedom of an adolescent who might himself enter only 40 per cent of the town's community settings, was measured in some degree by the 79 per cent which held for adolescents in general rather than by the 40 per cent which described him. Although only three or four adolescents regularly worked in the *Midwest Weekly* printing shop, this was generally known as a place where adolescents had an established place and it was undoubtedly an attribute of the position of adolescents in the eyes of most of them.

The territorial range map in Figure 4.10 shows the community settings

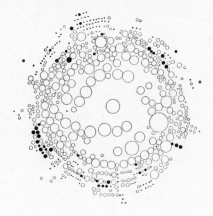

FIG. 4.10.—Children and Adolescents.

Territorial range map. The shaded circles are those settings not entered by children or adolescents.

occupied by children and adolescents of all ages; the territorial index is 87. These data mean that a child who lived to adulthood in Midwest would at some time during his childhood and adolescence have an opportunity to become acquainted with most of the community settings of the town. The curve of Figure 4.11 discloses that this increase in the area of freedom with age, was, on the average, a slow, regular one. Observations of individual children showed that it was a gradual process for the individual, too. A child usually added new, "older" behavior settings to his territorial range one at a time, and often his first entrance into a new setting was brief and on an apprenticeship basis. An adolescent girl was occasionally called upon to substitute for the regular teacher of a Sunday-School class of younger children. The lead in the Junior Class play had long experience on the stage of the school auditorium, beginning as one of the 25 first-grade children singing in the annual music program.

Another matter of importance in this connection which will be presented
in the next section of this chapter was the small amount of age segregation
in the behavior settings of the town. In most settings, a Midwest child
associated with people of a wide age range. He therefore continually experienced the ways and roles of younger and older persons. The gradual age
increments in the territorial range of children and the absence of age segregation in most settings meant that children grew into Midwest; there were
few sudden and radical shifts in their life situations.

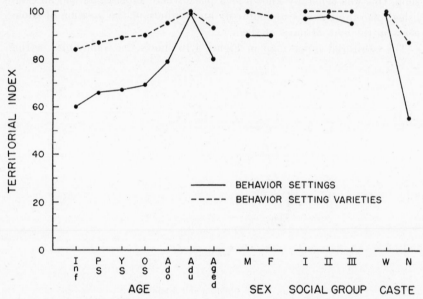

FIG. 4.11.—Territorial indexes of Midwest subgroups. Per cent of all community behavior
settings, and varieties of settings, inhabited by members of Midwest's population
subgroups.

Although children had a wide territorial range and one which increased
slowly and regularly, there were at every age community settings beyond
their area of freedom. This meant that there were new experiences awaiting
children at each succeeding age. Growing up in Midwest brought continually expanding opportunities and increased status. The 6-year-old had
privileges and opportunities not available to the 4-year-old, and the 8-year-
old had more freedom, more status, and more power than the 6-year-old.
Growing up was an advantage to the children of Midwest. This was not
so true for Lawton children. There, both 6-year-olds and 14-year-olds had
access to about 95 per cent of the community's settings. In the Lawton
School, age and increasing abilities broke down few barriers; growing up in
Lawton provided few advantages.

The data of Figure 4.11 show that there were no appreciable differences
in the territorial ranges of males and females or of the social groups.

However, the territorial range of the Negro citizens of Midwest was only a little more than half that of the white citizens.

Territorial range data provide no indication of the degree to which Midwesterners inhabited different settings within the various territorial ranges. As a matter of fact, the occupancy of community settings varied from 78,000 hours, or 7.5 per cent of the total occupancy time for the single setting Trafficways, to 3 hours, or .003 per cent of the occupancy time for the setting Cancer Control Committee Meeting. The 10 per cent of the community settings which were most heavily occupied accounted for 66 per cent of the occupancy time. Figure 4.12 which exhibits this relationship

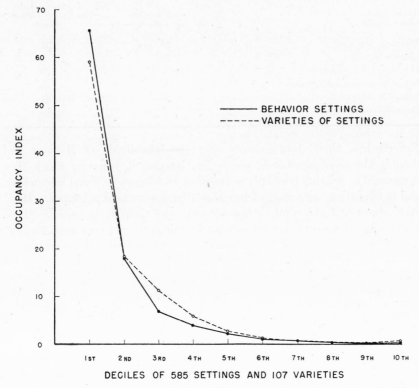

Fig. 4.12.—Occupancy indexes of deciles of behavior settings and varieties of settings, arranged in rank order of occupancy time.

in detail, indicates that most Midwest behavior settings were occupied for relatively small amounts of time.

We shall consider in the following sections the occupancy of various classes of behavior settings and of individual behavior settings.

KINDS OF BEHAVIOR SETTINGS

Community behavior settings can be classified in many ways. One classification which was common in Midwest is given in Table 4.1. For convenience we have called these the *kinds* of community settings. The names of these settings will identify them sufficiently for our present purpose. The lines between these kinds were not precise, and in classifying them we have followed the criteria used in Midwest. Later analysis will show that behavior in each of these kinds of community settings was complex and heterogeneous.

TABLE 4.1

TERRITORIAL INDEXES AND OCCUPANCY INDEXES OF KINDS OF COMMUNITY
BEHAVIOR SETTINGS

Kind of Community Behavior Setting	Territorial Index (Per Cent of 585 Settings)	Occupancy Index (Per Cent of 1,030,658, Hours)
Business Settings	20	51
Church Settings	20	4
Government Settings	7	9
Social Organization Settings	21	3
School Settings	26	24
Miscellaneous Settings	7	10

Nevertheless, these data indicate that the inhabitants of Midwest had roughly the same number of places for engaging in behavior which they designated as relating primarily to business, to religion, to social interaction, and to education, with many fewer places for government activities. However, about half the total occupancy time was spent in business settings, about a quarter of it occurred in school settings, 10 per cent took place in government settings, and 4 and 3 per cent of the occupancy time was spent, respectively, in church and social settings. As a first approximation, these data suggest that life in Midwest outside the families centered about business establishments, with schools as the main secondary focus, and government agencies, churches, and social organizations as active but distinctly tertiary centers of activity.

VARIETIES OF COMMUNITY BEHAVIOR SETTINGS

The classification of behavior settings according to varieties is systematically more adequate than classification by kind. The meaning of the S-30 varieties of behavior setting and of the procedures for identifying them have been described in Chapter III. In brief, settings which belong to the same variety could exchange locations, behavior objects, action patterns, and behavior mechanisms without greatly interfering with their functioning.

There were in 1951/52, 107 varieties of community behavior settings in Midwest. These are listed in order of occupancy time in the Behavior Settings Catalogue, and are represented in Figure 4.33. The subgroup territorial indexes based on varieties are shown in Figure 4.11.

The number of varieties of settings in a community is related to the variety of its behavior possibilities.   It has already been suggested that the range of behavior was limited in Midwest relative to the total range in American culture.   However, a reading of the names of the varieties of settings and a perusal of the settings which are included in each variety will make it clear that Midwest was by no means a primitive community, that it was in fact highly advanced technically.   The territorial indexes based on varieties show that the freedom of children to range over Midwest settings was not restricted to certain varieties of settings, and that, in fact, the territorial indexes based on varieties are greater for children than those based on individual settings.

As with the settings themselves, a few varieties consumed a great proportion of the total occupancy time; in fact, 70 per cent of the occupancy time was spent in 15 per cent of the varieties of settings.   These 16 most frequented varieties are listed in Table 4.2 together with their occupancy indexes and descriptions of their most prominent behavior characteristics. These are the 16 varieties of community behavior settings, from the 107 available, which Midwesterners preferred, as denoted by the way they distributed their available time.

TABLE 4.2

VARIETIES OF COMMUNITY BEHAVIOR SETTINGS WHERE MIDWEST
RESIDENTS SPENT THE GREATEST AMOUNT OF TIME

Variety Number and Name	Prominent Behavior Characteristics	Occupancy Index (Per Cent of 1,030,658 Hours)
1. School Classes	Formal teaching and learning	12.4
2. Trafficways	Traveling between behavior settings	7.5
3. Grocery, Locker, and Feed Stores	Buying and selling food	5.7
4. Motor Vehicle Sales and Service	Buying, selling, and repairing automobiles, trucks and equipment	5.4
5. Drug, Variety, and Department Stores	Buying and selling clothing, household accessories, and medicines	5.1
6. Indoor Entertainments	Attending and producing public entertainment	4.8
7. Restaurants and Taverns	Eating, drinking, and preparing food in public cafes and taverns	4.5
8. Government and School Offices	Office work	4.0
9. Home Appliance, Hardware, Implement, and Furniture Store	Buying, selling, and repairing home and farm equipment	3.8
10. Attorneys, Insurance, and Real Estate Offices	Legal work, buying, and selling insurance and real estate	3.3
11. Indoor Athletic Contests	Attending and participating in indoor athletic contests	2.9

Variety Number and Name	Prominent Behavior Characteristics	Occupancy Index (Per Cent of 1,030,658 Hours)
12. Building Contractors and Material Suppliers	Buying and selling building materials and equipment, and erecting and altering buildings	2.9
13. Hotels, Rooming Houses, and Nurseries	Providing temporary lodging	2.3
14. Telephone and Electric Offices	Providing and maintaining telephone and electric service	2.0
15. Barbers and Beauticians	Providing and securing hair dressing	1.8
16. Hallways and Cloakrooms	Going from one setting to another within buildings. Putting on and removing outdoor garments	1.3

According to these data, the preferred varieties of Midwest community settings were those where the standing behavior patterns were characterized by formal teaching and learning; traveling about the town; buying and selling food, clothing, medicines, machinery, automobiles, and building materials; repairing machinery; producing and attending entertainments and athletic contests; engaging in office and legal work; eating and drinking and preparing food for public consumption; supplying temporary lodging; and providing telephone, electrical, beauty, and barber service.

The varieties of behavior settings most frequented by children under 12 years of age are given in Table 4.3. In considering these, the assumption discussed in connection with territorial range should be kept in mind (see pp. 99–101).

It will be noted that the behavior setting variety County Jail and Sheriff's Residence was among the most prominent varieties of settings within the territorial range of children. This was due to the fact that Mr. Vey, the sheriff in 1951, had three children, that their home was on the ground floor of the County Jail, and that Mrs. Vey prepared the food for the prisoners. According to the K-21 ratings, Sheriff Vey's home and the county jail were subsettings of the same K-21 community setting. The view can be taken that since the relatively high occupancy time of this setting was to so great an extent due to three individuals, a biased picture of its importance in the lives of Midwest children results. However, against this view there are the facts that the jail was known to all Midwest children as a possible place for children to live, and that many of them had contacts with it because three of their friends lived there. We have proceeded on the assumption that the living conditions of any member of a population subgroup did, over a period of time, influence the living conditions of all the other members of the subgroup via acquaintanceship networks and group identifications. This is a matter which might be investigated in detail, although we have not done so. We have based our procedure, in this instance, on our general observation that Midwesterners were familiar with and interested in the behavior and living conditions of their subgroup associates, that they exhibited great pride in their associates' accomplishments, and defensiveness or humility when confronted with their associates' shortcomings. We have indicated

TABLE 4.3

VARIETIES OF COMMUNITY BEHAVIOR SETTINGS WHERE MIDWEST
CHILDREN SPENT THE GREATEST AMOUNT OF TIME

Variety Number and Name	Prominent Behavior Characteristics	Children's Occupancy Index*
1. School Classes	Formal teaching and learning	30.9
2. Trafficways	Traveling between behavior settings	7.4
6. Indoor Entertainments	Attending and producing public entertainment	6.4
21. Open Spaces	Playing	4.3
20. County Jail and Sheriff's Residence	Punishing law breakers	3.9
13. Hotels, Rooming Houses, and Nurseries	Providing temporary lodging	3.6
22. Sunday-School Classes	Formal teaching and learning	3.2
11. Indoor Athletic Contests	Attending and participating in indoor athletic contests	3.0
27. Shoe Repair Shop	Providing and obtaining shoe repair service	3.0
5. Drug, Variety, and Department Store	Buying and selling clothing, household accessories, and medicines	2.5
25. Rest Rooms	Washing, toileting	2.4
40. Classrooms: Free Time	Playing	2.3
30. Dining and Lunch Rooms	Providing and eating noon meal	2.3
31. Music Education Groups	Teaching, learning, and performing of music	2.1
16. Out-of-Door Athletic Contests	Attending and participating in athletic contests	1.9
19. Church Worship Services	Attending and participating in church worship service	1.6

* Per cent of total hours spent in community settings by infants, preschool, younger school, and older school children.

earlier in this chapter that the immediate psychological habitats of Midwesterners were limited to parts of the town, but that over a period of time they lived in the town as a whole. In 1951 the jail was, indeed, a living place for Midwest children in general.

According to the data of Table 4.3, the preferences of Midwest children with respect to varieties of behavior settings differed somewhat from those of Midwesterners at large; 7 of the 16 varieties in each list are common to both. The community behavior areas preferred by children were those where the standing behavior patterns were characterized by formal teaching and learning; traveling between settings; buying and selling clothing, household accessories, and medicines; producing and attending entertainments and athletic contests; eating, drinking, and preparing food for public consumption; supplying temporary lodging; playing; washing and toileting; practicing and performing music; taking part in church and Sunday-School services; punishing law breakers; and providing shoe repair service. The children of Midwest spent 80 per cent of their time outside their homes in settings where these patterns of behavior occurred. These varieties of settings differ from those preferred by the generality of Midwest citizens by a reduced prominence of business and work varieties, and by an increased prominence of educational, recreational, and religious varieties of settings. The nature of these differences will be examined in detail when the action patterns are considered.

INDIVIDUAL BEHAVIOR SETTINGS

The complete list of community settings with their occupancy times and most prominent action patterns and mechanisms are given in the catalogue of behavior settings. From this complete list, the 10 community settings with the highest occupancy times are presented below.

	Occupancy Index (Per Cent of 1,030,658 Hours)
Trafficways (26)	7.6
Midwest Theater (49)	2.9
Seventh- and Eighth-Grade Academic Activities (10)	1.9
Clifford's Drug Store (46)	1.8
Kane's Grocery and Feed Store (29)	1.7
Garnett's Grocery Store (34)	1.7
Telephone Company (156)	1.7
Gwynn Cafe (89)	1.7
Bank of Midwest (179)	1.5
Fifth- and Sixth-Grade Academic Activities (7)	1.5

These 10 preferred settings make up 1.7 per cent of the community behavior settings, and in them Midwest residents spent 24 per cent of the total time they were in community settings.

The 10 behavior settings preferred by the members of each age, sex, social, and race subgroup are listed in Appendix 10. These settings were the chief loci of the activities of the subgroup members outside their families.

A study of these lists shows that infants, aged inhabitants, younger school children, adolescents, older school children, and preschool children were, in this order, the most deviant of the subgroups in their behavior setting preferences.

SUMMARY

According to the data on the occupancy of community settings, the children of Midwest from infancy onward entered most of the town's behavior settings, and the area of their freedom expanded slowly and regularly as they grew older; at each succeeding age new behavior areas became for the first time accessible to them.   The community settings of Midwest were occupied with a high degree of selectivity by subgroups of Midwest's population; the preferences of the children differed from those of the population at large by a relatively greater emphasis upon educational, recreational, and religious varieties of settings, and by a greater uniqueness in the particular settings which they preferred.

Segregation in Community Behavior Settings

We shall turn in this and subsequent sections of this chapter from a consideration of the living conditions and behavior of children within the general context of Midwest's community settings to a more precise investigation of the nature of the settings the children actually inhabited and of their place in these settings.   We shall first look at the degree of segregation of population subgroups within behavior settings, and shall ask whether the behavior settings inhabited by the children of Midwest were populated by a limited segment of Midwest's citizens, or whether they were representative of the Midwest population in general.   Freedom to enter behavior settings has a special significance if these settings have a restricted population.

The data to be given describe the population characteristics of a behavior setting as these were observed by the field staff; they do not refer to the population subgroups for which the setting was officially intended.   Thus, the Presbyterian Women's Sunday-School Class was intended for adult women; however, one or two infants or preschool children were regularly present and are included in the report of those who inhabited the setting. Only regular attendants are reported; the unusual, irregular inhabitant of a behavior setting is not enumerated.   The segregation data to be reported were derived from the occupancy times, so the methodological comments made in connection with the latter are relevant.

AGE SEGREGATION

Data on the segregation of Midwest residents into limited age ranges within behavior settings are represented in Figure 4.13.   These data clearly show that there was little segregation of Midwest residents into narrow age groups.   In the case of children and adolescents, at least 67 per cent of the community settings they inhabited were also inhabited by all other ages. This means that throughout most of their territorial range, Midwest children associated with people ranging in age from infants to the aged.   Conversely, in less than 1 per cent of their territorial range were children of a single age group present with members of only one other subgroup (in all cases adults or aged persons). There was a regular increase in the number of segregated behavior settings until adulthood, with a reversal in old age.

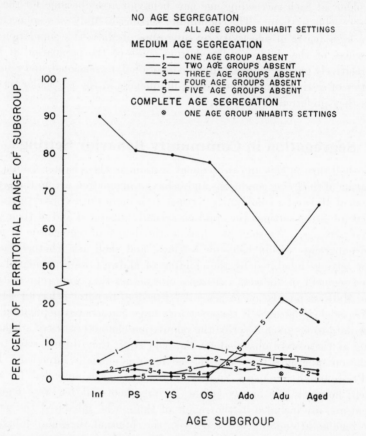

FIG. 4.13.—Age segregation in community behavior settings. Per cent of territorial range of subgroups in which age of inhabitants was limited to different degrees.

SEX SEGREGATION

Sex segregation within behavior settings was less frequent than segregation by age groups. The data are given in Figure 4.14. Throughout childhood and adolescence more than 90 per cent of the settings inhabited by each age group were inhabited by both sexes. The frequency of sex-segregated behavior settings increased slightly in adolescence and markedly in adulthood, with a reversal in old age.

One restriction on the data given in Figure 4.14, must be mentioned: the sex of children under four years of age was not considered. Until about four years of age, children in Midwest were socially asexual; any setting entered by children under four years of age was unsegregated with respect to sex so far as they were concerned. This was the case with all of the infant settings and most of the preschool settings marked as segregated in Figure 4.14.

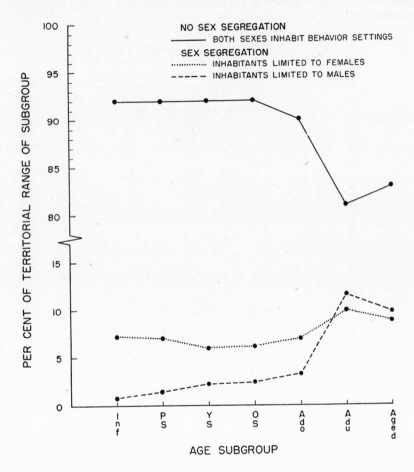

FIG. 4.14.—Sex segregation in community behavior settings. Per cent of territorial range of subgroups in which sex of inhabitants was limited to different degrees.

SOCIAL GROUP SEGREGATION

Segregation of social groups within behavior settings was almost non-existent for the children of Midwest. The data are presented in Figure 4.15. They show that 97 per cent or 98 per cent of the settings children and adolescents entered were inhabited by all social groups, and that for the adults and the aged these figures were 93 per cent and 94 per cent respectively.

Only 3 of the 585 behavior settings were inhabited by members of a single social group. These were all settings with such small numbers of occupants that chance factors might well have caused the segregation found in them during the survey year.

The absence of social group segregation has already been described generally in Chapter II, and it has been demonstrated in studies of individual children (7).

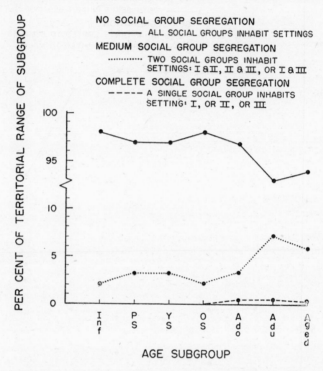

Fig. 4.15.—Social group segregation in community behavior settings. Per cent of territorial range of subgroups in which social group of inhabitants was limited to different degrees.

RACE SEGREGATION

Racial segregation within the behavior settings of Midwest was the greatest of all the kinds of segregation we have studied. Data are given in Figure 4.16. In childhood and adolescence, 60 per cent to 66 per cent of the settings were inhabited by both Negro and white residents, and in adulthood and old age 54 per cent of the settings were nonsegregated. Settings inhabited only by white citizens made up 40 per cent to 46 per cent of the territorial ranges of white Midwesterners at different ages, and settings inhabited only by Negroes comprised 2 per cent to 3 per cent of their territorial ranges.

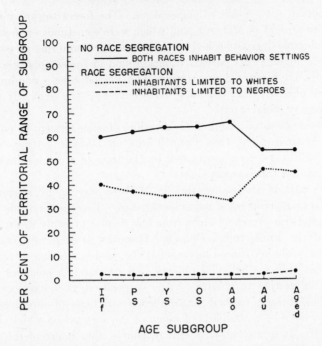

Fig. 4.16.—Race segregation in community behavior settings. Per cent of territorial range of subgroups in which race of inhabitants was limited to different degrees.

SOURCES OF SEGREGATION IN MIDWEST

The data on segregation in Midwest behavior settings disclose that Midwesterners were not often placed in limited social, age, or sex groups. Although systematic data are not available, our general observations showed that this was true, also, with respect to intelligence, education, political views, wealth, physique, and vocation.

The generally low level of segregation in Midwest was undoubtedly to an important degree, a reflection of the high Performance/Performer ratio of the town. Few K-21 behavior settings can operate with only a few occupants. A bridge club requires 12 or 16 persons, a ball team should have at least a dozen members, a scout troop needs 20 boys if it is to thrive, a grocery store must have a hundred regular customers. To secure suitable occupants with the requisite interests and skills, almost every setting in Midwest had to forego the luxury, which may often have been desired, of choosing its participants on the basis of sex, intelligence, age, social group, wealth, politics, education, or vocation. A store for the elite trade of Midwest would soon have failed in business, a ministerial association would have had only 3 members, a school class for crippled children would have had no pupils. In addition to the pressures for tolerance deriving from the Pa/Pe ratio there were in Midwest strong currents of a democratic ideology which opposed some kinds of segregation. The forces toward intolerance which were present in Midwest, and which were sometimes expressed, were to a considerable degree checked by these stronger countering pressures.

However, against this pervasive background of forces opposing it, some segregation did occur. Some settings had official rules excluding males, females, or children from entrance; no behavior setting explicitly excluded Negroes or any social group.

Unverbalized customs limited the freedom of some citizens to enter some behavior settings. The City Council was an all-male setting, and the churches of Midwest were segregated on the basis of race, despite considerable feeling that this was not right.

A great part of the segregation in Midwest was an expression of the differential attractiveness of behavior settings. There was no rule or taboo which excluded a preschool child from the regular monthly meeting of the Session of the Presbyterian Church. However, it is hardly conceivable that a preschool child would have found the Session meeting attractive; its time, its location, its behavior objects, and its standing behavior patterns were not interesting to children. Age segregation, therefore, occurred in the Session without explicit or implicit restrictions of any kind. This appears to have been the basis of much of the segregation which did occur in Midwest. It is undoubtedly true of course, that many of the interests which Midwest residents found so natural were the product of learned customs and taboos—learning which was so complete that alternative ways of behaving were not perceived.

In the case of the Negro residents and other subgroups with greatly restricted numbers, an unknown amount of the actual segregation was due to limited man-hours available for participating in behavior settings. Midwest's 35 Negroes would have found it taxing to attend all of the town settings, even if they had been freely able to enter them. Furthermore, 8 of the Negro residents were children and 10 of them were aged. Undoubtedly some of the apparent segregation of Midwest Negroes was an artifact of their small numbers and their peculiar age distribution.

SIGNIFICANCE OF SEGREGATION FOR THE CHILDREN OF MIDWEST

The important fact about segregation in Midwest behavior settings is that there was so little of it. Most of the settings which children inhabited contained persons of all ages, both sexes, both races, all social groups, all temperaments, all intellectual levels, and all physical characteristics to be found in Midwest. This required that children early learn to accommodate themselves to the whole range of social, physical, and behavioral differences in Midwest inhabitants. Midwest children had to acquire skills in adjusting to, and tolerance in accepting, a wide variety of people and behavior. They had to learn how to arrange a good game of "work up" which included both boys and girls, and all ages from the lower grades to high school. They had to be able to attend a 4-H club meeting without shock or embarrassment in the home of the Senator's son or the laborer's daughter. The Junior Class had to find a play with a part acceptable to the one Negro class member. Midwest children knew in terms of spontaneous, non-institutionalized contacts the whole gamut of the individual and social differences of the town.

Acceptable ways of incorporating these wide ranges of skills, interests, and temperaments within the same pattern of behavior were required. In some cases, special arrangements helped. In one case, a satisfactory ball game with nine boys ranging from 7 to 16 years of age was arranged by the 14-year-old and the 16-year-old "standing" the seven younger boys, with one "out" per inning for the older boys and six for the younger. A good game ensued, and the score of 29 to 22 in favor of the older "side" appeared to satisfy everyone as fairly achieved. Basically, however, a large measure of self-control and a large fund of tolerance were demanded of many persons. In the case of the Town Band, for example, the leader and the skilled performers had to limit their desires for good or interesting music to compositions suited to the abilities of all the band members whose ages ranged from 9 to 45 years and whose skills included those of the beginners and those of the ex-professional member of a circus band. The novices had to tolerate being pushed beyond their abilities on occasion, the skilled players had to live with the failures of the novices, and the audience had to appreciate fair music. The children and adults of Midwest learned to accommodate large individual differences within effectively functioning standing patterns of behavior. This can be done only with a generous supply of self-control and tolerance.

Such effectively functioning behavior patterns meant that success was achieved in Midwest at widely differing levels of performance. The fact that an 8-year-old and his father could both receive blue ribbons at the horse show, that the 6-year-old junior choir member and the septuagenarian preacher both gained social approval and self-esteem in the same worship service, and that the 9-year-old contractor's son operated the bulldozer when help was short undoubtedly gave a depth of meaning to much achievement which is absent where children's activities are limited to "children's" groups.

The wide individual participation in Midwest behavior settings meant, too, that many settings were learning situations where older children and adults unwittingly taught children the skills and social roles they had to learn. When 4-year-old Dutton Thurston regularly spent Friday morning with his father, brother, and two other mechanics in the machine shop of the Midwest Hardware and Implement Co., he was being educated in the ways of male adulthood and in the skills of a mechanic. The same was true of such settings as the 4-H Club which included boys and girls from 8 to 17 years, the Old Settlers' Amateur Program where contestants from 4 years to 65 appeared on the same stage, and the Sunday-School Christmas Program where individuals of all ages from infants to the aged participated. In this connection it is interesting to note that the school and the Sunday-School classes which contained the chief formal educational settings, were the ones where age segregation was most frequent. Other behavior settings of the town performed an educational function by abandoning the segregation principle. This points to the important fact that in evaluating the education of Midwest children it is necessary to look beyond the limits of the schools.

It seems clear that the relative absence of segregation in Midwest behavior settings did, in effect, maximize the variety and richness of life for the children of the town.

Penetration into Community Behavior Settings

The depth of a person's penetration into a behavior setting refers to his power over the behavior pattern of the whole setting. Depth of penetration varies from Zone 1 which is the position of the onlooker or tolerated visitor to Zone 6 where maximum power is vested in a single person. We have chosen to describe the penetration of population subgroups in terms of the maximal penetration of any group member. We have done this with the assumption that the maximal penetration of any group member has significance for most members of the subgroup, as in the case of territorial range and occupancy.

CHANGES IN MAXIMAL DEPTH OF PENETRATION WITH AGE

Table 4.4 shows the distribution of the maximal depths of penetration

TABLE 4.4

MAXIMAL DEPTHS OF PENETRATION INTO MIDWEST COMMUNITY
BEHAVIOR SETTINGS BY REPRESENTATIVES OF SEVEN AGE GROUPS

Age Group	Settings Not Entered	Zone 1	Zone 2	Zone 3	Zone 4	Zone 5	Zone 6	Total Entered	Q1*	Md*	Q3*
Infant	238	240	61	41	5	0	0	347	1.36	1.72	2.33
Preschool	204	211	82	70	18	0	0	381	1.45	1.90	2.88
Younger School	199	143	86	115	41	1	0	386	1.67	2.58	3.53
Older School	187	131	76	128	60	3	0	398	1.76	2.88	3.72
Adolescent	127	75	49	176	117	37	4	458	2.82	3.59	4.37
Adult	3	3	7	32	22	216	302	582	5.36	6.03	6.51
Aged	113	60	91	189	48	49	35	472	2.64	3.45	4.29

* Computed only for settings entered by representative of age group. The interval for Zone 1 is 1.00 to 1.99.

into the 585 community behavior settings by each of the seven age subgroups. The data are presented graphically in Figure 4.17. These data reveal a regular increase from infancy to adulthood in both the number of behavior settings inhabited, and in the maximal depth of penetration of inhabited settings. In old age there is a retrogression to approximately the adolescent level. These trends are revealed by the frequencies with which each maximal penetration depth occurred and by the medians. By inspecting Table 4.4 and Figure 4.17 it will be seen, for example, that infants entered Zones 4, 5, and 6, i.e., they were performers, in a few settings, and

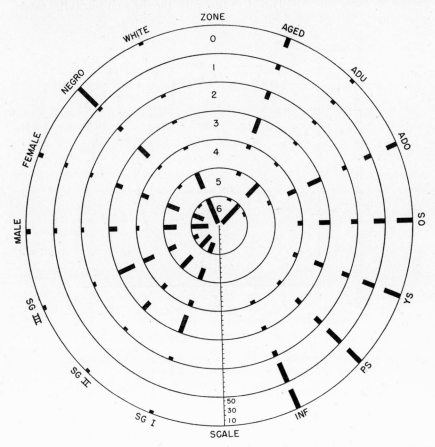

Fig. 4.17.—Penetration of community settings by Midwest subgroups. Per cent of all community settings which subgroup members entered to different maximal depths of penetration. Zone O in this figure represents the community settings not entered by any member of a subgroup. Data rounded out to nearest 10 per cent scale point.

that the number of settings in which these depths of penetration were achieved increased regularly to adulthood and declined in old age.

The frequency with which the age subgroups penetrated behavior settings to the performance zones is presented in Figure 4.18 for Midwest and for Lawton. It will be noted that in Midwest there was a regular increase during childhood and adolescence in the number of settings penetrated to the performance zones, and the data of Table 4.4 show that beginning with the younger school group, penetration extended to Zone 5, also. This was less true of Lawton. There, the younger school age group as well as the older school and adolescent age groups, had essentially the same status in behavior settings, and no settings were penetrated by these sub-groups to Zones 5 or 6. This is in line with the data on territorial range;

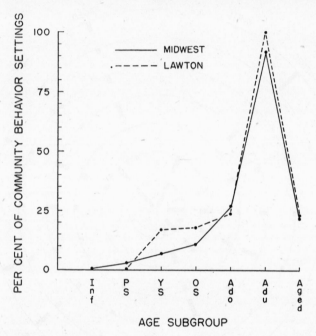

Fig. 4.18.—Age and performance. Per cent of community behavior settings in which members of age subgroups penetrated to Zones 4, 5, or 6.

both sets of data indicate that increasing maturity in Midwest was accompanied by benefits in the way of opportunities and status which did not accompany maturity in Lawton.

In connection with the penetration of children into Midwest behavior settings it is important to note that deep penetration was not limited to settings created specifically for children. Children or adolescents entered penetration Zones 4, 5, or 6 of 28 per cent of the community behavior settings. Of these, 45 per cent were designed specifically for children and existed because they were thought to be "good for" children, e.g., School classes, Scouts, the 4-H Club. However, 55 per cent of the settings in which children or adolescents were performers had no special reference to children; they were "adult" settings such as County Teachers Institute, Hopkins' Feed Store, County Welfare Office, Women's Club I, Regular Meeting. This meant much for the status and self-esteem of Midwest children and adolescents; their achievements were not disparaged by limiting them to children's settings. On the other hand, in Lawton 96 per cent of the settings were devised specifically for children.

Another fact of importance for the children of Midwest was the pre-eminence of adults in leadership positions. Adults or aged persons were joint or single leaders in 99 per cent of the community settings. Children and adolescents were free to range over most of Midwest, but they were not on the loose.

DIFFERENCES IN MAXIMAL DEPTH OF PENETRATION BY SEX GROUPS

Considering that generally in the American culture, homes are maintained by women and livings are earned by men, one might expect that the women of Midwest would not enter as many community behavior settings as men nor penetrate them as deeply. Yet, Table 4.5 and Figure 4.17 show that

TABLE 4.5

MAXIMAL DEPTHS OF PENETRATION INTO MIDWEST COMMUNITY
BEHAVIOR SETTINGS BY REPRESENTATIVES OF SEX GROUPS

| Sex | Settings not Entered | Settings Entered To | | | | | | Settings Entered | Q1* | Md* | Q3* |
		Zone 1	Zone 2	Zone 3	Zone 4	Zone 5	Zone 6				
Males	54	12	9	106	40	156	208	531	4.14	5.63	6.37
Females	56	9	32	92	101	161	134	529	3.99	5.19	6.01

* Computed only for settings entered by representatives of sex groups. The interval for Zone 1 is 1.00–1.99.

males and females inhabited and were performers in almost exactly the same number of community settings. However, males entered significantly more settings than females in Zone 6, and females entered more settings in Zone 4. Men were more often the single leaders of community settings and women were more often the active, operating functionaries. General observation suggested, too, that men inhabited the more powerful and prestigeful cytosettings, such as those of Mayor, Preacher, School Superintendent, Bank President. Nevertheless, women and girls were highly visible in positions of power and responsibility in the public behavior areas of the town. They were important in the schools as teachers, class officers, play performers, and band members; they held joint leadership positions in business settings; they were committee chairmen, club officers, and entertainers. Had the women and girls of Midwest suddenly returned to the homes of Midwest to let the men and boys run the community settings, the town would have suffered an economic and cultural collapse. The children of Midwest were presented with a picture of male and female roles in which there was little difference in the positions of the sexes in the community at large. The chief differences were in the action patterns and behavior mechanisms in which men and women participated within the settings. Data on this are presented in the next sections of this chapter.

In Lawton the situation was different. Males entered the performance zones of 56 per cent of the settings; females were performers in 87 per cent of the settings. Furthermore, the leaders of the more important Lawton settings were women.

DIFFERENCES IN MAXIMAL PENETRATION BY SOCIAL GROUPS

The data presented in Table 4.6 and Figure 4.17 disclose only one consistent difference between social groups in depth penetration. Positions of

TABLE 4.6

MAXIMAL DEPTHS OF PENETRATION INTO MIDWEST COMMUNITY BEHAVIOR SETTINGS BY REPRESENTATIVES OF SOCIAL GROUPS

Social Group	Settings not Entered	Zone 1	Settings Entered To Zone 2	Zone 3	Zone 4	Zone 5	Zone 6	Settings Entered	Q1*	Md*	Q3*
I	20	2	29	214	68	135	117	565	3.52	4.55	5.82
II	9	1	15	120	74	192	174	576	4.11	5.41	6.17
III	33	1	30	223	141	98	59	552	3.48	4.15	5.19

* Computed only for those settings entered by representatives of class groups. The interval for Zone 1 is 1.00 to 1.99.

power were more often held by members of Social Group II than by members of Group I or Group III. The total number of settings penetrated to the performance zones were 320 for Group I, 404 for Group II, and 298 for Group III.

As Midwesterners moved from setting to setting, they found Group II residents in responsible positions most frequently, but in over half of the settings members of Social Group I and III were in important positions also. Group III residents were found less frequently as presidents and proprietors than were members of Groups I and II, but they were considerably more often active as functionaries, subordinate club officers, store clerks, choir members, and performers in plays. The members of all three groups held vital positions in Midwest community settings. The less frequent penetration of Group I members to central positions in community behavior settings may be a function of their more limited numbers; in 1950 there were 80 Group I members, compared with 246 in Group II and 354 in Group III. It is obvious that members of Group I were busier in their positions as single leaders of 117 settings than were Group II members as single leaders of 174 settings. It may be that Group I residents did not have time for more leadership duties.

DIFFERENCES IN MAXIMAL DEPTH OF PENETRATION BY WHITES AND NEGROES

There were, at the time of the survey, 35 Negroes in Midwest. Data on their penetration into behavior settings are given in Table 4.7 and Figure

TABLE 4.7

MAXIMAL DEPTHS OF PENETRATION INTO MIDWEST COMMUNITY BEHAVIOR
SETTINGS BY REPRESENTATIVES OF CASTE GROUP

| Caste Group | Setting Not Entered | Settings Entered To | | | | | | Settings Entered | Q1* | Md* | Q3* |
		Zone 1	Zone 2	Zone 3	Zone 4	Zone 5	Zone 6				
White	7	0	11	13	6	215	333	578	5.53	6.13	6.57
Negro	217	7	47	178	26	5	5	268	3.07	3.45	3.82

* Computed only for those settings entered by representatives of caste groups. The interval for Zone 1 is 1.00 to 1.99.

4.17. These 35 Negroes, 8 of whom were children, entered 368 Midwest community behavior settings to a median depth of 3.45, i.e., to the membership-customer zone, compared with a median of 6.13 for white residents. We can characterize the penetration of the Negro into Midwest community settings as Zone 3 or greater in over half of the settings of their territorial range (36 per cent of all community settings), and as in the performance zones of 13 per cent of their territorial range (6 per cent of all settings). Negroes were joint or single leaders of 10 settings, all of which were in the African Methodist Episcopal Church, and they were active functionaries in 26 settings. Most of the latter were settings inhabited by both white and Negro citizens. Most Negro performances involved participation in school plays, musical programs, and athletic contests.

THE SIGNIFICANCE OF THE PENETRATION OF CHILDREN INTO MIDWEST
BEHAVIOR SETTINGS

The basic significance of penetration in Midwest derived from the fact that to keep Midwest functioning, children were essential both as performers and as members, spectators, and customers of settings. Children and adolescents did not often occupy the roles of house guests who had to be entertained, or of slightly daft characters who required special arrangements to "keep them busy." A modern Pied Piper would have left Midwest not only distraught, but crippled economically and socially.

There were many indications that the extra-family importance of children in Midwest had a great impact upon their experiences, particularly upon their self-perceived value and status. In Midwest the importance of children was a reality which rested upon more than intrafamily affectional relationships.

The picture of the penetration of children into the behavior settings of the Lawton School was quite different. The absence of a regular increase in depth of penetration with increasing age, the total absence of the penetration of children to Zones 5 or 6, and the almost complete absence of an opportunity for children to penetrate "adult" behavior settings call attention to the fact that this children's institution was, indeed, child centered. This may have occurred to such a degree that it offered its child inhabitants few opportunities to grow in status and self-esteem. To what extent this was a necessary product of the disablement of the children we do not know. However, this probably constitutes a common hazard of children's institutions. Lawton differed from Midwest, too, in the predominance of females in the central zones of its behavior settings.

Standing Patterns of Behavior in Community Settings

Having determined the number, the kinds, and the varieties of behavior settings in Midwest, and their degree of occupancy and depth of penetration by different subgroups, we are now in a position to consider their standing patterns of behavior, i.e., their persisting, extra-individual behavior configurations.

The standing patterns of behavior have been described in terms of 13 action patterns, namely Aesthetics (A), Business (B), Earning a Living (El), Education (E), Government (G), Nutrition (N), Orientation (O), Personal Appearance (PA), Philanthropy (P), Physical Health (PH), Recreation (Rec), Religion (Rel), and Social Contact (S). These action patterns and the rating scale for describing them have been set forth in Chapter III and Appendix 6. The ratings on the scale vary from zero (action patterns did not occur) to 14 (action pattern paramount in the setting). The meaning of the ratings can be briefly summarized in these terms: the highest ratings indicate that a large proportion of the behavior in a setting was judged to be involved in an action pattern in multiple ways, i.e., by directly participating in it, by supplying material and equipment for its occurrence in other settings, by learning and teaching the action pattern, and by appreciating it. Low ratings indicate that only a small proportion of the behavior was judged to be involved in a few of these expressions of the action pattern. A rating is, therefore, an indication of the degree of occurrence of an action pattern in the standing behavior pattern of a setting.

Few action patterns are mutually exclusive; the same setting may receive a high rating on a number of them; thus, Methodist Church: Women's Sunday-School Class Meeting was judged at the same time to be high on the action patterns Religion, Social Contact, and Education.

Distributions of Action Pattern Ratings

The distributions of the action pattern ratings of the community behavior settings are given in Figure 4.19. Action pattern ratings of 6 or more

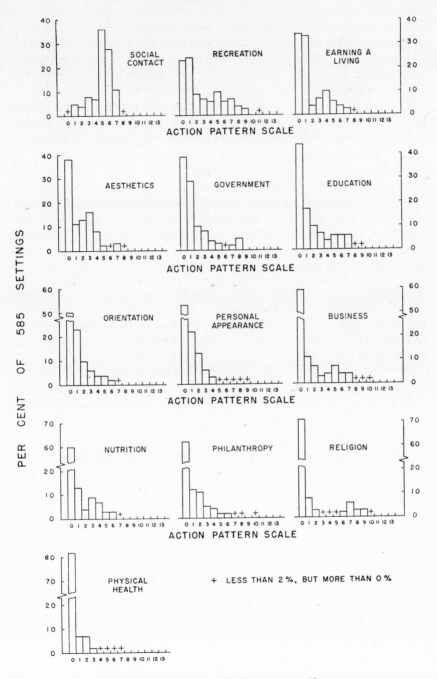

Fɪɢ. 4.19.—Distributions of action pattern ratings.

identify the action patterns which were commonly recognized by the citizens and the field workers as of primary importance in a setting. We have designated these action patterns as the *prominent* action patterns of a setting. This was a rather strict criterion of prominence; 11 per cent of all ratings were rated 6 or greater. The prominent action patterns of each behavior setting are identified in the catalogue of behavior settings.

The distributions given in Figure 4.19 show that action patterns differed greatly in the frequency and degree with which they occurred in the standing behavior patterns of Midwest's community behavior settings; in the following paragraphs, we shall consider various measures of their occurrence.

TERRITORIAL RANGE OF ACTION PATTERNS

Action patterns differed in the number of settings in which they occurred, i.e., in their territorial range. We have abstracted from the data of Figure 4.19 the territorial indexes of each action pattern, i.e., the per cent of all community settings which received any rating on an action pattern. These are listed below in order of their size:

Action Pattern	Territorial Index	Action Pattern	Territorial Index
1. Social Contact	99	8. Personal Appearance	48
2. Recreation	77	9. Business	41
3. Earning a Living	67	10. Nutrition	40
4. Aesthetics	60	11. Philanthropy	38
5. Government	60	12. Religion	29
6. Education	56	13. Physical Health	19
7. Orientation	50		

The territorial index of an action pattern is one indicator of its importance in Midwest. By analogy to a wildlife region, the territorial index is equivalent to the relative number of areas where grazing, watering, securing shelter, etc., occur in the whole region. It is an indication of the accessibility of the action pattern in the behavior areas of the town. According to this interpretation, Midwest provided its inhabitants with the greatest number of places to engage, or prepare to engage, in social interaction, and the least number of places for promoting physical health. Differences in the extents of the territorial ranges were great, varying from one action pattern whose territorial range embraced almost every setting in the town, to one which included less than one-fifth of the settings.

The territorial indexes indicate that the standing patterns of behavior in Midwest settings were characteristically a composite of a number of action patterns. If the settings had been specialized with each involving a single action pattern, the territorial range of each would have been 45 settings, and the territorial index 7.6. The list above shows that no action pattern had so limited a distribution; the median territorial index is 50.

The number of action patterns in a setting actually varied from 1 to 13; the median was 7.2. Like the behavior of the individual citizens of Midwest, the behavior in most behavior settings was highly varied.

MEDIAN RATINGS OF ACTION PATTERNS

The median ratings of the action patterns in the settings of Midwest are listed below:

Action Pattern	Median	Action Pattern	Median
1. Social Contact	5.71	8. Personal Appearance	.94
2. Recreation	2.31	9. Business	.85
3. Aesthetics	1.93	10. Nutrition	.83
4. Earning a Living	1.49	11. Philanthropy	.81
5. Education	1.37	12. Religion	.70
6. Government	1.36	13. Physical Health	.61
7. Orientation	1.00		

These medians are, in terms of our analogy to a wildlife region, equivalent to the median grazing potentialities of the whole region, including those areas where no grazing occurred.

As with the territorial index, there is great variation in the median ratings of the action patterns, and the rank order of the two is very similar. The rank order correlation (tau[3]) is .95, and significant beyond the .01 level. A determinative factor in this similarity is the large number of zero ratings which have the same kind of influence on both indexes; they enter the territorial index as zero occurrences and the median ratings as zero ratings.

MEDIAN RATINGS OF ACTION PATTERNS WITHIN TERRITORIAL RANGES

The median ratings of action patterns when considering only those settings which received some rating on an action pattern are given below.

Action Pattern	Median (Excluding Zero Ratings)	Action Pattern	Median (Excluding Zero Ratings)
1. Religion	6.19	8. Philanthropy	2.60
2. Social Contact	5.71	9. Physical Health	2.30
3. Business	3.82	10. Orientation	2.23
4. Recreation	3.73	11. Earning a Living	2.18
5. Nutrition	3.26	12. Government	2.16
6. Aesthetics	3.34	13. Personal Appearance	2.14
7. Education	3.14		

These data provide a different view of Midwest from that given by the medians which include the zero ratings. The rank order correlation between the two is .08 and not significant. The present medians which exclude the zero ratings are analogous to the median grazing potentialities of all the

[3] Tau: measurement of rank correlation; see Kendall (28).

grazing areas of a wildlife region.   They indicate the degree of occurrence
of an action pattern in the settings within its territorial range.   These data
show that the action pattern Religion, which had a low territorial index,
occurred in the greatest concentration within its territorial range; in fact, it
was a prominent action pattern in 50 per cent of the settings in which it
occurred.   On the other hand, Social Contact which had a wide distribution
also occurred in high concentration, being prominent in 40 per cent of the
settings in which it occurred.   Personal Appearance, Government, Earning
a Living, Orientation, Physical Health, and Philanthropy occurred with
great sparseness within their own territorial ranges, and the remaining action
patterns occurred with a low median degree of concentration.

OCCUPANCY TIMES OF BEHAVIOR SETTINGS WITH DIFFERENT ACTION PATTERNS

The people of Midwest spent varying amounts of time in behavior settings
with different action patterns.   The action patterns are listed below in
order of their occupancy indexes, i.e., the per cent of the total occupancy
time spent in the territorial range of each action pattern.

Action Pattern	Occupancy Index	Action Pattern	Occupancy Index
1. Social Contact	99	8. Aesthetics	62
2. Earning a Living	94	9. Nutrition	55
3. Government	90	10. Personal Appearance	44
4. Recreation	80	11. Physical Health	25
5. Business	77	12. Philanthropy	19
6. Orientation	73	13. Religion	12
7. Education	63		

The occupancy index of action patterns is analogous in a wildlife region
to the relative amount of time the species under study spends in grazing areas,
watering areas, shelter areas, etc.   Its rank order correlation with the
territorial index is .67 (significant beyond the .01 level), and with the median
rating within the territorial range is zero.

According to the occupancy index, Midwesterners spent most of their time
in behavior settings where the action pattern Social Contact occurred and the
least amount of time in settings where the action pattern Religion was present.
Settings with Earning a Living, Government, and Recreation action patterns
each consumed 80 per cent or more of the occupancy time of community
settings, while those with Physical Health, Philanthropy, and Religion action
patterns consumed 25 per cent or less.   The remainder of the action patterns
consumed an intermediate amount of the occupancy time of community
settings.

THE PROMINENCE OF ACTION PATTERNS IN MIDWEST SETTINGS

We have discovered three relatively independent indexes of the importance
of an action pattern in Midwest community settings, namely, (a) its terri-

torial index (or its median rating), (b) its median rating within its territorial range, and (c) its occupancy index. The rank order correlations between these three measures of the prominence of action patterns in community behavior settings are: (a) vs. (b), .03; (a) vs. (c), .67; (b) vs. (c), .00. We have combined these measures into a community-wide *prominence index* of an action pattern. The prominence index of an action pattern is the product of its occupancy index and its territorial index *for behavior settings which receive a rating of 6 or more on the action pattern.* In other words the prominence index of action pattern X=

$$\frac{100 \text{ (Number of settings rated 6 or more on X)}}{585} \times \frac{100 \text{ (Hours spent in settings rated 6 or more on X)}}{1{,}030{,}658}$$

Prominence indexes of Midwest action patterns and the data from which they are computed are shown in Table 4.8 along with the prominence

TABLE 4.8

OCCUPANCY INDEXES, TERRITORIAL INDEXES, AND PROMINENCE INDEXES
OF ACTION PATTERNS RECEIVING RATINGS OF 6 OR GREATER

ACTION PATTERNS	MIDWEST			LAWTON
	Occupancy Index	Territorial Index	Prominence Index	Prominence Index
Social Contact	27	39	1053	304
Recreation	14	21	294	1599
Business	30	9	270	0
Earning a Living	29	7	203	0
Education	15	13	195	104
Government	10	7	70	0
Religion	4	15	60	+
Aesthetics	6	8	48	36
Nutrition	9	4	36	264
Physical Health	7	1	7	63
Orientation	3	2	6	0
Personal Appearance	2	2	4	40
Philanthropy	+	4	+	0

indexes of action patterns in Lawton. The action patterns with the highest prominence indexes are those which were widely distributed in concentrated form and with which the people had extensive contact. With the prominence indexes before us, together with the distributions of the action pattern ratings, the medians, the territorial ranges, and the occupancy times, we are in a position to describe Midwest in terms of some of the major components of its standing behavior patterns.

Social Contact and Recreation. The most prominent action pattern in Midwest behavior settings was Social Contact (social interaction, fellowship, friendly conversation). Over 99 per cent of the settings received some rating for Social Contact, and 39 per cent received a rating of 6 or more. The latter settings consumed 27 per cent of the total occupancy time of community settings.

Next in order of prominence was Recreation (pleasurable activities, games, entertainments) with 77 per cent of all settings receiving a rating and 21 per cent receiving a rating of 6 or more. Settings in which Recreation was prominent consumed 14 per cent of the occupancy time of community settings.

Sociability and play formed the behavioral background of almost all the community behavior settings of Midwest. Midwest was, above all, a social town and one where "having some fun" was widespread. Midwesterners carried their social and recreational life into almost all behavior areas of the town. This can be verified and made more pointed by referring to the Behavior Settings Catalogue where the settings in which Social Contact and Recreation were prominent are identified.

Business, Earning a Living, and Education. Against the background of social and recreational action patterns, three behavioral figures stood out in Midwest, namely, Business (exchanging goods or services for profit), Earning a Living (hiring out for wages), and Education (formal teaching and learning). The profit-making and wage-earning settings were seen by Midwesterners as the places where people worked. Settings in which either or both of these work action patterns were prominent comprised 11 per cent of the community settings and consumed 35 per cent of the occupancy time. Most Midwest settings were not places to work, but work settings occupied more than one-third of the people's time outside their homes.

The action pattern Education occurred in 56 per cent of the community settings; it was prominent in 13 per cent of them, and 15 per cent of the total occupancy time was spent in settings where Education was prominent. It will be noted by referring to the catalogue of behavior settings that formal teaching and learning were by no means limited to the schools or to children; only 47 per cent of them were within the schools and only 60 per cent were created especially for children. Church organizations were the main secondary locus of educational settings, constituting 26 per cent of all settings in which teaching and learning were prominent. Most of the remaining educational settings were connected with the coöperative education program of the State College and Midwest County, although there were a few unattached, voluntary educational settings. Of the settings devoted to the education of children, 61 per cent were connected with the school, 26 per cent with the churches, and 7 per cent with the State-County program; 6 per cent were private music teachers.

We cannot describe here in detail the content, methods, and effectiveness of education in Midwest. It was clear, however, that with the schooling provided, Midwesterners succeeded in college and achieved the highest academic and professional levels. The school curriculum was undoubtedly limited, by many standards, but the total curriculum of the community was a rich one for most children and adolescents.

Much adult education was concerned with applications of the household arts, the mechanical and agricultural sciences, and with music. Extension classes in grain production, livestock management, and farm machinery maintenance were held regularly in the town. The musical education of the adults who were members of musical groups, about 10 per cent of the adult population, also took place regularly.

Aside from the practical arts, applied sciences, and music, the field of instruction in which most adults participated was religion. The Protestant conception of the good life was the concern of some adult group almost every day of the year, and most of these group meetings were educational settings where formal instruction was given by nonprofessional teachers. The textual material for most of this instruction originated with the central organizations of the churches and was excellently prepared by current educational and publishing standards. This material tended to represent the more liberal social and religious viewpoints of the denominations.

There was a continuous flow of speakers through Midwest bringing information and viewpoints on a great variety of subjects to the members of the Parent-Teachers' Association, the women's clubs, the Rotary Club, and the church, farm, and professional organizations. In the year under consideration these included an instructional film for women on the detection of breast cancer and a talk on education in Norway by a University graduate student.

Next to social interaction, recreation, and work, education was the action pattern of most prominence in the behavior settings of Midwest. Midwesterners frequently expressed the belief that education would solve social and personal problems and they viewed with disapprobation the occasional adolescent who stopped his formal education before completing high school.

Government, Religion, Aesthetics, and Nutrition. Following education, we find four action patterns in Midwest community settings of roughly the same order of prominence, namely, Government (creating, interpreting, and enforcing governmental laws and regulations), Religion, (worshipping, studying, and teaching religious matters), Aesthetics (beautifying surroundings), and Nutrition (dining in public places). These were prominent in from 4 per cent to 15 per cent of the settings which consumed from 4 per cent to 10 per cent of the occupancy time of Midwest community settings.

As the county seat of Midwest County, the town had a relatively heavy concentration of settings concerned with government activities. The City County, State, and Federal offices accounted for most of the settings in which government action patterns were prominent, i.e., 7 per cent of all community settings. It is interesting to note, however, that 60 per cent of all settings received some rating for government action patterns. Direct participation in government activities through collecting sales taxes, conforming to sanitary regulations, submitting to inspection of scales, restricting the sale of drugs and beer, reporting births and deaths, publishing financial reports, etc., were widespread.

Religion occupied the median position in the action pattern hierarchy. It fell in this high position because of its prominence in a relatively large number of settings (15 per cent) rather than because of the occupancy index of these settings (4 per cent). Midwesterners engaged in religious behavior in small, concentrated amounts in a number of specialized settings. Next to the action pattern Physical Health, Religion had the most restricted territorial range of any action pattern.

Midwesterners set aside 8 per cent of the town's community settings as places where the practice or promotion of art was prominent, and in 60 per cent of its settings aesthetic behavior patterns were present in some degree. Midwesterners' efforts to beautify their surroundings included such varied activities as the regular spring cleanup of winter debris, the oratorio given by the Methodist Choir, the exhibition in the Gilmah Implement Company windows of pictures painted by a former Midwest resident, the high-school Senior Banquet, and the large selection of greeting cards in the drug, variety, and department stores.

The art form most highly developed and most frequently practiced in Midwest was music. In 1951/52 five professional musicians practiced part- or full-time in Midwest and surrounding areas. Children's music groups practiced or performed almost every day in the year, and adult groups were active several times a week. Hardly a social group met without some musical activity performed either by the membership, or by outside vocal or instrumental entertainers.

Home decoration was actively pursued by many women and men of Midwest, and considerable pride was expressed in the products of these activities. Midwesterners had little hesitancy in planning and executing the decoration of their homes, from papering the walls to upholstering the furniture. The amount of building construction in recent years, though small, provided evidence of the acceptance of modern trends in Midwest home and office design.

Pictorial and plastic arts were not an active focus of behavior in Midwest. In the survey year no instruction in drawing, painting, or sculpture was available to Midwest children. In general, Midwesterners showed little concern about the pictures on the walls of their homes, although most of them had pictures. Despite the lack of activity in this area of the arts, Midwest's emigrant sons and daughters had achieved considerable success in the field. The prominent artist John Steuart Curry was born and reared in a neighboring rural area and received his first art instruction in Midwest.

A few of his pictures, gifts of the artist, were to be seen on the walls of Midwest homes. Two other Midwesterners had in more recent years become practicing artists and art teachers with considerable recognition for creative work. In 1951/52, however, the roots of such development could not be discerned in Midwest.

The drama and the dance were practiced in Midwest, but were, perhaps, seen more as a recreation than as art. Two plays were produced each year by high-school students, programs consisting of recitations by individual children were given by the members of each Sunday School, and occasional entertainments were presented by social groups. Characteristically these performances were presented with a minimum of preparation, with major dependence on the native skills and individual efforts of the performers. The difference in attitude toward dramatics and music was illustrated by the fact that the school provided a full-time music instructor, band instruments, music, and even elegant uniforms for the band members. When it came to dramatics, however, the plays were directed by a teacher who had another major responsibility, and the tradition was well established that the school could not afford plays for which a royalty had to be paid, or rented scenery or costumes secured.

The Midwest Theater exhibited about 150 different films during the survey year, most of them westerns, but including also a number of the best pictures. It has already been pointed out that the occupancy index of the setting Midwest Theater was next to the highest in the town, i.e., 2.9. Some Midwesterners attended theaters and entertainments in nearby cities regularly and many did occasionally.

The literary arts were not absent from the town. The *Midwest Weekly* published poetry of the residents of the town and vicinity quite regularly. Mr. Crowthers, the editor, had a distinguished literary style, when he could take time from getting out the next week's issue of the paper. The ministers of the town preached well-prepared sermons which were sometimes of high literary quality. Local residents regularly presented papers and gave speeches in a number of the social, educational, and religious settings. Midwesterners were regular readers of newspapers, magazines, and books. We have no data, however, on the amount or nature of this reading.

Eating and drinking were not prominent in Midwest community settings, but occurred to some degree in 40 per cent of them. Eating and drinking usually occurred in family settings. For most people, dining outside the home occurred only on special occasions. It was characteristically associated with recreation and with social interaction in large groups such as that of the Last Day of School Dinner, the African Methodist Episcopal Church Annual Homecoming Reunion Dinner, and the County Principals' Association Dinner. Refreshments were served at many social gatherings. An exception to this general rule was the school lunch. Almost all Midwest children ate their weekday lunches in the school dining room where a hot lunch was served, or in a specified classroom where lunches brought from home were eaten.

Physical Health, Orientation, Personal Appearance, and Philanthropy. Of the action patterns studied, Physical Health (promoting and maintaining physical health), Orientation (defining physical and social status), Personal Appearance (improving and appreciating personal appearance), and Philanthropy (giving to good causes) had the least prominence in Midwest. These action patterns were prominent in from 4 per cent to 1 per cent of the settings which consumed from 7 per cent to less than 1 per cent of the occupancy time.

The prominence index of the action pattern Physical Health, while a true representation of its occurrence within the borders of Midwest, is not a correct indication of its prominence in the lives of Midwesterners. We have stated in Chapter II that the more complicated and prolonged medical treatments were not available in Midwest. Behavior which had the purpose of promoting health in any way had the most restricted distribution of all action patterns, occurring in 28 per cent of the community settings.

We have speculated that community settings concerned with the maintenance of personal appearance might be of less prominence in Midwest than in a large community where individuals know each other less well, and where dress and grooming play an important role in establishing one's social position. Each person's status was so well established in Midwest that surface impressions affected it little. This does not mean that Midwesterners did not value their appearance; they spent 2 per cent of their time outside their homes in settings where behavior related to personal appearance was prominent, and in 48 per cent of the community settings behavior was in some degree involved with good personal appearance.

SUMMARY

We can summarize this description of the standing behavior patterns in the community settings of Midwest by saying that their most prominent components were social interaction and recreation, with work as the outstanding special behavioral figure, and with education next in prominence. The action patterns which were concerned with government, religion, the arts, and dining in public places were less conspicuous, but they were nonetheless clearly visible features of Midwest's behavior settings, and those concerned with health, orientation, personal appearance, and philanthropy were minor but not obscure elements of the behavior landscape of the town.

ACTION PATTERNS AT LAWTON

Some radical differences between Midwest and Lawton in the prominence of action patterns are apparent from the data presented in Table 4.8.

Action patterns which were much less prominent in Lawton than in Midwest were Business, Earning a Living, Government, and Religion, the first three receiving no rating as great as 6 in any Lawton setting. Action patterns which were of greater prominence in Lawton were Nutrition, Physical Health, and Personal Appearance. Social Contact and Recreation were of highest prominence in both communities, although their relative positions and magnitudes changed. One would have to say of Lawton that the most prominent components of its standing behavior patterns were Recreation and Social Contact with Nutrition, Education, Physical Health, Personal Appearance, and Aesthetics providing the most visible behavioral figures, and with Religion reaching prominence in only a single setting. Business, Earning a Living, Government, and Orientation were scarcely perceptible in Lawton. It seems apparent from these data that the children of the Lawton School were surrounded by quite a different behavioral milieu than the children of Midwest.

With a general view of Midwest before us, we next turn to the differential preference for these action patterns by different population subgroups.

Selection of Action Patterns by Population Subgroups

In the analysis which follows we have sought to determine how the community behavior settings inhabited by each subgroup of Midwest's population differed from Midwest as a whole with respect to action patterns. In this analysis we have included only the settings penetrated by a subgroup to Zone 2 or greater, i.e., to the position of audience and invited guest. We have eliminated settings in which members of a subgroup were only on-lookers or tolerated visitors. We have called the number of settings a subgroup entered to this degree the *participation range* of the group. This identifies the community settings in which the subgroup members had an established place.

We have used the *action pattern selectivity index* as a measure of the differential selection of an action pattern by a subgroup. This index is the per cent of the settings in the participation range of the subgroup with ratings on an action pattern greater than the median rating of that action pattern in all Midwest community settings. Thus, if the median rating of Midwest settings on action pattern $X = 2.0$, and if 50 per cent of the settings in the participation range of a subgroup A were rated above 2.0, the selectivity index would be 50 and we would conclude that subgroup A did not participate in Midwest settings selectively with respect to action pattern X. On the other hand, if 70 per cent of the settings in the participation range of subgroup B were rated above 2.0 on action pattern X, the selectivity index would be 70, and we would conclude that subgroup B participated in an excess number of settings involving action pattern X. The probability of a selectivity index deviating from 50 by chance was tested by chi square; deviations which would occur by chance with a probability of .01 or less are reported as significant. The median ratings used in computing the selectivity index are given on page 125.

The Selection of Action Patterns by Age Groups

The number of settings in the participation range of each age subgroup was as follows:

Infants	107
Preschool	170
Younger School	243
Older School	267
Adolescents	383
Adult	578
Aged	412

These were the settings in which each age group had more than an onlookers' or a tolerated visitors' position.

The action pattern selectivity indexes for the different age groups are presented in Figure 4.20. These data indicate that the participation ranges of all age groups except adults were not random samples from the action patterns of Midwest settings. They show the following kinds of selection:

1. The selective process more frequently involved the positive choice of settings than their avoidance. Action patterns were overselected 24 times and underselected 6 times.

2. The number of action patterns overselected or underselected was greatest in old age where 7 significant selectivity indexes occurred. The order of the other age groups with respect to number of significant selectivity indexes was: infant and preschool, 6 each; younger school and older school, 4 each; adolescents, 3; adults, none.

3. The degree of overselection and underselection, as indicated by the deviations from the expected 50 per cent if chance were operating, decreased from infancy to adulthood and increased in old age.

4. Three action patterns were overchosen by all child and adolescent age groups, namely, Aesthetics, Personal Appearance, and Recreation. Nutrition was overchosen by the preschool, younger school, and older school groups, and Religion was overchosen by preschool and infant groups. The underselected action patterns were Government at the infant and preschool ages and Education in infancy. In old age the overchosen action patterns were in all cases different from those in childhood; they were Physical Health, Business, Orientation, and Earning a Living; the action patterns

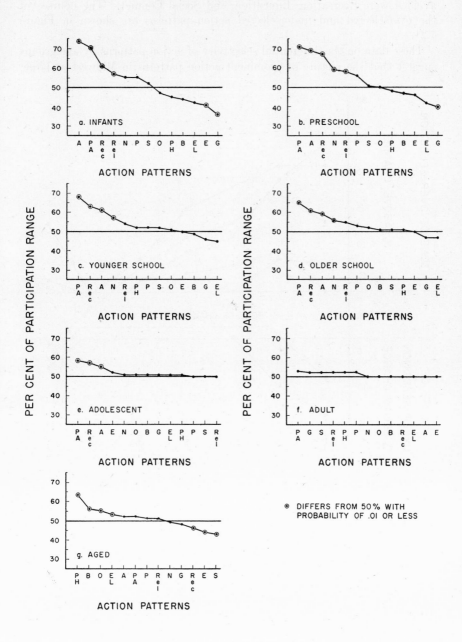

Fig. 4.20.—Action pattern selectivity indexes for age groups. Per cent of settings in participation range receiving ratings above the median of all Midwest settings.

avoided were Recreation, Education, and Social Contact. The courses of the overselected and underselected action patterns are shown in Figure 4.21.

These data on the differential selectivity of action patterns by age groups suggest that the picture of prominent action patterns in Midwest at large,

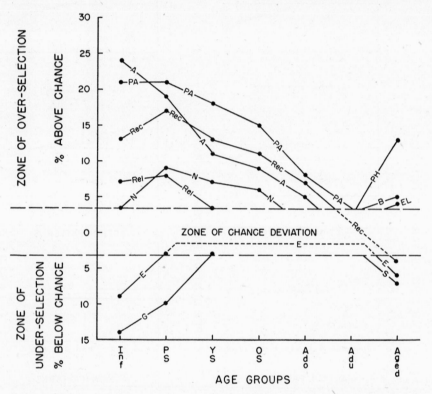

FIG. 4.21.—Degree of overselection and underselection of action patterns by age groups.

which was described earlier, is modified within the participation ranges of the children, the adolescents, and the aged. In Figure 4.22 the rank order of prominence of action patterns in the participation ranges of each age group are shown. The rank order within the participation range of an age group was determined by the same methods as those used to determine the rank order of prominence of action patterns in the total community. The lines mark those action patterns whose rank order of prominence changed markedly from infancy to old age. The rank order of action pattern prominence in the adult group is essentially that described for the community as a whole.

Action patterns which increased in prominence with age are Business, Earning a Living, and Government. Those which decreased are Nutrition, Religion (with a reversal in old age), and Personal Appearance. Social

Contact retained its primary position at all ages, and Recreation did so at all ages except old age. Philanthropy was least prominent at all ages.

The data on action pattern selection by age groups show that in infancy Midwesterners were introduced to a nonfamily world where social and

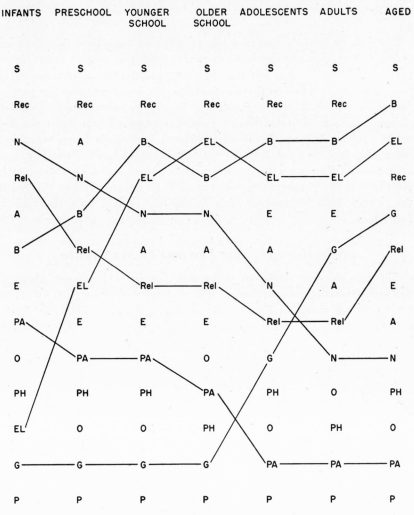

Fig. 4.22.—Rank order of prominence of action patterns in participation ranges of each age group.

recreational behavior formed an almost ubiquitous background for all other components of the standing behavior patterns, with Nutrition, Religion, and Aesthetics providing the dominant behavioral figures against this background. The pattern of prominence slowly changed with age until, in the participation range of the old inhabitants of the town, Recreation and

Nutrition had been superseded by Business and Earning a Living, and Government had taken a prominent place. One might characterize this shift with age in the chief components of the standing behavior patterns of Midwest participation ranges as tending from the less reality-bound action patterns in the youngest ages, considering that Nutrition, as defined, was usually a festive affair, to more reality-bound action patterns in old age.

The data on the selection of action patterns by the school-age subgroups of Midwest's population demonstrate that the different prominence of action patterns in Lawton was not due to the predominance of children in its population. The order of prominence of action patterns within the participation ranges of Midwest's younger school, older school, and adolescent citizens was quite different from the order of prominence in Lawton. The action patterns Physical Health and Personal Appearance had a lower rank order of prominence for Midwest children than for Lawton children, and Business and Earning a Living had a higher prominence for them. Only Nutrition in the participation range of Midwest school children differed in prominence from Midwest at large in the direction of its prominence in Lawton.

Selection of Action Patterns by Sex Groups

The participation ranges of males and females were almost identical, 519 and 520 settings, respectively. The selectivity of action patterns within these ranges is shown in Figure 4.23. Females showed a significant preference for the action patterns Aesthetics, Personal Appearance, Nutrition, and Recreation; males overselected Earning a Living and Government, and they underselected Personal Appearance and Aesthetics. The degree of selectivity was small, however, in comparison with that occurring in age groups, and it was not sufficient to make the rank order of prominence of action patterns different in the male and female participation ranges. Nevertheless, within the general order of prominence it indicates significant differences in emphasis.

Action Pattern Selection by Social and Color Groups

The participation ranges of the three social groups differed with respect to only a single action pattern. Social Group II significantly overselected settings with high ratings on the action pattern Government; the amount of overselection was only 1.5 per cent, however. The absence of differential action pattern selection by social groups is in accord with the data on social group segregation in Midwest.

White Midwesterners did not participate differentially in any of the action patterns. The selectivity of Negro residents within their participation

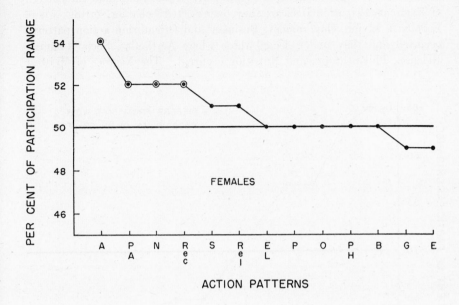

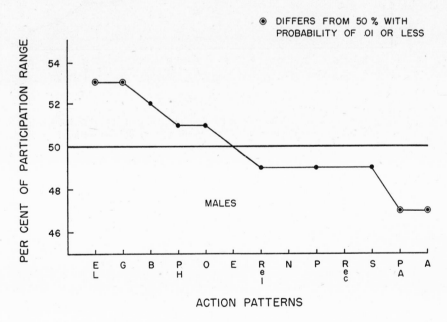

FIG. 4.23.—Action pattern selectivity indexes for sex groups. Per cent of settings in participation range receiving ratings above the median of all Midwest settings.

range of 270 settings is shown in Figure 4.24. From these data the pattern of Negro participation is clear; they overselected behavior settings where Earning a Living, Government, Business, and Orientation action patterns occurred and they underselected those where Aesthetics, Social Contact, Religion, Philanthropy, and Nutrition occurred. The Negroes of Midwest

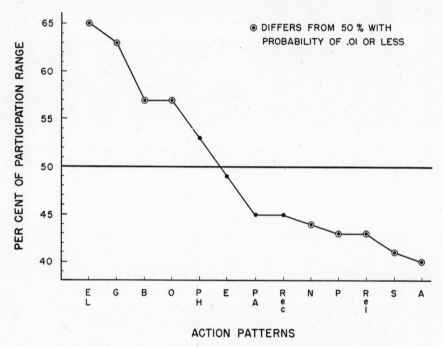

FIG. 4.24.—Action pattern selectivity indexes for Negroes. Per cent of settings in participation range receiving ratings above the median for all Midwest settings.

lived their social lives to a great extent within their own families, and their religious participation was largely limited to a few settings in which there was racial segregation.

The Mechanisms of Behavior in Community Behavior Settings

We turn now from the molar to the molecular characteristics of behavior in community behavior settings. We have called these the mechanisms of behavior. Seven mechanisms of behavior have been identified, namely, Affective Behavior (Af), Gross Motor Activity (GM), Listening (Li), Looking (L), Manipulation (M), Talking (T), and Thinking (Th). Ratings varied from zero (did not occur) to 10 (occurred during at least 90 per cent of the occupancy time of the setting with highest speed or sensitivity, and with greatest energy or concentration).

DISTRIBUTIONS

The distributions of Midwest behavior settings on the scales for the seven mechanisms are presented in Figure 4.25. Again a rating of 6 or greater

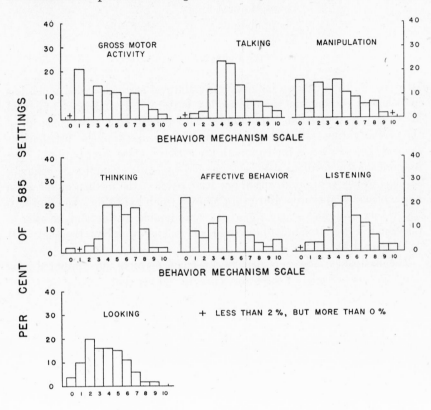

Fig. 4.25.—Distributions of behavior mechanism ratings.

designated a prominent behavior characteristic of a setting. The prominent behavior mechanisms of each behavior setting are given in the catalogue of behavior settings.

TERRITORIAL RANGES OF MECHANISMS

The distributions in Figure 4.25 disclose that the behavior mechanisms were much more widespread in Midwest than the action patterns. Five of the mechanisms occurred in over 95 per cent of the settings; only Manipulation and Affective Behavior were more restricted, and these occurred in 84 per cent and 77 per cent of the settings, respectively.

MEDIAN RATINGS OF BEHAVIOR MECHANISMS

The median mechanism ratings are:

Thinking	5.95
Listening	5.58
Talking	5.36
Gross Motor Activity	4.37
Manipulation	4.16
Looking	4.05
Affective Behavior	4.01

Here, again, the evidence indicates that Midwest settings varied much less in behavior mechanism than in action pattern. It indicates too, that Midwest was a "median" community with respect to mechanisms; all of the median ratings fall in the mid-ranges of the scales, and the distributions are less skewed than is the case with the action pattern distributions. The meaning of the medians can be suggested by scme examples of behavior settings which were rated within one scale point of the median on all seven mechanisms: Blanchard's Hardware Store, a small hardware where business was rather slow and where there was considerable loafing and viewing of television; Presbyterian Ladies Aid Food Sale; Father-Son Banquet; 4-H Achievement Day Banquet.

The occupancy indexes of behavior mechanisms were not computed inasmuch as they were in all cases very close to 100 per cent.

PROMINENCE OF BEHAVIOR MECHANISMS

The community-wide prominence of each mechanism was determined by the methods used with action patterns. The data are presented in Table 4.9.

TABLE 4.9

PROMINENCE INDEXES OF MIDWEST BEHAVIOR MECHANISMS RECEIVING
RATINGS OF 6 OR GREATER

Mechanisms	Occupancy Index	Territorial Index	Prominence Index
Thinking	46	49	2254
Gross Motor Activity	46	32	1472
Manipulation	41	26	1066
Listening	20	40	800
Talking	17	35	595
Looking	25	20	500
Affective Behavior	15	28	420

According to these data Midwest was a town where the most common standing behavior patterns required both brains and muscle. Almost half of the community settings in which Midwesterners spent almost half their time were places where thinking was at least on the level required to shop in stores or listen to a speaker at a banquet. Routinized behavior such as occurs in simple assembly work or picking corn by hand was not common in Midwest. There was, however, much heavy work done in Midwest. One-third of the settings in which the residents spent almost half of their time involved some work of the following sorts: changing automobile tires, unloading stock feed, playing baseball. The least prominent behavior mechanisms were Affective Behavior and Looking. In only 28 per cent of the settings in which residents spent 15 per cent of their time did the emotionality of a Grade-School Operetta or Presbyterian Worship Service occur. It is interesting to note that vision was rated less prominent in Midwest than hearing, and that both were relatively low on the prominence scale.

Selection of Behavior Mechanisms by Age Groups

The differential selection of behavior mechanisms by age groups has been determined by the methods used with action patterns. The mechanism selectivity indexes are given in Figure 4.26. These data show that the participation ranges of all age groups except adults were not random samples of the behavior mechanisms of Midwest. They show that:

1. The selective process more frequently involved the choice of settings with preferred behavior mechanism than the avoidance of settings with unattractive ones. Mechanisms were overselected 17 times and underselected 8 times.

2. The greatest behavior mechanism selectivity occurred at the older school and adolescent ages, with 6 and 7 overselected or underselected behavior mechanisms; at the younger school age there were 4 significantly selected mechanisms; there were 3 at the preschool and infant ages, 2 in old age, and none in adulthood.

3. The degree of overselection and underselection, as shown by the amount of the deviations from the expected 50 per cent, decreased from infancy to adulthood, with a slight increase in old age. Curves representing these changes are shown in Figure 4.27.

4. The behavior mechanism Affective Behavior was overselected at all child and adolescent ages, and Talking was overselected at all childhood ages. Gross Motor Activities were overselected by the younger school, the older school, and the adolescent groups, and Manipulation was overselected in the older school ages and adolescence. Looking was overselected in adolescence and old age. Underselected behavior mechanisms were Thinking at all child and adolescent ages, and Listening in the older school, the adolescent, and the aged groups.

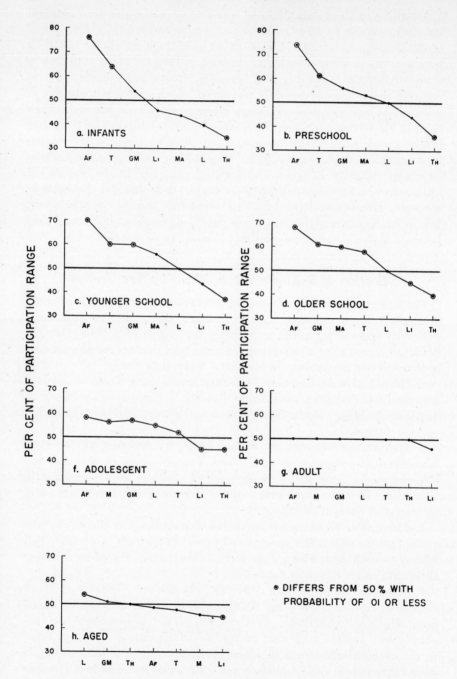

Fig. 4.26.—Mechanism selectivity indexes for age groups. Per cent of settings in participation range receiving ratings above the median of all Midwest settings.

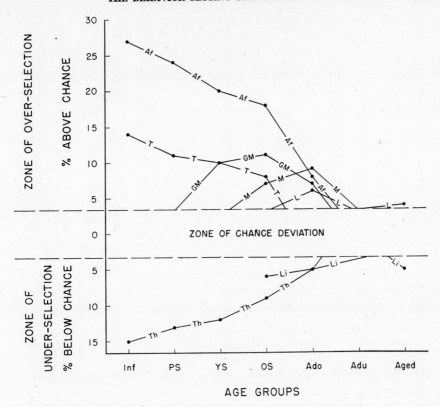

FIG. 4.27.—Degree of overselection and underselection of behavior mechanisms by age groups.

The data indicate that the order of prominence of behavior mechanisms was different in the participation ranges of different age groups. In Figure 4.28 the rank orders of prominence of behavior mechanisms are shown. The lines mark the mechanisms changing greatly from infancy to old age.

According to these data, Talking and Affective Behavior declined in prominence from infancy to old age; they were of highest prominence in the behavior settings in which infants participated and of lowest prominence in those in which the aged participated. On the other hand, Thinking, Gross Motor, and Manipulation mechanisms increased in prominence with age, and Looking did so between adolescence and old age.

Selection of Behavior Mechanisms by Sex Groups

Data on the differential selection of behavior mechanisms within the participation ranges of males and females are given in Figure 4.29. This makes it clear that such differential selectivity did occur. Males over-selected settings in which Gross Motor Activity, Manipulation, and Looking

INFANTS   PRESCHOOL   YOUNGER   OLDER   ADOLESCENTS   ADULTS   AGED
                     SCHOOL   SCHOOL

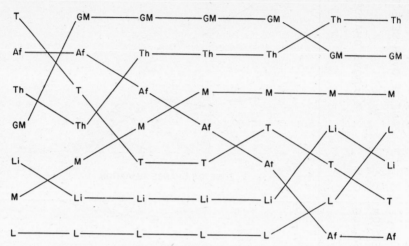

Fɪɢ. 4.28.—Rank order of prominence of behavior mechanisms in the participation ranges of age groups.

were strongly represented, and females overselected settings where Affective Behavior and Manipulation occurred. Males underselected Talking and Affective Behavior and females underselected Thinking and Listening mechanisms. Although statistically significant, none of these selective biases were large in absolute amount and did not change the rank order of prominent behavior mechanisms in the male and female participation ranges.

Selection of Behavior Mechanisms by Social and Color Groups

Significant selection of behavior mechanisms within the participation ranges of social groups occurred only in two cases: Social Group III overselected settings with both Gross Motor and Looking mechanisms.

The white citizens of Midwest did not participate differentially in behavior settings in accordance with their behavior mechanisms. The nature of the selectivity of the Negro citizens is shown in Figure 4.30. Here again, as with action patterns, the participation range of the Negroes was sharply biased with marked overselection of settings in which Affective Behavior, Looking, Manipulation, and Gross Motor Activities were highly rated, and marked underselection of settings with Talking mechanisms. Still however, Gross Motor Activity, Thinking, and Manipulation were the most prominent in the Negroes' participation range.

SUMMARY

Midwest was a community where the most prominent behavior mechanisms were those effective in coping with the real world, namely, Thinking, Gross

Motor Activities, and Manipulation.   However, these were modified in the
participation ranges of the young children, the old people, and the Negroes.
Mechanisms less bound by reality were prominent in the selections of the
youngest ages, while the more reality-bound mechanisms were selected by

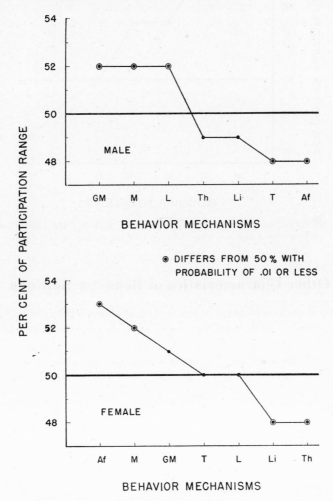

FIG. 4.29.—Behavior mechanism selectivity indexes for sex groups.   Per cent of settings in
participation range receiving ratings above the median for all Midwest settings.

the oldest ages.   The triad of mechanisms most prominent in the older ages,
Thinking, Gross Motor Activity, and Manipulation; are characteristically
used to actively cope with the real world, while Talking, Affective Behavior,
and Thinking, most prominent at the youngest age, are the mechanisms of
unreality.

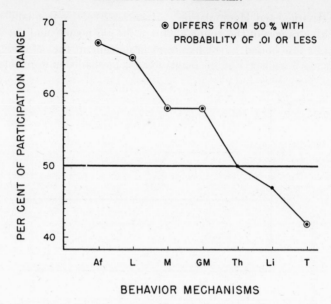

FIG. 4.30.—Behavior mechanism selectivity indexes for Negroes. Per cent of settings in participation range receiving ratings above the median for all Midwest settings.

Other Characteristics of Behavior Settings

We have described Midwest in terms of eight characteristics of its behavior settings, namely, their number, occupancy, kinds, varieties, degree of population segregation, penetration, action patterns, and mechanisms. Behavior settings have many other discriminable features. Some of these with which we have dealt in a preliminary way are the strength of coercive forces in settings, the variability of behavior in settings, the nature of the forces at the boundaries of settings, the tempo of behavior in settings, the emotional climate of settings, and the power relations between settings. We have collected data on factors associated with the birth, death, and transformation of behavior settings in Midwest. However, the only other characteristics upon which sufficient work has been done to justify a report at the present time is the *social weather* of behavior settings, and this was completed too late to be included in detail. Nonetheless, the approach is so promising that its general methodology and some sample results will be presented.[4]

Social weather refers to the social conditions which surround a particular child in a behavior setting. It is defined in terms of certain characteristics of the social responses toward the child by his associates. All of the people

4 The interested reader is referred to James E. Simpson's doctoral dissertation for details (53).

who are socially propinquitous to the child contribute to the total pattern of behavior which comprises his social weather in the setting.

The method of rating social weather is based upon the highly developed Fels Parent Behavior Rating Scales originated by Champney (15) and further developed by Baldwin and others (3, 4). The Fels scales were designed to measure the parents' attitudes and behavior toward a child and thereby evaluate the child's home environment. For our purpose, the scales were adapted to the rating of behavior settings on the basis of data supplied by specimen records.

Nine dimensions of the social weather surrounding a child in a behavior setting have been defined in terms of scales which are summarized by their cue-points in Table 4.10. Ratings can be made on these scales with a high

TABLE 4.10

BRIEF SUMMARY OF SOCIAL WEATHER RATING SCALES

SOCIAL WEATHER SCALES	CUE-POINTS DESCRIBING MEDIAN BEHAVIOR OF ASSOCIATES TOWARD CHILD				
	1	2	3	4	5
Approval	Is Hyper-critical	Disapproves	Is Impartial	Approves	Praises
Affectionate-ness	Is Hostile	Is Cool	Is Civil	Is Warm	Is Affect-ionate
Acceptance	Rejects	Resents	Is Non-committal	Warmly Accepts	Avidly Accepts
Attention	Ignores Child	Gives Minimal Attention	Gives Equit-able Attention	Is Child Centered	Is Fully Focused on Child
Assistance	Neglects	Withholds Help	Helps as Needed	Overhelps	Babies
Communi-cation	Withholds Conversation	Perfunctorily Converses	Routinely Converses	Actively Converses	Eagerly Converses
Adaptation	Is in Conflict	Has Friction	Is Indifferent	Is Harmonious	Is Keenly Empathetic
Privilege	Thwarts	Confines	Is Practical	Is Liberal	Allows Complete Freedom
Choice	Dictates	Dominates	Provides Options	Is Perfunctory	Is Passive

degree of agreement by different raters for a particular child in a particular setting. The data obtained provide the possibility of many kinds of analysis.

Here we present in Figure 4.31 only a single sample, namely the social weather ratings for the 12 Midwest and 2 Lawton children described in Chapter II. The ratings of Midwest children are presented separately for preschool and school children, and for community and family settings. The ratings of the Lawton children are presented for all settings combined. The data for each scale in Figure 4.31 are based upon 150 to 300 different ratings of social weather in the case of the Midwest children, and on approximately 75 ratings in the case of Lawton children. A rating was made each time a child entered a setting where there were associates who behaved in relation to him. The medians, first quartiles, and third quartiles represented in Figure 4.31 are the medians of these constants of each child's distribution of ratings.

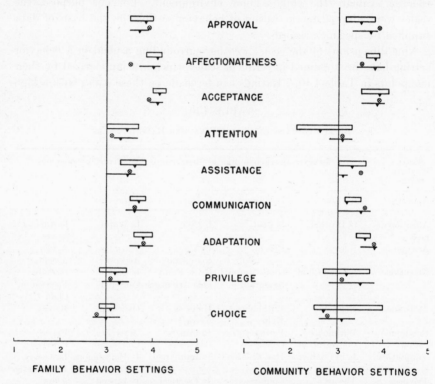

FAMILY BEHAVIOR SETTINGS   COMMUNITY BEHAVIOR SETTINGS

Fig. 4.31.—Social weather of behavior settings for 12 Midwest children and 2 Lawton School children. The vertical line is erected on the middle point of the social weather scales, the numbered points of which are described in Table 4.11. The arrowhead extending downward from the horizontal bar represents the median of the median ratings of the behavior settings each child entered. The bar extends from the median of the first quartile to the median of the third quartile of the distributions of ratings. The solid bar represents 6 school-age Midwest children and the open bar, 6 preschool Midwest children. The ⊗ indicates the median rating of the two Lawton children; the interquartile range of the Lawton rating is not represented. The same median Lawton ratings are placed with the family and the community settings for comparative purposes since the Lawton settings involve aspects of both.

If we consider that ratings between 3 and 4.5 are indicative, in general, of favorable social weather, and that the higher the rating in this range the more favorable, the data of Figure 4.31 signify that Midwest children were usually surrounded with favorable social weather by their fellows. Of the

36 medians, 34 fall in the favorable range, only those for Attention and Choice falling outside it in the direction of "Gives Minimum Attention" and "Dominates" in the case of preschool children in community settings. In 26 of the 36 cases, the entire interquartile range falls between 3 and 4.5.

There are indications that the social weather of the preschool and school children differed in family and community behavior settings. In family settings, the median social weather ratings of preschool children exceed those of school children on eight of the scales (Privilege being the exception), while in community settings this is true on only two scales (Acceptance and Assistance). It appears from this that within their own homes preschool children received more Approval, Affection, Attention, Assistance, Communication, Adaptation, and Choice, and less Privilege than school children did in theirs; and that outside their homes school children gained more Approval, Attention, Communication, Adaptation, Privilege, and Choice, equal Affection, and less Acceptance and Assistance than did preschool children.

In general, the social weather of family settings was rated more favorably than that of community settings. On 14 of the 18 comparisons, the median rating is higher for the family setting, on 2 the ratings are equal, and on 2 the median rating of community settings is higher (Privilege and Choice for school children).

The Lawton children were rated as receiving more Approval and Assistance and less Privilege, Choice, and Affection than the Midwest children.

Concluding Statement About the Behavior Setting Survey

It will be apparent to the reader that the description of the world of Midwest children which has been presented in terms of behavior settings has not been made in an evaluative vacuum. In presenting the facts and theories of behavior settings in Midwest, we have implied some of our own social values, and our own views of child development. Some will undoubtedly believe that we have painted too rosy a picture of Midwest as a living place for children. Others will consider the influence of behavior settings upon children to be minor in comparison with the forces involved in specific interpersonal relationships, particularly within the family situation. The implication for children of the richness and freedom of life, and of their low degree of segregation will, in particular, be differently interpreted. In fact, some citizens of Midwest do not agree with our evaluations, and strive for less freedom and more segregation for their children.

It is true that the authors do, in the present state of their knowledge of children, think that Midwest was, in general, a good kind of place for children, and they think the world as described in terms of behavior settings is important to the understanding of the welfare of children. However, this is incidental to the main significance of the materials presented which demonstrate the conceptualizations and methodology of the behavior setting

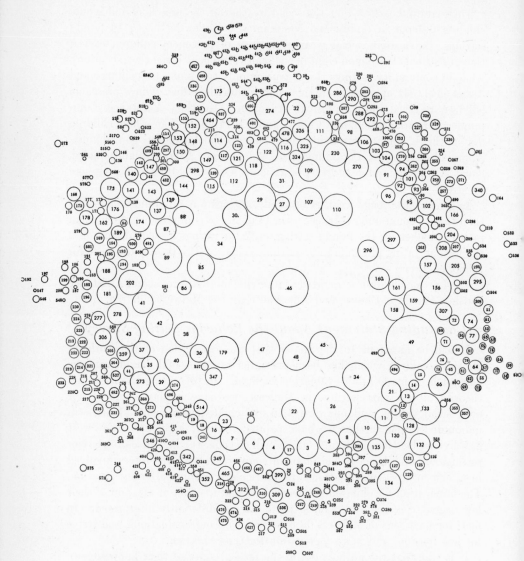

Fig. 4.32.—Base Map: Behavior Settings.   See pages 154–56 for explication.

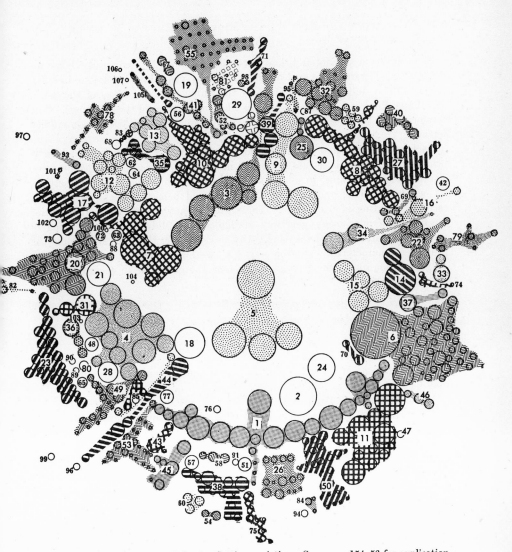

FIG. 4.33.—Base Map: Behavior Setting varieties. See pages 154–56 for explication.

survey and which present some facts which have been discovered about
Midwest. It may be that this will add another instrument to the armory
of those who are striving to discover what constitutes good psychological
living conditions for children.

Catalogue and Base Maps of Midwest Community Behavior Settings

The catalogue presented below lists all of the K-21 community behavior
settings which were discovered during the survey year, July 1, 1951 to June 30,
1952. It is a descriptive inventory of the public behavior areas of the town.
The maps, Figures 4.32 and 4.33 represent some features of these settings. The
catalogue and the base maps provide, together, an atlas of Midwest's community
settings.

Each setting is listed in the catalogue under the S-30 variety to which it
belongs, and the varieties are presented in order of decreasing occupancy time.
The catalogue contains, in addition to the name and variety of each setting,
its occupancy time, and its action patterns and behavior mechanisms which
received a rating of 6 or more. These are the action patterns and behavior
mechanisms which were generally recognized by Midwesterners as being of
primary importance in the setting. In the catalogue, they serve to define the
prominent characteristics of each setting's standing pattern of behavior.

Information about the settings is given in the catalogue in accordance with
the following form:

> *Variety Number*   *Name of the Variety*:   *Occupancy Time*
> Setting number   Name of the setting   Occupancy Time
> (Action patterns;
> Behavior mechanisms)

The limitations of the catalogue should be kept in mind. These limitations
may be enumerated as follows:

1. Code names of settings are used. These approximate the local significance
of the real names, and in some cases they are not very revealing of the nature of
the setting. It is hoped, however, that the name of the setting, in conjunction
with its variety and its prominent action patterns and mechanisms will be
sufficient to identify the setting for most purposes.

2. The occupancy time refers only to the time Midwest residents spent in the
behavior setting; it does not denote the total occupancy of the setting. Some
settings were occupied largely by persons from outside the borders of the town.
For example, most of the occupants of the settings belonging to the variety
Agricultural Extension Classes were farmers; only occupancy by Midwest
residents is reported for these settings.

3. The occupancy time is the estimated number of hours all Midwest residents
spent in the setting during the survey year without regard for the number of
persons involved, or the apportionment of the time among the occupants. Thus,
the Old Settlers' Reunion Amateur Show which occurred on two afternoons, had
an occupancy time of 1,400 hours distributed among approximately 500 Midwest
residents, with the amount of time per inhabitant ranging from about one-half

to 6 hours, whereas Garnett's Insurance Office, which occurred on 250 days, had an occupancy time of 1,550 hours distributed among about 100 persons, with one of them accounting for about 80 per cent of the total time.

4. The prominent action patterns which are listed with each setting must be interpreted in the light of the following conditions. An action pattern does not receive a rating of 6 on the basis of the participation subscale alone; i.e., because most of the behavior in a setting is directly involved in an action pattern. To be rated prominent in a setting, an action pattern must also receive some rating on one of the other subscales: supply, appreciation, or learning. Thus, the action pattern Earning a Living is listed as prominent in Clifford's Drug Store (rating, *6*), and as not prominent in Denton's Drug Store (rating, *5*). Earning a Living was given the maximum rating on the participation subscale in the case of both stores. However, Clifford's Drug Store received an additional rating of *1* on the learning subscale because of the strict training in salesmanship and merchandising its adolescent employees received, thus raising Earning a Living to the level of prominence. Circumstances such as this which are not superficially apparent account for many differences in the prominence of action patterns in otherwise similar settings. The same is true of behavior mechanisms.

In addition, the unreliability of the scales inevitably resulted in errors in the identification of prominent action patterns and mechanisms in individual settings. We were faced with three alternatives here: (*a*) to omit any mention of prominent behavioral features of individual settings; (*b*) to use a variable criterion of prominence in order to adjust for apparent rating errors; (*c*) to use a fixed criterion of prominence, with the resulting error in individual cases. We chose the last alternative. It should be clearly understood, therefore, that the prominent action patterns and mechanisms listed are gross indicators of the important characteristics of the standing behavior patterns of the settings. All other uses of action pattern and behavior mechanism ratings involve groups of settings where the errors due to unreliability of ratings are less serious.

In spite of these limitations, it appears that the Behavior Settings Catalogue is a useful survey of the behaviorally significant parts of Midwest. The abbreviations used for the action patterns and behavior mechanisms are as follows:

Action Patterns		*Behavior Mechanisms*	
Aesthetics	A	Affective Behavior	Af
Business	B	Gross Motor Activity	GM
Earning a Living	EL	Listening	Li
Education	E	Looking	L
Government	G	Manipulation	M
Nutrition	N	Talking	T
Orientation	O	Thinking	Th
Personal Appearance	PA		
Philanthropy	P		
Physical Health	PH		
Recreation	Rec		
Religion	Rel		
Social Contact	S		

Many features of behavior settings can be represented graphically. In the Base Maps we have attempted to denote in this way three variables which have general significance.

1. Each community setting is represented by a circle whose diameter is proportional to the General Richness Index of the setting.

2. The distance of each setting from the core setting at the center of the map, Clifford's Drug Store (46), is proportional to its K-value (interdependence) with this core setting.

3. The position of each setting is contiguous to other settings belonging to the same variety.

On the Base Map, Figure 4.32, the individual settings are numbered and can be identified by referring to the list of behavior settings in the catalogue. On Base Map, Figure 4.33, the varieties of settings are numbered and can be identified in the catalogue.

BEHAVIOR SETTINGS CATALOGUE

MIDWEST BEHAVIOR SETTINGS GROUPED BY VARIETIES

	Occupancy Time
1. School Classes:	*128,801*
1. Red Cross Home Nursing Courses (E; Li, Th)	27
2. County Teachers Institute (E, S; Th)	70
3. First-Grade Academic Activities (E, S; Li, L, Th)	7,014
4. Second-Grade Academic Activities (E, S; Th)	7,600
5. Third-Grade Academic Activities (E, S; Th)	7,290
6. Fourth-Grade Academic Activities (E, S; Th)	8,748
7. Fifth- and Sixth-Grade Academic Activities; Mrs. Nelson (E, S; Th)	15,400
8. Fifth- and Sixth-Grade Science and Mathematics; Mr. Phelps (E; Th)	6,516
9. Fifth- and Sixth-Grade Spelling; Miss Henning (E; Li, Th)	950
10. Seventh- and Eighth-Grade Academic Activities; Mrs. Garnett (E, S; Th)	19,810
11. Seventh- and Eighth-Grade Mathematics and Science; Mr. Phelps (E; Li, Th)	9,000
12. Seventh- and Eighth-Grade Home Economics (E, S; M, Th)	2,880
13. High School, Algebra and Geometry (E; Li, L, Th)	3,600
14. High School, Biology; Mr. Kero (E; Li, Th)	1,430
15. High School, Bookkeeping I (E; L, M, Th)	1,080
16. High School, English (E, S; Li, Th)	5,020
17. High School, General Mathematics (E; Li, L, Th)	900
18. High School, General Science; Mrs. Day (E; Li, Th)	1,430
19. High School, Home Economics (E, S; M, Th)	1,440
20. High School, Secretarial Practice (E; Li, L, M, Th)	360
21. High School, Social Sciences (E; Li, Th)	14,300

	Occupancy Time
22. High School, Study Hall and Library (; L, M, Th)	12,072
23. High School, Typing I and II (E; L, M, Th)	1,800
24. Eighth-Grade State Examination (; Li, L, Th)	40
25. University Extension History Course (E; Th)	20

2. Trafficways: *78,000*

26. Trafficways (; GM)	78,000

3. Grocery, Locker, and Feed Stores: *59,043*

27. Kerr's Frozen Food Locker (B; GM, M)	1,400
28. Kinglake Seed Corn (B, EL; GM)	30
29. Kane's Grocery and Feed Store (B, EL, N; GM, M)	18,000
30. Murray's Grocery (B, N; GM, M)	7,800
31. Poole's Grocery (B, EL, N; GM, M)	7,805
32. Hopkins' Feed Store (B, EL; GM, M)	5,800
33. Hopkins' Cream Station (; GM, M)	208
34. Garnett's Grocery (B, EL, N; GM, M)	18,000

4. Motor Vehicle Sales and Service: *56,242*

35. Kinglog Service Station (B, EL; GM, M)	3,300
36. Lohrman Blacksmith (B, EL; GM, M)	3,200
37. Swann Garage (B, EL; GM, M, Th)	4,300
38. Yeager Garage and Automobile Sales (B, EL; GM, M, Th)	7,890
39. Arkwright Garage (B, EL; GM, M, Th)	3,150
40. Bethel Service Station (B, EL; GM, M)	8,090
41. Chaco Service Station (B, EL; GM, M, Th)	5,512
42. Eastman Garage and Automobile Sales (B, EL; GM, M)	13,200
43. Eckman Service Station (B, EL; GM, M)	6,500
44. Corliss Blacksmith (B, EL; GM, M)	1,100

5. Drug, Variety, and Department Stores: *53,100*

45. Cabell Department Store (A, B, EL; GM)	10,500
46. Clifford's Drug Store (B, EL; Th)	18,525
47. Denton's Drug Store (B; Th)	13,750
48. Everging Variety Store (B; GM)	10,325

6. Indoor Entertainments: *50,205*

49. Midwest Theater (Rec; Af, L)	30,100
50. Midwest Theater Free Show; Christmas (Rec; Af, L)	220
51. Midwest Hardware: Films and Entertainment at High School (Rec; Af, Li, T)	640
52. Methodist Church: Sunday-School Christmas Program (Rec, S; Af, T, Th)	144
53. Methodist Church: Ladies' Aid Sunday Evening Film (Rel; Af)	70
54. Methodist Church: Movies by Mr. Jewett (Rel; Af)	140

Occupancy Time

55. Methodist Church and Presbyterian Church Sponsoring
The University Singers (A, Rel; Af, Li, L, Th)   148
56. Presbyterian Church: Movies (Rel; Af, L)   93
57. Presbyterian Church: Sponsoring the Spiritual Singers
from State City (A, Rel; Af, Li, T, Th)   105
58. Presbyterian Church: Sunday-School Christmas Program
(Rec, Rel, S; Af, T, Th)   264
59. Presbyterian Church: Women's Missionary Society Pictures and Program (Rel; Af, L)   93
60. African Methodist Episcopal Church: Annual Reunion
Afternoon Program at School (S; Af, GM, Li, T)   70
61. Midwest County 4-H Club Fashion Show (A, PA, S; L)   47
62. Primary-School Assemblies (Rec; Li)   100
63. Primary-School Christmas Program and Party (A, Rec,
S; Af, GM, T)   82
64. All-School Assemblies (Rec, S; Li)   1,365
65. Grade-School Operetta (A, PA, Rec, S; Af, Li, T)   460
66. High-School Assemblies (Rec, S; Li)   10,620
67. High School, Drama Club Meetings (Rec; Li, T)   110
68. High School, Junior Class Play (A, Rec, S; Af, Li)   600
69. High School, Junior Class Play Practice (A, Rec, S; Af,
Li, T)   270
70. High School, Pep Club Rally; to develop enthusiasm for
athletic contests (S; Af, GM, Li, T)   210
71. High School, Senior Class Night (Rec, S; Af, L)   403
72. High School, Senior Class Play (A, Rec, S; Af)   600
73. High School, Senior Class Play Practice (A, Rec, S; Af,
Li, T, Th)   180
74. School: Christmas Vespers (A, Rec, Rel, S; Af, Li, L)   700
75. School: Movie; all grades except 1 and 2 (Rec; Af, Li, L)   480
76. County School Music Festival (A, Rec, S; Af, Li, T)   348
77. School: Music Program (A, Rec, S; Af, Li, T)   700
78. All-High-School Party (Rec, S; Af, Li, T)   172
79. Halloween Celebrations: Movies at High School for
Younger Children (Rec; Af, L)   170
80. Music Recital at Home (A, Rec, S; Li, Th)   21
81. Music Recital at Methodist Church (A, Rec, S; Af, Li, Th)   150
82. Music Recital at Presbyterian Church (A, Rec, S; Af, Li,
T, Th)   150
83. Burris University Choir at Methodist Church (A, Rec;
Af, Li, T)   180

7. Restaurants and Taverns: *46,795*
84. Marlin Hotel Dining Room (; GM)   720
85. Pearl Cafe (N; M, T)   12,750
86. Beyet Dairy Queen; (ice cream store) (N, Rec;)   2,200
87. Corner Tavern (N, Rec;)   6,825

Occupancy Time

88. Hooker Tavern and Pool Hall (Rec;)   7,300
89. Gwynn Cafe (N; M)   17,000

8. Government and School Offices: *41,737*

90. Farm Home Administration Office (G; Li, L, Th)   4,730
91. County Clerk's Office (G; Li, L, Th)   6,745
92. County Clerk of the District Court, Office (G; Li, Th)   834
93. County Engineer's Office (G; Li, L, Th)   617
94. County Register of Deeds, Office (G, O; Li, L, Th)   1,155
95. County Superintendent of Schools' Office (E, G, O; Li, L, Th)   3,120
96. County Treasurer's Office (G; Li, Th)   2,605
97. County Weed Supervisor's Office (EL, G; Li, L, Th)   306
98. County Welfare Office (G; Li, L, Th)   8,040
99. U. S. Deputy Tax Collector at Courthouse (G; Li, L, Th)   16
100. U. S. Army Recruiting Officer (G, O; Li)   55
101. U. S. Army Selective Service Office (G; Li, L, Th)   1,892
102. County Agricultural Extension Office (EL, G, O; L, Th)   4,400
103. U. S. Production and Marketing Administration Office (G; L, Th)   2,418
104. U. S. Soil Conservation Office (G; Li, L, Th)   2,330
105. Ditto Room at School (; GM, L, M)   900
106. School Principal's Office (E, G; L)   1,574

9. Home Appliance, Hardware, Implement, and Furniture Stores: *39,725*

107. Sherwin Furniture Store (A, B, EL; GM, M)   10,500
108. Tilden Implement Co. (B, EL; GM, L, M)   250
109. Blanchard Hardware Store (EL;)   5,900
110. Midwest Hardware and Implement Co. (B, EL; GM, M, Th)   13,250
111. Gilmah Implement Co. (B, EL; GM, M)   9,825

10. Attorneys, Insurance, and Real Estate Offices: *34,255*

112. Hutchings, Attorney and Publishing Co. (B, EL, G, O, S; L, M, Th)   7,500
113. Lipmann, Real Estate and Law Office (; Th)   390
114. Deed, Farm Bureau Insurance Office (EL; Th)   4,060
115. Wiley Abstract Co. (B; L, Th)   3,200
116. J. Wiley, Attorney (B, G; Th)   1,600
117. Wiley-Deed, Real Estate (B; L, Th)   1,360
118. Wolf, Attorney (B, G, S; Th)   4,200
119. Metropolitan Life Insurance Co. Route (; GM, Li, Th)   25
120. Buchanen, Real Estate (B; L, Th)   1,320
121. Fowke, Attorney (B, G, S; Th)   1,600
122. French, French, French, Attorneys; Midwest County Abstract Co. (B, EL, G; L, Th)   7,200
123. Garnett Insurance Office (; Th)   1,550
124. Hardy, Insurance and Real Estate (B; L, Th)   250

	Occupancy Time
11. *Indoor Athletic Contests:*	**29,997**
125. Grade-School Boys' Basketball Practice (Rec; Af, GM, L, M, T, Th)	630
126. High-School Girls' Basketball Practice (Rec, S; Af, GM, L, M, T, Th)	197
127. Grade-School Boys' Intramural Basketball Games (Rec, S; Af, GM, M, T, Th)	550
128. Grade-School Basketball Program; in town (Rec, S; Af, GM, L, M, T, Th)	1,011
129. Grade-School Basketball Program; out of town (Rec, S; Af, GM, L, M, T, Th)	249
130. Grade-School Boys' Basketball Tournament (Rec, S; Af, GM, L, M, T, Th)	4,368
131. High-School Boys' Intramural Basketball Games (Rec, S; Af, GM, L, M, T, Th)	255
132. High-School Boys' Basketball Practice (Rec, S; Af, GM, L, M, T, Th)	2,685
133. High-School Basketball Program; in town (Rec, S; Af, GM, L, M, T, Th)	11,808
134. High-School Basketball Program; out of town (Rec, S; Af, GM, L, M, T, Th)	5,904
135. High-School Boys' Basketball Tournament (Rec; Af, GM, L, M, T, Th)	2,340
12. *Building Contractors and Material Suppliers:*	**29,964**
136. Mrs. Phillipson, Wallpapering (A; GM, L, M)	180
137. Trench Brothers Co., Plumbing (EL; GM, M)	4,530
138. Volney, Electrician (B; GM, L, M, Th)	425
139. Lambert Lumber Yard (B, EL; GM, L, M)	3,700
140. Bellows, Painter (A; GM, L, M)	2,530
141. Beyet & Trent Contracting Co. (B, EL; GM, M, Th)	3,200
142. Denham, Painter and Carpenter (; GM, L, M)	860
143. Hagedorn, Contractor (B, EL; GM, L, M)	6,400
144. Graham Lumber Yard (B, EL; GM, M)	5,015
145. Slack, Carpenter (; GM, L, M, Th)	414
146. Mrs. Woodale, Wallpapering (A; GM, L, M)	180
147. Astor, Carpenter (; GM, L, M)	2,530
13. *Hotels, Rooming Houses, and Nurseries:*	**24,241**
148. Mrs. Lawrence, Baby Care (S;)	5,040
149. Marlin Hotel, General (None rated 6 or over)	3,206
150. Berth Nursing Home (None rated 6 or over)	7,320
151. Mrs. Crowther, Roomers (None rated 6 or over)	1,000
152. Mrs. Denham, Baby Care (None rated 6 or over)	2,100
153. Mrs. Deland, Baby Care (None rated 6 or over)	3,075
154. Mrs. Price, Transient Roomers (None rated 6 or over)	1,000
155. Mrs. Eggleston, Transient Roomers (None rated 6 or over)	1,500

	Occupancy Time
14. Telephone and Electric Offices:	*20,900*
156. Telephone Co. Office (B, EL, S; GM, Li, T, Th)	17,100
157. Home State Power & Light Office (B; GM, M, Th)	3,800
15. Barbers and Beauticians:	*18,577*
158. Lent's Barber Shop (A, PA; T)	4,800
159. Burgess Beauty Shop (A, PA; T)	5,727
160. Broyer Beauty Shop (A, PA; T)	5,000
161. Dixon's Barber Shop (A, PA; T)	3,050
16. Hallways and Coatrooms:	*17,331*
162. County Courthouse: Halls (; GM, L)	2,870
163. County Courthouse: Annex Halls (; GM, L)	1,860
164. Primary School, Coatroom (; GM, L, M)	1,485
165. Primary School, Hall (S; GM)	186
166. High-School Building, Halls (; GM, L)	10,930
17. Out-of-Door Athletic Contests:	*15,589*
167. Men's Town Baseball Game; in town (Rec; Af, GM, Li, M, T, Th)	1,920
168. Men's Town Baseball Game; out of town (Rec; Af, GM, Li, M, T, Th)	960
169. Boys' Town Baseball Game; in town (Rec; Af, GM, Li, M, T, Th)	268
170. Boys' Town Baseball Game; out of town (Rec; Af, GM, Li, M, T, Th)	193
171. High School, Boys' Baseball Game; in town (Rec, S; Af, GM, Li, M, T, Th)	193
172. High School, Boys' Baseball Game; out of town (Rec, S; Af, GM, M, T, Th)	276
173. Grade School, Boys' Baseball Game; in town (Rec, S; Af, GM, L, M, T, Th)	168
174. High-School Football Game; in town (Rec, S; Af, GM, M, T, Th)	3,470
175. High-School Football Game; out of town (Rec; Af, GM, M, T, Th)	4,560
176. High-School Football Practice (Rec, S; Af, GM, L, M, T, Th)	2,568
177. High-School Track Meet; out of town (S; Af, GM, M, T, Th)	163
178. High-School Track Practice (; Af, GM, L, M, T, Th)	820
18. Banks:	*15,500*
179. Bank of Midwest (B, EL; L, M, Th)	15,500
19. Factories:	*14,600*
180. Wherry Window and Door Co. (EL; GM, L, M)	14,600

	Occupancy Time
20. *Church Worship Services:*	*14,535*
181. Methodist Church: Worship Service; regular (Rel, S; Af, Li, T, Th)	3,750
182. Methodist Church: Worship Service, Annual Laymen's Day Service (Rel, S; Af, T, Th)	125
183. Union Memorial Day Service (Rel, S; Af, Li, T, Th)	150
184. Methodist Church: Revival Week Services (Rel, S; Af, T, Th)	400
185. Methodist Church: Sunday-School Exercises (Rel, S; Af, T, Th)	1,222
186. Methodist Church: Children's Day Service (Rel, S; Af, Li, T, Th)	144
187. Union World Day of Prayer Service (Rel, S; Af, Li, T, Th)	50
188. Presbyterian Church: Worship Service; regular (Rel, S; Af, Li, T, Th)	3,750
189. Presbyterian Church: Sunday-School Exercises (Rel, S; Af, T)	1,222
190. Presbyterian Church: Children's Day Service (Rel, S; Af, Li, T, Th)	144
191. Presbyterian Church: Rally and Promotion Day Exercises (Rel, S; Af, Li, T, Th)	119
192. Presbyterian Church: Youth Fellowship Devotion at Pleasant Nursing Home (Rel; Af, Li, T, Th)	14
193. Weslyan Methodist Church: Worship Service; regular (Rel, S; Af, Li, T, Th)	694
194. Weslyan Methodist Church: Revival, Evening Meetings (Rel, S; Af, Li, T, Th)	875
195. Weslyan Methodist Church: Children's Revival Meetings (Rel, S; Af, Li, T, Th)	300
196. African Methodist Episcopal Church: Worship Service; regular (Rel, S; Af, Li, T, Th)	588
197. African Methodist Episcopal Church: Homecoming Reunion (Rel, S; Af, Li, T)	122
198. Vacation Church School: General Assembly (Rel; Li, T)	270
199. Vacation Church School: Closing Exercises for Parents (Rec, Rel, S; Af, L, T, Th)	358
200. Bible Auditorium Church Service (Rel, S; Af, Li, T, Th)	70
201. High-School Baccalaureate Service (Rel, S;)	340
21. *Jail:*	*14,415*
202. County Jail and Sheriff's Residence	14,415
22. *Open Spaces:*	*13,717*
203. County Courthouse Lawn (; Af, GM, T)	965
204. Primary-School Playground (Rec, S; Af, GM, Li, T)	2,330
205. High-School Playground (Rec, S; Af, GM, Li, T)	6,135

Occupancy Time

206. Football Field (; Af, GM, Li, M, T)   93
207. Cemetery (; Af, GM)   1,000
208. Lake (; GM, T)   2,012
209. Vacant Lot (; Af, GM, Li, L, T)   180
210. Rim Zone (; GM, Li)   1,000

23. Sunday-School Class Meetings: *13,526*

211. Mrs. Butler's Adult Bible Class (Rel, S; Li, Th)   320
212. Mrs. Butler's Children's Bible Class (Rel; Li, Th)   240
213. Methodist Church: Women's Sunday-School Class (E,
     Rel, S; Li, Th)   760
214. Methodist Church: Elementary Sunday-School Class (E,
     Rel, S; Li, Th)   1,200
215. Methodist Church: Infants Sunday-School Class (Rel, S;
     Li)   550
216. Methodist Church: Kindergarten Sunday-School Class
     (Rel, S; Li)   850
217. Methodist Church: Men's Sunday-School Class (E, Rel,
     S; Li, Th)   780
218. Methodist Church: Young Married's Sunday-School Class
     (E, Rel, S; Li, Th)   650
219. Methodist Church: Young People's Sunday-School Class
     (E, Rel, S; Li, Th)   600
220. Presbyterian Church: Nursery during Church Service
     (S; Li)   84
221. Presbyterian Church: Intermediate Sunday-School Class
     (E, Rel, S; Th)   650
222. Presbyterian Church: Kindergarten Sunday-School Class
     (E, Rel; Li, L)   600
223. Presbyterian Church: Men's Sunday-School Class (E,
     Rel, S; Li, Th)   750
224. Presbyterian Church: Primary Sunday-School Class (E,
     Rel, S; Li)   662
225. Presbyterian Church: Women's Sunday-School Class (E,
     Rel, S; Li, Th)   1,250
226. Presbyterian Church: Older Women's Sunday-School
     Class (E, Rel, S; Li, Th)   400
227. Presbyterian Church: Young People's Sunday-School
     Class (E, Rel, S; Li, Th)   450
228. African Methodist Episcopal Sunday School (E, Rel, S;
     Li, Th)   360
229. Vacation Church School: Junior-High Class (E, Rel, S;
     Li, Th)   280
230. Vacation Church School: Kindergarten Class (E, Rel, S;
     Li)   460
231. Vacation Church School: Intermediate Class (E, Rel, S;
     Li, Th)   540

Occupancy Time

232. Vacation Church School: Primary Class (E, Rel, S; Li)   440
233. Presbyterian Church: Junior-High Sunday-School Class
     (E, Rel, S; Li, Th)   650

24. Post Office: *12,870*
   234. U. S. Post Office (G; Li, L, M)   12,870

25. Dances: *12,540*
   235. Saturday Night Dance (S; A, GM, T)   11,900
   236. Halloween Celebration: Dance at Legion Hall (S; GM,
        Li, T)   320
   237. Old Settlers' Reunion: Dance (S; GM, Li, T)   320

26. Rest Rooms: *11,096*
   238. Methodist Church: Men's Rest Room (None rated 6 or
        over)   50
   239. Methodist Church: Ladies' Rest Room (None rated 6 or
        over)   50
   240. County Courthouse: Ladies' Rest Room (None rated 6 or
        over)   369
   241. County Courthouse: Men's Rest Room (None rated 6 or
        over)   720
   242. County Courthouse: Annex Ladies' Lounge (; L)   246
   243. County Courthouse: Annex Men's Lounge (; L)   720
   244. Primary School: Boys' Rest Room (S;)   222
   245. Primary School: Girls' Rest Room (S;)   650
   246. School: Girls' Basement Locker and Shower Room (S;
        GM)   154
   247. School: Girls' Basement Rest Room (S;)   2,930
   248. School: Boys' Basement Locker and Shower Room (S;
        GM)   805
   249. School: Boys' Basement Rest Room (S;)   2,810
   250. School: Home Economics Club Room (S;)   1,296
   251. School: Faculty Lounge (None rated 6 or over)   74

27. Social Organization Meetings, with Refreshments: *10,585*
   252. American Legion Regular Meeting (S;)   384
   253. American Legion Auxiliary Regular Meeting (S; T, Th)   828
   254. American Legion Auxiliary: School of Instruction Meeting
        (S; Li, Th)   39
   255. Homemaker Club Regular Meeting (Rec, S; Af, T)   900
   256. Bridge Club I Regular Meeting (Rec, S; M, T, Th)   750
   257. Bridge Club II Regular Meeting (Rec, S; M, T, Th)   683
   258. Bridge Club III Regular Meeting (Rec, S; M, T, Th)   512
   259. Cart and Saddle Club Regular Meeting (; Li)   32
   260. Women's Club II Regular Meeting (Rec, S; T, Th)   1,107

Occupancy Time

261. Eastern Star Past Matron's Club Regular Meeting (Rec, S;) 540
262. Rotary Club Regular Meeting (S;) 1,573
263. Rotary Club Farmers' Night (S;) 42
264. Rotary Meeting with Rotaryanns (S;) 356
265. Rotary Club Football Team Banquet (S;) 80
266. Rotary Meeting with Brownsville Rotary (S; T) 115
267. Rotary Meeting with Villiska Rotary (S;) 75
268. Rotary Club Entertainment for Foreign Students from University (S;) 50
269. Rural Letter Carriers' Association Meeting (S; T) 16
270. Women's Club I Regular Meeting (Rec, S; T, Th) 1,107
271. Home Demonstration Unit Regular Meeting (E, S;) 526
272. Parent-Teachers' Association Regular Meeting (; Th) 870

28. Shoe Repair Shop: *9,335*
273. Culver Shoe Repair (; GM, M, Th) 9,335

29. Newspaper: *9,200*
274. The *Midwest Weekly* (B, EL, E, G, O; GM, M, L, Th) 9,200

30. University Research Office: *9,121*
275. Child Study Project Offices (EL, E; M, Th) 9,121

31. Dining and Lunch Rooms: *8,841*
276. Primary School, Classroom Lunch (S; Af, T) 396
277. Grade School, Classroom Lunch (S; Af, T) 2,199
278. School Lunch Room (N, S; M) 6,246

32. Music Education Groups: *8,837*
279. Methodist Church: Adult Choir Practice (A, Rel, S; Af, Li, T, Th) 245
280. Methodist Church: Junior Choir Boys' Practice (A, Rel, S; Af, Li, T, Th) 22
281. Methodist Church: Junior Choir Girls' Practice (A, Rel, S; Af, Li, T, Th) 20
282. Presbyterian Church: Junior Choir Practice (Rel, S; Li, T, Th) 150
283. Presbyterian Church: Senior Choir Practice (A, Rel, S; Af, Li, T, Th) 544
284. Methodist Church: Junior-High Girls' Choir Practice (A, Rel, S; Af, Li, T, Th) 17
285. Primary-School Music Classes (A, E, S; Af, Li, T, Th) 1,218
286. Grade-School Music Classes (A, E, S; Af, Li, T, Th) 2,106
287. Seventh- and Eighth-grade Boys' Music Classes (A, E, S; Af, Li, T, Th) 495
288. Seventh- and Eighth-grade Girls' Music Classes (A, E, S; Af, Li, T, Th) 1,050

Occupancy Time

289. School: Band Marching Practice (S; GM, Li, M, Th)   112
290. School: Band Practice (A, E, S; Li, M, Th)   1,700
291. School: Band Trip to the University (; Af, GM, Li, M, T)   168
292. High-School Musical Groups (A, E, S; Af, Li, T, Th)   960
293. University Extension Course, Music at High School (A, E, S; Li, Th)   30

33. Government Garages: *7,530*

294. City Garage (; GM, L, M, Th)   1,485
295. County Garage (; GM, L, M, Th)   6,045

34. Doctors' Offices: *7,367*

296. Lewis Sterne, Dentist Office (PH; Th)   3,750
297. Frank Emerson, M.D. Office (PH; Th)   3,600
298. James Grayson, Veterinarian Office (EL; GM, L, M, Th)   17

35. Courts: *6,878*

299. City Court Chambers (G, S; Li, L, Th)   320
300. District Court Sessions (G, S; A, Li, Th)   910
301. District Court Judge's Chambers (G; Th, L)   38
302. Probate Judge's Office (G, S; Li, L, Th)   690
303. Sheriff's Office (G, S; Li, Th)   4,920

36. Laundries: *6,643*

304. Mrs. Matson, Home Laundry (; GM, M, L)   663
305. Mrs. Temple, Home Laundry (; GM, M, L)   1,600
306. Crowther, Laundry (; GM, M)   4,380

37. Heavy Truck Lines: *6,470*

307. Midwest Truckline (B, EL; GM, L, M)   5,420
308. Standard Oil Bulk Branch (B, EL; GM, L, M)   1,050

38. Church Group Meetings: *6,119*

309. Methodist Church: Ladies' Aid Regular Meeting (Rel; Th)   1,416
310. Methodist Church: Women's Evening Guild Regular Meeting (Rel; Li, T, Th)   800
311. Methodist Church: Youth Fellowship Regular Meeting (S; Li, T, Th)   325
312. Presbyterian Church: Ladies' Aid Regular Meeting (Rec, Rel; T, Th)   1,416
313. Presbyterian Church: Ladies' Aid Circle A Meeting (Rel; Li, T, Th)   132
314. Presbyterian Church: Ladies' Aid Circle B Meeting (Rel; Li, T, Th)   132
315. Presbyterian Church: Ladies' Aid Circle C Meeting (Rel; Li, T, Th)   225
316. Presbyterian Church: Ladies' Aid Circle D Meeting (Rel; Li, T)   16

Occupancy Time

317. Presbyterian Church: Youth Fellowship Regular Meeting
(S; Li, T) 130

318. Presbyterian Church: Evening Missionary Society Regular Meeting (Rel; Li, T, Th) 594

319. Presbyterian Church: Women's Missionary Society Regular Meeting (Rel; Li, T, Th) 360

320. Presbyterian Church: Women's Missionary Society All-Day Meeting (Rel; Li, T, Th) 55

321. African Methodist Episcopal Church: Missionary Society Regular Meeting (Rel; Li, T, Th) 365

322. Presbyterian Church: Missionary Study Meeting (Rel; Li, Th) 153

39. Outdoor Entertainments: 5,620

323. Grade School, Singing Carols on Square (A, Rec; Af, GM, Li, T, Th) 40

324. Old Settlers' Reunion: Amateur Show (Rec, S; Af, T) 1,400

325. Old Settlers' Reunion: Free Stage Show (Rec, S; A, Li, T) 1,300

326. Town Band Concerts (A, Rec; Af, Li) 2,880

40. Classrooms: Free Time: 4,655

327. First-Grade Classroom (S;) 716

328. Second-Grade Classroom (S;) 1,116

329. Third-Grade Classroom (S;) 916

330. Fourth-Grade Classroom (S;) 1,002

331. Fifth- and Sixth-Grade Classroom (S; Li) 530

332. Seventh- and Eighth-Grade Home Room (S;) 375

41. Door-to-Door Salesmen and Delivery Services: 4,335

333. Avon Products Sales Route (; L, T) 300

334. Milk Co. Route (B; GM, L, M) 180

335. Pearson Dairy Route (B, EL; M) 1,400

336. Grand Union Tea Co. Route (; GM, L, M) 450

337. Bakery Route (B; L) 1,400

338. Cleaners Route (; L) 300

339. Door-to-door Salesmen (; GM, Li) 305

42. Dairy Barn: 3,900

340. Pearson Dairy Barn (EL; GM, L, M) 3,900

43. School Shop Classes: 3,680

341. Seventh- and Eighth-Grade Shop; boys (E; GM, L, M, Th) 900

342. High-School Boys' Shop (E; GM, L, M, Th) 2,700

343. Veterans Vocational Agriculture Class (E; Th) 80

44. Circuses and Carnivals: 3,484

344. Boy Scout District Circus at Capital City (; Af, GM, M, T, Th) 90

Occupancy Time

345. 4-H Club: Carnival (Rec; Af, GM, M, T, Th)   189
346. Circus Performances (Rec; Af, GM, M, T, Th)   1,025
347. Old Settlers' Reunion: Midway (Rec; Af, GM, L, M, T, Th)   2,000
348. Circus Setting Up (Rec; Af, GM, L, M, T, Th)   180

45. Recreational Organization Meetings without Refreshments: *3,424*

349. Boy Scout Troop Regular Meeting (Rec, S; GM, L, T, Th)   1,600
350. Brownies' Regular Meeting (Rec, S; Af, GM, Li, M, T, Th)   344
351. Cub Scout Pack Meeting (Rec, S; Af, GM, Li, T, Th)   160
352. Cub Scout Regular Den Meeting (Rec, S; Af, GM, T, Th)   940
353. 4-H Club Regular Meeting (Rec, S; Af, GM, T, Th)   372
354. Rural Life Association Meeting (Rec; L, Th)   8

46. Masonic Meetings: *2,950*

355. Eastern Star Regular Meeting (S;)   900
356. Eastern Star Men's Night (Rec, S; Af)   300
357. Masonic Lodge Regular Meeting (S;)   1,750

47. School Janitor's Room: See Variety 81*a*

358. See Setting 545*a*

48. Watch Repair Shop: *2,675*

359. Tills' Watch Repair Shop (; Th)   2,675

49. Dinners and Banquets: *2,666*

360. Methodist Church: Mother-Daughter Banquet (Rec, S; T)   220
361. Presbyterian Church: Dinners (N; T)   370
362. Presbyterian Church: Women's Missionary Society Covered Dish Luncheon (; M, T)   114
363. African Methodist Episcopal Church: Annual Homecoming Reunion Dinner (N, S; T)   70
364. American Legion and Auxiliary Community Party (; T)   66
365. American Legion Auxiliary Father-Son Banquet (Rec, S; T)   260
366. Homemaker Club Family Dinner (; Af, T)   156
367. Homemaker Club Christmas Dinner (Rec, S; T)   72
368. The University Students of Midwest County Dinner (N, S; M, T)   10
369. County Principals' Association Dinner (S; M)   5
370. Fifth- and Sixth-Grade Thanksgiving Dinner (N; M)   40
371. High-School Home Economics Club Dinner (; M, T)   90
372. Boys "M" Club Banquet (Rec; M)   53
373. Last Day of School Dinner (N, Rec, S; Af, L, M, T)   540
374. Parent-Teachers' Association Penny Supper (Rec; Af, M, T)   430
375. Midwest High-School Alumni Reception (S; Af, T)   170

Occupancy Time

50. Parties: 2,538

376. Methodist Church: Junior Choir Party (S; GM, T)   20
377. Methodist Church: Women's Sunday-School Class Party
     (S; T)   32
378. Methodist Church: Fifth-Grade Sunday-School Class
     Party (Rec, S; GM, T)   8
379. Methodist Church: Young Married's Sunday-School Class
     Party (Rec, S; T)   84
380. Methodist Church: Junior-High Sunday-School Party,
     Boys (S; GM, T)   14
381. Methodist Church: Junior-High Sunday-School Party,
     Girls (S; GM, T)   21
382. Methodist Church: Senior-High Sunday-School Party,
     (S; GM, T)   30
383. Presbyterian Church: Men's Sunday-School Class Party
     (S; T)   40
384. Presbyterian Church: Primary Department Third-Grade
     Sunday-School Party (Rec, S; GM, T)   10
385. Presbyterian Church: Women's Sunday-School Class
     Party (Rec, S; T)   270
386. Presbyterian Church: Older Women's Sunday-School
     Class Party (Rec; T)   37
387. Presbyterian Church: Intermediate Department Sunday-
     School Party (S; GM, T)   78
388. American Legion Men's Party (S; Af, GM, M, T)   204
389. American Legion with Auxiliary, Mixed Party at Wolf's
     Home (Rec, S; Af, T)   105
390. American Legion Auxiliary: Card Party for Polio Fund
     (; M, T)   169
391. American Legion Auxiliary: Women's Party (Rec, S;
     Af, L, T)   207
392. School: Faculty Party (Rec, S; Af)   50
393. School: High-School Drama Club Party (Rec; T)   50
394. Baby Shower (; T)   308
395. Cosmetic Party; to sell cosmetics (A, PA; Af)   71
396. Halloween Celebration: Party at High School; Fifth—
     Eighth Grade (Rec, S; Af, GM, T)   160
397. Stanley Party; to sell household products (; T)   270
398. Wedding Shower (Rec, A, S; Af, T)   300

51. Gymnasium, Free Time: 2,382
399. High School, Gymnasium (S; Af, GM, M, T)   2,382

52. Special Holidays: 2,165
400. Easter Sunday (Rec; Af)   550
401. Fourth of July (Rec; Af, GM, T)   1,025
402. May Day (Rec; Af)   340
403. Valentine's Day (Rec; Af, L)   250

	Occupancy Time
53. Membership Business Meetings without Refreshments:	*1,923*
404. Methodist Church: Quarterly Conference (Rel; Li, Th)	276
405. Presbyterian Church: Congregation Meetings (Rel; Li, Th)	96
406. Cancer Control Organization Regular Meeting (P; Th)	98
407. Chamber of Commerce Regular Meeting (; Li, Th)	376
408. Farm Bureau Regular Meeting (; Li, Th)	8
409. Hospital Committee Meeting (P; Li, T, Th)	7
410. Production and Marketing Administration County Convention (; Li, Th)	4
411. Soil Conservation Annual Meeting (G, O; Th)	6
412. School: Annual Meeting (G; Th)	58
413. School: Fifth- and Sixth-Grade Citizenship Club Meeting (S; Li)	280
414. School: Seventh- and Eighth-Grade Class Meeting; Junior-High (; Th)	50
415. High School, Home Economics Club Meeting (; Li, T, Th)	20
416. High School, Freshman Class Meeting (S; Li, Th)	34
417. High School, Junior Class, Cub Reporter Meeting (Rec; Th)	44
418. High School, Junior Class Meeting (S; Th)	70
419. High School, Boys' "M" Club Meeting (; GM, Li, Th)	20
420. High School, Girls' Pep Club Meeting (; Af, GM, Li, T)	200
421. High School, Pep Club Drill on Football Field (S; Af, GM, Li, T, Th)	106
422. High School, Senior Class, Annual Staff Meeting (; Th)	73
423. High School, Senior Class Meeting (; Li, Th)	58
424. High School, Sophomore Class Meeting (S; Th)	31
425. High School, Student Council Meeting (S; Li, Th)	8
54. Home Rug Weaving:	*1,405*
426. Mrs. Knox, Rug Weaving (A; M)	205
427. Mr. Stanton, Rug Weaving (; M)	1,200
55. Executive Planning Meetings:	*1,392*
428. Methodist Church: Official Board Meeting (P, Rel; Li, Th)	150
429. Methodist Church: Board of Trustees' Meeting (P, Rel; Li, Th)	105
430. Methodist Church: Sunday-School Teachers' Meeting (E, P, Rel; Li, Th)	20
431. Presbyterian Church: Deacons' Meeting (P, Rel; Li, Th)	12
432. Presbyterian Church: Ladies' Aid Executive Committee Meeting (P, Rel; Li, Th)	26
433. Presbyterian Church: Session Meeting (P, Rel; Li, Th)	91

Occupancy Time

434. Presbyterian Church: Sunday-School Teachers' Meeting
(E, P, Rel; Li, Th) ... 13
435. Presbyterian Church: Trustees' Meeting (P, Rel; Li, Th) ... 24
436. African Methodist Episcopal Church: Annual Homecoming Reunion Planning Meeting (Rel; Li, Th) ... 40
437. African Methodist Episcopal Church: Junior Steward
Board Meeting (Rel; Li, Th) ... 20
438. Vacation Church School: Committee Meeting (E, O, Rel;
Li, Th) ... 20
439. City Council Meeting (G; Li, Th) ... 144
440. County Board of Commissioners Meeting (G; Li, Th) ... 75
441. City Library Board Meeting (; Li, Th) ... 14
442. City Volunteer Fireman Meeting (; Li, Th) ... 40
443. County Board of Social Welfare Meeting (G, S; Li, Th) ... 20
444. Cemetery Board Meeting (G; Li, Th) ... 12
445. Boy Scout, Adult Committee Meeting (P; Li, Th) ... 12
446. Cancer Control Committee Meeting (; Li, Th) ... 3
447. Chamber of Commerce Executive Board Meeting (; Li,
Th) ... 28
448. Cub Scouts, Adult Committee Meeting (O; Li, Th) ... 32
449. Farm Bureau, Executive Committee Meeting (; Th) ... 16
450. Infantile Paralysis Committee Meeting (P; Li, Th) ... 14
451. Extension Council Meeting (; Li, Th) ... 40
452. Agricultural Extension County Council, Election Meeting
(; Th) ... 11
453. Agricultural Extension Clothing and Textile Committee
Meeting (E; L, Th) ... 8
454. Agricultural Extension Family and Community Life
Committee Meeting (; Li, Th) ... 8
455. Agricultural Extension Food, Nutrition, and Health
Meeting (E; Li, Th) ... 6
456. County 4-H Club Council Meeting (E; Li, Th) ... 48
457. Agricultural Extension Housing and Furnishings Committee Meeting (; L, Li, Th) ... 8
458. Agricultural Extension Farm and Home Management
Committee Meeting (; Li, Th) ... 8
459. County School Boards' Meeting (G, S; Th) ... 5
460. School Faculty Meeting (S; Li, Th) ... 105
461. Grade-School Board Meeting (G; Li, Th) ... 144
462. High-School Board Meeting (G; Li, Th) ... 60
463. School: Parent-Teachers' Association Executive Board
Meeting (; Li, Th) ... 10

56. Horse Show: *1,310*
464. Old Settlers' Reunion: Horse Show (Rec; GM, M, T, Th) ... 1,310

57. Gas Service Man: *1,225*
465. Gas Service Co., Service (B, EL; GM, L, M, Th) ... 1,225

Occupancy Time

58. Paper Routes: 1,095

466. The City Paper Route (B; GM, L, M)   270
467. Capitol City Paper Route (B; GM, L, M)   415
468. State Journal Paper Route (B; GM, L, M)   410

59. School Classroom Recreation: 1,090

469. First-Grade Recreation (Rec, S; Af, GM, Li, M, T)   170
470. Second-Grade Recreation (Rec, S; Af, GM, Li, M, T)   223
471. Third-Grade Recreation (Rec, S; Af, GM, Li, M, T)   171
472. Fourth-Grade Recreation (Rec, S; Af, GM, Li, M, T)   198
473. Fifth- and Sixth-Grade Recreation (Rec, S; Af, GM, Li, M, T)   328

60. Individual Music Lessons: 1,062

474. Mrs. Wiley, Music Lessons (A, E, Rec; Li, T, Th)   225
475. Mr. Wiley, Music Lessons (A, E, Rec; Li, T, Th)   600
476. Mrs. Godfrey, Piano Lessons (A, E, Rec; Li, T, Th)   237

61. Parades: 1,062

477. Grade-School Halloween Parade (Rec, S; Af, GM, T)   120
478. Halloween Celebration: Parade (PA, Rec; Af, GM, T)   825
479. Old Settlers' Reunion: Parade (Rec; GM, L)   117

62. Home Bakery: 1,050

480. Mrs. Harbough, Bakery (B, EL;)   1,050

63. Bus Stop: 1,000

481. Bus Stop at Denton's (B;)   1,000

64. City Cleanup Campaign   1,000

482. Spring Cleanup Drive (; GM, L, M)   1,000

65. Engineer: 960

483. Pechter, Engineer (; GM, M, Th)   960

66. Recognition Programs: 939

484. Boy Scout Court of Honor (S;)   94
485. Eighth-Grade Graduation (O, S;)   245
486. High School, Senior Class Commencement (O, S;)   600

67. Camps: 915

487. Cub Scouts, Lads and Dads Camp (Rec; Af, GM, M, T, Th)   480
488. Boy Scouts, Summer Camp at Otis Camp (Rec, S; Af, GM, M, T, Th)   435

68. Recreation Room: 900

489. Masonic Lodge Recreation Room (S; GM, Li, T)   900

Occupancy Time

69. *Special School Days:* — 887

490. High-School Enrollment Day (O, S; Af, GM, Li, T) — 72
491. First Day of School (S; Af, Li, T) — 452
492. Last Day of School (; GM, T) — 363

70. *Public Drawings:* — 878

493. Christmas Merchandise Guessing at Stores (; Th) — 78
494. Treasure Chest Drawing (; Li, T) — 800

71. *Funeral Services:* — 837

495. Methodist Church: Funerals (Rel; Af, Li) — 357
496. Presbyterian Church: Funerals (Rel; Af, Li) — 357
497. African Methodist Episcopal Church: Funerals (Rel; Af, Li) — 70
498. American Legion Graveside Funeral Services (; Af, GM) — 26
499. American Legion Memorial Day Cemetery Service (None rated 6 or over) — 27

72. *Ice Company:* — 685

500. Ice House (B; GM, M) — 685

73. *Emergency Room and Board:* — 640

501. American Legion Auxiliary, Flood Disaster Headquarters (N; Th) — 640

74. *Town Elections:* — 594

502. Polling Place, North Side (G, O; L, Th) — 282
503. Polling Place, South Side (G, O; L, Th) — 282
504. School Bond Election (G; L) — 30

75. *Outings:* — 590

505. Methodist Youth Fellowship Picnic at Beyet's (N; Af, GM, T) — 39
506. Presbyterian Church: Annual Picnic at Rapture Ranch (S; Af, GM, T) — 361
507. Boy Scouts, Flaming Arrow Patrol, Horseback Trip (; Af, L, T) — 21
508. Boy Scouts, Patrol Cookout (Rec; GM, M, T) — 44
509. Brownies' Wading Party (Rec; Af, GM, T) — 34
510. Brownies' Summer Picnic (Rec, S; Af, GM, Li, M, T) — 43
511. 4-H Club Project Tour and Picnic (; Af, GM, Li, M, T) — 36
512. Midwest County Home Demonstration Garden Tour (; GM, L) — 12

76. *Public Library:* — 540

513. City Library (A; L, Th) — 540

77. *Public Emergencies:* — 500

514. Fires (; Af, GM, Li, M, T, Th) — 500

Occupancy Time

78. Agricultural Extension Classes: *473*

515. Agronomy School (E; Li, Th)   4
516. Artificial Breeding School (E; Li, Th)   4
517. Beef Cattle School (E; Li, Th)   4
518. Farm Price School (E; Li, Th)   8
519. Flood Rehabilitation Meeting (P; Li, Th)   6
520. Germination School (E; Li, Th)   4
521. 4-H Club Food Project Meetings (; L, M, Th)   101
522. 4-H Club Junior Leadership Meetings (E, S; Li, Th)   36
523. 4-H Club Project Leaders Training Day Meetings (E, S; Th)   15
524. 4-H Club Sewing Project Meetings (A, E; L, Th)   101
525. Home Demonstration Handicraft Meetings (A; GM, L, Li, Th)   80
526. Home Demonstration Lesson Leaders Meetings (E, S; Th)   90
527. Marketing Outlook School (E; Li, Th)   4
528. Tractor Maintenance School (E; GM, L, Li, M, Th)   12
529. Weed School (E; Li, T)   4

79. Fund Membership Drives: *471*

530. American Legion Auxiliary Poppy Day (P; GM, Li)   62
531. Cancer Control Fund Drive (P, PH; GM)   60
532. Children's Service League Fund Drive (P; GM, Li)   15
533. Infantile Paralysis Drive (P, PH; GM)   60
534. Red Cross Fund Drive (P; GM, Li)   122
535. Rotary Club Drive for Boy Scouts (P; GM, Li)   62
536. Midwest Home Demonstration Unit, Blue Cross Membership Drive (PH; GM)   90

80. Auctions: *450*

537. Auctions (; GM, L, Li, T, Th)   450

81. Food Sales and Rummage Sales: *426*

538. Methodist Ladies' Aid Rummage Sale (; Li)   21
539. Methodist Women's Evening Guild Food Sale (Rec;)   160
540. Methodist Youth Fellowship Ice Cream Social (N; T)   30
541. Presbyterian Ladies' Aid Food Sale (N;)   80
542. Presbyterian Women's Class Food Sale (N;)   40
543. 4-H Club Food Sale (N;)   40
544. 4-H Club Ice Cream Social (N, Rec; Af, T)   47
545. Rural Club Food Sale (N;)   8

81a. (47) School Janitor's Room: *399*

545a. (358) School Utility Room (; GM, L, M)   399

Occupancy Time

82. *Volunteer Work on Organization Buildings:*   382

546. Methodist Ladies' Aid Repair of Parsonage (; GM, L,
M, T)   270
547. Presbyterian Church: Work Night for Men (; GM, L,
M, T)   64
548. American Legion, Work Party at Legion Hall (; GM,
Li, M, T)   48

83. *Weddings:*   *371*

549. Methodist Church: Weddings (A, Rel, S; Af)   194
550. Presbyterian Church: Weddings (A, Rel, S; Af)   163
551. Civil Weddings (S; Af)   14

84. *Special School Trips:*   *336*

552. High School, Drama Club Trip to the City (Rec; Af, Li, T)   48
553. School: Senior Class Sneak Day Trip (S; Af, T)   240
554. School: Senior Class Trip to Capitol City for Pictures
(S; Af, T)   48

85. *Funeral Home:*   *319*

555. Sherwin Funeral Home (; Af)   319

86. *Initiations:*   *301*

556. High School, Senior Class, Freshman Initiation (PA,
Rec, S; Af, GM, M, T)   161
557. Charavarie (S; Af, GM, Li, M, T)   140

87. *Utility Pay Station:*   *260*

558. Gas Service Co., Pay Station (; Li, Th)   260

88. *Santa Claus at the Courthouse:*   *250*

559. Christmas: Santa at the Courthouse (; Af, GM, T)   250

89. *Coach's Room:*   *247*

560. School: Coach's Room (None rated 6 or over)   247

90. *Barn Play Space:*   *210*

561. Howell's Hayloft (Rec; Af, GM, Li, M, T)   210

91. *Class Dance and Banquet:*   *190*

562. High School, Junior Class Banquet for Seniors (Rec, S;
M)   190

92. *Flower Shows and Sales:*   *187*

563. Presbyterian Church: Ladies' Aid Flower Sale (A;)   137
564. Midwest County Home Demonstration, Flower Show
(A;)   50

93. *Fire Drills:*   *174*

565. Primary School, Fire Drill (S; GM)   30
566. High School, Fire Drill (S; GM)   144

Occupancy Time

94. *Radio Repair Service:*   125

  567. Bette, Radio Repair (; L, Li, M, Th)   125

95. *Clinics and Volunteer Health Aids:*   *109*

  568. Cancer Control Free Clinic (P, PH; Th)   12

  569. Red Cross Blood Donor Unit (P, PH;)   82

  570. Tuberculosis Chest X-Ray Unit (; Li)   15

96. *Farm Demonstration:*   *92*

  571. Midwest Hardware & Implement Co.: Terracing Demonstration (; GM, Li, M)   92

97. *Skating Party:*   *90*

  572. 4-H Club Skating Party (Rec, S; Af, GM, T)   90

98. *Extension Achievement Program:*   *88*

  573. Midwest County 4-H Club Achievement Banquet (Rec, S; T)   50

  574. Midwest County Home Demonstration Unit Achievement Day (S;)   38

99. *Swimming Party:*   *84*

  575. Boy Scouts, Swim at Longmont Pool (Rec; Af, GM, T)   84

100. *Ballet Classes:*   *50*

  576. Ballet Classes (A, Rec; GM, Li, L, Th)   50

101. *Teachers Association Meetings:*   *26*

  577. County Teachers' Association Meetings (E, S;)   22

  578. County Principals' Association Meetings (; Th)   4

102. *Child's Sales Stand:*   *25*

  579. Kool-Aid Stand (N; GM, T)   25

103. *Photo Contests:*   *21*

  580. Gilmah Implement Co.: Photo Contest (None rated 6 or over)   21

104. *Book Exchange:*   *20*

  581. Parent-Teachers' Association Book Exchange (; L, M)   20

105. *Political Meetings:*   *19*

  582. Midwest County Women's Republican Club (; Th)   12

  583. Taft for President Club Meeting (; Th)   7

106. *Qualifying Tests for Entrance:*   *16*

  584. Boy Scout Tenderfoot Test at Home (S; Li, Th)   16

107. *Field Trips:*   *16*

  585. High-School Biology Class Field Trip (S; GM, T, Th)   16

Chapter V

Behavior and Psychological Habitat As Targets of Description

Children Inside Midwest's Behavior Settings

THE behavior setting survey delineates stable extra-individual behavior patterns of Midwest and establishes some of their conditions; it exhibits characteristics of the behavior and living conditions of Midwest children en masse. But this survey does not disclose what individual children find and do inside Midwest's behavior settings. It does not bring to a focus the unique ways in which these children themselves see and relate themselves to Midwest and its parts. The methods of description before us now have been developed and applied for this purpose. Their aim is to exhibit some concrete details of children's behavior in Midwest, and to represent some related particulars of the psychological habitats in which individual Midwest children behave.

Raymond Birch is on his way to school. Margaret Reid is eating her lunch at home. Mary Ennis is reciting at school. Ben Hutchings is buying candy at Clifford's Drug Store. Douglas Crawford is saluting the flag at a scout meeting. We know from the survey of behavior settings what in general these children may be expected to find and to do in these places, times, and groups of Midwest. But what in particular *do* they find and do in them? With what behavior objects do Raymond, Margaret, Mary, Ben, and Douglas transact behavior? And how? How, in terms of intensity, efficiency, creativity, emotionality, outcome, and level of satisfaction? What sticks and stones, occasions, events, and persons register upon these children to invite, repel, excite, hinder, or command them? What, as far as an outsider can pretend to say, are the meanings to these children of the circumstances they meet, seek, or have forced upon them inside the behavior settings of Midwest? How did Raymond Birch go to school? Did he walk reluctantly or run eagerly? What did he notice on the way? Did he get into trouble or have any fun? Did Margaret Reid dawdle over her food or bolt it down? Did Mary recite well? And did the teacher approve? How did Mr. Clifford wait on Ben? Impatiently? Indulgently? In what kind of a group situation did Douglas salute the flag?

The task now before us is that of describing behavior and life situations on the level of questions like these. This task poses two broadly significant problems.

First, there is the problem of making naturally occurring human action a matter of scientifically adequate record.

Second, there is the problem of analyzing and of thereby reconstructing systematically the recorded behavior and its relevant context.

These problems define the assignments of the following chapters. Here, before going into the particulars of these assignments, we would like to consider some of their more general requirements and at the same time to bring into closer range the present targets of description.

"Behavior Qua Molar"

MOLAR VERSUS MOLECULAR UNITS

One way of setting off the behavior to be described is to identify it as primarily *molar* rather than *molecular*.[1] Consider the following comparisons:

Perspiration	versus	Hurrying to school
Salivation, chewing, swallowing, grasping	versus	Eating lunch at home or buying candy at Clifford's Drug Store
Elbow bending, extensor adjustments of the fingers, visual fixation	versus	Saluting the flag
Movements of the lips, tongue, vocal cords, arms, legs, trunk, and diaphragm	versus	Reciting at school

The units of behavior on the right necessarily implicate a person as carrier, seat, or agent. This is not true of the units on the left. They necessarily engage only subordinate and more or less independent parts or mechanisms of the person. A *child* in going about his business as a whole person never perspires in running to school or salivates in buying candy; and a child rarely, if ever, bends his arm in saluting the flag or wags his tongue in reciting a lesson. He runs to school, buys the candy, salutes the flag, and recites the lesson while, cotemporaneously, lesser systems do the sweating, salivating, bending, and wagging with greater or lesser independence of the person as a superordinate whole. The question here reduces to one of who or what does what; and the answers are given by straightforward recognition which is open to observers of naturally occurring behavior.

It is true that in common speech the parts of persons are sometimes the

---

[1] Since they were used first in psychology by Tolman (**57**), to whom we are indebted for the title above, these terms have acquired a somewhat bewildering variety of psychological meanings, as Littman and Rosen (**38**) have shown. Yet we know of no better words for the need at hand. Others who have dealt with this problem include Lewin (**33**), Murray (**43**), Muenzinger (**42**), and McDougall (**40**). We have developed in greater detail elsewhere (**61**) the distinctions made here.

subjects of sentences about behavior by the person as a whole. And the reverse also holds; persons are sometimes the subjects of sentences about behavior by their parts. "His hand shot up in answer to the question" and "Her eyes said, 'Yes'" are examples of the former construction. We recognize the elliptical nature of every such statement, however, and do not fail to find in a person the unit "source" of the behavior. On the other hand, when it is said of a person that "He sweat profusely," or of another that "He swept his eyes back and forth across the page while reading the book," we know again more or less explicitly that the statement leaves something out, and understand that the behavior is in fact an event of a subordinate mechanism.

Examine again the parallel lists of behavior units. Those on the right occur in relation to parts of the world with some kind and degree of meaning for the person: school; the hum in the classroom; the candy, Mr. Clifford, and the drug store; the flag. This is not true of the units on the left. They occur in essentially different contexts. They "go off" in relation to thermal and chemical conditions, light waves, sound waves, and physical impacts that are not organized by cognitive processes of the organism into meaningful things and events.

The units on the right exemplify molar behavior or *actions*, while those on the left exemplify molecular behavior or *actones* (cf. Murray: **43**). The molar units are molar in the sense that they occur in the context of the person as a whole and a molar environment. The molecular units are molecular in the sense that they occur in the context of subordinate parts or mechanisms of the person and a molecular environment. The size of a behavior sample, as defined by how long it lasts or how much of the physical organism it uses, cannot be made a test for this distinction. Bodily massive and long extended patterns of behavior, like the movements in walking, swimming, or dancing, can be molecular whenever they only mediate action by the person. Conversely, very small behavior samples are often molar. A footstep can be molar in the context of crossing a muddy street; and so can a wink in the context of a love affair. The determining context, as defined above, makes the difference in these and other cases.

Molar behavior has two additional main distinguishing features, both of which are implicit in the conception of action by a person. It is goal directed; and it generally occurs within the cognitive field of the person.

As for the first of these ascriptions, an action is always a "getting to" or a "getting from" a part of the molar environment (cf. Tolman: **57**). It is, in the language of Lewin (**34**), a locomotion or change in position of the person from a *starting region* to a terminal or subordinate *goal region* of the *life space*. Physical, social, and "intellectual" ("imaginal," "mental") locomotions are distinguished here by Lewin. A child goes from home to school, from bidding for attention to getting it, from *9 × 43* to *387*. Each of these behavior units is an action and, as such, each entails a particular directional

change in the position of the person.   Several available indices of directedness as a property of an action will be considered in Chapter VII.

To say that molar behavior generally occurs within the cognitive field of
the person is only to recognize that characteristically a person knows within
limits what he is doing.   There would seem to be no reason for doubting
that our own actions are known in the same way that other environmental
parts are known.   The action of the moment, actions of the immediate and
remote past, the "next thing to be done," simultaneously occurring or
alternative and mutually exclusive actions, and more or less remote, prospective things to do may all exist as cognitively separate units of a person's
situation.

Molecular behavior, on the other hand, is not comparably structured.
Turning a wheel is not generally perceived as a part of driving somewhere in
a car.   Neither are individual steps of the feet generally perceived as parts
of walking to a store, nor oculomotor movements as parts of reading a book,
nor laryngeal adjustments as parts of making a speech.   There is no boundary
line for the person between consecutive molecular units such as these.   The
individual actones are lost to the person.   They are not cognitively discrete
events in the behavior continuum or the total situation of the person.

As for actions by a person, these units of molar behavior are not all
differentiated cognitively with equal clarity.

At one extreme there are small molar units which occur as parts of larger,
including actions.   These involve the person in relation to minor subgoals.
Within the whole configuration of an including action unit, they can virtually
"go unnoticed," especially when they occur only as "means to an end"
under circumstances such that their own ends are not "valued" in themselves.   Opening a door on the way downtown, righting an easel in painting
a picture, saying during the delivery of a lecture, "With all of the foregoing
facts in view let us now turn and look at the other side of the matter,"
walking one block of three in catching a train, even scanning a paragraph in
reading a book sometimes are examples.

Like molecular units, actions on this level may lack discreteness as parts
of an own behavior sequence.   Such molar units have essentially the same
significance for behavior description as actones.   They can often be assimilated to actone manifolds which, to anticipate the argument of a later section,
mediate larger, including, and cognitively more salient actions.   Further, in
line with our definition of molecular behavior, one could refer these "inferior"
molar units to segregated and subordinate systems of the person by way of
some such formulation as that of dissociation theory.

At the other extreme there are inclusive units of molar behavior which
involve the person in relation to major long-range goals.   These also tend to
go unnoticed or to be only vaguely perceived.   Persisting actions which
unfold gradually over long periods of time have often been referred, in fact,
to unconscious processes.

We have already identified the action component of the episode, our basic unit of analysis for the description of individual Midwest children's psychological habitat and behavior, as a unit which occurs within the cognitively clear part of the behavior continuum (see p. 6). The action part of an episode conforms in all other respects as well to the characteristics of molar behavior. For this reason, further development of these minimal statements about behavior qua molar as against molecular behavior are required.

DEPENDENCY BETWEEN BEHAVIOR ORDERS

Molar and molecular behavior units are by no means phenomena of completely foreign orbits. On the contrary, they are inextricably joined by links homologous to those between the whole of a person and the subordinate parts of this whole. While partially independent as events on different levels, they are also partially interdependent as events of a larger system. Goldstein (21) in particular has shown that the interdependence works both ways; that "part responses" of the organism depend upon the processes of the whole individual and vice versa. Our knowledge and best understanding here requires a balanced conception and congruently balanced methods of investigation; descriptive and explanatory research in psychology must take into account both the interdependence between behavior levels and their residual independence.

As for the partial independence of actions, there is ample precedent in science for treating them as processes with some integrity. Precisely as the laws of wheels and levers, of planetary and trade winds, of ocean currents, and such laws for gases as those of Charles and Boyle, have been demonstrated without specific reference to subordinate arrangements and changes on the level of material particles, so uniform relationships and descriptive properties which hold for molar behavior without reference to molecular behavior units may reasonably be expected. The biological version of this position has been expounded by Novikoff, who states that each stratum of biological organization, whether that of the cell, the tissue, the organ, the organ system, or the whole organism, " . . . possesses unique properties of structure and behavior which, though dependent on the properties of the constituent elements, appear only when these elements are combined in the new system" (45, 209). He adds, "The laws describing the unique properties of each level are qualitatively distinct, and their discovery requires methods of research and analysis appropriate to the particular level" (45, 209). The common facts of biological research are in line with such a view. Thus, the biologist who studies the intact multicellular organism uses different techniques and a different set of explanatory concepts than the biologist who studies individual cells. Obviously, for example, the former would reap nothing but confusion if he applied the presently available methods of cytology to the problems of mammalian respiration.

There may be no real need to suppose that in the domain of any science the properties of a superordinate level or order are in some way "emergents" which, in theory, could never be revealed by study of relationships between elements of subordinate orders. The question as to whether or not this is true can be left open. In practice it holds either way that, of the different orders in many event hierarchies, each shows unique properties and raises special questions which, up to the present time in the history of science have required special methods. "Living cells present problems not to be encountered in the test tube or flask" (45, 210). Similarly the actions of persons present unique properties and problems not to be encountered in the behavior, the actones, of their parts.

This outlook, however, does not call for a kind of tubular viewing of molar behavior. Actones could not be ruled out of behavior description even if such were to seem desirable. This follows from the concurrence and interdependence of actones and actions. Not that one necessarily discriminates both molar units, on the one hand, and molecular units, on the other, in observing a behavior sequence. The whole complex is often perceived as a more or less unified pattern, much as one hears a symphonic phrase without discriminating its individual notes and measures. It may be observed only that the person as a unit is engaging in this or that unitary action; that a child is reading a book, or perhaps talking with a playmate. One may even perceive that a child is reading a book *eagerly* or talking *angrily* with a playmate without taking note of particular actones, although, to anticipate a point in our later discussion of behavior recording, actones are often highlighted by an interest in *how* a person does a thing. Since, in any case, actions do not occur apart from actones, molecular units of behavior are implicated at least implicitly in all that an observer can see in molar behavior. We need to ask more, therefore, about the interdependence of the units on these two levels in behavior samples. What is the essential nature of their interconnection?

ACTONES AS MEDIA

One feature of the relationship between molar and molecular behavior has major significance for behavior description. It is that actones and actions are related as mediating to mediated processes. Atmospheric conditions mediate weather phenomena. Processes in conductive substances mediate electrical current. Light and sound waves mediate visual and auditory perception. Comparably, actone manifolds mediate actions of the person. Steps mediate walking to school. Lip and tongue movements mediate reciting a lesson. Arm and finger movements mediate saluting the flag.

General characteristics of the relationship between mediated and mediating events have been treated intensively in a paper by Heider[2] (25). The main idea in the present suggestions relating to actones as media also is stated in

[2] The quotations from Dr. Heider's paper (25) are from an unpublished translation by the author and Grace M. Heider and are quoted with their permission.

this paper. Following Heider's analysis, we will indicate some characteristics of a mediating process and consider wherein they fit molecular behavior
in relation to actions as molar behavior units. Three of the major points
made by Heider and certain key examples will be paraphrased or quoted,
in italics.

*1. A mediating process is "conditioned externally"; its properties do not
arise from within, but depend upon the properties of a mediated process.*

*This holds for a configuration of sound waves that mediates between a
source of sound and the ears. Let the source be a tuning fork. The vibrations
that reach the ears are "forced vibrations." They are forced in the sense
that their form depends upon the form of the vibrations of the fork. The form
of the mediating wave configuration is not conditioned from within itself. It
is determined instead by the form of an internally conditioned process, namely,
the pattern of "free vibrations," which depends in turn upon the properties of
the sounding body.*

A manifold of actones evidently conforms in some degree to this first
characteristic of a mediating process.

Consider the steps of a child when he walks somewhere. Whether his
steps are high or low, slow or fast, constant or variable, to the right or the
left depends in part upon properties of the action in progress. His steps,
more precisely the steps of his locomotor apparatus, are high and fast when
he is going to the circus. They are low and slow when he is going to see the
principal to whose office he has been sent for misconduct. They bear to the
left if his destination is to the left of him; or to the right if his destination is
to his right. The form of the steps is not conditioned essentially from
within, but from without; it depends upon the form of the mediated action.

The same is true for the actones of speech. The words of a vocabulary
get organized into configurations only when they are "used" by an action;
and the form of the word pattern depends upon the properties of the action.
The language of a person may assume a primitive form, as when a scholar
talks to a baby; or it may have a form that is very complex, as when the
scholar talks to a colleague on a difficult subject. But the verbal actones
themselves are not primary determinants. They can be used or not used;
they can be used for any purpose and on any level of complexity up to the
maximum of which the person is capable.

Not all media are perfect. In general, other things being equal, the less
internally conditioned a mediatory process is the better the mediation it
provides. Heider uses as an example of a mediator the pointer of a recording
instrument. Like the column of mercury in a thermometer, it yields flexibly
to external influence. Under ideal conditions, "the successive positions
of the pointer are not connected in a way which is characteristic of the
pointer itself, but they are externally conditioned" (**25**). The conditions
are not always ideal, however, as Heider indicates. They are not ideal, for
example, if the shaft of the pointer is attached to a fulcrum in such a way

that friction is created. The movements of the pointer in this case are in part internally conditioned. They are affected by processes of the lower order context which includes the fulcrum and the shaft.

A manifold of actones is never a perfect mediating process in that it is altogether externally conditioned. The steps of a child may be low and slow partly because his legs are tired. He may talk without communicating what he means partly because his mouth is dry. He may read a story without understanding it well because his vision is impaired. Actones have their own context which can be secondarily coercive. It is nontheless true that changes in an actone medium apparently do not effect certain changes and no others in the mediated process. The child is not made to walk to a particular place, even to a bedroom, by the weariness of his legs. He is not made to say one thing or another by the dryness of his mouth. He is not driven to read a story meeting certain specifications as to content or even size of print by the impairment of his vision. Actions like these depend essentially upon needs, goals, and other conditions of the action context; they are not selected and coerced by the context of the mediating molecular units.

2. A mediating process consists of parts that are in a high degree mutually independent.

A source from which a mediating configuration of light waves issues is a real unit. Yet the configuration itself is only a "composite." It is an atomistic manifold and, as such, a "spurious unit." The same holds for a manifold of sound waves. The individual vibrations of every such complex are "guided by the external cause in each small section." The elements are not themselves internally united.

There is good evidence for high mutual independence of the units in a manifold of actones. First, the same actones can combine readily in many different configurations. The vast numbers of combinations and permutations of the actones of language are instructive here. The formation of a letter is ordinarily an actone when a person writes something. The composition of a sentence is invariably an action. Multitudes of sentence-writing actions are mediated by different combinations and permutations of the 26 letter-forming actones. Heider develops in his own terminology the essentials of this example and points out that the letters can be combined in many different ways only because they are independent of each other.

Also, mediating actones do not of themselves invariably "require" one another. An abundance of evidence has been brought against the reflex chain construction in which each movement of a series unfailingly calls up the next; the tool systems of the person do not in themselves independently bring and keep actones together. Molecular behavior units could not be so readily recombined and they would more characteristically organize themselves independently of actions if they were strongly united internally. It appears, therefore, that the unity of an actone manifold is essentially spurious; it has the spurious unity of a composite.

Heider shows that media are by no means all equally good insofar as their efficiency is determined by mutual independence of parts. Thus, as he mentions, pliable bodies, whose parts are relatively independent of one another, mediate certain processes better than solid bodies, whose parts are less mutually independent. A piece of cloth, for example, will mediate better between the fingers and the contours of an object than a piece of equally thin but less flexible paper.

An actone manifold is never a perfect medium in this respect; its parts are not wholly independent of one another. Links in the chain of a "habit" are sometimes hard to separate, as Guthrie (23) and others have shown. A learned motor configuration, like swimming a certain way, tends to be self-maintaining and may not be easily changed. Semantic studies have shown that this can be equally true of word patterns. Yet all such composites are open enough to change that "relearning," formulated as reorganization of actone manifolds, is never impossible; even the oldest dogs *can* be taught new tricks. This is understandable when the great "adaptability" of molecular behavior mechanisms is considered. The system of the hand, with its separate and independently movable fingers, excels in this respect (25). So does the vocal apparatus. All carriers of molecular behavior lend themselves in varying degrees to the formation of differing actone combinations; and the members of these combinations show commensurate mutual independence.

3. A mediating process is an "offshoot" which generally constitutes a sign of the mediated process.

"The light rays which meet the eyes are messengers from the object and represent it." *These processes, however, like the vibrations from a source of sound, "spend themselves, so to speak, in the process of mediation."* *The same does not hold for all mediators.* *Thus, "The barometer which informs us of the air pressure appears in consciousness as something on its own account."* *So appearing, moreover, it stands for the atmospheric processes which it mediates.*

Similarly, the actones of another person serve as signs of molar behavior. Just as we learn of changes in an electrical system through observation of mediating pointer excursions, so we may see what another person is doing in part through observation of his molecular behavior. It is significant here that many actones, such as gestures and postural adjustments, have often been classified as "expressive movements." We cannot think of any that should not be.

The sign character of actones derives from their partial dependence upon actions. Our recognition of this dependency has been reënforced here by the principle that a molecular behavior manifold as a mediating process is in itself a more or less neutral composite whose form and organization depends in part upon the forces in the context of molar behavior. Again, whether the steps of a child when he walks to a destination or his vocalizations when he says something are thus and so or otherwise depends significantly upon properties of the action in progress. The form of the action affects the form of the actone pattern in such a way that it represents in some degree the properties of the action.

The dimensions of actones per se are limited to such directly observable variables as amplitude and velocity as these are manifested, for example, in variations from large to small and quick to slow of locomotor, manual, laryngeal, and facial adjustments. Changes in these variables, however, are so correlated with changes in molar behavior that they provide essential information about the characteristics of actions. Here, in the sign function of actones as media, lies much of their pertinence to description of molar behavior, as we will try to show more fully when the problem of recording molar behavior and its context is discussed.

ACTIONS AS UNIQUE EVENTS

When all has been said concerning the interdependence of actones and actions, their partial independence of one another remains. They are not interconnected in a one-to-one way. Instead, a kind of transposability holds for the relationship between the units of the two orders.

First, an action is transposable from one to another manifold of actones. There are different ways to skin a cat. A child can memorize the rule for dividing fractions by writing it, reading it, or speaking it. Different letters and words might have been used for this paragraph.

Second, the same actones can be used for different actions. The same molecular manifold in walking or looking or speaking can mediate numberless different molar behavior units. Grasping with the hand can serve a thousand "purposes." So can saying *yes, no, why, I agree with you*, or almost any word or word combination. Different actions can be mediated even at one time by essentially the same actones. Walking, as a manifold of locomotor adjustments, can simultaneously mediate exercising, strolling for fun, and going to a particular place. Talking, as a set of laryngeal adjustments, can simultaneously mediate giving information and earnestly seeking a friend.

These observations are important here by reason of the support they give to earlier indications that the description of molar behavior requires special procedures. They imply that the most thoroughgoing scrutiny and reporting of actones by methods suited to the characteristics of behavior on the molecular level will not yield an adequate description of actions. Insofar as the same action can be mediated by different actones and the same actones can mediate different actions, this must be true.

Reduction statements which designate actone correlates of actions have sometimes been made for the sake of simplicity and objectivity in descriptions of behavior on the molar level. One proponent of this strategy has stated, for example, that the " . . . response which we call 'fear' . . . *is* a catching of the breath, a stiffening of the whole body, a turning away of the body from the source of stimulation, a running or crawling away" (**59**, 8; italics ours). "His body stiffened" is probably more credible as raw fact than "he drew back in fear." "John's fist swung upward through an arc of about 30 degrees and landed on Henry's chin" may be less assailable on the same basis than "John hit Henry hard with apparent intent to hurt him." One way in which description of molar behavior has moved toward objective, or operational, definition is offered here. Yet how far it can or how fast it should be pushed in this direction is an open question. The limiting condition is the absence noted above of a univocal, one-to-one, relationship between molar and molecular units of behavior. There must be many hundreds of ways in which the parts of a 10-year-old boy can behave while *he* is behaving avoidantly or aggressively, and these possible correlations are complicated by the fact that the same parts can behave in many of the same ways while the boy is behaving nurturantly or submissively. Experimental indications (**52**) that one kind of molar behavior cannot be distinguished reliably from another when its context is unknown cannot be surprising for this reason. The truth is that we now have little information as to what actone patterns go with such and such kinds of molar behavior. It is therefore impossible for an observer or analyst to approach action by a person with a comprehensive set of coördinating definitions which give molecular indices of behavior on the molar level. Any reliable criteria of this kind have to be worked out while investigation proceeds.

One way to begin to describe action by a person is to record it as fully as possible in the idiom and by techniques which, in the light of our common social experience, now seem best adapted to the range of its own special characteristics. The idiom of common language and techniques which utilize common observation appear to have the needed breadth and flexibility. One can include in what is recorded as data of interest in their own right and as material with sign significance for molar behavior all that can be observed of correlated molecular details. This wide line of attack, which will be developed in the following chapter, has the advantage of encompassing at least partially and provisionally what there is to be reduced, where eventual reduction statements promise anything in the way of credibility and simplification; and it has the advantage of leaving open the problem of relationships between the two orders of behavior units.

Actions differ greatly in kind and they have a multiplicity of dimensions. Different *modes* of action which correspond to commonly recognized "needs," "desires," "propensities," "urges," and the like occur in differing degrees. These include, as examples, aggression, dominance, submission, nurturance, avoidance. Actions vary in energy level, tempo, efficiency, and persistence. They differ in manifest affectivity, in level of satisfaction or dissatisfaction, and in emotional quality. Actions differ also in outcome. Some, for example, issue in failure, others in success.

Actually, psychology is by no means prepared to name systematically all of the kinds and dimensions of molar behavior. It has had no adequate taxonomy of actions. As for the variables which we can now distinguish, our knowledge of their manifestation under naturally occurring conditions, of the frequency with which they occur, of their relationships with one another, and of their situational correlates, even of the conditions under which particular kinds or characteristics of molar behavior units may be expected to appear, is greatly limited. We do not know enough about the natural history of actions to collect them for study by rigidly systematic techniques. These considerations, also, argue for a method of behavior recording with breadth and flexibility. As for the later stages of the descriptive process, in which the recorded material is subjected to analysis, development of criteria for analytical categories again requires reliance upon everyday knowledge and perception. Fortunately, ordinary social intercourse continually demands skill in identifying and assaying the actions of our associates on the level of everyday behavior episodes. It seems reasonable to expect much from the coupling of this skill with suitable descriptive categories.

Psychological Habitat

HABITAT DESCRIPTION AND WHAT THE PERSON SEES

Psychological habitat can now be defined as the relevant context of naturally occurring molar behavior. A fact requiring attention at the outset in any attempt to describe this complex is that its environmental parts generally are perceived in some way by the person. One must also face the additional fact that the consequences for behavior of these perceived contents of the environment depends crucially upon their properties as objects of perception. Here is a matter of major concern for ecological studies in psychology. We would like to consider it here with a view to the whole task of recording and analyzing conditions in the situation of a person. "Observation" of these conditions as they are seen by another will refer to this total process.

One might propose, against the perils of subjectivity, to describe the surroundings of a person as they are perceived by people in general. This one can do efficiently with the help of a standard dictionary to establish what the surroundings mean. This indeed is essentially what we have done, with special regard for the perceptions of Midwest people in general, in studying Midwest behavior objects. But one cannot describe the psychological habitat of Midwest children by such a procedure. The inescapable reason for this is that these children do not uniformly transact behavior with the parts of Midwest as invariants on a list of behavior objects. They behave in relation to their surroundings, not necessarily as the generality of people in Midwest or elsewhere see them, but always as they themselves see them. A Midwest child could see, and interact with, a motto as only what the dictionary says it is, "an inscribed sentence, phrase, or word." But he might see it and interact with it at a given time as, say, a welcome birthday present or a stern reminder to be good or a familiar patch on a bedroom wall. A Midwest child could see, and interact with, his mother as no more or less than a "female parent," although this seems improbable. It is not improbable that he will see her and interact with her at a given time as a person in a good mood or a bad mood or an in-between mood who is presently helpful or hindering or bossy or demanding or protective or generous.

Margaret Reid's mother urges some noodles upon Margaret in the behavior setting, Home Meal. The mother smiles and is gentle, but very insistent. It seems clear that Mrs. Reid, from her point of view, is behaving nurturantly; and it might be added correctly that she is behaving in a nurturant way from the dictionary's or Midwest's point of view, and from the observer's point of view. But more has to be added if we are to describe adequately Margaret's psychological habitat at the time. We have to tell how Mrs. Reid is behaving from Margaret's point of view. As Margaret sees it, is the behavior of the mother nurturant? *Or*, as the urging and insistence might suggest, is it not nurturant, but dominating? Or both? Or neither? Here, in such alternative characteristics of physical and social facts as they are perceived by the person, are critically important properties of environmental habitat parts. Adequate description of psychological habitat requires, then, an assay of these properties. It requires in practice that data be gathered and processed from the beginning within a frame of reference which includes some form of the question: What does the person see and how does he see it?

One thing to be said for inquiry of this kind is that our social transactions require us to practice it daily. Within limits, too, we learn to have confidence in the information it yields. We identify casually the things others notice or do not notice, and see, within limits, how others look at, feel about, or "take" things, recognizing often that the viewpoint of another differs from our own. Within limits, we see what the actions of Y mean to X. Our confidence in the correctness of such observation is strengthened by our finding that, very much more often than not, X sees our own behavior as we do. We often observe with confidence also the characteristics of "things in general" as they are for another person. Even when it appears to us that the "actual" circumstances of X are favorable, we may see that, "as far as he is concerned," his situation as a whole is confused or unhappy or threatening; and the reverse can occur. In these cases, moreover, we generally act in relation to X as much in terms of his situation as we observe it to be for him as in terms of what we know about the "actual" state of affairs.

The ability to see what another sees in his habitat is a necessity of social intercourse. It alone enables us to deal with our associates on the basis of their goals, obstacles, paths, and values, and thereby, to adapt ourselves appropriately to the actions of others. Errors in observation of circumstances as they are perceived by our associates do, of course, occur. Doubtless they are frequent on the level of conditions which correspond to very long behavior units and deeper motives. But everyday experience suggests that they are rare on the level of the behavior episodes with which we are concerned in the present research. Such misperception can be made the rule by the presence of psychopathology in either or both of the interacting persons or by lasting maladjustment in their relationship. Yet that it is not frequent normally on the episode level is implied by the fact that, in the long run of minute by minute social interplay with others, we *do* generally adapt ourselves appropriately to their actions, which means that we *must* generally deal with them on the basis of their goals, obstacles, paths, and values, which is possible only in the degree that we *do* observe what they see in their situations. Ways of bettering such observation will be considered later. We suggest, meanwhile, that what is required here is only the adaptation to research procedures of sufficiently reliable everyday practice.

How one observes the parts of another's habitat as he sees them is yet another problem for studies of social perception which cannot be met in any detail here. We would like only to add to what has been said about this problem in Chapter I (see pp. 10–14) by noting as cues to such observation the present behavior of the person, the *sequential context* of the behavior, and the characteristics of present behavior objects and settings.

One may observe that a dog is a threatening or fearsome creature in the eyes of Henry Miller, in part because one now sees Henry run from the dog (the present behavior cue), in part because one saw the dog bite Henry an hour earlier (the sequential context cue), and in part because one notes that the dog is big and fierce by common Midwest standards (a behavior object cue). The present-behavior index is probably the most sensitive and decisive. We observe that, as a child sees it, a thing is liked because he approaches it, or disliked because he withdraws from it, or funny because he laughs at it, or sad because it makes him cry. This lead alone obviously lands us in a circle. We get the characteristics of the environmental object from the behavior that we want to understand by relating it to the object. Fortunately, however, the present behavior cue generally does not stand alone; settings or behavior objects and sequence indices provide stimulus information which is in some degree independent. In Midwest, for example, one may be moderately safe in asserting that a swarm of bees nearing a boy on his way to school is perceived by him to be menacing and dangerous even if, at the time, one can observe little or nothing of the boy's behavior. And, going by sequential context, one who momentarily loses sight of the same boy at home with his mother can have some confidence that, to him, her mood is unhappy if one knows that a minute before, he found her weeping over bad news. The behavior cue is needed to check the other cues which, nonetheless, can be independently revealing.

Observation of another's situation in terms of what he perceives in it can be devoid of rational inference where such inference means that one weighs criteria and deduces their consequences. It can be essentially direct. One may observe at once, without deliberation of any kind, that one or another aspect of a situation is now seen to be good, bad, indifferent, threatening, inviting, hot, cold, or whatever. As examples above suggest, however, such observation may always involve inference on some level. However this may be, it seems correct to generalize that the process of observing the facts with which we are now concerned does not differ in principle from observation of other complex phenomena. Further consideration will be given to the role of inference in description of both psychological habitat and behavior in the succeeding chapter.

There is one possible overinterpretation of the emphasis placed here upon the importance of getting at perceptually derived attributes of habitat parts. It is that adequate description of psychological habitat requires a mirroring of "private worlds." We have not meant to imply such an assumption. Whatever the potentialities in some phenomenological procedures, one who uses naturalistic methods of observation and analysis from without cannot hope to break into the consciousness of a person and to come out with a description which duplicates its content through the shortest period of time. Only novelists who are free to improvise and to use deliberately the stratagem of filling in another's experience with their own would seem to be in a good position to do this. The most we have aimed to do in any such direction has been to represent the public side of private experience to the extent of exhibiting some properties which parts of a person's psychological habitat have because they are objects of perception.

The "private world" conception of the end sought in description of psychological habitat is open to another exception. The relevant context of molar behavior includes by definition all of the conditions that make a difference to action by the person. But one cannot assume that these conditions are all represented in conscious experience. It would be superfluous to review here the common reasons for holding that many are not. Proof that an object or condition has entered the psychological habitat of a person is established by effectiveness rather than awareness: whatever has effects upon the molar behavior of the person exists in his psychological habitat. One can even doubt that the person is continually aware of habitat parts which derive from present behavior settings. It seems safe to say that Raymond Birch, whose mother works in the Midwest County Courthouse, can traverse unerringly all of the corridors in this largest building of Midwest with his "thoughts" preëmpted by things that completely exclude the walls to his left and right. Yet the walls must continually make a difference to his behavior at the time. Otherwise, he would not continually avoid them. He must be less continually aware of them. Midwest children at school do not think to themselves all of the time, "I must not talk out loud without permission, I must not talk out loud without permission, I must ... " Yet talking out loud without permission is a relatively rare exception to a rule of the Midwest school setting. The children "conform" to the rule, and thereby demonstrate its effectiveness, most of the time while the teacher who embodies it is present. One can doubt that they are aware of the rule through the whole of this time.

It is common practice in psychology to test the behavioral effectiveness of an observed condition in the situation of a person without any reference to private experience or to perception. One can do this in the case of the rule against talking out loud, for example, by observing the children both with and without the teacher in the room. On the same basis, one can compare the effects upon behavior of different conditions and use the observed differences in behavior to establish by deduction the psychological properties of these conditions. This procedure, too, is common and probably offers the only available means of determining the particular characteristics of some facts in the context of behavior. It is no less true that the primary conditions in relation to which a person behaves at a given time are structured by and get their psychologically relevant properties from the processes of perception. Adequate effort to describe these conditions requires, therefore, a frame of reference and specific methods which enable one to identify these properties with the greatest possible clarity and directness.

The "investigatory set" proposed here is based upon the position that psychological studies demand a choice as to the standpoint from which facts in the surroundings of a person are to be described. One can take the standpoint of the observer, of the culture, or of the person. And there are other possibilities. In some studies, often identified as "behavioristic," and featured always by environmental description in terms of "objective" stimulus conditions, the choice has been the standpoint of physical science. One frame of reference or another has to be chosen, in any case, or the results of inquiry about the psychological environment must be completely ambiguous. Our choice for study of behavior objects has been the standpoint of the culture. Our choice for study of behavior settings has been the standpoint of the observer, a standpoint close to that of Midwest people in general. Our choice in the part of the research under consideration now has been the standpoint of the person. This choice was crucial to our decision to undertake description of psychological habitat. The standpoint of the person can be defined in differing ways. We have meant to define it broadly in conceiving psychological habitat to be the total relevant context of behavior by the person at a given time. This leaves as the crux of the present requirement, however, the fact that the conditions of this context include the properties of habitat parts which have to be identified in terms of what the person perceives at that time.

There can be no getting around the fact that some "screening" and bias stemming from one of the standpoints mentioned here, namely, that of the observer, can never be entirely escapable.   All that we have to report on the parts of Midwest as they are seen by its children obviously will have to be accepted or rejected as *our* perceptions of what the children see.   Psychology, where it undertakes representation of this kind, is in practice, very much worse off as a descriptive discipline than many other sciences; but its position outside the facts is not unique in principle.   An ideal view of a plant or a rock is biased and imperfect.   This is true even of the view which reduces either to proton-electron aggregates as nearly ultimate realities, for these, to face the paradox of all searching investigation, are in fact only inventions by the observer.   Ultimately, the only advantage on the side of being "scientific" which one investigation can have over another lies, not in any corner it has on reality, but in its better intersubjective tests.   It follows that, our descriptions of psychological habitat and of behavior, however they stack up against the "true facts," should at least be as objective as reporting in this area will allow.   This is to raise again the problem of reliability which will recur at several points later.   No special measures to solve the greater validity problem will be offered.   Our case here will have to rest upon the degree in which the descriptive findings on both habitat and behavior show internal consistency and otherwise make sense.

THE TASK OF CONCEPTUALIZING HABITAT CONDITIONS

We have suggested in first referring to psychological habitat as a target of description that the greatest present need here is for adequate concepts by means of which to identify and to relate different habitat conditions.   In the absence of such concepts, one of two unsatisfactory alternatives must be chosen.   The first is to link behavior directly with nonpsychological facts, i.e., with the physical and social conditions which only supply raw materials for the psychological habitats of individual persons.   Precisely this has been attempted in correlational studies of behavior and age or sex; behavior and climate; behavior and social class or caste; behavior and urban, as against rural, life.   It should not be surprising that the correlations obtained in these studies are generally low and often contradictory; for it is known that lawfulness and stability are to be found only in relationships between events and facts of the same order.   Modern physics, for example, does not use in its derivations biological, economic, or psychological quantities.   The best one can expect from linking behavior directly with nonpsychological conditions is an indication as to where some psychological truth may lie.

There remains the alternative of bridging the gap between behavior and nonpsychological habitat with the wisdom of common sense and art in the manner of the novelist or the biographer.   One can go beyond a statistical correlation of behavior with birth order, for example, and describe the psychological habitat of, say, *the only child* in terms of his loneliness, the overindulgence of his parents, and the oppressiveness of an atmosphere that is overcharged with adult interests and standards.   Representation of this kind has been condemned as subjective. The way out, the way to secure objectivity, has often been seen as just that of relating behavior to non-psychological facts. But it may be asked whether, for the purposes of understanding molar behavior, the facts of this order are rightly to be accepted as objective. Objective conditions are generally held to be those which actually exist, unviolated by the biases or special viewpoint of the observer, in the context of the phenomena under investigation. It is by no means clear that, for example, social class or race or climate, as these are defined and measured by the sociologist, the anthropologist, and the meteorologist, do actually exist for a child in the relevant determining context of his behavior. On the other hand, it is clear that conditions vaguely identified by words like "loneliness" and "parental overindulgence" and the "oppressiveness of adult standards" do exist in the contexts of children's behavior as coercive facts. A primary task of psychological ecology where it is concerned with psychological habitat is the one of conceptualizing such facts with enough precision that they can be related to behavior in an orderly way. We have aimed to do this in applying the schemata and descriptive categories which are later to be presented. First, however, material for analysis must be gathered. This is the problem of recording habitat and behavior, to which we now turn.

Chapter VI

Recording Behavior and Psychological Habitat

Naturalistic Recording in Psychology

NARRATIVE BEHAVIOR RECORDS

On June 2, 1949, four-year-old Margaret Reid spent 28 minutes in the Midwest behavior setting, Home Meal (Lunchtime). The physical and social raw materials of Lunchtime are quite highly standardized in Midwest. In homes like Margaret's they invariably include a room of moderate size (sometimes a part of the kitchen), a table with a cloth or mats on it, chairs with hard bottoms and straight backs, durable tableware, food in dishes to be passed, and parents. These physical and social behavior objects are generally so deployed in relation to children, with their hungriness and other needs, as to require of them the actions of sitting down at the table, eating some of the food, and engaging in preponderantly amiable conversation with tablemates. As Midwest behavior settings go, this one is rather strongly coercive; much more so, for example, than the settings Vacant Lot or Presbyterian Church Picnic. Yet a very great many enormously differing circumstances and actions of children can occur in it; like even the most demanding and limiting of Midwest behavior settings, it has an immense tolerance for variability in psychological habitat and behavior.

On the date mentioned, Margaret "ate very well," and her behavior was otherwise consistent with the standing behavior pattern of the lunchtime setting. But this is by no means all. Margaret did 42 clearly discriminable and different things on the level of behavior episodes during the 28 minutes. Here, identified by a participial phrase that alludes to the situation in which each action occurred, are 21 of the 42 actions, just half of the total:

> Rejecting Lemonade
> Recollecting Pancakes Eaten for Breakfast
> Cutting Tomato
> Helping Self to Noodles
> Forecasting Bible-School Picnic
> Challenging Little Brother to Lunch Eating Race
> Appraising Combination of Lemon Juice and Milk
> Inquiring About Valentine's Day
> Coping with Dropped Napkin
> Commenting on Play of Neighbor Friend
> Playing on Words About Bible-School Picnic

195

Wiping Something Out of Eye
Reporting Little Brother's Capers
Dunking Cookies in Cocktail Sauce
Telling About Imaginary Friends
Putting Box of Kleenex on Bench
Inviting Parents to Look Into Stomach
Soliciting Mother's Opinion on Brother's Eating
Using Spoon as Airplane: With Sound Effects
Chanting "Bones to Be, Bones to Be"
Reporting on Birthday Greetings at Bible School

This breakdown demonstrates the great dispersion to be found in actions of individual Midwest children from the modal behavior which defines a Midwest behavior setting. It indicates the richness and variety in what we have wanted to record.

Such a listing of things done by the children of Midwest in all of the town's behavior settings would be useful without elaboration, especially if one were to line up beside it similar inventories from other communities in other cultures. Yet any itemization of this kind would leave untold vastly more of psychological interest than it would tell. We know from carefully recorded observation that this is true of the present sample. It represents only the content of Margaret's behavior and psychological situation. It tells nothing of how Margaret did what she did. One can score it on scarcely any of the variables—intensity, efficiency, creativity; aggression, submission, dominance; failure, success; or whatever—that figure significantly in current psychological theory and research. It leaves out all of the emotional overtones and motivational undertones. It exhibits none of the continuity that we commonly ascribe to behavior. And it tells very little about the conditions under which Margaret behaved. These behavior items only point in the direction that psychology has to go for its vital statistics in ecological studies.

How can one record molar behavior and its context in such a way as to preserve for study the continuity, the qualitative refinements, and the observable conditions of everyday human action? We have concluded that there is now open only one practicable way to do this; and that is to observe what a person does together with the situation of the person and then to narrate and set down what has been observed in common language. Common language has much to recommend it for the purpose. It has been adapted by centuries of daily practice to the variability, the complexity, and the richness of human conduct. It should not surprise us therefore that, in the judgment of Lewin: "The most complete and concrete descriptions of [behavior and] situations are those which writers such as Dostoevski have given us. These descriptions have attained . . . a picture that shows in a definite way how the different facts in an individual's environment are related to one another and to the individual himself." (**33**, 13). In the hands of a Dostoevski, conventional speech can make us see subleties in behavior beyond the range of our ordinary daily perceptions and far above the level of our best statistics and experiments.   We have collected narrative records in the belief that, in the hands of trained observers, the same medium can preserve some of the essential facts of children's naturally occurring behavior and psychological living conditions.

Take *Cutting Tomato* from the list, above.   Margaret has a glass of milk and a glass of lemonade before her, and she has on her plate some noodles with beef, some peas, some applesauce, some buttered bread, and a slice of tomato, which her mother has just acknowledged to be "stringy."   Here is what we have recorded.

Margaret began cutting her tomato with difficulty because she had the knife upside down.

Her mother said, critically to direct, "Now, you're doing that all wrong."

Margaret looked up at her mother curiously, apparently not realizing that she was cutting with the blunt side.

She immediately admitted softly, "Oh, yes," and turned the knife over.

Then she changed the knife from her right hand to her left, and the fork from her left hand to her right.

She continued cutting rather awkwardly, holding the tomato steady with the knife and cutting with the fork, which was quite blunt.

The mother said, "Now, you should be cutting with the knife, not the fork."

Margaret giggled as if suddenly accepting this as a joke.

She changed back to cutting with the knife quite matter-of-factly.

The mother suggested to the father, "You help her."

Margaret continued trying busily to get the tomato cut, her industry suggesting that she meant to resist any help.

The father was occupied with something just then and made no comment or move to help.

Margaret turned briefly and looked at me, not self-consciously.

She turned back around and again cut industriously on the tomato.

Then Mr. Reid took the knife and fork and cut the tomato, while Margaret sat passively waiting.

Below, to expand one more of the listed behavior units, is what we saw in *Telling About Imaginary Friends*.

Margaret started to talk with food in her mouth.

Her mother shushed her by firmly stating, "Now don't talk when your mouth's full.   Wait until your mouth isn't full."

Margaret impassively finished chewing and swallowing.

Then she announced as if presenting an excellent plan, "Jimmy said to come to his house."

The mother asked curiously, "Jimmy who?"

Margaret hesitated a moment to consider.

She replied, "Jimmy," simply.

The mother said, with fairly good-natured persistence, "Jimmy who? I don't know what Jimmy you're talking about."

Margaret again hesitated while considering the answer.

Then a little grin came across her face, and she stage whispered, "Jimmy Roy."

The name evidently was fictitious and probably two first names thrown together.

The mother laughed appreciatively.

The father forced a laugh, and asked, "Now what's all the big secret about?"

12:23   Margaret took a bite of fruit.

She giggled about the funny thing she had said.

Then she whispered across the table to her mother, "Jimmy Sarah," and seemed to expect laughter.

Getting no response, she whispered again, "Billy Sarah."

The mother looked at her in annoyance and commanded, "Well, quit whispering."

Although she had been cut off quite shortly, Margaret, apparently not minding or noticing the reproval, asked eagerly, "Did you hear me, mother?"

The mother, trying to be patient with her, said, smiling wearily, "Well, not hardly."

Margaret happily said, "Jimmy," then whispered, "Sarah."

Immediately she repeated, saying, "Jimmy," and whispering, "Sarah."

> She seemed in general to be trying to tantalize her parents, I thought.
> She seemed more to be impish than to be merely amusing herself.

Our record of Margaret's behavior and situation during the 28 minutes of the lunchtime setting extends through 16 pages. It provides a continuous, running account of what Margaret did in relation to the parts of her situation at the time. It is one part of an unbroken narration, 379 pages long, which begins at 8:04 a.m., when this child woke up, and ends at 10:16 p.m., when she went to bed, on June 2, 1949. This is the *specimen record*, introduced in Chapter I. The one on Margaret is a *day record*. Using the narrative method which it employs, we have made also a shorter *settings record*, which describes the behavior of a child in a particular Midwest behavior setting. The present chapter deals with the rationale and the preparation of these word specimens of naturally occurring behavior and psychological life situation.

SPECIMEN AND OTHER RECORDS

Other methods of recording behavior directly, i.e., of describing the naturally occurring behavior of persons without interviewing them or testing

them, have been used in psychology.   These include (*a*) time-sample procedures, (*b*) behavior surveys and tabulations, and (*c*) case studies and biographies.   We cannot review these methods in any detail here; but comment
upon each of them with some regard for their advantages and limitations may
help to differentiate the method of the specimen record.

Time-sample techniques generally use rating scales or check lists which
require on-the-spot judgments along prescribed dimensions of habitat or behavior.
These devices were developed originally to meet the commonly attributed shortcomings of anecdotal descriptions of behavior.   They allow behavior and situations to vary in their full complexity and try to achieve objectivity and efficiency
in recording and analysis by limiting with precision the aspects and the temporal
lengths of the behavior continuum which are to be observed and studied.   They
also try to secure representativeness and reliability by recording large numbers
of observations.   These procedures are efficient.   They incur a minimum of
interference with the subject.   They regulate systematically the aspects of
behavior and situation to be recorded.   They are left, however, with the one
great deficiency that such procedures do not preserve the complexities, the
interdependencies, and the continuity of behavior and situation.   The patterns
of simultaneous and sequential variation are not recorded.   Instead, as indicated,
single variables are selected and defined in advance; then, aspects of the behavior
or the situation which fit the definitions of these variables are abstracted from
the observed constellation; the actual events and their context are not saved
for study.   It appears to us that this weakness is serious for many problems.
Adequate conceptualization of a particular person's behavior and its conditions
is possible only if one has both before him for deliberate examination.   A geologist cannot determine the full significance of a particular rock formation until
he has placed it in relation to the geological structure of the surrounding region.
Neither can a psychologist be expected to get the full meaning of a behavior
unit until he has placed and studied it in the sequence and context to which it
belongs.

Another shortcoming of the time-sample method is that usually it segregates
arbitrary sections of the behavior continuum.   Meaningful units of behavior
joined with habitat are of all lengths; they do not come in predictable sizes.
The result is that arbitrarily limited samples of behavior are often like a part of
a page torn from a book.   Again, extended sequences of behavior in context are
required for correct determinations.   The advantages of time-sample records
should not be minimized.   Whether these can be combined with adequate
breadth, richness, and adherence to the actual structure and context of behavior
is a matter for study.

Surveys and tabulations are similar in principle to time-sample procedures
and have most of the advantages and disadvantages of the latter.   They give
records of the frequency of occurrence of various behavioral and situational
factors in convenient form upon many subjects.   Here, for example, one finds
tabulations of books read, language used, jobs liked, games played, and opinions
held for differing populations of children.   Such investigations have omitted
almost entirely, concrete description of the contexts in which the reported items

of behavior or situation have occurred. For this reason, they give only a very rough and partial base for the reconstruction of actions and conditions of life.

Many case studies and biographies are essentially descriptions of psychological habitat and behavior. As such, they are of great potential value for ecological purposes. Practically, however, they have serious limitations. As a rule, the data for these records are gathered long after the events to which they refer have occurred, with the result that they are subject to the omissions and distortions of memory. Also, many of the facts in case studies are based upon reports of emotionally involved informants, which include usually the subject or patient and such other persons as parents, teachers, friends, and enemies. Another limitation is that records of this kind can give little indication as to the commonness of the reported conditions and events. They provide an inadequate basis for normative generalizations because they report mainly the behavior and situations of highly selected (deficient, maladjusted, gifted, famous) individuals. Finally, case studies and biographies describe segments of the life span which are so long-extended as to present very difficult problems of description and conceptualization. Such documents are useful to ecological studies chiefly as sources of supplementary, background data.

Specimen records also have advantages and disadvantages. Their advantages can now be quickly summarized. They give a multivariable picture of the molar and molecular aspects of behavior and situation. They save for study interrelations between simultaneous and successive conditions. They preserve the continuity of behavior. They do not violate natural boundary lines between different actions. They gather and report behavior phenomena at the time of their occurrence. They present undissected specimens of behavior and psychological situation.

Permanency and stability can be added to the advantageous features of specimen behavior records. Barring a revolution in written English and in the social conventions of western mankind, our recorded day in the life of Margaret Reid will have the same meaning in 2055 that it has now in 1955. No one could be confident that a time-sample or survey report based on scale judgments geared to current psychological jargon, such as we will use later in the analysis of specimen records, would retain its original meaning for so long a time. This seems to us a matter of no small importance. One cannot investigate adequately the changes which have occurred during the last century in the rearing and behavior of children. No scientific records of children's life situations and behavior have been kept. Meanwhile, technological, economic, and political changes have been quite thoroughly recorded in a way consistent with scientific standards. It seems safe to assume that valuable psychological findings would be forthcoming from a comparison of change in these milieu phenomena with change in children's habitat and behavior. The best psychology can do in providing data for such studies is to call upon lay writings and reconstruct from them in some degree the behavior and psychological situations of the past. If records like the one on Margaret Reid had been made in 1855 we would be in a much better informed position; and those available now should be of like value in the equally distant future.

There remains as the central, distinctive asset of specimen records their theoretically neutral character. They are biased only by the predilections of common sense which is here taken to be the sense most of us have in common. They are not ruled by any special set of notions held in advance as to the characteristics or conditions of behavior. They are open to study in behalf of greatly differing interests, to placement in widely divergent theoretical frames of reference, and to analysis by means of a great variety of qualitative and quantitative techniques. They can be divided as one pleases, and scrutinized part by part; or they can be reviewed and interpreted intact. Their word by word content demands no particular conceptual reformulation. Anyone can make what he likes, for example, of the ordinary facts that Margaret had trouble cutting her tomato, that her mother said, "Now, you're doing that all wrong," that Margaret promptly replied to this, "Oh, yes," that her father finally cut the tomato for her, and that at another time Margaret reeled off to her parents a number of fictitious names. Material in these records is often like behavior observed first-hand in the number and variety of both the questions it raises and the answers it suggests.

Specimen records have many limitations. These include, to mention now only their most evident shortcomings, a lack of built-in provisions for quantification, dependence upon observations without instrumental aids, and sheer bulk. In making these records, moreover, we have come up against a number of difficult problems. Our experience indicates that these problems can be met and that the recording process can be made equal to its major purposes by certain techniques. These problems and techniques will now be discussed in terms of practicalities and some theoretical questions that we have had to face and that others who make similar records seem likely to encounter. This will require at some points, review in a more concrete context of problems touched in the preceding chapter.

Making Specimen Records

MOLAR AND MOLECULAR DESCRIPTION

It is possible to make a record which describes only molar behavior units like the one that follows:

George went berry picking for his mother.

Or one can make a record which includes subordinate molar units like those in italics below:

George *took a basket from the kitchen table* and *walked outdoors* where he *mounted his bicycle* and went to pick berries for his mother.

Finally, one can bring into a record molecular details like the actones italicized in the following description:

> George, with his *lips quivering,* his *brows knit,* and the *corners of his mouth turned down,* took a basket from the kitchen table, and, with the *fingers of his left hand wound limply around the handle of the basket,* his *shoulders hunched,* his *chin sagging against his chest,* and his *feet dragging,* walked outdoors, where he mounted his bicycle and, with his *head still bent,* went to pick berries for his mother.

Note that molar and submolar details of the *situation*—the mother and the berries, the basket, the bicycle, and the kitchen table—are included in these descriptions. One could add molecular detail to the situation by mentioning, for example, that according to a thermometer on the front porch of the house, the temperature stood at 81.5 degrees.

Consider the first description. It identifies a complete episode. In this respect, it is like our listed behavior items from the lunchtime behavior of Margaret Reid. We have suggested that an adequate sample of episodes, so identified, would be useful. It would indeed tell us quite essentially *what* the individuals concerned had been observed to do. We have seen also, however, that a specimen record which did no more than this would be deficient in that it could tell us relatively little about *how* the individuals concerned did what. But the critical point here is that, as anticipated in the preceding chapter, the *hows* of actions are signified by actones. This is demonstrated by the third example. Thus, we know with some confidence from the quivering lips, the knit brows, and the dragging feet, that George went to pick the berries *unwillingly* and *unhappily.* This is one kind of information that we want to put in a specimen record if only because the *hows* of what persons do hold important clues to the meaning for them of their actions and the conditions of their lives.

Even the correct identification of an action, let alone a "reading" of its qualitative characteristics, often is facilitated by the recording of molecular detail. Here is another episode:

> Henry, while sitting behind Susan in school, pulled Susan's pigtail.

Nothing is said in this description about the how of the action. But that is not all; questions may be raised as to what Henry was really doing. Was he hurting Susan? Was he only signalling her? Or was he teasing her? Information about the implementing actones would be pertinent. To consider only one possibility, the observation that, at the time, Henry's jaws were firmly clenched while also his lips were drawn in a sharp line, would support the first judgment. Remaining alternative identifications of the action are reserved for later mention.

Information about actones and molecular components of situations is useful then as a basis for diagnosing actions. Yet the necessity for the further step of including this information in specimen records might still be questioned, as it has been from time to time by some of our beginning observers. We gathered from the several recorded molecular details that George undertook the chore for his mother unwillingly and unhappily. But the observer could have inferred the unwillingness and the unhappiness from these same data on the spot, in which case he might then have saved for recording only the generalization that George was unwilling and unhappy in facing the task. Similarly, an observer of the pigtail incident could report only that Henry intentionally hurt Susan by pulling her pigtail, and not report that Henry's jaws were clenched or that his lips were drawn tight. It might be proposed, in short, that only generalizations about actions from molecular details, but not the details themselves, need to be recorded. Freedom on the part of the observer to make and to record such synoptic judgments seems desirable. Often, there is accessible on the scene of an action more or better data on which to base valid statements about events of any sort than can later be reproduced. It is urged, however, that a record which includes the molecular details by which characteristics of molar units are inferred will be a better record than one containing only the inferences.

For one thing, generalizations by the observer from molecular to molar particulars of behavior can be in error. Only a record with adequate information about actones will make it possible for one to check upon the observer's generalizations from them to action characteristics. Further, such a record allows for conceptualization which is impossible for the observer. In order to describe behavior in adequate conceptual terms, one must have available for study more than an observer can integrate while events are unfolding before his eyes.

Language limitations also are important here. Often it is impossible to hit upon words that adequately sum up inferences about actions from actones. To do this one must ordinarily use adverbial expressions as direct qualifiers of verbs denoting molar units: George went *unhappily*; David ate his cake *with obvious relish*; Martha answered the question *as if she were afraid of the teacher*. But these direct qualifiers of actions often are unequal to subtleties which, nonetheless, may be expressed by mention of mediating actones. It is hazardous for a nonliterary person to stake much here on examples; but probably, "William looked *with great wonder* at the gibbon" conveys less of consequence about molar behavior than, "William looked wonderingly at the gibbon with his neck thrust out, his body rigid, his mouth wide open, and his eyes bulging." Short of bringing in these actones, a gifted reporter might be able to improve upon our "with great wonder"; it is doubtful, though, that any one could do much better without referring to molecular behavior units.

Novelists and poets have turned the present point to good advantage. Typically Victorian novels often represent actions in somewhat abstract terms. They lay molar units of behavior end to end and describe them frontally by means of generalizing qualifiers which strain with only moderate success to show what the characters are doing. Richer novels, while they are no less essentially concerned with molar behavior, do not try to make actions stand without support from actones. They weave in molecular details of behavior and situation and in this way achieve the end of describing actions concretely. The reader is given at least a fair chance to infer from actones qualitative aspects of molar behavior that cannot easily be generalized in words.

In the face of these arguments on behalf of the significance of molecular behavior units for description of molar behavior, we have found it important to emphasize that the sharpest observer may not always perceive and be able to report actones upon which judgments as to the what or the how of an action are based. The judgments may stem, not from "rational inference," for which the actone criteria are known, but from "perceptual inference," for which all such criteria are wholly implicit (cf. **26**). An observer may see only that John did thus and so wistfully or sheepishly or in a kind way or thoughtfully; and he may be unable to specify any of the molecular details behind the observation. The best observer cannot state all of the criteria by which he sees a stick; and an observer may not be able to state any of the criteria by which he sees the wistfulness of an action. Yet in either case, the observer's perception may be entirely right. Consider, again, the pulling of the pigtail. In this instance, it was easy to muster actone criteria for the judgment that Henry meant to hurt Susan. But it is harder to think of such criteria for the judgment that he was teasing her or signalling her. One might nonetheless have observed with confidence and correctly that Henry was in fact teasing or signalling.

Molecular behavior and the molecular aspects of situations, whatever their significance for the correct identification and description of actions, certainly do not outweigh the leads to the same end within the molar order itself. Here, critically important clues to what a person is doing and how he is behaving and what the parts of a situation mean to him are given by the sequential context of an action, as mentioned in Chapter V. One cannot generally bring into a narrow focus the person and only the most immediate parts of his situation and either infer from perceived actones, or observe directly, the meaning of his behavior in progress. Take the following item of a field report: "John ate all of the spinach on his plate with a fork in his right hand going up and down between plate and mouth at top speed." Question: Did he enjoy it? From this description alone one could not say. Knowledge of the larger situation, however, might enable one to decide. Let the situation be one in which John was completely free to do as he chose. We would report confidently in this case that he saw the spinach as good. But let the situation be one in which he was under strong pressure from a mother who had made him promise to clean his plate. Applying universal, implicit molar behavior theory, we would weigh the possibility that, in the pressure situation, John saw the spinach as bad and, therefore, to be gotten out of the way as quickly as possible.   Probably, additional molecular clues would help one to perceive the behavior correctly; but, alone, they might not be sufficient.

Perhaps the most reliable and valid observations of molar behavior are those made upon the basis of facts gleaned from an inferential shuttling back and forth between molecular details and the larger contexts of actions.   Our observers at any rate have made their observations and reports under the assumption that a good behavior record is one which reflects and facilitates such a process.

THE PROBLEM OF OBJECTIVITY

The question of objectivity is raised by the aim of specimen records to describe *molar* behavior and *psychological* habitat.

Phenomena of the molar order do indeed call for observation which is in some degree inferential.   It is true also that they rarely yield to the instrumental recording which is common in the physical sciences.   The result is that, if objectivity means a simon-pure empiricism which brooks no venturing beyond directly observed facts, molar behavior and its context cannot generally be studied objectively either in the laboratory or in field research. But the same criteria obviously would hold, then, for many phenomena of nature which have in fact been investigated by putatively objective methods. It is well known, actually, that objectivity means something more and other than sticking in a Baconian way to directly observed facts.

On the negative side, objective inquiry means correcting against biases and special viewpoints which limit and misrepresent reality.   On the positive side, it means describing conditions in the context of whatever one is trying to be objective about as they really are in that context.   It follows that, if one is to be objective in describing actions and psychological situations, one must often break through a wall of directly observed conditions and events by means of inference, and must see things as the other person sees them from his viewpoint, and as they really are for that person.   If, instead, the student of molar behavior sticks to the facts as he sees them from his own viewpoint, and as they are for him, he will not be objective, but subjective in a bad sense, biased—and wrong.   This is to reapply earlier argument for diagnosing the parts of psychological habitat as objects of perception by the person under study.

What the student of molar behavior has to do, whether his methods are ecological or experimental, is to reconstruct the psychological world of the person.   Anyone who is concerned about the objectivity of specimen records must face this fact.   He must recognize that in studying behavior on the molar level it is necessary to deal with the goals and intentions of the person and the meaning to the person of his behavior and situation; and it has to be acknowledged that these cannot always be directly perceived.   By recording sequences of both perceived and inferred events and conditions, the best basis for a final "true" record is laid.

The reconstruction of habitat and the description of behavior by means of specimen records is based upon a wide collection of data. The process only begins when the immediate perceptions and impressions of the observers are reported. Single observations are always fallible and, for this reason, once a record has been drawn up, its parts have to be corrected in the light of evidence as to their internal consistency. All of the data may then be interpreted with the help of coördinating definitions that relate behavior and habitat with constructs and theories. In general, the problem of objectivity reduces to one of intersubjective testability, which appears to be no different in principle for the phenomena of molar behavior than for physical phenomena not open to direct observation. Coördination between what is observed and theoretical constructions must at last be made in both cases.

THE TASK OF THE OBSERVER

Because specimen records are made by watching and describing in words the behavior and situation of a subject, the observer has to function as a recording instrument. Careful consideration must be given, therefore, to the requirements of good observation for specimen records. We have boiled these requirements down to one of developing the sort of observation that adult persons must do well if they are to interact effectively with others. The task of the observer calls for no tricks, formulas, rules of thumb, or any special devices. If only for the sake of consistency, our observers have been called upon to side with the main intentions of this chapter. But these main intentions demand no more of them than that they go on doing, with more vigilance and thoroughness than are common and with rare self-effacement, what they have long been doing as a matter of course in their everyday lives. Beginning instructions, passed from old to new observers run something like this:

> You have watched many children with an interest in what children do, and you have formed judgments at the time about what they were doing and about the things of consequence to them in their situations. This is all you have to do now. Go to it.

Inferences differing in kind or level from those of ordinary social intercourse are not required here. Technical interpretations, moreover, like those in the reports of the clinican and the social psychologist have no place in specimen records. The observer is not asked to theorize; he is asked not to theorize. He is asked to suspend biases from formal psychological training, and to fall back upon the elementary, garden variety, spur-of-the-moment notions and hunches about behavior which are common to man as a socialized being, which rule most of the interpersonal observations of the most sophisticated psychologists, which could never be abolished or appreciably suppressed if this should seem desirable, and which, while they are not without error, cannot help but astonish anyone who stops to reflect upon them with their accuracy.

At this point, a rough three-level classification of psychological descriptions may be useful.

There are, first, running accounts of what a person is doing and of his situation on the level of direct perception or immediate inference. Here are some samples from one of our records. What we take to be immediate, not studied or methodically rational, inferences are italicized here.

Suddenly Raymond ran *eagerly* to another tree.

He started climbing the tree with great energy.

He remarked *in an offhand way*, but with slight emphasis on the second word, "I hope I can climb this tree." *He seemed to say this to himself as a form of encouragement.*

In a high pitched, soft sing-song he said, "I hope, I hope, I hope."

Raymond continued climbing the tree, *cautiously* grasping one branch and then another, and fixing his feet firmly.

He called out to Stewart in a *playfully boastful manner*, "Stewart, this tree is harder to climb than the other one."

Stewart called back *very firmly and definitely*, "No, it isn't."

When Raymond was as high as it seemed safe to climb, he settled in a crotch of the tree with his hands gripped tightly around the branches.

Exuberantly he sang out, "Owww, owww, wheee. Do you see me?" (**8**, 392–93).

Statements like these make up the great bulk of our specimen records.

Second, there are minor interpretations, made "off the cuff," which occur in the form of statements *about* rather than descriptions *of* the behavior or situation of the person. Usually these are based upon observations covering a more or less extended sequence of behavior. Always they are couched in the idiom of everyday social experience. The following are examples:

I had the feeling that although the story wasn't especially interesting, he liked this restful part of the day when he could just sit (**8**, 220).

In handing his father the sugar bowl and salt shaker, Raymond was helping. Of course, he would have helped more if he had gotten up and put them in [the cupboard] himself. . . . I think Raymond wanted to be in on what was going on, that he wanted his father's continued attention more than to help. But the efforts were accepted as help (**8**, 27).

[In crossing the street] . . . He didn't seem to be worried or frightened but, rather, very cautious. It might be pertinent to mention that one of Raymond's closest playmates, Fred Wecker, had recently been in an accident on the square. Fred's bicycle had crashed with a truck (**8**, 52).

Minor interpretations like these often may be included advantageously in a specimen record when the behavior and situation of the subject would otherwise remain obscure. Actually, they appear rather infrequently in our reports, and the observers are not pressed to offer them. When any such interpretation does occur in a record, it is set apart by indentation from the rest of the account where it can be considered for what it may be worth.

Finally, there are the technical or professional interpretations. We mean here generalizations based upon quite explicit theories about behavior. Possible examples follow:

The evidence suggests that in "accidentally" breaking the new briar pipe, after listening in on the argument between his parents, Tom was manifesting repressed aggression against his father.

The fact that Jim stopped working on his May basket as soon as the teacher left the room suggests that his earlier enthusiastic work upon this task was largely a product of induced forces stemming from the social power field of the teacher.

These statements exemplify the theorizing that our observers are asked not to do. Although, again, he may occasionally offer minor interpretations, chiefly with the aim of clarifying the observed behavior and situation, the observer is never expected to take time out to propose answers to these questions: What kind of a person is this? What are the underlying dynamics of that behavior? The psychology of the observer in making a specimen record is not a depth psychology, or a textbook psychology, but whatever psychology there is in common understanding of behavior.

Technical interpretation is required by the larger task of psychological ecology. We have considered, however, that its time comes after a record has been made. It is then possible to study the recorded behavior and situations in context and, by applying appropriate concepts, to get some quantified and conceptual understanding of what the reported facts mean. To theorize in making the record would be like theorizing about the movements of the stars without at some time independently photographing their actual positions. The main difference here is that in psychological field studies the observer has to be the camera. We are not indifferent to the significant role which hypotheses and theories have often played in guiding scientific observation. But the fact remains that at some stage in all empirical research unbiased description of phenomena must occur. Studies of naturally occurring behavior would seem to demand such description in the beginning stage of data collection.

Raising again the question of objectivity, one might ask if all inferential description should not be left out of a specimen record, as it certainly would be if the observer were the astronomer's kind of a camera. All we can say is that in this case the record could never make available for study what it aims to record. Even if sound motion pictures were to be taken of the subject's activities, any attempt to theorize about the recorded actions and their context still would have to be preceded by inferential description. John throws a ball toward Jim. A motion picture would show this plainly. But it would not show whether John was trying to hurt Jim or to engage him in a game of catch in the same positivistic sense that a photograph can show the position of a star. Only observation involving explicit or implicit inference would enable one to say what John was really doing. Trying to hurt Jim or to play catch with him and, to lift other examples from our records, saying things "proudly and with definiteness," showing "evident surprise," being "motherly," speaking in an "authoritative tone," talking "firmly and with agitation," acting as if one had a "bright idea," and "ominous quiet" go to make up the minimal phenomena of molar behavior; and any recording instrument which will not register them is no good for the purposes of ecological studies of molar behavior. We see no cause for discouragement on this score, for every normal adult has the needed instrument built into him.

The observer of the actions of persons cannot be as precise as the observer of the movements of physical bodies. It is doubtful, though, that he needs to be or that precision has the same meaning for both observers. On the descriptive level, in any case, neither has to run the risks of speculation or theory. Essentially unbiased description of phenomena is possible here as it is in other scientific discipline because the raw facts of molar behavior, rather than being accessible only through speculation or theory, are open to common and straightforward, even though partly inferential, observation. If anyone still wants to challenge the objectivity of such description he must give up all hope that psychologists in their research or laymen in their daily affairs can ever be objective in considering what other persons do, for the objectivity of the naked eye, while it is suited to the facts of actones and their contexts, is not equal in or out of science to the data of behavior on the molar level.

The line between partly inferential description of molar behavior and interpretation or theorizing about it probably can never be as sharp as the line between the former and the description of behavior in terms of direct perception. Where does the partly inferential description leave off and the outright interpretation or theorizing begin? There is hardly a dichotomy here, although we have not found this distinction difficult in practice. One working rule which has proved to be helpful follows. In observing and reporting, the observer should think in terms of the *intentions* of the subject and the things tied in with each intention, leaving the *dynamics* of his situation for later study. A record which does not permit eventual description in terms that refer to the causal texture of psychological habitat must be of relatively limited value; but we have hoped to get this from the completed record by systematic analysis of the simultaneous and sequential facts of behavior and situation, though never with any purpose to get down to the deeper levels which "dynamics" is sometimes understood to imply, especially in personality theory.

One cannot consider the task of the observer whose reports are recorded in specimen records without giving some thought to the qualifications which he should possess as a field worker.

We would like to emphasize that observing for specimen records does not exact the knowledge and skills of the trained psychologist. Actually, quite the opposite is true in our experience. Persons with advanced training in psychology can become excellent observers, but they are handicapped at the outset, and almost invariably it takes them longer to learn how to do it. They theorize. Their first three or four reports usually have to be thrown away. Persons without any psychological training, on the other hand, often do very well from the first.

We have not found that special talent along the line of "intuitiveness" or something like "clinical insight" is a necessary qualification. The observer does not have to work at this level; he does not have to commune with anyone or to make searching diagnoses. He must have first rate general competence, if only because of the demands made for clear, thorough, and vivid reporting. This probably is the main requirement. Some experience in the routines of observing and reporting is necessary. But the sum of the observer's experience with other persons is more important. It is clearly desirable that these other persons shall have included individuals of the sort to be observed; observers of children who have known some children will probably do better than those who have not. It seems advantageous that the observer be one who fits in the culture of his subjects; but we hope that, as the accomplishments of some anthropologists would suggest, it is possible for Kansans to get good specimen records on Africans, New Yorkers, or Eskimos.

In general, the practicability of the specimen record as a research tool is not limited by a scarcity of persons who can learn how to do the necessary observing. Observers undoubtedly vary in their perceptiveness; and some verbalize better than others what they have seen and heard. But we have been impressed less by these differences than by the uniform quality of the reports in our records.

THE PROBLEM OF OBSERVER INFLUENCE

The task of making specimen records is subject to a serious technical complication, namely, one of interference by the observer with the phenomena to be observed and recorded. When a geologist surveys and describes an area he does not appreciably change the geology of the region. But the presence of an observer may well change the psychological situation and hence the behavior of the person observed. How can one keep the habitat of the person natural and so observe naturally occurring behavior when it is not natural for an observer to be present? It is probable that the interference by the observer in psychological field studies can seldom be reduced to zero. The problem, then, is one of making the interference minimal, of defining it, and of keeping it as nearly constant as possible.

There is, of course, the possibility of concealed observation. In the larger situation of field research in psychology, however, this recourse is questionable on grounds of consideration for others and public relations. The practice is dubious, to say the least, if the behavior to be observed is not public and therefore open to scrutiny by all. It is clear that people living in a community have the right to say when and by whom their privacy is to be invaded. They differ in this respect from subjects who have consented to be guinea pigs behind one-way vision screens in psychological laboratories. Only a policy of openness and candor, moreover, seems likely to insure in the long run, confidence in a field worker. In line with this policy, we have informed our subjects of each plan for observation in terms suitable for their various levels of maturity, with these exceptions: Children in public situations are observed without our first asking for their consent, although the notebook of the observer often tips them off to his presence. Also, children below the age of five are observed without their knowledge in an unrestricted variety of situations. In both instances, however, the consent of adults is secured.

Instead of resorting to concealment, the specimen record maker can do quite the opposite; he can get to know and be known by his subjects and their associates and, during his time at work as an observer, build for himself the role of a friendly, nonevaluating, nondirective, and nonparticipating person who is interested in what people do. We have adopted this tactic in Midwest, and our experience has indicated that it goes far to obviate the guinea pig feeling. Scientific observers of children in nursery schools and other like settings have long since found the same to be true. Their experience, like ours, has shown that most children "get used to" the presence of onlookers who, though friendly and not entirely anonymous or unresponsive, let what one is doing take its course and rarely if ever interfere. This holds especially if, as with many of our specimen records, observations are long enough to permit adaptation to any new or uncertain elements of the situation which have initially been disturbing. A child cannot stop being himself for long, if at all, just because someone is watching him; and forces of the psychological habitats which arise in the behavior settings he enters must often be stronger than those induced by any mere onlooker. Beyond this, a kind of reassurance from example can occur; we have found that, when a prospective subject has seen a record in the making, he is not so likely to be bothered when his turn comes.

It is clear that age is correlated significantly with the degree in which behavior is natural in the presence of an observer. Children of Midwest under 10 years do not generally show appreciable symptoms of sensitivity or self-consciousness under direct observation; and for this reason our specimen records are currently restricted to subjects of this age range. We have not secured records on adolescents. There are indications that it is possible to obtain valid descriptive accounts of behavior by adolescents or, possibly, willing adults; but it now seems clear that special methods must be used for this purpose.

The strategy of the observer is important for this problem. His task must be to stay in the background as much as possible. Inactivity and unresponsiveness sometimes make an observer stand out as a stationary figure against a moving background; but activity and responsiveness may at other times have the reverse effect. A good field observer is one who has mastered the technique of varying his behavior as the situation varies in such a way that he is not prominent and yet neither elusive nor secretive.

Whatever the extent to which the observer may complicate the psychological habitat of the subject, his influence need not be left unknown and unmeasured. Several checks upon how much and what kind of difference this complication makes are possible. The behavior of the subject while the observer is likely to be most disturbing, as when he is alone with the subject, can be compared with his behavior while the observer is least disturbing, as when in a school classroom, for example, many others are present. Reports from parents, teachers, and others as to deviations from characteristic behavior during periods of observation can be secured. Also, the behavior of the subject in relation to one observer can be compared with his behavior in relation to other observers and to other adults. Specific findings on the social role and psychological effects of the observer will be presented in Chapter XII.

Our evidence indicates that such influence as the observer may have is constant through long periods of observation. If one observer is replaced by another, this constancy obviously is reduced. It is pertinent, therefore, to consider that when a record covering several hours is made, and efficiency requires the use of a number of observers in turn, one probable result is a tendency for the different effects of different observers to cancel one another. At least, if several observers take turns, the behavior of the subject is not bent in one direction by a single, unique, interpersonal relationship between himself and a particular onlooker.

A final consideration here is the important one that any interaction between a subject and an observer is real behavior with significance in its own right. It is, moreover, behavior which shows as well as any other how a given person in a particular setting of a particular community reacts to a definable situation.

THE RELIABILITY OF SPECIMEN RECORDS

Two facts about the reliability of specimen records are paramount in the present state of their development as a scientific technique. First, specimen record reliability is not a single problem; it is a whole series of problems.

Specimen records do not have a single reliability coefficient, as a mental test does; they have as many reliability coefficients as they have attributes which mirror the subject's behavior or situation.   They have different reliabilities for example, as sources of data on the games of children, on the amount of time children spend outdoors, on the ways children are disciplined, or the number of overlapping episodes in which children engage, and on the occurrence of daydreaming in the behavior of children.   We have already identified several score of such features of specimen records, and the reliability of each has to be separately determined.

This introduces the second of the paramount issues mentioned above. Before specimen record reliabilities can be determined, it is necessary to devise techniques for analyzing the records and to establish the reliabilities of these analytical techniques.

For these reasons, viz., the extent of the problem and the prior necessity of developing analytical techniques, we are unable at this time to present data directly bearing on the reliability of specimen records.   Our time has run out.   However, we have felt justified in using specimen records in our research without waiting for systematic studies of their reliability because of the following indirect, general evidence.

We have already pointed out that specimen records are essentially the method by which behavior is observed and reported for the purposes of ordinary social intercourse.   The whole experience of mankind indicates that this method is sufficiently reliable for many kinds of interpersonal understanding.   Specimen records are not a new instrument; they are, in fact, the oldest means of collecting behavioral data.   This indicates, at least, that the reliabilities of specimen records for assessing important characteristics of another's behavior are not zero.

One source of evidence of the reliability of specimen records is provided by records of the same subject made by different observers during consecutive observation periods.   The reader can experience this reliability directly, as we have, by reading a published day record (8).   No one can doubt that the observers in these cases were seeing the same child and describing the same continuum of behavior.

The data we shall present are the pooled observations of a number of observers.   This arises from the facts that no period of observation lasted more than 30 minutes, that the order of the observers was random, that the identity of the observers was not considered in analyzing the data, and that all tables of data contain episodes reported by a number of observers. Whatever increment in reliability arises from averaging the observations of a number of observers occurs in these data.

The picture of the behavior and psychological habitat of Midwest children which is revealed by specimen records is confirmed by other, independent evidence such as the behavior setting survey and the social weather ratings.

The data from specimen records provide a generally consistent picture of the psychological habitats and behavior of the children studied. In the presentation of results, numerous meaningful, congruent relationships between independent analytical categories applied to the content of the records will be discussed. These are relationships which would occur very infrequently if the reliabilities of specimen records were very low.

It seems probable to us that the reliabilities of specimen records are closely related to the reliabilities with which they can be analyzed for different behavioral properties. Characteristics of behavior which are observed and reported unreliably will almost certainly appear in the records with indefiniteness, ambiguity, and inconsistency, and in consequence the reliabilities of the analyses will be low. The reliabilities of all the analyses are reported, and those which are too low have been discarded.

We do not discount the importance of systematic studies of the reliabilities of specimen records. We can only say that we have not had the time to do this. Although we do not offer it as a defense, we are nonetheless reassured by the fact that, according to our reading of the history of science, the introduction of new methods usually follows the pattern we have had to follow here, namely: first, use of the methods in research, and, if the results are promising, detailed study later of the limits of their accuracy.

PROCEDURAL ROUTINES

In making specimen records, as in administering psychological tests, some standardization of routines is necessary. The following are suggested as practices which now appear to be advantageous.

1. Observational Period. The length of each period of observation should be limited. The observer must perceive and remember a multitude of simultaneous and sequential occurrences. This task is fatiguing, and no one can maintain for long the steady alertness it requires. *We have found that the maximum length of time for efficient observation is 30 minutes. This means that long records necessitate a corps of observers who take turns; at least six are needed for a day record.*

2. Notes. The observer should take notes on the scene of the observed behavior. Sufficiently detailed and accurate reporting of events and circumstances in their true order is otherwise impossible. Our observers have not recorded verbalizations verbatim; but they have aimed to get down enough of the words spoken by the subject and his associates to permit near duplication of all verbal behavior.

3. Timing. Observations should be timed so that the duration of reported episodes may later be determined. Indications of the time at intervals of approximately one minute are sufficient for most purposes. For note taking and timing, our observers use a 10 inch by 14 inch writing board with a metal clasp to which a watch is attached. We have not found the use of a stop watch practicable.

4. Dictation. Observations should be recorded by dictation immediately after each observational period. It is probable that, when ratings and general summaries of behavior and situation are made, an interpolated interval allowing for perspective and insight is desirable.   But when the emphasis is placed upon concrete details, as in making specimen records, immediate recording is essential. Following his notes, the observer narrates sequentially what he has observed. Not infrequently, an action or circumstance will remind him of something which occurred earlier.   In this case, the observer should dictate a description of the earlier occurrence at the point of the recollection.   Strictly sequential ordering of the material can come later.

5. *Interrogation.*   We have found it valuable to provide an interrogator who listens to the original dictation and, upon the conclusion of the report, questions the observer on unclear points and asks for elaboration where the account is lean.   This allows both for spontaneity in the original narration and for subsequent corrections and additions.   It usually requires at least an hour to record the observations of a 30-minute period, and often a longer time.   With a team of observers, a schedule can be arranged whereby each observer serves also as an interrogator.   Interrogation benefits both the observer's report and the interrogator's subsequent observations; it provides for a better record and for continuous training.

6. *Written Revision.*   After the dictated report has been transcribed, it should be revised by the original observer as soon as practicable.   The revision should include deletion of duplications, correction of unclear or inaccurate statements, placement of all incidents in their proper order and, above all, filling in of newly recalled details which did not occur to the observer at the time of the dictated narration.   This step is of the utmost importance.   Often we have found that it makes the difference between a clear and rich report and one that is unclear and poor.

7. *Supplementary Interrogation.*   Our experience has shown that further interrogation is indispensable after the observer has revised his report.   This we have found to be even more profitable than interrogation when a report is first dictated. The interrogator raises questions about parts of the account which remain unclear or still appear to call for elaboration.   When the report has been modified to meet these questions, it is ready for final typing.   Even during the subsequent analysis of the record, however, the observer may be called upon to fill in gaps or to clarify unclear statements.

Probably these procedural routines can be improved.   Meanwhile, they give a basis for making specimen records in an orderly way.

SOME RULES OF REPORTING

Our experience, especially in analyzing the records, has uncovered aspects of the task of reporting which need special emphasis.   These we and the observers have generalized in the subjoined "rules."   In part they only restate points that have been made already; but they bring together in one place a list of things to do and not to do which, in our practice, have turned out to make the difference between a good record and a poor one.   Some of the rules are concerned mainly with the content of the report, others more with its form.   All of them pertain in some degree not alone to reporting but also to observing itself, for obviously the two processes are not entirely separate.

The imperative form is used here for emphasis and convenience. Also, the rules are stated with special reference to children as observees.

Content Rules

1. Focus upon the behavior and the situation of the subject. This is one of the many points at which reporting certainly cannot be separated from observing.

The observer is up against a tough assignment in perception. What he has to do is see behavior and the situation that gives rise to it all at once. This means that his perceiving must be widely inclusive. At the same time it must be sharply exclusive; for no analysis of behavior and psychological habitat can use anything that falls outside the range of the subject, his behavior, and his situation. The situation of the subject includes only things that exist for him and in any way make a difference to what he does. Our analytical procedures sift out everything else.

Actually, the subject and his situation are big and complicated and important enough to give the observer more than enough to deserve his undivided attention. It might seem otherwise at times. Observe a child in school while he only sits and reads a book for several minutes. Other children and the teacher are behaving, meanwhile, in more interesting ways. It is easy and tempting to turn and attend to these other children and the teacher, and later to add what they did to the report upon the behavior of the subject. But if the observer digresses in this way, the content of the record is almost sure to be weakened.

What one must keep in mind is that, at least for the purpose of analyzing a record, everything the subject does is interesting. The most common behaviors can be of as much consequence and have as many observable facets as the most unusual behaviors. A child can read a book, even a schoolbook, in a great many different ways. If that is what he is doing, it is important to know whether he is reveling in the book, just tolerating it, bored by it, fascinated by it, hating it, amused by it, saddened by it, *or* is sleepily indifferent to it; and the observer cannot see such things well and report them if he lets his attention wander to more intriguing actions by other persons.

There are two cases in which information about events or circumstances outside the range of the subject—*his* behavior and *his* situation—are pertinent. Each calls for careful consideration.

a) It is in order to report an action of someone other than the subject or a circumstance which apparently does not exist for him if the action or the circumstance is one that would *ordinarily be expected* to register upon and somehow make a difference to the subject. Suppose that, while Jimmy Vey, the subject, is drawing a picture, other children in the same room with him are making a lot of noise. As far as can be observed, Jim is utterly oblivious to everything but the picture; it appears that he might as well be all alone in the room. The observer should nonetheless report the noise, for one would ordinarily expect it to register upon and somehow make a difference to Jim. Clearly, in this instance, the information about the noise is useful. It tells something about the behavior of the subject, for it can be used as evidence that Jim was *concentrating* upon his picture. The need for exclusion of the extraneous remains. If something happens which evidently could not strike a spark in the subject it should be ignored and suppressed.

b) It is in order to report an action of someone other than the subject or a circumstance which apparently does not exist for him if the action or the circumstance is one that leads up to a change in the situation of the subject. A visitor walks into a schoolroom where Jim is seated and takes a seat. Jim is busy and cannot see, touch, hear, or otherwise experience the newcomer. Later, though, he talks with her. The least one can say is that it would be disconcerting to the reader of a report about this conversation were the visitor to appear from nowhere. We would suggest only that in his report the observer get her into the room. Looking back, he can bring her in at the point where she entered. But that is all that he need do with her—up to the point where she interacts with Jim. If, meanwhile, she does 10 interesting things to or with other children or the teacher, so long as these actions do not break into Jim's situation or if they do not lead later to a change in it, they do not belong in the record.

2. Observe and report as fully as possible the situation of the subject. The principle of exclusion in Rule 1 would be disastrous if it should be construed as requiring neglect of anything which does in fact enter the situation of the child under observation. If an associate of the subject talks with him, we are just as interested in what the associate says as we are in what the subject says. If an associate smiles at the subject, we want to know that and how he smiles. If the subject looks at a picture or sings a song, we want to know something about the picture or the song. We have to know, above all, and as best we can by inferential description, what the picture, the song, or whatever, is like for the child.

3. Never make interpretations carry the burden of description. There is a place for interpretations which go beyond inferential description and generalize *about* the behavior or the situation of the subject. But interpretation cannot take the place of good description. One cannot conscientiously analyze an interpretation. All one can analyze is the behavior of the subject or some aspect of his situation. Interpretative comments are of value principally as means to the better understanding of what the observer *describes*. The least the observer can do is push as far as possible away from interpretation as a substitute for concrete description. Any interpretations which he does offer should be expressed always in the idiom of everyday usage. Technical theorizing is out! (See p. 208.)

In the written revisions, all interpretative comments should be bracketed. The same should be done with statements about happenings or circumstances that only lead up to a later change in the subject's situation. The bracketed material is indented in the final copy of the record.

4. Give the "how" of everything the subject does. It is assumed that everything a child does is done some*how*. No child ever just walked, for example. The first time the subject walked he walked slowly, haltingly, awkwardly, unsteadily. Five years later, on his way downtown to get a haircut, he walked reluctantly. Ben smiled. How? Ducking his head with embarrassment? Coyly? Politely? Complacently? Contentedly? Proudly? Impishly? William said, "No."

How? Uncertainly? Crossly? Curtly, like a depot agent? Brooking no argument? Petulantly? Aggressively, with his chin out? Resignedly? Roy raised his hand. How did he raise it? One observer said, "as if maybe he knew the answer and maybe he didn't." Roy walked to school. The how is given by this sentence from one report: "He swaggered as he used his entire body to hurry." Earlier, Roy had lingered in bed. The following effectively tells how. "He began kicking off the covers in a slow, leisurely fashion, raising one knee and slowly bringing it down, taking a long time as if savoring the lying in bed for a moment."

Often the answer to the one question, "how?" meets the requirements of our analytical procedures. In the "how" of the child's behavior, there is its constructiveness, its intensity, its social maturity level, its efficiency, the affect that accompanies it. Beyond this, one often can infer from the "how" of his behavior much about the situation of a child.

It may be that occasionally it is impossible for an observer to see at all or to interpret how a child does a thing. When such is the case, when the observer cannot give the "how" of an action, he should say so. It is true that children do not do everything dramatically, in some way that stands out—as tearfully, rapidly, gaily, gloomily, angrily. They do many things in just an ordinary, average, middling, routine, neither-this-nor-that way. But, again, when this holds, the observer should say so.

5. *Give the "how" of everything done by any person who interacts with the subject.* We have tried to state this rule carefully. The intention is to ask for the "how" of every action by a person who is in the psychological habitat of a child. This excludes the actions of all who are only in the child's physical situation. If, however, anyone talks to, smiles at, winks at, pushes, trips, hits, beckons, runs toward or away from, leads, follows, caresses, teases, joshes . . . the subject, the content of the behavior should be given absolutely as fully as the content of the subject's behavior. This rule develops Rule 2, which requires full description of the subject's situation.

6. *Report in order in the final version all of the main steps through the course of every action by the subject.* The main point here is that continuous, unbroken records must be secured. All hands that go up must come down. A subject is said to be on his way to the school basement. Up to this point, he has been sitting at his desk in the schoolroom. How did the behavior start? A child is at the front of the room talking to the teacher. The next thing we know, he is in his seat. How did he get there? In some analysis of the records, we try to mark off every smallest molar "phase" in each course of behavior. This can be done correctly only if the present rule is applied.

7. *Wherever possible, state descriptions of behavior positively.* It is possible to study only what the subject did do, not what he did not do. "Ben didn't say the words very loud." Then, did he say them "softly?" "He was not disturbed about being late." This tells something. But, should the following be correct, it would tell more: "Despite being late, Ben was calm and relaxed."

8. *Describe in some detail the scene as it is when each period of observation begins.* Even good novelists have trouble in keeping their readers abreast of the main parts of physical and social situations. It seems best to meet this problem by

asking each observer to sum up what he finds before him when he arrives on the scene of each observational period. Nothing elaborate is needed here. The observer can go about it as a playwright does in setting up the scene of a play. Who are the main characters? What are their positions? What are the chief features of the physical layout? Just where, of course, is the subject? Where is the observer?

9. Put no more than one thing the child has done in one sentence. This rule should be kept in mind only through the work on the written revision. It doubtless would inhibit dictation.

Some of our methods of analysis separate from one another all distinguishable actions by the child; and it helps if the units come to the analyzer with no more than one of them in a single sentence. If the observer does refer to molecular units of behavior, any number he prefers may as well be packed into a sentence, so long as the intention is to study the molar units of the record. For, in this case, actones need never be separated from one another to be analyzed one by one; they can be strung together as qualifiers in statements describing molar behavior units.

10. Put in one sentence no more than one thing done by a person in the situation of the child. This is Rule 9 applied to associates of the subject.

11. Do not report observations in terms of time intervals. The time is noted and reported at intervals of approximately one minute, but this does not mean that the reported actions are to be time bound. The observer should let the behavior set its own limits; he should not mark off a unit himself by referring to clock time. The following sentence illustrates time-bound delimiting. "He was concentrating on his work during this whole minute from 3:41 to 3:42." If, by coincidence, the child does begin concentrating on his work at 3:41 and goes on concentrating until 3:42, at which time he turns to something else, the observer should report:

> 3:41   He started concentrating. . . .
> 3:42   He turned away from his work. . . .

Often, when this rule is broken, we get lean, generalizing statements.

However correct and useful these rules may be, they are less important than the basic aim of the observer. The observer must approach the task of making a specimen record with the intention of seeing as nearly as possible everything the child does and everything in his situation, and of determining as truly and completely as possible the meaning to the child of his actions and the parts of his situation. He must aim to achieve a rich and full account of the concrete situations and the actual behavior of the subject. We have said that the best model for the observer is a good novelist.

Specimen Records and the Sampling Problem

EPISODES AS SAMPLING UNITS

Our unit for study of individual Midwest children's behavior and habitat is the episode. A specimen record, therefore, can be viewed as an episode collection. One of the earliest findings of the Midwest study was that very great numbers of these units occur even in a small community. Analyses of our records indicate that, with only the children of the town contributing to the count, there occur in Midwest 75 thousand to 100 thousand episodes each day, roughly 3 million each month and 36 million each year. Means have to be found for sampling a population so great. This is made the more urgent by the requirement that the procedures of a psychological field study be repeatable in different communities and at different times.

In setting out upon the Midwest research we did not fully anticipate this problem. There was originally in the minds of the proponents the hope that a great number of casual observations, made and recorded over a period of years, would provide the material for an adequate description of the behavior and life situations of the children in the community. We counted first upon the fact that the total number of subjects whose behavior was to be studied would be small. We considered further that the children would be living near one another in a cage surrounded by the limiting boundary of open farm land, and we made much of this slogan: Every time we see a child we will see a subject. We anticipated that it would be easier to keep track of the ongoing behavior than if the actions of the same number of children were to be studied in a larger community. It appeared that, in a city, one would be led in an ever widening circle to different neighborhoods, schools, clubs, and cliques until a halt would be enforced at a point determined less by requirements of the problem than by the limitations of available facilities. Nothing like this seemed likely to happen in Midwest. We reasoned that, because the children of the town would be limited as to range of movement, their paths would continually cross, and that our observations, rather than leading us in an ever widening circle, would repeatedly bring us back to the same subjects and the same behavior settings.

Most of these expectations have been fulfilled. The children of Midwest do live in a cage, for virtually all of their activities occur within the geographical limits of the town; we do see a subject every time we see a child; and the paths of the different children do continually cross and recross. These circumstances are important. They permit intensive repeatable field procedures which would otherwise be impossible. They insure also a degree of familiarity with the subjects and their conditions of life which increases greatly the richness of recorded observations. Owing to one error in our calculations, however, they leave the sampling problem unsolved. The error lay in underestimation of the sheer volume of human action which occurs in a small community. There is so much child behavior going on around us in Midwest that we can in no way record all of it or observe and report without the guidance of some sampling plan a sufficiently representative part of it. It is necessary that we select upon some basis a number of episodes to represent without bias the total for our subjects. This problem must be faced in any similar ecological study.

PERSONS AND SETTINGS AS SAMPLING GUIDES

There are as guides to a stratified sample of behavior and habitat such stable, nonpsychological characteristics of individuals as age, sex, and social group. Factors associated with variations in each of these influence behavior in more or less characteristic ways. The behavior settings of a community also can be used as sampling guides. Their suitability and importance for this purpose are immediately evident. It follows from the synomorphic relationship between behavior settings and coördinate systems of psychological habitat and behavior that one way to tap the different kinds of actions and psychological living conditions in a community is to collect episode units from its different settings. In all, then, a field investigator is in a position to make a two-way stratified sampling of an episode population if he has available a census of the individuals in a community with their age, sex, and social group, and such an inventory of behavior settings as the one represented here in the Behavior Settings Catalogue.

Some determination of the relative weight or importance of different settings for different classes of subjects must be made if a settings inventory is to be used to guide a stratified sample. But what should importance be made to mean here? We have concluded that the basic question which the needed weighting criterion must answer comes to this: How preoccupying is each setting in the life of the person? To how much of the person's total psychological world does it contribute? The amount of time spent in a setting gives an answer to this question. Accordingly, occupancy times, as expressed by the measurements reported in Chapter IV, provide a convenient guide to the sampling of children's episodes from different behavior settings.

Settings records have been obtained from continuously maintained settings, such as the soda fountain of Clifford's Drug Store, and from relatively short, periodic, or occasional settings, such as the regularly scheduled meeting of an organization, an athletic event, a school program, or a children's party. To secure one of these records the observer goes to the setting at a time when a child of a given age level and sex is known or expected to be present. The social group of the child is, in most instances, left to vary on a chance basis. Also, when the setting offers two or more children who are equally eligible in terms of the sampling schedule, a chance selection procedure is used to single out a particular child for observation. Where a setting is of limited duration and its standing behavior pattern has a clearly defined beginning, course, and end, as in the case, say, of an organizational meeting, the behavior of the observed child through the entire time span of the setting may be recorded. This has not always been practicable. In every case, however, the intention is to secure a record which does not violate either the integrity of the setting or the continuity of the child's behavior.

The behavior setting survey and the settings records are the keys to the proposed sampling plan. Coördination of these two methods with determinations of age, sex, and social group as standard behavior correlates appears to provide for an efficient survey of the psychological situations and behavior of individual children of Midwest or other communities. Limitations of the settings record, however, require that it be supplemented for some purposes by the day record, as suggested below.

We have not as yet filled in completely a precise design on the basis of the proposed guides to an adequate sample of individual Midwest children's habitat and behavior. These guides have nonetheless been used in the securing of our present record collection. As for behavior settings, it is stated in Chapter IV that there were 107 varieties of community settings in Midwest, and that children under 12 enter settings in 98 of these variety groupings; as the reader will recall, children do not enter lodge settings, for example. We have specimen records which represent 36 of the 98 varieties. The 36 varieties of community settings which have been sampled, moreover, are high in importance as measured by occupancy time. Thus, they account for 745,415 hours per year, whereas all 62 of the varieties which have not been sampled account for the lower figure of 277,039 hours per year. In addition, we have sampled by day and settings records all of the major home settings, as opposed to community settings. This is to report data on the sample provided by our total record collection. Special sampling designs involving the use of day records have also been used for the analytical studies to be reported in later chapters.

SAMPLING BY THE DAY RECORD

A person is characteristically on the go throughout his waking hours from one behavior setting to another—from bed to breakfast to school to a ball game and so on through a lifetime. Children and others do not begin over again in each setting. Behavior with habitat forms a continuous chain; and probably the chain often has about as much integrity between as within temporally contiguous settings. A result of this is that an observer who stays in a setting and takes a series of episodes from it may inevitably go away with a length of chain that never should have been broken at either end.

It is clear that a field investigator is forced to cut the chain of behavior and habitat somewhere, and to use only a part of it. But he is not compelled to go to one and then another part of a community and to take from each whatever comes in the way of habitat and behavior. It is possible instead to go to a person and to follow the chain of his behavior and habitat through a sequence of settings. In this case, though, a decision as to where to break the chain still has to be made. The section through a setting is not necessarily arbitrary and also is clearly delimited operationally. In addition, a settings record usually provides for analysis a manageable block of material. Are there lengths of the behavior chain running through a number of settings which satisfy these criteria?

The continuum from which a part has to be taken is extended in time. How much of it comprises a sequence that is not arbitrary, that is operationally well defined, that provides material within the reach of practicable methods of analysis? The part through an hour? A month? A week? Ten minutes, as in some time samples? A day? Considerable experimenting has led us to conclude that a day from the life of a child in the settings of a community gives a sample of behavior and habitat that is meaningfully limited, readily identified as a discrete part of the behavior continuum, and analytically feasible. We have accordingly secured a number of day records of the behavior of children in Midwest. Our chief aim in this has been to collect some specimens of the actions and situations of the children in the community which do justice to the continuity of behavior.

A day in the life of a person is not a whole without tag ends. For grown-ups, certainly, it is often bound remorselessly to days before and after. These lines are being written against a deadline and, for their writers, the days of the past two weeks have coalesced. There has been 1 course of behavior, not 14. Fortunately, though, people do not always behave so compulsively. Each of our 14 days, moreover, has had something of a new beginning, and each has been pushed until late to a moderately fit stopping place. The degree in which these consecutive days have merged and the degree in which the same generally occurs for others depends clearly upon past and future time perspective. It is pertinent, therefore, that the time perspectives of children are relatively dim and short; impotence and brevity of the past and future have to be counted among important features of the world as it is for a child (cf. 19). Children under 12 have relatively little to do with Tuesday or Thursday on Wednesday. They can heed the Biblical admonition here without trying because their plans and retrospections are relatively hazy and little extended. Our day records themselves suggest that a day in the life of a child under 12 is generally in itself something of a model behavior continuum.

Naturalistic descriptions in psychology usually have violated the continuity of behavior. To summarize: our settings records have done this in some degree by recording limited sequences of episodes; the earlier anecdotal records did the same by reporting single incidents; time-sample records have done this by reporting only fractional aspects of behavior or situation; case studies and biographies usually retain the rough temporal order of the reported events, but they leave many gaps. All of these methods have selected from the continuity of behavior with habitat, material of value. But they have generally left out the vitally important factor of the continuity itself. It may be that this aspect of behavior is preserved effectively by the day record. A related consideration is that the possibility of a biased selection of episodes is reduced as the length of a recorded sequence is increased. We find that a record covering the behavior of a child through a day contains from 6 to 13 hundred episodes. A day record, therefore, as compared to a shorter record, is equivalent to a larger rather than smaller population sample.

We have selected each subject for a day study by referring to a sampling schedule in which provisions are made for the variables of age and sex.

Despite its several advantages, the specimen day record is limited as a research tool for a thorough and efficient survey of the behavior-habitat units of a community. The process of making it is demanding. It requires the concerted efforts of a staff of 8 to 12 trained persons, including secretaries, over a period of no less than two weeks. The coöperation of several individuals of the community, including the subject, his parents, and his teachers, must be secured; and all of these persons must be carefully prepared for the procedure by interviews and visits before observations begin. It is obviously impossible to get a sample of behavior-habitat units that is balanced as to the age, sex, and other stable characteristics of the subjects and that represents adequately all of the behavior settings of a community by this one method alone. The day record, however, does appear to be of unique value for work upon a number of problems. We believe that it and the settings record complement one another in a productive way.

Concluding Statement

One way to use specimen records scientifically would be to deposit them in museums. They qualify as science end products insofar as they are true records of what they aim to record. Another way to use them scientifically is to subject their content to conceptual and quantitative analysis. We have done this. We have experimented with different kinds of such analysis among many other kinds that are possible. The following chapters, in which the procedures and results of this experimental work is reported, may show at least that the recorded material has significance for certain varieties and levels of psychological problems.

Chapter VII

Dividing the Behavior Stream

Episodes as Action-and-Situation Units

A SPECIMEN record collects episodes; in the present research, it is made for this purpose. Yet, because it describes the sequential flow of behavior without any systematic reference to parts of the ongoing stream, each record leaves undone the task of delimiting episodes as targets of description. This task defines the central problem of the present chapter which contains also some discussion of the general significance of recorded episodes in psychology and preliminary discussion of what we have done with them toward description of individual Midwest children's psychological habitat and behavior.

We can go to a Midwest child with the problem of bounding these units.

Margaret Reid was wakened by her mother at 8:10 on the morning of June 2, 1949. The first thing she did was to mutter sleepily to her mother something about going to Bible School that day. Then, while continuing to talk with her mother about Bible School, she stretched, groaning and extending her arms "way out." Next, she proceeded to get dressed, and while this action was still in progress, she (a) said sleepily, "I want to lie down," and did so, (b) stretched again, this time "raising up and wiggling," (c) playfully pulled several bobby pins out of her hair, (d) conversed about her curls with her mother, entering upon this action while still fiddling with the bobby pins, and continuing it after pulling out the last bobby pin, (e) hugged her mother in response to the latter's sally that she, Margaret, walked "like an old lady," (f) went to the bathroom, and, on the way to this morning rite, (g) took note for the first time of a lady who stood holding a writing board.

These are things Margaret was observed to do by a trained observer. They are actions, every one of which might have been seen by Margaret's mother, who was on hand most of the time. They might have been discriminated by any present and normally perceptive adult. Every one of them, we assume, was perceived by Margaret herself as something she was doing. They have all been recorded in detail in a specimen record. Each of them, together with the psychological life situation in which it occurred, is an episode.

These episodes are presented below as we have marked them off on the record, with each delimited by a marginal bracket and identified by a number and title. As indicated already, Margaret's behavior here was not, throughout, entirely a matter of one thing after the other, but also a matter now and again of two or more things at the same time; during parts of the sequence, two episodes and, at one time, three, occurred at once. We call such concurrence of episodes *overlapping*, a common phenomenon to be considered later in detail. Overlapping is graphed on the records by parallel placement of episode brackets which shows here, for example, that the whole of *Lying Down* (5) overlaps with an early part of *Getting Dressed* (4). Note by referring to the pertinent brackets that the forepart of *Discussing Curls with Mother* (8) overlaps with the concluding part of *Taking Out Bobby Pins* (7), and also with an intermediate part of *Getting Dressed*. Note also that the sequential course of the record has nowhere been transgressed, so that each of the episodes can be studied in its larger context. Mrs. Reid has just entered Margaret's bedroom, which opens off the Reid's dining room.

1

COMING AWAKE

Mrs. Reid went into the bedroom and said, "Margaret, Margaret, it's time to get up; you have to go to Bible School," coaxingly calling Margaret out of her sleep.

Margaret muttered very, very sleepily, "I hope they don't start," as if she didn't want Bible School to be.

I took this to mean that if Bible School didn't start she wouldn't have to get up.

The mother said very pleasantly, "Yes, dear, it does start."

Margaret rolled over.

Mrs. Reid walked out of the room.

Margaret was still seemingly sound asleep.

2

EXCHANGING REMARKS WITH MOTHER

8:11 Returning, the mother said a little more firmly, "Margaret, get up so you can get to Bible School on time."

Then she turned to me and said, "She's sleeping so soundly I hate to wake her."

Turning to Margaret, she said coaxingly and in a loving tone of voice, "Come on, honey, get up; you have to get ready for Bible School."

3

STRETCHING

Margaret groaned and stretched way out.

The mother pulled down the covers.

Margaret put her arms clear above her head and raised herself by using her heels and her head as supports, wiggling as she did so.

The mother then said, "Well, how do you feel?" in a very pleasant tone of voice, as she sat on the edge of Margaret's bed.

Margaret said very, very sleepily, "O.K.," and the mother absently murmured, "Huh?"

Margaret said, "O.K., I don't have a cold."

This was said a little less sleepily in the tone of one who is telling something of great interest.

The mother asked, "You don't have a cold?"

Margaret muttered, "Huh," still rather sleepily, lapsing back to her former sleepy state.

The mother asked pleasantly, "Do you want to go to Bible School?"

Margaret murmured, so sleepily as hardly to say a word at all, "Yes."

4

8:12 The mother urged, "Well, let's get dressed."

As Margaret started to slide off the bed, her mother said quickly, "Wait." Then she explained, "Get your shoes and socks so you won't have to get your feet dirty."

Margaret sat on the edge of the bed where she was before her mother's voice arrested her slide to the floor.

5

As the mother reached for her foot, Margaret said sleepily, "I want to lie down."

The mother laughed and said, "So you want to lie down and go to sleep again."

She let Margaret lie down.

Margaret lay with her head at the foot of the bed this time.

6

Margaret then stretched as far as she could with her arms back, raising up and wiggling.

It was almost as if she were shedding her sleep like a snake sheds its skin.

Her mother laughed at her pleasantly, almost with her.

7

Margaret said cautiously, "A hairpin came out."

Her hair was done up in bobby pins for curling purposes.

Then she asked with a great deal more interest, much more animated than she had been, "Do you see a curl?"

She wiggled some more.

The mother didn't say anything.

"I took a hairpin out," said Margaret with firmness, almost with a note of defiance.

The mother said, "So you took a hairpin out," as if "so what." It seemed as if Margaret were pestering her mother. Since saying the hairpin came out had brought no reprimand, she seemed to be trying to get one by saying she took it out.

Margaret took out several more hairpins, reaching rather lazily up to remove them.

She looked cautiously at her mother.

Getting no response, she didn't bother to look at her mother anymore.

Margaret watched her mother's hand as if to make sure she was keeping the hairpins safely.

8

8:13 She took several more hairpins from her hair and said to her mother, "Do you see a curl?" rather eagerly.

The mother said, "I see a lot of them that are going to be curls."

Margaret took a few more bobby pins out and said again, "Do you see a curl now?" a bit more eagerly.

The mother answered, "Yes, I see a curl," as if she knew she had to say so before she would have any peace.

The mother finished putting on the shoes and socks for Margaret and told her to take off her pyjamas and put on her panties.

Without saying anything, Margaret put her feet off the bed rather lazily.

She slid slowly to her feet.

9

Margaret kind of wobbled and took several steps toward her mother.

Mrs. Reid laughed and said, "Think you can walk this morning, honey?" in a very pleasant, loving tone of voice.

She added, "You walk like an old lady."

Margaret giggled and laughed.

She put her arms affectionately around her mother's neck.

As her laugh subsided, the mother said, "Take off your pyjamas and I'll put your panties on you," in a pleasantly firm tone of voice.

The mother unclasped Margaret's arms from her neck and let them slide down.

The mother pulled Margaret's panties on rather snugly but in a loving way.

She gave Margaret a little pat on her rear.

10

Margaret came out of the bedroom and into the dining room, prepared to go to the bathroom.

11

GETTING DRESSED | GOING TO BATHROOM | NOTING OBSERVER

She finally noticed me.

The observer was sitting in the dining room near the door to Margaret's room.

She opened her mouth in surprise.

She really seemed surprised to find me there.

She almost stopped, but didn't, and walked on to the bathroom.

8:14 The mother followed her and asked, "About through, honey?"

I thought I had better not go into the bathroom at this point.

There were sounds of splashing water as the mother helped.

8:16 Margaret came out of the bathroom, through the kitchen, and into the dining room.

As she stood there, she pulled on the housecoat which her mother had left on a chair for her.

Two parts of every episode stand out, here, as in every episoded specimen record. These are an action and a situation.

The action of an episode is in some instances single and undivided, as in *Noting Observer*. It is in other instances divided into subordinate parts, steps, or *phases*, as in *Getting Dressed*. It is always, whether divided or undivided, an essentially unitary thing done by a person. The situation is the person's psychological habitat when the action occurs. It includes the needs and working abilities of the person and the habitat objects of the environment which coexist and interact to determine the action. Where the action is divided, the situation also is divided; habitat objects change, working abilities change, and needs change as the person goes from one phase of an action to another. Yet the total situation, like the action, has unity. Its parts belong together. They are interdependent and they form on the environmental side one set of outer conditions to be dealt with in some way at one time for one purpose.

Take *Lying Down*. This title identifies the action. The situation includes the need state signified by Margaret's sleepiness and the inviting bed. It includes also the friendly mother as a carrier of psychological effects and all of the other parts of the behavior setting that entered Margaret's psychological habitat and so made a difference to her behavior while she was lying down, as these are represented in the record.

One obviously cannot hope to find in a specimen record a complete description of either the action or the total situation of an episode. The state of the person and the content of the psychological environment cannot be completely determined by presently available methods for the diagnosis of either naturally occurring or experimentally created situations; nor is it possible to describe fully by any available means the content and properties of an action by the person. We nonetheless hope to demonstrate that some essential dimensions of the molar behavior unit and its context in an episode can be reconstructed on the basis of material in a specimen record.

Life Incidence and Research Values of Episodes

One thing which must now be clear is that there is nothing esoteric about an episode. To the contrary, these links in the chain of molar behavior are in their nature above board to the person in whose life they occur and, as a rule, to any reasonably observant associate of the person at the time. This holds as a corollary of the specification that episodes fall within an intermediate behavioral range of magnitude, whose limits are set by the normal behavior perspective, identified in Chapter I. We will later define this range more precisely and specify in greater detail other empirical and conceptual traits of episodes. Meanwhile, we would like to indicate the place of behavior-and-situation units on this level in the economy of naturally occurring behavior, to enlarge familiarity with them, and to suggest some of their advantages for research on psychological problems which exceed the limits of the present naturalistic studies.

Naturally occurring episodes are the happenings people write home about, if they write daily. They are the entries in diaries. They are, as a rule with exceptions, too small, vestigial, and numerous for annual letters; and they are relatively rare for the same reasons in biographies, novels, and histories; but they generally form the plot units of short stories and plays. They are the molar behavior phenomena that parents, teachers, neighbors, storekeepers, and others note as a matter of course in the daily lives of children, and which they praise or blame, abet or hinder, delight in or deplore, but, at all events, must get along with as best they can. This does not mean that behavior units of children and others which fall outside the size range of episodes always go entirely unobserved. Both shorter and longer lengths of behavior sometimes command attention. At times, for example, a mother will notice a subepisodic unit, most often, perhaps, to scold it, as when she entreats her child to stop absent drumming with his fingers. Rather frequently, also, a mother will take note of superepisodic units, especially to encourage some very long ones, as when she urges upon a recalcitrant fiddler the advantages in a musical career. For the greater part, however, mothers and the like attend to and get concerned about only the intermediate behavior parts, episodes, which also are perceived while they occur by children themselves in their own behavior.

The practical daily management of human affairs is for everyone most essentially a matter of coping, with greater or lesser involvement as spectator or participant, with episodes. These are the behavioral events that set the clock, crawl out of bed in the morning, eat breakfast, go to the office (to the kitchen, to a sandbox, to school), wait on a customer, bake a cake, stand

and recite, pile blocks, answer the phone, vote, and go to church on Sunday. These are the personal and interpersonal incidents of preëmptive hour by hour and minute by minute concern on the part of the behaving person and his associates. They do not use up all the energy available to the person for molar behavior. Some of this energy is consumed by longer running parts of the behavior stream, like getting ahead of the Smiths, which however, an observer or the person himself can see only by stopping to look far back or ahead. Episodes remain alone as the never dormant and characteristically perceived links in the event chain of behavior.

Episodes have practical significance and consequent research importance on many counts. Traumas and other crises in personality formation, and the rudimentary frustrations, failures, and successes of life, center in these primary behavior units. They are the arenas for all face to face social interactions. Lasting interpersonal relationships, group processes, and group structures can originate in them and are continually regulated by them. They both mediate and determine superordinate trains of action. They are the root sources of learned behavior patterns. They reflect and express characteristic, enduring properties of the individual.

Basic laws of molar behavior are manifest in the observable action-to-situation relationships within episodes. At least, a presumption to this effect is implicit in the fact that, undertaking to test hypotheses about interdependencies between situation and action, experimental psychologists commonly create episodes, which they often call "trials," in the laboratory. Particular experimental conditions often are manipulated for this purpose in such a way that the experimenter establishes trial by trial a situation which engenders one or another action. These manipulated conditions bring about, in short, a particular episode in which, say, a cat escapes from a puzzle box; or an ape rakes a banana into his cage; or a child strives to reach a playhouse on the other side of a screen; or a man makes a hatrack out of two poles and a table clamp.

These and many other laboratory episodes give us empirical access to lawful relationships between the parameters of molar behavior. But their analogues are abundantly available in naturally occurring units of the same order whose variables of action and situation are no less subject to the same uniformities. For example, the frustration paradigm of a child, something the child wants, and an interposed obstacle occurs many times over in our specimen records on Midwest children. It is possible to collect from such records an adequate sample of episodes in which individuals of any chosen age, sex, social group or other nonpsychological classification behave in situations that present in one or another degree a particular type of frustration, freedom, failure, success, social pressure, conflict, or the like. It also is possible in forming every such sample to hold other situational variables essentially constant with the end result that one can determine relationships between the selected, independent, situational variable and such dependent variables of behavior as, say, energy level, efficiency, or constructiveness.

What this comes to is that a planned collection of naturally occurring episodes from the pages of specimen records can permit in effect an experiment in nature in which each of the sample units of action and situation amounts to an experimental trial. Such an experiment, moreover, has some advantages over comparable procedures of the psychological laboratory.

Outstanding here is the advantage that one can find in recorded life episodes, situations whose elements cannot be contrived easily, if at all. Consider among situation variables the properties of other persons as carriers of psychological effects. For example, warm and earnest *affection*, an observable, reliably measurable, and frequently occurring property of a parent in a home or of a playmate, as data later to be reported here may show, cannot readily be simulated by or discovered in a laboratory associate of a laboratory subject. The same holds for intense aggression, which occurred, for example, in one of our records as a psychological property of a girl when she hit her brother hard over the head with a bucket. These and other such determinants of molar behavior operate often as a matter of course in the episodes of specimen records.

Another advantage in recorded episodes for research toward laws of molar behavior is that they provide a unique opportunity for investigation of sequential interdependencies. The situations and actions of consecutive episodes can be rated in terms of selected variables, and curves can be drawn to represent change from unit to unit in the continuing behavior and its context. Using a collection of episoded specimen records as source material, one also can do experiments of a kind on interunit relations. It is possible to set up almost any constellation of situational variables or behavior variables, or both, to find the constellation in particular episodes and then to determine the situation, the behavior, or both, in flanking, antecedent and subsequent, episodes. Here is an opening for many hypotheses and a way to test them.

The experiments in nature upon which one can capitalize through study of episoded behavior records have apparent limitations for research on general psychological laws. They obviously do not permit the efficient accommodation of conditions to hypotheses, the positive separation of independent variables, and the elimination of extraneous factors which are characteristic of good laboratory procedures. Yet they offer possible corroboration of laboratory findings and they stand to turn up new hypotheses. They do provide, also, a means to the study of relationships between properties and conditions of molar behavior which cannot be captured easily in the laboratory.

Recorded episodes clearly have greatest significance for *behavior problems* on the level of particular actions and their more immediate contexts. As suggested earlier, many *personality problems* clearly require identification and study of long biographic units whose determining contexts include lasting and characteristically stable needs and goals of the person. Yet units of action-and-situation on the episode level are used in clinical practice and research. The diagnostic interview, for example, often discloses particular "incidents" which are judged to be pivotal and decisively revealing parts of a life history. So do associated testing procedures. Some of these procedures elicit verbalizations of episodes which are used as signs for the diagnosis of enduring behavior traits and for the prediction of like behavior units in daily life. We have considered that the episodes of specimen records could be used to strengthen tests of such prediction. Clinical psychologists have recognized and have themselves helped to fill a need for validation measures that cross the lines between clinical practice and related enterprise in psychology. Major steps in this direction have been taken across the boundary that separates clinical from experimental psychology. But it seems probable that important steps with a like purpose also can be taken across the boundary between clinical psychology and a psychological ecology. This is the more true because of the vital interests of clinical psychologists in naturally occurring behavior. Specimen records, divided for study into episodes or, for that matter, treated in some other way, provide one means of going about such a project.

Episodes as Ecological Population Units

The foregoing review leaves as the primary research value of the episodes in specimen records their store of information about the actual distribution of different kinds, properties, and conditions of molar behavior outside the laboratory and clinic.

One can take recorded episodes much as a medical student takes the slides of a series, and study them one by one from the standpoint of their action and situation *content*. But they also have significance for our natural history problem from an entirely different point of view.

To episode a record is to find boundaries between the parts of a whole behavior sequence. One can then inquire into the relations of part to whole and part to part within the sequence without any reference to what the parts contain. This is to ask about the structure, anatomy, or geometry of the behavior continuum. The problem is analogous to the one presented by relations of part to whole and part to part of a skeleton, a plant, or a rock formation, except that, in the case of behavior with its context, the whole is extended in time as well as space.

Given a behavior sequence through a known period of time, to what extent, in the first place, is it differentiated into parts? How many episodes does it include? How many "things," for example, does a normal Midwest two-year-old do in a day? A Midwest four-year-old? How are the episodes of a behavior sequence related interpositionally, whatever the degree in which the total sequence is divided? To what extent do they occur one by one in single file? To what extent, on the other hand, do they overlap? And what variations occur in the form and complexity of such overlapping? This line of inquiry raises in turn a number of questions about factors associated with the anatomy of behavior. What conditions in the habitat of a person act at the beginning of an episode to get it underway or at its end point to break it off? Under what conditions does the behavior stream bifurcate so that episodes overlap? One can ask also about cross-effects between different units of a sequence. When episodes overlap, for example, in what degree may they interfere with, complement, or reënforce one another? Such questions identify the problem of *behavior structure*.

We have analyzed both the action and situation content of individual episodes in specimen records on Midwest children and also their structural and related dynamical properties. Results of these different kinds of analysis are presented in succeeding chapters. Meanwhile, the problem of behavior structure points back directly to the groundwork task of discriminating episodes in specimen records. Because this task is crucial for all phases of the present method, its conceptual framework, working principles, and technical requirements must be dealt with here in considerable detail.

To meet this practical problem we were compelled to work out something of a theory of behavior unit formation. The theory, which owes most to Lewin (**34**), may have pertinence for general questions of behavior perception, or other problems. Also, some developments of it that are stated in the following discussion may say something about behavior structure on the side of results for the reason that these developments represent, to some extent, discoveries made in work with specimen records. We have stated several of the main ideas in a more formalized way elsewhere (**61**).

Plotting Behavior Structure
Episoding With and Without Special Criteria

Some circumstantial observations on our experience with episoding may now be helpful.

We have found by careful checking that on the average it takes a trained episoder 12 minutes to divide one page of a specimen record. On this basis, 54 minutes were used in episoding the excerpt, above, from the day record on Margaret Reid. A part of the actual time was spent only in reading through the material and in inscribing episode brackets and titles. Most of it, however, was spent in applying to the material, criteria for telling episodes apart. This may seem out of line with our statement that each of the episodes in the sequence might easily have been discriminated at the time of its occurrence by any present and normally perceptive adult. We have said even that such action and situation units in the life of one person are characteristically open to ordinary perception by others. What is the need, then, for the special criteria?

As a matter of fact, we had virtually no explicitly formulated guides to episoding at the time of setting out to divide the records. We began instead with little more than the word "episode" as a name for a commonly recognized or recognizable unit of action with its context. Yet, lacking substantially more than this to go upon, we were nonetheless able to find in the records units of action and situation that stood out clearly to us and that seemed likely to have been open to easy discrimination by others when the recorded behavior occurred. Also, we agreed among ourselves more often than not in marking off these units. Some of them were "spotted" without hesitation or any dissent. For example, we can now say with confidence that no one of the pilot episoders would have missed *Going to Bathroom* of the Margaret Reid record if it had occurred on the first page of our first episoded record.

Despite agreeing more often than not in this earliest dividing of the records, we did not agree often enough to meet adequate standards of reliability. One episoder would see a particular part of a sequence as a discrete and entire unit while another would see it as only a part of a larger unit. A third might see the same part as two or more episodes. Certain nodal points, each denoting the end of one unit and the start of another, were marked in extended sequences with firm unanimity among as many as three independent episoders. Yet, between these nodal points, discrepancies occurred rather often. Also, there were frequent instances in which units seen to be concurrent or overlapping by one analyst would be seen by another to form only subordinate parts of a single episode.

These disagreements led us to consider that, while there are easily and commonly recognized units of action and situation within a certain behavioral range, this range includes different and more or less equally perceptible units. Consistency in episoding required, therefore, some positive specifications which could be used to judge whether a given unit was or was not to be marked off as an episode. The need for the subsequently developed criteria is, first, a need for such consistency. An episoder has to go by what he sees, no less than anyone else, which means that these criteria cannot take the place of common perception. They probably do not even make common perception more than ordinarily correct. Perhaps the best they can do is increase its stability within the range of ordinarily recognized behavior units. In any case, evidence will be set forth to show that the episoding of a specimen record with the help of these criteria is a reliable and repeatable process.

A second advantage gained by the criteria at last developed has been the one of clarifying the properties of episodes as objects of study. This would seem desirable apart from the objective of consistency or reliability in episoding.

Proximal Episode Cues

Study of episoded records suggests that the following cues have figured in our marking of the beginning and end points of episodes:

1. Change in the "sphere" of the behavior from verbal to physical to social to intellectual, or from any one of these to another.

2. Change in the part of the body predominantly involved in a physical action, as from hands to mouth to feet.

3. Change in the physical direction of the behavior. Now, a child is walking north to a sandpile; next, he is going up a tree; later, he climbs down the tree.

4. Change in behavior object "commerced with," as from a knife to a watch to a dog to a person.

5. Change in the present behavior setting. A storm comes up, a fire whistle blows, a teacher says, "Pass," and the child goes from one action to another.

6. Change in the tempo of activity, as when a child shifts from walking leisurely to running toward a friend.

These and other like indicators, many of them doubtless subliminal necessarily are implicated in the discrimination of episodes. Yet such empirical marks are by no means bound univocally to behavior units on this level. The changes noted under 1, 2, and 3 are, in fact, often only changes in the actone manifolds that mediate continuing units of molar behavior (see pp. 182–86).

The situation is like that in perception where the recognition of a geometrical form, such as a circle, is possible under a great variety of stimulus conditions. In the case of the form, the necessary conditions do not have to be defined for the person who sees it. Three-year-olds who know nothing about the laws of object constancy can identify a circle, for example, whether you lay it on a table or pin it to a wall. Similarly, persons in real life or episoders can recognize episodes under enormously varied, molecular, phenotypic, or "proximal" conditions, which no one has defined for them, and which, moreover, we are in no way prepared to define for the present purpose. Our problem, then, is to find indicators which remain essentially invariant while these conditions change. It is to find criteria that sustain to all such indices something of the relationship which the distal form properties of the circle sustain to its changing proximal characteristics.

Primary Criteria of Episodes

Constancy in Direction. The centermost criterion of an episode derives from a principal characteristic of molar behavior, directedness. It provides that the behavior from the beginning to the end of an episode is constant in direction. This means that for every change in the direction of behavior a change in episode occurs. Muenzinger (**42**) has made direction constancy the most essential feature of a *start-end unit*, which has other features in common with an episode.

Another episoded sequence will now be useful; we will refer back to it repeatedly. It is taken from a day record on Dutton (Chuck) Thurston. The sequence begins at 7:32 in the evening on November 3, 1950, in the back yard of the Thurston home, where Chuck is sitting on the hood of a truck, while his father stands nearby.

GOING INSIDE

7:32 The father called good-naturedly, "Come on, Chuck. Come along, boy."

Chuck jumped down easily and quickly.

He trotted a few steps ahead of his father.

Mr. Thurston caught up at the back door of the house. There he said briskly, as he opened the door, "Come on; let's get inside."

Chuck bounded into the house.

He walked quickly through the kitchen and dining room into the living room, where his mother sat resting on a couch.

TAKING OFF WRAPS

COMMENTING ON COLD

He started to peel off his jacket.

At the same time, he remarked companionably to his mother, "It's cold outside. It's really cold out there." He said this in a very adult way.

Only smiling pleasantly, his mother seemed to take it that way.

GETTING MITTENS OFF

7:33 Chuck pulled his jacket down from his shoulders; but it stayed on because the sleeves jammed against the bulky gloves he was wearing.

Chuck demanded of no one in particular, "Mittens off!"

His mother said nothing and made no move to help.

Chuck resolutely walked over to his mother.

Standing before her with his coat sagging, he soberly held out his hands.

The mother reached over toward him.

Then, while he helped by pulling back a little, she tugged off his gloves.

Chuck wriggled on out of his coat, letting it drop where he stood.

PUTTING WRAPS AWAY

His mother said firmly, "Chuck, put your hat and coat away."

He just stood there.

His mother repeated her command, this time very firmly.

Chuck asked, looking impish, "Shall I get the ruler, Mommie?"

> Earlier in the day Chuck had refused to put away his wraps, whereupon his mother had said threateningly, "Now, where is my ruler?" So, in asking now if he should get the ruler, Chuck evidently was just beating his mother to the draw.

Chuck did not press the question about the ruler. Before his mother could answer it, he picked up his hat and coat.

Then he carried the wraps into the bedroom. He was smiling.

He returned to the living room at once.

The direction criterion is exemplified by the judgment that, so long as he behaved in the episode, *Going Inside*, Chuck was engaging without a break in the action which took him from a starting position—outdoors, on truck, near father—to a new position, inside the house, which he had intended to reach from the starting position. It is exemplified also by the judgment that, when Chuck began to take off his wraps, his behavior took a new directional "tack," whereupon a new episode began; and so on through the marked units of the sequence.

Several marks of directedness as a property of behavior have been proposed in the psychological literature. Certain of these are applicable, especially in conjunction with one another, as guides to the recognition of both change and maintenance of direction in a behavior sequence. Representative clues of this kind are listed below, each with a psychologist who has advocated it and also with an example, adapted in most instances from our specimen records.

1. Action persists in the absence of instigating conditions (McDougall: **40**).

> Mrs. Logan, the second grade teacher in Midwest says, "Turn, stand, pass," and Ben Hutchings proceeds to walk out of the classroom, to go on out of the building, and to continue walking a distance of three blocks until he reaches his home.

The instigating conditions act more like a goad than a continuing push from behind. They set the action off; then, in a sense, the action maintains itself, not in a situational vacuum; yet without the continuance of the initial stimulus factors.

2. Change in position toward a part of the environment is renewed after forced digression or delay[1] (McDougall: **40**).

> Raymond Birch uses his wagon to haul a large and wobbly old crate across a lot. The crate falls from the wagon repeatedly, and, each time it does, Raymond stops pulling the wagon, hurries to one side of it, works the crate back onto the wagon, *and* goes on his way.

3. "Preparatory adjustments" appropriate to imminent situational change, toward which the observed action contributes, accompany the action (McDougall: **40**).

> A Midwest 11-year-old "primps" often and turns repeatedly to look at her reflection in store windows while she half runs to a birthday party.

Here, there is a getting-readiness for the very state of affairs, or change in situation, which the action itself is tending to bring about. This getting-readiness in the behavior confirms the observation that the child is indeed, as a matter of psychological fact, going in the direction of the party.

McDougall gives as a classical example the postural and pointing adjustments of a predatory animal, stalking its prey.

4. Sustained locomotion is abruptly discontinued after an *end*, provisionally identified by the observer, has been reached (McDougall: **40**).

---

[1] Our version of what McDougall says about "variation in the direction of persistent movements."

Jimmy Hebb, observed across a street, is wandering somewhat lacka-daisically in his front yard, and has been so doing for several minutes. His head is bent. Every now and then he gets down on his hands and knees and runs his fingers through the grass. What *is* he doing? It begins to look as if he might be looking for a four-leaf clover. Confirmation is finally given to the best guess that all of the behavior does add up to an action toward this end when Jimmy looks at something in his left hand, audibly counts "1-2-3-4," and then flops down, stretches out on the grass and lies still for a few seconds.

It is as if the end sought had been the reason for the action's being, so that, with the end reached, the action loses its dynamics. Actually, however, one need not suppose, as we do not, that the end somehow causes the action; it appears, rather, only to be one of its necessary conditions.

5. Action between observable beginning and end points shows continuity (Koehler: **29**).

This holds for each of the foregoing examples. Throughout the length of such behavior segments there are no gaps. Differing individual, subordinate molar units of behavior occur. But these are scarcely seen singly, as a matter of course; one often has to search for them. The whole action, however, appears as a good figure. The distinguishable lesser actions show a connectedness that arises from their implementing progress toward the point of cessation.

6. Action between beginning and end points follows the shortest available path (Wheeler: **60**; Adams: **1**).

Ben Hutchings on his way home from school cuts across a vacant lot.

Ben might have gone "the longest way around," say, with a friend. In this case, however, we doubtless would have marked two overlapping episodes, the one: *Going Home from School*, and the other: *Walking with Friend*. Ben's continuously maintaining closest possible connection with *home* by taking the shortest available route implies directedness as a feature of the behavior and, beyond that, helps to establish the true action in progress.

There is considerable experimental evidence to show that this sign of directed action is a basic characteristic of molar behavior. Such evidence has been generalized by Adams (**1**) in terms of "parsimony," by Gengerelli (**20**) in the principle of "maxima and minima," by Bingham (**13**) in the rule of "easiest means," and by Wheeler (**60**) in the "law of least action."

7. Variance in behavior is concordant with variance in the position of an environmental object (Baldwin: **2**).

Stella Town is rushing pell mell back and forth across the school playground. What is *she* doing? Her behavior looks quite random and aimless—until the observer discovers Sammy Sherwin on the other side of a grouping of children, and finds that every time Sammy runs north or south, so does Stella. Now, the behavior looks thoroughly directed. And the particular directed action in progress is now evident. Stella is chasing Sammy, or, at least, as some other noted facts suggested, putting on a good show of doing same.

All of these indices are available alike to observers and to analysts of molar behavior and its conditions.   We cannot profess to their intentioned, systematic use in episoding.   Yet we do assume that these and probably other equally important signs of behavioral direction are used almost inevitably, both as evidence that an action by a person is in progress and as a means of telling one action from another, in common social intercourse and similarly in dividing a specimen record.   The degree in which the differing signs are effective presents a problem in social perception which is open to objective study.   The main point here in any case is that these indicators establish the empirical manageability of direction as an attribute of molar behavior units.

Notions that we have found particularly useful for the determination of both constancy and change in direction are those of *present position, change in position*, and *terminal intended position*.   Synonyms of terminal intended position are *goal* and *end*.   The episoder continually looks ahead to diagnose the end or the position intended from the present position of the person. Once a particular end has been fixed, all behavior seen to bring the person nearer to it is considered to lie in the same direction.   The observed progress can be great or small or in the limiting case it can be zero.   Also, a change in position can occur when there is no observable movement in physical space.   The person can move in a social sphere of action, as when a child speaks a piece, or in an intellectual sphere, as when a child solves a mathematical problem.

The behavior theory from which the episode stems is that an action changes the position of the person on a path in a space formed by a situation; the person locomotes on this path to or toward a sought end, a new, intended position.   The test, then, of whether a particular action proceeds at a given moment in the same direction as a preceding, simultaneous, or subsequent one is this: Does the action carry the person nearer to the end diagnosed for any one of the compared actions?   If it does not, its direction is different and the uniqueness of the action is established.   Two processes in episoding are implied here.   The first consists in diagnosing the end toward which the person is moving; and the second consists in judging whether the "movement" brings the person nearer to that end.   The total process is clearly circular.   The new position is determined from the behavior of the person and the direction of the behavior is determined from its relation to the new position.   In reality, however, the required judgments usually are not analytical.   The direction of the behavior in relation to the new position and vice versa generally are immediately apprehended; the unity of the action in an episode generally is perceived almost as immediately as the unity of a visual form or an auditory pattern.

In episoding, continual rediagnosis of the terminal intended position is essential.   A principle to be heeded here is that change in the position of a person can bring about a realignment of psychological forces such that, at any point, a new goal or end can arise.   Wesley Mead, in a darkened room, turns on a light. Then, at once, he goes to a wall and stands before it, looking at a picture. Is *Turning on Light* a separate episode or is it only the first phase of a larger episode, *Looking at Picture?* This question can be answered only by establishing whether or not, in turning on the light, Wesley intended to view the picture. If so, there is only the one larger episode; if not, there are the two smaller ones. We have found generally in such cases that the facts needed for a reasonably confident decision are available, although the alternatives are sometimes about equally cogent.

While, in episoding, sensitivity to change in direction is important, it must be balanced by sensitivity to maintenance of the same direction. Consider the following excerpt, which we have abbreviated slightly for the present purpose, from our day record on Chuck Thurston:

Mr. Thurston came to the doorway into the living room and said loudly, "Chuck, come here." This was a command.

Chuck went directly into the dining room.

His father said concisely, "Put your jacket up."

The jacket was on the floor by the stove where Chuck had earlier dropped it.

Chuck promptly took his jacket to the kitchen and hung it up.

Two possible ways of handling this sequence present themselves. The first is to divide it into two episodes: *Going to Dining Room*, and *Hanging Up Jacket*. The second is to discriminate only one episode: *Complying with Father's Command*. The critical requirement here is the one of diagnosing Chuck's terminal intended position, his goal, at the starting point where the father said, "Chuck, come here." Our decision was that the position intended at this point was not simply the one to be reached by standing in the dining room, but the one to be reached by doing what the father wanted done. We therefore chose the second of the alternatives. The meaning of the command to Chuck, as we read the record, was essentially, "My father wants me to do something. I'd better go do it." We took it that the command did not mean to Chuck merely: "My father wants me to go and stand beside him. I'd better do *that.*" The forces in the situation might have changed radically on Chuck's arrival in the dining room. These forces could have engendered a new terminal intended position, possibly even the one to be reached by *not* doing what the father wanted done. We judged, however, that no such change occurred; that, instead, essentially the same constellation of forces was maintained throughout the sequence, so that Chuck did one thing, i.e., moved in one direction, in one developing, yet relatively stable, situation. The judging by the episoder in this case may have been completely wrong. Only a principle, however, is at issue; namely, the one that an episode runs through the total length of an action toward a particular, terminal intended position. This principle is a cardinal feature of the method; for it reduces in fact to the criterion of constancy in direction.

A further complication here is that the goal of an episode is not necessarily reached. It can be relinquished, as in failure. Theoretically, however, if not always demonstrably, an episode never ends so long as the goal sought when it began persists. This provision we have generalized in the statement that the action in every episode extends through its issue, where issue means outcome, whether the outcome be failure, success, satiation, or some other terminal development in the behavior. Issue is defined more fully in Chapter VIII. When the person does fail or is forced to quit an action by pressure or blocking from without, and the goal is not relinquished, an interruption occurs, in which case the episode at stake may or may not be subsequently resumed. Pertinent examples will be reviewed when, at a later point, special consideration is given to the problems of episode interruption.

One secondary indicator of behavioral direction is expression of intent. This clue can be quite direct when the expression is verbal. Often, a person *announces* a terminal intended position which is then established by other behavior. Intention signals have to be used with care, however, as indicators of directional change. A principal reason for this is that they are not perfectly synchronized with the initiation of behavior in a new direction. Here in a slightly abbreviated excerpt, is a case in point from our day record on Raymond Birch.

Raymond picked himself up and started pulling the wagon westward, along the side of the Vocational Training building.

7:34 As he walked along, he muttered to himself, "I'll go get my crate."

He ran around the back of the building and headed for the pit, where he had been playing with the crate in the afternoon.

When he reached the pit, he crawled down into it and went straight to the crate.

He began tugging and pulling at the crate, trying to raise it up to the level of the vacant lot. He worked hard (8, 411).

The point where the episode begins seems clear. First, Raymond started after the crate. Then, later, he verbalized his intention to get it. He moved along toward the goal after telling us what was afoot; but he had, in fact, started earlier to do so.

There are a number of different circumstances under which expression of intent, whether verbal or nonverbal, does not lead into behavior in the direction which it suggests. Four that we have found in our records are as follows:

1. The child indicates an intention but at the same time shows realization of inability to carry it out.

2. The child indicates an intention, but outside pressure forces him to do other things. For example, Walter Kane states that he is going to climb a tree, but his mother makes him practice his music lesson.

3. The child indicates an intention but realizes that time must elapse before action toward it can be effective, as when Ben Hutchings announces a decision

to listen to "The Lone Ranger," but knows that the program will not be on the air until 30 minutes have passed.

4. The child indicates an intention, but sees the goal as relatively permanent and equally accessible at a later time, whereupon he seizes the opportunity to enjoy a more fleeting opportunity, as when Roy Eddy picks up the evening paper to read the "funnies," but puts it down when the radio announcer says that the "Jack Armstrong Program" is about to start.

In each of these cases the expression of intent is in itself an episode. But in none of them does it point to directed action beyond itself.

In using the present criterion, the episoder has to recognize that direction is a genotypic factor in behavior which can be clothed in diverse phenotypes; there are no behavioral specifics for either constancy or change in this behavior factor. One must recognize also that direction refers to an attribute of behavior as it is for the behaving person. This means that the observation of its constancy or change must always be tentative. One continually tests such observation in daily life by questioning the other person or by trying out various responses which prove more or less conclusively what the other person is "driving at" or aiming to get done. A similarly experimental approach must be followed in the episoding of a record. The same tests cannot be literally applied. Yet somewhat equivalent hypothetical tests are possible. Would the child feel interrupted if I broke the behavior here? Would the loss to the child be the same if I broke it here or there? We have found such probing useful. The major requirement of episoding from the standpoint of the direction guide, however, is considered to be a mastery of the genotype and wide familiarity with its differing manifestations.

OCCURRENCE WITHIN THE NORMAL BEHAVIOR PERSPECTIVE

Our second primary criterion of an episode concerns its size. We have seen that there is great variation along this dimension. To illustrate further, legitimate molar behavior units can differ in size from minimal ones, like *Stepping Down From Curb*, to short ones, like *Crossing Street*, to rather extended ones, like *Walking to School*, to long ones, like *Working to Pass From the Third Grade*, through still longer ones, like *Getting an Education*, to very long ones, like *Climbing to the Top in Life* or, if some psychologists are right, *Getting Revenge on Father*. All of these, with the probable exception of the last, could comprise for a child at one time a hierarchy of molar behavior units corresponding to a hierarchy of goals.

The importance of this factor for episoding derives in part from the fact that size of behavior unit and direction of behavior are related. A Midwest six-year-old who has been ordered sternly by his mother to stay at home first runs off to the school playground and then goes to the house of a friend. We would mark *Running to School Playground* and *Going to House of Friend* as separate episodes on the grounds that the two actions differ in direction.

But, within the compass of such a behavior cycle as *Breaking Away from Parental Domination*, for example, both could have the same direction and consequently belong to the same unit. This does not mean that the one judgment would contradict the other. Both could be true. The direction of flow of the Missouri River is 14 degrees south of east between Kansas City and St. Louis; it is 37 degrees east of south between the more inclusive points of Rapid City and New Orleans. Both statements are correct.

Some designation of limiting points on the continuum of behavior analogous to zone restrictions on a geographical map is needed here to fix the size range of episodes. How long is an episode? It is never the most extended detectable unit nor yet the shortest; episodes are somehow intermediate in size; they are the size of an entry in a diary, not the size of a chapter in a novel. This much we have considered. But more stable range indicators are required. We have tried to meet this need by defining an episode in terms of size as a molar behavior unit which the person himself perceives to be in progress. This specification designates the points on the behavior continuum within which episodes fall by means of a perceptual coördinate. It eliminates as subepisodic, molecular and short molar units that "run off" with no or only vague awareness by the person; and it eliminates also as superepisodic long units that are maintained outside the limits of clear perception. The span of attention or clear perception by the person of his own behavior-in-progress we have called the *normal behavior perspective*. Our second primary criterion places episodes within this span. As indicated in Chapter I, close correspondence between the action units within the normal behavior perspective of a subject and the action units seen by an observer is considered to hold. We will come back to this point after first developing some essentials of the basic concept.

The idea of behavior perspective brings to bear upon the perception by a person of his own behavior three characteristics of perception in general:

1. Selective awareness. The part of the action continuum within the behavior perspective is that part of it which stands out as figure against an undifferentiated behavioral background. Other parts of the continuum are in the peripheral zone of faint perception, while still others are presumed to lie entirely outside the perceptual field.

2. Limen of sensitivity. Just as the resolving power of sensory surfaces for visual, auditory, and other stimuli are finite, so that limens exist below which discrimination is impossible, there are corresponding limits of perception by the person of his own behavior. Some molecular units or actones cannot be perceived at all, as earlier suggested (see pp. 6 and 180), and some extended molar units are taken to be equally imperceptible.

3. Range of sensitivity. The range of stimuli for any sensory modality within which a person can discriminate is wider than the range within which he does discriminate. This also appears to hold for the behavior continuum. The range in size of the behavior segments which a person *can* perceive, from the largest episode in progress to the smallest perceptible actone, is greater than the size range of the segments which he normally *does* perceive. The maximum behavior perspective with the total range of sensitivity is achieved only by special techniques, as in cases of "insight" under clinical direction. This does not mean that the normal behavior perspective is rigidly fixed. It varies instead from moment to moment, although its limits appear to be quite sharply defined. The behavior units outside this range are real and legitimate. They are left out of direct account in episoding, however, for the reason that, by definition, a behavior unit which falls outside the perspective by the person on his own behavior is not an episode. Considered as a device of the present method, the behavior perspective is an aperture past which the continuum of action by a person must pass and through which one can see episodes of behavior. This perceptual coördinate, in other words, is a range finder. One can use it to say how big episodes are, to identify units of the prescribed size, and to exclude those which are either larger or smaller. On the other hand, it says nothing about the essential nature of an episode. Nor should it be taken to imply that episodes have only an heuristic, perceptual significance. An episode is rather a natural unit of action and situation with an integrity which depends first upon its dynamical and structural properties.

As the most generally perceived behavior units, episodes might reasonably be considered to have fundamental evolutionary significance. Just as there probably is survival value for man in the normal range of his visual acuity for size and distance, there also may be adaptive value in the normal behavior perspective. We might be grateful to see neither more nor less that it discloses of our own behavior. Self understanding and guidance would be inadequate if we saw much less, while stressfulness and confusion in living would seem likely to be increased if we saw much more. One cannot face cheerfully the prospect of a personal world always full of muscle twitches and lifetime undertakings any more than one can like the prospect of a physical world crowded by visible whirling atoms and planets. Insight into the longer parts of the behavior stream and into the ordinarily "hidden" motives which underlie them can occur and is now generally thought to be hygienic. But such insight comes only in "flashes" with the fortunate result that we do not have to live continually with its revelations. It seems a good thing also that we do not have to live any more continually with the small and the large behavior units outside the behavior perspectives of our associates.

How, in the dividing of a behavior sequence, are the limits of the behavior perspective to be set? What secondary guides can be used in the application of this primary criterion of an episode?

The nub of the problem here is that the behavior perspective of a person, like the direction of his behavior, is defined at bottom in terms of what exists for the person which means that, like direction, it cannot be observed directly. No observer can pretend to get into private worlds in using this or any other test for an episode. Yet certain marks of action limits are perceived no better by the person than by an observer. The observer sees from the outside what the person sees from the inside. The result is that we all are able to detect in the continuing behavior of our associates, units that evidently match well their behavior perspectives. Even children are remarkably sensitive to the intended boundary lines between the actions of their mothers, fathers, and teachers; children of five and six years know rather well, many exceptions to the contrary notwithstanding, when to break in or hold back on occasions when adults are intermittently busy.

Persons could not hope to get on well with others without ability to discriminate their intended actions. We have to know with a good deal of precision when the things our associates do and mean to do, begin and end. This ability seems as indispensable to our social relations as is object discrimination to our nonsocial relations. Without it, to say the least, we and others would be continually interrupting one another. But others do not generally cut in on our actions as we see them; nor do they generally complain of the reverse. On the other hand, persons do not commonly see in the daily lives of their associates, long trains of behavior which encompass lesser actions that differ in direction, and are thereby analogous to the direction from Rapid City to New Orleans. It is only when one deliberately adopts the characteristic orientation of the psychiatrist, the counselor, or the biographer that this happens.

The upshot here is that, in applying the criterion of occurrence within the normal behavior perspective, the episoder of a specimen record has available another one of the common skills which at the present stage in the development of psychological methods must be used in naturalistic studies. We have considered that factors with some effect upon this skill must include acquaintance with the subjects whose behavior sequences are to be divided, and commonality of cultural background as between the episoder and the subject.

Our experience indicates that facility in reading behavior perspectives in a record is influenced also by familiarity with the behavior settings entered and the behavior objects used by a child. The movies, scout meetings, basketball games, assigned chapters in school books, pencil sharpeners, ball bats, eating utensils, comic books, and skidovers (unknown outside the city limits) of Midwest provide at times, objective gauges of children's episodes. They often tell what Midwest children are about and signal intended beginning and end points of actions. These guides are useful because of their common meanings for persons who share the same milieu. This is not to say that there is no danger in admitting such meanings as psychological. A mother looks from her living room window toward the Midwest school yard, a block away, to discover her seven-year-old son there with a group of classmates. Suddenly, the boy jumps high into the air and flays his arms about with great vigor. Observing from her point of vantage, the mother might see in this behavior an exuberant celebration of the additional milieu fact that school has just been dismissed for the summer. But were she to become aware of the actual nonpsychological supports for the behavior, namely, a swarm of small red ants, her observation would be radically altered. Not that knowledge of the physical presence of the ants would alone establish their psychological significance. Yet this knowledge together with what one can see of the boy's behavior provides a basis for determining what occurs within his behavior perspective.

Change in behavior perspective is coördinated generally with change in the direction of behavior. The perspective of the person on his own behavior accommodates itself, so to speak, to his goals, which depend upon dynamical as well as perceptual conditions. We have seen that a person can be involved at one time in a hierarchy of behavior units corresponding to a hierarchy of goals. In every such case an episoder must answer this question: At the end of which behavior segment in the hierarchy does the subject's present behavior perspective end? The unit alignment in the case of the child who, while *Stepping Down From Curb*, might also have been doing some other bigger things, can be represented as in Figure 7.1.

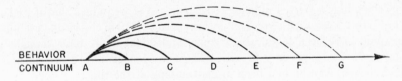

BEHAVIOR
CONTINUUM   A   B   C   D   E   F   G

A TO B: STEPPING DOWN FROM CURB
A TO C: CROSSING STREET
A TO D: WALKING TO SCHOOL
A TO E: WORKING TO "PASS" FROM THE THIRD GRADE
A TO F: GETTING AN EDUCATION
A TO G: CLIMBING TO THE TOP IN LIFE

FIG. 7.1.—An action hierarchy. The shading of the arcs from left to right stands for progressive diminution in the perceptual clarity of the behavior units. Each broken arc represents a unit judged to lie outside the behavior perspective.

If the assumption be made that each of these behavior units is in progress at point A, we can be sure that, at this point, the behavior perspective of the subject ends at one of the positions B, C, D, E, F, or G. This at least limits the possibilities. Our rule in practice has been to fix the end of the behavior perspective at that position beyond which there is no *positive* evidence for perception by the child of a more remote terminal intended position. We have used as a test query, the question: What, *at the most*, is the child doing as far as he is concerned? To strengthen this test, we have asked: What, now, is the *longest* action which the child could name if one were to confront him directly with the inquiry: What are you doing?

A sequence from the record on Raymond Birch parallels closely parts of the fictional one, above.   At 8:26 a.m. on April 22, 1949, Raymond's mother notified him in a pleasant way that he should be off for school.   Immediately:

Raymond went down the steps to the street level (**8**, 50).

At 8:33, seven minutes later:

Raymond walked very briskly onto the schoolgrounds (**8**, 55).

Next, he just stood a while watching two snarling dogs.

We have marked off as an episode the segment of behavior and situation which began when, at 8:26, Raymond "went down the steps," and ended when he set foot on the schoolgrounds.   We had positive evidence from Raymond's demeanor at the time and from subsequent developments that, at 8:26, he saw reaching the schoolgrounds as a terminal intended position. But we could find no positive evidence that at the time he was moving toward *and also* looking ahead to a position beyond the schoolgrounds.   We judged that, if we had asked Raymond at 8:26—What are you doing?—he *might* have said: "I'm getting down these steps."   We judged, however, that if this question had been pressed at all, Raymond probably would have said something like: "Why, I'm going to school."   Yet we judged that if we had asked—But, look, aren't you really working to pass from the second grade?— he would have been taken aback some, and might easily have thought in some way suited to seven-year-olds: "Those psychologists *are* deep," meaning much deeper than he had been in his thinking at the time.

In the judging of Raymond's behavior perspective here, another assumption was made.   We assumed that, if Raymond had been engaged at 8:26 in the pursuit of a goal, *which he saw*, beyond the schoolgrounds, some evidence to this effect quite probably would have been put in the record, which was made with intent to get down everything Raymond paid any attention to or showed concern about.   To be sure, the chances are high that if, beginning at 8:27, we had had a heart-to-heart talk with Raymond, or had called in a clinician to interview him, positive evidence might have been found that, at 8:26, below the surface, he was in fact working to "pass," really getting an education and even, say, breaking away from parental domination.   But such evidence could not have been used to extend the judged length of his behavior perspective, which is limited precisely to what lies on the surface.

In general, whatever the actual margin of error in our judgments of behavior perspective, we have found that these judgments usually can be made with high confidence on the basis of material in a specimen record. A protocol from a clinical interview probably would be more difficult to handle from this standpoint for the reason that it would contain both surface and "depth" description.   We can only say on this that a major aim of the present method is to try to make the most of description on the surface level.

Once the behavior perspective of a subject has been determined, episodes, by definition, must be marked within its limits. Yet it can include more than a single episode. This holds when, but only when, overlapping occurs, in which case the beginning and end points of each overlapping unit are set by limits deriving from constancy in direction, or from the third major determinant of an episode, which remains to be defined. Our episoding to date has not turned up instances in which a behavior perspective was judged to include more than four simultaneously overlapping episodes.

The idea of behavior perspective is related in some respects to the concept of *time perspective* (cf. Frank: **19**). Both refer to perception by the person of processes within the continuum of behavior. Time perspective, however, is broader in scope. It embraces all of the psychological present, past, and future as these are seen by the person. Behavior perspective extends through only a part of the person's *behavior in progress*, namely, the part within the span of clear perception. Actions which have been carried out or which are yet to be undertaken may also be perceived by the person in virtue of time perspective; but, as units not in progress, these fall outside the behavior perspective.

Figure 7.2 may clarify the foregoing on behavior perspective in relation to time perspective. Every arc in each figure represents an episode. The changing

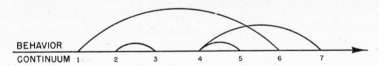

A. CONSECUTIVE AND SIMULTANEOUS EPISODES

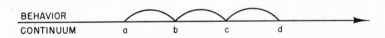

B. CONSECUTIVE BEHAVIOR UNITS

Fig. 7.2.—Relationships between units of the behavior continuum.

behavior perspective through the sequence of Figure 7.2*A* is such that the person sees *in progress:*

> one unit from *1* through *2*;
> two overlapping units from *2* through *3*;
> one unit from *3* through *4*;
> three overlapping units from *4* through *5*;
> two overlapping units from *5* through *6*; and
> one unit from *6* through *7*.

Only a single one of the units represented in Figure 7.2B can exist at one time within the behavior perspective of the person inasmuch as there is no point from a through d at which more than one action is in progress. The behavior perspective, then, never extends through successive behavior units. This does not hold for the time perspective of a person which, in the case of the sequence in Figure 7.2B might encompass all three of the indicated units at any point from a through d. For example, at point a, the person could see all of the units as lying ahead; or, at point d, each unit could be seen as lying behind—within time perspective limits. Also, time perspective could conceivably include all of the units in Figure 7.2A at any point from 1 through 7.

What is the child now doing, at the most, as he sees it? The behavioral range sought by this question, later formulated in terms of behavior perspective, was our first explicit guide to episoding. We applied it at the outset to specimen day records. Our case for it was that a day of episodes, defined from this standpoint, would represent the parts of a child's day as they were for him. Such representation provides a defined base of one kind for work on a variety of psychological problems.

SUPERIOR WHOLE POTENCY

Episodes are sometimes *undivided*, single-molar-unit events, as when a child answers only "Yes" or "No" to a question. *Commenting on Cold* of the Chuck Thurston sequence, above, is another example of an undivided episode. More often than not, however, an episode is *divided* into consecutive parts. The reader can easily find in *Going Inside* from Chuck's day (see pp. 236–37), for example, such episode divisions as *jumping down from truck, trotting ahead of father*, and *bounding into house*. These parts of the total episode are all lesser action-and-situation units. It holds for every divided episode, moreover, that the person is "involved in" one of its part units or another at every moment while he is involved in the whole. The whole and the part coexist as units with some degree of independence, with each part both an action and a minor, dependent, included situation.

As a subordinate complex, every part unit of an episode makes a greater or lesser contribution while it is in progress to the whole of the ongoing behavior; each, compared with the whole, has a greater or lesser degree of importance for the total behavior of the person. To say this with better conceptual language developed by Lewin (cf. **34**, especially), every part, relative to the whole, has a greater or lesser degree of *potency* or *weight*. The potencies of the whole unit and any part unit are by definition relative to one another, so that when the weight of either goes up, that of the other goes down. A presently important feature of this relationship is that the relative weights of part and whole can differ from one segment of an episode to another. One might judge, for example, that as a part of *Going Inside*, *bounding into house* had a greater potency when it took place than just *trotting ahead of father* at the earlier time of its occurrence.

Our third primary criterion of an episode refers to the potency relationship of part to whole within the total episode unit. It provides that *an episode as a whole has greater potency than any of its parts.* Consider in this connection a group of persons. The unity of a social group depends in part upon group action in some one direction. But it depends also on potency relationships. The unity of a group can be destroyed in some cases if one of its members "outweighs" the entire group as a whole. It is the same with an episode. Its unity and integrity depend, not only upon constancy in direction of the included action, but also upon *superior whole potency.*

A corollary of this principle has decisive importance for the structure of behavior. The corollary follows: *If any part unit of a behavior sequence with a constant direction either exceeds or equals the whole in potency that unit becomes a separate episode.* It is as if a social group member were to achieve "overweening importance" and so become an "isolate." The basic rationale of the principle is that when a part unit in the stream of behavior does equal or exceed in potency an including whole unit, established as such by constancy in behavioral direction, it takes precedence over the whole, (a) in the behavior perspective of the person, and (b) in the total dynamics of the continuing behavior.

In the Chuck Thurston sequence, the action in *Getting Mittens Off* was considered to have the same direction as the action in *Taking Off Wraps.* But the episoder judged that, while Chuck was involved with the troublesome mittens, this lesser, included unit had at least as much weight as the whole of the larger, containing segment of behavior. *Getting Mittens Off* was therefore singled out as a separate episode. Units which are individuated in this way by superior *part* potency we have called *contained.* In terms of direction, every such unit is "enveloped" by a larger behavior segment. Yet, because of its superior relative potency, every such unit is made to stand alone in some degree as a part of the total stream of behavior. Every contained episode overlaps with the containing *parent* unit, for it necessarily occurs while the latter is in progress. Yet coexisting contained and containing episodes differ from other overlapping episodes in that they have the same direction, with the result that they leave the behavior continuum less widely split.

Superior whole potency and behavior perspective are conceptually independent of one another. Their behavioral indices are nonetheless correlated. In general, as the potency of a behavior unit goes down, it tends to move toward the periphery of the behavior perspective; and obviously a unit with zero potency could not be perceived at all by the person. Yet we have assumed that action units with relatively high potency can occur outside the behavior perspective. This might be considered to hold, for example, in the case of a somnambulistic trance.

In episoding, we have used as indicators of high potency (a) wide involvement of motor, verbal, and other behavior mechanisms, (b) "indifference" to potentially distracting conditions, and (c) high energy level of the behavior. We have found also that certain factors in the situation of the person are associated with high potency. These include (a) high resistance or obstruction and (b) strong interpersonal stimulation.

Relatively high potency, then, can segregate as an episode a *part* of a parent episode. One might well ask whether this principle applies to *any* part whatsoever of the latter. Our answer has been that it does not. The particular parts to which it does apply will be indicated in the succeeding section.

Secondary Complications in Behavior Structure

Episoding consists mainly in using the ideas of constancy in direction, behavior perspective, and superior whole potency as guides to the discrimination of episodes in a specimen record. But the method takes into account also a number of complications in behavior structure arising from special characteristics of episodes.

EPISODE PARTS

There are, again, both undivided and divided episodes. We have found in divided episodes three classes of parts. Although these are not marked off in episoding, they have significance for the process of dividing a record and for the larger problem of behavior structure.

1. *Phases.* An action hierarchy, such as the one shown in Figure 7.2 presents a scale of varying inclusiveness. From top to bottom in every such hierarchy the behavior units decline in size, where size is defined by the number of subordinate units each includes. A phase is the smallest behavior segment in an action hierarchy. As such, it is a minimal unit of action in the sense that descriptive subdivision of it would break it into actones (see pp. 179–80). A phase, then, is an irreducible part of an episode.

Take Chuck Thurston's *jumping down from truck* as a part of *Going Inside*. This we see as a phase. We find in it something Chuck did in relation to molar parts of his environment. *Bounding into the house* is taken to be another phase in this episode which, as such, also presents something Chuck did. But we can find no recorded evidence of *actions* by this child within these phases. Divide the jumping unit and you get movements of the arms, trunk, and legs. Divide the bounding unit and you get comparable molecular adjustments. Divide either unit and you get, not actions, but actones.

The phase, like an episode, contains an action and also its own minor set of conditions or context. Dynamically, it differs from an episode principally in that the action in a phase is directed toward a subgoal, whereas the action in an episode is directed toward a goal which, within the limits of the behavior perspective, is terminal. As a minimal molar unit of behavior toward a subgoal, a phase action contributes one step in the direction of the terminal goal of an episode.

A practical complication in episoding concerns what we have called *precursory* and *sequent* phases. Both are irregular in that the action in a phase of either class differs in direction from the action in the larger episode unit. Otherwise, both are like any other phase. It is emphasized especially that both are regular as to potency, which means that a unit of each type always is lower in weight than the including episode. In the face of the stated irregularity, a precursory or sequent phase is considered to belong with an episode as an integral part unit.

A precursory phase amounts to a step which takes the person up to that point at which the prevailing action of an episode begins; it is linked functionally with the prevailing action as a necessary antecedent. A sequent phase, on the other hand, amounts to a step out of an episode; it is linked functionally with the prevailing action as a necessary or at least "natural" sequel. Likely examples of precursory and sequent phases, respectively, are the entrance before and the exit after a speech.

Examining Scrap of Rubber, which overlaps with *Going to School* of the Raymond Birch sequence, begins with a precursory phase, reproduced below:

Then he kicked the dirt and dust lying in the street by the curb.

The same episode ends with a sequent phase, as follows:

He tossed the piece of rubber aside, not noting where he threw it.

Note that kicking at dirt and examining rubber must not be directed toward the same terminal intended position; as far as one can tell from the record, Raymond did not even know the rubber was there when he did the kicking. Note also that tossing the rubber aside just as clearly diverges in direction from examining it. Further, the potency of each unit is judged to be lower than the potency of the episode to which it is assimilated. Otherwise, each would be made an episode in itself. If, for example, Raymond had stubbed his toe severely in kicking the dirt, probably the kicking would have been made to stand alone perceptually for an observer; and probably, in this case, it would have stood alone, both perceptually and with dynamical independence, for Raymond, even if he had nonetheless gone on to pick up the rubber and examine it. Picking up the rubber, incidently, we judge to lie as a means toward an end in the same direction as the examining.

Precursory and sequent phases are not highly frequent. They occur often enough, however, that some systematic provision for them is necessary. In the absence of such provision, the direction principle would often require the marking off as episodes of units with very meager content which, moreover, probably are seldom real units in the behavior perspective of the person.

At one stage in the dividing of our records, phases were marked (each by a line extending to the vertical part of an episode bracket). This has some advantages, especially for the study of behavior structure. We concluded, however, that discrimination of phases is unnecessary for most purposes in later work with episodes. Yet we have found it clarifying in episoding to think in terms of phases. Having first gained familiarity with a record as a whole and with the section of it at hand, one reads phase by phase and asks concerning each one: Is this, or is it not, the same in direction as the one before it? We have found that this practice makes for reliable identification of episodes (especially relatively short, overlapping ones) which would otherwise be missed.

2. *Stages.* Once begun, the prevailing action of an episode continues until a new action begins. This follows from constancy in direction as a primary criterion of an episode. We have left implicit until now a further consequence of the direction principle, the one, namely, that an episode characteristically encompasses not only the behavior in getting to the region of a terminal intended position or goal, but also the behavior in going through the goal region. Each of these two behavior segments, with its context, we have called a *stage*. The behavior and situation in "getting there" extend through a *transitive stage*, while the behavior and situation in "being there" extend through a *consummatory stage*. A transitive stage is illustrated by getting an ice cream cone, through the point of handing the clerk a nickel, while eating the cone illustrates a consummatory stage.

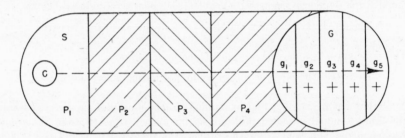

FIG. 7.3.—Transitive and consummatory stages of an episode. The small circle represents the child, *C*. *S* is the starting region of the episode, *G* the goal region. *S*, as the starting region, is the first part (P_1) of the *path* to the goal; while P_2, P_3, and P_4 are interpolated path regions. *G* is differentiated into parts g_1, g_2, g_3, g_4, and g_5. Also, all parts of *G* are homogeneously plus, or equally *valent*, as shown by the plus signs of equal size. The cross-hatching of the interpolated path regions represents resistances, which are lacking in the goal area.

The part of the broken arrow through P_4 represents behavior through the transitive stage, while the part of it in *G* represents behavior through the consummatory stage. All of the conditions outside the large circle make up the transitive part of the total situation; all of the conditions inside the circle make up the consummatory part of the situation.

To illustrate: At *S*, *C* asks for and receives a nickel for an ice cream cone. Through P_2, he gets his bike out of the garage; through P_3 he rides downtown on the bike; through P_4, he extends a nickel to the clerk with one hand, and takes a cone with the other. *C* encounters some resistance in each part of the whole path, beginning with the first, in which his mother is reluctant.

Through *G*, *C* eats the cone. At g_1, he takes the first lick; at g_2, the second; at g_3, the third; etc. All of these licks are fine; the next one is not appreciably better than the present one; there are no bigger plusses ahead to be struggled toward. Also, in *G*, resistances are virtually zero and distances to be traversed are minimal. In all, *C* can relax and enjoy himself, in *G*.

Strictly, the shift from a transitive to a consummatory stage of an episode incurs change in direction of the continuing behavior. The behavior in a transitive stage is directed from one part to another more or less distant part of the person's situation. The behavior in a consummatory stage, as action in relation to a goal area which the person has entered, is directed toward the present region. This difference, however, is not as great as it might at first seem; for, in every observable case of consummatory action, the present region, i.e., the goal area, is differentiated into parts from one to another of which action is continuously in progress, which means that in a consummatory stage the present position and the intended terminal position of the person are not identical. Yet the person is at each moment in a "plus" area; and, characteristically, as in a game played purely for fun (so that "the running is as good as the winning"), all parts of this area are homogeneously *plus*. One is not "spurred on" or "attracted," and meanwhile made more or less miserable, by something better at a distance. Also, resistances and distances to things seen ahead are virtually zero in a consummatory stage whereas, in a transitive stage, they can be maximally high. These points are represented in Figure 7.3.

In theory, both of these consecutive stages occur generally in a complete episode. It does not hold, however, that both always appear in behavior. Often, as far as one can see, the goal is only a point reached rather than an area enjoyed. A consummatory stage cannot be observed so long as this is true. When Raymond walked briskly onto the schoolgrounds, he reached the goal in *Going to School*. But there was nothing in the record to show that the region of this goal was differentiated. As far as one could observe, a new goal was instigated at once by those barking and snarling dogs with the outcome, for the observer, at least, that the terminal position in *Going to School* was an undifferentiated area or *point region* which Raymond reached and passed through at one and the same time.

Conversely, it is sometimes impossible to observe a transitive stage. Shortly before crossing the busy street, Raymond digressed from his path to school to the extent of behaving through the following episode.

ROCKING BENCH

He sat down on one of the benches [on the Courthouse yard] with a pleasant, relaxed expression.

He rocked the bench back and forth for a few seconds, sitting with his hands stretched out and holding the edges of the bench to brace himself. His feet were out in front of him, flat on the ground.

He hummed a little to himself, very softly, contentedly.

He jumped up and began rocking the bench as he stood on the ground at one end of it. He held onto the seat and the back and pushed the bench back and forth.

He gave me the feeling of his having lots of energy ready to spill over, although he was going about all this rather quietly (**8**, 51).

We can find here only a consummatory stage, with the possible exception of the first phase, in which Raymond sits down on the bench.

In line with the foregoing, on the basis of what has appeared in our records, we have distinguished transitive episodes, consummatory episodes, and episodes which are both transitive and consummatory. Here are titles of some transitive episodes from a day record on Mary Ennis:

> *Looking for Socks*
> *Getting Milk from Refrigerator*
> *Making Own Bed*
> *Working Problem on Blackboard*

The following are titles of consummatory episodes from a day record on Jimmy Sexton:

> *Bouncing on Bed*
> *Drinking Milk*
> *Singing to Self*

Below are representative titles of episodes with both a transitive and a consummatory stage:

> *Hanging and Admiring Picture*
> *Retrieving and Bouncing Ball*

We have said that an episode includes characteristically both a transitive stage and a consummatory stage, but that one or the other may not be evident to an observer. We have said further that, when only a transitive stage can be seen, we mark off a transitive episode; and that, when only a consummatory stage can be seen, we mark off a consummatory episode. Beyond this, in a number of cases, special considerations have led us to discriminate *as separate episodes* consecutive behavior segments *both of which are seen* and respectively look like transitive and consummatory stages.

It is important for these cases that the transition from a transitive to a consummatory stage does incur a shift in direction of the continuing behavior, with this shift consisting in a change from behavior toward a goal region to behavior through, or from part to part within, a goal region. In some instances, once this shift has been made, the region of the goal "expands." The person appears to find more in it than he can be presumed to have expected in moving toward it as a terminal, intended position. It looks to be a goal region, clearly enough, with parts about homogeneously plus; and apparently it presents no appreciable resistances to be overcome or distances to be traversed. But it also looks to be more than *the* goal region which the person sought through the antecedent transitive part of the behavior. One doubts that, during this antecedent segment, the expanded goal area did exist in the behavior perspective of the person as a part of the total action in progress. For these or whatever reasons, the two units do not look to the observer as if they belong together. This, we have considered always, is the paramount fact to be weighed by the episoder; his perceptions, when they are clear and confident, must be better than any formal notions at the present stage of our stupidity in the systematic part of social psychology. Yet there are the indicated reasons of principle as to why the two units are not parts of one whole for the child and therefore should not be expected to look as if they were to the observer. Confronted with sequences of the indicated sort, at any rate, we have marked off two episodes.

Our day record on Chuck Thurston presents a case in point. Chuck spent the morning playing in and around the Midwest Hardware and Implement Store, where his father and brother were employed. He amused himself for some time with a miniature scale model tractor and several matched accessories. At last, he noticed some new toys on a shelf five feet above the floor level. He set out at once to get one of these, a truck, which was still in its box. First, Chuck asked his brother, Al, who was working nearby, to give him the truck. Then, while waiting for Al to act, Chuck made a half-hearted effort to climb up and get the toy himself. Al refused to help. Next, Chuck begged for help from George Grim, another employee, but George went to the front of the store, leaving Chuck alone with his problem. At last, Chuck managed to climb up to the shelf. He could barely reach the truck, but finally did get it down. Eagerly, he drew the truck out of the box. It had taken him nearly six minutes of sustained effort to reach this goal. Then, what? Chuck put the truck on the floor with his other toys and played happily with it for another five minutes before turning to something new. During this period, he did many different things with the truck. He pushed it along the floor, raised and lowered its dump bed, scrutinized its parts carefully, and experimented with it in a great variety of ways.

We saw in this sequence two courses of action, the first transitive, and the second consummatory. The possibility of treating these as consecutive stages of one episode was carefully considered. But we at last made them two episodes, *Getting Truck* and *Playing with Truck*. In the first place, this is how we confidently saw the two units. Perceptually, the first did not run smoothly into the second; not as in *Getting and Eating Cone*, *Hanging and Admiring Picture*, or *Retrieving and Bouncing Ball*; not for the episoder, nor, as we judged, for the child. The two units *appeared* to belong apart. The reasons, in principle, for setting them apart, as episodes, we have anticipated.

A transitive or a consummatory stage may or may not be divided into subordinate phases. A person can reach a goal by one unified action, a minimal molar unit, as in taking a glass from a tray; or he may have to go through a number of steps, as in working most mathematical problems. Also, to turn from a transitive to a consummatory stage, one can move through a goal region in one minimal action, as in drinking the water in the glass with one tilt; or one can go through the goal part of a situation stepwise, as in eating through the courses of a holiday feast.

Ordinarily, divided consummatory action presents no difficult problems. Sometimes, however, a sequence may at first appear to present several short episodes, whereas its further study in context leads to the recognition of one continuous behavior unit in an activity area with the characteristics of a goal; a child first seen to be flitting from one thing to another may be seen on a second view to be just where he wants to be and to be doing what he wants to do while he enjoys the different parts of one activity region. Here is a pertinent sequence, also from the Raymond Birch record:

He ran swiftly to the flag pole.

He picked up the baseball bat which was lying nearby.

He leaned leisurely against the flag pole and tapped it softly a few times with the bat, holding the bat behind him.

He wandered a few steps from the flag pole. As he walked along, he swung the bat from side to side in front of him a few times, cutting a wide half-circle in the air each time.

Then he energetically swung the bat up and down, straight above his head and down in an arc through his legs, as he leaned forward.

The movement involved his whole body.

He took hold of the bat with both hands, one hand grasping the head of the bat and the other hand the base.

He held it out horizontally in front of him and knocked it against the flag pole several times, making a louder noise than he had before.

Next he clutched the bat with his left hand and banged at the flag pole even harder.

He looked up questioningly at the top of the pole as he struck at it (**8**, 169–70).

Monkeying Around With Bat

It is our guess that, if someone had asked Raymond at any time during this sequence—"What are you doing?"—his reply would have been close in meaning to the title of the episode, *Monkeying Around with Bat*. It seems unlikely that he would have listed discriminable subordinate actions. Raymond, we judge, was just having fun with a bat. The total unit, accordingly, becomes a one-stage, consummatory episode.

3. *Sections.* We have seen that a phase is directed toward a subgoal on the way to the terminal goal in an episode. A transitive stage can include also any number of superordinate subgoals to which the lesser goals in a series of phases are subordinate. The behavior directed toward such a superordinate subgoal, together with the context of this behavior, we have called a *section*. Such a unit always is made up of more than one, but fewer than all, of the phases in a divided transitive stage. Structuring of this kind does not occur in a con-summatory stage, where all phases, as steps in a terminal goal region, are on the same valence level, with the result that a superordinate subgoal cannot occur. But for its high potency, *Crossing Street* of Raymond's going-to-school sequence would be a section.

These intermediately large parts of an episode have theoretical importance for study of the hierarchical structuring of behavior. Also, they have a practical application in episoding for the reason that episodes individuated by potency are almost invariably units which, were it not for their relatively high weight, would be sections, the only exceptions being contained episodes which, but for the same reason, would be phases. What this comes to follows: *Given a behavior sequence with a constant direction toward a terminal goal, no part of that sequence is ever segregated as a contained episode unless it has integrity based upon constant direction toward the superordinate subgoal of a section* (or in some rare cases, the minor subgoal of a phase). It turns out, then, that a contained episode, like any other, has its own beginning and end, from which it follows that, within the frame of the parent unit, it is unique in direction. *A contained episode may therefore be said to conform in principle to uniqueness in direction as the pivotal test of an episode*:

This qualification of the potency criterion is an important episoding guide. Without it, sequences of behavior are sure to be broken into fragments without integrity. Here, to illustrate, is the middle part of an episode from a day record of Wally Wolfson, through the earlier course of which Wally has been trying to get his mother to give him a cooky; over and over again he has been asking the mother to give him the cooky.

> Wally wheedled, "Ben wants one, too. We just want two cookies." He was trying to make this sound very reasonable.
>
> Wally's mother did not answer.
>
> Again Wally asked in a very whiny voice, "Can Ben and I have cookies?"
>
> The mother answered from the kitchen, still pleasantly, "No."
>
> Now Wally dropped his head onto the arm of the chair which stood near the door.
>
> He cried very mildly as he said, "Mommy, can't I have just one?"—very plaintively.
>
> His mother didn't answer.
>
> "Just a cooky? Just *one* cooky?" Wally pleaded, sounding heartbroken.
>
> His mother said, "No, I'm getting supper," in a reasonable tone of voice.

As the episode continued, Wally calmed down considerably, but went on repeatedly begging for the cooky, essentially as he had been doing from the first, going step by step, with each step like the last and the one ahead in turns of apparent intent, and with no point on the whole behavior course outstanding as a superordinate subgoal, until at last his mother gave in.

We considered tentatively the possibility of discriminating as an episode that part of the sequence marked by the bracket on the grounds that, beginning with the whining, it was of greater potency than the whole. This possibility was rejected, however, for the reason that the segment does not form an integral subwhole; it does not end with a superordinate subgoal; it does not have a self-contained subordinate beginning and end; it certainly is not just a phase, and it is not a section. It is an essentially unbounded part of a continuous course. It has some qualitative uniqueness because of the high emotional involvement while Wally whines and pleads; but it is in no way unique directionally as a behavior unit. It does not stand out alone *structurally* on any basis. One can hardly suppose that Wally saw it as an independent whole. To segregate it as a separate unit would be to leave for analysis, emasculated first and last halves of the parent episode. Contrast this segment with *Crossing Street*, by Raymond, or *Getting Mittens Off*, by Chuck Thurston. *Crossing Street* is a well defined subwhole. It does end with a superordinate subgoal; it has a self-contained beginning and end; and, in short, it would be a section but for its high relative weight. All of the same is considered to hold for *Getting Mittens Off* in relation to *Getting Out of Wraps* for four-year-old Chuck.

Episode parts are themselves real integral units of a behavior sequence. Because of their limited content little could be gained and, because of their dependence upon the including episode, probably much would be lost by singling them out for separate analysis. Yet it may now be evident that it is necessary to consider these subordinate units with great care in any attempt to divide a behavior sequence validly or to understand its structure.

OVERLAPPING

Overlapping can be defined now as a complication in behavior structure such that different episodes occur, wholly or in part, at one time. A length of the action stream within the behavior perspective of the person bifurcates so that one segment of behavior with its context intersects in time with another. These statements imply that each of any two or more overlapping episodes has a potency greater than zero. We have touched on overlapping at several points in the chapter. Here, particulars stated earlier will be reviewed and others will be added.

Overlapping episodes differ in purely geometric interrelationships. Chapter VIII will reëxamine these different interrelationships as they have been demonstrated in specimen records. They must be considered here, however, for the reason that all are critically important for the theory and process of episoding.

We have distinguished three major types of overlap, the *coinciding*, the *enclosing-enclosed*, and the *interlinking*, each of which is graphed by episode brackets in Figure 7.4. Examples of the enclosing-enclosed type are abundant in the episoded sequences which have been presented in the chapter. One instance of interlinking occurs in the Margaret Reid sequence, on page 228. A common example of the coinciding type, which we have found to be rare in our records, is that of the man who starts to read the morning paper on beginning to eat breakfast and lays the paper aside on swallowing a last sip of coffee.

For some purposes, it is useful to focus on the relationship which a given single episode sustains to one with which it overlaps. From this point of view, four types of overlapping episodes can be distinguished in line with the statements, above, and in line with the diagrams of Figure 7.4:

A *coinciding episode* (CND) is one such that the whole of it intersects with the whole of another.

An *enclosing episode* (ENG) is one such that a part of it overlaps with the whole of another.

An *enclosed episode* (END) is one such that the whole of it intersects with a part of another.

An *interlinking episode* (ITG) is one such that a part of it overlaps with a part of another.

To this list there must be added the *isolated episode,* which is defined as one that does not intersect at any time during its course with any other unit.

As many as four, though very rarely more than three, episodes have been found to overlap at one time in our records. One consequence of simultaneous overlap involving more than two units is that, in terms of the structural relationships which it sustains to others, a particular episode can

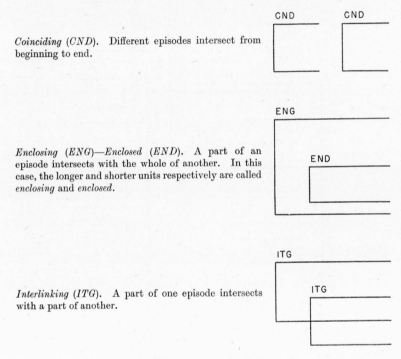

Coinciding (CND). Different episodes intersect from beginning to end.

Enclosing (ENG)—Enclosed (END). A part of an episode intersects with the whole of another. In this case, the longer and shorter units respectively are called *enclosing* and *enclosed*.

Interlinking (ITG). A part of one episode intersects with a part of another.

FIG. 7.4.—Different types of episode overlap.

be of mixed type. At one time, for example, one unit can be enclosed in relation to a second while it is enclosing in relation to a third, and interlinking in relation to a fourth.

These statements have dealt entirely with simultaneous overlap. It has to be considered further that, as some of the illustrative episoded sequences here have shown, different episodes can overlap sequentially with a given episode in progress, as shown in Figure 7.5*A*.

Also various complications are possible in a sequence of simultaneous overlaps. More or less extended linkages of overlapping episodes can occur, as in Figure 7.5*B*, which includes also an isolated episode, from a record on two-year-old Mary Chaco.

The gap between a *linkage* and another linkage or an isolated episode we have called a *break*.   In this relation, it also is convenient to identify an isolated episode as a *link*.

Further development of these specifications is left to Chapter VIII.

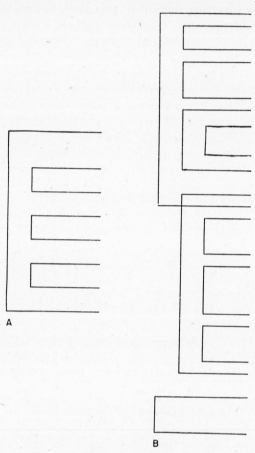

Fig. 7.5.—Types of overlapping episodes.

RELATIVE WEIGHT

A centrally important feature of the dynamical relationship between episodes which overlap is their weight or potency in relation to one another.

While it is convenient to refer to the potency of an episode as such (or one of its parts), potency is more strictly a characteristic of the situation *in* an episode.   This concept refers specifically to the degree in which the total behavior of a person is determined by the forces of a situation which the person has entered and in which the person is presently behaving.   To say that a person is in a situation is to say that its forces are now operative in some degree, so that it has some importance for the total ongoing behavior.

Thus, each situation of any two or more that overlap has a potency greater than zero.

The weights of overlapping situations are always relative, so that, if the weight of one increases, that of the other must go down commensurately. If a person is in only one situation, as in the case of a single undivided episode, it has by definition a potency of 1, which implies that, at the given time, the potency of all other situations is zero. Stating that a person is in only one situation or saying that a situation the person is in has a potency of 1 are different ways of saying the same thing. When more than one present situation exists, as in the case of overlapping episodes, the potency of each must vary between .9 and .1.

The problems of scaling potency values and of establishing criteria for their determination is left for later consideration (see pp. 278–79). Meanwhile, it will be necessary to use this concept in dealing with the following complication in behavior structure.

INTERRUPTION

It does not hold, as mentioned in our discussion of constancy in direction, that the action in every episode necessarily reaches its goal. This is to recognize that an episode can be discontinuous or incomplete. Using here a common term which refers to any "break in an otherwise continuous course" (American College Dictionary), we say in all such cases that the episode is interrupted. Interruption in this sense is a common psychological event. We have found that it occurs appreciably in the behavior in our records (see pp. 294–95). Also, it has figured significantly in experimental research, especially in the studies by Rickers-Ovsiankina (48) and Zeigarnik (65) of certain consequences of unfinished tasks. If only for these reasons, we have tried to develop clearly the meaning of interruption for episoding.

We have defined interruption by a drop in the potency of an interrupted episode to zero before the person has reached his goal in the prevailing action. This criterion is taken to imply that need tension corresponding to the unreached goal persists after the interrupting break. We have considered further that such persisting tension can undergo diffusion in time or that it can act to "bring the person back" to the interrupted behavior unit. This means that an interrupted episode may or may not be resumed. We have marked interruption in episoding, however, only when resumption does occur. This arbitrary practice has been followed because, throughout an extended period of experimenting, we were never able to establish clearly, in the absence of resumption, the persistence of unreleased tension following an interrupting break.

Here, in a sequence from Wally Wolfson, is how interruption looks in a record. Wally, a disabled four-year-old, is trying hard to coast in his wagon during a period of play with two older boys, Jim and Ben.

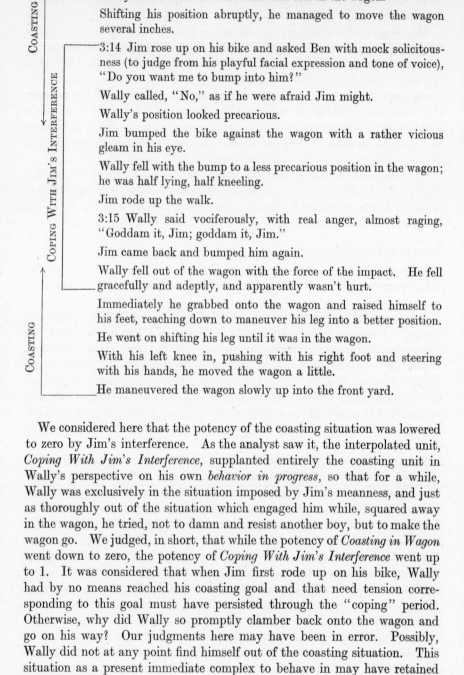

Wally raised himself on his arms and feet in the wagon.

Shifting his position abruptly, he managed to move the wagon several inches.

3:14 Jim rose up on his bike and asked Ben with mock solicitousness (to judge from his playful facial expression and tone of voice), "Do you want me to bump into him?"

Wally called, "No," as if he were afraid Jim might.

Wally's position looked precarious.

Jim bumped the bike against the wagon with a rather vicious gleam in his eye.

Wally fell with the bump to a less precarious position in the wagon; he was half lying, half kneeling.

Jim rode up the walk.

3:15 Wally said vociferously, with real anger, almost raging, "Goddam it, Jim; goddam it, Jim."

Jim came back and bumped him again.

Wally fell out of the wagon with the force of the impact. He fell gracefully and adeptly, and apparently wasn't hurt.

Immediately he grabbed onto the wagon and raised himself to his feet, reaching down to maneuver his leg into a better position.

He went on shifting his leg until it was in the wagon.

With his left knee in, pushing with his right foot and steering with his hands, he moved the wagon a little.

He maneuvered the wagon slowly up into the front yard.

We considered here that the potency of the coasting situation was lowered to zero by Jim's interference. As the analyst saw it, the interpolated unit, *Coping With Jim's Interference,* supplanted entirely the coasting unit in Wally's perspective on his own *behavior in progress,* so that for a while, Wally was exclusively in the situation imposed by Jim's meanness, and just as thoroughly out of the situation which engaged him while, squared away in the wagon, he tried, not to damn and resist another boy, but to make the wagon go. We judged, in short, that while the potency of *Coasting in Wagon* went down to zero, the potency of *Coping With Jim's Interference* went up to 1. It was considered that when Jim first rode up on his bike, Wally had by no means reached his coasting goal and that need tension corresponding to this goal must have persisted through the "coping" period. Otherwise, why did Wally so promptly clamber back onto the wagon and go on his way? Our judgments here may have been in error. Possibly, Wally did not at any point find himself out of the coasting situation. This situation as a present immediate complex to behave in may have retained some potency throughout. If our opinion had been that it did, we would have marked the two units as overlapping; such always is the alternative to the marking of interruption. Our best guess here, in any case, was that an interruption did occur.

Judging the occurrence of interruption is one of the most difficult requirements in episoding. One more example from our records, this one from a record on Sue Dewall, may help to clarify part of the problem.

Sue is in the sitting room at the Lawton Foundation. She has been watching television for 15 minutes. While she continues to do so steadfastly, Clara, an aide, steps into the room and tells Sue to go to the bathroom and wash for supper. Slowly and reluctantly, Sue gets up from her chair and edges her way out of the room, keeping her eyes on the screen as long as possible. Following a brief stay in the bathroom, she returns purposefully to the living room, where she sits down, turns again to the screen, and goes on watching television for 11 additional minutes.

This sequence clearly presents two episodes, *Watching Television*, and *Washing For Supper*. Yet it leaves the episoder with the question as to whether *Washing For Supper* interrupts or overlaps with *Watching Television*. With the occurrence of each episode assumed, only these two possibilities are open. What one has to do in choosing between them is to decide whether the relative weight of *Watching Television* is zero or greater than zero while *Washing For Supper* proceeds. Only a "unity supply" of potency, expressed by the value of 1.0, is available for the psychological situations of a person at any one time. Is this supply shared here, so to speak, by the two situations, or is it all used up by only one of them? While she behaves in the washing situation, is Sue also in the watching situation? These are like ways of stating the problem.

One thing to be noted is that *Washing For Supper* did take Sue outside the range of the necessary physical behavior supports for the other activity. It put her in a position such that appropriate "television action" was difficult on any level. Yet this is not decisive. Two other things stand out. One is that Sue left the television set with reluctance and the other is that she hurried back to it. Both might be taken to indicate something like an intervening continuance for Sue of the watching situation. But both can be viewed in the very opposite way. As the episoder saw it, the reluctant leaving meant, "Oh, now I have to move *out*," while the hurried returning meant, "I want to get back *in*"—the television situation. Our best guess was that, if we could have asked Sue what she was doing during the break period, she might have said something like this: "I'm washing my hands. I *was* watching TV, though, and I'm hurrying to get *back* to it as fast as I can. Clara interrupted me." The disjunction indicated here between a present immediate situation and a removed situation which the person has had to leave, but wants to reënter, appears to be the distinctive feature of interruption which, to conclude the example, we have marked on the record in the present case.

We have found it useful in dealing with this problem to think in terms of three levels on a continuum, as follows:

1. One-unit continuance : An isolated episode E_1 proceeds continuously. Its situation, as the only one existing for the person, has a potency of 1. The person behaves toward one terminal intended position.

2. Overlapping : At this level, episodes E_1 and E_2 occur simultaneously. The situation in each has a potency greater than zero, but less than 1. The person behaves toward different terminal intended positions, each in a different direction.

3. Interruption: An interrupting episode E_2 proceeds continuously between the forepart and the latter part of an interrupted episode E_1. The situation in E_1 has a potency of 1, while the situation in E_2 has a potency of zero. The person behaves again toward one terminal intended position.

It is evident from this analysis that the relationship which an interrupting episode sustains to an interrupted one has some kinship with the relationship between different overlapping episodes. One way to state the essential difference between the two relationships is to say that in the case of the first, i.e., the relationship between an interrupted and an interrupting episode, there is within the behavior perspective of the person, understood as perspective on *behavior in progress*, only one unit, whereas in the second, there are two. This is not to propose that there are no cross-effects of situation upon behavior as between interrupted and interrupting units. No such proposal is tenable with respect to the relationship between any two units of a behavior sequence. Such cross-effects must certainly connect consecutive units; yet we are not therefore inclined to consider them overlapping. Owing, however, to the peculiarly close dynamical and structural connectedness between interrupting and interrupted episodes, for certain purposes, to be developed in Chapter VIII, we have considered the relationship between them to be one of *secondary overlap*. Thus, for these purposes, *Coasting in Wagon* and *Coping With Friend's Interference*, by Wally Wolfson, as also *Watching Television* and *Washing For Supper*, by Sue, become instances of secondary overlap. This leaves interruption open for study as a special psychological phenomenon.

One important line of inquiry about interruption which we will only mention concerns the factors in the situation of the person which tend to bring it about. We judge that, in the sequence from Sue, the interrupting factor was *social pressure*. Other interrupting factors which we have found in our records include the arising of *new positive valences*, as when a child is pulled away from a sandbox by a flight of planes; the intrusion of *negative valences*, as when a child is moved to stop making a mud pie by the nipping of a stray dog; and *environmental cessation*, as when the projector at the Midwest movie breaks down. These changes come in upon the child from the outside.   There are also interrupting factors, such as failure, which are in some degree intrinsic to the ongoing behavior.

We have left implicit the fact that any number of interrupting episodes can occur between the forepart and the resumed, latter part of an inter- rupted episode.   This in itself presents a question for study: Through how many interrupting behavior units can children, and especially children differing in age, sustain their need tensions, as established by eventual resumption?

There is to be considered here also a technical matter of importance for the use of episodes as analytical units.   It is that all interrupted units which are later resumed confront the analyst with segments separated by one or more episodes.   These separate segments can be analyzed independently or treated together as a single unit.   We have done the latter on the grounds that our standard descriptive target is a whole episode whose limits are defined by the beginning and end points of an entire action toward a goal.

SOCIAL INTERVENTION

The structure of a behavior sequence can be greatly complicated by the associates of a person.   This follows as a consequence of inducing forces that stem from the *social power field* of an associate (cf. Lewin: **32**).   Obvi- ously, other people have much to do with the steering of behavior in this or that direction, with the relative potency of action units, and with the determination of what behavior shall or shall not fall within the behavior perspective of the person.   A parent or a teacher, for example, may act virtually as the creator and custodian of a child's behavior structure through long periods of time.   This is a broad and extremely complex problem which we cannot hope to deal with adequately in the available space.   We shall consider only briefly one aspect of the problem which bears directly upon discrimination of behavior units.

Three ways in which the intervention by an associate can affect the formation of action units in the behavior of children have shown up con- spicuously in our episoding of specimen records.

1. Obstruction.   An associate creates resistance to locomotion toward the goal in an episode.   The restraining forces which act upon the child in this case are no different in principle from those deriving from nonsocial barriers.

Lewis Hope goes to the real telephone at home and begins to make a pretend call.   His mother comes along and urges him to shorten the call out of her wish to save the phone for more serious business.   Lewis is only a little deterred, although he does look up at his mother.   He continues to talk with his imaginary friend right through the admonition.

Some thought was given to the possibility of blocking off the interaction with the mother here as a separate episode.   It was decided, however, that there was only one episode in which the mother figured as a person who briefly stood in the way of the prevailing action, much as a chair might have stood between the child and the phone.

2. *Potency segregation.* An associate steps up the relative weight of an episode part in an amount such that the part becomes a contained episode, individuated by potency. Generally, this complication differs only in degree from that in which the associate exerts restraining forces.

Lewis asks his mother if he can go with Stanton, his brother, to deliver some milk. The mother throws Lewis into a bad state by saying, "No." Against this prohibition, however, he runs to the door and away from the house with Stanton.

Again, here, an associate creates resistance. But the interaction between the mother and child incurred by this resistance was judged to wax in importance for Lewis' behavior above the level or, at least, up to the level of the larger, including off-with-Stanton unit. Accordingly, we marked *Leaving Against Mother's Protest* as a contained episode that overlaps with *Going With Stanton*. Because Lewis' goal in pushing through the "No" was seen as a subgoal on the path toward the goal in joining Stanton, the actions in the two units were taken to be the same in direction, for which reason *Leaving Against Mother's Protest* had to be marked as contained.

3. *Redirection.* An associate stirs up an action in a direction differing from that of the behavior in an ongoing unit. Here, the child is doing something "for its own sake." The associate intervenes, usually as a resistance maker. "Objectively," i.e., in terms of actones or observable mechanisms, the original action persists, but no longer toward its original end as an end in itself; rather toward an end to be reached only by behavior in relation to the associate. The action is bent so far from its original course that in terms of molar rather than molecular behavior it is converted into a new action in a new direction.

Lewis sits happily banging his dinner plate with a table knife. Mrs. Hope forcefully orders him to stop, whereupon Lewis earnestly bangs the plate harder.

At first, as we took it, Lewis was banging just for the fun of *it*. But we judged that, following his mother's intervention, he banged, still for fun, but not just for the fun of banging; rather for the fun of teasing, aggravating, tantalizing, or perhaps, somehow getting the better of, his mother. There arose as the analyst saw it a new and entirely different goal. The actones stayed the same; so did the prior action of banging just for banging; but a second, new action arose in a new direction. In short, therefore, a new episode supervened. What we did was to mark off *Banging Plate to Tease Mother* as an episode overlapping with, not contained by, but rather, only enclosed by, *Banging Plate For Fun.*

It must be clear that these kinds of social intervention only sample a great many ways in which the social environment can effect behavior unit formation. Yet they may suggest the adaptability of our main episoding guides to complications of this variety.

RESTLESS BEHAVIOR

Fragments of restless behavior often are found within the limits of an episode. The subject's legs may twist and turn while he reads a book, for example. These behavior elements, usually actones, are not integral parts of an episode; they only go along with it. Each discriminable restless pattern within episode limits is marked with a bracket and a horizontal line, labeled *R*.

We have occasionally encountered somewhat moderately extended blocks of restless behavior which do not overlap with an episode; that is, they occur between the end of one episode and the beginning of the next. For all such pseudo-units, the marking is the same as for a regular episode, except that the vertical bracket line is broken, and the unit is labeled, *R*.

Practical Routines in Episoding

Most of the conventions in episoding have been introduced by way of illustrative, episoded sequences. There remain, however, some procedural requirements that we have found to be of some importance.

Reading the record. Our experience shows that, on undertaking to episode either a day or a settings record, one should first read the whole of it. A need for this follows from the fact that the task in episoding is essentially the one of finding boundary lines which inhere in the whole.

Reading ahead. The episoder will save a great deal of erasing by making sure that he knows clearly and definitely what is coming next in the record. Reading a whole record is not enough, alone, to guarantee this. Our practice has been to episode in blocks of 30 to 40 pages. The material of every such block should be studied intensively before any marks are drawn. Mental notes can be made on the main units while the reading continues. Usually, we have set down rough episode lines between such notes and the final bracketings.

Rule of maximum inclusiveness. An episoder is sure to experience ups and downs of confidence as he works through a record. He will be in doubt most often in trying to decide whether a minor segment is an integral part of a given episode or in itself a shorter, overlapping episode. When, in all such cases, there has appeared to be about as much justification for treating a piece of behavior in the one way as in the other, we have included it in the more extended unit. This practice is recommended because it seems better to err on the side of contaminated wholes than with abstracted parts, and because it makes for consistency. The rule is not restricted to cases in which the alternatives are integral parts or complete wholes. It is applicable also wherever unresolvable doubts arise as to whether one or more than one episode ought to be distinguished.

Episode titles. Participial phrases are used invariably in wording episode titles. The requirement here is to describe as concisely and concretely as possible what the child is doing in the episode. Whenever the episoder finds it difficult to hit upon a title that identifies without ambiguity some one thing the subject is doing, he generally will do well to reconsider the segment in question, to make sure he is dealing with an integral behavior unit. The title has little significance in later stages of the analysis, but we have found that a clear and fitting one usually gives partial proof of a correctly discriminated episode.

Numbering. We have numbered the episodes of a record according to the order in which they start, placing the number in every case over the episode bracket. Wherever overlapping episodes start together, they are numbered according to the order in which they end. In the rare instances of coinciding overlap an arbitrary choice is made. Episode numbers are indispensable for machine coding where episodes are used as descriptive units. They are essential especially for study of sequential interdependencies in behavior.

Weight designation. The relative weight or potency of every overlapping episode can be designated by a number over the episode bracket. We have done this in all of our episoding. A numerical scale for the rating of relative weight is presented in the following chapter.

Contained overlap. We have given every contained episode a special notation, namely, the letters CTD, placed to the left of the episode bracket. Otherwise, the markings themselves are left to show type of overlapping.

Applications and Reliability of Episoding

The present method has been applied to day records, partial day records, and settings records of the Midwest collection as shown in the breakdown of Table 7.1. The table shows that this work has made available for study 19,654 episodes, 14,417 of them in records of Midwest children, and the remaining 5,237 in records on nearby disabled children. We look upon these episodes as a file of resource materials for psychological studies.

Most of the episoding was done during one year by a team of five analysts which included a supervisor who reviewed all of the work by the other four. The supervisor made some changes in the original episoding. Usually such changes were made only after consultation with the analyst concerned so that continuous training was provided.

TABLE 7.1

MIDWEST COLLECTION OF EPISODED RECORDS

Subjects	Type of Record	Number of Records	Pages	Episodes
Midwest Children	Day	12	4627	11567
	Partial Day	1	192	480
	Settings	130	948	2370
	All	143	5767	14417
Disabled Children	Day	4	1393	3482
	Partial Day	4	322	805
	Settings	52	380	950
	All	60	2095	5237
ALL	ALL	203	7862	19654

Throughout, application of the method has been supplemented by procedures to test its reliability. We shall report here findings obtained by use of these procedures on 14 day-records.

Sequences varying in length from 30 minutes to 90 minutes and covering approximately one-fourth of the subject's waking time during the recorded day were marked off in each record. There were 50 sequences in the total sample. These were chosen from different parts of the records to give variety in kinds of behavior and situation.

Fifty pairs of episoders were formed by pairing eight analysts under a rotation scheme which minimized disproportionate teaming of any two persons. One of the 50 sequences was assigned to every pair, each member of which independently divided into episodes a transcript of the sequence. Following work on a sequence, the members of every pair jointly compared the independently divided transcripts. They recorded the title of every episode which either analyst had discriminated, and checked all instances of agreement and disagreement. Agreement was credited whenever an episode marked by one analyst was essentially the same in span, content, and identifying participial phrase as an episode marked by the other. Differences in the marking of units as isolated or overlapping were not scored as disagreements. As a rule, however, where there was agreement upon the identity of an episode, there also was agreement with respect to its position. Other characteristics of episodes were not considered in the comparisons.

In every case, the paired analysts reconciled their differences and, leaving the independently marked transcripts intact, jointly episoded a third copy of the material on the basis of their pooled best judgments. Finally, the leader of the episoding team reviewed the joint product and made some, though never extensive, changes in the markings. Because it represents a best effort to apply the method correctly, we shall refer below to the final outcome of these several steps as the *criterion version*.

For each of the episoded sections in the sample an *estimate of accuracy* was secured by means of the following formula:

$$\text{Estimate of Accuracy} = \frac{\substack{\text{Number of Episodes} \\ \text{Discriminated by X} \\ \text{Discriminated also by Y}}}{\dfrac{\substack{\text{Total} \\ \text{Number of Episodes} \\ \text{Discriminated by X}} + \substack{\text{Total} \\ \text{Number of Episodes} \\ \text{Discriminated by Y}}}{2}},$$

where X and Y are any two independent analysts.

The numerator of this formula is the number of episodes upon which the two independent analysts agreed. But it is not necessarily the true number. On the contrary, this value is open to two errors. First, it may include units incorrectly identified as episodes by both analysts. Second, it may not include units correctly identified as episodes by one analyst, but not so identified by the other. The denominator is the best available estimate of the true number of episodes. It is the mean number discriminated by both analysts. Its rationale is based upon the assumption that any competent analyst, trained in the method, will approximate the correct total number of units which the method defines as episodes. Actually, of course, every analyst will make errors of two kinds. He will identify two or more episodes where there should be one (overestimate the true number) and he will combine into a single unit, two or more episodes where there should be more than one (underestimate the true number). If these are chance errors, the averaging of the judgments of more than one judge should provide a better estimate of the true number of episodes than the judgments of a single judge. In any case, the quotient gives that proportion of the "true" number of episodes "correctly" discriminated independently by each analyst.

Application of this formula to the 50 sequences of the sample yields estimates of accuracy ranging from a low of 72 to a high of 92. Table 7.2 presents a frequency distribution of these measures. An overall estimate was computed by summing for all 50 sequences and then substituting in the formula. This computation gives a value of 81.11, which represents the central tendency shown in the table.

TABLE 7.2

ESTIMATE OF ACCURACY OBTAINED BY COMPARING THE
EPISODING BY INDEPENDENT ANALYSTS OF 50
SEQUENCES IN 14 DAY RECORDS

Estimate of Accuracy	f
72–74	3
75–77	4
78–80	16
81–83	11
84–86	10
87–89	5
90–92	1
Total Number of Sequences	50

One can classify as *major* all episodes rated primary in relative weight and as *minor* all rated secondary and tertiary in weight. See the scale for judgment of relative weight on page 278. An estimate of accuracy was computed independently for the major episodes, the minor episodes, and, finally, all of the episodes in each of 10 sequences, 4 from one day record and 6 from another. For this purpose, the weight ratings of the episodes in the criterion version were used. It is emphasized that episodes of lower than primary weight were characteristically overlapping, enclosed, short and usually undivided units which we have eliminated in most instances from later analysis on the grounds that there is not enough in them to justify special study. The data obtained from these different classes of episodes are presented in Table 7.3, which shows that, for *all* of the different episodes discriminated in the various sections of the two records, the estimates of accuracy range from 72 to 87, and that for major episodes they range from 87 to 98.

TABLE 7.3

ESTIMATES OF ACCURACY OF EPISODERS ON MAJOR
EPISODES, MINOR EPISODES, AND ALL EPISODES IN 10
SEQUENCES OF 2 DAY RECORDS

SECTION	EPISODERS	ESTIMATE OF ACCURACY			NUMBER OF EPISODES		
		Major	Minor	All	Major	Minor	All
1	A, B	87	41	76	72	35	107
2	C, D	91	72	84	50	34	84
3	B, A	92	50	84	68	24	92
4	D, C	93	70	86	79	37	116
5	B, C	91	35	73	38	19	57
6	A, B	92	67	80	36	28	64
7	B, D	94	62	80	29	20	49
8	C, D	95	64	87	32	19	51
9	D, A	96	47	73	35	21	56
10	C, A	98	42	72	23	23	46

The question of how to test statistically the significance of these data on interanalyst agreement presents a difficult problem in sampling theory. Some progress has been made in this area by Guetzkow (22) in his treatment of reliability problems met in "unitizing" the qualitative data in interviews, autobiographies, and the like. But now we prefer to leave the reported estimates as they stand.

Chapter VIII

Behavior Structure

Problem and Source Material

THIS chapter[1] is about the structure of children's molar behavior. It will summarize procedures and results of an attempt to explore this problem. The data of the study are based upon analyses of 16 episoded day records, including 12 on Midwest children and 4 on disabled children of nearby communities. Pertinent information about these children is presented in Chapter II and in Appendix 1 and Appendix 2.

For certain purposes, which will be considered later, all of the episodes in the 16 records were used. For other purposes, however, efficiency required a sampling of the total episode population. We adopted a method of sampling randomly the episodes in the behavior settings entered by these children. Earlier analysis had established for every entry into a behavior setting the number and name of the setting, the identifying numbers of all included episodes, the total number of these episodes, and the time of occurrence and duration of behavior in the setting. There was available, then, a comprehensive minute by minute breakdown of each recorded day in terms of behavior settings. We chose to include in the episode sample from every record all the episodes that occurred during alternate entries into each setting.

This selection procedure had to be modified in order to avoid disruption of naturally occurring behavior sequences. If any part of a linkage[2] fell in a sample, the entire linkage was either assimilated to it or excluded; a linkage was included if only a few episodes outside the sampled setting were involved. These modifications made relatively small net differences in the number of selected episodes.

A major advantage in this basis of selection is that it gives approximately proportionate representation to behavior settings of widely differing degrees of importance, as measured by time spent in them by the children. Thus, nearly 40 per cent of the behavior in the 16 records occurred in Home Indoors. The sampling scheme gives a similar proportion of episodes from this setting. Another advantage in the plan is that it preserves the natural continuity of extended behavior sequences.

These procedures give a total sample of 7,749 episodes from nearly all of the different behavior settings entered by the 16 children. This is 51.6 per

[1] The chapter is based on the doctoral thesis by Phil H. Schoggen (51).

[2] Readers are referred to Chapter VII for definitions of those concepts not defined in this chapter.

274

cent of the entire episode population. The size of the samples range from 45 per cent to 56 per cent of the episodes in each record.

Method

With exceptions to be noted, the data reported in the section on results were obtained by applying special descriptive categories to all episodes in the sample from the 16 records. Some of these categories deal with purely structural characteristics of episodes, while others are concerned with dynamical factors or conditions related to behavior structure. Each category will now be itemized and defined.

Structural Characteristics of Episodes

1 Episode Length

1. 15 sec	7. 5 min
2. 30 sec	8. 6–7 min
3. 1 min	9. 8–10 min
4. 2 min	10. 11–14 min
5. 3 min	11. 15 or more min
6. 4 min	

Category 1 provides a measure of length of episode in clock time. Each episode in the sample was rated on this variable. The judgments are made on a "nearest to" basis. For example, when an episode is checked One Minute, this means that, of the time intervals itemized in the category, a minute is nearest to the judged duration of the episode.

In judging length of episode, the analyst is guided by the time notations and description of the child's behavior recorded by the observer. The estimates required of the analyst here were considered to be such as to obviate necessity for systematic agreement tests.

2 Total Number of Overlapping Episodes

1. 1	6. 6–8
2. 2	7. 9–11
3. 3	8. 12–14
4. 4	9. 15 or more
5. 5	10. DNA (Isolated Episode)

As stated in Chapter VII, an important aspect of behavior structure is the overlapping of episodes. This category is used to record for the target unit the total number of other episodes which overlap with it throughout its entire course. In Figure 8.1, for example, we find by counting that episode *1* has five other episodes overlapping with it. Episode *1* is tabulated, therefore, under item 5 of the category. Episodes *4* and *5* are both tallied under item 2, since each has two others overlapping with it. Every remaining episode in Figure 8.1 has only one other overlapping with it; hence, each is tallied with item 1. Episodes that have no others overlapping with them at any time are tabulated under item 10, Does Not Apply.

For this category, as for categories 3 through 6, below, the evidence of reliability in application is indirect. Each of these categories deals with an aspect of behavior structure identified in the episoding process. The task of the structure analyst was only a matter of inspecting episode brackets or of counting episodes; interpretations which had been made previously as a part of the episoding process were noted and recorded. Thus, the question of reliability goes back in each case here to the episoding process itself, the reliability of which was tested by procedures described in Chapter VII.

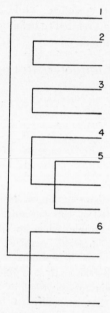

Fig. 8.1.—Overlapping phenomena. See text, categories 2 and 3.

Our tests of episoding reliability, as may be recalled, measure only agreement between independent analysts on presence or absence of episodes. Such determinations as the position of units in relation to others were not considered in the agreement computations. It is clear, therefore, that the episoding agreement per cents can be taken as only indirect and partial evidence of the reliability of the present categories. We have considered, however, that where the reported agreement levels were high, agreement on episode interrelations is likely to have been satisfactory. It has seemed highly improbable that two episoders could agree acceptably in identifying particular episodes and yet disagree seriously on such variables as number of overlapping episodes or type of overlap. In view of these considerations, we have not subjected categories 2 through 6 to special reliability tests.

3 Maximum Number of Simultaneously Overlapping Episodes

1. 1
2. 2
3. 3
4. DNA (Isolated Episode)

Category 3 is used to record for the target unit the largest number of episodes which overlap with it at any one time during its course. Reference to Figure 8.1 will clarify the difference between this variable and Total Number of Overlapping Episodes. We noted above that episode *1* in Figure 8.1 has a total of five other episodes overlapping with it and that it is tallied, therefore, under item 5 of category 2. However, it will be seen that the largest number of episodes which overlap with episode *1* at any one time is two. Accordingly, item 2 of the present category applies to episode *1*. On the same basis, item 1 applies to episodes *2*, *3*, and *6*, and item 2 applies to episodes *4* and *5*.

4 Type of Overlap

1. Coinciding
2. Enclosing
3. Enclosed
4. Interlinking
5. Interpolated
6. DNA (Isolated Episode)

Attention is turned now from quantitative to qualitative aspects of overlapping phenomena. Category 4 is used to describe the structural form of relationships between overlapping episodes.

Except for item 5, Interpolated, the several types of overlap have been defined and illustrated on pages 260-62. Item 5 applies wherever the target episode occurs "between the arrows" used to indicate interruption of a previously begun and subsequently resumed episode. An example of this can be found in Figure 8.2. In this figure, each bracket represents one episode. Item 5 of the present category applies to episodes *11c* and *d*, *12c*, *d*, and *e*, and *13c*, *d*, *e*, and *f*. This item makes possible the segregation of episodes involved in occurrences of secondary overlap, as defined on page 266.

Wherever a target episode sustains more than one type of overlap relation to others, each type is checked. Thus, in Figure 8.2, episode *6a* is interlinking in relation to episode *6b*, but enclosing in relation to episode *6c*. For episode *6a*, therefore, both items, Enclosing and Interlinking, are checked.

5 Form of Transition

1. Abrupt
2. Merging

Category 5 is concerned with the structural relationship between the target unit and other episodes at its terminal point, i.e., at the point of transition to the immediately subsequent behavior segment, which can be a new unit or the remaining part of a more extended overlapping episode. The category might be said to measure smoothness of behavior flow. Where an abrupt transition occurs, the target unit is immediately succeeded by a break in the behavior sequence. Where, on the other hand, a merging transition occurs, the target unit ends while an overlapping episode is still in progress. Looking again at Figure 8.2, we note that, among others, episodes *1*, *2a*, *6b*, and *12c* are characterized by abrupt transitions. Examples from this figure of merging transitions include episodes *2b*, *6a*, and *12b*.

6 Continuity of Episode Course

1. Continuous
2. Discontinuous

Category 6 is used to record the frequency with which episodes are broken into more than one segment. It measures, in other words, the frequency of interruption when resumption follows within the limits of the record.

Item 1 applies where the target episode proceeds continuously from its beginning to the point of final termination, whether or not the goal in the episode is reached. In terms of conceptual criteria described earlier, an episode is considered continuous if it is judged to maintain potency greater than zero throughout its course.

Item 2 applies where an episode is interrupted *and* resumed one or more times during its course. As many as 20 separate interruptions have been found to break the course of an episode in our records. Note that the category is in no way concerned with ultimate completeness of an episode. A judgment is not made here as to whether the child ever reaches his intended terminal position. The question of completion or incompletion is raised by a later category.

Every bracket in Figure 8.2 represents a continuous episode except for episodes *11a, 12a,* and *13a* which, as the arrows indicate, are discontinuous.

Conditions Related to Behavior Structure[3]

8 Basis of Episode Discrimination

1. Direction
2. Potency (Contained Episode)

Category 8 differentiates between contained episodes discriminated solely on the basis of their relatively high potency, and episodes discriminated on the basis of unique direction.

The analyst merely notes whether the target unit has been marked a contained episode during the episoding process. Thus, the question of reliability again goes back to agreement on episoding. In this case, however, no evidence of interanalyst agreement is available; differences between independent episoders as to whether a given episode was contained were not considered in the episoding agreement tests.

9 Relative Weight

1. Primary	6. Primary, Tertiary
2. Primary, Tied	7. Secondary, Tertiary
3. Secondary	8. Primary, Secondary, Tertiary
4. Tertiary	9. Does Not Apply (Isolated Episode)
5. Primary, Secondary	

[3] Category 7, *Actone Interference Between Overlapping Episodes,* is concerned with the mechanics of the molecular implementation of two or more simultaneously overlapping episodes. Neither the category nor the results of its application to the records will be presented here. The interested reader is referred to reference **51** where the problem is discussed and results are reported in detail.

Category 9 is concerned with the potency, or relative importance to the total behavior of the child, of different simultaneously overlapping episodes. The weight of every episode among two or more involved in an overlap at one time is ranked in order from primary through tertiary. Occurrence of more than three simultaneously overlapping episodes has been found so rarely in our records that no provision was made for this in itemization of the category.

Item 1 applies when the target episode clearly outranks the other overlapping units in potency throughout its entire course. Item 2 applies when the first rank in potency is shared by the target unit and another episode at some point during the course of the target episode, i.e., when neither episode appears to have greater potency than the other. Actually, an episode of secondary weight could be equaled in potency but our experience has not required provision for this possibility. Whenever three episodes were found to overlap simultaneously, one of them was always clearly tertiary.

The remaining items represent combinations of items 1, 3 and 4. These are used when an episode of some length is judged to have different weights at different times during its course.

The relative weight of a long, enclosing episode is not necessarily constant throughout its course but may vary from time to time, depending upon the characteristics of the episodes which it encloses. Thus, for example, item 5 applies when the target episode is primary in potency through a part of its course but is secondary at one or more points.

As indicated earlier, the indicators of high potency which we have used in episoding the records include (a) wide involvement of motor, verbal, and other behavior mechanisms, (b) indifference or potentially distracting conditions, (c) high energy level of the behavior, (d) high resistance to obstruction, and (e) strong interpersonal stimulation. Judging episodes on relative weight becomes a matter of deciding which of the overlapping units makes the most difference to the total behavior of the child in terms of these indices.

The category was judged on the basis of relative weight markings which were placed on the episode lines as a final step in the episoding process by the leader of the episoding team. Since no agreement checks were conducted, the results from this category must be offered on this qualified basis.

10 Episode Initiation

1. Spontaneous
2. Instigated
3. Pressured
4. Can Not Judge

Category 10 stems from an interest in the extent to which the structure of naturally occurring behavior is self-regulated rather than regulated from without.

Item 1, Spontaneous, applies whenever the action of an episode begins in the apparent absence of external instigation, defined as any observed and reported change in the child's situation. In these cases, the child is seen to behave as if he "just happened to think of something to do"; i.e., action is initiated without evident dependence upon active behavior objects. When, in the case of social behavior objects, the child is seen to react to the presence, as opposed to the activity, of an individual, the initiation is considered spontaneous, as when Lewis Hope was observed to interrupt his paper-reading father long enough to get some information about a camera. In all cases of spontaneous initiation, the essential element is an apparently voluntary "selection" of action by the subject. One clearly can not assume in any such case anything like complete detachment from environmental conditions. Yet we have found that behavior with the *appearance* of spontaneity stands out in the records, and believe that sense made by findings to be reported has justified special consideration of this behavior.

Item 2, Instigated, applies when the child is seen to respond to some observable event or change in his situation, provided only that the event or change does not constitute "pressure," as this is defined below. An event or change here means any observed and reported occurrence referable to some source other than the subject. Someone enters the subject's presence; a tractor drives past on the street; someone speaks; a paper flutters; a whistle blows; a clock chimes; a book falls. This item aims to measure the extent to which the child behaves in response to such incitement.

Item 3, Pressured, applies when an episode appears to begin as the result of any form of pressure upon the child. Pressure means here external influence of any kind which is in any way inconsistent with the child's own momentary needs and goals. Although social pressure accounts for a majority of these cases, other kinds of pressure are included, as when Raymond Birch was "forced" by rain to leave his play and go indoors. *Practicing Piano Lesson*, which began when Raymond's mother called him in from his play to carry out this apparently unpleasant ritual, exemplifies the more common, socially pressured, initiation.

This is one of four categories upon which specific agreement tests were made. An assistant applied each of these categories to a number of episodes which the principal analyst had previously judged. In all, there were eight blocks of 50 episodes each in the agreement sample. These blocks were taken from eight different records. They were selected, moreover, from different behavior settings in order to provide a variety of target material.

Results of the agreement tests on this category show exact agreement between independent analysts in 91 per cent of 400 episodes. Taken separately, the agreement per cents for each of the eight blocks of episodes range from 80 to 98. The median of these values is 91.

11   Episode Issue

This category is used in an attempt to describe some aspects of the psychological significance of the target episode for the child at the point of episode termination. It seems important to ascertain the frequency with which such psychological outcomes of behavior units as "success" and "failure" occur in any attempt to study the structure of behavior.

In applying the category, a decision was made first as to whether the episode was complete or incomplete. In the case of transitive or goal-seeking behavior, this amounted to deciding whether or not the child reached his goal. In the case of consummatory behavior, i.e., behavior within a goal region, the analyst judged only whether or not satiation occurred. When confident judgment as to the completeness of an episode could not be made, the analyst marked the unit,

Can Not Judge. If, however, the analyst was able to make a judgment as to episode completeness, the category was applied as it is itemized below:

Complete Episodes	*Incomplete Episodes*
1. Acquittance	7. Nonattainment
2. Attainment	8. Frustration
3. Gratification	9. Failure
4. Success	10. Consummation: Not Satiated
5. Consummation: Satiated	11. Other
6. Other	12. Can Not Judge

A set of criteria was adopted for each item. Any given item applies only when all of the stated criteria are met. These items, together with the criteria and references to examples from specimen records, are shown below:

1. Acquittance

   a) The action consists of a single minimal molar unit.

   b) The action is characteristically brief.

   c) Resistance against action is virtually zero.

   d) The episode is "unimportant." If involved in an overlap, its relative weight is secondary or less.

   Example: At 9:48 in the morning of the Ben Hutchings record, Ben was busily occupied at his desk with the reading lesson for the day which involved reading, coloring, and some writing. While doing this, he glanced up momentarily to look at the first-graders who were reciting orally to the teacher. This episode, *Noting First Graders*, meets the stated criteria for the issue, Acquittance.

2. Attainment

   a) The goal in the episode is reached only after the child has overcome appreciable resistance.

   b) The child does not attribute credit to himself or to anyone else for reaching the goal; there is satisfaction, but neither pride nor gratitude.

   Example: At 6:03 p.m., Douglas Crawford climbed high up in a large elm tree in his yard. After finding a suitable perch, he worked vigorously in cutting a small branch from the tree with a knife. After about two minutes of engrossed work, he cut through the branch and threw it to the ground, satisfied with the accomplishment.

3. Gratification

   a) The goal is such that the child could not reach it, if he were to do so by his own efforts, without overcoming appreciable resistance.

   b) The child attributes credit for reaching the goal to someone besides himself or to external circumstances.

   Example: When Dutton Thurston's brother, Al, spontaneously offered him a piece of chewing gum, the episode *Getting Gum from Al* was considered to meet the above criteria.

4. Success

   a) The goal in the episode is reached only after the child has overcome appreciable resistance.

b) The child attributes credit to himself; there is satisfaction and pride in accomplishment; the child feels that he has "done something."

Example: On the evening of the Margaret Reid record, she, her mother, and her grandparents spent more than an hour in the yard enjoying the pleasant June evening. At 8:05, Margaret's grandfather noted that her 18-month-old brother had wandered off to the back part of the yard. Margaret at once caught up with him and gave him a couple of swats with a small stick. She then returned to the adults announcing, "I gave him a big spanking." She seemed very proud of her accomplishment which she justified by crying, "He did something wrong once."

5. Consummation: Satiated

    a) Resistance against locomotion is virtually zero; the child is free to move about with little or no difficulty.

    b) All activity regions are homogeneously positive; there is virtually no valence differential between any present position and any next step.

    c) Distance to ends sought is virtually zero.

    d) The episode terminates because the child becomes satiated with the goal activity; the activity becomes neutral in valence.

Example: At 8:07, Roy Eddy sat down to breakfast with his older siblings, two sisters and one brother. The breakfast consisted of prepared cereal, buttered toast, and hot chocolate. These foods seemed to be Roy's favorites, for he ate heartily and with obvious pleasure. He appeared to be just where he wanted to be and to be doing just what he wanted to do for the next 15 minutes. That the episode terminated in satiation is indicated by Roy's comment as he pushed himself away from the table with a big sigh, "Whohh, I'm plumb full now."

6. Other (Complete)

This item is used when a judgment of "complete" seems correct, but when the criteria for no one of the above issues are met.

7. Nonattainment

    a) The child gives up only after overcoming appreciable resistance.

    b) The child does not place any blame for not reaching his goal; the non-attainment is taken for granted.

Example: At 7:40 p.m., Margaret Reid, with the assistance of her mother, tried to learn how to whistle. Her mother demonstrated whistling and Margaret tried several times to imitate her mother's action. After about a minute of this experimentation, Margaret gave up, apparently tired of the effort, without making a whistle which suited her. This episode, *Trying to Whistle*, exemplifies this issue. Item 9, Failure, would have applied in this case if Margaret had blamed herself. There is no evidence that she did. Rather, she apparently decided that this skill was only to be mastered by older persons; thus, she did not feel "badly" about her own inability to whistle.

8. Frustration

    a) The child gives up only after overcoming appreciable resistance.

b) The child places blame for not reaching the goal upon someone besides himself or upon external circumstances.

Example: In the afternoon after school on the day of the Ben Hutchings record, Ben and his friend, Morris, were playing "war" with toy soldiers and airplanes on the floor of the kitchen in the Hutchings' home. At 4:30, the boys got into a quarrel about the rules of their game. The quarrel deteriorated into a scuffle which ended only with the intervention of Ben's mother. Since Ben failed after considerable effort to reach his objective in this *Quarreling Over Rules* episode, and since it was clear that he blamed Morris and his mother, the episode exemplifies the issue, Frustration.

9. Failure
  a) The child gives up only after overcoming appreciable resistance.
  b) The child places blame for the failure upon himself; he feels not only dissatisfaction, but also some shame.

Example: Raymond Birch went out in the yard to watch his father practice casting with a fishing rod. When he had a turn at casting, Raymond tried three times to make the plug land in a basket some distance away. He missed the first two times and produced a backlash on the third try. Raymond commented, "I *can't* put it in the basket." (**8, 33**.)

10. Consummation: Not Satiated
  a) *b*) *c*) Same as for item 5, above.
  d) The episode terminates because of a factor other than satiation, e.g., new positive valence, social pressure.

Example: About 10:39 a.m., Mary Chaco, who was playing with first one thing and then another in her yard, picked up the rope tied to the handle of her wagon and pulled the wagon a short distance, apparently just for the fun of it. Then, as though struck by a new idea, she dropped the wagon handle and went to her tricycle. The episode, *Pulling Wagon*, is representative of many episodes involving essentially consummatory behavior which terminate, not as a result of satiation, but of an environmental change, such as a new positive valence, as in this case.

11. Other (Incomplete)
  This item is used when a judgment of Incomplete is made, but when the criteria for no one of the above issues are met.

Results of the agreement tests show that exact agreement between independent analysts occurred in 56 per cent of 400 episodes. The agreement per cents for each of the 8 test blocks range from 26 to 74, with a median of 59. These data for the individual items of this category are not reassuring. They leave open to question findings on the precise termination of individual episodes. However, it is important to remember here that we are dealing with large numbers of cases. If the errors of judgment are random, as there is reason to believe they are, considerable confidence can be placed in the frequency of occurrence of different kinds of episode issue. Separate agreements were computed for judgments on episode completeness. They show that the analysts agreed on 81 per cent of the 400 episodes.   The per cents on each block of 50 range from 64 to 98, with a median of 83.   This means that judgments as to whether episodes terminated, in general, either satisfactorily (complete) or unsatisfactorily (incomplete) were made with a good degree of agreement.

12   Episode Termination

1. Spontaneous
2. Instigated
3. Environmental Cessation
4. Pressured
5. Can Not Judge

This category complements and is patterned after category 10, above, on episode initiation.   Item 1, Spontaneous, applies where the action of the episode appears to terminate from within.   If the child apparently just quits upon reaching his objective or tiring of the action, termination is judged to be spontaneous.   Ruled out here are all cases of termination in response to observed and reported change in the child's situation.

Item 2, Instigated, applies where termination of the episode appears to occur in response to an external change or event provided that this change (*a*) does not consist in reaching the goal of the episode, and (*b*) does not conform to items 3 and 4 which, as will be seen, are only special cases of instigated termination.   This item is directly analogous to the one of the same name under category 10; the definitions and examples cited there are applicable here as well.

Item 3, Environmental Cessation, applies where the episode terminates owing to withdrawal of necessary behavior supports, as when one stops watching a movie because the film breaks.   This, as anticipated above, may be considered a special type of instigated termination.   Not all instances of environmental cessation are as clear cut and obvious as that of the cited example.   This kind of termination occurs wherever the behavior of the episode is sustained by forces external to the child and then brought to an end by disappearance of these forces. Dutton Thurston is playing with his truck on the floor.   He looks up to answer a question put by his mother only to find that she has left the room.   Here, the terminating factor in *Answering Mother's Question* was judged to be environmental cessation.   A somewhat different example of the same kind of termination is given by the episode, *Watching Observer*, which terminated when the observer left the room.

Item 4, Pressured, applies where the episode terminates as a result of external pressure on the child.   The definitions and examples given for the item of the same name in category 10 can be adapted here.

Agreement tests show that independent analysts achieved exact agreement on this category in 82 per cent of 400 judgments.   The per cents for each block of 50, range from 70 to 94, with a median of 82.

Special Pattern Factors

The marking conventions used in episoding a specimen record hold information about the patterning and differentiation of behavior sequences which can be obtained readily by simple inspection and counting procedures.

We have used such procedures to obtain data on both episodes and linkages as behavior parts. These data are based upon study of all episodes and linkages in each of the 16 episoded day records. They are derived partially from distinctions as to kinds of linkages, which we shall identify briefly before turning to the section on results.

A linkage is a sequence of episodes connected with each other by overlapping. The minimal sequence is an isolated episode, otherwise identified as a link. Linkages range upward in complexity to those including as many as 50 or 60 episode links. Figure 8.2 illustrates some of the more common patterns formed by these linkages. The columns show different complexity levels of simultaneously overlapping episodes, ranging from the isolated episode or single link to the pattern of four simultaneously overlapping episodes. The examples in each row are intended to show that the number of episodes which overlap sequentially is variable for each pattern of simultaneous overlap. Thus, in the case of linkages at the level of triple overlapping, exemplified in the third column, the total number of episodes may vary from a minimum of 3, as in the first row, through 6, as in the last row, on up to as many as 50 or 60. Data on these different patterns have been tabulated and are reported in the section on results which follows.

Results and Discussion

Findings of this study will be presented under (a) purely structural characteristics of behavior, and (b) conditions related to behavior structure. In the case of each variable, we will consider the basic results for the 12 Midwest children, any evidence on relationships with age, and comparisons between the physically normal children of Midwest and the 4 disabled children. The data on disabled children are too limited to permit definite conclusions; but it is hoped that they may provide leads for later and more extensive studies.

The results to be reported will represent only a part of the available data. Problems not considered include questions of relationship between structure variables and the sex, social group, and family situations of the subjects, and also questions of relationship between major variables of the descriptive scheme. These problems must await a later report.

Aspects of Behavior Structure

NUMBER AND DURATION OF EPISODE LINKAGES

Table 8.1 shows some of the results from the study of linkages in the 16 records; the spatial groupings separate the 12 physically normal Midwest children, Mary Chaco through Claire Graves, from the 4 physically handicapped children, Wally Wolfson through Verne Trennell. Within each

Fig. 8.2.—Common linkage structure types.

group, the children are listed here and in subsequent tables in order of increasing age.

The first column shows that the number of linkages in each record varied from 135 to 683, with a median for the Midwest children of 428. In order to make valid comparisons between the different children, it was necessary to adjust the figures in Column 1 for differences between children in the length of their day records. The difference in time between the longest record (Mary Ennis; 14 hours, 27 minutes) and the shortest (Lewis Hope;

TABLE 8.1

NUMBER, PARTITION, AND DURATION OF EPISODE LINKAGES

CHILD	AGE TO NEAREST MONTH (YRS.-MOS.)	COLUMN 1 Actual Number of Linkages	COLUMN 2 Adjusted Number of Linkages *	COLUMN 3 Average Number of Episodes per Linkage	COLUMN 4 Average Duration (Minutes)
Mary Chaco (MC)	1-10	667	626	1.65	1.06
Jimmy Sexton (JS)	1-11	656	653	1.56	1.02
Lewis Hope (LH)	2-11	683	683	1.95	0.98
Dutton Thurston (DT)	3-10	544	471	2.13	1.42
Margaret Reid (MR)	4-6	427	357	2.48	1.87
Maud Pintner (MP)	5-0	499	491	2.39	1.36
Roy Eddy (RE)	6-2	249	206	2.80	3.24
Ben Hutchings (BH)	7-4	296	264	2.28	2.53
Ray Birch (RB)	7-4	430	353	2.32	1.89
Mary Ennis (ME)	8-7	370	285	2.62	2.34
Douglas Crawford (DC)	9-2	307	240	3.06	2.78
Claire Graves (CG)	10-9	135	105	3.66	6.37
Range		135-683	105-683	1.56-3.66	0.98-6.37
Median		428.5	355	2.35	1.88
Wally Wolfson (WW)	4-3	390	381	2.32	1.75
Sue Dewall (SD)	7-1	138	113	5.59	5.66
Bobby Bryant (BB)	7-4	225	193	3.03	3.45
Verne Trennell (VT)	7-5	307	238	3.18	2.80

* Adjusted for differences between children in length of day

11 hours, 8 minutes) was 3 hours and 19 minutes. Obviously, such differences must be taken into account in comparisons which are, in part, dependent upon the duration of the record. Therefore, the figures given in Column 1 were adjusted for these time differences by applying the formula below to the data from each record. This reduced all records to the temporal base of the shortest day, i.e., 11 hours, 8 minutes.

$$\frac{\text{Adjusted N of linkages}}{\text{in record X}} = \frac{\text{Duration of shortest record}}{\text{Duration of record X}} \left(\frac{\text{Actual No. of}}{\text{linkages in record X}} \right)$$

The adjusted numbers of linkages are given in Column 2, which shows a range from 105 to 683. The differences between children are not distributed randomly; there is a relationship with age, as shown by a rank order correlation coefficient between adjusted number of linkages and age, of −.67, significant beyond the 1 per cent level.[4]

[4] Throughout this section, the term "level" as used in connection with tests of statistical significance refers to an absolute probability, P, i.e., a "two tailed" test of significance. For example, the phrases "5 per cent level of significance" and "P equals .05" are synonymous.

In Column 3 of Table 8.1, the average number of episodes per linkage is given for each child. Here, Jimmy had the smallest average, 1.56, and Claire the largest, 3.66. The median for the Midwest children is 2.35. Again, relationship with age is apparent from inspection of the table; and this is demonstrated by a rank order correlation of .73, significant well beyond the 1 per cent level.

Finally, the data on average duration of linkage are shown in Column 4. For these values, the range is 0.98 minutes to 6.37 minutes, the median duration is 1.88 minutes, and the correlation with age +.67, again definitely significant. The data in Columns 3 and 4 are not, of course, independent of those in Column 2; for with length of record held constant, where the total number of linkages in a record is smaller, each linkage must include more episodes and last longer.

YOUNGER   OLDER

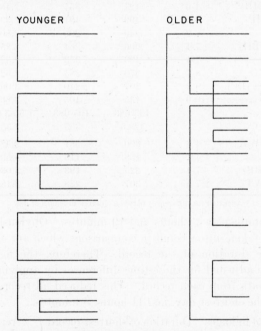

FIG. 8.3.—Typical sequences of episodes for younger and older children.

These data indicate that for the older children there is consistently a higher degree of connectedness among the episodes; the older children tend to keep more activities going at a given time; they more frequently begin a new action while still finishing an earlier one. On the other hand, the younger children are more often completely absorbed by a single action and do not as frequently begin a new one without ceasing the earlier action. Typical sequences for younger and older children are shown in Figure 8.3. Five linkages are shown for the younger child and one for the older; the data in Column 2 show that in some cases, as in that of Lewis (2–11) versus Claire (10–9), this ratio is more than 6 to 1.

There is no suggestion of a difference in the linkage patterns of disabled and normal children. This is of some importance for its suggestion that peripheral disablement does not necessarily interfere with behavior complications of the kind occurring in long linkages. Of especial significance in this regard is the fact that Sue Dewall, despite severe motor disability, had the highest number of episodes per linkage.

NUMBER AND DURATION OF EPISODES

Table 8.2 presents, for episodes, data comparable to those shown in Table 8.1 for linkages. The actual number of episodes in each record is given in Column 1. Just as with linkages, the original number of episodes is not directly comparable from record to record owing to differences between the children in length of day. Consequently, these figures were adjusted by a formula analogous to that used with the number of linkages. The adjusted figures are shown in Column 2.

TABLE 8.2

NUMBER AND AVERAGE DURATION OF EPISODES

CHILD	AGE	COLUMN 1 Actual Number of Episodes	COLUMN 2 Adjusted Number of Episodes *	COLUMN 3 Average Duration (Minutes)
Mary C.	1-10	1103	1036	0.64
Jimmy	1-11	1027	1022	0.65
Lewis	2-11	1335	1335	0.50
Dutton	3-10	1159	1004	0.66
Margaret	4-6	1059	885	0.75
Maud	5-0	1196	1178	0.57
Roy	6-2	699	579	1.15
Ben	7-4	675	603	1.11
Ray	7-4	1000	821	0.81
Mary E.	8-7	969	746	0.89
Douglas	9-2	940	735	0.91
Claire	10-9	494	383	1.74
Range		494-1335	383-1335	0.50-1.74
Median		1013.5	853	0.78
Wally	4-3	907	887	0.75
Sue	7-1	771	629	1.01
Bobby	7-4	683	587	1.14
Verne	7-5	977	759	0.88

* Adjusted for differences between children in length of day.

It will be seen that the actual number of episodes for the Midwest children ranges from a low of 494, for Claire, to 1335, for Lewis, with a median of

1013; when length of day is reduced to the shortest day (11 hours, 8 minutes), the range is from 383 to 1335. These figures for Claire and Lewis represent a striking difference in the behavioral partitioning of the two days. Claire's day was made up of a relatively small number of large parts. Several of Claire's episodes lasted as long as 50 minutes, one of them 2 hours. Lewis, on the other hand, engaged in few long episodes. His day consisted of many small parts. Comparisons of other older and younger children reveal similar differences.

The age relationship suggested by inspection of these data is borne out by a rank correlation coefficient of $-.61$, significant beyond the 1 per cent level. Column 3 presents the same results in different terms. These figures were obtained by dividing the total number of minutes in the day by the actual number of episodes for each child. The age relationship for Column 3 is, of course, identical with that of Column 2 with the sign reversed. A finding of fewer episodes of longer duration as age increases is clearly established for these children.

From inspection of Table 8.2, it is apparent that the four disabled children do not differ significantly from the Midwest children in differentiation of their days into episodes. On a plot to show relationship with age, the curves for the two groups are scarcely distinguishable.

LENGTH OF EPISODES

Beginning with Table 8.3, all reported results are based not upon the entire record on each subject, but upon our sample consisting of about one-half of the episodes in each record.

Looking first, in Table 8.3, at the overall distribution of the per cents of episodes with different temporal durations, perhaps the outstanding finding is that, with every child, more than 70 per cent of the episodes lasted less than two minutes. The number of episodes lasting two or more minutes totals no more than 26 per cent in any case, and those of one minute duration amount to less than 8 per cent. These findings are consistent with those in Table 8.2 on average duration of the total number of episodes in each record. We have noted that the mean duration ranged from half a minute to a minute and three-quarters. These data can be said to show that, on the average, the children set out toward a new goal once every 45 seconds. Table 8.3 shows that this average is heavily weighted by many very short episodes and that relatively few of the episodes lasted more than five minutes.

The two rows immediately below the data for the Midwest children record rank correlations with age, together with significance measures. The coefficients show that correlation between age and length of episode is significantly negative for the shortest episodes, and gradually shifts to positive for longer episodes until it reaches a highly significant positive value with the longest episodes. Change from a negative to a positive correlation occurs between the time intervals of 30 seconds and one minute. The generally prevailing reversal was implied earlier by figures on average episode duration for each record; but the point at which the shift occurs is shown here. So also are relatively high correlations with age for the very short episodes at one extreme, and the longest episodes at the other. Again there is no evidence that the disabled children differed from the Midwest children.

TABLE 8.3

PER CENT OF EPISODES WITH STATED LENGTH

Child	Age	N	$\frac{1}{4}$ m	$\frac{1}{2}$ m	1 m	2 m	3 m	4–5 m	6–10 m	11 m or more
Mary C.	1-10	615	50	20	21	4	2	1	1	+
Jimmy	1-11	490	54	22	18	4	1	1	1	+
Lewis	2-11	653	53	20	17	6	1	1	1	+
Dutton	3-10	633	58	19	12	4	2	2	2	+
Margaret	4-6	582	39	33	18	4	2	2	1	2
Maud	5-0	607	51	21	18	5	2	1	1	1
Roy	6-2	326	29	22	31	8	3	2	2	3
Ben	7-4	358	32	23	25	9	4	1	3	2
Ray	7-4	511	42	18	24	9	2	2	2	1
Mary E.	8-7	545	41	18	27	5	2	3	2	2
Douglas	9-2	422	42	20	22	7	2	2	1	3
Claire	10-9	233	27	20	28	11	4	4	3	4
Correlation with age			−.45	−.21	.48	.54	.44	.62	.59	.74
Significance level			.05	.37	.04	.02	.06	.01	.01	.001
Wally	4-3	499	45	18	25	5	3	2	2	1
Sue	7-1	423	40	21	26	4	2	2	2	3
Bobby	7-4	337	30	20	30	9	3	3	3	2
Verne	7-5	513	36	24	27	5	2	2	2	2

These data on the number and duration of episodes are basic data on the partitioning of behavior in naturally occurring situations. They show that the children of Midwest did from about 500 to about 1300 "things" in a day, that the average duration of these commonly discriminated units of action was from half a minute to one and three-quarters minutes, that the number of episodes was negatively correlated with age, that the duration of episodes was positively correlated with age, and that there was no suggestion of evidence that the disabled children differed from the normal children in these respects.

FREQUENCY AND COMPLEXITY OF OVERLAPPING

Data on episode overlapping are presented in Tables 8.4 through 8.6. They supplement and refine some of the information from analysis of linkages.

To what extent did overlapping of episodes occur in these recorded days? Table 8.4 answers this question in terms of the per cent of all episodes in each record which were found to overlap with one or more other episodes. The table shows that, of the Midwest children, Jimmy behaved in the smallest and Douglas in the largest proportion of overlapping episodes, as indicated by per cents of 51 and 83 respectively. The median per cent of overlapping episodes is 73. A relationship between amount of overlapping and age is

TABLE 8.4

PER CENT OF EPISODES WHICH ARE OVERLAPPING

Child	Per Cent of Episodes	Child	Per Cent of Episodes
Mary C.	53	Roy	77
Jimmy	51	Ben	75
Lewis	67	Ray	63
Dutton	64	Mary E.	76
Margaret	75	Douglas	83
Maud	71	Claire	78
Wally	66	Bobby	80
Sue	89	Verne	74

demonstrated by a rank correlation coefficient of .61, significant beyond the 1 per cent level. It appears, then, that only about one-fourth, and never more than one-half, of the episodes in the days of these children occurred in isolation. For the most part, the children did not do one thing at a time; they were involved during a greater part of their time in multiple-track action. In general, moreover, this was true more frequently of the older than of the younger children.

Although Sue, one of the disabled children, has the highest per cent of overlapping episodes, the four disabled children as a group do not appear to differ greatly from the Midwest children on this variable. The relatively high per cent for Sue may be a function of the ubiquity of social behavior objects in her life situation (see p. 397). From the earlier description of these children, it may be recalled that Sue spent her entire day at the Lawton School where solitude was not often possible.

Overlapping episodes differ with respect to the number of episodes that overlap with them. This difference has been measured in two ways. We have determined for each overlapping episode, first, the total number of other episodes which overlap with it throughout its course and, second, the largest number of episodes which overlap with it at any one time during its course (see categories 2 and 3, above). Results of these measurements indicate that most of the overlapping episodes intersect with only one other episode. The occurrence of more than one episode overlapping sequentially (category 2) with the target episode comprised no more than 27 per cent of the overlapping episodes for any child. A clear relationship (Tau = .50, P = .03) was found between age and the per cent of overlapping episodes having more than five others overlapping sequentially with them.

Simultaneous overlapping (category 5) of two or more episodes with the target unit accounted for per cents of overlapping episodes ranging from a low of 1, in the Jimmy Sexton record, to a high of 20, in the Ben Hutchings record, with a median of 9. These per cents are somewhat higher for the older than for the younger children. A rank correlation of .38 suggests relationship in the expected direction but the significance of this coefficient is doubtful (P=.10).

There is no evidence to suggest that the disabled children differ from the nondisabled with respect to overlapping.

TYPE OF OVERLAP

Overlapping episodes differ with respect to their interpositional relations. This is the variable we have attempted to measure by means of category 4, Type of Overlap. Results from classification of overlapping episodes according to this category are summarized in Table 8.5. The table shows that, for every child, most of the overlapping episodes were of the enclosed type. These and enclosing episodes account for about 90 per cent of the

TABLE 8.5

RANGE AND MEDIAN PER CENTS OF OVERLAPPING EPISODES
OF STATED TYPE, MIDWEST CHILDREN

	Coinciding	Enclosing	Enclosed	Interlinking	Combinations
Range	0–+	13–28	65–78	0–4	2–11
Median	0	18	72	2	5

overlapping in the 16 day-records. Interlinking episodes are relatively rare; and all combinations of differing types of overlap taken together total no more than 11 per cent of the overlapping units in any case.

Our data from 12 Midwest children indicate that the frequency of occurrence of both enclosing and enclosed episodes is correlated with age. Rank order coefficients for these two types of overlapping respectively are −.45 and .52, with corresponding significance levels of .05 and .03. These findings, taken together, give further evidence that the behavior of the older children occurred in units of longer duration, which means that the older children managed to maintain goal directed actions with greater persistence in the face of potentially interrupting action units. The findings are consistent with those reported above on number and duration of episodes and linkages. No evidence was found that the disabled children differed from the nondisabled.

FORM OF INTEREPISODE TRANSITION

Results from category 5, Form of Transition, are summarized in Table 8.6. The per cents in this table are based upon the total number of episodes in the respective samples, not only the overlapping episodes, as in the immediately preceding tables. These data are not entirely independent of other results presented above, nor are they duplicative. They represent a somewhat different approach to the general problem of describing the structural interrelationships of episodes.

Table 8.6 shows that the different transition forms occur with varying frequencies in the behavior of different children. In Jimmy Sexton's record, 67 per cent of the episodes were characterized by abrupt termination, while only 33 per cent were characterized by merging transitions, i.e., were linked by overlapping with a continuing episode. With the older children in general, these per cents are reversed. For example, they are 37 and 63 respectively for Claire. The median per cent of merging transitions for the Midwest children is 55. A rank correlation of .64 (P=.01) was obtained

TABLE 8.6

RANGE AND MEDIAN PER CENTS OF EPISODES WITH STATED FORM
OF TRANSITION AT POINT OF TERMINATION, MIDWEST CHILDREN

	Abrupt	Merging
Range	34–67	33–66
Median	45	55

between age and per cent of episodes marked by merging transition. These data substantiate earlier evidence that the behavior of the older children was less broken or saltatory than that of the younger children. The younger children tended to do things sequentially, one at a time; the actions of the older children were more interlaced. There is no consistent pattern of difference between the disabled and the nondisabled children.

CONTINUITY AND INTERPOLATION

The final results on structural characteristics of behavior are data on the continuity of episode course and on the incidence of interpolated episodes, i.e., episodes occurring between segments of discontinuous units.

It was found that discontinuous or interrupted episodes comprise a very small proportion of the total number, the largest value being 3 per cent for Bobby Bryant. There is no correlation between age and the per cents of discontinuous episodes.

The per cents of interpolated episodes range from 1 to 9 with a median of 4.5. A weak relationship between age and per cent of interpolated episodes is indicated by a rank correlation coefficient of .42 with a P of .07. Thus, there is indication that, while the proportion of discontinuous episodes remains roughly constant from record to record, the proportion of units interpolated between the different segments of these discontinuous episodes tends to be somewhat larger for the older children. This finding could be taken to suggest manifestation under naturally occurring conditions of an increase with age in ability to sustain need tension corresponding to an incomplete action.

The findings on these two variables for the disabled children differ little from those for the nondisabled. A weak tendency was found toward more interpolated episodes for the disabled children than for their nondisabled age-mates. Bobby Bryant had more interpolated episodes than even the oldest nondisabled child. A possible psychological correlate of peripheral motor disability suggested here is an increased ability to maintain tension toward the goal of an incomplete action through a number of interpolated episodes.

Conditions Related to Behavior Structure

Turning now from purely structural characteristics of behavior, we will consider some related factors and conditions.

INCIDENCE OF CONTAINED EPISODES

The incidence of contained episodes in each record was measured in terms of the per cent of the number of overlapping episodes. For the Midwest children these per cents range from a low of 4 for Margaret to 14 for Claire, with a median value of 8. There is no correlation between these data and age. Among the four disabled children, the range is as great as that for the Midwest children, i.e., 2 to 12. These results are important to a study of behavior structure because contained episodes constitute a special source of overlapping. Each episode contributing to these per cents is a part of a larger, unidirectional unit from which the part is segregated solely on the basis of its high relative potency. The data indicate that the frequency with which parts of episodes become so segregated varies from child to child. It may be that equal or even greater variation occurs for the same child in different situations. An adequate accounting for these variations could be made only by a special investigation.

RELATIVE WEIGHT

Table 8.7 summarizes the results from classifying overlapping episodes according to relative weight. These data show that between 65 per cent and 85 per cent of the overlapping episodes were of primary weight for at least a part of their duration. Or, conversely, only 15 to 35 per cent of the overlapping episodes never reached a rank order potency higher than secondary. Episodes which were never less than *primary tied* (1′ in table) total between 55 and 72 per cent of the overlapping units. There are no significant relationships here with age, nor do there appear to be group differences between the disabled and the nondisabled children.

TABLE 8.7
Range and Median Per Cents of Overlapping Episodes With Stated Relative Weight, Midwest Children

	RELATIVE WEIGHT							
	1	1′	2	3	1, 2	1, 3	2, 3	1, 2, 3
Range	22–51	12–42	14–35	0–2	7–18	0–1	0–+	+–3
Median	38	25	22	1	12	+	0	2

EPISODE INITIATION

Table 8.8 gives data on episode initiation. The results for the Midwest children form a clear pattern. For all but two children the per cent of spontaneous starts is greater than the per cent of instigated starts which is, in every case, much greater than the per cent of pressured starts. Ignoring the size of the differences, it is possible to measure the consistency of this highest, next highest, and lowest pattern for spontaneous, instigated, and pressured starts respectively among these 12 children by Kendall's coefficient of concordance, W (**28**, 81). This coefficient for the Midwest children was found to be .862, significant well beyond the 1 per cent level. This statistic indicates that consistency of the initiation pattern among these children is greater than could be expected on the basis of chance alone. The data show that observable instigation from without operated in a lesser degree than spontaneous initiation of episodes in the days of these children.

TABLE 8.8
Per Cent of Episodes with Stated Type of Initiation

Child	Spontaneous	Instigated	Pressured	Can Not Judge
Mary C.	59	35	5	+
Jimmy	58	40	2	+
Lewis	62	35	2	1
Dutton	62	34	4	+
Margaret	49	43	8	+
Maud	56	42	2	+
Roy	49	45	+	6
Ben	40	50	7	3
Ray	56	40	3	1
Mary E.	53	42	3	2
Douglas	60	34	3	1
Claire	42	54	0	5
Range	42–62	34–54	0–8	
Median	49	41	3	
Wally	50	47	2	2
Sue	45	54	1	+
Bobby	36	63	1	1
Verne	44	53	2	1

There is a weak negative relationship between age and per cent of spontaneously initiated episodes, as shown by a rank correlation coefficient of $-.33$. Although it does not meet customary standards of significance ($P = .16$), this coefficient suggests greater spontaneity in the initiation of action units among the younger children. It does not follow, however, that this is necessarily a function of age per se. We have shown elsewhere in the book that children of different ages enter different behavior settings and that different behavior settings require different kinds of behavior. One possibility is that many behavior settings entered by the older children, e.g., school settings, organized group meetings, are more directly coercive with regard to particular molar actions than are the settings in which the younger children spend much of their time, e.g., Home Indoors. An analysis of episode initiation in different behavior settings might very well produce more definitive trends than those suggested in the present data.

The data in Table 8.8 on the disabled children provide an interesting contrast with the data on the Midwest children; the pattern mentioned above is partially reversed in that, for three of the four disabled children, the per cent of instigated starts exceeds the per cent of spontaneous starts. The coefficient of concordance, W, for this pattern is .813, significant at the 5 per cent level, which means that its consistency among the children is greater than chance allows. Thus the Midwest children tended to have consistently higher per cents of spontaneous starts and the disabled children tended to have consistently higher per cents of instigated starts.

In interpreting this reversal, differences in behavior settings again seem important. Sue Dewall spent her entire day, and Verne Trenell spent a large part of his day, in the Lawton School where individual freedom was necessarily limited by group routines. Bobby Bryant, who has the highest per cent of instigated starts, was constantly surrounded by associates.

EPISODE ISSUE

Table 8.9 summarizes the results on category 11, Issue of Episode. In accordance with the original itemization of the category, issues are grouped in the table according to whether the episode was judged to be complete or incomplete.

In view of the results of the agreement tests on this category perhaps the most dependable finding is the one on completeness of episodes. Complete units make up between 72 and 83 per cent of all episodes for the Midwest children, with a median of 76 per cent. The per cents of incomplete episodes range from 4 to 17, with a median of 11. The data indicate, further, a negative relationship between age and per cent of incomplete episodes, shown by a rank correlation coefficient of $-.74$, significant well beyond the 1 per cent level. These data indicate, therefore, that all of the children usually finished things they started, but that the younger children stopped short of the goal more frequently than the older children.

TABLE 8.9

RANGE AND MEDIAN PER CENTS OF EPISODES WITH
STATED ISSUE, MIDWEST CHILDREN

	ISSUE OF COMPLETE EPISODES							
	Acquittance	Attainment	Gratification	Success	Consum. Sat'd.	Other	Total Completed Episodes	Can Not Judge
Range	8–18	3–15	+–4	+–4	+–8	32–63	72–83	9–16
Median	11.5	7.5	2	1.5	2.5	50.5	76	11

	ISSUE OF INCOMPLETE EPISODES					
	Nonattain.	Frustration	Failure	Consum. Not Sat'd.	Other	Total Incomplete
Range	+–8	0–3	0–+	2–6	1–7	4–17
Median	1	1	0	4	3	11

A somewhat surprising result shown in Table 8.9 is the low frequency of occurrence of success, frustration, and failure. Summing the per cents for these three issues for each of the children, the resulting values range from less than 1 per cent to 7 per cent, with a median of 2 per cent. Life for these children appears to have been less a matter of high ups and low downs than one might be led to expect from the amount of attention often given to these outcomes of action in research and writings on children's behavior.

It is interesting to compare the per cents of "good" outcomes, i.e., attainment, gratification, and success, with the per cents of "bad" outcomes, i.e., nonattainment, frustration, and failure. For every child, the per cent of good outcomes or endings is higher than the per cent of bad endings; for the Midwest children, the median per cents are 11 and 2, respectively. While the differences between the per cents of good and bad endings are not great (median difference=7 per cent), the consistency of this relation from child to child is striking.

Both good and bad endings show weak negative correlations with age. The rank correlation coefficient between age and per cent of good endings is .36 (P=.11), and is −.42 (P=.07) for bad endings. Note that the decrease with age is slightly more pronounced for bad than for good endings.

A somewhat similar trend is apparent in the data on consummatory episodes. The rank correlation coefficient between age and per cent consummatory episodes is −.45, significant at the 5 per cent level. Considering the nonsatiated consummation issues alone, the rank correlation with age is −.53, significant at the 2 per cent level. Activity valued as an end in itself evidently declined with age.

Finally, we note the relatively high frequency of occurrence of the issue, acquittance. This issue is checked, it may be recalled, for very short and unimportant episodes. The table shows that acquittance issues account for between 8 and 18 per cent of all episodes. This would indicate that a sizeable portion of the episodes in these records consists of units best described as brief distractions from the main course of events.

Once again there is no suggestion of difference between the disabled and the nondisabled children. It is noted especially that these data offer no evidence to support a contention that motor disability necessarily implies more frequent occurrence of bad episode endings.

EPISODE TERMINATION

Table 8.10 presents findings on episode termination. The overall pattern shown by these data is even more consistent than that for the data on episode initiation. For every child the rank order is the same, viz., spontaneous, environmental cessation, instigated, and pressured in order of mention. Thus for the Midwest children, this pattern yields a coefficient of

TABLE 8.10

PER CENT OF EPISODES WITH STATED EPISODE TERMINATION

Child	Spontaneous	Instigated	Environmental Cessation	Pressured	Can Not Judge
Mary C.	62	11	18	6	4
Jimmy	62	11	22	2	2
Lewis	65	8	19	4	4
Dutton	65	10	16	3	6
Margaret	57	11	21	6	5
Maud	62	11	18	4	6
Roy	51	11	26	2	10
Ben	59	10	21	4	7
Ray	67	8	19	1	5
Mary E.	66	5	22	2	6
Douglas	63	9	17	5	6
Claire	59	6	23	0	12
Range	51–67	5–11	16–26	0–6	
Median	62	10	20	3.5	
Wally	54	14	24	2	6
Sue	55	8	26	1	10
Bobby	56	9	29	1	6
Verne	52	13	27	2	6

concordance, W, of 1.0. Although this coefficient leaves out of account the size of the differences between the four possible kinds of termination, the table shows large differences between columns. These findings, together with those reported above on episode initiation, indicate that these children displayed marked independence in starting and stopping their action units; they were not often forced to start or stop their activities.

In general, the data for the disabled children follow the pattern of these for the Midwest children, i.e., the per cents have the same rank order. The disabled children, however, have somewhat lower per cents of spontaneous and pressured terminations than the Midwest children. This trend is in the same direction as that noted above for episode initiation, but here the difference is less clear cut. The two sets of data suggest, however, that behavior structure was determined more by external forces among the disabled children.

Discussion

The larger significance of the data on behavior structure is necessarily limited at the present time because few other facts about the structure of naturally occurring behavior are known and because most current theories do not focus on behavior structure. However, some suggestions arising out of the data are presented below.

In this connection, the most important result of the study is the demonstration that the stream of behavior has fundamental characteristics which can be reliably described in terms of behavior structure, as here defined. The evidence supporting this conclusion is of four kinds, namely, (a) the degree of agreement with which records can be episoded, (b) the degree of agreement with which descriptive categories can be applied to episodes by independent workers, (c) the internal consistency of different aspects of the structure data, and (d) the concordance of the findings with theories of behavior which have wider confirmation.

The results of the episoding reliability tests ranging, as they do, from 72 to 92 per cent agreement by independent episoders, mean that the behavior of children, as reported in the specimen records used in the study, displays structural characteristics of sufficient clarity to permit quite highly consistent discrimination of episodes as units of behavior structure.

Direct agreement tests for 4 of the 12 categories which specify structural characteristics of episodes (categories 7, 10, 11, and 12), and indirect evidence for 5 of them (categories 2, 3, 4, 5, and 6) provide evidence that some precise structural features of episodes can be consistently identified by different analysts. Further evidence along this line is provided by the reliability of social interaction characteristics presented in Chapter X.

Data on the internal consistency of the behavior structure findings come from the age relationships discovered. Different indices of behavior complexity show the same trend toward greater complexity in the behavior of older children and none of the findings are at odds with this trend. Thus, the younger children did more things in a day and their action units were, on the whole, shorter than those of the older children; i.e., the number of units (both episodes and linkages) was negatively correlated with age and the average duration of units was positively correlated with age. Furthermore, the older children as compared with the younger showed:

> more episodes in each linkage;
> more overlapping episodes;
> more instances of three or more simultaneously overlapping episodes;
> more instances of five or more sequentially overlapping episodes;
> more episodes which ended by merging into the subsequent behavior units;
> more episodes interpolated between the segments of discontinuous episodes;
> more completed episodes.

These findings are mutually supporting. They produce an overall picture of marked differences in structural characteristics of behavior between younger and older children. The younger children tended to do things sequentially, one at a time, to shift frequently from one action to another, and to persevere in a given activity a relatively short time whereas the older children tended to engage in actions of longer duration, to pursue more than one action at a given time, and to carry to completion a higher proportion of their episodes.

The data on the relationship between behavior structure and age present points of affinity with theories of development offered by Lewin (**32, 33**), Kounin (**31**), and Baldwin (**2**). In terms of the theory of development presented by Lewin and Kounin, which we will review only in outline here, the psychological person is structured into parts or regions which are coordinated to different behavior possibilities for the person. According to this theory, the degree of differentiation of the person increases with age. Thus an older person normally has more possibilities for action in a given situation than a younger one. The regions of the psychological person necessarily have boundaries. One postulated property of these boundaries is their rigidity, defined as the inverse of communication between neighboring regions of the person. Thus, the more rigid the boundary between two regions, the less a change in one affects neighboring regions. Further, the degree of rigidity of the person increases with chronological age. The psychological structure of the person is characterized, therefore, not only by a higher degree of differentiation into parts with increasing age but also by a higher degree of independence as between these parts.

The findings, reported above, that the older children had more long episodes and that they completed a higher proportion of the things they started than the younger children appear to be consistent with this theoretical formulation. The longer average duration and more frequent completion of episodes in the days of the older children could be conceived as a function of a higher degree of rigidity; for, since the theory provides that change in one region as a consequence of change in neighboring regions decreases with increase in rigidity, and that rigidity increases with age, one can derive from this representation lesser susceptibility to distractions and diversions in the older children. Greater ability on the part of the older children to maintain simultaneously different courses of behavior, as shown by the increase with age in frequency of overlapping episodes, also can be derived from the greater rigidity of the boundaries which separate their need and ability systems.

Baldwin (2), in his description of the maturity continuum, holds that expansion of the psychological world is one of the major characteristics of the developmental process. One feature of this expansion, in Baldwin's formulation, is an increase with development in the temporal and spatial remoteness of objects with which the child is concerned. This means that the older child is to a lesser degree subject to the coerciveness of the immediate situation, the here and now, than is the younger child. One implication of this formulation, as far as behavior structure is concerned, might be that the older child, with his ability to relate himself to more remote objects, would have longer episodes and would show more persistence in reaching his goals than would a younger child. Such differences between the behavior structure of older and younger children were clearly demonstrated for the subjects of this study.

The data of this part of the study demonstrate quite conclusively that naturally occurring behavior has structural properties which can be reliably identified and which are related to both empirical variables and theoretical formulations in ways that hold promise of wide significance.

Chapter IX

The Behavior Objects of Midwest

ANY investigation of the behavior of Midwest children must inevitably deal with bicycles, balls, flowers, spoons, comic books, Easter eggs, jump ropes, valentines, and other objects in seemingly endless variety. Even a cursory reading of specimen records reveals how completely the behavior of the children of Midwest is entangled with things.

Behavior Objects and Habitat Objects [1]

We have analyzed data only in terms of *behavior objects*; however, the definitions and methods make it necessary to define habitat objects as well.

BEHAVIOR OBJECTS

Behavior objects are the counterparts with respect to things, of behavior settings with respect to regions. Like behavior settings, behavior objects consist of a part of the nonpsychological milieu and an associated standing pattern in the behavior of men, en masse. They differ from behavior settings by being seen as points around which the behavior occurs rather than regions within which it takes place. In the case of behavior objects, the behavior pattern is circumjacent to the associated milieu while with behavior settings the milieu is circumjacent to the behavior. The prototype of a behavior object is a Maypole around which the pattern of the dance occurs; while the prototype of a behavior setting is a park within which the dance occurs. As a matter of fact, behavior objects are generally located within behavior settings; they are spatially related to behavior settings as stage properties are related to the scenes of a play.

Behavior objects may be exemplified from an episode of Chuck Thurston's specimen record.

> After the evening meal, Chuck Thurston had helped his father fix the family truck; they came into the house together.

7:34 Chuck's mother said firmly, "Chuck, put your coat and hat away."

Chuck just stood in the middle of the kitchen.

His mother repeated her command, this time very firmly.

[1] This chapter is based in part on the M.A. Thesis by Phil H. Schoggen (**50**).

Chuck asked, looking somewhat impish, "Shall I get the ruler, Mommie?"

Earlier in the day, Chuck had refused to put away his wraps, whereupon his mother had said, threateningly, "Now, where is my ruler?" So, in asking now if he should get the ruler, Chuck evidently was beating his mother to the draw.

Chuck did not press the question about the ruler.

Before his mother could answer it, he picked up his hat and coat.

He carried them into the bedroom. He was smiling.

He returned to the living room at once.

This episode occurred within the behavior setting Thurston Home, Indoors, and it conforms to the standing pattern of behavior associated with this setting. The following behavior objects are mentioned in this episode: *Chuck, Mrs. Thurston, Coat, Hat, Ruler.* These are all behavior objects by virtue of three characteristics which each possesses: Each is (*a*) a part of the nonpsychological milieu and (*b*) a standing pattern of behavior which (*c*) is circumjacent to the milieu. These characteristics of behavior objects are found in their official definitions. The behavior object *Hat*, for example, is defined by Webster as follows (parentheses ours):

> a shaped object made of various materials (milieu) and used as a covering for the head and worn by men and women (behavior, circumjacent to milieu).

Every other definition of a behavior object includes these three features either implicitly or explicitly.

Behavior objects differ in many ways. Two important kinds of behavior objects which are represented in this episode are, *social* behavior objects (Chuck and Mrs. Thurston) and *nonsocial* behavior objects (coat, hat, and ruler). Chuck and Mrs. Thurston are, on the milieu side, parts of the social-physical world: they have size, age, social group, sex, and family membership characteristics which are completely independent of their behavior. On the behavior side, they are, in Midwest, the focus of unique patterns in the behavior of others. The nonsocial behavior objects can be identified and described in purely physical terms, and on the behavior side discriminable patterns of behavior are anchored to them. Rulers are not worn on the head nor are coats used to draw straight lines.

Behavior objects differ greatly in their frequency of occurrence and in their distribution throughout society. Some are culture-wide in their occurrence and are, in fact, so well established that they are found in the dictionaries of a society. This is true of all the nonsocial behavior objects mentioned in the episode above. Webster provides the following definitions (parentheses ours):

> Coat: a layer of material usually made of cloth or skin, shaped as a garment (milieu) and worn over the upper part of the body (behavior).

Ruler: a straight or curved strip of wood, metal, etc. with a smooth edge (milieu) used for guiding a pencil or pen in drawing lines (behavior).

Some single behavior objects are known to a large population; this is true, for example, of the behavior object Liberty Bell. Other behavior objects are less widely distributed and less widely known. The behavior object, *Senior Color Cane* is very restricted on both counts. It is defined as follows:

a walking stick located in the trophy case of the Midwest High School (milieu) to which each Senior Class ties its colors in a ceremony on Class Day (behavior).

So far as the authors are aware there is only one Senior Color Cane, and knowledge of it is largely restricted to the community of Midwest. Within a local dictionary, however, Senior Color Cane would have as definite physical characteristics and behavioral attributes as hat, coat, ruler, and Liberty Bell have in the dictionary of a wider culture.

Chuck Thurston, like the Senior Color Cane, is a unique behavior object in Midwest. He is recognized as a particular person by most of the people of the town, and around him there occurs a pattern in the behavior of others which differs in its details from the behavior attached to any other person. Outside of Midwest, Chuck Thurston would become only a little boy, and the unique standing pattern of behavior associated with him in Midwest would be modified to that of the more general and widely distributed standing pattern of behavior attached to the behavior object, Little Boy.

Local cultures sometimes attach a unique behavior pattern to a widely discriminated part of the milieu. This happens in Midwest with the milieu side of the behavior object, *ruler*. It will be noted that Chuck and his mother in the episode reported above do not use the term, "ruler" to refer to the behavior object defined by Webster. In Midwest, "ruler" denotes Webster's behavior object and, in addition, an entirely different behavior object, namely:

a light, flexible piece of wood or plastic, one or two feet long (milieu), used to paddle children for misbehaving (behavior).

The part of the milieu discriminated by Webster is used, in Midwest, for this very different behavior object, in addition to the one defined by him.

As with behavior settings, the source of the connection between a behavior object and its pattern of behavior is not well known. However, all of the factors mentioned in connection with behavior settings undoubtedly operate with behavior objects, too. Behavior objects have physical and social properties which influence the behavior connected with them, and they are perceived by innate and learned processes as appropriate for some patterns of behavior and not for others.

Furthermore, behavior selects and creates behavior objects which sustain its prevailing pattern.   For the behavior "counting out," Midwest children select dandelions which have gone to seed.   They select these particular flowers from the hundreds of others available because the physical properties of dandelions fit this behavior.   Children also make behavior objects to support their behavior; they make hopscotch designs, and they make swings in order to have the behavior objects essential for playing hopscotch and for swinging.

Behavior objects represent the prevailing culture.   By definition, the standing pattern of behavior attached to a behavior object is a property of the behavior of men en masse.   This pattern must, therefore, be either a universal characteristic of the behavior of all men with reference to the object, or it must be an attribute of a particular culture.   Since it is questionable whether universal behavior patterns unmodified by local cultural influences ever occur, we are safe in considering almost every behavior object as a piece in the total prevailing culture mosaic—a resultant of universal, regional, and local patterns.   Behavior objects are carriers of culture and they are products of culture: the prevailing patterns of behavior select and create appropriate behavior objects which, in turn, coerce behavior in the likeness of the behavior for which they were created.   People of Midwest who cannot afford "modern conveniences" may complain of the behavior imposed upon them by behavior objects made for another era.   However much the outdoor privy, the wood-burning kitchen range, and the oil lamp may be decried, they dominate behavior if they are used as behavior objects. The only way to be free from their authority is to replace them.

HABITAT OBJECTS

Every behavior object in addition to its involvement in a standing pattern of behavior is also implicated in the unique, ongoing molar actions of particular individuals.   In the context of an individual's actions a behavior object becomes a habitat object; it becomes a part of his psychological habitat.   The behavior object *Hammer*, for example, is "an instrument consisting of a head, usually of iron or steel, fixed crosswise to a handle (milieu) for driving nails, beating metals, and the like (behavior)." However, at the time a hammer is involved in such a standing pattern of behavior, it is also participating in the actions of a particular person, actions which often extend beyond the behavior of hammering.   In these longer, individual behavior sequences a hammer carries a multiplicity of psychological effects.   It may be a means of making a playhouse, or of cracking walnuts for candy; it may be a source of frustration to a child too weak to "hammer" effectively; or, to a three-year-old who for the first time successfully drives a nail, it may be the way to an important goal successfully achieved.   In these cases, the characteristic standing pattern of behavior (hammering, pounding, driving, beating) defines the *behavior object*; while the behavior unit arising within the context of each individual's unique action, e.g., "building a playhouse," "making walnut fudge," defines the *habitat object*.

The patterns of the individual's behavior in which the habitat object is involved will usually be consonant with the standing pattern of the behavior object, merely including the latter as one phase of a sequence of behavior which originates outside the standing pattern and continues beyond it. However, when any behavior object enters the psychological habitat of a particular person, the standing pattern of behavior is stamped by the unique characteristics of the particular action under way. This is why the behavior which is anchored to behavior objects has a general, patterned identity rather than a precise, particular form. The standing pattern of a behavior object must accommodate within itself the multiplicity of individual actions and unique psychological significances attaching to it as a manifold of habitat objects. And occasionally the action in which a habitat object participates will differ widely from the standing pattern of behavior. Thus, a hammer might conceivably be fastened to the wall and used for hanging coats; it might be used for a paper weight or a table decoration. The existence of a discriminable standing pattern of behavior in connection with a behavior object indicates, however, that such radical deviations are not sufficiently frequent to destroy the perceived patterning.

Habitat objects in the episode presented above are: Chuck's mother, Chuck's coat, Chuck's hat, and the ruler. All of these objects affected Chuck's actions and therefore entered into his psychological habitat as carriers of psychological effects. Some of the significances of these habitat objects for Chuck may be tabulated as follows:

Habitat Object	Psychological Significance for Chuck
Chuck's mother	Center of coercive power requiring Chuck to engage in the negative action of putting away his hat and coat.
	Target of humorous, deprecating, hostile, counterthrust, "Shall I get the ruler, Mommie."
Chuck's hat	Source, via his mother, of region of activity of negative valence, putting hat away.
Chuck's coat	Same.
Ruler	A basis of mother's power and/or a means of assaulting her and showing independence.

There are many ways in which habitat objects may be analyzed and classified. In fact, the psychology of habitat objects overlaps with much of the material covered by individual psychology. It includes the problem of how "things" come to have a psychological significance for a person, i.e., perception and learning; it includes, also, the problem of the adjustment of the person in his psychological world, however it arises.

SUMMARY

Behavior objects lie at the intersection of the nonpsychological and the cultural worlds; they are simultaneously parts of the nonbehavioral milieu and of the prevailing culture pattern. They are, therefore, crucial for studies of culture and of its relation to the physical and social environment. Behavior objects have the same values for social psychologists as artifacts have for anthropologists and archeologists. Habitat objects lie at the intersection of the nonpsychological milieu, the prevailing culture pattern, and an individual's psychological habitat; they are, therefore, crucial for studies of personality and its relation to culture and to physical and social conditions.

The Behavior Objects Used by Three Children

The behavior objects recorded in the three day-long specimen records of Mary Ennis, Raymond Birch, and Bobby Bryant have been analyzed. These children are described in Chapter II and Appendix 1 and Appendix 2. These particular subjects were chosen for this first attempt to study the natural history of behavior objects because they involved sex differences, urban-town differences, and differences in physique within a limited age and culture range. They appeared likely to furnish a varied sample of behavior objects.

There are approximately 1,200,000 behavior objects in Midwest. This estimate is based upon sample counts in representative behavior settings. On an ordinary weekday, about half of these behavior objects are accessible to most citizens. The other behavior objects are the private possessions of particular individuals or families, or are available only on special occasions, such as the meetings of organizations. On Sundays the number of behavior objects which are freely accessible is reduced to approximately 200,000; and on some holidays the available behavior objects are further restricted. In addition to these, there is an unlimited number of potential behavior objects which can be selected or created at any time. The figures given above refer to objects which are generally available and generally perceived. Thus in these counts each tree is included as a behavior object because, in Midwest, trees are discrete perceptual units with associated standing patterns of behavior; however, each branch and twig is a potential behavior object, although they are not usually discriminated as such.

SAMPLING BEHAVIOR OBJECTS

In view of the large number of behavior objects in Midwest, some system was necessary to select them for study. There were a number of ways of doing this, among them the following: (a) one might sample the total population of behavior objects; (b) all, or a sample, of the behavior objects in a particular behavior setting or other community unit might be studied;

(c) the behavior objects used by a particular person during a particular period might be investigated. The availability of material especially suited to the last method, and the relevance of such data to our concern with the living conditions of individuals within the general context of Midwest led us to use it.

We can define the universe of behavior objects included in this study, then, as those which entered the psychological habitats of Mary Ennis, Raymond Birch, and Bobby Bryant. It should be emphasized that although we limited our attention to objects which entered the psychological habitats of these subjects, we were not, at this point, concerned with them as habitat objects; we were concerned only with their characteristics as behavior objects. Limiting our consideration to behavior objects which were also habitat objects was a device for defining the universe of behavior objects to be investigated.

Specimen records provided the necessary data. A day-long specimen record includes virtually all the behavior objects which participate as essential supports in the behavior of the child during the course of a day; i.e., it includes the objects which enter the child's psychological habitat. A specimen record includes, in addition however, many other behavior objects which are mentioned for purposes of general orientation. We were faced, therefore, with two technical problems: (a) the identification of the behavior objects mentioned in the record, and (b) the further identification of those behavior objects which entered the subject's psychological habitat.

In connection with the first problem, the procedures and conventions which were followed may be outlined as follows:

1. The basic criteria for identifying behavior objects were contained in their definition. In practice one looked for (a) parts of the nonpsychological milieu with which there was regularly associated in Midwest (b) a standing pattern of behavior which was (c) circumjacent to the milieu.

2. Physical, social, and cultural milieu parts and their standing patterns of behavior were included in the census of behavior objects. Included as parts of the social and cultural milieu were any discriminable features of the environment which could exist independently of the associated behavior. This covered such things as songs, arithmetic problems, the rules of a game, fictional characters, stories, and radio programs. In all of these cases there was, or there could be, a milieu aspect of the behavior object which existed independently of the behavior. A song, for example, is a product of behavior, like a box or a path; like them too, after it has been created, i.e., written down or recorded, it becomes an independent feature of the milieu.

3. The occurrence of a standing pattern of behavior was judged in terms of Midwest culture. The identification of behavior objects, therefore, required judges thoroughly familiar with local mores.

4. Behavior objects which were far removed in time and/or space from an action were often, nevertheless, implicated in the behavior. These were usually

cases where verbal behavior was prominent. The following episode is an example:

Bobby Bryant was in the kitchen with his aunt making cookies.

The aunt referred to a story about milk.

Bobby broke in excitedly, "Yeah, she gave the milk to the teddy bear."
He said this in a disparaging way as if the girl in the story should have known better.

In this episode, *milk* and *teddy bear* were both marked as behavior objects, although neither was physically present.

5. Behavior objects which were involved in behavior via their symbols or representations were enumerated only once if the symbol itself did not enter the habitat as a separate behavior object; if it did, both the symbol and that for which it stood were included. The following example will illustrate this problem:

Bobby was playing with his brother Kenny.

Bobby stepped over to Kenny who was sitting down, stood squarely in front of Kenny, and crooked his finger dramatically as he exclaimed, "See, this is a hook."

The episode continues with Bobby demonstrating further with his hooked finger.

In this case, both *finger* and *hook* were included as behavior objects.

6. Both generally recognized behavior objects and unusual behavior objects which were selected or created by the subject were included in the enumeration. Thus, twigs, flower petals, and the fender of an automobile were included, although they would not be enumerated in a general survey of behavior objects in Midwest.

The problem of identifying the behavior objects which enter a subject's psychological habitat is easily solved in principle, but presents difficulties in practice. The psychological habitat of an individual is the naturally occurring life space, in Lewin's system. Lewin describes the life space in terms of such noncultural constructs as need, goal, path, barrier, region, and force. Every behavior object which enters the psychological habitat carries these and other psychological properties in the life space of an individual, i.e., it becomes a habitat object. The fact that a particular behavior object enters a person's psychological habitat cannot be as directly perceived as some other features of the subject's situation, e.g., whether an object is physically close to the subject. The line between those objects that enter his habitat and those that do not is indefinite. As practical guides, we may say that the child must look at, listen to, speak to or about, manipulate, approach, withdraw from, or otherwise indicate overtly that the object is inextricably implicated in what he is doing, and that it is an essential psychological support for his behavior. This clearly eliminates from the analysis, objects which are mentioned for background purposes as well as some objects which are merely on the fringe of psychological significance. However, the line is a narrow one and in using these guides there were doubtless errors made in both directions. In the final analysis, the basic criterion is that the observer and the analyst perceived an object to have entered the subject's psychological habitat. This did not completely coincide with the psychological reality for the subject, but it was the best we could do. An excerpt from the specimen record will illustrate the point.

The following episode, called *Talking to Shirley*, occurred at 11:15 a.m. in the third- and fourth-grade classroom of the Midwest School. Mary Ennis, the subject of the observation, had just asked permission to leave her seat.

Mary immediately stood and with quick, almost furtive little steps she scooted up to Shirley's seat.

In her effort to be quiet, she swung her body as she walked.

After a brief, very business-like conversation with Shirley, Mary returned directly to her own desk.

In terms of the guides stated above, there is little doubt that *Shirley*, as a behavior object, entered Mary's psychological habitat during this episode. It is equally clear that the behavior objects *own body* and *Shirley's seat* were not part of Mary's psychological habitat. The position of the behavior object *own desk* is not so clear. In this case the analyst, basing his decision on the whole context of the behavior judged that the object *own desk* should be included.

GUIDES FOR ENUMERATING BEHAVIOR OBJECTS

Certain conventions were adopted for dealing with a number of particular problems. The first relates to objects which recurred frequently throughout the record. In the course of a day, a child interacted with certain objects many times. This posed the problem of how many times such objects should be considered. Two procedures were followed: First, each behavior object was enumerated and analyzed once, independent of the number of times it entered a child's habitat. This constitutes a census of behavior objects entering a child's psychological habitat. Second, each object was enumerated in every episode it entered. This constituted a survey of *object transactions*, an object transaction being defined as the occurrence of a particular behavior object in one episode of behavior. The sum of the object transactions of all behavior objects provides an index of the rate of flow of behavior objects through the child's psychological habitat.

Another convention is concerned with the handling of *collective objects*. When a child interacted with two or more objects as though they were a single object, the collective object was analyzed as one. For example, the record states that "Mary called happily, 'Hey kids, come over,' to her friends, Ben and Sarah." Here Ben and Sarah comprise a single collective object. In another episode the record says that "Mary gathered up a stack of things from her desk and went toward the door with this rather awkward load. Included in this stack of belongings were a paint box, three or four small rocks, two or three books, and a few pencils." Here Mary behaved with reference to her belongings as a group, not to each object separately. Hence, these belongings make up one collective object.

The last convention relates to behavior settings. A behavior setting was never counted as a behavior object, even though in the episode under consideration, the child behaved toward it as to a behavior object, i.e., as a point rather than as a region. One might, for example, consider a "picnic" as a behavior object when Mary talks about the fine time she had there, but this was not done.

RELIABILITY OF BEHAVIOR OBJECT IDENTIFICATION

Two questions arise about the degree of confidence which can be placed in the identification of behavior objects in a specimen record. One question asks whether the rules for identifying behavior objects and for selecting those which entered the psychological habitat were so stated that they could be followed by others, and the other asks whether the rules were consistently followed by the analysts. To answer these questions, two assistant analysts were trained by the chief analyst in the principles and practice of identifying behavior objects. In each case the theory of behavior objects and the guides for identifying them were thoroughly explained. The assistant analysts practiced applying these principles, and their work was checked and criticized by the chief analyst until little evidence of further improvement was apparent. Every effort was made to avoid training the assistants to unwittingly make the errors the chief analyst made. The aim was to educate the assistants to judge consistently with the principles, regardless of the chief analyst's biases.

The final test material consisted of a section of a record in which the chief investigator had identified 100 behavior objects. This section covered about 20 pages of the record and 40 minutes of time. The assistants checked their identifications on unmarked copies of the record. The results are as follows, by the *estimate of accuracy* method previously described (p. 271):

Assistant A *vs.* chief analyst, per cent accuracy = 92

Assistant B *vs.* chief analyst, per cent accuracy = 93

These agreement checks are taken to mean that the principles of identifying behavior objects are adequate to permit independent investigators to achieve a satisfactory level of agreement in this operation, and that the principles, as communicated to the assistants, were followed by the chief analyst.

NUMBER OF BEHAVIOR OBJECTS AND FREQUENCY OF OBJECT TRANSACTIONS

A total of 1,950 different objects occurred in the psychological habitats of the children. The objects used by each child are listed in Appendix 11 where they are classified into 13 broad categories called *kinds*, and 509 subordinate, narrow categories called *varieties*. Here the number of objects and object transactions are given for each kind of behavior object, and the prominent varieties are designated.

Basic data from the analysis of the number of behavior objects and the frequency of object transactions are:

	Mary	Raymond	Bobby
Duration of record in hours	14.50	13.55	12.95
Number of behavior episodes	920[2]	1000	683
Number of different behavior objects	571	671	749
Number of object transactions	1882	2282	2490

These data show the high degree to which the behavior of the three subjects was involved with things. Mary's behavior made use of a *different* behavior object every 1.5 minutes, Raymond's every 1.2 minutes, and Bobby's every 1.0 minutes. These figures indicate the average rate of "flow" of different behavior objects into the habitats of the children. This is only part of the story, however, for more than one episode of behavior was transacted with most behavior objects. The average number of transactions per object was for Mary, 3.3, for Raymond, 3.4, and for Bobby, 3.3. Behavior was transacted with *some* behavior object, either a new object or an old object, every 28 seconds by Mary, every 21 seconds by Raymond, and every 18 seconds by Bobby, on the average. The temporal distribution of behavior objects and object transactions of these children during one half-hour period are represented in Figure 9.1. The points represent object transactions with old behavior objects and the bars represent transactions with new objects. This half-hour was not atypical of other parts of the day; it provides a picture of the rate at which the world of things flowed through the psychological habitats of these children.

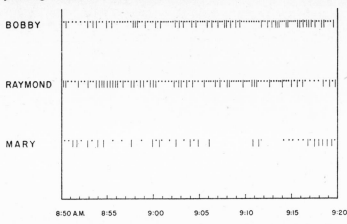

FIG. 9.1.—Temporal spacing of object transactions and new behavior objects entering the psychological habitats of Bobby, Raymond, and Mary during a half-hour interval. Points (....) represent transactions with old behavior objects; bars (|||||) represent transactions with new behavior objects.

[2] The discrepancy of 49 between the number of episodes in the Mary Ennis record as shown here and elsewhere in the book is the result of certain minor revisions in the episoding of this record after the analysis of behavior objects had been completed. Since the results of the behavior objects study would not have been appreciably changed, they have not been corrected for this discrepancy.

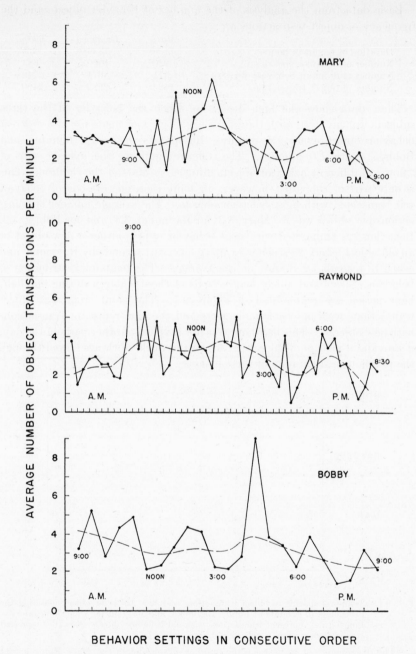

Fig. 9.2.—Rate of object transactions in consecutive behavior settings during the day for Mary, Raymond, and Bobby.

The rates of object transactions in consecutive behavior settings throughout the three days are shown in Figure 9.2. In this figure each point represents the average number of object transactions per minute in each setting. Behavior settings which were inhabited by the subject for less than two consecutive minutes have been omitted because of the instability of the transaction frequencies for short periods. These data indicate a trend in the three cases for the rate of object transactions to decline throughout the day; the rate is from one to two transactions less per minute for the last five settings of each day than for the first five settings. In each curve, too, the peak of object transactions frequency occurs in the middle parts of the day. There appear to be superimposed shorter and longer cyclical fluctuations in each case.

KINDS AND VARIETIES OF BEHAVIOR OBJECTS

Neither the kinds nor varieties of behavior objects represent a systematic classification based upon definite criteria, as was the case with varieties of behavior settings. Both are commonly recognized classifications in Midwest. We claim no more for them than convenience and accordance with common Midwest ways of seeing things. They provide one way of presenting the 1,950 behavior objects which the three children discriminated and selected as supports for their behavior from the millions available.

The kinds of behavior objects and their rank order with respect to frequency of object transactions are given in Table 9.1. Kinds of behavior

TABLE 9.1

KINDS OF BEHAVIOR OBJECTS PRESENTED IN RANK ORDER
OF PER CENT OF TOTAL OBJECT TRANSACTIONS BY THE SUBJECT*

KIND	MARY		RAYMOND		BOBBY	
	Rank	Per Cent	Rank	Per Cent	Rank	Per Cent
People	1	46.1	1	45.1	1	43.5
Reading Writing and School Supplies	2	10.7	2	10.5	5	6.2
Furniture, etc.	3	10.4	3	7.7	2	14.3
Plants	4	6.1	8	3.3	12	0.2
Clothing	5	5.4	7	4.2	7	4.9
Playthings	6	4.7	4	6.3	3	9.5
Physique	7	2.4	6	4.7	6	4.9
Food	8	2.4	10	2.4	4	7.0
Animals	9	2.2	9	2.5	8	2.0
Outdoor Equipment	10	1.8	5	5.0	11	0.3
Earth Materials	11	1.8	11	1.4	13	0.1
Vehicles	12	0.2	12	1.0	9	1.7
Money	13	0.2	13	0.3	10	0.6
Miscellaneous		4.2		4.3		3.6

* In this and the following tables observers are included as behavior objects unless otherwise indicated.

objects which rank high for all subjects (rank of 5 or higher) are People; Reading, Writing, and School Supplies; Furniture. Those which rank low for all subjects (rank of 9 or lower) are Earth Materials; Vehicles; Money. The most variable varieties of behavior objects as to rank order of object transactions are Plants, Food, and Outdoor Equipment; and the most stable kinds are People, Furniture, and Animals.

Preferred varieties of behavior objects, i.e., varieties with which the subjects transacted behavior most frequently are listed below. They are the varieties which occur among the upper 15 in the rank order of at least one of the subjects. The figures in parentheses give each object's position in Mary's, Raymond's, and Bobby's rank order respectively; an X indicates that the object does not fall among the 15 varieties of behavior objects most preferred by the subject. Preferred varieties of behavior objects in terms of frequency of transactions with them are: women (1, 2, 1), boys (3, 1, 2), girls (2, 4, 13), men (12, 3, 5), books (4, 7, 11), dogs (8, 8, X), trees (5, 12, X), desks (9, 9, X), papers (X, 6, 12), cap guns and caps (X, X, 3), cookies (X, X, 4), bicycles (X, 5, X), flowers (6, X, X), radios (X, X, 6), swings (7, X, X), chairs (X, X, 7), doors (X, 11, 15), hats (X, X, 8), boxes (11, 14, X), records (X, X, 9), sofas (X, X, 10), dresses (10, X, X), arithmetic problems (13, X, X), hands (X, 13, X), pencils (14, X, X), batons (15, X, X), miniature cars (X, 15, X), and coats (X, X, 14).

ATTRIBUTES OF BEHAVIOR OBJECTS

The behavior objects used by Mary, Raymond, and Bobby have many attributes. A few of these have been analyzed. In all cases the analysis is in terms of behavior objects, i.e., as they participated in standing behavior patterns in Midwest, not in terms of their use by the subjects. Thus, although Raymond used a retaining wall for a path as he went to school, in the present analysis this is analyzed as a retaining wall.

Social and Nonsocial Behavior Objects. Table 9.2 presents data on social and nonsocial behavior objects.

TABLE 9.2

SOCIAL AND NONSOCIAL BEHAVIOR OBJECTS

Behavior objects (BO) and object transactions (ObT) in terms of per cent of total for each subject. Average number of object transactions with each behavior object (ObT/BO).

	MARY			RAYMOND			BOBBY		
	BO	ObT	ObT/BO	BO	ObT	ObT/BO	BO	ObT	ObT/BO
Nonsocial Behavior									
Objects	80.9	51.8	2.1	78.2	51.9	2.2	84.9	55.7	2.2
Pets	0.3	2.0	18.5	2.4	2.4	3.4	1.6	0.5	1.0
Social Behavior									
Objects	18.8	46.2	8.1	19.4	45.7	8.0	13.5	43.8	10.8

The data from the three children agree in indicating that nonsocial behavior objects were more than four times as frequent in the habitats of the subjects as social behavior objects, and that the transactions per social behavior object were about four times as great as those per nonsocial behavior object. The result is that total object transactions were about equally divided between social and nonsocial behavior objects. The position of pets in the days of Raymond and Mary, comprising as they do 2.0 and 2.4 per cent of the object transactions, is worthy of notice.

Characteristics of Social Behavior Objects. Some characteristics of the social behavior objects used by Mary, Raymond, and Bobby are given in Table 9.3.

TABLE 9.3

CHARACTERS OF SOCIAL BEHAVIOR OBJECTS AND
OBJECT TRANSACTIONS

Number of behavior objects (BO) and frequency of object transactions (ObT) in terms of per cent of total social behavior objects and object transactions.

	MARY		RAYMOND		BOBBY	
	BO	ObT	BO	ObT	BO	ObT
Family membership						
Family	5.6	19.5	1.5	18.5	11.8	60.3
Nonfamily	94.4	80.5	98.5	81.5	88.2	39.7
Age						
Children and						
Adolescents	68.3	40.5	53.9	42.7	30.7	28.6
Adults	28.0	59.0	41.5	56.7	56.4	69.4
Unspecified	3.7	0.5	4.6	0.6	12.9	2.0
Roles						
Mother	0.9	14.1	0.7	10.5	1.0	13.7
Father	0.9	2.1	0.7	7.9	1.0	1.8
Aunt	0	0	0	0	1.0	22.6
Teachers	2.8	11.1	3.9	13.2	0	0
Fictional and						
Historical Persons	0	0	9.2	1.2	23.7	2.4
Neighbors	3.7	1.0	3.1	0.9	1.0	0.3
Observers	9.4	29.1	6.9	20.7	4.9	22.2

With all subjects, nonfamily persons constituted by far the greater number of social behavior objects. These seven- and eight-year-olds had interactions with many persons beyond the borders of their families. This was even true of Bobby who reached beyond the family circle, to which he was physically confined, to many behavior transactions with prominent contemporary, historical and fictional persons such as Jessie James, Little Orlie, Bugs Bunny, Bing Crosby, Dagwood, the Lone Ranger, and Roy Rogers. Mary and Raymond had more behavior transactions with non-family than with family persons; but this was not true of Bobby.

The limited number of persons within the families of these children meant that each family member participated in many of the subject's behavior transactions. For particular family members, the number of transactions during the day was high. Mary had 137 transactions with her mother and Raymond had 110 with his mother. Bobby had 245 transactions with his aunt and 150 with his mother. Mary and Bobby each had 20 behavior transactions with their fathers; Raymond had 82 transactions with his father.

More different children than adults entered the lives of Mary and Raymond and fewer entered the life of Bobby. However, transactions with adults were more frequent than with children. In addition to the heavy load of transactions carried by family members, teachers were participants in many object transactions. Mary's classroom teacher participated in 58 of her transactions and Raymond's teacher participated in 99 of his.

CHARACTERISTICS OF NONSOCIAL BEHAVIOR OBJECTS

Some features of the nonsocial behavior objects used by subjects are presented in Table 9.4. The items of this table may be defined as follows:

TABLE 9.4

Characteristics of Nonsocial Behavior Objects

Number of behavior objects (BO) and frequency of object transactions (ObT) in terms of per cent of total nonsocial behavior objects and object transactions.

	MARY		RAYMOND		BOBBY	
	BO	ObT	BO	ObT	BO	ObT
Natural	24.9	22.8	22.1	21.3	13.5	12.5
Man-made	75.1	77.2	77.7	78.7	86.0	87.2
Unspecified	0	0	0.2	0.8	0.5	0.3
Apparel and Adornment	9.5	10.1	4.0	7.2	9.9	9.9
Aesthetics	10.0	10.1	3.8	2.4	1.3	0.6
Education	14.1	17.2	14.1	16.0	6.1	5.7
Health and Cleanliness	3.9	3.4	4.9	3.3	1.9	1.2
Nutrition	6.5	5.2	9.0	5.5	14.5	13.3
Recreation	5.4	10.7	10.7	16.3	19.5	25.7
Religion	0.2	0.3	0	0	0.3	0.2
Other and Ambiguous	50.4	43.0	53.5	49.3	46.5	43.4

Natural Behavior Objects: objects which occur independently of man's activities. *Examples*: tree, rock, flower.

Man-made Behavior Objects: objects which are fabricated or directly processed by man. *Examples*: book, shoe, button, money, steak.

Behavior objects used primarily for Education: objects with which a pattern of behavior is associated that is generally seen in Midwest as increasing knowledge and scholarly attainments. *Examples*: textbook, school bell, work-book, school desk.

Aesthetics: objects which participate in the creation or enjoyment of beauty as locally defined. *Examples*: drawing, paint brush, flowers.

Apparel and Adornment: objects involved in the behavior of dressing or adorning the person. *Examples*: dress, barrette, necklace.

Nutrition: objects used for food or drink. *Examples*: salad, milk, or popsicle.

Recreation: objects used in play, sport, games. *Examples*: bicycle, comic book, merry-go-round.

Health and Cleanliness: objects used in the behavior of promoting health and cleanliness. *Examples*: tooth brush, soap, toilet.

Religion: objects used in religious behavior. *Examples*: Bible, psalm, perfect attendance pin.

Other and Ambiguous: objects not clearly belonging to one of the other categories.

Behavior objects have many characteristics not included in this analysis. The intention here was to classify only those objects clearly falling in one of the seven classes. For this reason the class "other and ambiguous" was provided.

A few facts are quite clear from these data: (*a*) Mary, Raymond, and Bobby lived predominantly in a man-made world. Over 75 per cent of the behavior objects were manufactured or processed, and over 75 per cent of the object transactions were with such man-made things. (*b*) Educational and recreational behavior objects tended to rank high with respect to both object frequency and transaction frequency, comprising from 5.7 per cent to 17.2 per cent of objects and transactions in the case of educational objects, and from 5.4 per cent to 25.7 per cent in the case of recreational objects. (*c*) Religious behavior objects and objects with health and cleanliness functions ranked low. Religious behavior objects entered the weekday behavior of these children in no more than 0.3 per cent of their transactions in any case; objects concerned with health and cleanliness comprised a maximum of 4.9 per cent of the behavior objects and 3.4 per cent of the transactions.

(*d*) Objects having to do with nutrition, aesthetics, and apparel and adornment fell in the intermediate ranges of occurrence.

The ownership of the behavior objects used by the subjects is shown in Table 9.5. Approximately one-fourth of the behavior objects used by the

TABLE 9.5

OWNERSHIP OF BEHAVIOR OBJECTS

Number of behavior objects (BO) and frequency of object transactions (ObT) in terms of per cent of total nonsocial objects and object transactions.

OWNER	MARY		RAYMOND		BOBBY	
	BO	ObT	BO	ObT	BO	ObT
Subject	27.7	39.0	28.2	43.5	27.3	33.9
S's family	32.2	25.9	18.5	13.8	37.9	40.5
Other person	5.0	4.3	15.0	10.5	15.1	11.9
Public	9.3	12.0	22.1	20.0	3.0	3.0
Ambiguous	25.8	18.8	16.2	12.2	16.7	10.7

subjects were their own property, and about half were owned by the children or their families. Transactions with objects belonging to other persons varied from 4.3 per cent to 11.9 per cent of all object transactions, and transactions with public property varied from 3 per cent to 20 per cent.

COMPARISONS OF MARY, RAYMOND, AND BOBBY IN THEIR USE OF BEHAVIOR
     OBJECTS

In the absence of a promising theory of the selection and use of behavior objects it would seem sensible to expect that these would be related to such characteristics as the subject's age, sex, intelligence, physique, social class, and living conditions, and to the season of the year. Our three subjects were essentially equivalent in age, intelligence, social class, and general culture. They differed, however, with respect to some other characteristics:

Mary and Raymond differed in sex.

Raymond and Bobby differed with respect to physique, season of the year in which the observations were made, and urbanization of the communities in which they lived.

Mary and Bobby differed with respect to the same variables as Raymond and Bobby, and in addition they differed in sex.

We have asked of our data whether differences in the selection and use of behavior objects are in the order given above with Mary and Raymond exhibiting the fewest differences, and Mary and Bobby the greatest.

Before considering intersubject differences, however, we shall point out some obvious agreements between subjects. Probably the most surprising agreement is found in the average number of transactions per behavior object used, viz., 3.3, 3.4, and 3.3 for Mary, Raymond, and Bobby, respectively. We are unable to cast any light on whether this similarity is a chance occurrence or whether this is, in fact, a behavioral constant. Other agreements may be listed:

All subjects exhibited preferences for particular kinds, varieties, and individual behavior objects. There was a heavy concentration of transactions on relatively few objects.

Behavior was transacted with a greater number of nonsocial than of social behavior objects.

Each social behavior object participated in more transactions on the average than did each nonsocial object.

The total number of transactions with social and nonsocial objects was approximately equal.

Nonsocial behavior objects with which behavior transactions were relatively frequent were objects to which educational and recreational behavior patterns were attached; objects belonging to the class Furniture, Household and Office Equipment and Parts of Buildings; man-made objects; and objects owned by the subject or his family.

Among social behavior objects a relatively large number of transactions occurred with adults and with the subject's mother.

The trend of object transaction rates was downward throughout the day with peaks, however, occurring in the middle of the day.

We have determined for each of 63 variables presented above in the tables and the text, that one of each triad of intersubject pairs which was the most similar and that one which was most different. The method can be illustrated with the first item on Table 9.1, viz., People. The per cent of all the object transactions which involved people was 46.1 for Mary, 45.1 for Raymond, and 43.5 for Bobby. With these data, the following triad of differences in the per cent of all object transactions which occurred with people can be set down:

Differences

Raymond *vs.* Bobby	1.6
Raymond *vs.* Mary	1.0
Bobby *vs.* Mary	2.6

Raymond and Mary were most similar, and Bobby and Mary were most different in the degree to which people entered their psychological habitats as behavior objects.

The results of this kind of analysis of 63 variables are given in Table 9.6.

TABLE 9.6

NUMBER OF VARIABLES ON WHICH EACH PAIR OF SUBJECTS
WAS THE MOST SIMILAR AND THE MOST DIFFERENT OF EACH TRIAD

POSITION IN TRIAD OF DIFFERENCES	Mary and Raymond	Raymond and Bobby	Mary and Bobby
Most similar	35	16	12
Most different	8	21	34

These data comprise all the intersubject comparisons previously mentioned except items which obviously were largely overlapping, such as the item People, and the item Social Behavior Objects. However, we have not tested the statistical significance of the relation depicted in Table 9.6 since the degree of independence of the remaining items could not be tested. Nevertheless, the data strongly suggest that the order of similarity of the subjects in their selection and use of behavior objects is as conjectured above, with Mary and Raymond being most similar, and Mary and Bobby most dissimilar.

Concluding Statement

We have been able to make only the merest beginning in our analysis of the behavior objects of Midwest and physically disabled children. Every reader will think of many analyses which might be made, and the inventory of objects in Appendix 11 will allow him to make some of these if he desires. Our time was necessarily devoted, first, to methods of defining and identifying behavior and habitat objects. These proved to be difficult problems and consumed most of the available time. Perhaps what has been done is sufficient, however, to demonstrate the method, to indicate its possible fruitfulness, and to give a glimpse of the world of things of Midwest children. In the latter connection, the behavior object analysis confirms the behavior setting survey in indicating richness and variety, and in pointing to the importance of social behavior, recreation, and education.

Chapter X

Social Action and Interaction I : A Descriptive Instrument

THE preceding chapter has pursued behavior objects of Midwest into the psychological habitats of individual children. But it has not taken the further step of asking about the characteristics of, and behavior in relation to, these environmental units as habitat objects. One attempt in this direction will be reported in the remaining part of the book.

Forthcoming data suggest the estimate that 60 to 80 per cent of the episodes of Midwest children involve them in active relationships with mothers, fathers, teachers, neighbors, peer friends, pets, and other social habitat objects. Here in the associates of these children are vitally important carriers of psychological effects. What are their psychological properties? This is largely a question of action properties; it is a question of how others behave in relation to individual children of Midwest. But how also do the children behave in relation to others? And what kinds or patterns of social interaction occur as between these children and their associates?

Toward answers to these questions we have used a set of categories to deal with certain aspects of psychosocial habitat and behavior that appear to be elemental in social action and interaction.[1] Most of these categories are thought and talked in one idiom or another in the everyday management of human affairs. Parents and teachers have had to use them to solve problems in their everyday dealings with children; and so have child, social, and clinical psychologists in their practice and in their experimenting and theorizing about human social behavior on all developmental levels. The categories are commensurable and therefore give a basis for systematic study of interdependencies in the context of social behavior. But of first importance here is the fact that these analytical guides provide a scheme for description in a critically important area of children's naturally occurring behavior and its conditions.

[1] Jack Nall participated in the development of these categories in connection with an independent research project. Also, he contributed as an analyst of specimen records and as a supervisor of analytical work with the records to the study of Chapter XII. John Luback has contributed similarly in the later stages of this part of the Midwest research.

This chapter contains definitions of the categories, a summary of data on their reliability, and consideration of technical problems met in applying them to the episodes of specimen records. Chapter XI presents an episode exhibit which exemplifies the principal categories, and pictures concretely psychosocial behavior and situations of individual children. Finally, Chapter XII describes in terms of quantitative data, yielded by application of the categories to recorded episodes, certain aspects of social action and interaction in both Midwest children and a compared group of physically disabled children.

Categories for Psychological Description

The categories are named and classified in the subjoined outline. They comprise an instrument with six parts each of which treats a cluster of variables identified briefly below the outline.

Outline of Categories

Matrix Factors

Associate Complexity
Sociality of Episode
Action Circuit
Social-Field Potency
Action Sequence
Relative Power
Strength of Motivation
Centrality of Motivation
Episode Weight
Behavior Setting

Action Modes

Dominance
Aggression
Resistance
Submission
Nurturance
Appeal
Avoidance

Action Attributes

Pressure
Affection
Mood
Evaluation

Interplay Variables

Interplay Type
Accord

Subject Constants

Age
Sex
Social Group

Associate Constants

Age and Sex
Social Group
Role Classification

Matrix Factors include such basic variables of the total action field as behavior setting and the habitat factor of motivation strength. They include also relative power and other central aspects of the relationship between S and A, the subject and associate in a target episode. Action Modes, as common words under this heading in the outline suggest, are qualitatively different kinds of action by S in relation to A and also by A in relation to S; each mode of action by subject and associate is identified and rated as to strength.   Action Attributes are primary aspects of social behavior, like affection, which enter into every kind of interpersonal action. Here, also, ratings are made on both action by the subject and action by the associate.   Interplay Variables are factors in interaction as a process supraordinate to the behavior of A and the behavior of S.   Included here, for example, are such kinds of social interplay as coöperation and conflict. Subject Constants are stable characteristics of the subject, and Associate Constants are stable characteristics of the associate as a social behavior object.   Role Classification refers to such *associate classes* as parent and teacher.

Each category will now be itemized and defined.   Throughout, the itemizations are adapted to the Hollerith card, which we have used in conjunction with a worksheet to record and tabulate all analytical findings.   An item of every category, though one very rarely used with most, is *cannot judge*, or indeterminate.   We shall append to each definition, with certain of the simpler matrix categories excepted, references to illustrative episodes of the exhibit in Chapter XI.

Matrix Factors

Associate Complexity
1. Simple: one alone
2. Simple: one of two or more
3. Compound

An associate is defined as any social behavior object that gets into the psychological habitat of a subject and so becomes a habitat object.   But one can demonstrate this development only if the subject acts in relation to the object. An associate is defined empirically, therefore, as a physically present social behavior object O in relation to which the subject acts.   Any kind of directly observable action that involves or requires O in any way or degree, such as striking O, pushing, pulling, talking to, smiling at, or only listening to or looking at O, is used to satisfy this criterion.   The social behavior object can be a single individual, called a *simple associate*; or it can be a complex social unit, formed by any number of individuals, called a *compound associate*.   This is the essential distinction made by the present category.

Where the subject acts consecutively in relation to two or more individuals or complex social units during the course of an episode, the one of these judged to have the greatest effective strength or influence as a carrier of psychological effects, is designated as the associate.   Correct choice in these cases is by no means always obvious; but we have found that associate designation is reliable as shown by agreement between independent analysts (see p. 354).

A secondary distinction is made here between the case in which a simple associate is alone with the subject (item 1) and the case in which at least one social behavior object other than an associate is present as a part of the immediate milieu (item 2). A present social behavior object other than an associate is defined in every such case as either (a) a physically present individual in relation to whom the subject now could, but does not, act or (b) a physically present individual in relation to whom the subject does act, but whose effective strength is below maximum for the given episode.

In establishing present social behavior objects, a qualifying provision is applied to the observer as a virtually never-absent part of the physical situation. If judged to be in the background throughout an episode, like a wall behind the subject or an unused piece of furniture, the observer is not classed as either an associate or a present social behavior object. Obviously, this rule is difficult. In applying it, we have assumed that the observer is lost in the background so long as there is no positive evidence to the contrary. In effect, a judgment has been made here as to whether or not the subject "pays any attention" to the observer. It would have been desirable to segregate all cases in which the observer was the only present social behavior object in addition to an associate; but we were too far along when need for such an adjustment was discovered to do this in the analyses to be reported.

The observer may indeed be an associate. We have segregated as *observer episodes* all in which the observer is either a simple associate or a member part of a compound associate. This leaves as *standard episodes* all in which the observer is in no way implicated as a social behavior object.

A subject hurries to greet a lone friend on the street, leaving the observer out of sight and, as far as one can say, for lack of contrary evidence, out of mind. The friend is a simple associate, and item 1 applies. A subject in a classroom, where he is surrounded by other children, whispers to a classmate. Again, the associate is simple; but, owing to presence of individuals other than the associate, item 2 applies. Another subject sits with his parents at home. Looking from one parent to another, he solicits from both, as he might from one alone, permission to go fishing. The parents constitute a compound associate, and item 3 applies. A subject makes an "activity report" to the members of his class at school. These other class members as a collective social whole constitute, again, a compound associate.

As applied to the records, this category distinguishes compound associates differing as to number of individuals in the complex social unit and, wherever this total does not exceed 3, as to presence or absence of other individuals, as follows: 2 alone, 2 of 3 or more; 3 alone; 3 of 4 or more; 4 through 7; 8 through 15; 16 or more. These differentiations are not itemized above inasmuch as they are not used in the study of Chapter XII, for reasons to be stated.

Sociality of Episode

1. Social
2. Potentially Social
3. Nonsocial

The analysis of an episoded record by means of the instrument begins with the application of this category.

A social episode is one in which the subject has an associate, in virtue of action in relation to a social behavior object. A potentially social episode is one in which, although the subject does not have an associate, at least one other person is present, in the sense stated under Associate Complexity, above. A nonsocial episode is one in which the subject is alone.

Only social episodes are analyzed by other categories of the instrument. Social episodes are quite readily identified. It is fortunate that they alone are analyzed, because the distinction between potentially social and nonsocial episodes proved to be difficult. Our best surmise now is that we have erred on the side of finding too few nonsocial episodes, even though overall item by item agreement on the category is good, as later data will show.

Action Circuit

          1. Open
          2. Closed

An associate, by definition, is an individual in relation to whom the subject acts. But an associate may or may not act in relation to the subject. If action by A in relation to S does not occur, the action circuit of the relationship between the two is left *open*. If, however, A does act in relation to S, this circuit is *closed*. In practice, a closed action circuit generally has been scored only if A does something which is so described in a record that it can be rated on a majority of the instrument variables. Active ignoring of S by A has been considered to meet this criterion.

An open action circuit obviously limits greatly the range of psychological effects which can be carried by an associate. It eliminates operation of all variables of social *inter*action, and of all variables in the instrument which pertain to the associate's behavior, with the exception of *mood*. Accordingly, our analyses have dealt principally with social episodes in which the action circuit was found to be closed.

Social-Field Potency

          1. Low
          2. Medium
          3. High
          4. Unity

Mary Ennis, in *Telling Mother Goodbye* on leaving for school, transacts behavior only with her mother. This episode is all social; nonsocial behavior objects are in no way required for the action unit or used in it. Later, in *Playing With Paints*, at home, Mary gets "absorbed" in a behavior transaction with a box of water colors, a brush, water in a glass, and a bathroom washbowl. The most she does in relation to a social behavior object during the episode is to mumble indifferently to the observer about her activity in progress. This episode is almost entirely nonsocial.

Social-Field Potency refers to the degree in which the behavior of an episode is transacted in relation to social behavior objects. *Unity* holds when the required and used objects are exclusively social, or virtually so, as in *Telling Mother Goodbye*. *Low* applies when, as in *Playing With Paints*, the required and used objects are predominantly nonsocial, *high* when the reverse is true, and *medium* when nonsocial and social objects are required and used about equally. In essence, two fields of situational content, the social and the non-social, are distinguished by the category, which gives a rating of the relative weight or potency of the social field.

Findings to be reported on this category discriminate between just minimum and above minimum. Only this gross distinction proved to be meaningful when target episodes and recorded scale judgments were compared. The category is nonetheless useful as a means to segregation of episodes in which interpersonal action is subordinated to action in relation to nonsocial aspects of a situation.

Action Sequence

1. S–A
2. S cycle
3. A–S
4. A cycle
5. Does Not Apply

Action Sequence has two dimensions, one concerned with order, and the other with complexity of interaction. It applies only where S and A are involved in a bilateral action relationship.

Interaction initiated by S (items 1 and 2) and interaction initiated by A (items 3 and 4) account for the order possibilities. As for complexity of inter-action, two levels are differentiated. On one level, there occurs an initiating action followed by a concluding reaction (items 1 and 3), while on the other and more complex level there occurs an initiating action, a reaction, and at least a subsequent action by the initiating participant (items 2 and 4).

In passing Jim Hebb on the street, Roy Eddy says, "Hi, Jim," and Jim says "Hi," to end this episode. Here, Roy, the subject, acts in relation to Jim. Jim responds, and that is that; item 1, S–A, applies. Had Roy acted in relation to the response by Jim, a cycle of interaction would have occurred here, and item 2, *S cycle*, would apply. This example can be accommodated to items 3 and 4 of the category only by making Jim, as A, take the initiative.

Relative Power

1. $A < < < < < S$
2. $A < < < < S$
3. $A < < < S$ Items 1–5: A has less power than S
4. $A < < S$
5. $A < S$
6. $A = S$ Item 6: A has power equal to that of S
7. $A > S$
8. $A > > S$
9. $A > > > S$ Items 7–11: A has more power than S
10. $A > > > > S$
11. $A > > > > > S$

Relative Power is by far the most difficult category, conceptually and from the standpoint of clear empirical indices, of all categories in the instrument. Power, here, means ability on the part of A, as this ability is perceived by S, to change the behavior of S. As perceived potential to change behavior, power may or may not be used: it may not be actualized in social pressure (see pp. 339–40) during an episode, or it may be so actualized in any degree. Each item of the category expresses a ratio. The analyst undertakes to compare the degree in which A is able to change the behavior of S with the degree in which S is able to change the behavior of A. This comparison is made on the basis of what S is judged to see of the total interpersonal relationship.

To try to rate, not the overt behavior of S, but the way in which S sees, not the behavior A, but only the ability of A to change the behavior of S as compared with the ability of S to change the behavior of A, must be near the height of temerity. This effort will have to be valued chiefly on two grounds: (a) the reliability of the ratings; and (b) the sense made by findings on relative power reported in Chapter XII. This is indeed the better part of our case, not only for the present category, but also for others that follow.

Empirically, power is defined *in part* by correlations with relatively stable characteristics and appurtenances of A and S which signify ability or lack of ability on the part of each to affect action by the other. Often, these are marks of "influential position" which means in effect that power is here made to include status. On the side of high power, definitive characteristics and appurtenances are taken to include, throughout a wide range of differing cultures, large physical size, known skill or wisdom, adulthood, parenthood, grownupness, any kind of leadership role, repute for difficult or heroic accomplishment, belongingness to or "connections" with the elite, with officialdom, with the "varsity," with "the gang," or the like, uniforms of rank, and various titles, degrees, badges, and medals. Owing to its derivation from such relatively stable properties of individuals, the power ratio between A and S at the time of a particular episode depends, first of all, upon who A and S happen to be. Thus, by and large, our ratings on relative power show that, for Midwest children, mothers have more power than brothers, teachers more than schoolmates, bigger and older playmates more than smaller and younger playmates, adults more than other children.

Linked though it is with stable person characteristics, the ratio of power between A and S can change from episode to episode with no change in associate. We have built this tenet into our definition of relative power by arbitrarily using as guides such model paradigms as these: Midwest teachers generally have greater power over their pupils in the classroom than almost anywhere else in Midwest. Midwest mothers generally have greater power over their children at home when guests are not present than at home when guests are present. Of three similar Midwest children, A, B, and C, A has more power over B if C is A's pal than if C is B's pal.

One can generalize from the foregoing that the power ratio between A and S can vary according to the degree in which present conditions call for, permit, or foster display of ability by each individual to change the behavior of the other. Important conditions here include milieu supports for influential position in the present behavior setting, as in the case of the teacher in her classroom, and group reënforcements, as in the case of the child fortified by guests or the child with an ally. This means that a certain power level cannot be ascribed to a particular associate of S, say a playmate, teacher, or a mother, and then be assumed to hold for every episode in which that associate occurs. An analyst must look for signs of relative power episode by episode. One must continually ask the following: as far as S is concerned, to what extent is A now able, under all of the prevailing circumstances, to change the behavior of S? At the same time, because these circumstances do include characteristics of A that exist and may be known to S outside the limits of any one episode, sequential context is decisively important for correct judgment.

"Situational factors" here, important though they are, leave relative power more stable for a given associate than other variables of the instrument. This follows from the basic correlations between ability to change another's behavior and relatively unchanging characteristics of individuals. Our ratings generally place mothers, fathers, and teachers in the A>S part of the scale, peer friends or siblings near the A=S part, and pets, younger children, and infants somewhere in the A<S part. Generally, for a particular associate, the situational factors only bring about fluctuations within a certain range. It has seemed important, however, to try to measure these fluctuations and their cumulative outcomes; and this can be done only if ratings are made an episode at a time.

Illustrative episodes: 3 through 5.

Strength and Centrality of Motivation

Strength and Centrality of Motivation, which are dynamical habitat variables, are not used in the study of Chapter XII, for which reason neither will be elaborated here. However, in order to indicate possibilities in this direction of analysis, we have put episodes to illustrate both categories in the exhibit of Chapter XI.

These situational factors were worked into the present descriptive scheme in the first place as basic determinants which may advantageously be taken into account in an attempt to describe any dimension whatsoever of molar behavior or its context. Both categories have been applied along with others of the instrument to all records that we have processed. The resulting data have pertinence for description of social action and interaction chiefly as a means to the reclassification of findings from other categories. For example, these data enable one to distinguish social conflict under conditions of weak and peripheral motivation from social conflict under conditions of strong and central motivation. Such refinement has raised difficult problems of analysis and interpretation which we have judged it best to reserve for additional study.

Illustrative episodes: 1 and 2.

Episode Weight

       1. Primary
       2. Below Primary

Episode Weight refers to the potency or relative weight of the target episode. This variable has been anticipated in Chapter VII and defined more fully in Chapter VIII. Here, special and restricted use is made of it.

Item 1 applies under either of two conditions: (*a*) the target episode is isolated, with the consequence that its potency from beginning to end is necessarily primary, in the meaning stated in Chapter VII; (*b*) the target episode overlaps with another, but is of primary weight during all or any part of its course.   Item 2 applies to every episode which, throughout its course, is of less than primary weight.

This category is used especially as a means to the selection for study of social episodes whose importance for the total ongoing behavior of the child is not subordinated to that of overlapping units.   But it is employed also, as in Chapter VIII, for investigation of episode weight as a factor in social behavior.

Behavior Setting

Behavior Setting, which is contingently itemized, provides for identification of the K-21 setting in which each target episode occurs.   We will not report data from this category in the study to be presented for two reasons.   First, the number of episodes in different settings common to all of the subjects proved to be rather small.   Second, where common settings did occur, these were found to be highly correlative with common social habitat objects, which are here of central concern.   For example, as it turned out for the records we have used, to describe social interaction with a mother, a father, or a sibling usually is to describe social interaction in the home setting.

Action Modes

These variables have their analogues in certain of the *needs* distinguished by Murray (**43**).   However, we are concerned here, not with needs or other determinants of action, but with qualitatively different ways of behaving.   Murray's exegeses on needs have nonetheless contributed directly to the ensuing definitions; for, in defining these *action modes* we have used a modification of his scheme for need analysis and also have taken the liberty of extensively paraphrasing descriptive particulars in his treatment of related needs.   Indebtedness here to Murray for his comprehensive and perceptive need descriptions is large.   Yet our aim throughout has been to develop criteria with special pertinence for momentary actions as against enduring needs or wants.   Accordingly, the definitions have undergone repeated and often substantial revisions in the light of problems raised by and criteria found in the records.   Our names for modes are the same as Murray's for needs in the instances of dominance, aggression, and nurturance; and modes that we have called submission, resistance, appeal, and avoidance respectively, have criteria in common with his needs of deference, defendance, succorance, and rejection.   One other point relating to our indebtedness here to Murray must be mentioned.   It is that he himself recognized the possibility of de-conceptualizing his needs to kinds of action (**43**).

We do not have here anything like an exhaustive inventory of significantly differing kinds of social action.   But we do have seven ways of behaving by any person, X, in relation to another, O, which have to be considered fundamental.   The rationale for selection of these and no more reduces to this claim plus the fact that dominance, aggression, resistance, submission, nurturance, appeal, and avoidance have met better than other discriminable kinds of social action, the test of reliable and fruitful diagnosis upon the basis of behavior description in specimen records. In this we see something of a discovery, the history of which, however, is too long for the present space.

Every definition begins with a general statement as to the way of behaving characteristic of the given mode. A presumed end sought by the person, X, as an effect (cf. Murray: **43,** 55–58) of the behavior is then specified. There follow specifications as to the occurrence of the mode in relation to action by the other person, O. Here, both of two possibilities are open. First, the behavior can be *spontaneous* in that it is not activated necessarily by a particular kind of action on the part of O, as in nurturance, for example; and, second, the behavior can be *reactive* in that it does presuppose a particular kind of action by O, as in submission, which implies instigating dominance or aggression (cf. concept of *press* in Murray: **43,** 115–23). Where the behavior is held to be reactive, commonly observed kinds of activating or instigating O behavior are noted. Also, whether the behavior is classified as spontaneous or reactive, or both, ways of behaving which it commonly activates are mentioned. Common variants of each mode and, in this connection, both motor and verbal indices of its occurrence are then indicated. Descriptive terms frequently used in referring to the characteristic behavior and emotional states which are commonly ascribed to one who exhibits it conclude each analysis. Following Murray's example, we have aimed to work into the definitions a variety of clues to correct identification. *These clues often rest upon untested theory about the concomitants and correlates of the behavior concerned,* but at this stage better leads to follow are not available; we have had to use some primitive theory here to direct search for facts.

Although every action mode is conceived to vary in intensity or strength, a continuum above zero has in no case been posited. We take it, for example, that an action may be aggressive in some degree or not aggressive at all. As for the variations in degree, where a mode is judged to obtain of the target behavior, its strength is rated on a scale of three points. We have used, then, for each of these mode categories the following items.

> 0. Zero: absent
> 1. Lower range
> 2. Middle range
> 3. Upper range

It is mentioned again that every action mode is applied to both the subject S and his associate A. A rating on the side of A refers always to the behavior of A as S sees it. With this provision understood, the definitions will refer to any individual, X, in relation to any other individual, O, so that each statement can be adapted to the subject or the associate.

Dominance

X rules or seeks to rule O by exerting social pressure in an arbitrary way. Dominance presupposes some power; it is power used in the form of authoritarian pressure.

End sought: To influence, direct, or control O by gaining ascendance over O; to gain such ascendance as an end in itself.

Occurrence relative to action by O: Spontaneous or reactive. When reactive, instigating O behavior includes dominative action itself. Instigated O behavior includes submissive action, resistance, counterdominance, aggression, and avoidance.

Common variants: To sway, lead, boss, prevail upon, direct, regulate, govern. To organize or supervise. To pass judgments, set standards, lay down principles, give decisions, settle things. To prohibit, restrain, confine. To demand an audience, exact imitation, command a following. To impose conditions or requirements.

> *Motor indices*: Vigorously beckoning, pointing the way. Pushing, pulling, holding a person.

> *Verbal indices*: Commands, such as: Sit down! Come here! Stop that! Hurry up! Get out! Give me that! Shut up!

Common descriptive terms: Masterful, forceful, assertive, authoritative, disciplinary.

Emotional concomitants: Not consistent enough to serve as signs. Can include feelings of superiority; also, feelings of insecurity, inferiority.

The verbal model for dominance is the order, "You do that" or "Do not do that," especially when a "because I say so" is expressed or implied. A less pure form occurs when reference to a rule qualifies an order. Here, by invoking the rule, X personifies power which, although it is otherwise impersonal and one step removed from him, is still essentially arbitrary. Any "explanation" of an order or a rule generally reduces the degree of dominance.

Illustrative episodes: 6 through 8.

The desiderata of these mode definitions may have been clarified by this one example. The idea, as already mentioned, is to accumulate a variety of indices. Consider, for example, the *common descriptive terms*. Often, these are like or the same as words used by an observer to describe behavior in specimen records. The emotional concomitants obviously can give only very roundabout clues at best. Yet they help to round out the total pattern. The specifications of occurrence relative to action by O are definitely and absolutely not intended to be exhaustive. No one knows, for example, all of the different kinds of behavior which can be instigated by dominance. We are willing to say flatly that here is a kind of behavior which sometimes instigates resistance or counterdominance, and this helps a little to place dominance in an inventory of types of social action. But the field is left open for an unlimited number of other possible reactions to dominative behavior. We went so far as to put on the wall of the room where our analyzing was done, a motto stating that the same holds for all modes of action. Actually, to try to give benefit from experience, here is one point at which our ideal preference would be to start over. The section on occurrence in relation to action by O has to be included here in each definition inasmuch as it was used throughout in getting data that are to be reported. With a few exceptions, however, it will be knocked out before we do more analysis with the categories because the specifications tend to be too limiting. The exceptions are modes which cannot be defined without reference to action by O. For example, what we choose to look for under submission is a kind of behavior that occurs in its very nature as a reaction to dominance or aggression.

Our policy at first in experimenting with mode categories was to stay clear of elaborate definition. We considered the basic concepts to be fairly concise and believed that judgments could be made least equivocally on the basis of statements limited to minimum essentials. Murray's need definitions seemed unnecessarily intricate. But experience with the records made us change our minds. We were forced by the great complexity of naturally occurring behavior, with its never ending variations on the same themes, to use somewhat equally complex specifications for the named kinds of action.

Aggression

X attacks and tries to injure O or any object forming a unit with O. Included among objects which may form a unit with O are things or persons owned by, related to, liked or made by, or "in league with" O. The idea of unit formation that we have in mind here has been developed for treatment of interpersonal relations by Heider (27).

End sought: To make O suffer. Subsidiary ends include revenge, punishment, defense. The suffering which X aims to inflict upon O may be any undesirable experience or state of affairs such as pain, discomfort, loss, embarrassment, or frustration.

Occurrence relative to action by O: Spontaneous or reactive. When reactive, instigating O behavior includes aggressive action, dominative action, and resistance. Instigated O behavior includes submission, avoidance, resistance, counteraggression, and dominance.

Common variants: To move or speak in a hostile or threatening manner. To willfully aggravate or annoy; to tantalize. To "pick a fight." To frighten. To be "mean."

> *Motor indices*: To strike, kick, scratch, bite. To break things.

> *Verbal indices*: Belittlement: to criticize, depreciate, slander; censure: to reprimand, blame, scold; ridicule: to make fun of or to tease.

Common descriptive terms: Aggressive, combative, belligerent, pugnacious, quarrelsome; malicious, revengeful; destructive, cruel, vindictive, ruthless; accusatory, abusive; severe.

Emotional concomitants: Anger, rage, irritation, resentment, hatred.

Illustrative episodes: 11 through 15.

Resistance

X "holds out against" dominance, aggression, appeal, or action of any kind in which O exerts social pressure.

End sought: To withstand coercive social influence or to ward off harm and consequent suffering.

Occurrence relative to action by O: Reactive only. Instigating O behavior includes aggressive action, dominance, appeal. Instigated O behavior includes dominance, aggression, or a resurgence of pressure in one or another form.

Common variants: With aggression as instigating O behavior: X defends himself physically; he defends himself verbally, as in protesting criticism. With dominance or social pressure as instigating O behavior: X witholds compliance;

he "gets his back up"; he actively ignores demands or requests; he "takes a stand" and "sticks to it" in the face of appeals or arguments.

Motor indices: To ward off blows. To stand firm.

Verbal indices: Saying: No. I won't! Try and make me! Not now. I don't want to. Saying: I am not (a liar, a dope, a dumbell, a coward).

Common descriptive terms: Unyielding, disobedient, refractory, stubborn, recalcitrant.

Emotional concomitants: Often unclear. May include anxiety, indignation, "feelings of obstinancy."

Illustrative episodes: 9 and 10.

Submission

X "gives in" to dominance, aggression, appeal, or action or any kind in which O exerts social pressure.

X perceives pressure from O. He sees that O is trying in some way to get him to do something or to get him to refrain from doing something and he lets O have his way. He is in some degree coerced; he "takes" action by O upon him. His behavior is essentially negative; he is nonresisting.

The behavior of X in submission always has for him this significance: "I am being coerced. O is in some degree pushing or pulling me."

Submissive action can occur as an immediate response to pressure or it can follow some degree of resistance. This means that, within the total course of an episode, a subject or his associate may exhibit both resistance and submission.

End sought: To eliminate or meliorate stressful interaction between X and O. In submitting, X does not aim to benefit O, as in nurturance, but only to ease the pressure on himself.

Occurrence relative to action by O: Reactive only. Instigating O behavior can include dominance, aggression, appeal. Instigated O behavior varies greatly. Submission can invite dominance or attack. Another possibility is instigation of nurturance "out of sympathy" when submission has occurred as a reaction to dominance or aggression.

Typical behavior: To "take" injuries, blame, criticism, punishment, or bossing without defense, resistance, or retaliation. To resign oneself to imposed conditions. To adopt a passive, meek, humble, or servile attitude. To let others push and get the better. To allow oneself to be "talked down," bullied, or dispossessed. To give things up or relinquish own aims in favor of another.

Motor indices: To bow. To sag all over. To stand aside. To take a back seat.

Verbal indices: To say: 'Nuff. I surrender. I'm licked. You win. "I'm 'umble." You are better (stronger, smarter, etc.). Oh, all right, you can have your way. I quit.

Common descriptive terms: Submissive, acquiescent, pliant, meek, humble, servile, abasive, resigned, patient, passive.

Emotional concomitants: Resignation; humility; inferiority feeling.

Submission and avoidance differ. Both can occur within the same episode.

In submission, however, X does not move away or hang back from O with fear or dislike. Instead, he stays and "takes it."

X can react compliantly to pressure so low that the meaning of being coerced is not realized in his behavior, for him, or for one who perceives what he does. This appears to hold most often in passive and immediate reactions to mild appeal. All instances of such ordinary *compliance* are segregated from submission. Accordingly, in Chapter XII, data on compliance are given independently of data on submission.

Illustrative episodes: 16 and 17.

Nurturance

X extends himself to benefit O.

X sees that O has a need. He tries to meet this need. He does something in a positive way for the sake of O. He actively does give or tries to give O something, to help O, or to protect O.

Nurturance holds when the behavior of an associate A is rated if it is judged that, as the subject S sees it, A is doing or trying to do something for S.

End sought: To meet or gratify the needs of O.

Occurrence relative to action by O: Spontaneous or reactive. Instigating O behavior includes appeal. In the absence of appeal, any perceived evidence of need may instigate nurturance.

Nurturance always entails positive action to benefit O. This holds no less when it is reactive than when it is spontaneous. Thus, there can be no nurturance in only passive giving in to appeal or any kind of pressure. This holds even when the effect of the giving in is beneficial to O. Nurturance is action by X for the sake of O. The passive behavior of giving in is generally action by X for the sake of X; its purpose is merely to free X of pressure from O. Whether the behavior of X is spontaneous or reactive, it is nurturant only if X in some way *extends* himself to benefit O.

Instigated O behavior can include resistance.

Typical variants: To react *and* administer sympathetically to the needs of a weak, disabled, tired, inexperienced, infirm, deflated, humiliated, lonely, depressed, ill, or helpless O. To be "moved" by distress. To prove an increase in affection when O exhibits weakness, inability, unhappiness, or any negative state or position. To support, console, comfort, nurse, heal. To extend lenience or indulgence. To give freedom. To condone. To be protective when O is maltreated. To encourage, pity, console, or sympathize with an unhappy O. To assuage, calm, appease, or pacify. To give things to O; to help O; to protect O. Just to be nice to O.

Common descriptive terms: Nurturant, sympathetic, compassionate, maternal, paternal, benevolent, altruistic; indulgent, merciful, charitable, lenient, forbearing, forgiving, tolerant; generous; helpful, supporting; protective.

Emotional concomitants: Tenderness; sympathy, pity, compassion.

Illustrative episodes: 18 and 19.

Appeal

Reliable judgments proved to be more difficult with this mode than with any of the others. Thus, the extended formulation, which was adopted only after many unsuccessful attempts to define appeal so that it meant essentially the same thing to different analysts. This was a struggle.

X solicits benefit from O.

X behaves with the purpose of expressing a need or want. He indicates somehow to O that this is his purpose. He points to the specific need or want in some way. He asks O by some means, more or less direct, to meet or to help him meet the need.

Satisfaction of the need expressed by X in appeal is in some degree "put up to" O; X confronts O with a chance to do or not to do something for him. Thus, in appeal, X places himself in or exploits a position which is in a degree dependent.

Appeal presupposes at the moment of its occurrence some incongruity between O's behavior at this moment and the goal of X for O's behavior. It necessarily entails, therefore, at least minimally strong social pressure.

The essence of appeal is a direct bid for need satisfaction. To be scored on appeal an action must have this significance for X and it must be such that X evidently expects it to have this significance for O. Any action not cast in a form which directly signifies, "I have a need" does not conform to the definition of appeal. The action must mean to X and he must expect it to mean to O: "I am behaving as I do now to express a need to you. This is my purpose. I want you to meet or to help me meet the need. I want you to benefit me—to give me something, to help me or protect me. I am telling you this directly. In so doing, I acknowledge some dependence, for the time being, at least, upon you. At the same time, I am putting you on the spot, where you can do what you will about the need. You can turn me down or not. I have to depend on you. It's up to you."

The conditions stated here can be realized in a high degree, as in begging; or conditions having the same qualitative characteristics can be met in a very low degree, as in many mild requests. It remains true that *routine, casual, matter-of-fact inquiries made in the ordinary course of conversation quite generally do not meet these conditions.* Two men meet on the street. One says, "It sure is a fine day, isn't it?" and the other says, "It sure is. Who, do you think, is going to win the election?" There is no appeal in either of these queries. Neither means outside of a dictionary: "I am announcing a need. You will understand that I am. You will see that I have put myself on the receiving end. Are you going to benefit me or not?" One can safely judge that neither interrogator here expected that his offhand question would strike the other person in this way. Yet the equally casual question, "What time is it?" does express appeal *if* the asker clearly really needs to know the time and is intentionally giving the other person an opening to be a nice person and tell him the time.

When the behavior of an associate A is rated, appeal holds only when it is judged that: the subject sees the action by A as one having, to A, the meaning of a bid for need satisfaction; S sees the action as one which A expects S to see as a bid for need satisfaction.

End sought: To have own needs gratified by the sympathetic action of O. To be supported, sustained, helped, protected, nursed, advised, guided, indulged, forgiven, consoled. To be benefited in any way by another.

Occurrence relative to action by O: Spontaneous or reactive. The situation giving rise to appeal can be simply one in which O is not at the moment meeting a need on the part of X. Thus, instigating O behavior can include abandonment, "pointed" unconcern, aggression, dominance, or any kind of pressure; in such cases, X asks O to refrain from what he is doing.

For the reason that appeal involves pressure, it is a kind of action to which O can react with any of the reciprocals to pressure. These reciprocals include resistance and submission. O can *hold out against* appeal or, without doing anything for the sake of X, i.e., without being nurturant, simply give in to it. A remaining possibility is that, in response to appeal, O can actively extend himself in behalf of X; O can react to appeal with nurturance.

Common variants: To seek out a nurturant O, one in a position to give help, gratuities, or protection. To ask, with dependence, for information or understanding. To bid for tenderness and affection, as in exhibition of a wound. To invite sympathetic attention by telling of misfortunes, hardships, accidents, or failures; by exaggerating difficulties or injuries, by complaining of discomfort, anxiety, sadness, or depression. To call upon the good nature, generosity, understanding, tolerance, mercy, or forbearance of an O.

> *Motor indices*: To adopt a supplicant attitude; to weep; to look forlorn; to enact a "hang dog."

> *Verbal indices*: To cry out for help. To speak plaintively or wistfully.

Common descriptive terms: Succorant, dependent; helpless, suppliant, petitioning, begging, pleading, entreating.

Emotional concomitants: Feelings of dependence or inadequacy or insecurity; anxiety.

Illustrative episodes: 20 and 21.

Avoidance

X increases or keeps his distance from O in the face of aggression or any negatively valent feature or effect of O's behavior or of O; X hangs back or draws back or withdraws from O.

End sought: To avoid any dissatisfying effects of O's company, of O's behavior, or of any part or aspect of the situation which forms a unit with O.

Occurrence relative to action by O: Generally reactive. Can be spontaneous, in effect, when X is shy or apprehensive in a situation such that no danger or threat can be identified by the observer. When reactive, instigating O behavior includes aggression, dominance. But, any dangerous, threatening, unpredictable, or unpleasant action or characteristic of O can instigate avoidance. Instigated O behavior can include nurturance, "out of pity."

Typical behavior: To stand still and make no noise so as to be unobserved; to "freeze up" in the company of an O. To hide. To steer clear of unpleasant or threatening O's or of O's who create unpleasant or menacing conditions. To flee from attack. To just shy away.

> *Motor indices*: Running away. Trembling. Standing immobilized. Pallor. Ducking head, with finger in mouth.

> *Verbal indices*: Saying: I'm going home because—you hurt me, I don't like you. Keeping very silent. Saying: I don't want you to take my picture.

Common descriptive terms: Timorous; afraid; hesitant, wary, careful.

Emotional concomitants: Apprehension, fear; disgust, displeasure (in the rejective sense of "being displeased with" a person).

Illustrative episodes: 22 and 23.

Action Attributes

Say that the behavior of X in relation to O shows the action mode of dominance. In this case, X can exert strong or weak *pressure* and exhibit plus or minus *affection*, good or bad *mood*, and positive or negative *evaluation*. Each of these dimensions is an attribute of every kind of social behavior. If only in this sense, action attributes are like attributes of sensation, while modes of action are like sensory modalities.

Pressure

		X is now acting to change the behavior of O
0.	Zero	in no degree
1.	>0	very little—lowermost range
2.	$>>0$	little
3.	$>>>0$	moderately—middlemost range
4.	$>>>>0$	much
5.	$>>>>>0$	very much—uppermost range

Pressure is actualized social power; it is used ability to change the behavior of another individual. X exerts social pressure on O by acting in any way to effect any kind of change in O's behavior. Pressure occurs only if there is some incongruity between O's behavior and some goal which X has for action by O.

Pressure can occur in different forms, depending on the mode of action by X in progress. An authoritarian kind of pressure occurs with dominance; hostile pressure occurs with aggression. Equally strong pressure can occur with appeal, as when X begs O to do something. Also, pressure can occur with nurturance, as when a host urges more pie upon a guest.

Pressure presupposes some degree of power. We have assumed, however, that an individual whose power is relatively low, as he and his associate see it, can exert high pressure. For example, in begging for food or a toy, a baby can act intensively to change the behavior of a parent, who is presently withholding the object. One might say that in these cases *pressure is high in proportion to a necessity of compensating for low power*. On the other hand, with power high, pressure can be low. The Dean always has high power for this writer, whether he only passes the time of day in a corridor, without exerting pressure at all, or calls for a delayed report of grades, thus exerting pressure which may go up to point five—to drop down to flat zero again during a pleasant drive to and from Midwest.

We may be incorrect in using here a dichotomy of absence (0) and presence (>0). Perhaps, so long as two individuals interact, each acts in some degree to change the behavior of the other. Practically, however, the records have compelled us to recognize cases in which the degree of pressure is at least virtually zero. Pressure loses its meaning if, for example, it is ascribed to a father who only answers a child's question promptly and in a nice way.

Illustrative episodes: 24 and 25.

Affection

1. $-----$
2. $----$
3. $---$ Items 1–5: The momentary feeling of X toward O is negative
4. $--$
5. $-$
6. N   Item 6: The momentary feeling of X toward O is neutral
7. $+$
8. $++$
9. $+++$ Items 7–11: The momentary feeling of X toward O is positive.
10. $++++$
11. $+++++$

Affection here means momentary feeling on the part of X toward O as a social habitat object. This variable forms a U-shaped continuum with a negative segment, a neutral break, and a positive segment.

Positive affection refers to momentarily favorable feeling toward O. It is commonly denoted by such words as *affectionate, friendly, tender, fond, loving, sympathetic*. Negative affection means momentarily unfavorable feeling toward O, as denoted by words like *hostile, cross, irritated, spiteful, antagonistic*. Minus affection is "bad feeling" in the sense that it always carries an element of hostility. Thus, even "coldness," so long as it is not in some degree mean or hostile, is not negative on this scale. In minus affection there is always some "feeling against." In plus affection there is always some "feeling for."

Neutral affection refers to absence of either plus or minus feeling. It is denoted by words like "indifferent" and "unconcerned." It includes "coldness" so long as this is not active in the sense of involving in any degree hostility or "feeling against."

There are some cases in which, through the total course of an episode, both minus and plus affection toward O are discernible. Extended experience with the records has shown that, when this holds, confident judgment of equality as between plus and minus elements is rarely possible, whereas judgment of preponderance on one side or the other can generally be made. In all such instances, therefore, either plus or minus affection has been marked.

Occurrences of plus or minus affection in the same episode, whether these are judged to be equal or unequal, will be marked and counted in later analyses. Such ambivalence clearly is worth special study for a number of reasons. This did not become clear to us, owing to the nature of our target material, until analysis of the results was in midstream.

A person generally liked by X often becomes for him an object of positive affection, and the reverse holds for a person generally disliked by X. But, at the time of a particular interaction, X may have plus affection for a person whom he generally dislikes or minus affection for a person whom he generally likes. Baldwin (2) has suggested that the frequency of such imbalance rises with increasing maturity.   Affection in any case should not be confused with like or dislike as a relatively stable attitude toward a person.   A child, especially an older child, may like his mother and know full well she is a person whom he likes through the time of an unpleasant quarrel while, at the same time, his momentary feeling for her, in the present sense of affection, is negative.   It may be necessary to go to adults of high maturity and sophistication for cases in which X dislikes O as a person, knows it at the time, and yet momentarily has positive feeling toward O.   This leaves the point that, in rating affection here, one must not try to measure like or dislike as a generally prevailing attitude.   The rating is shifted up and down with any change from one episode to another in evidence as to the momentary feeling of X toward O.

Hostile feeling presumably is always an emotional concomitant of aggressive action.   But this does not mean that, in the absence of aggressive action, negative affection never occurs.   On the contrary, X may feel strongly hostile toward O while, at the same time, instead of attacking O, he yields abjectly to attack by O upon him.   There might well be grounds for the judgment in such a case that, in the life space of O, while the perceived affection of X contains hostile feeling, the action of X in relation to O is not aggressive, but submissive: "Hold, see the eye of malice in yon cowering knave."   Yet it does seem correct to assume that the perception of hostile feeling generally carries with it the perception of potential aggression.   Probably this is why Nero (or whoever might have said what we have just made up) ordered his guard to lop off the knave's head (according to the phantasy).   The point remains that hostile feeling and actual aggressive action, either as these occur in X or as O perceives them, are independent behavioral properties.

Illustrative episodes: 26 through 29.

Mood

1. $- - - - -$
2. $- - - -$
3. $- - -$ Items 1–5: X is unhappy
4. $- -$
5. $-$
6. N   Item 6: X is neither happy nor unhappy
7. $+$
8. $+ +$
9. $+ + +$ Items 7–11: X is happy
10. $+ + + +$
11. $+ + + + +$

Mood means a momentary state of X which exists without any special reference to O as an object.   Negative or unhappy, and positive or happy moods are distinguished.   These form a U-shaped continuum broken by a neutral zone.

Mood can change suddenly, although a "bad" or a "good" mood often "hangs on" through an extended time.   It is generally necessary in any case to study a somewhat extended sequence of episodes in order to judge validly the mood of S or A in any unit of the sequence.

As diffuse affectivity, mood can vary qualitatively over a wide range of positive or negative states.   Terms denoting qualitative variations in both unhappy and happy moods are given below. In some instances, the indicated distinctions refer at least in part to differences in degree. The clues to mood in a specimen record include words like these and also explicit references to the common behavioral signs of the affective states which they name.

> *Terms denoting unhappy mood*: anxious, troubled, worried, fretful, distressed, disturbed, discontented; irritable, riled, angry; annoyed, vexed, cross; despondent, miserable, bitter, despairing; dejected, sad, depressed, gloomy, melancholy.

> *Terms denoting happy mood*: gay, merry, glad, gleeful, elated, joyous, blissful, delighted; cheerful, comfortable, gratified, contented.

It is clear that the words in each of these groupings refer to feeling states which are by no means all the same. For some purposes, too, it would be desirable to measure the different variants of happy and unhappy mood. Probably the material in specimen records would permit reliable judgments upon certain of these. In the present context, however, more refined distinctions have not seemed profitable.

Neutral mood means absence of either plus or minus affectivity. It is denoted by words like *impassive, wooden,* and *apathetic*. For example, we have judged the mood of a very compliant and flexible kitten to be neutral for a child when the child plays with the kitten as he might with a pillow.

Mood and affection are presumed to be positively related. Yet they are considered to vary independently, as our ratings show. Minus mood with plus affection, especially, is not uncommon. For example, a Midwest mother, in tears because a hail storm is destroying her husband's wheat, can clasp her child warmly while the hail falls.

This category obviously only touches a very complex class of phenomena, which include such feeling states as excitement and calm, and many, differing, emotional qualities. An entire instrument could be devoted to affective and emotive aspects of social interaction.

Illustrative episodes: 30 and 31.

Evaluation

> 1. – – – – –
> 2. – – – –
> 3. – – –   Items 1–5: X is disapproving S's behavior
> 4. – –
> 5. –
> 6. N   Item 6: X is not judging S's behavior
> 7. +
> 8. + +
> 9. + + +   Items 7–11: X is approving S's behavior
> 10. + + + +
> 11. + + + + +

Evaluation means critical assessment by X of O's behavior. A U-shaped continuum is formed by negative evaluation, absence of evaluation, and positive evaluation. Approval of behavior and disapproval of behavior, respectively, are the plus and minus segments of the continuum.

Evaluation is a behavioral property of X as judge or critic. The target of the judgment made by X is what O is doing or how O is behaving. X also may judge O as a person. These two assessments, the one of O and the other of O's behavior, may occur independently and yet at one time. Thus: "What you are speaks louder than what you say." And: "The doer is often better than the deed." But evaluation of O is not rated here. Where it and judgment of O's behavior both appear to occur, and to differ, only the latter is counted. Actually, it cannot be assumed that young children ever distinguish evaluatively the doer from the deed either when they judge others or when others judge them. It can be doubted, for example, that this distinction gets across to the five-year-old miscreant when his mother says, "I love you but not what you do." One source of equivocation is eliminated at any rate by making behavior alone the target of evaluation, as here.

Evaluation can occur either explicitly or altogether implicitly. X can look very sternly at O and say, "That was a naughty thing to do," or imply minus assessment by what he says to a third person or by merely behaving grumpily. Both explicit and implicit evaluations are rated. Thus, in applying the category, the analyst does not look only for evaluative acts, i.e., for outright administerings of praise or blame. The apparent mood or manner, intimations and innuendoes of X also are considered. There is no "does not apply" here. It is assumed that, so long as X has an associate, the category applies; that, in other words, evaluation in one form or another is always a behavioral property of X as an associate of O. This, of course, does not mean that it always is manifest in the episode of a record, for which reason a judgment of evaluation is not always possible. We believe now that the category might advantageously be itemized in future analyses to provide for the distinction between explicit and implicit evaluation.

Model words for plus and minus evaluation are *praise* and *blame*. Verbs like blame which occur in the records, or whose meanings are conveyed in the records by other words, include: censure, criticize, reproach, accuse, rebuke, chide, reprove, berate, reprimand, castigate, scold, upbraid, decry, depreciate, belittle, disparage, condemn, scoff at, sneer at, derogate. Verbs like praise include: esteem, admire, value, appreciate, commend, compliment, applaud, flatter.

Illustrative episodes: 32 through 35.

Interplay Variables

Many different kinds of social interplay obviously are possible as consequences of differing interaction frameworks and differing modes of action and variations in action attributes. Some of these are treated under Interplay Type; and the level of interpersonal harmony or disharmony is rated under Accord.

Interplay Type

The actions of X and O are:

1. Conflict	incompatible and mutually opposed
2. Disjunction	only incompatible
3. Unfriendly Rivalry	incompatible and competitive
4. Coöperation	compatible and mutually supporting
5. Conjunction	only compatible
6. Friendly Rivalry	compatible but competitive
7. Juxtaposition	divergent

Interplay Type means kind of congruence or incongruence between the actions of X and O. The items of the category are discrete. With the exception of Juxtaposition they are based upon the dichotomy of incompatible as against compatible actions, and the trichotomy of mutually opposed, mutually supporting, and competitive actions. Each kind of interplay will be defined with reference to these basic distinctions.

X and O are engaged in compatible actions when the behavior of each is consistent with the goal or wishes of the other. Neither dislikes what the other does. X and O greet one another pleasantly; they exchange smiles; they converse agreeably; they walk arm in arm; a "meeting of minds" occurs. Neither blames, prohibits, opposes, or injures the other or does anything else "out of line" with the wants of the other. Conjunction (item 5) occurs as the type of interplay where, without being congruent in any other sense, the actions of X and O are compatible. The behavior on the one side need not necessarily facilitate that on the other in conjunction; yet this may occur, as when X gratuitously helps O. But merely conjunctive actions are never *mutually* supporting; X and O do not act together and help one another.

X and O are engaged in incompatible actions when the behavior of each or of one alone is inconsistent with the momentary goal or wishes of the other. Each or one dislikes what the other does. *Disjunction* (item 2) occurs where, without being otherwise incongruent, the actions of X and O are incompatible. In disjunction, the action on the one side need not hinder that on the other. A unilateral opposition may occur, however, as when a mother says "stop" to her child, and the child stops. But X and O do not contend against one another. Merely disjunctive actions are never *mutually* opposed.

X and O are engaged in mutually opposed actions when the behavior of each hinders or counteracts the behavior of the other. X strikes and O defends himself or strikes back; X commands and O resists or countercommands; X prohibits and O defies or actively ignores. A model for interplay of this kind is a fight or a quarrel. Mutually opposed actions are always incompatible. Conflict (item 1) occurs when the actions of X and O are incompatible *and* mutually opposed. Reciprocated hindering or opposition is the essential feature of conflict. For this reason, conflict is characteristically cyclical (see Action Sequence, above). X does something O dislikes; then, O opposes X; next, X opposes O; and so on.

X and O are engaged in competitive actions when both elect the same or comparable things to do and each tries independently to outdo the other. To outdo here means to reach a particular goal or a higher goal from which the one person is excluded if and when the other enters the goal region. X and O try to win the same girl, get the same job, or find the same wildflower; or each tries to outrun, outwit, outspell, outwhistle, or otherwise do better than the other.

Competitive actions can be compatible or incompatible. Where they are compatible, each participant wants the other to try to outdo him. Where competitive actions are incompatible, each participant wants the other to desist from trying to outdo him. Competition is mutually invited in the one case and shunned on both sides in the other. Competitive actions are commonly compatible when "winning is its own reward," as in a game; they are often incompatible when X and O seek a goal which, like the girl, the job, or the wildflower, is valued more as an end in itself than as a mark of attainment.

Friendly Rivalry (item 6) occurs when the actions by X and O are competitive and compatible. Unfriendly Rivalry (item 3) occurs when the actions of X and O are competitive and incompatible. Rivalry, whether friendly or unfriendly, can lead to mutually opposed actions. When this holds within the course of an episode, conflict is scored.

It has to be considered that X may compete with O under conditions such that O does not reciprocate; an interaction may be competitive on only one side. X, in other words, may try to outdo O in an activity which O undertakes without meaning to compete with X. For example, a child who is working with another on an arithmetic problem, *towards which the latter shows indifference,* mutters to a bystander, "I'm going to get the answer first," and clearly works hard with this intention. One can speak in such cases of *unilateral rivalry.* Unilateral rivalry can be friendly or unfriendly. It is friendly so long as the competitive action by X is not contrary to the wishes of O, i.e., so long as the action does not bring about a disjunctive type of interplay. It is unfriendly, however, if the competitive action is contrary to O's wishes, so that the form of interplay is disjunctive—as when O is "annoyed" or in any way displeased by the efforts of X to compete with him.

The distinction between unilateral rivalry and bilateral rivalry, while it seems clear in the abstract, turned out to be difficult in practice. We found that it was not possible to segregate reliably the cases in which competitive action was not reciprocated. Also, testing indicated that the relative frequency of such cases is low. For these reasons, items to cover unilateral rivalry were at last excluded from the category.

X and O are engaged in mutually supporting actions when both elect the same thing to do, when each adopts the sought end of the activity as a goal held in common with the other, and when each tries to facilitate the behavior of the other toward the common goal. Mutually supporting actions generally entail some subordination of extraneous individual goals to the "joint undertaking." X and O act together and help one another in building a bird house, in carrying a load, in planning a picnic, in repairing a bicycle. Mutually supporting actions, as implied by their definition, are compatible. Coöperation (item 4) occurs when the actions of X and O are compatible *and* mutually supporting.

Coöperation can occur with rivalry, as when the members of a *team*, in a game or the like, coöperate with one another and yet compete with the members of an opposing team. In these cases the analyst scores the kind of interplay which is judged to be the more important or to have the greater weight for the subject at the time of the episode.

This leaves Juxtaposition (item 7). Here, the actions of X and O are in no sense either congruent or incongruent, but divergent. Neither participant in the transaction is behaving in relation to an action by the other person. X says, "Look at my new coat," and O says, "Pull my sled." Piaget's examples of "collective monologue" (46), in which children converse in such a way that each apparently disregards what the other says, appear to be instances of juxtaposition. One finding which can be reported now is that juxtaposition has been found to occur in only a negligible number of the episodes in our records. For this reason, it is not used as an item of the present category in the study of Chapter XII.

A synopsis of the principal features of each interplay type with the exception of juxtaposition will be given in Chapter XII. Readers may wish to refer now to this summary, which begins on page 452, in connection with the following illustrative episodes: conflict: 36, 37; disjunction: 38; unfriendly rivalry: 39; coöperation: 41, 42; conjunction: 40; friendly rivalry: 43.

Accord

1.	– – – – –	
2.	– – – –	
3.	– – –	Items 1–5: X and O are at odds
4.	– –	
5.	–	
6.	N	Item 6: X and O are neither at odds nor at one
7.	+	
8.	+ +	
9.	+ + +	Items 7–11: X and O are at one
10.	+ + + +	
11.	+ + + + +	

This category provides an overall estimation of the degree of harmony or disharmony in the interaction between subject and associate. Interplay Type tells whether the actions of X and O are compatible or incompatible, and specifies the prevailing kind of interaction. Accord brings out the *degree* of compatibility or incompatibility. It gives a generalizing measure of how well or how poorly X and O are getting along together.

This continuum is U-shaped, with maximum disharmony at one end, maximum harmony at the other, and a centermost neutral break for indeterminate accord, in which A and S cannot be considered either definitely at odds or definitely at one.

The core dimension here is unity of the interactive relationship. The degree of unity can be viewed as an outcome of relationships between behavior of the associate and behavior of the subject. Thus, for example, plus affection, plus mood, and plus evaluation in both A and S are conducive to plus accord, which presumably shifts in the direction of minus accord with every substitution of a minus for these action attributes. It is on this basis that accord is classified as an interaction product. Such interrelationships are not considered in any systematic way, however, in rating accord. To the contrary, an across-the-board estimate is made on the basis of the analyst's direct perception of the harmony or disharmony in the relationship.

Illustrative episodes: 44 through 46.

Subject Constants

Only a minimal treatment of subject characteristics is provided, in line with considerations in Chapter VI.

Conventionally itemized categories on *age*, *sex*, and *social group* are used.

Associate Constants

Essential characteristics of the associate as a social behavior object are covered by associate categories on *age, sex, social group,* and *role* classification, the first three of which are itemized below:

Age of A	Sex of A
1. infant	1. male
2. preschool	2. female
3. younger school	3. male and female
4. older school	
5. adolescent	*Social Group*
6. adult	1. I
7. mixed ch	2. II
8. ch and adol	3. III
9. ch and adult	4. I–II
10. adol and adult	5. I–III
11. ch adol adult	6. II–III
	7. I–II–III

The combination items in each of these categories provide for compound associates. A child speaking a piece at a school program, for example, could have as a compound associate an audience made up of children, adolescents, and adults of both sexes and all three social groups, in which case items 11, 3, and 7, respectively, under age, sex, and social group would apply.

Role classification, otherwise designated as *associate class,* refers to the common, role assignment of the associate. Is the associate a mother, father, sister, brother, neighbor, teacher, grocer? The category is contingently itemized, and it allows for any role combination when the associate is compound.

Applying the Categories

We can summarize the foregoing presentation and show how the method works in practice by reviewing application of the categories to an episode of a day record. Comment on what the analyst saw will be added to the ratings where this seems likely to be clarifying. The episode is reproduced below. Its subject is five-year-old Maud Pintner whom we find sitting beside her mother at the fountain counter in Clifford's Drug Store.

"What do you want, Maud?" Mrs. Pintner asked.

"I want a soda," Maud answered promptly, turning to Ruth Dunner, the clerk at the counter.

"Oh, you don't want a soda," Mrs. Pintner said at once.

"Yes, I want a soda," Maud insisted vehemently.

Mrs. Pintner assured her with determined emphasis, "No, you don't get a soda."

"What *do* you want, then," she asked, impatient for Maud's answer.

"I want a soda!" Maud repeated belligerently, for the clerk's benefit.

"You don't want a soda," the mother said again. "Besides, you wouldn't drink it if you had it."

"Bet I would!" Maud snapped back.

"Do you want a coke? You can have a coke." Mrs. Pintner's voice carried urgency and impatience.

"No!" was Maud's quickly fired answer.

"Do you want an ice cream cone?" Mrs. Pintner seemed anxious to settle Maud's mind for her. "I think we can afford one," the mother said to the clerk. The clerk smiled at her, sharing in a pleasant way Mrs. Pintner's attempts to cope with the situation.

"Do you want an ice cream cone?" The mother put a great deal of pressure into her question.

Maud nodded her head, settling abruptly for the ice cream cone.

The clerk asked Maud what flavor of ice cream she wanted.

Maud said thoughtfully, "Chocolate. No, I want strawberry. No, I want vanilla."

Ruth Dunner explained, "Well, that's the white one."

She handed Maud the ice cream cone.

The analysis follows.

Subject Identity

> *Age*: 5-0
> *Sex*: Girl
> *Social Group*: I

Associate Identity

> *Age*: Adult
> *Sex*: Female
> *Social Group*: I
> *Role Classification*: Mother

Interaction Matrix

> *Behavior Setting*: Clifford's Drug Store
>
> *Time*: December 11, 1950; 2:48 p.m.
>
> *Action Circuit*: Closed. Maud behaved in relation to her mother, and the mother in relation to Maud.
>
> *Associate Complexity*: Simple *A*, rather than compound *A*; one person of two, the second being Ruth Dunner, the clerk.

Social-Field Potency: *High* (.7–.9); short of unity (1.0) owing to considerable involvement of nonsocial behavior objects, viz., the soda, the cone, etc.

Interaction Sequence: *A cycle.* A initiates the interaction by asking, "What do you want, Maud?" whereupon Maud speaks up, and a back-and-forth interchange proceeds.

Relative Power: *A>S* (7). Mrs. Pintner is somewhat less powerful than in her own bailiwick at home. For one thing, the clerk as an appraiser of parental demeanor, puts her at some disadvantage, seized by Maud. Maud is no pushover under the prevailing circumstances and knows it. She knows, for example, that Midwest mothers generally refrain from disciplining children at soda fountains. We know this, at least, and take it that Maud does. Note that the rating goes by what evidently registers upon Maud in her habitat. This must be understood to hold for all of the subsequent ratings on the behavior properties of Mrs. Pintner, the associate.

Episode Weight: *Primary.* The episode is isolated, in fact, which means that its relative potency necessarily is 1.0.

Action Modes

Dominance: *A, present* (3); *S, present* (2). Mrs. Pintner rules, but Maud gets in some counterbossiness.

Aggression: *A, absent*; *S, present* (1). Maud "insisted vehemently" and "repeated belligerently." She "snapped back" one of her retorts and "fired" another. But there was no manifest meanness on the part of the mother. All who rise up here have to remember that we are not aiming to diagnose needs or motives under action modes, but only to detect ways of behaving that get to the surface.

Resistance: *A, present* (3); *S, present* (2). Each holds out against the other, but Maud resists less firmly and steadfastly than her mother.

Submission: *A, absent*; *S, present* (2). Maud gives in only after a stand, to be sure, and not at all abjectly; yet she "takes it."

Nurturance: *A, present* (1); *S, absent*. Maud could have found her mother nicer, but this was nonetheless a treat which, as we saw it, the mother extended to Maud for Maud's benefit, *as Maud saw it.*

Appeal: A, *absent*; S, *present* (2). On the mother's side, there is no asking in the sense of "asking for." There is only ordering plus a little interrogating which, though, is directive. On Maud's side, there is some brave assertiveness, scored above under dominance; but there is also some dependent putting it up to a mother. Maud says, "I want——" three times. She could have said "give me——!" under conditions in no way indicative of entreaty with dependence.

Avoidance: A, *absent*; S, *absent*. Neither hangs back, draws back, or shies from the other.

Action Attributes

Pressure: A, *strong* (5); S, *strong* (4). Each uses power to change the behavior of the other; but the mother bears down the harder. Mrs. Pintner, if one can rely upon the observer, as we must, managed even to put pressure into, "Do you want an ice cream cone?"

Affection: A, *minus* (4); S, *minus* (4). One has to keep in view in rating affection that it means *momentary* feeling for or against. Adding up, we judged that Mrs. Pintner in Maud's habitat, was preponderantly put out with Maud, although not strongly so; and that Maud had, overall, about the same amount of minus feeling for her mother. (Judgment in this particular case is difficult. Yet independent analysts have generally agreed acceptably in using the category.)

Mood: A, *negative* (3); S, *negative* (4). The mood of both is taken to be minus, with Mrs. Pintner's the more strongly so, in Maud's situation. We will come back to this.

Evaluation: A, *disapproving* (3); S, *disapproving* (4). The mother says, for example: "Oh, you don't want a soda." ... "You *don't* want a *soda*." ... "Besides, you wouldn't drink it if you had it." Maud is only somewhat less explicit in evincing a dim view of her mother's conduct.

Interplay Variables

Interplay Type: *Conflict.* Mutual opposition as between Maud and her mother is an outstanding feature of the episode; each opposes action by the other.

Accord: *Negative* (2). There is disharmony rather than harmony in the social relationship, as established by the finding of conflict; and this rating gives an estimate of how much the conflicting mother and child are at odds.

One rule that we have followed and would like to stress now is violated by this sample analysis, as it has been presented here. The rule provides that each episode must be studied in context. Thus, it requires that the whole of any episoded record must be at least scanned before any episode within it is analyzed, and that the analyst continually read ahead intensively as analysis of consecutive episodes proceeds. The objective in applying a category to a particular episode is to represent exclusively behavior or a condition within the time limits of that episode. In order to see clearly the characteristics of the behavior or of the condition, however, generally it is necessary to use all available information on preceding and succeeding behavior and conditions. This follows from the fact that every episode, although it presumably has integrity as a natural unit, is a part of a larger continuum. A geologist identifies marks on a rock as stratification lines by seeing the rock, at least in his mind's eye, as a part of a larger formation. Similarly, our judgment, recorded above, of minus mood, scale point 2, on the part of Maud's mother as Maud saw her at the time, was clarified by knowledge that, through several episodes preceding, Mrs. Pintner had shown the stressful effects of a hectic shopping tour. Here, and in every case, the target episode is viewed only as a center of focus.

The training of an analyst begins with intensive study of the categories. Three or more analysts generally have worked together during this preliminary stage, which has been reinstated from time to time with change in the analysis staff, in the instrument itself, or in methods of application. We have meant and tried accordingly, to make the most of group activity in developing the categories and in learning how to apply them. At the time of each learning period, every category has been studied in terms of its conceptual definition; and empirical criteria for the different discrete items and scale points have been sought, first, in common experience and, then, in the records. Permanently recorded ratings have been preceded always by "agreement checks" in which, after working independently, analysts have compared findings on particular episodes and have resolved differences in judgment. These checks have been used as a means to both interanalyst training in the method, and tests of readiness to apply it. At times they were too skimpy, especially in the earlier analyzing. Even so, our reliability tests, soon to be reported, have generally been reassuring.

The categories certainly are not all alike in their demands upon an analyst. Those under Subject Constants and Associate Constants require only recording of filed information. Action Relationship, Associate Complexity, and Action Sequence require essentially that attention be paid to directly observed facts, which can be noted readily if they have been supplied by the observer. This leaves Relative Power, Social-Field Potency, the Action Modes and Attributes, Interplay Type, and Accord. Analysis by means of these *core categories* presents special problems.

Early experience led us to distinguish two differing *sets* in application of the core categories. These we have called for want of better words the *rationalistic* and the *perceptual*. Both presuppose mastery of the conceptual criteria for each variable. Both presuppose accumulation through experience with the records of examples to fit the different scale points and other category items. The two approaches differ as indicated below:

An analyst who maintains the rationalistic set :	*An analyst who maintains the perceptual set :*
reads the record as he would a graph or table;	reads the record as he would a first-rate novel;
maintains a critical detachment from the subject and his associate;	empathizes with the subject and his associate freely;
probes methodically for significant details and scrutinizes them one by one as evidence for stepwise "rational inference" (see p. 204);	maintains a sharp lookout for significant details which, however, are generally only sized up collectively as clues toward immediate "perceptual inference" (see pp. 204, 207);
makes issues out of alternative interpretations and weighs exhaustively all differing possibilities;	quickly adopts the most likely one of alternative interpretations *even when this means forcing a judgment*;
strives to keep in focus strict empirical criteria for each variable;	depends upon an unformalized array of criteria from everyday social perception and from experience with the records;
exacts of himself rational grounds for every rating;	relies freely upon his hunches;
intends primarily to be logical.	intends primarily to be perceptive.

The perceptual set is by no means all negative; it is more than the absence of a methodical, critically deductive approach. It is not characteristically lax, careless, or passive. It includes on the positive side alert concentration and involvement, like that required of an effective interviewer, therapist, salesman, teacher, diplomat, social worker and, for many purposes, of a good laboratory psychologist. Probably it requires more alertness and steady concentration than the rationalistic set. It has to make up with these assets what it lacks in meticulous logic.

For better or worse we have cast our lot with the perceptual set. There is some evidence, moreover, that from the standpoint of reliability, this choice has not been for the worse but, if there is any difference, for the better. Specifications for the two sets, precisely as they are stated above (except for minor editing), were studied by three analysts who had helped to formulate them and who had been trained in all essentials of the instrument.   Then, following a period of practice in the maintainance of first one set and then the other, agreement between independent analysts under the conditions of each was tested in an experiment, the essential procedures and results of which will be reported later in the chapter.

As anticipated in the preceding chapter, it is impossible at the present stage of our groping ignorance of social behavior variables to draw up hard and fast empirical rules and particulars to go with the items of categories like Social Pressure, Dominance, Nurturance, Appeal, Affection, Mood, and Evaluation.   We have tried very hard to do this in some cases, only to find every such effort grossly unequal to the staggering variety of phenotypes in which differences along these dimensions, differences agreed upon by independent judges, are manifest in the descriptive material of specimen records. It is therefore impracticable and, we now believe, only confounding and a mummery to proceed here as if strict operational guides were now available. The observer could never state rigorously the empirical criteria for what he puts in a specimen record.   No more can an analyst know rigorously the empirical criteria for what he finds in a record, with the consequence that he is up against a stone wall in holding himself to task for such knowledge. The analyst can be at best only the long arm of the observer.   Both work under much the same operational limitations and both, on the other hand, are free to capitalize upon the same capacities to see what everyone must in judging the behavior of others.   The main difference, perhaps, is that the observer records what he sees first-hand by using a great many relatively small words, but no numbers, while the analyst records what he sees second-hand by using a few relatively large words, to some of which numbers (for scale points) are attached.   Fundamentally, both are observers; only the analyst's observations are more selective, orderly, and synoptic.

It might be objected that progress toward rigorous empirical definition of social behavior variables cannot be made so long as a position like the one taken here is maintained.   This is an understandable objection with a real bite in it.   The perceptual set, however, is not inconsistent with operational rigor; it merely sees futility, cramping restraint, and artificiality in pressing too fast to achieve it in the face of present lack of systematic knowledge about the kinds of phenomena that we would like to describe.   Another way to meet the situation, of course, would be to turn to simpler phenomena. But the variables used here seem to be about as simple as variables of molar-and-social behavior get; one cannot ask much less about a thing done by one person in relation to another than whether or not the action was aggressive, for example.   In any case, progress cannot be made by this way around the difficulties, either.

A major feature of the perceptual approach in application of the core categories is its greater economy.   We would not have been led to make it explicit and to test it but for this. The Action Modes, Affection, Mood, and Interplay Type, applied as one battery, were found to require approximately 7.5 minutes per episode under the rationalistic set, maintained through a block of 105 regular social episodes, 45 of which were analyzed before, and 60 of which were analyzed after, processing of roughly 5000 episodes under the perceptual set, at the rate of approximately 4 minutes per episode. The greater economy of the less methodical procedure does have to be counted as one of its advantages, although this asset alone clearly would not be enough to justify it.

Reliability of the Method

Principal Findings

We shall report here findings from tests of agreement between independent analysts on the major categories of the psychosocial instrument and also on contingent selection procedures. The tests were so spaced as to represent all stages of the investigation reported in Chapter XII. For each, the critical score is an *agreement per cent*, defined as per cent of analyzed episodes meeting a specified criterion of agreement. In a few instances, we shall report also nonparametric correlation measures.

Target episodes were selected to provide samples of raw material from all major behavior settings and from subjects distributed representatively as to age, sex, social class, and disability status. For reasons of operational convenience, however, both the test material to be analyzed and the analysts who took part in the agreement procedures were not the same for all categories. Table 10.1 gives the N and source of the episodes used to test different categories, or selection routines and, in the case of each, identifies the participating analysts by letter symbols. The analysts were paired in rotation for all tests to minimize disproportionate comparisons of ratings by any two persons. Full item by item agreement was reached on Sociality of Episode, as this category is itemized on page 326, in 95 per cent of the test units.

Once it has been established that an episode is social, the analyst must designate the particular associate of the subject. This becomes a special problem, as indicated earlier, when the subject behaves in relation to more than one individual during an episode, in which case two possibilities must be weighed: a single individual with preëminent effective strength exists as a simple associate, or two or more individuals constitute a compound associate. The data show that the same, simple or compound, associate was designated by analysts X and Y in 91 per cent of the 234 test episodes. In 6 per cent of these episodes, X chose a particular simple associate while Y saw the same individual as a member of a unitary social complex. Complete disagreement in designation of associate occurred, then, in only 3 per cent of the test units.

The matrix variables of Associate Complexity, Action Circuit, and Social-Field Potency can now be considered.   Full agreement was reached on these three categories, respectively, in 95, 91, and 95 per cent of the test episodes. This means in the case of social-field potency, discrimination of minimum from above minimum on the scale itemized on page 327.

In applying the instrument, we have excluded from analysis beyond the determination of sociality all *irregular episodes*, each a unit the reported content of which is incomplete (owing to such observational misadventure as the disappearance of the subject into a bathroom), or a pseudo unit of restless action (see p. 269), or a unit with acquittance as its issue (see p. 281).

TABLE 10.1

TARGET EPISODES AND ANALYSTS FOR AGREEMENT TESTS

		EPISODES	
CATEGORY OR SELECTION PROCEDURE	N	Source	Analysts
Sociality	380 ⎤		
		5 Day-Records;	A, B, C
Selection of Associate	234 ⎰	4M, 1D	
Episode Selection	339 ⎦		
Associate Complexity ⎤			
Action Circuit ⎬	160 ⎤		
Social-Field Potency ⎦			
Interaction Sequence	106 ⎬	5 Day-Records;	A, B, C, D.
		4M, 1D	
Relative Power ⎤			
Pressure ⎬			
Evaluation ⎬	200 ⎦		
Accord ⎦			
Action Modes ⎤			
Affection ⎬	210	11 Day-Records;	E, F, G
Mood ⎬		8M, 3D	
Interplay Type ⎦			

NOTE.—M, record on Midwest child; D, record on disabled child.

Also, we have used the categories of Sociality, Associate Complexity, Social-Field Potency, Action Circuit, and Relative Weight to select episodes for analysis by all of the remaining categories.   Complete analysis, to summarize, is given only to *regular social episodes*, each a unit of directed action, sufficiently described, with an issue other than mere acquittance, in which the associate is simple, the action circuit closed, the social-field potency high, and the relative weight primary.   Regular social episodes which do not meet all of these criteria are subjected to *secondary analysis* consisting only in the application of the categories under Subject Constants and Associate Constants in the outline on page 324.   It obviously becomes important to test the reliability of this selection process. The part of the process involving elimination of irregular episodes and episodes of less than primary relative weight falls to the episoder. As for the remaining steps, agreement between independent analysts in selecting units for complete analysis occurred in 33 per cent, while agreement in the selection of units for secondary analysis occurred in 58 per cent of the test episodes, which means that the overall agreement per cent for the critical stages of the selection process was 91.

Agreement data on Action Sequence, another matrix variable, are presented in Table 10.2, which contains, in addition to agreement per cents,

TABLE 10.2

AGREEMENT BETWEEN INDEPENDENT ANALYSTS ON
ACTION SEQUENCE

PAIRED ANALYSTS	S INITIATION VERSUS A INITIATION		CYCLICAL INTERACTION VERSUS NON-CYCLICAL INTERACTION		EXACT DISCRETE RATING	N
	Agreement Per Cent	Tb	Agreement Per Cent	Tb	Agreement Per Cent	
A:B	83	.54	76	.50	66	41
A:C	87	.75	74	.48	69	39
B:C	88	.74	81	.49	73	26

NOTE.—Tb, dichotomous *tau beta* coefficient of rank correlation. See Kendall (28).

rank order coefficients of correlation between the ratings of identified analysts, as seemed desirable in this case, owing to the somewhat borderline magnitude of the agreement measures. Note further that secondary groupings of the category items, to be found as originally itemized on page 328, are represented. The data are taken to indicate fair agreement on the distinction between initiation by S, the subject, and initiation by A, the associate, and also on cyclical versus noncyclical interaction. They were found to show rather poor item by item agreement, however, for which reason only the grosser breakdowns represented in the table are used in Chapter XII.

We come to the categories of Relative Power, Evaluation, Affection, Mood, and Accord, each of which requires a rating on an 11-point scale. Disparity between independent analysts of no more than one scale point on these categories was as follows, with the first figure referring to the associate and the second to the subject, wherever ratings were made on both: Relative Power, 94 per cent; Evaluation, 71 per cent and 76 per cent; Affection, 83 per cent and 83 per cent; Mood, 86 per cent and 81 per cent; and Accord, 84 per cent. If the criterion of substantial agreement is stretched to admit a disparity of 2 points, these values become 98 per cent on Relative Power,

82 per cent and 86 per cent on Evaluation, 95 per cent and 94 per cent on Affection, 97 per cent and 93 per cent on Mood, and 96 per cent on Accord. The Evaluation ratings show lower reliability than those on the other scales. Concerning this, a finding with pertinence is that, as later data will show, markedly high variability is characteristic of this category; associates, especially, proved to be mercurial in expression of plus and minus evaluation.

Social Pressure presents another continuum variable, although it was treated as such by a scale of only 5 points. It was rated also, however, as to virtual absence or measurable presence. Agreement on presence or absence of pressure by the subject and pressure by an associate respectively occurred in 75 per cent and 81 per cent of the test episodes. Disparity on the scale ratings no greater than one point occurred in 91 per cent of these episodes on the subject side, and in 89 per cent on the associate side.

It will be recalled that the Action Modes call for judgment as to presence or absence, and also a rating of strength. Since the strength ratings will not be used in Chapter XII, only measures of agreement on presence or absence will be given here. These are, on associate and subject respectively: Dominance, 86 per cent and 90 per cent; Aggression, 89 per cent and 92 per cent; Resistance, 88 per cent and 92 per cent; Avoidance, 96 per cent and 96 per cent; Appeal, 92 per cent and 88 per cent; Nurturance, 85 per cent and 94 per cent; Submission, 92 per cent and 85 per cent; Compliance, 84 per cent and 82 per cent.

One conclusion drawn from our work with the mode categories has special significance in relation to these data. It is that judgment errors in the identification of action modes are most characteristically errors of omission rather than errors of commission. On comparing their judgments on the same episodes, analysts have quite often held out against one another tenaciously for differing assignments of modes to an action. One may say, for example, "There is a plain case of aggression," while the other says, "No, come on now, it's nothing but strong dominance." Such disagreement, however, was found to be relatively rare. When two analysts compare work sheets, a very common remark by either is in the nature of "Whoops, I missed that." Very often, a particular mode is outstanding in an action, or as many as three or four stand out, while, nevertheless, others can be detected. It is the weak mode, in the background of stronger ones, which brings about the most frequent disagreements; one analyst sees it while the other misses it; one fails to note what is there but, to judge from final judgments often reached jointly when comparisons are made, *neither sees frequently what is not there.* In all, then, we have considered that the mode identifications probably do not tell the whole truth and yet do not often tell mistruths. It is our strong impression, moreover, that the frequencies on the different modes are not undershot disproportionately; we cannot pick out any kind of action which tends to be missed more than others, unless an exception be made for aggression, which has been marked by a given analyst fairly often, but not marked by a second who, however, has promptly acknowledged its occurrence on having it called to his attention.   If this is correct, findings from the instrument as to the relative frequencies of action modes are to be trusted, although the absolute frequencies may be short of actual occurrence.   Here, at all events, are some method problems for further careful study.   Probably, too, these problems are open to quantitative procedures which, though, it has not been possible for us to explore to date.

There remains one category, Interplay Type.   The three analysts varied somewhat in agreement on this category.   Exact item by item agreement per cents from three pairings of raters are 91, 83, and 71.   Agreement per cents on *compatible* interplay (coöperation, conjunction, and friendly rivalry) vs. *incompatible* interplay (conflict, disjunction, and unfriendly rivalry) are 96, 86, and 84.   On conflict vs. no conflict, the values for the three analyst pairings are 99, 100, and 94.

Rationalistic Set versus Perceptual Set

We have referred to evidence on reliability of the psychosocial instrument under each of the two analysis sets, the rationalistic and the perceptual. Here is that evidence.

In each of 6 day-records on subjects distributed representatively as to age, sex, and social group, 20 consecutive regular social episodes were marked off.   The episodes in each block of 20 were comparable in that: with minor exceptions, they occurred in the same behavior setting; most of them involved the subject in relation to the same associate; they occurred during the same part of the day.   One sample, P, of 60 episodes was formed by massing the first 10 of the 20 episodes in every block; while another sample, R, of 60 episodes was formed by massing the second 10 of the 20 episodes in every block.   We have considered that, by reason of the indicated common features of all units in each of these blocks, the two samples were matched.

Paired analysts, working under the perceptual set, applied a battery of core categories, the Action Modes, Affection, Mood, and Interaction Type, to the episodes of the P sample in the ordinary course of processing 11 day-records, including the 6 used for the present comparison.   Subsequently, after all of the 5,640 regular social episodes in these 11 records had been analyzed, the same analysts applied the same categories to the episodes of the R sample, which had purposely been withheld from analysis.   One objective in this design was to weight the rationalistic set by any advantages in experience on the part of the analysts.   Special precautions were taken throughout to guarantee analysis in context of every episode in each sample. If anything, the R units were favored from this standpoint, inasmuch as they were analyzed only after intensive reading and processing of every record concerned.   The source records, blocks of target episodes, and analyst pairs are shown in Table 10.3.

TABLE 10.3

SOURCE RECORDS, TARGET EPISODES, AND ANALYST PAIRS FOR EXPERIMENT
ON RELIABILITY OF ANALYSIS UNDER PERCEPTUAL AND RATIONALISTIC SETS

SOURCE RECORD	TARGET EPISODES		ANALYST PAIR	
	P Sample	R Sample	P Sample	R Sample
JS: B,2	10	10	AB	AB
MC: G,2	10	10	AC	AC
DT: B,4	10	10	BC	BC
MR: G,5	10	10	AB	AB
VT: B,7	10	10	AC	AC
DC: B,9	10	10	BC	BC

NOTE.—B, Boy; G, Girl.   Each number following B or G gives approximate age.   P, perceptual set
R, rationalistic set.

Agreement per cents were computed for both the P units and the R units on six of the Action Modes (Dominance, Resistance, Aggression, Nurturance, Appeal, and Avoidance), the Action Attributes of Affection and Mood, and Interplay Type.   The following criteria of agreement were used:

Action Modes: Analysts X and Y both find the given mode absent or find it present with a strength disparity no greater than 1 scale point.

Attributes: Compared ratings by X and Y differ by no more than 1 scale point.

Interplay Type: X and Y agree on the exact item designation.

Data for the 6 modes and 2 attributes respectively, as applied to both the behavior of the associate and the behavior of the subject, were massed to give 360 ratings and 120 ratings as basic N totals.   That is, each of the 6 modes was judged on each of the 60 episodes to give a total of 360 ratings; and each of the 2 attributes was judged on each of the 60 episodes to give a total of 120.

The agreement findings are presented in Table 10.4.   A Chi square test for significance of difference between groups, based on the N's for agreement and disagreement, shows in the case of each comparison that the hypothesis of no difference in reliability as between the two sets cannot be rejected. Only in the instance of Interplay Type does the obtained difference approach significance; and here the agreement per cent is higher for the perceptual set.   These findings are without any exception consistent with results yielded repeatedly by less formalized and controlled comparisons, one of which involved P and R samples of 45 episodes each, in 3 day-records.   Wherever any appreciable difference has been found, it has indicated greater reliability of the perceptual set.

TABLE 10.4

AGREEMENT IN PER CENT BETWEEN INDEPENDENT ANALYSTS
ON ACTION MODES, ATTRIBUTES OF AFFECTION AND
MOOD, AND INTERPLAY TYPE UNDER PERCEPTUAL AND RATIONALISTIC SETS

CATEGORIES		PERCEPTUAL SET Agreement Per Cent	N:E	N:R	RATIONALISTIC SET Agreement Per Cent	N:E	N:R	DIFFERENCE Chi²	P
Modes	A	88	60	360	91	60	360	.71	> .05
	S	91	60	360	91	60	360	—	—
Attributes	A	80	60	120	83	60	120	.44	> .05
	S	78	60	120	80	60	120	.10	> .05
Interplay		87	60	60	78	60	60	1.45	> .05

NOTE.—A, behavior of associate; S, behavior of subject.   N:E, number of episodes;
N:R, number of ratings.

Concluding Statement

The reported agreement measures are taken to indicate variable but
generally satisfactory reliability of episode analysis by means of these
categories. It remains true, of course, that many of the judgments made
in applying the categories cannot be operationally precise. Yet, in support
of these judgments, we would like to raise one further point. They are
made always upon the concrete material in, or in the recorded context of,
a single behaviour episode. Similar judgment have long been secured via
personality rating scales and inventories, *on* whole persons. It has appeared
to us that, generally, episodes may provide more definite and more clearly
circumscribed target material. When an analyst is called upon to rate a
trait of a person, he must somehow weigh a multitude of widely ranging
facts and events, with many of which he has had no direct acquaintance.
The rater of an episode, on the other hand, has everything to be considered
before him. Also, in treating the material of a specimen record, he repeats
these judgments on every episode of an extended sequence, so that much
cancelling out of error should occur.

We have no direct evidence on validity of the method. Any case for
its validity has to rest now on the meaningfulness and tenability of such
results as those reported in Chapter XII.

Chapter XI

Social Action and Interaction II: An Episode Exhibit

THIS chapter has two aims. The first is to present in the form of episodes in specimen records an exhibit of social action and interaction in Midwest children and disabled children of nearby communities. The second is to strengthen empirical definition of the psychosocial categories. Necessarily the exhibit is small; and because it shows individual episodes out of context it is nowhere equal in richness to the originally recorded material. Yet it gives a view that we could not hope to open in a less direct way; and it provides a needed bridge between the check lists and scales of the preceding chapter and the charts and tables of the chapter to follow.

Each episode has been chosen to illustrate clearly an item or scale segment of a particular category. Clear illustration of a scale segment, such as negative mood or positive mood, generally has required examples of manifestation in a high degree, although we have included some episodes to suggest degree variation. In every case, the item designation or precise scale rating by the analyst is indicated. Very often an episode suited to one variable conspicuously represents others as well. Cross-indexing, however, is left to the reader. A particular category item or part of a scale often is illustrated by more than one episode where this has seemed desirable for clarification or to show variety.

Episodes to represent Matrix Factors other than Relative Power, Strength of Motivation, and Centrality of Motivation are not included; but examples that fit these omitted categories, which ordinarily require easy and unequivocal judgment, so long as the pertinent data have been reported in a record, can be found readily in the exhibit.

A majority of the episodes are from Midwest children. Yet a sizeable number from disabled children who do not live in Midwest are included for comparative purposes and, often, for the sake of clear illustration. Children differing in age, sex, and other subject characteristics are represented.

For every episode, its title, the subject, the behavior setting, the associate, the date and time of day, and the rating are given. Each subject is identified as a Midwest child, M, or a nearby disabled child, D, and placed also as to sex, social group, and age.

In several instances, the original text of the source record has been abbreviated slightly to save space and, in a few cases, overlapping episodes without pertinence for the present purpose have been eliminated. Where necessary, a brief statement is made about the context of an episode.

Social Behavior Episodes

Throughout here the classification headings and category titles of the instrument are followed. Also, subheads are used under Action Modes and Action Attributes to distinguish between behavior by the associate and behavior by the subject.

Matrix Factors

Strength and Centrality of Motivation

1. Strength of Motivation

Subject:	Dutton Thurston (M, M, 3, 3-10)
Episode:	Getting Ready to Go Outdoors
Setting:	Thurston Home, Indoors
Associate:	Mother
Time:	November 3, 1950; 7:15–7:17 p.m.
Rating:	4

Note:
M, Midwest child
M, Male
3, Social group 3
3-10, 3 years 10 months

Dutton, nicknamed Chuck, has just been given permission by his mother to go outdoors where his father is working.

Chuck slammed the door and ran back into the dining room.

He asked his mother where his gloves and jacket were. He was breathless and in a hurry to get outside.

His mother smiled and told him where to find his things.

Chuck raced to the back door. On the way, he yelled, "Wait a minute."

He opened the back door and screamed as loudly as he could, "Wait a minute, Daddy."

He tore back into the kitchen and into his bedroom. Somewhere along the way he located his jacket and gloves and cap.

He darted back into the dining room, carrying his outdoor clothes.

In a shrill, excited voice he said, "Mamma, he'll wait."

He stood directly in front of his mother and turned so that she could put his jacket on him.

While Mrs. Thurston buttoned up the jacket, Chuck bounced up and down and wiggled around in an excited way.

Then he quickly turned to face her and held out his right glove.

While his mother was putting the glove on, Chuck moved his hand about to help her.

He shoved out the left glove.

Then while the mother put it on, he wiggled around impatiently.

Mrs. Thurston chuckled and said, as if to calm Chuck down a little, "Well, he's just going out to drain the tractor."

Chuck said, "Can I go, too; can I go, too?"

He didn't seem to be asking for her permission now.
This was more of a statement than a question.

As soon as he was dressed to go outside, Chuck whirled around and started on his way.

2. Centrality of Motivation

Subject:	Sue Dewall (D, F, 4, 7-1)
Episode:	Talking to Olivia About Letter
Setting:	Lawton Free Time, Indoors
Associate:	Olivia, Occupational Therapist
Time:	June 5, 1951; 1:27 p.m.
Rating:	5

Olivia is reading a letter to Lila, Sue's roommate at Lawton. The letter is from Lila's parents.

Olivia noticed Sue listening intently to the letter.

Right away, looking wise and kind, Olivia pretended to read from the letter. "How is Sue?" Then Olivia paused and looked at Sue to get her reaction.

Sue smiled happily.

Olivia finished the letter and laid it on the table.

Sue, looking pleased at being mentioned in Lila's letter and wanting to talk about it said, "Now, why did they put me in there?"

Olivia, still seated, turned around to face Sue.

Sue took two steps and threw her arms around Olivia and embraced her affectionately.

Olivia fondly put her arms around Sue and playfully slapped her on the rear once or twice.

Sue said to Olivia happily, "I didn't know I was in there." She was very pleased.

Olivia stood up and walked away.

Relative Power

3. Relative Power: $A > S$

Subject:	Margaret Reid (M, F, 3, 4-6)
Episode:	Obeying Instructions
Setting:	Vacation Church School, Kindergarten Class
Associate:	Adult Leaders (Compound A)
Time:	June 2, 1949; 9:22 a.m.
Rating:	9

Margaret and several other children are being lined up to practice an exercise for a program.

At this time, Mrs. Hebb, the music teacher, and some of the other leaders of the Vacation Church School, decided to sort the children, telling the shorter ones to go to either end of the row and the taller ones to stand toward the center of the line on the platform.

Margaret stood passively and watched the shuffling process.

While she watched, the adult leaders came closer and closer.

Margaret had been about fourth or fifth in line. Then, suddenly, she was switched to third from the shortest at one end.

Margaret very carefully put her toes right on the exact edge of the carpet as all the children had been instructed to do.

4. Relative Power: $S > A$

Subject: Mary Ennis (M, F, 2, 8-7)
Episode: Jollying Little Brother
Setting: Ennis Home, Indoors
Associate: Timothy, her baby brother
Time: May 12, 1949; 7:59 a.m.
Rating: 3

Mary is roaming about with a hairbrush in her hand, rather aimlessly brushing at her hair.

Mary went slowly over to her brother's crib and poked him gently, playfully, with one end of the brush.

He giggled heartily.

This made Mary laugh, so she poked him again.

Again Timothy chuckled, curling himself up in a little ball as he did so, pulling his knees way up to his tummy and pushing his hands toward the place where Mary had poked him with the brush.

Mary laughed again and then said in a babyish tone of voice, as if to come down to Timothy's level, "Does that tickle you, honey?"

This tone came very close to mimicking the mother's tone when she talked to the baby.

5. Relative Power: $S = A$

Subject: Maud Pintner (M, F, 1, 5-0)
Episode: Playing Horse With Otto
Setting: Pintner Home, Indoors
Associate: Otto Chaco, four-year-old playmate
Time: December 11, 1950; 10:40–10:42 a.m.
Rating: 6

Otto and Maud are in the midst of talk about what to play.

Maud, with Otto following, circled back to the children's room and stopped just inside the doorway.

She started away, as though to lead Otto again.

Otto asked in a serious tone, "Can I be the horse?"

Maud immediately agreed in an equally serious tone, "O.K."

In a loud, commanding voice Maud yelled, "See, you run away and I catch you." This was a new angle to the game.

Otto matter-of-factly gave Maud the rope and immediately darted through the hall and into the living room.

Maud stood quietly for a moment and watched him, letting him get a good start.

Then she started after him, trotting along at a fairly swift pace, but not as fast as she could have if she had really wanted to catch him.

Holding one end of the rope in her hand, she let it dangle over her shoulder, as though planning to use it as a whip.

She followed Otto through the living room and back into the children's room.

When she caught up with him, she slipped the rope around his waist.

Otto looked down at the rope with a frown on his face and reprimanded her, "You're not supposed to do it that way—*this* way," and he pulled it down a bit.

> I don't know whether Maud had the rope too tight or whether it was too high on his waist. Anyway, she was doing something that Otto didn't like.

Maud received the decision with a calm, "O.K."

The children galloped through the hall and into the living room with Otto, the "horse," leading Maud.

Otto knelt down on the living room floor; his attention was caught by a toy car which lay on the floor.

He picked up the car and began playing with it.

Maud dropped the rope.

> Otto was responsible for ending the "horse" game. Maud showed no particular disappointment.

Modes of Action

Dominance

6. Dominance: Associate

Subject:	Verne Trennell (D, M, 3, 7-5)
Episode:	Reacting to Saline's Orders
Setting:	Lawton, Younger Children's Classroom, Academic
Associate:	Saline Cutton, a teacher
Time:	June 21, 1951; 9:22 a.m.
Rating:	3 (element of aggression)

The teacher, Saline Cutton, is centering her attention on Verne who has just torn a sheet of paper from his notebook. He hands it to the teacher at her sharp request.

Saline proceeded to explain to Verne what his next assignment was to be. In a comparatively calm and well modulated voice she said, "Now, you do this. You have done this kind of thing many times before."

Abruptly she raised her voice in an ultimatum, emphasizing every word, "*Will you read your instructions, please. Read your instructions, please.*" Slapping the paper down on the table before Verne, she continued after the slightest possible pause in a little less vehement tone than before, "You've done this so many times."

Verne listened with a puzzled frown on his usually bland face. He sat so still that I couldn't see a muscle move.

After Saline had finished her tirade, Verne continued looking at her in a stunned way.

7. Dominance: Associate

Subject:	Douglas Crawford (M, M, 3, 9-2)
Episode:	Obeying Mother's Command
Setting:	Crawford Home, Meals
Associate:	Mother
Time:	April 18, 1949; 7:21 p.m.
Rating:	3

Douglas, his father, mother, and sister, Norah, are at the dining room table having an animated conversation while they eat supper.

Douglas stood, shoved his chair back, and marched away from the table, taking short steps and wobbling from side to side. He was through with his meal and was ready to go outside and play.

His mother, in no uncertain terms, commanded, "Sit down." She left absolutely no room for argument or appeal.

Douglas slowly, matter-of-factly, came back and sat down.

8. Dominance: Subject

Subject:	Margaret Reid (M, F, 3, 4-6)
Episode:	Ordering Mother About Bucket
Setting:	Reid Home, Outdoors
Associate:	Mother
Time:	June 2, 1949; 8:15 p.m.
Rating:	3

Margaret has been riding in a wagon, pulled by her grandfather. Enroute she grabs up an empty bucket from the ground.

Margaret abruptly called out authoritatively, "Mother, here."

When her mother apparently paid her no attention, she added impatiently, "Mother, have that ready."

As she finished talking, she threw the bucket forcefully toward her mother.

Resistance

9. Resistance: Associate

Subject: Margaret Reid (M, F, 3, 4-6)
Episode: Trying to Get Permission to Go to Ellen's House
Setting: Reid Home, Outdoors
Associate: Mother
Time: June 2, 1949; 1:02 p.m.
Rating: 3

Ellen Thomas, an older neighbor girl, lives across the street from the Reids. It is Ellen's birthday. Margaret appears to like Ellen very much.

Margaret followed behind her mother.

She was suddenly intent on getting her mother's permission to go over to Ellen's house. She asked, "Mother, can I go over to Ellen's?"

The mother said flatly, with no hesitation, "No."

Margaret tried to talk her mother into letting her go by whining and arguing.

But Mrs. Reid was final and definite, answering with another, "No." Then she added, "Ellen isn't home, anyway."

Immediately, Margaret seized the opening. "Yes, she is; she's home now."

Her mother wouldn't even listen. "No, you cannot go over there now," she said, and stamped into the house.

10. Resistance: Subject

Subject: Wally Wolfson (D, M, 3, 4-3)
Episode: Protesting Being Carried to Auto Seat
Setting: Wolfson Home, Outdoors
Associate: Ben, six-year-old playmate
Time: August 9, 1951; 2:57 p.m.
Rating: 3

Wally is playing with Jim and Ben, two older boys, in a shed behind the Wolfson house. Ben has just asked Wally to play with them on an old auto seat.

Ben came to Wally and said shortly, "I'll carry you."

He picked Wally up by the arms and proceeded to drag him across the debris and wire to the auto seat.

Wally squirmed and protested loudly, "I don't want over there."

He cried out repeatedly and firmly that he didn't want to go "there."

Wally's reluctance seemed to make Ben more insistent.

Ben dragged Wally over and dumped him on the end of the auto seat.

Aggression

11. Aggression: Associate

Subject:　　Margaret Reid (M, F, 3, 4-6)
Episode:　　Responding to Bradley's Blow
Setting:　　Reid Home, Outdoors
Associate:　Bradley, 18-month-old brother
Time:　　　June 2, 1949; 6:33 p.m.
Rating:　　2

Margaret is sitting on the front porch playing rather roughly with a young puppy.

Bradley came from around the corner of the house. He walked deliberately over to Margaret where she sat playing with the puppy and hit her on the head twice, just as hard as he could hit.

It appeared that Bradley didn't like what Margaret was doing with the dog.

Margaret looked very surprised and annoyed. The expression on her face showed definitely that she wanted to return the blow.

She looked at me in a rather questioning way.

Then she just rubbed her head while looking belligerent.

12. Aggression: Associate

Subject:　　Roy Eddy (M, M, 3, 6-2)
Episode:　　Responding to Geoffrey's Blows
Setting:　　Midwest Hardware and Implement Company
Associate:　Geoffrey, seven-year-old playmate
Time:　　　February 22, 1949; 3:43 p.m.
Rating:　　3

Roy is playing in the Hardware store with Thomas and Geoffrey, peer playmates, both sons of employees in the store.

Geoffrey went behind the counter and got an old pair of overalls. He came up to Roy and Thomas, who stood near the counter, and swung the overalls hard against Roy.

Roy gave no sign of minding.

Geoffrey swung again, obviously to hit Roy. The expression on his face showed that he was swinging the overalls as hard as possible.

This time one of the buckles hit Roy across the hand. Roy showed irritation. He was hurt and glared at Geoffrey.

Geoffrey swung once more, hitting Thomas; and then he left rapidly.

Roy stared after Geoffrey with a hurt and hostile look.

13. *Aggression: Subject*

Subject: Maud Pintner (M, F, 1, 5-0)
Episode: "Fixing" Freddy
Setting: Pintner Home, Indoors
Associate: Freddy, 20-month-old brother
Time: December 11, 1950; 7:05 p.m.
Rating: 3

Maud is in the kitchen where her father is tying a tea towel around her head turban-style, at her request. Maud stands very still. As Mr. Pintner ties the towel, he calls to Freddy in the dining room, "You'd better put those up." Freddy is playing with Maud's crayons in the dining room. Mrs. Pintner agrees that Freddy should put the crayons up since they are Maud's.

Maud asked, "What?" curiously, not moving at all since her father was still tying the scarf. She was standing very still, with her back to Freddy.

Without moving, Maud warned, "I'll fix you!"

As soon as the towel had been tied, she dashed into the dining room.

With the palm of her hand she hit Freddy hard and vehemently in the belly several times.

Freddy seemed surprised at the vigor of these blows but apparently was not hurt. The basket of crayons fell to the floor.

14. *Aggression: Subject*

Subject: Wally Wolfson (D, M, 3, 4-3)
Episode: Throwing Rock at Maud
Setting: Wolfson Home, Outdoors
Associate: Maud, two-year-old sister
Time: August 9, 1951; 10:04–10:07 a.m.
Rating: 3

Wally has been having a brief but vigorous argument with Maud about who brought their Easter baskets, declaring that the Easter Bunny rather than Santa Claus had done so. His strong statements have reduced Maud to whimpering.

Wally coolly put the basket down. He reached down quickly, picked up a large piece of gravel, and cocked his arm. His facial expression was immobile, but it struck me as coldly angry.

Maud, evidently gathering Wally's intention, ran toward the step at the north end of the porch.

It appeared that she wanted to get inside the house to the protection of her mother before Wally threw the gravel.

Wally waited as if stalking his prey, until Maud was near the door so that the post on the corner of the porch wouldn't be in the way. Then, as Maud ran through the door, Wally threw the stone, which hit Maud just above her hip.

It appeared that Wally threw as hard as he could, although that actually wasn't very hard.

When the stone hit Maud, her whimpering immediately turned into loud crying. She ran on into the house where I could hear her saying something to her mother, who comforted her.

15. Aggression: Subject

Subject:	Margaret Reid (M, F, 3, 4-6)
Episode:	Hitting Bradley
Setting:	Reid Home, Outdoors
Associate:	Bradley, 18-month-old brother
Time:	June 2, 1949; 1:03 p.m.
Rating:	3

Margaret has been teasing her mother to go to the neighbor's to play; but Mrs. Reid goes into the house, having firmly refused Margaret's pleas. Bradley is wandering about the yard while Margaret and her mother argue.

Bradley picked up a tin bucket that Mrs. Reid had taken from Margaret. He swung it, rattling a stone in the bottom of the bucket.

Margaret went over and started pounding on Bradley's legs, his back, and the back of his head.

Bradley seemed to expect this. When she came toward him, he knew what was coming. He cowered as if it were rather a regular occurrence for her to hit him.

Margaret hit Bradley again and again.

He cried a little each time she hit him and, finally, started crying seriously.

Seeing that Bradley was really going to cry in earnest, Margaret let him alone. But she taunted, "I can hit you and I can throw you," as she left him.

Submission

16. Submission: Associate

Subject:	Mary Ennis (M, F, 2, 8-7)
Episode:	Directing Sarah in Swing
Setting:	Ennis Home, Outdoors
Associate:	Sarah, 11-year-old playmate
Time:	May 12, 1949; 4:10 p.m.
Rating:	3

Sarah came out of the house.

Immediately, Mary suggested that the two girls swing together in the long, rope swing which hung from a high branch of a tall, elm tree.

Sarah was easily persuaded.

Mary guided her and instructed her exactly in the position she should take in the swing.

Sarah followed Mary's instructions passively.

As Sarah sat in the swing, Mary climbed on the board so that she stood facing Sarah.

Suddenly, holding to the ropes with her hands, Mary kicked her feet straight out so that she fell, kerplunk, into Sarah's lap, practically knocking the wind out of her.

Sarah was unable to speak. She obviously wasn't very enthusiastic about this, but said nothing.

Mary showed no awareness of Sarah's disapproval. She was having a wonderful time.

Then both of the girls stood up, facing each other in the swing. They discussed the exact positions of their feet until, at the end of the discussion, Mary had both of her feet on the outside with Sarah's feet on the inside. This clearly was as Mary wanted it.

Mary maneuvered Sarah's feet, using her own to kick Sarah's out of the way until she had enough room.

Sarah did not protest in any way. As the two girls swung back and forth, Mary continued to shriek and laugh.

At last, the two girls coasted to a stop. Sarah appeared glad to stop and Mary too exhausted to continue. Again Mary commanded Sarah to sit down. She was still shrieking and laughing and giggling at the top of her voice.

Sarah complied and sat down.

Again Mary climbed into the swing and abruptly sat down on Sarah's lap with all her weight.

This time Sarah was prepared for the shock. She endured in silence, but did not suffer from the jolt as she seemed to have previously.

The two girls attempted to swing while still seated. Sarah sat on the swing seat while Mary sat on her lap facing her, her legs extending out at each side of Sarah.

When they came to a stop, Mary climbed vigorously right over Sarah to the ground. Looking at Sarah, she grinned and beamed, "Now, are you glad?" Then she added, "Or would you rather be murdered?"

Sarah said she was glad they had swung together. But she did say, "I'd rather be murdered." Then, she corrected herself quickly, "No, I'd rather do this."

17. Submission: Subject

Subject:	Wally Wolfson (D, M, 3, 4-3)
Episode:	Responding to Jim's Reprimand
Setting:	Wolfson Home, Outdoors
Associate:	Jim, eight-year-old playmate
Time:	August 9, 1951; 1:16 p.m.
Rating:	3

Wally is playing cars with Jim and indulging in much imaginary play and conversation about roads and cars.

Jim glanced at Wally and said sharply, "You're messing the road up." Then he ordered Wally brusquely, "You have to go back and fix 'em. Go on."

Wally obediently turned around and began to make the road more distinct and clear.

Jim commanded, "That's enough. Turn around and come back."

Wally obediently turned around and started to come back over the road.

Jim admonished him, "Don't go too fast. You'll get your leg in it again." Hardly stopping, he said, "There, you did get your leg in it again," as Wally's foot touched a side of the road.

Wally carefully lifted his leg over the road without touching any more of it. He said reassuringly, "I'll fix it up."

Nurturance

18. Nurturance: Associate

Subject:	Verne Trennell (D, M, 3, 7-5)
Episode:	Letting Father Dress Him for Bed
Setting:	Trennell Home, Indoors
Associate:	Father
Time:	June 21, 1951; 9:14 p.m.
Rating:	3

Verne has just been bathed and dried by his father. The urinal bag worn by Verne in the day time has been removed. This bag has to be replaced by absorbent diapers for night wear.

Verne's father got two diapers from the drawer in the same cupboard in the bathroom where the towels were. He wrapped a towel around Verne, picked him up in his arms, and carried him out to the bedroom and laid him on his bed.

Verne lay passively on the bed with the towel wrapped around his shoulders.

His father went to a chest of drawers behind Verne and took out a can of talcum powder. He returned to the bed and powdered Verne's genitals. Then he placed the diapers under Verne and fastened them, using safety pins.

Verne passively permitted his father to do this.

Throughout, Verne seemed to play the role of an infant and his father treated him like one.

The father turned around and straightened the light woolen blanket on Verne's bed.

Verne slept in a crib with iron sides on it. The side away from the wall was lowered; the side next to the wall was raised.

Mr. Trennell turned back to Verne. He picked up the tops of a pair of pajamas that were on the bed and asked Verne kindly, "You want to put these on?"

Verne sat up and helped his father put the tops of the pajamas on him by lifting his arms and pulling his hands through the sleeves.

19. Nurturance: Subject

Subject: Maud Pintner (M, F, 1, 5-0)
Episode: Responding to Fred's Fall
Setting: Pintner Home, Outdoors
Associate: Fred, 20-month-old brother
Time: December 11, 1950; 11:06 a.m.
Rating: 3

Maud and Otto, a four-and-one-half-year-old playmate, are swinging, with Maud doing the pushing. Fred, Maud's young brother, is wandering about near the porch swing.

Accidentally, Fred skidded on the floor so that he fell with his body partially under the swing as it swooped back from the library doors. He yelled, "Whoops," and then lay still since he saw the swing coming back over him.

Maud noticed his fall and at once gripped the swing chain tightly, halting it as quickly as possible. Her face showed real concern about her brother as she held firmly to the chain of the swing until he could get out from under it.

As soon as the swing stopped, Otto got out to check on Fred's welfare.

Appeal

20. Appeal: Associate

Subject: Douglas Crawford (M, M, 3, 9-2)
Episode: Responding to Blake's Coaxing
Setting: Eddy's Home, Outdoors
Associate: Blake, six-year-old playmate
Time: April 18, 1949; 6:24 p.m.
Rating: 2

Douglas and Blake are playing Indians.

Douglas picked up his bow and arrow and then started to get ready as though he were going to shoot it.

In a wheedling tone of voice, Blake said, "I'd like to shoot it."

There was no response.

"Can I shoot it once? Please?" Blake sounded even more wheedling. He coaxed again, "Please, can I shoot it just once?"

Graciously, although not very promptly, Douglas handed the bow to Blake.

I thought that Douglas was going to give it to him all along, but that he enjoyed being asked and having someone else want so much to shoot it.

21. Appeal: Subject

Subject: Maud Pintner (M, F, 1, 5-0)
Episode: Questioning Mother About Going to Game
Setting: Pintner Home, Indoors
Associate: Mother
Time: December 11, 1950; 3:51 p.m.
Rating: 3

Maud is apparently intensely occupied with coloring as she kneels on the floor and bends over a coloring book.

Maud suddenly jumped to her feet and raced to the breakfast room where her mother was ironing.

She said in a rather plaintive tone, "Mom, are we going to the ball game?"

Her mother answered rather vaguely, "I don't know. You can ask your daddy. But you didn't get any rest, so I don't know."

Maud said, "I'll lay down now."

Her mother continued, "Well, I don't know about daddy, either; he's awfully busy. Maybe not tonight."

Maud kept on, "Well, if I just closed my eyes, could I go?"

The mother said, more firmly, "Well, we'll go to some game but not tonight. We don't have a good team this year. Let's go to a good game."

Maud asked plaintively, "Well, when is basketball going to come?"

Her mother replied, "Well, this is a basketball game tonight."

Then Maud began to squeal and cry.

She said, between squeals, "Well, I want to go to a basketball game; that's what I want to go to."

Avoidance

22. Avoidance: Associate

Subject:	Douglas Crawford (M, M, 3, 9-2)
Episode:	Teasing Charlotte
Setting:	School, Third Grade Classroom
Associate:	Charlotte, classmate
Time:	April 18, 1949; 8:58 a.m.
Rating:	2

Douglas has just come to school and is sitting at his desk gazing rather idly about the room.

He called to Charlotte as she came in the door, "Hey, Charlotte."

Charlotte ignored him.

Douglas watched her while she walked all the way back to the back seat in the front row, which was just at my right.

Charlotte sat down and another girl, Shirley Vey, sat on her desk and began to talk to her.

Douglas called back, "Did you wear them pigtails yesterday?"

Charlotte said something to Shirley Vey, another classmate, that sounded like, "I'm not listening to him."

Douglas kept on saying, "Those are like tails off pigs—tails off pigs—tails off pigs," to no one in particular, but making sure that it was loud enough that Charlotte could hear him.   He definitely was teasing.

23. Avoidance: Subject

Subject:	Margaret Reid (M, F, 3, 4-6)
Episode:	Objecting to Getting Picture Taken
Setting:	Thomas Home, Festive Occasion
Associate:	Mrs. Thomas and party guests (Compound A)
Time:	June 2, 1949; 3:12–3:14 p.m.
Rating:	3 (element of apprehension)

Margaret is at Ellen Thomas' birthday party.   Ellen and all of the other guests are older girls; they range in age from 8 through 12.   Margaret has been invited because of her special fondness for Ellen.

Mrs. Thomas called out cheerily to Margaret, "Come on.   Come on and stand with the group and have your picture taken."   One or two of the girls joined in the call.

Margaret stood, sober and silent.

Mrs. Thomas spoke persuasively, "Well, come on and get your picture taken with everybody and then after that we'll have something to eat."

Signs of not knowing what to do came over Margaret's face; but at last she started slowly forward, obviously reluctant to stand for the picture.   Evidently, though, the idea of something to eat appealed to her.

She moved shyly and with pouting lips toward the group.

I felt that her shyness was not the sole cause of this reluctance; that she also felt some fear or uncertainty.

As she reached the group, Margaret was lined up on the front row.

She held her face downward.   She pouted.   Twisting a balloon in her hand, she looked genuinely unhappy.

Several of the taller girls in the front row were asked to squat down to make a better arrangement.

Then Mrs. Thomas snapped the picture.

Margaret frowned downward and chewed on her balloon.

Pressure

Attributes of Action

24. Pressure: Associate

Subject:	Douglas Crawford (M, M, 3, 9-2)
Episode:	Resisting Out-of-Bed Demand
Setting:	Crawford Home, Indoors
Associate:	Mother
Time:	April 18, 1949; 7:30 a.m.
Rating:	4

Douglas lay asleep on one of the two cots in his room.

Douglas' mother walked casually into the room.

She turned to Douglas and straightened out the covers, which were somewhat tumbled, and began shaking him, saying in a rather sharp voice, with an urgent tone, "Douglas, Douglas."

She repeated his name several times, loudly, and then said, "Wake up, wake up," in the same pressing tone of voice.

Douglas did not respond.

After another urging by his mother, Douglas grunted a very sleepy, but certainly a genuine, "Uh."

He lay still; he was lying on his face.

He wiggled a little as his mother called his name again.

Douglas said, "Well, all right," in a very grumpy, sleepy, reluctant tone.

Mrs. Crawford said, "Get up," three times, with a commanding, sharp, but not angry expression.

She said, "Wake up, Douglas, it's time to go to school." Her voice was more pleasant.

Douglas continued to lie still. After a few seconds he began wiggling around.

He slid down in his bed.

He slipped his head from the pillow.

He gradually rose on his knees.

He said, "I'm getting up," in a grumpy, sleepy voice, as though really reluctant to part with his slumber.

> When she saw that Douglas was really aroused, Mrs. Crawford left the room.

25. Pressure: Subject

Subject:	Mary Chaco (M, F, 2, 1-10)
Episode:	Getting Salad
Setting:	Chaco Home, Meal
Associate:	Father
Time:	October 10, 1950; 12:10 p.m.
Rating:	4

> The family is seated around the kitchen table eating the noonday meal. Mary has been eating heartily.

Mary indicated that she wanted something else to eat by a string of words apparently unintelligible to her parents.

She pointed toward the table, raising her voice slightly as she spoke.

Her father started to give her some meat.

She became more upset than before. The meat definitely was not what Mary had in mind.

Her voice changed to a whine. She kicked her feet against the foot rest on the highchair. She was demanding and impatient.

By lifting each dish in turn, Mr. and Mrs. Chaco found it was jello salad that Mary wanted.

Her father immediately gave her a helping of salad.

Mary seemed pleased, but took this as a matter of course.

Affection

26. *Minus Affection: Associate*

Subject: Verne Trennell (D, M, 3, 7-5)
Episode: Taking Reprimand from Marilyn
Setting: Lawton, Rest Period
Associate: Marilyn, Aide
Time: June 21, 1951; 1:00 p.m.
Rating: 2

Verne has earlier been ordered by Marilyn to lie still and nap.

Verne picked up his crutch and inspected it busily from top to bottom. He held the crutch high in front of his face.

Marilyn walked into the room just at that moment and shouted to him sternly, "Verne, will you put that down and leave it alone?"

Verne obediently dropped the crutch immediately, a momentary trace of fear in his expression.

Marilyn walked over and picked up both of Verne's crutches. She placed them out of his reach, then turned around and walked away.

As she disappeared, Verne's right foot moved sharply and briskly as if he were kicking something hard in anger. His lips moved quickly. He frowned. Verne appeared to be very angry. He closed his eyes as if wanting to shut out the world. Then he opened them again. He muttered to himself angrily. He made a fist with his right hand.

27. *Minus Affection: Subject*

Subject: Wally Wolfson (D, M, 3, 4-3)
Episode: Protesting Ben's Tipping Wagon
Setting: Wolfson Home, Outdoors
Associate: Ben, six-year-old playmate
Time: August 9, 1951; 2:55 p.m.
Rating: 2

Wally is sitting in his wagon on the walk in front of his home. Ben ambles into the Wolfson's yard from his home next door.

Ben turned his attention to Wally. He purposely lifted the wagon high up in front, pulling the handle up so that Wally almost fell out.

Wally held on tightly to the wagon. He said heatedly, "Stop, goddam it, stop."

Ben continued to tip the wagon. He was teasing.

Wally protested, "Quit, Ben," in a plaintive complaining tone.

Mrs. Wolfson called from the kitchen, from which she could see through a front window, "Ben, be careful."

Wally called a final, annoyed, "Goddam it," at Ben.

28. Plus Affection: Associate

Subject: Jimmy Sexton (M, M, 2, 1-11)
Episode: Responding to Father's Attention
Setting: Sexton Home, Indoors
Associate: Father
Time: February 8, 1951; 7:10 p.m.
Rating: 10

Jimmy and his father are in the Sexton's living room where Mr. Sexton has been reading and Jimmy has been playing about the room.

Mr. Sexton gazed fondly at Jimmy; in fact, he had been doing so for some time, although Jimmy had seemed unaware of the attention.

Suddenly, Jimmy turned his face toward his father and looked at him with contentment and satisfaction.

As though unable to contain his admiration any longer, Mr. Sexton picked Jimmy up and held him close on his lap. Then, laughing in a playful way, he turned Jimmy face down across his knees.

Grinning with pleasure, Jimmy wiggled himself off his father's lap and landed with feet flat on the floor.

29. Plus Affection: Subject

Subject: Sue Dewall (D, F, 4, 7-1)
Episode: Whispering to Celeste
Setting: Lawton, Times to Eat
Associate: Celeste Beloit, Director of Lawton
Time: June 5, 1951; 10:04 a.m.
Rating: 10

Between lessons in the schoolroom is a brief refreshment period. Celeste Beloit passes through the room, stopping for a moment to drink a glass of water.

Celeste walked past Sue, set her glass down on a nearby table and then came back past Sue again.

Sue looked up at her and all of a sudden impulsively held out her arms, with a happy smile on her face.

Celeste leaned down, putting her head close to Sue's lips.

Sue whispered something into Celeste's ear.

Celeste smiled companionably.

Sue laughed quietly about the secret. She looked very pleased.

Mood

Mood on the part of the associate will be omitted. It cannot be exemplified well by an episode out of context.

30. Minus Mood: Subject

Subject: Sue Dewall (D, F, 4, 7-1)
Episode: Responding to Theresa's Teasing
Setting: Lawton, Younger Children's Classroom
Associate: Theresa, older classmate
Time: June 5, 1951; 1:32 p.m.
Rating: 2

Sue has been alternating between acting sleepy, sober, happy, and grumpy since lunchtime. She is seated now among other classmates at a table in the schoolroom, apparently awaiting the next period in the day's schedule.

Theresa, sitting next to Sue, reached over and ran her hands through Sue's hair in a teasing way.

Sue said crossly, "Don't, Theresa."

Theresa continued as before.

Once again Sue said, with more firmness and irritation, "Don't, Theresa."

Theresa persisted tenaciously.

Sue almost cried. She was obviously unhappy and upset.

She protested once again, "Don't, Theresa," and this time raised her head and turned it from side to side, trying to evade Theresa's overtures.

Then Theresa took her hand away, smiling broadly.

Sue remained sitting at the table and looked around the room with a very forlorn expression on her face.

31. Plus Mood: Subject

Subject: Dutton Thurston (M, M, 3, 3-10)
Episode: Making Noises in Truck
Setting: Thurston Home, Outdoors
Associate: Father
Time: November 3, 1950; 7:30 p.m.
Rating: 10

Chuck is "working" in the yard with his father, who has turned on the motor of the truck.

Chuck apparently enjoyed the noise of the motor for he squealed with delight. He let out several squeals in quick succession, seeming to enjoy both process and result.

He did quite a bit of jabbering which I could not understand; Chuck was making noise rather than communicating.

He squealed again, in the same tone of voice as before.

I had the impression that he was really enjoying himself.

He combined a real laugh with a squeal, throwing back his head in a quick, abandoned movement.

Evaluation

32. *Minus Evaluation: Associate*

Subject:	Margaret Reid (M, F, 3, 4-6)
Episode:	"Painting" Porch Pillar[1]
Setting:	Reid Home, Outdoors
Associate:	Mother
Time:	June 2, 1949; 11:37 a.m.
Rating:	1

Using a small branch with leaves on it as a brush, Margaret has just finished "painting" a tree trunk, using dirty water in a bucket as paint. Her mother, taking a very unfavorable view of this enterprise, has scolded Margaret for it.

Mrs. Reid brushed some dirt from Margaret's dress, slapping her hands down the skirt. Bradley, the baby brother, started howling in an abandoned way for "Mommy." His mother was too busy to go to him. Instead she scolded Margaret for getting dirty.

Margaret hopped onto the porch with her pail and "brush."

She started painting the porch pillar in a flustered way, wildly and carelessly daubing with the branch.

I felt that Margaret painted on the pillar partly because of what her mother had said about painting the tree. Margaret knew, I think, that spreading ditch water on the pillar would make her mother crosser than if she painted on the tree trunk.

With the baby still howling, the mother scolded loudly again, "Don't do that on the porch. Do it on the tree if you have to, but do it on the tree."

This was a modification of her first command, which was to desist from all painting.

The baby cried so hard that the mother's attention finally turned to him. While Bradley continued to cry, Mrs. Reid tried to get Margaret to hush him. "Why do you always paint? Why don't you play with Bradley?" she asked petulantly. But at last she went inside the house with a shrug of her shoulders as if giving up.

Bradley kept on crying loudly.

Margaret calmly painted the porch pillar, giving no indication of disturbance.

Mrs. Reid came out in answer to Bradley's cries, but ignored him after a brief look.

[1] This rather long episode strikes us as some kind of a classic in child-and-mother behavior. Readers probably will agree that there is much more in it than minus evaluation by the associate.

She said to Margaret, "I don't *want* you to paint there. *Stop it!*" She was definitely giving an order.

Margaret did not stop. She painted on, putting on an air of unconcern.

The mother tried another tactic. She said, "I bet daddy won't like what you're doing when I tell him." Then she paused, apparently expecting Margaret to obey at last.

Margaret brushed her wet, muddy hands over the pillar.

> This action, I thought, was more purposeful naughtiness, directed at the mother.

"Don't wipe your hands all over the porch," the mother insisted with exasperation.

Margaret kept right on painting the porch pillar, poker-faced, but a little jittery in her movements.

"Why can't you play with your dolls and let that go?" her mother asked with much disgust.

Margaret kept on painting the pillar as before, neither looking at her mother nor answering her.

"Listen, Margaret, don't you go to that ditch and get any more water. You hear?" Mrs. Reid spoke emphatically, thoroughly aroused.

Margaret nodded affirmatively this time, meaning apparently to acknowledge the query, "You hear?"

The mother said, "O.K., you said you wouldn't and now you mustn't," and went back into the house.

Bradley still howled.

Margaret muttered half under her breath, with great determination, "Well, I'll have to get done with this, anyway."

> In other words, she simply was not going to stop just because her mother wanted her to stop.

She said, "Well, I have to get this much done."

> She seemed to be speaking to herself, but at the same time about her mother's command.

After a time she crouched down so that she could scrape and stir around in the bucket.

Then she went right on, alternately dipping the twig brush and painting the pillar. She was very much involved in this and was enjoying herself thoroughly.

> I took it that she found pleasure in this activity for two reasons: The play itself was fun, and going counter to orders was fun.

She spoke to herself, saying approximately these words, "No, don't you touch this, 'cause you'll get it on your hands."

After a while she said, "It's a long time before I paint."

I couldn't tell from her sentence or her manner whether she meant that it had been a long time since she had painted or that it would be a long time before she would paint again.

Then she added, "I'm going to get done forever again."

I think she meant that she was going to keep on painting and painting and painting, never stopping. She spoke from the bottom of her heart, as if she simply was never going to stop painting, and I did feel that this was a direct answer to her mother's command not to paint.

She poured some water onto the porch with a very pleased expression on her face. She said, "This is dry, maybe," and gingerly poked at the freshly "painted" porch floor.

Then she said, "That'll dry," and poked another place on the porch with an experimenting finger. She repeated, "That'll dry."

"This stuff," she said, and paused as if inhibiting her thoughts. Then her voice took on emphasis and emotionality of a sort as she continued under her breath, "This stuff will be dirty for a hundred days."

She sounded very pleased.

33. Minus Evaluation: Associate

Subject:	Ben Hutchings (M, M, 1, 7-4)
Episode:	Seeking Praise from Sister
Setting:	Hutchings Home, Indoors
Associate:	Sarah, 10-year-old sister
Time:	November 23, 1948; 12:09 p.m.
Rating:	3

Sarah and Ben are home for lunch. While waiting, Ben is playing a phonograph. Sarah is wandering about rather aimlessly.

Noticing a picture of a turkey on the ironing board, Sarah picked it up and inspected it, but said nothing.

Benjamin was sort of surreptitiously watching her out of the corner of his eye. He said, "Sarah, look at the other side."

She turned it over and said, "Ha, I see. You made this one by putting the paper over it, copying through it, didn't you?"

Ben said, "Yeah."

Sarah said, "Well, the tail's not very good, though."

Ben said, "Oh, isn't it?" This was in a very plaintive tone, as if he thought, "She's going to brag about it—but, no, she didn't."

He left the phonograph and followed Sarah into the kitchen where he said to his mother, "Don't you think it's a pretty good . . . tail?" He seemed to be seeking reassurance from his mother.

Sarah said, "Oh, well, you'll learn as you get older."

Ben looked quite crestfallen, as if she had reacted quite differently than he had expected. He had obviously thought his work pretty good and deserving of praise.

34. *Plus Evaluation: Associate*

Subject: Verne Trennell (D, M, 3, 7-5)
Episode: Keeping Up With Tommy
Setting: Neighbor's Home, Outdoors
Associate: Tommy, eight-year-old playmate
Time: June 21, 1951; 6:07 p.m.
Rating: 11

Verne and Tommy have been playing in Tommy's front yard, near the front porch.

Tommy dashed up the steps and ran to the far end of the porch.

With a beaming face, Verne hurried after Tommy on his crutches as if nothing in the world could be more important than keeping up with Tommy.

He managed, by hanging on to the porch post and supporting himself partially on the step in front of him, to drag himself up the steps to the porch floor.

Verne's face showed some surprise, evidently at the speed with which he navigated the steps.

Tommy apparently had the same idea, for he stopped short in his cavortings and said, "Why, Verne, you can walk *pretty good.*"

This was an entirely spontaneous remark and Verne's expression showed that he took it as acclaim.

Standing close to the porch pillar, Verne asked Tommy in all seriousness, "Does it hurt when you fall off?"

He looked down at the grass before him and seemed to measure the distance from the porch to the ground in a tentative way as if he were tempted to fall off as Tommy earlier had done.

35. *Plus Evaluation: Subject*

Subject: Sue Dewall (D, F, 4, 7-1)
Episode: Complimenting Theresa
Setting: Lawton, Trafficways, Downstairs
Associate: Theresa, older classmate
Time: June 5, 1951; 12:11 p.m.
Rating: 10

Sue is watching while Theresa, a child who walks with difficulty by using two canes, goes slowly and patiently to the schoolroom.

Sue said to Theresa in an adult-like fashion, patronizingly, yet in a very complimentary tone, "That's a girl!"

Sue continued in the same tone, "I'm proud of you, Theresa."

Interaction Products
Interplay Type

36. *Interplay Type: Conflict*

Subject: Roy Eddy (M, M, 3, 6-2)
Episode: Responding to Boy's Teasing
Setting: Trafficways
Associate: Douglas Herne, 11-year-old playmate
Time: February 22, 1949; 3:34

Roy and Thomas have just come out of the Midwest Hardware Store.

The boys met Douglas Herne walking past the hardware store.

Without apparent provocation, Douglas reached out antagonistically and ruffled Roy's hair. There had been no preliminary conversation, nor any action which might have led to hostility.

Roy seemed to take this very seriously. He squared off angrily at big, red-headed Douglas.

Douglas backed off a little, although he obviously had nothing to fear. Despite his retreat, he seemed to be threatening Roy.

Roy held his ground and didn't give an inch.

Although he did not attack, he stood alert, cautiously prepared for any eventuality.

Even though Roy remained poised and prepared for action, the older boy turned and left; and that was all.

37. *Interplay Type: Conflict*

Subject: Dutton Thurston (M, M, 3, 3-10)
Episode: Trying to Get Kitten from Sister
Setting: Thurston Home, Indoors
Associate: Shirley, 15-year-old sister
Time: November 3, 1950; 5:32 p.m.

Shirley is trying to open the door of a toy truck into which Chuck has mischievously shoved Inky, a kitten.

When he saw the truck door opening, Chuck reached in and grabbed the kitten out, grabbing hold of part of its tail and part of its rump, and yanking the cat away from Shirley.

Shirley lunged forward to grasp Chuck's hand, saying that he was mean. She succeeded in taking Inky away from Chuck.

Chuck said, "Uh, uh, uh, uh," in a whiny protest and stamped after her.

Shirley hurried to the divan and sat down on it for leverage, holding the kitten to one side.

Chuck scurried after her, apparently chagrined to have her winning.

Then they had a tussle on the divan with Chuck reaching and stretching to get the kitten.

Shirley grabbed his hand and held it, while she held the kitten further on the other side of her. Shirley said with certain rebuke that she was going to take the kitten outside if that was the way he was going to treat it. She hurried determinedly toward the kitchen.

38. Interplay Type: Disjunction

Subject:	Wally Wolfson (D, M, 3, 4-3)
Episode:	Saying "Hi" to Jim
Setting:	Wolfson Home, Outdoors
Associate:	Jim, eight-year-old playmate
Time:	August 9, 1951; 1:08 p.m.

Wally is playing in his yard with small cars, running them on the ground. Jim lives next door.

Jim came over.

Wally said in a friendly manner, "Hi, Jim."

Jim didn't reply.

Wally repeated insistently, "Hi, Jim."

Jim still didn't answer.

Wally said, "Hi, Jimmy," once more, but he seemed to understand that Jim was not going to play with him.

Jim picked up the bike that was lying on the ground nearby and rode away.

39. Interplay Type: Unfriendly Rivalry

Subject:	Roy Eddy (M, M, 3, 6-2)
Episode:	Retrieving Chair
Setting:	School, First Grade Classroom
Associate:	Seven-year-old Jimmy Vey, eight-year-old Betty Reeves, schoolmates (compound A)
Time:	February 22, 1949; 12:29 p.m.

The children are free to do almost anything they please after they have eaten their lunches. Roy is seated at a long, low table modeling with clay. Children are rough-housing all around him but he seems to be concentrating on his clay modeling.

Jimmy Vey suddenly pulled the chair on which Roy was sitting out from under him.

Roy quickly reached out to get the chair back. Grabbing hold of it, he pulled hard.

Jimmy at last gave in, but Betty Reeves took hold of the chair, saying she did not have one.

Roy, determination, not hostility, in his face, would not give in one bit. He battled over the chair with Betty for a moment.

Roy won. He took the chair, placed it firmly and with satisfaction where it had been, and sat down.

He had been quiet, but persistent and a little annoyed at the interference.

40. Interplay Type: Conjunction

Subject: Jimmy Sexton (M, M, 2, 1-11)
Episode: Looking at Book
Setting: Sexton Home, Indoors
Associate: Father
Time: February 8, 1951; 4:23–4:25 p.m.

Jimmy is looking for his own, small book and suddenly spies it on the arm of a chair. His father is reading in a nearby chair.

Picking up his book, Jimmy ran quickly to the davenport.

I had the impression that for the past few minutes he had been looking for his book so he could read, too, like his daddy.

He made a very contented little sound as he opened and leafed through the book.

Suddenly, Jimmy sneezed loudly.

He caught his daddy's eye as he sneezed.

Jimmy and his father grinned happily although neither spoke.

Jimmy immediately returned his glance to his book.

41. Interplay Type: Cooperation

Subject: Claire Graves (M, F, 3, 10-9)
Episode: Making Bed With Sister
Setting: Graves' Home, Indoors
Associate: Frances, nine-year-old sister
Time: January 28, 1949; 8:06–8:08 a.m.

Claire is standing in the front room near the stove while her sister, Frances, is in the kitchen.

Claire went to the doorway and called pleasantly to Frances, "Come on, Frances, let's go and make our bed."

Frances went into the bedroom followed by Claire.

They started to make the bed together, talking as they worked, with Claire on one side and Frances on the other.

Claire took the leading role momentarily.

She said, "Now, this cover." She went on, working all the while, "Now, that one. Let's smooth out that one; here is a bumpy place."

She chatted along pleasantly with Frances.

Claire smoothed the covers out with both hands and was very professional about putting the spread on.

Frances breathed heavily to see her breath in the cold room.

The room was quite cold, for the door to the front room, the only heat source, was closed.

Claire and Frances proceeded to put on the spread and Claire said, "Oh, it goes this way," after looking at it.   She was directing Frances and helping her at the same time.

Frances didn't mind Claire's direction.   Rather, they coöperated on this project.

They got the spread on and smoothed it out.

42. Interplay Type: Cooperation

Subject: Dutton Thurston (M, M, 3, 3-10)
Episode: Putting Wood in Stove
Setting: Thurston Home, Indoors
Associate: Mother
Time: November 3, 1950; 5:33 p.m.

Chuck is standing on the porch outside the kitchen watching the kitten drink milk.   His mother is standing near a pile of wood on the porch.

Chuck saw his mother picking up some wood to take into the house.

He grabbed up a piece of wood and shot back into the kitchen.

He went in by the dining room stove and waited patiently a moment until his mother got there.

Both put some wood in the stove at the same time and each was polite about allowing the other enough room.

His mother spoke pleasantly, asking Chuck not to get his hands too close to the stove.

Chuck mumbled communicatively about the wood burning.   He seemed quite satisfied and gave his stick of wood a final vigorous push.

43. Interplay Type: Friendly Rivalry

Subject: Dutton Thurston (M, M, 3, 3-10)
Episode: Having Play Fight with Brother
Setting: Thurston Home, Indoors
Associate: Al, 18-year-old brother
Time: November 3, 1950; 6:42 p.m.

Chuck is just back in the house after going out on the porch with Shirley to feed the kitten.

Chuck dashed through the kitchen into the dining room to Al who was seated on the divan.

Chuck ran into Al's legs and pounded playfully, yet hard, on them.

Al ordered Chuck with mock sternness, "Cut that out," as he stood to defend himself, assuming a boxer's pose.

Grinning, Chuck backed away.

He extended his left hand in front of him as if he were going to take a haymaker swing at Al.

With mock ferociousness Chuck acted as though he would kick Al on the leg.

Al warned him playfully that he had better not kick him, only to give Chuck further incentive.

Chuck gamely tried to kick Al on the leg.

He finally slipped close enough to kick Al but didn't kick as hard as he might have; he was being entirely playful.

Al made out that he was greatly offended. He seized Chuck by the arms and briefly lifted him off the floor.

As Al put him down, Chuck landed on his hands and feet.

Al playfully kicked Chuck in the seat of the pants. Both were enjoying the game a great deal.

Still playful, Al tried to seize Chuck.

Chuck fled into the kitchen as fast as he could go.

Then Al sat down in a rocking chair.

Chuck sauntered back into the dining room, mockingly nonchalant.

He circled around Al, showing that he had dared to come back.

Accord

44. *Minus Accord*

Subject:	Ben Hutchings (M, M, 1, 7-4)
Episode:	Quarreling About Rules
Setting:	Hutchings' Home, Indoors
Associate:	Morris, six-year-old playmate
Time:	November 23, 1948; 4:30 p.m.
Rating:	2

Ben and Morris are playing with toy soldiers, having a pretend battle. Ann, Morris' sister, is seated nearby looking at a book. One rule that Ben has made is that no plane may go up without a man in it.

Then Ben said, "Let's stay in our places; let's not move the other soldiers around. Move the airplanes."

Morris objected, "Heck, no. I'm going to send up planes without men."

Ben countered, his voice raised, "Not with my men." (Meaning, not while you're playing with my toys.)

Morris stated loudly, "These aren't yours."

Ben yelled, "Yes, they are; these are Sarah's," referring to the ones he was playing with, and "those are mine—you aren't going to take a plane up with my men."

Suddenly both boys were rolling around on the floor. They fought quietly.

Morris reached out and knocked Ben's soldiers all over the floor.

Ben knocked Morris' men helter-skelter.

Ben got the upper hand and sat on top of Morris.

Morris almost began to cry.

Ann left the kitchen hastily and went to find Mrs. Hutchings.

Mrs. Hutchings came in and said, "What's the matter here?"   She spoke with curiosity, showing little concern.

Ben got off Morris very slowly; he didn't jump up as if he were frightened.

> ### 45. *Plus Accord*
> | | |
> |---|---|
> | Subject: | Jimmy Sexton (M, M, 2, 1-11) |
> | Episode: | Playing with Father |
> | Setting: | Sexton Home, Indoors |
> | Associate: | Father |
> | Time: | February 8, 1951; 4:42 p.m. |
> | Rating: | 11 |

Jimmy and his father are standing side by side at a dining room window, companionably munching dates.

Mr. Sexton bent down, lifted the boy up in the crook of his arm and gazed warmly at him.

Jimmy placidly returned the look and moved his face close to his father's cheek.

Suddenly Jimmy grinned from ear to ear as he watched each move of his father's jaws.

Mr. Sexton said, "Well," and turned toward the living room.

He bounced the boy in his arms, holding him stretched out full length, supported beneath his neck and his knees.

Jimmy alternately laughed aloud and giggled softly; he was having a good time.

Mr. Sexton laughed, too.   Then he held Jimmy at the knees, not supporting him anywhere else.

Jimmy adjusted his weight so as to sit with nothing under him.

The father slowly and carefully raised Jimmy by the knees until his head touched the ceiling.

With deliberate care he moved Jimmy backwards until his head hung downward at his father's back.

All this time, Jimmy laughed hilariously; he was fully enjoying both the companionship with his father and the acrobatics.

Mr. Sexton carried Jimmy into the dining room, twisting him around so that he straddled his father's neck, relaxed, and not holding on to anything at all.

Jimmy laughed aloud, surveying the world from his high perch.

> ### 46. *Plus Accord*
> | | |
> |---|---|
> | Subject: | Claire Graves (M, F, 3, 10-9) |
> | Episode: | Joking About "John" |
> | Setting: | Graves' Home, Indoors |
> | Associate: | Frances, nine-year-old sister; Stanley, teen-age brother |
> | Time: | January 28, 1949; 4:40 p.m. |
> | Rating: | 11 |

> Frances and Claire are warming up in front of a glowing base burner after coming from school. Stanley enters, stamping off snow, after shoveling a narrow path, and is preparing to warm himself before going back to more work on the path. Charles, the four-year-old brother, also is on hand. The air outdoors is sharp.

Stanley, Frances, and Claire gathered about the stove, while Charles stood upon a chair near the telephone.

Stanley and Charles began talking about a person or thing called "John." It was evidently something they had a secret about. Frances and Claire were trying to discover who or what "John" was. There was a great deal of joking.

Claire said teasingly, "Who is John?"

Stanley said, "Don't you tell, Charles."

Claire looked merry.

> The merriment was not extreme, but there was a comfortable family feeling about the whole situation. Stanley and Charles lined up against Frances and Claire and everybody recognized this. I had the feeling that it was all done for Charles' benefit.

Charles became quite boisterous. He laughed as if he were getting a big kick out of it all.

The two girls smiled broadly. They giggled.

Then Claire and Frances began to wheedle Charles, trying to get him to tell.

Stanley interrupted to say, "Don't tell; don't you dare tell, Charles."

Frances suddenly walked over and picked Charles up and whirled him around as best she could and both she and he giggled and walked into the kitchen.

This left Stanley and Claire standing contentedly by the fire.

Concluding Note

These episodes answer some questions about the psychosocial habitat and behavior of these children. Yet they also raise questions about the same.

How common among Midwest mothers is dominance, such as Mrs. Crawford's when she flatly ordered Douglas to sit down? And with what frequency do Midwest children submit to someone as, in this case, Douglas did? How frequent is aggressive behavior like Geoffrey's (with the overalls as a whip) against Roy? As far as we know, nothing of this kind has ever been counted episode by episode. How often does minus evaluation by a mother or anyone, such as Mrs. Reid's disapproval of Margaret's "painting," fall in a day on a Midwest child? And with what frequency in a day do Midwest children resist pressure from others as, in resolving to paint on and on, Margaret did? Is social conflict, like that between Roy and Douglas in front of the hardware store, common in Midwest? And how often is every-thing fine between children of Midwest and their associates, as between Claire Graves, Stanley, Frances, and Charles, before the fire?

How about relationships between social behavior and age in Midwest? And what about differences between these physically normal Midwest children and disabled children? But easier, though still important, questions are raised by this material. We have wanted to know merely how often these children get involved with others. And we have wanted to know who these others are, and how large a part different kinds of individuals play in the social lives of the children.

Questions like these started us on the present line of study, and they will do as well as any others to lead up to the following chapter. No one could give answers for all Midwest children or any children on all of their days, or for all of their associates, obviously. But we have gone to some pains in the belief that answers here based on a few days in the lives of a few children should be instructive.

Chapter XII

Social Action and Interaction III
Quantitative Findings

Problem and Source Material

THE categories of Chapter X have been applied to 10,406 episodes of 11 day-records whose subjects are eight children of Midwest and three nearby disabled children. The total episode populations for the Midwest and disabled children, respectively, are 7,751 and 2,655. Below, in Table 12.1, with the number of episodes from each record and with essential information on each child, are the 11 subjects.

TABLE 12.1

MIDWEST CHILDREN				
	Episodes	Sex	Group	Age
Mary Chaco (MC)	1103	F	II	1-10
Jimmy Sexton (JS)	1027	M	II	1-11
Dutton Thurston (DT)	1159	M	III	3-10
Margaret Reid (MR)	1059	F	III	4-6
Raymond Birch (RB)	1000	M	II	7-4
Mary Ennis (ME)	969	F	II	8-7
Douglas Crawford (DC)	940	M	III	9-2
Claire Graves (CG)	494	F	III	10-9

DISABLED CHILDREN				
	Episodes	Sex	Group	Age
Wally Wolfson (WW)	907	M	III	4-3
Sue Dewall (SD)	771	F	IV	7-1
Verne Trennell (VT)	977	M	III	7-5

The eight Midwest records give a balanced sample with respect to age, sex, and social group of the subjects. There are four preschool children and four children of school age. Boys and girls are equally represented, as they are approximately in the total child population of Midwest, while also a boy and a girl are paired at the younger and older preschool levels, and at the younger and older school levels. The children are equally divided between social Groups II and III, which account for 88 per cent of the Midwest child population.

Wally Wolfson, Sue Dewall, and Verne Trennell have been identified earlier as children with severe orthopedic disabilities. For particulars on the behavior settings and social behavior objects unique to these children when their records were made, and also for comparable information on the Midwest children, readers are referred to the biographical sketches of Appendix 1.

The assignment before us is to describe in terms of the psychosocial categories some aspects of social action and interaction in episodes of the 11 records on these children. The relation between child and associate is basic for all phases of the description. This relation will be considered with reference to associates en masse of the children and often with reference also to different classes of associates. Relationships between age of the Midwest subjects and different aspects of their social behavior and its conditions are to be explored; so also are indications of difference between the Midwest and disabled children, although we shall be concerned primarily with the children of Midwest. Data on the days of Wally, Sue, and Verne will be used mainly for comparative reconnaisance.

Readers will recall that sex and social group are included among Subject Constants of the present instrument and that the eight Midwest children are equally divided as to both. Attention will be confined here, however, to relationships with age as a subject constant. This simplifies a crowded picture and leaves for later special study the social group and sex of the subjects as social behavior correlates.

We begin now with a survey to determine the relative frequency of social and potentially social episodes, to identify associates of the children, and to get background information about some basic characteristics of the recorded situations and social relationships. This survey also will select for extended analysis social episodes with significant common features.

Note on Statistics. It will be convenient to anticipate by general comment some of the statistical problems of this chapter.

Our sample consists basically of individual episodes. These episodes, however, occur in 11 blocks; there is one block for every child, day, or record. Independent variation in psychological situation and behavior from episode to episode within any one of the 11 blocks cannot be assumed. On the contrary, there are at least two sources of interdependence as between the episodes of every record. First, there is the child. Each of the 11 children is a persisting source of influence upon all his episodes. Second, there is in every case the set of circumstances unique to the day of the record. This set of circumstances constitutes a probable source of influences common to the episodes of each record. These considerations are not seen to count against the episode as a primary descriptive unit. Interdependence of the episodes in each record imposes nonetheless the requirement that, in employing the present data to deal with the particular problems raised in this volume, we use as our N the total number of records (children, or days) rather than the total number of episodes.

The use of a subject-N rather than an episode-N doubtless has a number of advantages. One apparent advantage is that it eliminates "buried" weighting of the results with scores from the episodes of any atypical children (days, or records). The subject-N has nonetheless at least one disadvantage: It incurs necessarily a loss in sensitivity to intrasubject variance. Much of this variance we believe to be legitimate and significant for the present purpose. Yet satisfactory ways to reveal and express it in statistical indices do not appear to be available at this time.

Inspection of the data indicates that certain of the distributions are not normal and that the variances are in many instances heterogeneous. Therefore, and also because the maximum N is 11 (Midwest children: 8; disabled children: 3), nonparametric methods have been used throughout.

We shall be concerned at several points with differences obtained in the case of each subject by comparing certain measures, X and Y. The binomial test was used to assess the consistency from subject to subject in the direction of all such differences. Here, in every case, the number of differences in each of the two possible directions ($X > Y$ and $Y > X$) was determined, and the probability that a split of the observed magnitude could occur by chance was computed by expanding the binomial $(P+Q)^n$. Following Walker and Lev (57a), we have ignored ties in getting this statistic.

Various relationships with age of the children are to be reported in terms of rank order correlation coefficients. The coefficient used here, as in Chapter VIII, is Tau (28).

The study is purely descriptive; it asks open questions instead of making predictions. Accordingly, two-tailed tests have been applied in obtaining all probability measures.

As in earlier chapters, we leave for comment where they are used additional statistics required by special problems.

Survey of Episodes

FREQUENCY OF SOCIAL UNITS

To what extent did other individuals figure in the days of these children? Table 12.2 answers this question with a breakdown of the total episode population in terms of Sociality.[1]

It shows the per cent of social, potentially social, and nonsocial episodes respectively in each day, and gives median per cents for the Midwest and disabled children. Regular and irregular standard and observer units are distinguished among social episodes. It will be convenient in some contexts to identify individuals in the standard episodes as *participant associates*.

---

[1] Readers are referred to Chapter X for definitions of the categories and principal concepts of the present report.

TABLE 12.2

Per Cent of Social, Potentially Social, and Nonsocial Episodes in Records of Midwest and Disabled Children

Episodes		Midwest									Disabled			
		MC	JS	DT	MR	RB	ME	DC	CG	Mdn	WW	SD	VT	Mdn
SOCIAL — Standard	R	64	53	54	66	52	51	45	54	54	62	62	66	62
	I	2	2	6	3	7	6	4	8	5	4	8	4	4
	T	66	55	60	69	59	57	49	62	61	66	70	70	70
SOCIAL — Observer	R	15	18	18	16	17	23	31	21	18	11	13	18	13
	I	1	0	2	2	3	2	2	3	2	2	4	2	2
	T	16	18	20	18	20	25	33	24	20	13	17	20	17
All		82	73	80	87	79	82	82	86	85	79	87	90	87
Potentially Social		18	26	19	12	16	16	17	14	16	21	12	10	12
Nonsocial		0	1	1	1	5	2	1	0	1	0	1	0	0
TOTAL N		1103	1027	1159	1059	1000	969	940	494	7751	907	771	977	2655

NOTE.—R, regular episode; I, irregular episode; T, total (R + I)

Let us look at the Midwest days. The median per cent of standard episodes is 61. The median per cent of observer episodes is 20, while the corresponding median for standard plus observer units is 85. Inspection of the values for each day shows that these medians are quite representative. Overall, the per cents of potentially social and nonsocial episodes cluster, respectively, near medians of 16 and 1. In line with discussion in Chapter VI of observer influence there is a trend toward an increase with age in per cent of observer units, as suggested by a rank order correlation of .57 ($P < .10$). Otherwise, these measures seem to us remarkably stable. Per cents of like magnitude hold, moreover, for the three disabled children.

Regular, adequately described, and otherwise substantial social action units predominate in every record. Concerning the irregular episodes, we note only their generally low frequency. As anticipated in Chapter X, these are not used in subsequent stages of the analysis.

One would like to know what the relative frequency of social episodes might have been with the observer an invisible man. The per cent of standard social units does not tell us this because it leaves open the possibility that the observer, despite efforts to stay in the background, may often have displaced someone else as a social habitat object. Special analysis from the standpoint of Associate Complexity shows that an observer became an associate while alone with the subject in only 3 per cent of the 7,751 Midwest episodes. During a great majority of the observer units, then, other individuals were available to the children. But there is no telling how frequently associates would have emerged from among these others in the absence of observers. It seems certain that this would not have occurred in every case; for we know from the proportion of potentially social episodes, for which the median per cent is 16, that the children did not always act in relation to available associates. One can do no more here than conclude that, with the observer unavailable as a behavior object, the proportion of social units probably would have fallen somewhere between the proportions for standard social and all social episodes. For the Midwest subjects, accordingly, we can place this value between the median per cents of 61 and 85.

The observer could not and did not stay out of the situations of these children. But what kind of a social habitat object was the observer? Although it is secondary to our main interest, this question will be given considerable attention at several points to follow. Properties and effects of observers have central importance for work with specimen records and for other procedures in psychological ecology; here is a source of influence upon behavior that needs measurement in studies of this kind. Also, we have found the observer useful as a comparison figure in relation to whom characteristics of participant associates are clarified by contrast.

It is clear that social habitat objects played a large part in the days of these children. Frequency of involvement with others does vary from child to child. As our biographical sketches of the children in Appendices 1 and 2 and forthcoming data to identify associates indicate, this variability is attributable in part to differences between the subjects in availability of social behavior objects. For example, one is not surprised to find that for Verne Trennell, who spent the greater part of his day at Lawton School, and for Sue Dewall, who spent all of hers in this home with 24 children plus 14 staff members, including therapists, teachers, aides, custodians, and a director, the per cent of standard social episodes was 70, whereas for Jimmy, an only child, who spent the greater part of his day at home alone with Mrs Sexton, the equivalent per cent was 55. But we find it arresting that this difference is no greater. It is almost as if there had been in these children a certain amount of socializing which had to come out and did, all episodes counted, at a level no lower than 73 per cent, no matter who the children were or how old, verbal, or whatever else they were, and no matter how few, varied, or abundant the social behavior objects around them. The possibility of testing further the stability of these measures by comparative study immediately suggests itself. One would like to know, for example, whether there may be no great difference in relative frequency of social behavior episodes, despite great difference in number and variety of social behavior objects, as between children of small families on farms and children of large families in crowded urban areas.

ASSOCIATE COMPLEXITY

There were 4,286 regular standard social episodes in the days of the Midwest children, and 1,689 in the days of the disabled children. It is important now that an acquaintance be struck with the particular social habitat objects in these behavior units. Table 12.3, which is based on the category, Associate Complexity takes a step in this direction by showing for each record the per cent of episodes with simple and compound associates. The member parts of a compound associate sometimes include an observer. Supplemental provision is made in this table, accordingly, for observer episodes, of which there were 1,512 and 375 respectively for the Midwest and disabled subjects.

We call attention first to the standard units. A marked preponderance of standard social episodes with single individuals as associates will be seen to hold for every record. The per cent with compound associates, each a grouping of two or more individuals, is as low as 4 in two records and in none does it exceed 21.

For the Midwest children, there is a positive relationship between per cent of standard episodes with compound associates and age, as shown by a rank order correlation of .82, significant beyond the 1 per cent level. One might gather from this that these children show with increasing age greater ability to "take in" a group of two or more individuals at one time in their social transactions. It has to be considered, however, that the older children, if

TABLE 12.3

PER CENT OF STANDARD AND OBSERVER EPISODES WITH SIMPLE AND COMPOUND ASSOCIATES

EPISODES		MIDWEST									DISABLED				ALL
		MC	JS	DT	MR	RB	ME	DC	CG	Mdn	WW	SD	VT	Mdn	Mdn
Std	Simple	96	96	86	90	82	84	84	79	85	86	85	92	86	86
	Compound	4	4	13	9	17	16	15	21	14	14	14	7	14	14
	Total N	704	538	629	705	520	498	424	267	4286	566	479	644	1689	5975
Obs	Simple	92	96	98	96	92	98	92	85	94	94	93	94	94	94
	Compound	8	4	2	4	8	2	8	15	6	6	7	6	6	6
	Total N	166	188	207	167	170	219	292	103	1512	102	97	176	375	1887

NOTE.—Std, standard episodes; Obs, observer episodes. The residue from 100 per cent opposite Std and under DT, MR, RB, DC, and VT is a per cent of episodes on which the analyst could not judge Associate Complexity. These indeterminate units are excluded from the 5,272 simple associate episodes reported on the following page.

only as a consequence of the hours they spent at school, were more often confronted with relatively large numbers and especially with preformed groups of other persons; groupings of individuals to be taken in at one time were more often available to them. Here, in any case, is one kind of evidence that there goes with growing up in Midwest an increase in the complexity of social behavior.

Readers will find on turning to the observer units in Table 12.3 a preponderance of simple associates generally greater than that in the standard episodes. This holds for 9 of the 11 days and, for one record, the standard and observer per cents are equal. It thus appears that, when observers did get involved with the children, they were less frequently linked with others on the scene; they behaved more as isolates in their dealings with the children. This can be understood if it is considered that, in making the records, all observers tried to minimize mixing with individuals in the children's situations.

We do not find consistent or accountable differences here between the disabled children and Midwest children on their age levels.

Social episodes with compound associates are to be eliminated from this point forward. They are relatively infrequent, as indicated above. But also they are not uniformly comparable; the associate can be a couple in one, a trio of friends in another, and an audience in a third. Consequently, an indiscriminate sample of such episodes lacks precise meaning. It would be interesting to study episodes with different types of compound associates, but preliminary experimenting has shown that the available material does not justify analysis so refined.

The elimination of episodes with compound associates leaves a total of 5,272 regular standard social episodes in which the associate was a single individual. But who were the single individuals in relation to whom these children behaved in the standard episodes? This is our next problem.

PRINCIPAL ASSOCIATES

Table 12.4 shows the per cent of standard units in which specified individuals or classes of individuals were associates of the subjects. Some of these data are represented graphically in Figure 12.1.

An adult friend is any grownup other than a parent or other relative, a teacher or, for the records on Sue and Verne, any member of the Lawton staff. Guardian refers to a supervisor of Lawton who was considered to fill for Sue the role of a mother surrogate. An adolescent friend is any adolescent or young adult other than a sibling. A child friend is any child under 12 other than a sibling. In Midwest (or at Lawton), if you are not a relative, you are a friend.

A number of points about associates of the Midwest children come out of these data at once. Adult associates entered more episodes than did child

TABLE 12.4

PER CENT OF REGULAR STANDARD EPISODES WITH SPECIFIED ASSOCIATES

Associates		MC	JS	DT	MR	RB	ME	DC	CG	Mdn	WW	SD	VT	Mdn
		MIDWEST									DISABLED			
ADULTS	Mothers	70	52	42	51	13	25	11	20	34	24	0	15	15
	Fathers	11	38	13	3	7	3	3	0	5	3	0	10	3
	Relatives	+	1	0	4	0	0	0	0	0	2	0	0	0
	Teachers	0	0	0	5	24	16	18	21	10	0	19	14	14
	Friends	3	1	13	3	5	4	21	5	4	1	0	2	1
	L Guardian	—	—	—	—	—	—	—	—	—	—	14	0	—
	L Director	—	—	—	—	—	—	—	—	—	—	3	0	—
	L Aide	—	—	—	—	—	—	—	—	—	—	21	9	—
	ALL	84	92	68	66	49	48	53	46	59	30	57	50	50
ADO	Friends	0	0	0	+	+	7	2	1	2	+	14	3	3
	Siblings	0	0	21	0	0	0	0	7	0	0	0	0	0
	ALL	0	0	21	2	+	7	2	7	2	+	14	3	3
FRIENDS	Infant	0	0	0	+	1	0	0	0	0	0	0	0	0
	Preschool	0	7	0	8	3	4	0	0	0	2	0	1	1
	Younger School	0	+	0	4	30	24	22	3	6	56	7	30	30
	Older School	0	0	0	9	11	9	13	17	9	+	20	9	9
	All	0	7	0	21	45	37	35	20	21	58	27	40	40
SIBS	Younger	0	0	0	8	0	3	7	27	2	7	0	4	4
	Older	14	0	0	0	0	0	0	0	0	0	0	0	0
	All	14	0	0	8	0	3	7	27	6	7	0	4	4
CHILDREN	ALL	14	7	0	29	45	40	42	47	34	65	27	44	44
	Male	25	39	36	19	43	24	35	21	30	63	13	46	46
	Female	73	60	53	78	51	71	62	79	67	33	86	51	51
	Animals	2	1	11	3	5	3	2	0	3	3	+	3	3
	Indeterminate	+	0	0	0	0	2	1	0	0	1	1	0	1
	TOTAL N	681	517	540	632	429	419	355	211	3784	484	409	595	1488

NOTE.—ADO, adolescents; L, as in L Guardian, staff member of Lawton Foundation. Adults plus Children plus Animals plus Indeterminate add to 100 per cent.

associates in seven of the eight days.   This is emphasized by the curves of
Figure 12.1 which show also, however, that adult and child associates
differed relatively little in frequency for the four older subjects.   Other
children outrank adults as associates of the oldest child, Claire Graves.   But
it has to be considered here that Claire's father was not at home on the day
of her record, and that her family had the largest number of child siblings.
Among adults, mothers ranked highest in five of the eight days and were
preceeded only by teachers in two days and by teachers and adult friends
in the one day remaining.   Mothers figured in the social situations of every
child much more often than fathers—from nearly 2 to about 17 times as

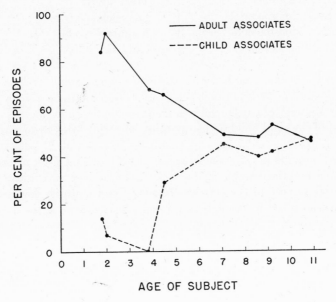

Fig. 12.1.—Per cent of regular standard episodes with adult and with child associates.

often in six of the eight Midwest days.   Yet fathers were second to mothers
in frequency of episodes in which they were associates of two of the four
younger children, and, except for Claire again, they played a part in an
appreciable number of episodes of each child.   Mothers, teachers, and
fathers—these three classes of adults go far toward accounting for all
grownups in the days of the Midwest children.   Note too that, of these
three, mothers alone played a substantial part in the day of every child.

The Midwest children had adult relatives other than parents as associates
in an almost negligible number of episodes.   The same holds for adult friends,
although every child did transact some behavior with grownups outside his
family or the school.   Overall, these transactions with adults abroad in
Midwest occurred in 238, or 6 per cent, of the Midwest standard units;

and here, with the per cent of episodes entered by each, are the people concerned:

Next-door neighbor	2.5	Passing motorist ("Hi")	.1
Hardware store clerk	1.1	School superintendent	.1
Bible-School leader	.7	School janitor	.1
Hardware store mechanic	.3	Field Station photographer	.1
Sitter	.2	Cafe manager	.03
Casual acquaintance	.2	Cafe cook	.03
Bible-School assistant	.2	Service station attendant	.03
Farmer	.1	Soil conservation worker	.02
Drugstore customer	.1	Truck driver	.02
Service station operator	.1	Lady school visitor	.02
Hardware store bookkeeper	.1	Neighbor's cook	.02
Bakery route salesman	.1	Lady sick in bed	.02

The median actual number of episodes in which adult friends became associates of the Midwest children is 19. Most of these people were at work in Midwest when the children made contact with them.

Seven of the eight children had nothing, or rather little, to do with adolescents. As for the remaining child, Dutton Thurston, all 21 per cent of his social action units in this associate class put him with a sister or brother.

Inspection of the data on child associates shows that: the subjects differed much with respect to the relative frequency and maturity levels of other children who entered their episodes; infants figured little in the days of the children; episodes with child siblings as associates did not occur at all in three of the eight days and varied greatly in frequency among the remaining five.

Table 12.5 shows for each of the children the per cent of all standard social

TABLE 12.5

Per Cent of All Standard Episodes With Younger,
Same Age, And Older Child Associates

CHILD ASSOCIATES	MIDWEST									DISABLED				ALL
	MC	JS	DT	MR	RB	ME	DC	CG	Mdn	WW	SD	VT	Mdn	Mdn
Younger	0	0	0	6	13	15	17	32	10	10	2	9	9	9
Same Age	0	0	0	7	28	16	14	14	10	0	3	2	2	3
Older	14	7	0	7	5	9	11	2	7	56	22	33	33	9

episodes in which child associates, including child friends and siblings, were younger than, of the same age, and older than the subject. For this purpose, we have considered a subject and another child to be of the same age wherever their actual ages differed by no more than one year. It may be seen that, with the exceptions of Mary Chaco and Jimmy Sexton, whose child associates were all older, and of Dutton Thurston, who had no contacts with other children, the Midwest subjects acted in relation to some children who were younger than they, to some of the same age, and to some who were older. For the subjects en masse, 31, 33, and 34 per cent respectively of all child associates were younger, of the same age, and older. Considered together, then, these children were not closely tied to children on their own age levels in social transactions with contemporaries, as data of Chapter IV have led us to anticipate; about one-third of the children in relation to whom the subjects behaved were more than a year above them in age and about one-third were more than a year younger. These proportions, however, do not hold by any means for every child. There is great variation among the children; but the differences are not without direction. A rank order correlation of .71 with a P beyond .05 indicates here an age relationship such that the older the child, the greater the preponderance in per cent of younger child associates.

Comparison and analysis of the values opposite Male and Female in Table 12.4 shows that the children engaged in 8 to 59 per cent more episodes with girls or women than episodes with boys or men, the median of the differences being 32 per cent. These Midwest children had female associates just over twice as frequently as male associates. Further analysis shows that mothers and teachers account for 75 per cent of the entire number of episodes with female associates. Women figured much in the days of these Midwest children. Cultural anthropologists (41) have claimed for women and for mothers in particular a paramount place in the rearing of American children. Our Midwest episode by episode data on female associates are consistent with this observation.

Animals got into seven of the eight days as associates at the rate of 1 to 11 per cent of the episodes in each record, with Claire's the one exception. Overall, animals account for 3.6 per cent of the Midwest standard social units. These creatures, with the per cent contribution of each, are listed below:

Own pet cat	1.5	Stray dog	.14
Own pet dog	1.4	Bug	.02
Dog neighbor	.3	Fly	.02
Cat neighbor	.2	Pig	.02

There is a clear case in data of Table 12.4 and in Figure 12.1 for maturity level as an associate selector. The per cent of episodes with adult associates goes down against minor reversals with increase in age of the subjects as shown by a rank order correlation of − .79, significant beyond the 1 per cent level. Coefficients of − .71 and − .64, both significant at the 5 per cent level, show that mothers and fathers, respectively, contribute strongly to this trend. Teachers, of course, stand against it. We have found it interesting that fathers as well as mothers were involved more in the days of the younger children than in the days of the older children. Episodes with child associates go up with age, as shown by a correlation of .64, also significant at the 5 per cent level.

Two things are apparent at once when one turns from the Midwest to the disabled children. One is the occurrence of Lawton staff members as associates unique to Sue and Verne; and the other is the relatively low frequency of adult associates, complemented by high frequency of child associates, in the case of four-year-old Wally. Otherwise, no well defined differences between the Midwest and disabled children are evident here. As for the high frequency of child associates in Wally's episodes, we can only report that his mother left him free to play outdoors with two school-age cousins during a large part of his day; note that 58 per cent of his episodes were with child friends, and that in 56 per cent of his episodes the children were of school age. A fact to be considered here is that this record was made during school vacation, whereas all of the others were made during school days.

A number of questions are to be raised about different classes of associates in episodes of the Midwest and disabled children. Meanwhile, however, we go back to the standard social units en masse and to the observer episodes to look at both from the standpoint of matrix variables with basic importance for social situations and behavior. Tables 12.6, 12.7, and 12.8, which present respectively, data from the categories of Action Circuit, Social-Field Potency, and Episode Weight, serve this purpose. Some of the data in these tables will help especially to clarify the significance of the observer as a social habitat object.

ACTION CIRCUIT

Table 12.6 shows for each record the per cent of standard and observer units with a closed rather than open circuit.

TABLE 12.6

PER CENT OF STANDARD AND OBSERVER EPISODES
WITH CLOSED ACTION CIRCUIT

| EPISODES | MIDWEST | | | | | | | | | DISABLED | | | | ALL |
	MC	JS	DT	MR	RB	ME	DC	CG	Mdn	WW	SD	VT	Mdn	Mdn
Standard	89	75	78	86	81	80	87	80	80	88	76	83	83	81
Observer	64	22	41	87	58	62	88	53	60	74	58	78	74	62

Behavior by the child in relation to an associate occurs by definition in every social episode. Inspection of the first row in Table 12.6 shows that there occurred also behavior by an associate in relation to the child in a large majority of the standard episodes of all 11 days; the overall median per cent is 81, and it does not fall in any case below 75.   There is no evidence of any relationship here with age; or of difference as between the Midwest and disabled children.   In fact, from two-year-old Mary Chaco through the row to disabled seven-year-old Verne the per cents show an average deviation from the median of only 4.5 points.

Frequency of closed action circuits can be used as an index of social responsiveness, for the interpersonal transaction in an episode is closed only when an associate does something in relation to the child.   One can say, then, that all of these children, the younger and the older, those who went to school and those who did not, the physically normal and the disabled, were responded to as social habitat objects on about the same frequency level—as expressed in a per cent of episodes neighboring 80.   This leaves the reciprocal per cent of episodes in which the action circuit was open.   It can thus be said that the individuals in relation to whom both the Midwest and disabled children behaved did not respond to things these children did, questions they raised, "Hellos" they spoke, or whatever, in something like 20 per cent of the standard social episodes.

Closed action circuits are much less frequent among the observer units for every day but Margaret Reid's and Douglas Crawford's, in each of which, however, there is a perverse difference of only 1 per cent.   Owing to these two reversals, the binomial test for significance of the trend toward less bilateral action among observer episodes than standard episodes is not satisfied if only the Midwest days are considered.   But for all 11 days this trend is significant beyond the 1 per cent level.   In general, relatively low frequency of action by the observer in relation to the subjects is indicated; and this is consistent with the observer's intent, in making a specimen record, to stay in the background as much as possible.

Marked variability in the per cent of closed action circuits among observer episodes is apparent.   The range here for all 11 days is from 22 to 88, with a median of 62 and an average deviation of 14.   But these per cents do not go up or down with age, nor do they differ consistently between the Midwest and disabled children.   Personality differences seem likely to be of decisive importance for the conspicuous variation.   Our observers want it said about this that they would like to see anyone not be responsive to Douglas Crawford or to Margaret Reid for whom the per cents on bilateral action with the observer soar to 88 and 87.   They report, on the other hand, that it was easy to steer away from involvement with two-year-old Jimmy Sexton, for whom this per cent is 22, and who showed consistently a fine preference for old friends and relations.   It also must be considered here that some responsiveness to the subject was a part of the observer's strategy, in the interest of avoiding an unnatural and consequently disturbing detachment. Yet it is important that this responsiveness was supposed to be kept meager and shallow.   We shall see whether it was or not.

POTENCY OF SOCIAL FIELD

Table 12.7 shows the per cent of standard and observer episodes of each child in which potency of the social field was superior. It answers this question: Are behavior transactions with social habitat objects within the limits of an episode of greater importance to the child than transactions with nonsocial habitat objects? The answer for the great majority of both standard and observer units in all 11 days is, yes. For none of the records, whether the associate was an observer or someone else, does the per cent of episodes with superior potency of the social field fall below 88, and it ranges up to 99. We conclude that, when the children did get involved with other individuals the social transaction was not often subordinated to involvement with nonsocial parts of the situation; when individuals got into these episodes, sociability tended to "take over." Low variability here from child to child is conspicuous; and there is no suggestion of relationship with age or difference between the Midwest and disabled children.

But one substantial difference does appear in these data; and it might be thought surprising. For seven of the eight Midwest children, observer episodes exceed standard episodes in per cent of units with superior potency of the social field. This also holds for two of the three disabled children. These differences are small, but their consistency satisfies the binomial test at the 1 per cent level.

What is the meaning of this? Our interpretation turns on the point that potency of the social field is a relative, not an absolute, value; it is relative to potency of the nonsocial field. Thus, *unity* weight (cf. scale on p. 327) on the social side of a situation can occur when involvement of the subject with an associate is weak and peripheral. Only a casual reading of our records suggests that high social potency with low interpersonal involvement was indeed characteristic of many transactions between subject and observer, as in the following verbal starts and quick stops, each representative of an observer episode.

What a funny watch (on the writing board)	Yes, isn't it?
What are you writing?	Oh, my lesson.
Will somebody else (another observer) come soon?	Yes, Mrs. Hebb, I think.

Such action units are all social and are therefore rated maximum on the social potency scale. In the degree that they have contributed toward the difference in question, this difference obviously does not imply relatively strong or central action relationships between subjects and observers. It is true that when the observer did join with the subject in activity geared to nonsocial behavior objects, as in helping a child to open a stubborn door, an effort was made to damper the social interplay, with consequent high relative weight of the nonsocial field. But a first law of observing for specimen records is the law of minimal participation in any and all activities of the child; with exceptions forced by emergencies, the observer left the child to open his own doors. For the most part, observers behaved in relation to subjects, not as coparticipants in their activities but only as respondents to their words. Perhaps reasons for the relatively high social potency of observer episodes reduce largely to this fact. In any case, we are left with a need for additional direct evidence as to the actual social significance for the child of the observer. The following section gets further into this.

TABLE 12.7

Per Cent of Standard and Observer Episodes
With Superior Potency of Social Field

Episodes	Midwest									Disabled				All
	MC	JS	DT	MR	RB	ME	DC	CG	Mdn	WW	SD	VT	Mdn	Mdn
Standard	95	96	94	94	96	92	88	90	94	94	94	97	94	94
Observer	96	98	97	93	97	93	96	97	96	98	93	99	98	97

EPISODE WEIGHT

By far the greater number of the social action units of these children were of first order relative weight. This holds by a large margin for the standard episodes of all Midwest and disabled subjects, as shown in Table 12.8, which gives for each record the per cent of standard units and observer units with a weight rating on the primary level. The per cent of the former with

TABLE 12.8

Per Cent of Standard and Observer Episodes
With Primary Relative Weight

Episodes	Midwest									Disabled				All
	MC	JS	DT	MR	RB	ME	DC	CG	Mdn	WW	SD	VT	Mdn	Mdn
Standard	92	93	86	94	84	83	88	84	87	89	86	84	86	86
Observer	74	88	56	90	64	55	86	68	71	72	70	83	72	72

primary weight may be seen to range from 83 to 94. This means that a large majority of the episodes involving these children in relationships with participant associates stood alone, with no others overlapping with them, or outranked overlapping units in potency. In short, these episodes generally were important episodes in terms of relative weight.

Table 12.8 shows that social episodes were preponderantly of first order weight even when observers were the associates. But the per cent of primary weight observer units is lower by comparison for every one of the 11 days. Episodes involving the children with observers, then, were judged to be of lesser relative importance than those involving the children with participant associates. The median of the actual differences here is 15 per cent.

Another thing to be noted about the potency of the observer units is that it varies much more from child to child. The per cent of standard social episodes with primary weight ranges, again, from 83 to 94. There is an average deviation from the median value in this range of 3 per cent. On the other hand, the corresponding values for observer episodes range from 55 to 90, with an average deviation from the median of 10 per cent. Age evidently has nothing to do with this variability, nor does it differ consistently between the Midwest and disabled children. As in the case of the divergence between standard and observer units on action circuits, personality differences are suggested.

How do the social episodes of these children compare in potency with episodes of the 11 days in which the children behaved in relation to things instead of individuals? To answer this question, Table 12.9 shows for each

TABLE 12.9

PER CENT OF STANDARD SOCIAL, OBSERVER SOCIAL, AND EXTRA-SOCIAL
EPISODES WITH PRIMARY RELATIVE WEIGHT

EPISODES	MIDWEST									DISABLED				ALL
	MC	JS	DT	MR	RB	ME	DC	CG	Mdn	WW	SD	VT	Mdn	Mdn
Standard Social	92	93	86	94	84	83	88	84	87	89	86	84	86	86
Extra-social	92	81	95	53	85	65	75	96	83	65	21	57	57	75
Observer Social	74	88	56	90	64	55	86	68	71	72	70	83	72	72

record the per cent of extra-social (i.e., potentially social and nonsocial) units along with the per cent of standard and observer units with a primary weight rating. Comparatively great variability in weight of the extra-social episodes immediately stands out.

The per cent of primary units ranges for these units of behavior and situation without social habitat objects all the way from 21 to 96; it rises above the per cent for standard episodes in three cases and falls below that for observer episodes in six. There is no indication that this variation is linked with age. And, although the values on the disabled children are all low, there is no clear difference here between these children and the Midwest subjects; only for Sue is the per cent of primary units so low as to fall under that for any Midwest child.

We find, then, that the social episodes of these children were neither lower nor higher in weight than the extra-social episodes as far as the data tell. But it is clear that the former were very much more stable in this respect. They were consistently high in potency relative to other action units.   To be clear about what this means, one has to keep in view the criteria for relative weight.   In terms of the most important of these criteria, as they are stated in Chapter X, one can generalize that, with good consistency from child to child, a large majority of the standard social units of the Midwest children, and of the disabled children as well, were rated primary rather than secondary or lower with respect to how much the recorded behavior showed immunity to potentially distracting conditions and high energy level.   One would hesitate to make any prediction on the basis of these data as to whether or not a bat or a ball or a bicycle would hold the "attention," "interest," or "concern" of one of these children to the extent of crowding out or subordinating behavior with other habitat objects.   But it looks much safer to predict that an individual—a mother or father or teacher, or perhaps a pet—would be preëmptive in this way.

SUMMARY OF EPISODE SURVEY

Excluding observers as associates, and assuming validity of the ratings and judgments, one can draw from the foregoing episode survey the following statements as to the social situations and behavior in the days of the Midwest children.

The episodes of all days were preponderantly social.   A substantial majority of them can be so classified in the sense that they confronted the children with individuals in relation to whom the children behaved.   Also, most of the remaining episodes were potentially social in that they occurred in behavior settings which made social behavior objects available.

Much more often than not others of Midwest played their parts as associates of the children one at a time.   Groupings of two or more individuals did occur as compound associates, however, in 4 to 21 per cent of all social episodes in the different days.   One indication of increase with developmental changes in the complexity of social behavior appears here inasmuch as the per cent of episodes in which behavior was transacted with these complex social units increased with the age of the children.

Single individuals as associates of the children included mothers, fathers, teachers, relatives in addition to parents, grownups exclusive of all relatives and of teachers, pets, and other children.   But above all, these associates were Midwest adults.   Among adults, mothers entered the largest number of episodes.   Teachers participated in the next to the most.   Teachers, in fact, had a part in more episodes than mothers in the days of three children among the four of school age.   Fathers were associates much less frequently than mothers and, for the four older children, much less frequently than teachers. Although parents and teachers account for a large majority of the children's behavior transactions with adults, while relatives who were not parents formed a small minority of associates, other Midwest grownups entered some episodes of every child. There remain chiefly other children as associates. The four younger subjects had few child associates. Episodes entered by child associates increased, however, with age of the children. At the same time, episodes with adult associates were most frequent among the younger children. One could say that, in general, the younger children were reared more by their elders, and the older more by their contemporaries. Child associates were about equally divided overall among older, same age, and younger children, the older decreasing and the younger increasing in frequency with age of the subjects.

The children behaved in one way or another in relation to all of their associates. This holds by definition. But the associate did not always reciprocate. Action in only the one direction occurred overall in approximately one-fifth of the children's episodes. In those remaining, however, the action circuit, opened either by the child or an associate, was closed, with behavior occurring on both sides. Thus, in something like four out of every five episodes, associates demonstrated responsiveness to the children by "going along" in a social interchange.

Again, social episodes greatly outnumber nonsocial episodes in the days of the children. This is to say that the social activity of the children was extensive; there was more commerce with individuals than with things. But this is not all. We have seen two ways in which the social activity of the children was also intensive. First, the parts of their social episodes involving them with associates generally were superior to the nonsocial parts in potency. Things and relations with things were subordinated to individuals and relations with individuals in something like 9 out of 10 episodes in the day of every child. Second, in a ratio near nine to one, the social episodes themselves either occurred alone with no other action units running along beside them, or outranked overlapping episodes in relative importance for all of the ongoing behavior; the social units of each day were not often crowded out by others or left subordinate to others in relative weight. The latter happened much more often to extra-social episodes in four of the eight days.

Observers who made the records became associates of the children in roughly one-fifth of all social and extra-social episodes. There are indications, however, that involvement of observers with the children was relatively restricted and lacking in depth. First, the action circuits of episodes with observers were much less frequently closed than those of episodes with participant associates in six of the eight days. Also, the frequency of observer episodes with high relative weight was lower in each day. The relative potency of the social field was consistently greater with observers as associates; but this can be attributed to restriction of action by the observer to mainly verbal behavior short of participation with the child in activities involving nonsocial behavior objects.

The disabled children of Lawton necessarily are found to differ in important ways from the Midwest children in the makeup of their associate realm. Despite this fact and the additional fact of their physical limitations, no evidence is found of consistent differences between them and the Midwest children in other variables of the present survey. There is no evidence that physical disability and its immediate consequences in terms of social behavior settings and objects influence psychosocial habitat and behavior on this basic level.

CONSOLIDATION OF SURVEY : INTERACTION EPISODES

Gains made toward selection of social action units for further analysis can now be consolidated.

We began with 10,406 episodes of 11 specimen day records. These episodes have been sorted by the categories of Associate Complexity, Action Circuit, Potency of the Social Field, and Relative Weight. Below, expressed in per cents based upon pooled standard and observer episodes of all 11 records, are data that represent the main steps of the sorting process and sum up the broader findings yielded by it:

1. Eighty-two per cent of these episodes are social, in that they involved the children with associates.

2. Of these social episodes, 92 per cent are regular, adequately recorded and substantial action units.

3. Ninety per cent of these regular social episodes involved children with single individuals, called simple associates, rather than groupings of individuals, called compound associates.

4. Of the regular social episodes with simple associates: (a) 77 per cent are marked by social action on both sides of the relationship between associate and child; (b) 95 per cent are characterized by superior importance of social as against nonsocial habitat objects; (c) 84 per cent are of first order relative weight.

One more step shows that 4,661, or 66 per cent, of the regular social episodes with simple associates have *in common* the features of closed action circuit, superior potency of the social field, and primary importance in relation to simultaneously occurring episodes. This is to say that these units are comparable in fundamental ways. They alone have been analyzed by categories remaining in the present descriptive scheme, and attention will be confined to them in all that follows. For study of the psychosocial habitat and behavior of these children, their most important common feature is two-sidedness of action relationship for which reason we shall call them *interaction episodes*.

Table 12.10 presents a breakdown of these interaction units into standard and observer episodes of the Midwest and disabled children. The N counts

TABLE 12.10

NUMBER OF STANDARD AND OBSERVER
INTERACTION EPISODES OF MIDWEST
AND DISABLED CHILDREN

Episodes	Midwest	Disabled	Total
Standard	2696	1065	3761
Observer	675	225	900
Total	3371	1290	4661

in this table give the major totals upon which all results to follow are based. Note that these totals range from 225 for observer episodes of the disabled children to 2,696 for standard episodes of Midwest children. Episodes with observers as associates make up 19 per cent of the total for all subjects, 20 per cent for Midwest children, and 17 per cent for disabled children. Comparison of these values with those of Table 12.2 shows that they are of the same order of magnitude as the per cent of all social units with observers as associates among both social and extra-social episodes in each record.

Table 12.11 lists the different associate classes common to the children in numbers of episodes large enough for statistical purposes. Here are the principal groupings of individual Midwest people, Lawton residents, and others who behaved in relation to the children and in relation to whom the children behaved in episodes of high social potency and primary relative weight.

Included among *all* adults here is every grownup in the total associate realm of the subjects, not just mothers, fathers, and teachers. Similarly, *all* participant associates include every individual, all mothers, fathers, teachers, brothers, sisters, schoolmates, neighbors, store clerks, pets, and others, in the total associate realm. Various comparisons are to be made as between adult associates en masse versus the generality of child associates, and as between the other listed associate classes. Associates in toto of the children also will be treated in terms of their psychosocial properties and behavior and in terms of the children's behavior in relation to the totality of social habitat objects which they form.

Study of our data has shown that the essential findings yielded by the survey of associates in standard social episodes of these children, as reported on pages 399–404, hold also for the interaction episodes classified in Table 12.11. This appears to be true at any rate of all such findings with pertinence for the data to follow. It is true with unimportant qualification for the proportions of adult and child associates, for relationships between age of the children and frequency of different classes of associates, for the proportion of *adult friends* among adult associates en masse, and for the relative frequency of younger children, children of the same age, and older children among child associates. For these reasons, a comparable associate survey of the standard interaction episodes will not be reported. We present only the data of Table 12.11, to show the N totals upon which subsequent analysis is based.

TABLE 12.11

NUMBER OF INTERACTION EPISODES WITH SPECIFIED ASSOCIATES

PARTICIPANT	ASSOCIATES	MIDWEST									DISABLED				ALL
		MC	JS	DT	MR	RB	ME	DC	CG	All	WW	SD	VT	All	
ADULTS	Mothers	378	184	164	289	40	75	25	30	1185	83	48	69	200	1385
	Fathers	69	135	40	16	22	9	9	—	300	11	—	41	52	352
	Teachers	—	—	—	25	77	47	35	32	216	—	53	61	114	330
	All	458	327	235	369	152	136	124	62	1863	102	168	212	482	2345
CHLDRN	Friends	—	20	—	88	121	101	103	21	454	221	70	172	463	917
	Siblings	68	—	82	24	—	6	17	33	230	27	—	16	43	273
	All	68	20	—	112	121	107	120	54	602	248	70	188	506	1108
	All Participant	533	348	359	501	293	281	252	129	2696	368	280	417	1065	3761
	All Observer	76	35	66	121	63	73	206	35	675	60	46	119	225	900

NOTE.—The entries opposite **All** are not in every case column totals, for the reason that the associate classes represented in the table are not all-inclusive.

Gaps in Table 12.11 will be noted; certain associate classes are not represented in some of the records. Most of those missing are accounted for in the sketches on children prepared in connection with their day records and presented in Appendices 1 and 2. Concerning this it is mentioned further that, since the basic N for all of the comparisons and correlations (with age) is the number of subjects, these gaps count against findings beyond chance expectation. The same holds, of course, for classes of associates which are in some cases meagerly represented, as in the instance of the father for Mary Ennis and Douglas Crawford.

A few of the entries call for brief comment.

In the episodes of Sue, opposite mother, the associate was an aide at Lawton who, in view of the role she filled in relation to Sue, was considered a mother equivalent. For Margaret Reid, one of the preschool children, the associate in the episodes opposite teacher was a teacher of the Vacation Church School. It has to be recognized that, in both of these cases, the individual designated is not strictly comparable to others of the same class. Yet, in each, the degree of comparability has seemed sufficient to make the particular findings to be reported on Midwest teachers and on mothers of the disabled children meaningful.

The total number of sibling associates is relatively low; and it may be seen that for Jimmy Sexton and Raymond Birch, both "only" children, and for Sue Dewall who had no contacts with family members on the day of her record, associates of this class are lacking. Furthermore, the siblings remaining differ so greatly as to age and sex that, for many purposes, it becomes questionable to group them. Yet, for other purposes, we have thought it worthwhile to compare the 230 sibling units with those involving other associates, as in asking whether the brothers and sisters of these children differed from their parents in frequency of nurturant behavior. For the reasons indicated, this grouping will be given separate consideration only in special cases. Special attention is called to the 82 sibling episodes in the day of Dutton Thurston which are entered in Table 12.11 in italics to set them apart from others of this class. In all of these, the sibling was a brother or a sister, both of whom we have classified in Chapter II with adolescents, although the brother was a young adult. These episodes are excluded from those in the total for child associates en masse. For purposes to be represented later, however, it has seemed profitable to group them with episodes in which the sibling associates were children.

We are confronted now at the end of this episode survey with a defined population of social action units in which these children interacted with social habitat objects. Thus far, however, nothing has been said about the nature of the person to person relationship per se between associate and child. Some characteristics of this relationship are now to be considered.

Power and Sequence Relations

RELATIVE POWER

Figure 12.2 presents a graph based on the ratio scale for measurement of Relative Power. To recapitulate from Chapter X: $A < S$ means power of associate less than power of subject; $A = S$ means power of associate equal to power of subject; A>S means power of associate greater than power of subject. Mary Ennis in episode 4 of Chapter XI humors her baby brother, mimicking Mrs. Ennis' tone. Maud Pintner and Otto Chaco in episode 5 play horse with equal give and take. Margaret Reid in episode 3 literally toes the line while "adult leaders" come closer and closer. Here, in person to person relations of these episodes, are the major variants of relative power.

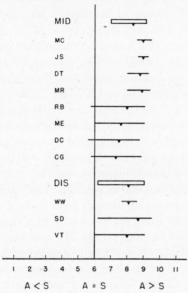

FIG. 12.2.—Relative power of Midwest and disabled children in relation to all associates. *A* designates power of associates, *S* power of subjects. The vertical line is erected on the middlemost point of the power scale, represented by the base line. It stands for equality of power as between *A* and *S*. The individual children of the Midwest (*MID*) and disabled (*DIS*) groups are listed in the order of their ages to the left of this line. Each horizontal bar extends through the interquartile range of the power ratings for a single child or for one of the two groupings of children. The mean rating in each case is indicated by an arrowhead extending downward from the bar.

Figure 12.2 shows for each child in relation to his or her total realm of participant associates the median and interquartile range of all ratings on this continuum. It tells us one thing as positively as the ratings can, namely, that these children lived the socially interactive parts of their days in action relationships with individuals generally more powerful than they, with individuals whose ability to change the behavior of the children usually exceeded the ability of the children to do the reverse. This anyone probably would take to be a sample from the fate of children everywhere. These data, therefore, have to depend much for their significance on the particular A>S scale placements for the eight children of Midwest, as against comparable children of other communities and cultures; and they depend similarly on the corresponding determinations for the disabled subjects. The actual measures of central tendency and dispersion are put on record with this in view. For the Midwest and disabled children, the median ratings are 8.4 and 8.1.

Age and power of the Midwest children are related. Age makes a difference here in two ways. First, the older the Midwest child, the greater his relative power, as shown by a rank order correlation of .93, significant at the 1 per cent level. Second, the older the Midwest child, the more variable his relative power. Evidence of continuous increase with age in power fluctuation is no better than a rank correlation of .57, with a P value of .10. But inspection of Figure 12.2 leaves no doubt that the power relations of the four younger, preschool children were more stable than those of the four older, school children, nor does it leave any doubt that, in the long run of their episodes, greater power fell to the older children.

These correlations and differences are clarified by reference back to dependence of relative power upon stable characteristics of associate and child. All power ratings here were guided by an expectation that, given a child C, his power with an associate A generally will depend in part, though not entirely, upon how much bigger or smaller, stronger or weaker, and higher or lower in enduring status position A is than C (see p. 329). It follows that earlier tables which identify associates of the different children as to age and role classification are consistent with these data on power and age. So also are earlier findings on the Midwest children of increase with age in frequency of child associates and decrease with age in frequency of adult associates. The older children interacted more with children and less with adults; therefore, their relative power was greater. The older children divided their interactions more between children and adults; therefore, their relative power was less stable. The latter of these two interpretations may touch a quite universal source of stress and strain in growing up. Later data, moreover, bear upon this possibility as it applies to Midwest children.

Dependence of the associate to child ratio of power upon difference in maturity level between child and associate is confirmed by Figure 12.3. Note first the graph on the left. The medians and measures of dispersion which it represents state a plain case. They indicate that in interactions with adults the Midwest and disabled children had to put up with a greatly inferior power position which varied little from episode to episode. Surprisingly enough, this position evidently varied scarcely at all from child to child, for the medians from Mary through Verne form a nearly straight vertical line. Generalized, these data would say among other things that neither growing up from 2 to 11 nor being physically normal within this age range will gain you anything in power relations with adults if you live in Midwest or its vicinity.

The graph on the right states a quite different case about children with children. The medians here do show a gain in power with age, confirmed by a rank correlation of − .71, significant beyond the 5 per cent level,[3] between age of subject and power of associate. The quartile deviations appear to be similarly related with age; although the coefficient in this case (.57, with a P of .10) is low and of doubtful significance. It obviously is pertinent to both of these age relationships that growing up necessarily carries with it a gain in the person-anchored correlates of power in relation to a constantly increasing number of children.

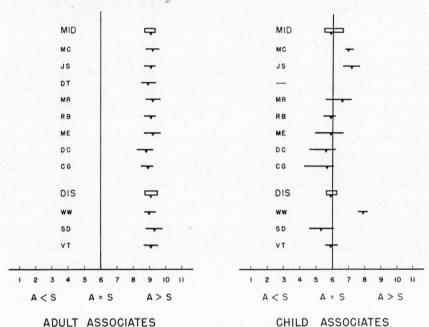

FIG. 12.3.—Relative power of Midwest and disabled children in relation to adult associates and child associates. Cf. FIG. 12.2.

Comparison of the graphs in Figure 12.3 shows that each of the children had higher relative power in interactions with children than in interactions with adults. The median of the actual differences is 3.2 scale points for the Midwest subjects. There is a correlation of .67, significant at the 5 per cent level, between these differences and age, which means that the degree in which power with other children outranks power with adult associates increases with age.

A canvass of likely power differences as between different principal associates shows that in their relations with the children, (a) mothers had greater power than child friends, (b) mothers had greater power than siblings, and (c) adults en masse had greater power than observers, according to the

[3] The magnitude and significance of this coefficient are reduced by loss of a case owing to Dutton's day without child associates.

ratings. The first two of these differences satisfy the binomial test at the 5 per cent level, and the third at the 1 per cent level. A tendency toward greater power on the part of teachers than child associates is suggested by a binomial P value of .10.

Outstanding among these differences is the evidence of relatively low power of observers as compared with other adults. Observers, no less than these other mature persons, had many characteristic power traits that go with being grown up. Yet they evidently managed to place and keep themselves in relatively powerless positions, as it was their aim to do. This fact goes to show that adulthood in itself was not the only factor in the higher relative power of adults. Yet it apparently was a large factor. Two findings indicate this. First, different adults among participant associates, no matter who they were, were not found to differ in relative power. Second, even the observer was rated as having higher power in relation to the children than child associates, with this difference significant by the binomial test at the level of 5 per cent.

No consistent or clear differences in these power ratings are evident as between the Midwest and disabled children. Minor divergencies of one or another disabled child from Midwest children on the same age level can be found on inspection of Figures 12.2 and 12.3. But these we can do no more than attribute to idiosyncrasies unconnected with physical disability or its consequences for social situations.

So much for the power relations of these children. The main findings represent a central part of the social matrix for interaction between the children and their associates, for which reason they will be revived at several later points in the description.

INTERACTION SEQUENCE

We are concerned here with two questions about the sequential character of the interaction between associate and child: Who started it? And how far did it go? Answers to each of these questions will be presented separately.

TABLE 12.12

PER CENT OF STANDARD AND OBSERVER INTERACTION
EPISODES IN WHICH INTERACTION WAS INITIATED BY THE SUBJECT

EPISODES	MIDWEST									DISABLED				ALL
	MC	JS	DT	MR	RB	ME	DC	CG	Mdn	WW	SD	VT	Mdn	Mdn
Standard	50	56	52	50	40	51	56	46	50	50	54	47	50	50
Observer	77	82	83	85	76	82	91	62	82	93	89	85	89	85

Initiation by subject versus initiation by associate. Table 12.12 records for each day the per cent of standard and observer episodes in which interaction was initiated by subjects rather than associates. It shows that, for both the Midwest children and the disabled children, "starting it" in relations with participant associates was precisely or approximately a fifty-fifty matter.   One might have expected from the data on relative power a quite different result.   It seems reasonable to anticipate from greatly superior power on the side of participant associates that they would far outdo the children in "taking the lead."   But evidently, for these children, initiation of social interplay has nothing to do with relative power, or, at least, with the use of it.   Apparently, too, initiation of social interplay, unlike relative power, has nothing to do with age.   There is no evidence either that it has anything to do with differences between the Midwest and disabled children. Nor, finally, is there any evidence that it has anything to do with differences between different classes of associates.   We have compared adults with children on this variable, mothers with fathers, mothers with siblings, fathers with siblings, mothers with child friends, teachers with child friends. We have looked for differences wherever they might conceivably be expected to occur and, throughout, the result is the same: These children initiated about half of their social transactions with others of Midwest and its vicinity. Things which cannot be said, then, of children in this culture on the basis of these data, are that, here: children wait to speak until spoken to (or characteristically speak first); children are more (or less) reticent than their associates; children seek others more (or less) than others seek them.   As far as order of action with others is concerned, these 11 children with all of their differences in age, sex, social group, and physique, acted in relation to everyone on a basis of equal give and take.

It is emphasized that all of this applies only to participant associates. The observer is again in a class by himself.   In no case does the per cent of observer episodes in which interaction was initiated by the child fall below 62; it reaches 93 for disabled Wally Wolfson, with the median 82 for the Midwest children, and 85 for the disabled children.   As for nearly every variable treated thus far, the observer episodes show greater variability, although the per cents do not vary in relation to age of the subjects or differ consistently as between the Midwest and disabled children.   Once more, personality differences are suggested.   We are not prepared to go into detail on this; but we can say that some of the child to child variation here is consistent with our knowledge of the children.   Douglas Crawford, for example, whose bilateral action relationships with the observer exceeded those of all other subjects, is famous among field workers of the station as an irrepressible seeker and dispenser of information whose outgoing approach to all observers was beyond any shushing tactics, whereas Claire Graves, for whom the per cent of subject-initiated interactions with the observer is lowest, stands out among subjects of our day studies as a child so reserved and uncommunicative that, on the day of her record, observers were moved at times to speak to her to break an awkward silence.   These observations leave one to wonder why personality differences which may account for differences in initiation of observer contacts do not also effect differences in initiation of contacts with participant associates. On this question we have no answer, although later discussion of the observer's special significance for individual subjects relates to it.

Cyclical versus noncyclical interaction. In a noncyclical interaction, to summarize the definition in Chapter X, X does something, Y reacts—and that is all; whereas, in a cyclical interaction, there occurs in addition at least an action by X in response to the reaction by Y. If only in terms of total amount of social behavior, cyclical interplay is the more complex.

Table 12.13 gives for all records the per cent of standard and observer interaction episodes in which cyclical interaction occurred. It shows first

TABLE 12.13

PER CENT OF STANDARD AND OBSERVER INTERACTION
EPISODES IN WHICH INTERACTION WAS CYCLICAL

EPISODES	MIDWEST									DISABLED				ALL
	MC	JS	DT	MR	RB	ME	DC	CG	Mdn	WW	SD	VT	Mdn	Mdn
Standard	64	72	65	57	62	62	50	56	62	70	65	70	70	64
Observer	60	39	57	40	54	57	40	32	47	47	58	62	58	54

that, for every Midwest child but one, and for the three disabled children, action relationships with participant associates were preponderantly cyclical, with the median per cents for the Midwest and disabled children respectively 62 and 64. Continuance of interaction with participant associates beyond one act and a response occurred, then, definitely more often than not.

The range here for the Midwest children extends from 50 to 72. But variation within this range is not haphazard. It is age related as shown by a rank order correlation of − .68, significant at the 5 per cent level, between age and per cent of cyclical interactions. This result was entirely surprising to us. Why should the relative frequency of the seemingly more complex versus the seemingly less complex interactions go down with age? Toward an answer to this question we have run correlations between age and per cent of cyclical interactions with different classes of associates, to find that: the negative relationship holds only for adults; there is no relationship at all between age and relative frequency of cyclical interactions with other children en masse or with other children of any associate class. For adult associates en masse, the coefficient is − .93, significant at the 1 per cent level; for mothers, it is − .54, with a P of .10; for fathers, it is − .52, with a P of .15. Generalized, these data would mean that, for whatever reasons, there goes with growing up in Midwest a tendency toward curtailment of social interaction with grownups to simple action and reaction; that the more adult in point of age Midwest children become, the more noncyclical are their interactions with adults. Here is an episode from our record on Claire Graves, the oldest child of the study—who has been helping Mrs. Graves get breakfast:

Claire said to her mother, "Did you forget about the cocoa?"

Her mother said pleasantly, "You know, I haven't forgotten, but I guess it should be moved," and then she took the cocoa off the fire.

And here is an episode from the record on Douglas Crawford, next to the oldest child, who is reading in the living room of his home.

Mrs. Crawford came into the room and said, "Well, you found your *Ben Hur* book."

"Oh, no," Douglas said, while he went on reading, "I'm not looking at that."

These X, Y rather than X, Y, X . . . exchanges are typical of noncyclical interactions with adults which, if the present data are representative, occur increasingly with advance in the maturity of Midwest children. Now that we look at them on the child side they strike us as rather adult.

Noncyclical interaction may be more generally characteristic of social interplay between mature persons than its simplicity at first suggests. Much social intercourse between adults is in fact of the noncyclical variety; and it could be argued that this is often both a consequence and a requirement of social efficiency, if not of sociability, as when a conductor says, "your ticket, please," and a passenger only hands over the ticket. On the other hand, much social intercourse involving very young children with adults is in fact cyclical, often out of a kind of echolalia, sometimes owing to the child's wish to socialize, as in saying "Goodnight, mother" 20 times running, or in engaging conductors in drawn out repartee, and often as a result of social inefficiency, as when, in episode 25 of Chapter XI, two-year-old Mary Chaco wound up her parents with her in a tedious effort to identify a wanted dish of salad, whereas an older child might well have asked for and received the salad in an easy noncyclical transaction. It would be out of the question certainly to use frequency of noncyclical interaction in an unqualified way as a measure of maturity. Obviously, extended social give-and-take is characteristic of mature persons under some conditions, as in examination of a witness, while one give followed by no more than one take is characteristic of immature persons under other conditions. For this reason among others, it would be desirable to investigate conditions under which these two levels of interaction occurred in these children. For the time being, however, we can only report this unexpected relationship for further study.

In line with everything learned here until now about observers in relation to the children, the per cent of cyclical interactions with the observer is consistently below the same with participant associates and, also, the per cents for observer episodes vary greatly from child to child, and yet are not related with age. No significant differences in this variable as between different classes of participant associates were found.

Action by Associate and Child

Except for information to identify associates, everything reported thus far on the social behavior and situations of these children has been concerned primarily with formal characteristics of social episodes or of person-to-person relations within these episodes. Qualitative characteristics of the actual behavior in the interactions between associate and child have been left out of account. Helping, attacking, resisting, submitting, praising, blaming, and other distinctive kinds of social behavior occurred on both sides in these interactions. This much we have learned from episodes of the foregoing chapter. But our problem now is to quantify such phenomena.

How, in terms of ratings and counts made episode by episode, did the children behave in interacting with others? And how, on the same basis, did these others behave in interacting with the children? These questions state the twofold problem at hand. Answers to the second question are aimed toward description of psychosocial habitat, while answers to the first are aimed toward description of behavior in that habitat.

As anticipated by the outline on page 324 of categories in the instrument, action by associates and subjects will be described under the two headings, Modes of Action and Attributes of Action, both of which refer to qualitative aspects of social behavior. Episodes of the Midwest children in which they interacted with participant associates are to get first and most attention in each case. Consideration will be given supplementally, however, to observer episodes and to differences as between the Midwest and disabled children.

Modes of Action

BEHAVIOR OF ASSOCIATES

Relative frequency of action modes. We can begin here by looking into the relative frequency of different modes of action by participant associates en masse of the Midwest children. Figure 12.4 serves this purpose.

All action modes were ranked in order as to frequency in terms of the per cent of episodes in which they occurred on the associate side in the standard interaction episodes of every record. Each bar of the graph in Figure 12.4 shows the mean of the ranks obtained for a given mode by this procedure. The graph as a whole consequently gives a synopsis of the more and increasingly less common ways of behaving on the part of others in relation to these children. But it leaves open the question of whether particular modes differ in rate of occurrence with significant consistency from record to record. Binomial tests were made, therefore, to answer this question for all possible comparisons of each mode with every other mode. Symbols explicated in the legend of the figure are placed over the bars to show the findings of these tests. Finally, the median per cent of interaction episodes in which every mode was judged to occur, i.e., the computed median of the eight per cents for all records, is entered in each case beneath the appropriate bar.

In the greater part of all that follows on modes of action we shall consider mainly differences in rank without referring often in the text to magnitudes of the differing values. However, the approximate level of every such

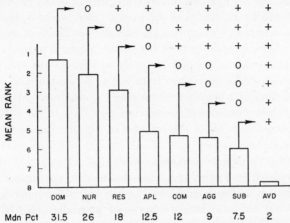

	DOM	NUR	RES	APL	COM	AGG	SUB	AVD
Mdn Pct	31.5	26	18	12.5	12	9	7.5	2

FIG. 12.4.—Relative frequency of different modes of action by all participant associates of the Midwest children. Names of the modes are abbreviated as follows: *DOM*, dominance; *NUR*, nurturance; *RES*, resistance; *APL*, appeal; *COM*, compliance; *AGG*, aggression; *SUB*, submission; *AVD*, avoidance. Each mode is represented by a bar whose height expresses the mean of the ranks established by first determining for each record the per cent of standard interaction episodes in which the given mode was judged to occur, and then arranging the obtained per cents in order of magnitude. For every mode the median per cent (*Mdn Pct*) is entered under the appropriate bar. Attention is called to the symbols, + and 0, and to their placement in relation to the bars and arrows. A plus (+) over one bar and opposite the arrow extending from another denotes a difference in mean rank significant beyond the 5 per cent level between the modes represented by the two bars. For example, the + over *RES* and opposite the arrow extending from *DOM* shows that dominance significantly outranks resistance, with the P value of this difference beyond .05, while the 0 over *NUR* and opposite the arrow extending from *DOM* shows that nurturance and dominance do not differ significantly in rank.

magnitude will be indicated precisely as it is in the present figure by a median per cent on each mode. These measures of central tendency are important inasmuch as they will say most of all that our data show about the actual frequency of the different action modes. For this reason, close attention by readers to these values is suggested.

Figure 12.4 exemplifies a method of data presentation and analysis that will be used to represent also the relative frequency of these different modes of action by both child and adult associates and by the children in relation to different groupings of associates. The array of ranks in each case poses as another reliability problem the question of the degree in which the total frequency pattern is consistent from child to child. To meet this problem we have computed the coefficient of concordance, W, for each array. W is .81, with a P of .01, in the present case; and it is significant well beyond the 1 per cent level for all of the other distributions as well. There is some variation, however, in magnitude of the coefficient from one pattern to another. This variation is not without interest insofar as it shows varying uniformity among the children in action by, and in behavior of the children in relation to, different classes of associates. But we have been unable to discover a satisfactory way to test the significance limits of such variation. Further, the apparent differences here have raised a number of baffling problems which push us beyond presently available data and which, also, would require extended digression from our major assignment of describing habitat conditions and behavior common to the children. We are therefore going to use these measures of consistency now only to the extent of citing them as evidence that all of the pictures in Figures 12.4 through 12.9 are substantially representative.

One finds on turning to particular modes of action by all associates as these are depicted in Figure 12.4, that dominance, nurturance, and resistance rank highest, and avoidance lowest, while appeal, compliance, aggression, and submission are of relatively low and insignificantly differing rank. Special attention is commanded by the high frequency of dominance. The median per cent of 31.5 indicates that these children were subjected collectively to authoritarian pressure in something like 30 of every 100 episodes involving them in interactions with individuals other than observers. But note also that the median per cent on nurturance stands at 26 and that frequency of dominance greater than that of nurturance is not consistent enough to satisfy the binomial test. Evidently, although individuals of Midwest were given much to arbitrary ordering, bossing, ruling of the children, they tended about as strongly to help the children, to protect them, or to give them things. Yet resistance is prominent in the picture. This kind of behavior, consisting in a holding out against pressure of any kind, is outranked significantly only by dominance and it ranks with consistency above every other mode but nurturance and appeal. Avoidance is all but out of the picture. The median per cent of episodes in which it was found in the behavior of participant associates falls to 2, and this kind of associate action ranks significantly below all others, with appeal as one exception.

Aggression by others against these children is indeed low on the list. Some readers may find this surprising. But one must keep in view here that our aim throughout has been to describe social action, not social motivation, above the threshold for perception of behavior by these children themselves. To what extent *as the children saw it* did others get mad at them and hurt or try to hurt them? This is the question answered as best the observers and analysts could answer it on the basis of what *they* saw by the low median per cent and the low mean rank on aggression.

Modes of action by adults, represented in Figure 12.5, may be seen at once to differ little from the same by associates in toto. Adults got into the social episodes of these children more often than others, as Table 12.4 has shown us. But it is now clear also that they were far from being neutral agents. Near identity of Figures 12.4 and 12.5 suggests that, rather, the children's total social scheme of things bore their stamp.

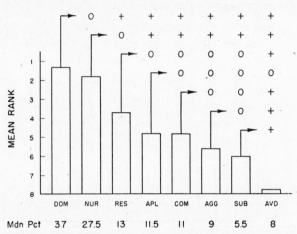

Fig. 12.5.—Relative frequency of different modes of action by all participant adult associates of the Midwest children. Cf. Fig. 13.6.

Only one notable difference between the frequency pattern of action modes for all associates and the one for adults alone is apparent. Resistance ranks lower in the latter. Its relative frequency consistently exceeds only that of avoidance in the adult picture, whereas this kind of behavior significantly outranks compliance, aggression, submission, and avoidance in the one for associates at large. Yet it cannot be said that grownups avoided contention with the children. Contention with them in the more positive form of dominance stands, rivaled only by nurturance, as the most frequent kind of social action by adults.

Figure 12.6 shows the mode hierarchy for child associates. Here, resistance surpasses all other ways of behaving. Its occurrence rate among children who interacted with the subjects exceeds significantly that of appeal, submission, aggression, and avoidance. Nurturance follows next in order, although it consistently outranks only compliance and avoidance. Other divergencies of child associates from adults in mean rank of the modes will be noted. There is no further evidence, however, that any one of the kinds of behavior by other children, dominance, appeal, submission, aggression, compliance, or avoidance, occurred more or less often than another with consistency among the eight subjects. Dominance, though, is in the foreground part of the picture. It is next to nurturance in mean rank and the median per cent of episodes, 15, in which it was found is relatively high.

Differences between classes of participant associates. Comparison of Figures 12.5 and 12.6 raises the question of dissimilarity in frequency of particular action modes as between different classes of associates by suggesting such dissimilarity in the case of grownups versus children. Actually, only one difference between all adult and all child associates satisfies the binomial test beyond a P of .05, namely, that in the direction of more frequent dominance by adults. But there remain subordinate classes of grown-

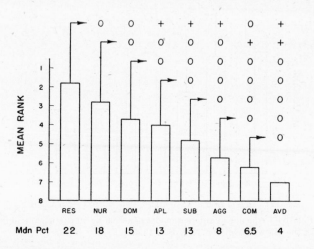

Fɪɢ. 12.6.—Relative frequency of different modes of action by all child associates of the Midwest children. Cf. Fɪɢ. 13.6.

ups and children which are found to differ. Differences here, significant beyond the 5 per cent level, in per cent of episodes scored on different modes confront us with:

> **dominance** by all adults *more* frequent than that by children;
> **dominance** by mothers *more* frequent than by child friends;
> **avoidance** by child friends *more* frequent than by mothers.

The evidence noted last that mothers shunned the children less frequently than various classmates, playmates, and chums, would seem to give some support to the adage about a boy's best friend. But one is impressed more here by the greater prominence among adults, and mothers in particular, of dominative behavior. However one looks at these data on kinds of action, this directive, authoritarian, ruling, ordering, you-do-that, or do-not-do-that kind of social action stands out in the behavior of Midwest grownups with the children. Yet the high rank of nurturance among these same adults also should be kept in view.

Age relationships. Does age of the children make a difference to kind of social behavior by participant associates in relation to the child?   There is evidence that it does, and that this holds specifically for appeal, resistance, and avoidance.

Rank order correlations, each with the coefficient and probability index in parentheses, show that with increase in age of the children:

appeal by associates en masse *increases* in frequency (.82,P<.01);
appeal by all adults *increases* in frequency (.68,P<.05);
resistance by all adults *decreases* in frequency (−.61,P<.05);
resistance by mothers in particular *decreases* in frequency (−.71,P <.05);
avoidance by all adults *decreases* in frequency (−.71,P<.05);
avoidance by mothers *decreases* in frequency (−.71,P<.05).

Tendencies toward a decrease in dominance by associates en masse, an increase in appeal by all child associates, and an increase in submission by child friends with increase in age of the children are suggested by coefficients of .46 to .57, each with a P beyond .10.

Here are measurements of some intelligible consequences of growing up for psychosocial habitat. It seems understandable, for example, that others would more often solicit benefit from the older Midwest children, with their greater size and strength, higher mental ages, wider knowledge, and better skills, than from the younger children of Midwest.   It also makes sense that the older children, if only because of a lesser proclivity for "getting into everything" should meet lesser resistance from others, especially from adults and especially, indeed, from mothers.   Why the older children should be avoided less by adults in general and by mothers in particular is not so immediately apparent, but this will be clarified when correlations between age of the subjects and their own modes of action are considered.   Meanwhile, these age relationships contribute, as will later data in a like way, toward a kind of developmental psychology of the social environment in Midwest.

One cannot help but note kinds of action by adult associates that are not seen to change with age of the children.   This holds notably for nurturance and dominance, both of which have appeared above as the most frequent kinds of adult behavior in relation to all of the children.   There is no evidence that, as might be predicted, nurturance by adults declines with age; and there is no evidence that, as some might expect and be pleased to discover, dominance by adults declines with age.   Through the whole span of years from 2 to 11 represented by the children, these two ways of behaving on the part of interacting grownups are found on inspection of the raw data to be remarkably constant in frequency at the levels shown by the median per cents of Figure 12.5.   This we will later reconsider.

So much for modes of action on the associate side. Let us turn, then, to the side of the children themselves.

Figure 12.7 represents the relative frequency of action modes on the part of all Midwest children in relation to all of their associates. It tells a new and different story.

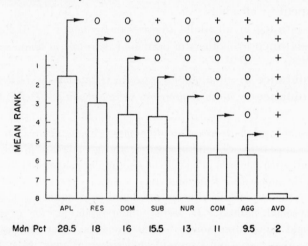

FIG. 12.7.—Relative frequency of different modes of action by the Midwest children in relation to all participant associates. Cf. FIG. 13.6.

Appeal, among all on our list, definitely appears to have been the preëminent kind of social behavior by these Midwest children. The median per cent of interaction episodes in which appeal by a child to an associate was scored stands at 28.5. Moreover, appeal significantly outranks all other modes on the child side but resistance, dominance, and nurturance. Resistance is the nearest in frequency to appeal, although the only kinds of behavior which it consistently outranks are avoidance and aggression. Avoidance, again, is significantly exceeded by every other mode and, as with behavior of all associates, the median per cent of episodes in which it was found, stands at only 2. This leaves dominance, submission, nurturance, compliance, and aggression, no one of which can be said to have occurred more or less often than another in the episodes of all subjects.

Modes of action by the children in relation to adults alone are represented in Figure 12.8. As indicated by both the stated median per cents and by comparison as to rank of each mode with every other, appeal remains at the top, and avoidance at the bottom of the hierarchy. Submission, though, replaces resistance as the mode nearest to the top. Its frequency closely rivals that of appeal. Yet resistance, the very opposite of submission, is next in order, although this kind of action with adults does fall below submission in the number of other modes which it consistently outranks. Again, nothing more can be said with confidence about the relative frequency of nurturance, compliance, dominance, and aggression.

Soliciting benefit, giving in to pressure, and withstanding pressure, are the salient kinds of behavior by the children with adults. Special attention will be given later to the first and second of these, appeal and submission.

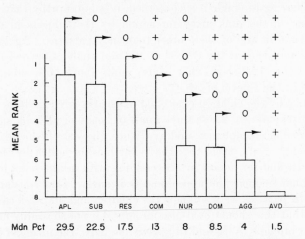

Mdn Pct	APL 29.5	SUB 22.5	RES 17.5	COM 13	NUR 8	DOM 8.5	AGG 4	AVD 1.5

FIG. 12.8.—Relative frequency of different modes of action by the Midwest children in relation to all participant adult associates. Cf. FIG. 13.6.

We reach now in Figure 12.9 modes of action by the children with children. Two points stand out when one compares this figures with the one just

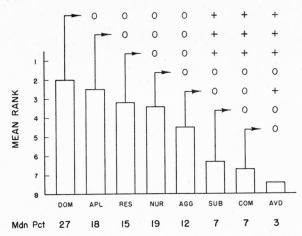

Mdn Pct	DOM 27	APL 18	RES 15	NUR 19	AGG 12	SUB 7	COM 7	AVD 3

FIG. 12.9.—Relative frequency of different modes of action by the Midwest children in relation to all child associates. Cf. FIG. 13.6.

above it. First, whereas submission is one of the most frequent kinds of behavior by the children in relation to adults, it is one of the least frequent by the children in relation to children. Second, whereas dominance is one of the least frequent kinds of behavior by the children in relation to adults, it is one of the most frequent by the children in relation to children. Giving in to grownups, but dominating or seeking to dominate peers, appears to have been a rule of the children's social behavior. As far as the part of this rule referring to children is concerned, it is noteworthy that aggression ranks higher in the rank array for action by the subjects in relation to associates than in any of these other frequency patterns. Aggression out-ranks avoidance here at the P level of .05; and analysis beyond that repre-sented in Figure 12.9 shows that it also ranks above both submission and compliance at the P level of .10.

Dominance by the children over child associates is virtually in a tie with appeal and resistance. These three kinds of behavior all rank significantly above submission, compliance, and avoidance, the last of which is again the least frequent. Note, then, that the hierarchies for action by the children with children and for action by the children with adults have in common relatively high frequency of appeal and resistance. That resistance should loom in both pictures we who know the children and Midwest can appreci-ate. But that this should hold also for appeal is not so readily understood. Figure 12.8 brought to us, and to readers, perhaps, the image of grownups, with their superior height, weight, strength, wisdom, pretensions, and the like, as authentic solicitees of benefit; child associates seem unequal to a role so lofty. One might wonder with some justification also at the high rank of dominance by the children with children, for earlier data which show dominance moving downward, so to speak, from adult to child leave us without readiness to see it moving horizontally from child to child.

One possible explanation for these results which somehow do not fit well in the presently unfolding pattern of these children's relations with grownups and peers comes easily. It is that child associates of the subjects included children a large proportion of whom were not strictly peers. Child associates were younger than the subjects in 31 per cent of their inter-action episodes and older than the subjects in 34 per cent of their interaction episodes. May it be that the relatively high frequency of appeal by the subjects to child associates stems from their relations with older children? And may it be also that relatively high dominance by the subjects over child associates stems from their relations with younger children? It could hold further, to weigh a chance obverse to these, that relatively high nurturance by child associates derives from relations of the subjects with older children.

We are not prepared by the data at hand for statistically adequate analysis on the breakdown level required by these questions. The entire important problem of social interaction in Midwest between children and other children of differing maturity levels must be left for later study. Meanwhile, on the basis of the foregoing, one is encouraged to state the hypothesis that with respect to certain action modes, interaction between Midwest children and child associates who differ in level of maturity is similar to interaction between Midwest children and adults. From older contemporaries, children of Midwest may get chiefly dominance, nurturance, and resistance, as our subjects do from bonafide grownup associates, while they reciprocate these with submission, appeal, and resistance, as our subjects do in transacting behavior with adults; and the reverse may hold for Midwest children in their relations with younger contemporaries.

This leaves the present picture of behavior by the subjects in relation to adults and by adults in relation to the subjects sharp and intelligible. Also, it leaves well marked certain features in the corresponding picture of social behavior on both sides of the relationship between these children of Midwest and all other Midwest children. Foremost here is the finding that the subjects and the whole realm of their child associates in relations with one another were given more to resistance, but *no* more to submission, than to any other action mode. By partial contrast, in their relations with adults, again, the children were given more to submission than to any other mode but appeal, and more to both of these than to resistance. The comparatively high frequency of dominance on the part of both the children and their child associates also stands out clearly. The fact is that, whereas dominance stands near the bottom in the picture of how these children behaved with adults, it ranks near the top in the picture of how they behaved with the generality of other children; and dominance stands comparatively high in the picture of how other children in general behaved with the subjects. There was frequent ordering and directing on both sides when the children were with children, but only on the taller side when they were with adults.

One other point can be made about the children with children versus the children with adults. It is that additional clear differences do appear when comparisons are made here, not of one mode with another, but of the same mode in behavior, on the one hand, by or toward child associates and in behavior, on the other hand, by or toward adult associates. This we have seen already in action on the associate side. Then, are there like differences on the subject side? The section to follow includes answers to this question.

Differences in behavior toward different classes of associates. All possible comparisons of particular modes of action by the children in relation to our distinguished classes of associates disclose differences significant beyond the 5 per cent level which show:

> **submission** to adults en masse *more* frequent than to children;
> **submission** to mothers *more* frequent than to child friends;
> **submission** to mothers *more* frequent than to siblings;
> **compliance** with all adults *more* frequent than with children;
> **resistance** against mothers *more* frequent than against child friends.

Differences with a P value beyond .10 suggest that:

compliance with mothers is *more* frequent than with siblings;
resistance against mothers is *more* frequent than against teachers;
dominance over child friends is *more* frequent than over mothers;
dominance over child friends is *more* frequent than over teachers;
aggression against mothers is *more* frequent than against teachers;
nurturance of siblings is *more* frequent than that of mothers.

These comparisons show above all what one might reasonably expect to find on the reverse side of the coin that we saw on comparing modes of action by different classes of associates. More frequent dominance by adults (than children) is complemented now by more frequent submission to adults, and by more frequent compliance with adults, especially with mothers as associates. On the other hand, as if to balance accounts with elders by subjugating youngers, the children evidently dominated child friends more than mothers, who so often dominated them, and also more than teachers. Teachers appear to have evoked more than mothers a kind of "treading easy" policy to judge from the trends indicating lesser resistance and aggression against them. That the children were bolder in resisting their mothers than their child friends goes a little against the prevailing drift of the data, but note that this holds only for mothers, not for any other class of adults, and not for adults en masse. Perhaps mothers generally have learned not to expect reciprocation of their nurturant behavior. Yet they might be surprised to find the evidence reported last above that these children acted less often to benefit mothers than to benefit brothers and sisters, of all people—among our Midwest classes of associates.

Age relationships. Earlier evidence of change with age in frequency of modes of action by associates in relation to the children raises the reverse question as to whether the same holds for modes of action by the children in relation to associates. The data indicate that such is the case, especially in the instances of appeal, compliance, and nurturance.

Going by rank order correlations, we find that, with increase in age of the children:

appeal to all associates *decreases* ($-.61$, $P < .05$);
compliance with all associates *increases* ($.67$, $P < .05$);
compliance with all adult associates *increases* ($.71$, $P < .05$);
nurturance of all associates *increases* ($.64$, $P < .05$);
nurturance of all adult associates *increases* ($.64$, $P < .05$);
nurturance of all child associates *increases* ($.67$, $P < .05$).

Tendencies toward an increase in nurturance of mothers, an increase in dominance over siblings, a decrease in resistance against teachers, and an increase in submission to adults with increase in age are indicated by coefficients ranging from .51 to .80, and all with a P beyond .10.

What we see in these data are in greater part measurements of increasing psychosocial maturity in terms of indices which, at least in Midwest, are widely recognized and endorsed as signs of growing up. Midwest adults to whom we have shown these data tell us that they do expect children to ask for benefit from others less as they grow older, to comply more with requests, especially when these are made by grownups, to help, protect, or give things to others more, to resist their teachers less, by all means, and also to submit (though not in a servile way) to adults more. Some of them have expressed surprise that we do not find aggression decreasing with age of the children. But their advice is that, in general, the rest of this seems about right; and they should know, if anyone without any episode-by-episode data does. There is, in any case, congruence between these data and expectation norms of Midwest's culture.

Yet it remains true that, as in the behavior of associates, certain relationships with age of the children are conspicuous by their absence—or lack of strength. This holds especially for two modes of action which have been prominent in the behavior of the children. We refer to resistance and submission. Resistance against associates in general, against all adults, against mothers, against fathers, against child friends, against siblings varies little in frequency through the age span of the children. It stands in every case in the records of all subjects near the levels represented by the median per cents in Figures 12.7 through 12.9. The same holds for submission to the total realm of associates, to mothers, to fathers, to teachers. There is some indication that, in relating themselves to adults in general, the older children submitted even more often than the younger. With a later purpose in view, however, we note only that, evidently, with increasing age of these children, submission does not go down, and resistance does not go up—or down.

ASSOCIATE BEHAVIOR VERSUS SUBJECT BEHAVIOR.

We have considered in turn action by associates and action by the children. Indications of difference as between the children and their associates have appeared at several points. These indications stand to be clarified and extended by direct comparison of associate behavior with subject behavior.

Figure 12.10 shows the median per cent of all standard interaction episodes in which every mode was judged to occur on each side in the interaction between associate and child. Symbols denote also the significance level of differences found on each comparison.

The picture clearly revealed here is one of more frequent dominance by associates, more frequent submission by subjects, and more frequent appeal by subjects, plus a trend toward greater frequency of nurturance by associates. Otherwise, there are no consistent dissimilarities between the children and all individuals of their total associate realm.

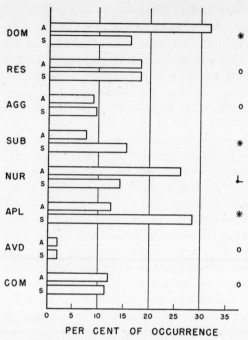

Fig. 12.10.—Modes of action by all associates versus modes of action by the Midwest children. *A* denotes action by associate; *S* action by subject. The symbols on the right refer to significance levels of the represented differences as follows: *, P<.01; L, P<.10; 0, no significant difference.

All possible comparisons of action by our subordinate classes of associates with action by the children reveal differences, with P values as indicated, which demonstrate or suggest that:

dominance by subjects is *less* frequent than by

adults en masse (P< .01),
mothers (P< .05),
fathers (P< .05), or
teachers (P< .10);

submission by subjects is *more* frequent than by

adults (P< .01),
mothers (P< .01),
fathers (P< .05), or
teachers (P< .10);

appeal by subjects is *more* frequent than by

adults (P< .01),
mothers (P< .05), or
fathers (P< .05);

nurturance by subjects is *less* frequent than by

adults (P < .10),
mothers (P < .01),
fathers (P < .05), or
teachers (P < .10);

resistance by subjects is *more* frequent than by

adults (P < .10),
mothers (P < .10),
all child associates (P < .05), or
child friends (P < .05).

This breakdown still leaves dominance, submission, and appeal in the foreground as kinds of behavior in which these Midwest children differed from individuals with whom they interacted. But it also points in each case to adults on the associate side. The children evidently got from adults, and most of all from parents, a good deal more than they gave in dominative behavior, and gave a good deal more than they got in submissive behavior and dependent asking, soliciting, requesting behavior. Not to be overlooked here is the evidence of more frequent nurturance by associates. The children consistently got more than they gave in action for the sake of benefit, again, from adults in particular. Their parents especially were more generous than they with helping, protecting, and outright giving behavior. Finally, there is the evidence of more frequent resistance on the part of the subjects. This appears in the relations of the children with adults, mothers especially, and even more clearly, as earlier data have led us to expect, in their relations with other children.

SUMMARY: PATTERNING OF THE ACTION MODES

The findings now reported on dominance, nurturance, appeal, submission, resistance, compliance, aggression, and avoidance by these eight Midwest children and their associates will not be summarized in serial order. An attempt will be made, instead, to use the main results toward a description of the habitat and behavior pattern involving the children with others of Midwest. Clues to a nuclear part of this pattern are found in certain complementary relationships which appear if one reviews the relative frequency of action modes in the behavior of the children and of grownups with whom they interacted during their recorded days. In examining these and other comparable relationships, we are going to make some inferences about reciprocity of action, i.e., about how the children behaved when adults behaved thus and so. These inferences can be checked only in a later stage of the research begun here when kinds of action by children and their associates are interrelated episode by episode. Meanwhile, however, we want to take beginning steps toward understanding of action interdependencies by building on straight analysis of, first, associate behavior and, then, child behavior in the present total episode population. A background for a more dynamical type of analysis may be developed in this way. The mentioned complementary relationships follow.

Frequent appeal by the children complements frequent nurturance by grownups. It was above all the part of the children to ask, one could say, and about equally often the part of adults to give. There is evident here a dependency relation, with the child as solicitor, petitioner, supplicant, and the adult as grantor, helper, and protector.

Frequent submission by the children complements frequent dominance by grownups. Adults preeminently ordered and directed. The children on their side deferred to adult interdictions and requirements only a little less often than they appealed to adults. There appears in this case a control relation.

These two relations of dependency and control are taken to be fundamental in the pattern of action relationships involving the children with adults.

With a number of qualifications to be stated shortly, we add up only this much plus earlier findings on child power versus adult power to the conclusion that these children lived their days with adults in a benevolent authoritarian regimen, in a complex of social relations with the common authoritarian features of superior power to benefit and dominate realized in actual beneficence and directiveness, on one side, and of inferior power and dependence realized in submission and solicitation, on the other. This regimen had also the characteristic authoritarian feature of centralization, chiefly in mothers and subordinately in teachers among those grownups whose kinds of behavior we have compared, of actualized power, of power actually used in nurturance and dominance. So it appears to have been with these children. But no one can suppose that there has been discovered here a state of affairs unique to Midwest. Any to whom the main outline of the pattern looks strange must live a long way from Midwest. One hypothesis with considerable evidence to support it already is that Midwest adults are on a pipeline of authoritarianism in child rearing which runs through a very much wider culture.

This regimen of the children with adults evidently was not one in which the children were held in close subjection. Its machinery for managing, regulating, supervising, for giving decisions and settling things, for prohibiting and restraining, for imposing conditions and requirements evidently ran smoothly much of the time, for adults often accomplished control, as we know from the high count on submission to them. Yet there was secondary resistance. The children held out against adults only a little less frequently than they gave in to them. This they did most often indeed with mothers, who dominated them most. Frequent resistance, however, need not be considered at odds with the prevailing authoritarian pattern. There are grounds, instead, for confident prediction of such behavior from a social situation of this kind, as experimental studies have shown (cf. Lippitt: **37**).

There is evidence that this regimen of the children with adults was not a highly conflictive one, as more autocratic social arrangements are sometimes found to be. Resistance by the children complements dominance by adults in a negative sense. As what you do to reciprocate if someone else dominates you first, resistance is a kind of contention equivalent to dominance. Yet contention by the children with grownups in the more positive form of dominance itself rarely occurred. These children did not often try to tell their elders what or what not to do. The control relation evidently was too restraining for that. Interactions between grownups and the children were in any case less conflictive because dominance on the child side was relatively infrequent than they would otherwise have been.

This regimen of the children with adults evidently was not narrowly restrictive, muzzling, or oppressive. What we have seen of resistance by the children implies as much. But there is more direct evidence to the same effect under Interaction Sequence in data which have shown that the children behaved with social initiative, that they demonstrated and used freedom to begin things with others as often as their associates in toto, and as often as any grouping of their associates, including adults, and including the most frequently present and dominative of these adults, their mothers. Grownups evidently left to the children freedom to approach them, to lead off, to speak up, to have a say, to call upon them.

Baldwin, Kalhorn, and Breese (**3, 4**) have pointed in a naturalistic study of parental behavior patterns to different types of autocracy in adult to child relations. They distinguish family autocracies in which the elements of indulgence, hostility, and rejection are prominent. We can say that the authoritarian regimen of these Midwest children with adults evidently was not characteristically indulgent or hostile or rejective. As for the first of these possibilities, perhaps it is enough to consider only the finding that resistance by grownups against the children was next in frequency to nurturance in their behalf. Direct evidence against the second possibility will be given under Attributes of Action; but we have already some data to show that adults were not characteristically mean or unkind to the children in the long bar on nurturance of Figure 12.5 and in the short bar there on aggression. Finally, rejection is minimized in the pattern by near absence of adult avoidance.

To summarize, there is in this description of how grownups behaved with these Midwest children, and of how the children behaved, the picture of a beneficent, yet dominative, but not characteristically subjugating, bridling, conflictive, hostile, indulgent, or rejective situation. There is the picture of an authoritarian social regimen which was at the same time a benevolent one.

Some core features of this pattern changed little with increase in age of the children while other more or less central parts of it were modified considerably by the forces of psychological change with development.

The children did not outgrow essentials of the control relation with their adult associates, not in gaining nine years on adults.[4] Dominance by grownups did not go down during these years, and neither did submission to them go down. Nor did resistance by the children against adults go up. Claire Graves at 10 years and 9 months was ordered and directed by grownups as much, while at the same time she gave in to them as much, as Mary Chaco at 1 year and 10 months; nor did Claire resist her elders more. Resistance on the adult side did decrease with age of the children. We cannot say whether this was because the older children ran counter to the wishes of adults less or because adults let them "get away with" more. There is indicated here in either case something of an increase in the liberality of adult control as the children grew older. In its essentials, nonetheless, the basic control relation evidently held firm through the age span of the children.

There remains the dependency relation with its major complementary components of nurturance by adults and appeal to adults by the children. Increase in maturity evidently did not alter it on the associate side, for adult help, gratuities, and protection were extended to the older children no less than to the younger. Claire was acted upon by grownups for the sake of benefit to her as much as Mary for her good. But the behavior of the children here did yield to developmental change. While adults sustained fully their nurturant role with increase in age of the children, appeal to them and others by the children diminished. It appears that the older children got more than they asked for; that adults kept saying in effect, "You need our help, protection, and the things we give you," while the older children were telling them, by not appealing as often as the younger, "We can get along better without you now. We are growing up." Meanwhile, as they gained in maturity, the children gave more to adults instead of asking more from them. The children grew up enough within the span of 2 years to 11 to reciprocate nurturance by grownups while not yet giving them measure for measure of dominance. Their actions apparently began to say as they grew older, "You are still too big for us to boss you, but we can benefit you now." This developing altruistic kind of behavior was not rebuffed. Let alone being receptive to it, the grownups on their side appealed increasingly for benefit from the children, evidently recognizing growth in ability to nurture them and without doubt wanting to avail themselves of this ability, as in getting dishes washed and having playthings put away.

In general, while the pattern of action relationships in which these children were involved with adults apparently did vary in some particulars with increase in age of the children, it appears to have been much the

---

[4] We suppose that it can do no harm here to write for convenience as if the study had been a longitudinal one.

same with respect to the key features of authority and benevolence for all of the children. This brings us, then, to a remaining important question. How is the pattern modified by the substitution for adults of other children as associates? We have indicated reasons to believe that the social regimen of children with children cannot be represented adequately without quite exact specifications as to difference in age between child and child associate which we are not prepared to make with the data at hand. However, some distinctive characteristics of the behavior transactions involving the subjects with their child associates can be briefly reviewed.

In the first place, a control relation is not found in the pattern of action of children with children. Dominance by child associates occurred comparatively often. But it was not complemented on the side of the children by frequent submission. Submission was rather one of the least common kinds of behavior on both sides of the child to child relation. We note at once that one of the *most* common kinds of behavior on both sides of this relation was, *instead*, resistance. And dominance, relatively frequent among child associates, also ranked high among the subjects. So, these children did not give in to other children; they resisted them, or met dominance with dominance. And, vice versa. There is no relation of control on the part of other children over the subjects, or of the subjects over other children. But there would seem to be a well defined social relation here nevertheless, namely, one of conflict. It is a horrible thought that in the long run of human relations conflict is a sure alternative to control, and we do not propose this. Yet these alternatives can be seen in the two patterns here of action relationships involving children with adults versus action relationships involving children with their child friends and siblings. More on this will be said when we reach Interplay Type.

The height of dominance in the pattern free of adults is arresting. It is as if these children took the dominance they got from adults and passed it on when the chance arose, as a fair chance did arise when they got involved with their contemporaries, who in turn seized their equally fair chance to return it or to resist it. As for resistance, there is some indication that the subjects held out against other children more than adults. This one could try to understand as an outcome of the fact that they controlled other children less, with the further consequence that other children tried to dominate them more.

The action pattern involving these children with children does exhibit the dependency relation, with its reciprocals of nurturance and appeal; there is frequent appeal by the children and comparably frequent nurturance by their child associates. Any attempt to interpret this finding is postponed, however, until later study has clarified the consequences for child-to-child action relationships of differences in age between the interacting children.

It is hoped that two purposes have been realized by this review. One purpose has been simply to recast and so to clarify our description, only quantitative *description*, of different kinds of social action by the associates of these Midwest children and by the children themselves. Description is the main aim here, as everywhere in the book. The second purpose of the review has been to derive from the descriptive facts some preliminary conceptions of interdependencies between qualitatively differing actions by associate and child.

A next step, as suggested at the outset, must be to link actions by associate and child an episode at a time. When Midwest adults dominate in episodes, a, b, c, . . . n, what do Midwest children do? With what relative frequency in this case do they submit? Resist? Appeal? Dominate back? Behave aggressively? The same questions can be asked for Midwest mothers, fathers, teachers, for Midwest younger children, older children, children of the same age, etc. One can at least feel somewhat better prepared to attack such questions, with the many complications they are sure to bring, on the basis of the more purely descriptive kind of approach here represented.

MIDWEST VERSUS DISABLED CHILDREN

We have used the Festinger method (18) to test the consistency of differences between the Midwest and disabled children in per cent of episodes scored on each mode of action by associates and subjects.

Differences significant beyond the 5 per cent level show that on the associate side mothers of the disabled children were more often nurturant, and that child friends of these children were more often aggressive while child friends of the Midwest children were more often avoidant. Equally consistent differences show that on their side the disabled children appealed more frequently than the Midwest children for benefit from mothers and also from adults in general, and that the disabled children were more frequently aggressive and resisting, yet more often submissive in their reactions with child associates. The magnitudes of these differences are generally substantial, as indicated by the median per cents of Table 12.14, which restates the per cent comparisons.

Relatively great dependence upon others on the part of the disabled subjects appears here in more frequent action by mothers to aid or protect them and in their own more frequent soliciting of benefit from mothers and other adults. In short, the dependency relation with grownups which we saw in the days of the Midwest children evidently was even more pronounced for the disabled children. Additional inspection of our data indicates, further, that the control relation, with dominance on the adult side and submission on the child side, also held for the disabled children.

We find particularly interesting the findings summarized in Table 12.14 on action relationships between the disabled subjects and their child associates. These results indicate that Wally, Sue, and Verne did not get along with other children as well as the physically normal subjects of Midwest.

They attacked and were attacked by other children, resisted other children, and yet gave in to other children more frequently. All of the child associates of Sue were disabled; all in Wally's day were physically normal. Verne's child associates were about equally divided between the normal and the disabled. In general, these comparisons are suggestive of action relationships in social interactions involving disabled children which invite further investigation.

TABLE 12.14

PER CENT OF INTERACTION EPISODES OF MIDWEST AND
DISABLED CHILDREN IN WHICH DESIGNATED MODES OF
ACTION OCCURRED

Action by Associates	Nurturance by Mothers	Midwest	32
		Disabled	52
	Aggression by Child Friends	Midwest	6
		Disabled	20
	Avoidance by Child Friends	Midwest	5
		Disabled	2
Action by Subject	Appeal to Mothers	Midwest	34
		Disabled	54
	Appeal to Adults	Midwest	30
		Disabled	44
	Aggression Against Child Associates	Midwest	12
		Disabled	19
	Resistance Against Child Associates	Midwest	15
		Disabled	24
	Submission to Child Associates	Midwest	7
		Disabled	12

ACTION MODES AND THE OBSERVER

What modes of action were characteristic of observers in their relations with the subjects? And vice versa? We will use here only data from the Midwest children.

Figure 12.11 shows the relative frequency pattern for modes of action by observers. In mean rank, nurturance stands above all other modes, whereas it stood second in the pattern for participant adults. Compliance is second in rank, whereas it outranked avoidance only in the pattern for participant adults. Dominance is one of the three least frequent modes, whereas it was the most frequent in the pattern for participant adults. These two frequency arrays, the one for observers and the other for participant adult associates, are notably similar in but one particular: in both, resistance is third in mean rank.

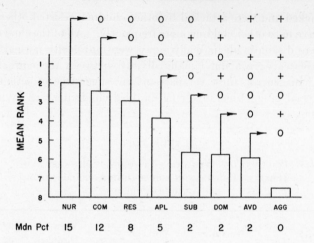

Fɪɢ. 12.11.—Relative frequency of different modes of action by observers in relation to Midwest children. Cf. Fɪɢ. 12.4.

The frequency pattern for action by the subjects toward observers is presented in Figure 12.12. Appeal holds the top position, as it did for behavior toward participant adults. Also, resistance is again third in mean rank. There remain, however, two conspicuous differences. First, whereas submission ranked next to the top among modes of action toward other adults, here it falls to the bottom. Second, whereas nurturance ranked near the bottom among modes of action toward other adults, here it stands next to the top.

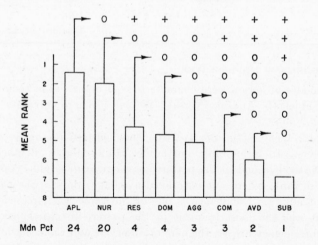

Fɪɢ. 12.12. Relative frequency of different modes of action by the Midwest children in relation to observers. Cf. Fɪɢ. 12.4.

The dependency relation evidently occurred in interactions with observers in that the children in these interactions were given most to appeal while the observers were given most to nurturance.   But the control relation breaks down: observers rarely confronted the children with dominance, and the children rarely submitted to observers.   The high place of dominance in the pattern for participant adults is taken by compliance in the pattern for observers, which suggests greater control of observers by the children than the reverse.   At the same time, frequent submission to participant adults is supplanted by frequent action to benefit observers.   One notes that the children tended more to be helpful and beneficent to observers, who dominated them little, than to participant adults, who dominated them much.

Before considering further these relative frequency patterns, we can compare observers with other grownups mode by mode as to the per cent of episodes in which each kind of action occurred on the associate side and the subject side.   Differences with significance levels as indicated show on the associate side that:

> **dominance** by observers is *less* frequent than by participant adults ($P < .01$);
>
> **nurturance** by observers is *less* frequent than by participant adults ($P < .01$);
>
> **resistance** by observers is *less* frequent than by participant adults ($P < .05$);
>
> **aggression** by observers is *less* frequent than by participant adults ($P < .01$);
>
> **avoidance** by observers is *less* frequent than by participant adults ($P < .05$).

Comparisons on the subject side show that:

> **resistance** against observers is *less* frequent than against participant adults ($P < .01$);
>
> **compliance** with observers is *less* frequent than with participant adults ($P < .05$);
>
> **submission** to observers is *less* frequent than to participant adults ($P < .01$).

In general, these differences fit the role which the observers aimed to play.   Note especially that nurturance, although it ranks highest among modes of action by observers, was found more often in the behavior of other adults, and that resistance, although it ranks near the top among modes of action by and toward observers, was found more frequently on both the associate side and the subject side when the associates were other adults.

A thorough canvass of possible correlations between age of the subjects and either action by or action toward observers reveals no significant relationships which differentiate observers from participant associates.

Also, only one dissimilarity appears when episodes with the observer of the Midwest and disabled children are compared: appeal to an observer was found more often in the episodes of the disabled children. Greater dependency of these physically handicapped children upon others apparently extended even to their relations with the observer, whose place in their situations we now know to have been quite peripheral.

Attributes of Action

AFFECTION, MOOD, AND EVALUATION

Our descriptive scheme defines affection, mood, and evaluation as dimensions of all social behavior that vary independently of the action modes. Each is understood to operate with aggressive or submissive or nurturant action, or any other distinctive kind of interpersonal behavior as a factor in social interplay and climate. Findings on these behavior attributes will be used now to expand and qualify the pattern of behavior relationships which the mode analysis has revealed. We will consider the three variables together, first on the associate side and then on the child side, in the Midwest and disabled children's days.

Behavior of associates. As explained more fully in Chapter X, each variable here confronts us with negative, neutral, and positive behavior on a U-shaped continuum represented by an 11-point scale. Figure 12.13 shows for each of the Midwest and disabled children the median and interquartile range of the ratings on each variable in the behavior of all participant associates. It shows chiefly that associates en masse gravitated generally in their relations with the children to high positive affection, mood, and evaluation: individuals by and large with whom the subjects interacted evidently were given more to feeling for than to feeling against the children, more to happiness than to unhappiness, and more to approval than to disapproval of the children's conduct. For none of the variables does the median rating fall even to the neutral part of the continuum. Only for evaluation, moreover, do we find values of the interquartile range in the minus part of the scale, and this occurs in only 4 of the 11 days. Evaluation shows generally greater variability than affection or mood. This is apparent from inspection for all of the disabled children. The same difference among the Midwest children is significant beyond the 1 per cent level for the comparison with mood, and beyond the 5 per cent level for the comparison with affection. It appears, then, that associates of the children were more steady in affective attitude and in general feeling tone than in approval or disapproval of what the children did.

For the Midwest subjects, the graphs of Figure 12.13 are closely representative of the ratings on different classes of participant associates. All possible comparisons as between different associate classes reveal only two differences, both of them significant beyond the 5 per cent level: child friends consistently exceed mothers in mean score on affection; mothers exceed child friends in variability of affection.

There is scant evidence in the data that affection, mood, and evaluation on the part of the children's associates varied with age of the children. Figure 12.13 gives no such evidence from the behavior of all participant

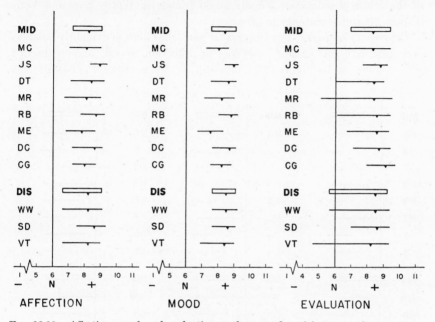

FIG. 12.13.—Affection, mood, and evaluation on the part of participant associates en masse in relation to the Midwest and disabled children. The scales used to measure these attributes of action are represented by the baselines of the three graphs. Points *1* through *5* extend through the negative part, while points *7* through *11* extend through the positive part of each continuum.   The vertical line erected on point *6*, the middlemost value of each scale, stands for behavior classified as neutral with respect to the given variable.   The individual children of the Midwest (*MID*) and disabled (*DIS*) groups are listed in the order of their ages to the left of this line.· Every horizontal bar of each graph extends through the interquartile range of the ratings for a single child or for one of the two groupings of children, with the median rating denoted by an arrowhead which points downward from the bar.

associates.   But the same appears to hold also for subordinate classes of associates, with one exception. There is a tendency, indicated by a rank order correlation of − .62, with a P of .10, toward increasingly negative evaluation by fathers with increase in age of the children. Barring this exception, the Midwest subjects evidently encountered actions by others that were similar along these three dimensions throughout the age span of the children.

It seems reasonable in view of the findings on modes of action to expect differences here between the Midwest and disabled subjects. And there

are dissimilarities, all of which satisfy the Festinger test beyond the
5 per cent level. First, in line with their more frequent nurturant behavior,
mothers of the disabled children show stronger plus affection than mothers
of the Midwest children. Also, mothers of the disabled children show more
highly positive mood. Stronger approval of conduct holds for child friends
of the Midwest subjects. Finally, child friends of Wally, Sue, and Verne
display greater variability in affection.

Behavior of subjects. For the greater part, the children evidently balanced
accounts with participant associates in affection, mood, and evaluation.
This is borne out by Figure 12.14, especially by the medians which it presents.

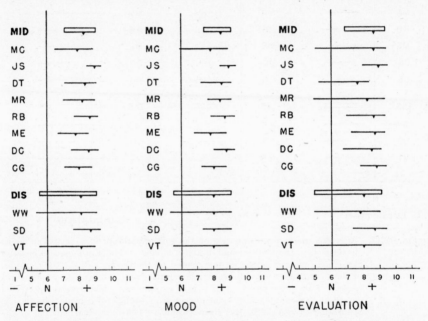

Fɪɢ. 12.14.—Affection, mood, and evaluation on the part of the Midwest and disabled
children in relation to participant associates en masse. Cf. Fɪɢ. 12.15.

The dispersion values on affection and mood do appear to be larger than on
the associate side. So they are for two (Wally and Verne) of the three
disabled children. There is no consistent difference in this direction, however, for the Midwest children. Variability of evaluation stands out less
here than on the associate side. Yet that it varied more in behavior of the
Midwest children than either affection or mood is suggested by a binomial
P of .10.

We found in the behavior of associates greater plus affection for the
Midwest children by child friends than by their mothers. Now, something
of a reciprocal to this appears, for a P of .05 indicates greater plus affection
by the children for their child friends than for their mothers. Two other

differences, each with a P of .05, are found on comparison of different associate classes. First, the subjects show more happiness with other children than with adults. Second, greater happiness with fathers than with mothers appears in behavior of the children with adults.

There is one firm relationship in this area with age, namely, a decrease with age of the children in feeling for child associates: the older the child the lower the mean rating on affection for other children, as demonstrated by a rank order correlation of $-.60$, with a P of .05. A correlation of $-.62$, with a P of .10, suggests also a decline with age in plus evaluation of fathers' behavior, which reciprocates the tendency noted above toward decrease with age in plus evaluation by these fathers of the children's behavior.

Again, there are significant differences between the Midwest and disabled children, each indicated by a P beyond .05 on the Festinger test. This holds, however, only for episodes with child associates. The disabled subjects, like the children with whom they interacted, show greater variability in affection for other children than the Midwest subjects. Also, they show in episodes with child associates greater fluctuation in both mood and evaluation. Further, the Midwest children display higher plus evaluation of conduct by their friends than do the disabled children.

Relations with observers. Observers are found to differ from participant adult associates as to affection, mood, and evaluation in only one way: the ratings indicate greater stability of observer behavior. Comparison of the quartile deviations shows for episodes of the Midwest children in which an observer was the associate, lesser variability in affection, with the significance level of this difference beyond .01, and suggests a like difference in mood and evaluation, with a P in each case beyond .10. Corresponding comparisons show very much the same for behavior of the children toward observers, with the P, .10 for affection and .01 for evaluation and mood.

Observers tried to maintain with the subjects an evenly tempered relationship, free of extremes in emotive behavior of any kind. These data indicate something like this.

PRESSURE

Pressure is a summarizing variable. Subsuming all kinds of used social power, it measures without reference to quality of influence only the amount of influence that one person brings to bear upon another. In what degree did the associates of these children act, whether by commanding, denying, begging, suggesting, cajoling, arguing, teasing, tempting, or doing anything whatsoever, to change the children's behavior? And in what degree did the children act to change the behavior of their associates? These are the present questions. Both have been answered by episode ratings on a scale of five points, plus a zero for all instances in which pressure was not detectable. The answers below should help to consolidate some earlier data. Readers should keep in mind in considering these data that pressure need not be authoritarian. It can be just the opposite, as in begging. It can take any form so long as social influence is wielded in some way.

Figure 12.15 presents for the individual Midwest and disabled children the mean and per cent of the ratings above zero on pressure exerted by all

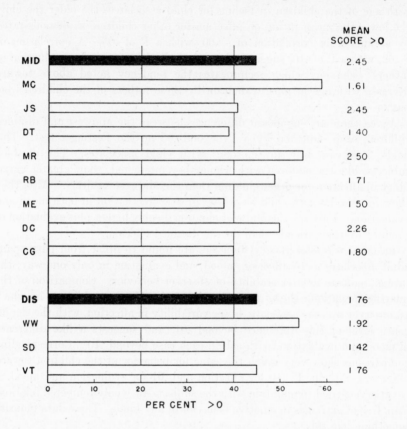

FIG. 12.15.—Pressure by participant associates en masse on the Midwest and disabled children. *MID*, Midwest children; *DIS*, disabled children.

participant associates. It shows that pressure from the associate side was found in 45 per cent of the episodes of the Midwest children, with the per cent for each child ranging from 38 through 59. It shows also that, for those episodes in which pressure greater than zero was detected, the mean rating is 2.4, with the mean for each child ranging from 1.4 through 2.5. Corresponding values of like size hold for the disabled children. One can say that at least minimum pressure was exerted by an associate in a proportion rather near half of the interaction episodes per day of each subject.

We have compared different classes of participant associates as to per cent of episodes in which pressure greater than zero was brought to bear by an associate to find evidence that:

pressure from adults was *more* frequent than from children (P < .05);
pressure from mothers was *more* frequent than from child friends (P < .05);
pressure from mothers was *less* frequent than from teachers (P < .10);
pressure from mothers was *more* frequent than from siblings (P < .10);
pressure from teachers was *more* frequent than from child friends (P < .10).

One is not surprised to discover adults outdoing other children in pressure upon the subjects; nor, in view of earlier findings on relative power, on modes of action, and on evaluation, is one surprised to find mothers prominent among these adults, with none to challenge them but teachers.

Here is one behavior variable for which there is lacking on the associate side any indication of relationship with age of the children. As far as the data tell, pressure on the Midwest subjects from associates of every class was constant through the age span from 2 to 11 years. Apparently, no matter how grownup you are in Midwest, so long as you stay a child, action by others of one kind or another to change your behavior does not waver, up or down. Also, there is no evidence of any consistent difference here as between the Midwest and disabled children.

The mean and per cent of the ratings above zero on pressure exerted by the individual subjects on participant associates en masse are shown in Figure 12.16. This picture will be seen to differ considerably from the corresponding one of behavior by associates. For the Midwest subjects, the mean pressure rating is 1.6, whereas it was 2.45 on the associate side. As for the per cent of episodes in which pressure was judged to occur, differences with P values as indicated show that:

pressure from all associates is *more* frequent than pressure by the children upon all associates (P < .01);
pressure from all adults is *more* frequent than pressure upon all adults (P < .01);
pressure from mothers is *more* frequent than pressure upon mothers (P < .01);
pressure from fathers is *more* frequent than pressure upon fathers (P < .05);
pressure from teachers is *more* frequent than pressure upon teachers (P < .10).

Essentially, the sum of this is that adults brought greater influence to bear upon the Midwest children than the children brought to bear upon adults. Note that the same was not found to hold for child associates.

On the subject side, no consistent differences are found in pressure upon any class of associates as compared with any other. Again, there are no relationships with age of the children; and there are no differences as between the Midwest and disabled subjects. The children evidently got pushed and pulled about by others in varying degree, depending upon who the others were; but they would seem to have distributed their influence about equally among all associates.

There remains the question of pressure exerted upon the subjects by, and by the subjects upon, observers. The data here are clear and simple.

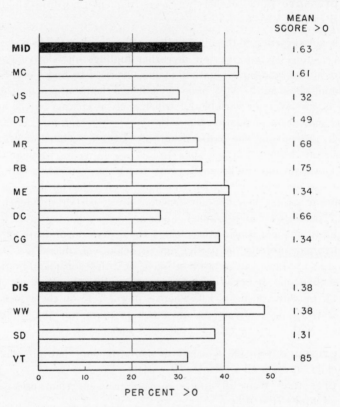

Fig. 12.16.—Pressure by Midwest and disabled children on all participant associates. *MID*, Midwest children; *DIS*, disabled children.

A difference significant at the 1 per cent level shows first, that, observers put less pressure than other adults upon the children. There is no evidence that the children exerted either more or less pressure upon observers than upon other associates of any class. A difference significant at the 1 per cent level does indicate, however, more pressure by the subjects upon observers than by observers upon the subjects—whereas, as we have seen, the reverse held for all classes of participant adults. The bystander position of the observer is demonstrated as clearly here as at any other point.

SUMMARY

The data on action modes revealed a social situation of the Midwest children with grownups which, despite central features of adult control and child dependence, was beneficent. So it appeared to be in the sense that Midwest adults were solicitous of the children's needs. We found in the mode data, moreover, indications that the adult sector of the children's world was not hostile, oppressive, or rejective. But there are grounds now for more positive ascriptions. The data on affection, mood, and evaluation include evidence that the situation of the children with grownups and everyone else was preponderantly friendly, agreeable in feeling tone, and approving. These data include as well evidence that, in general, the same was true of the children's behavior. Marked stability of affection and mood appears in the behavior of both the children and their associates, with approval or disapproval of conduct characteristically more erratic, especially on the associate side.

Some variations in these action attributes with change in associate and with age of the subjects was found on both the associate and child sides in the episodes of the Midwest children. On the associate side, child friends showed more plus affection and greater stability in affection than mothers. The subjects on their side displayed more plus affection for child friends than for mothers. The subjects also showed more happiness with other children than with adults and more happiness with fathers than with mothers. The younger the children the greater was their plus affection for other children. These differences and relationships are well substantiated by the data. Otherwise, except for questionable ups and downs with change in associate and with age of the subjects, affection, mood, and evaluation as attributes of action by Midwest associate and child are remarkable for their stability.

These variables turn out to be sensitive at several points to differences in social situation and behavior as between the Midwest and disabled children. Mothers of the disabled children displayed more plus affection and better mood than mothers of the Midwest children. Child friends of the disabled children showed lesser approval of conduct and greater instability in affection. The disabled children themselves showed, in relations with child associates, greater variability than the Midwest children in affection, mood, and evaluation; and, like their child friends, they showed in these relations lesser approval of conduct by the other person. A general impression created by these data together with earlier findings on modes of action is that other children tended to be storm centers for the disabled children and that, in line with behavior widely expected of mothers, the mothers of Wally, Sue, and Verne were warm and pleasant storm ports. Concerning the last point, we mention again that one of the "mothers" here, Sue's, was in fact a staff member at Lawton, selected as a mother surrogate.

The findings on pressure point again to a control relation between Midwest adults and the Midwest children. Also, they bring us back full circle to the data on relative power by showing that associates of the children who had the greatest power used the most. These associates were adults in general and, in particular, mothers and teachers. Adults surpassed other children in pressure, mothers and teachers surpassed all other classes of associates, and all of these brought more influence to bear on the children than the children on them. On neither the associate side nor the child side does there appear to have been change in this factor with increase in age of the children or any difference as between the Midwest and disabled children.

Findings on behavior by and toward observers in terms of affection, mood, evaluation, and pressure conform generally to the role of nonparticipant onlooker which the maker of a specimen record is expected to fill.

Social Interplay

In what ways did these children and their associates *interact* and with what relative frequency did different kinds of interaction occur? We have drawn answers to this question from parts of the foregoing data on behavior of the children and behavior of their associates. But there remain more direct findings on the process of interaction between associate and child as a special object of description.

Conflict, disjunction, unfriendly rivalry, coöperation, conjunction, and friendly rivalry are the kinds of interaction on which we have data—from the category, Interplay Type. The principal features of each of these may be summarized as follows from discussion in Chapter X. Where associate and child are involved in

conflict	the action of each disagrees with the wants of the other, and the two actions are mutually opposed;
disjunction	the action of each or of either one is contrary to the wants of the other, but the two actions are not mutually opposed;
unfriendly rivalry	both jointly elect the same activity or comparable activities, each tries to outdo the other, and the action of each disagrees with the other's wants, so that neither wants the other to compete;
coöperation	both jointly elect the same activity, each adopts the end of this activity as a common goal, both subordinate other goals, the action of each agrees with the wants of the other, with the total effect that the two actions tend to be mutually supporting;

conjunction   the action of each agrees with the wants of the
                    other, and the action of one may, yet need not,
                    support that of the other (as in gratuitous help-
                    ing), but the two actions are not mutually
                    supporting;

friendly rivalry   both elect the same activity or comparable
                    activities, each tries to outdo the other, and the
                    action of each agrees with the wants of the
                    other in such a way that each wants the other
                    to compete.

This listing overrides the fundamental dichotomy of compatible and incompatible actions on the part of interacting individuals. There are incompatible actions in conflict, disjunction, and unfriendly rivalry as against
compatible actions in coöperation, conjunction, and friendly rivalry. As
for the different forms of rivalry, we have combined them in the analysis
represented in Figure 12.17 below. It has seemed meaningful to do this
in view of the competition element which they have in common. Also,
the frequency of each form proved to be so low as to make the more refined breakdown unprofitable.

Figure 12.17 shows the relative frequency of the interplay types in all
interaction episodes of the Midwest children. It can be said, to begin with,

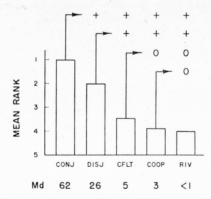

FIG. 12.17.—Kinds of interplay between Midwest children and all participant associates.
CONJ, conjunction; *DISJ*, disjunction; *CFLT*, conflict; *COOP*, coöperation.
For other conventions, see FIG. 12.4.

that the total frequency array is quite consistent from child to child. This
is demonstrated by a W coefficient of .88, significant beyond the 1 per cent
level. Here, then, is a fairly representative picture of some important ways
in which the Midwest children got involved with others.

Conjunction is definitely foremost among the different kinds of interaction.
This ordinary social intercourse without joint enterprise but with "a meeting

of minds" ranks first in frequency in all of the eight days, and the median per cent of episodes in which the analysts found it stands at 62. Disjunction ranks second, with the median per cent down to 26, while conflict ranks third, with a median of only 5. Readers may be surprised to note that conflict was found in no more than about 5 of every 100 episodes. Coöperation follows in mean rank. It is not outranked by conflict, however, with significant consistency from child to child. This leaves friendly and unfriendly rivalry, both of which together account for less than 1 per cent of all interactions involving the Midwest children.

One sure indication of these data is that episodes in which the actions of Midwest associate and child were compatible exceeded by far those in which the contrary was true. Added, the per cents for conjunction, coöperation, and friendly rivalry, show that approximately two-thirds of all standard interaction episodes in the eight days of the Midwest subjects were judged to involve the children in compatible action relationships. Yet there are to be considered as far from negligible the episodes of the remaining near one-third, some 900 of them, more than 100 per recorded day, in which incompatible actions were found.

We have drawn pictures like that of Figure 12.17 for interactions of the Midwest children with adults and for their interactions with children. Both resemble Figure 12.17 so closely that their reproduction here would serve no purpose. The frequency pattern for interplay with associates in general, then, can be taken to represent our findings on the Midwest subjects' relations with both grownups and contemporaries.

In exploring relationships between kind of interaction and associate identity, age of the Midwest children, and physical disability, we have confined attention after some experimenting to the special dichotomy of conflict and harmonious interplay, with the latter combining conjunction, coöperation, and friendly rivalry. Comparisons and correlations made on this basis yield some results of interest.

As for comparison of different associate classes, trends are found in differences with a binomial P beyond .05 which suggest that:

> **conflict** with children is *more* frequent than with adults;
> **conflict** with mothers is *more* frequent than with teachers;
> **conflict** with child friends is *more* frequent than with teachers;
> **harmonious interplay** is *more* frequent with fathers than with mothers.

We have been prepared for the data here on conflict by findings on modes of action. One could expect greater frequency of conflict with adults than with children from the evidence for more frequent counterdominance and less frequent submission by the subjects in their relations with child associates. One could expect greater frequency of conflict with mothers than with teachers from the evidence for more frequent aggression and resistance against mothers than against teachers; and the lesser conflict with teachers than with child friends is understandable on similar grounds. The greater frequency of harmonious interplay with fathers than with mothers also seems consistent with earlier data, inasmuch as mothers of the Midwest children have stood out repeatedly as carriers or recipients of relatively stressful social action.

There is a clear case for decrease in conflict with child associates with increase in age of the Midwest children. This relationship is demonstrated by a rank order correlation of -1. Also, a correlation of $-.57$, with a P of .10, suggests a decline with age in conflict between the children and adults. These findings can be added to earlier evidence, especially in the data on action modes, of greater psychosocial maturity in the older children.

Only one difference is found here on comparison of the Midwest and disabled children: greater frequency of harmonious interplay with child associates appears among the former. This difference, which is significant beyond the 5 per cent level, strengthens evidence from the data on action by child and associate that the Midwest subjects got along better with other children.

One would expect relatively little conflict and at least hope for comparatively harmonious relations between observers and the children. So it turns out consistently. Differences significant beyond the 1 per cent level show less frequent conflict and more frequent harmonious interplay in observer episodes than in episodes with participant adults. In five of the eight days of the Midwest children, conflict with observers did not occur at all, and in no case did it occur in more than 3 per cent of all interaction episodes. The median per cent of harmonious interactions with observers was 88.

ACCORD

Accord provides a synoptic measure of harmony or disharmony in social interaction by means of an 11-point scale which extends from maximally disharmonious relations through a neutral point to maximally harmonious relations.

Figure 12.18 shows the mean and interquartile range of the ratings on accord with all participant associates for each of the Midwest and disabled children. The mean ratings, which do not fall below point 8 on the scale or rise above point 9, restate in terms of degree the evidence just seen for predominantly harmonious interaction. They indicate also high uniformity among the children in average level of accord. Spread of the ratings into the minus part of the scale is conspicuous, however, for 5 of the 11 subjects, 2 of whom are disabled children. One finds on turning back to Figures 12.13 and 12.14 that a similar spread on both evaluation by associates and evaluation by the child hold for each of the same 5 subjects. In fact, these two figures and the one at hand are generally so much alike as to indicate that *accord* between child and associate and *evaluation* by each of the other's behavior are closely related.

No significant differences or sizeable indications of difference are found on comparison of associate classes in terms of this variable. However, a rank order correlation of .61, significant beyond the 5 per cent level, indicates increasingly harmonious interaction with child friends with increase in age

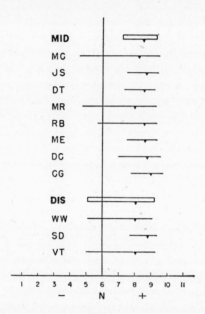

FIG. 12.18.—Level of accord on the part of Midwest and disabled subjects with all participant associates. *N*, neutral relationship; –, minus accord (subject and associate at odds); +, plus accord (subject and associate at one). See FIG. 12.2 for other conventions.

of the Midwest subjects. Also, a difference with a P of .05 points to more harmonious interaction with child friends in the episodes of the Midwest children than in the episodes of the disabled children. These findings are in agreement with those on harmonious interplay and conflict which were reported under interplay type. So also, finally, are comparisons of observers with participant associates in terms of accord.

SUMMARY

The data on social interplay from the categories of Interplay Type and Accord present a picture of predominantly, yet by no means exclusively, harmonious relations between these children and others. Friendly interchange short of coöperation and discord short of conflict respectively were judged to occur at the rates of roughly 60 and 25 episodes per hundred in the days of the Midwest children. In order of mention according to frequency, conflict, coöperation, friendly rivalry, and unfriendly rivalry all were found in small minorities of the Midwest children's episodes.

The data on the Midwest children suggest more frequent conflict with child associates than with adults, with mothers than with teachers, with child friends than with teachers, and more frequent harmonious interplay with fathers than with mothers. They indicate further that: with increase in age of the Midwest children, conflict declined in frequency and interaction became increasingly harmonious in episodes with child associates, while also conflict occurred less often in episodes with participant adults; conflict with child associates occurred more often, and interactions with child friends were generally less harmonious in episodes of the disabled children than in episodes of the Midwest children. All of these results agree with implications of earlier findings on behavior of the children and behavior of those with whom they interacted.

The data include evidence that observers got into trouble with the subjects less often and maintained more harmonious relations with them than other adult associates; the occurrence of conflict evidently was almost negligible and the frequency of harmonious interplay was very high in observer episodes.

Concluding Statement

A resumé of our main findings on social action and interaction is afforded by the summaries beginning on pages 409, 435, 451, and 456 of this chapter. Special attention is drawn to the discussion of patterning of the action modes in the summary which starts on page 435. We believe that an internally consistent picture of psychosocial habitat and behavior in the days of these Midwest and nearby disabled children emerges from these summaries, which will be drawn together in the chapter to follow.

Chapter XIII

Psychological Ecology of Midwest: A Summary

OUR aim in this research has been to describe the psychological living conditions and behavior of the children of the town of Midwest and of some children with physical handicaps living in neighboring communities.

In 1951/52, Midwest was a rural, trading, and government center of 721 people in the central part of the United States. Since its founding almost 100 years before, it had not been directly influenced by cultural forces from outside the country. In this sense it was old American. The town was within one hour's automobile ride of a number of industrial and cultural centers, but few residents commuted to these cities to work. The town had a unity and a completeness of its own; it was the center of life for its inhabitants. Midwest was highly literate and had an advanced level of technological development; it was possible to live a "modern" life within the borders of the town.

In pursuing our aim we have become involved in many problems of methodology. These will not be reviewed in detail here. We shall only mention that it has been possible to discriminate reliably, naturally occurring behavior-situation units of both individual and extra-individual behavior phenomena. These are behavior episodes, each a unit of behavior and situation in the life of an individual person, behavior settings, each an enterable part of the community with a standing pattern of behavior, and behavior objects, each an object with which behavior is transacted in a characteristic way. These three differing foci of description all appear at this time to have a unity and a psychological integrity which make them appropriate for studies in psychological ecology.

Behavior Settings

Behavior settings are perceptually segregated units of extra-individual behavior. They are also community areas which individuals enter and in which they behave in accordance with forces that produce the characteristic behavior pattern. During the survey year there were 585 community behavior settings, and 1,445 family settings in Midwest. The community settings were classified into 107 varieties. During an average weekday about 205 community behavior settings of 70 different varieties occurred in the town. Midwest's residents spent about one-third of their waking time in these community settings, most of the remaining time being spent in the family settings. The amount of time spent in community settings increased from infancy to adolescence, where it amounted to almost half of the waking time of adolescents; it declined in adulthood and old age. The present survey is concerned almost entirely with the community behavior settings of Midwest.

The picture of psychological living conditions and behavior of Midwest children which is provided by the behavior setting survey can be summarized in a number of paragraphs.

In 1951/52, the variety of behavior settings available to Midwest children was limited; it was only a part of the total range occurring in American culture. This is, of course, true for the children of every community. Nevertheless, the children of Midwest had a smaller portion of the total range of American life within their maximal area of locomotion than did many American children. A Midwest child on a Sunday afternoon could not visit an aquarium, ride in a subway, eat pizza in an Italian restaurant, or attend a chamber music concert. Opportunities for highly specialized training and experience were not available in the town.

The actual variety of psychological situations and behavior in which individual Midwest children engaged was, nevertheless, great. It may have been greater than that of children living in cities. A highly literate and technologically advanced segment of American life was represented in Midwest. Because this rich segment occurred within a small geographical area, because there was relatively little specialization within the behavior settings, and because there was pressure to enter many settings, Midwest children participated in a wide range of psychological situations and they engaged in a great diversity of behavior.

The factor of pressure was especially important here. The community behavior settings of Midwest were not neutral behavior areas, but demanded in different degrees the participation of Midwest citizens. However, the 585 behavior settings had the "use" of only 721 people; the average Midwesterner was, therefore, under pressure to participate in a number of settings. In fact, during 1951/52, he participated in positions of trust and responsibility in 7 community settings. This is what we have called the town's ratio of performances (responsible positions) to performers (total population), i.e., the Pa/Pe ratio. It is a measure of the responsible participation of the citizens of a community in nonfamily activities, and, considered in connection with the variety of behavior settings, it is a measure of the multiformity and richness of life for the individual citizens.

Incomplete evidence provides a basis for the hypothesis that the Pa/Pe ratio declines in American society as community size increases beyond that of Midwest. In Midwest, at least, the Pa/Pe ratio of 7 indicated that most citizens participated responsibly in a wide variety of the behavior patterns of the town. This was true not only for adults; it was also true for children. Each child of Midwest engaged in an average of 9 performances during the survey year.

The levels of accomplishment of Midwest children were usually lower than those of which they were capable. Because they were under pressure to take part in so many diverse activities, Midwest children were able to attain in few of them the maximal levels of which they were capable. For this same reason Midwest children were valued for general competence, versatility, and willingness to assume responsibilities as much as for outstanding achievement. Midwest's functioning was so dependent upon the coöperation of a relatively large proportion of the eligible population that Midwest value systems could not give highest status to the specialist who restricted his range of activities. Not only did Midwest provide no specialized training at advanced levels for its children, but it probably did not provide as much encouragement to excel as would some subgroups of a city.

Midwest children had to tolerate a wide range of individual differences in the inhabitants of most of the behavior settings they entered, and they had to develop skill in making diverse people fit into the same behavior patterns. The need for participants was so great in relation to the number of inhabitants that selection on the basis of sex, age, social group, intelligence, personality, political beliefs, or wealth was virtually impossible. This tendency was supported by a pervasive democratic ideology. The low degree of segregation meant, further, that most behavior settings had to accommodate a wide range of abilities, motives, and personalities within their standing patterns of behavior. This, in turn, required that children learn early to adjust to a wide range of individual differences. Such adjustment was accomplished partly by special rules and arrangements, but basically it required a great measure of self-control and tolerance.

The lack of segregation in Midwest behavior settings was a factor adding to the richness of life for Midwest children. Not only did they participate in many independent settings with different standing patterns of behavior but, within most of these settings, a wide range of Midwest citizens was present. The old and the young, the rich and the poor, the bright and the dull rubbed shoulders in most settings.

The children of Midwest occupied positions of power and prestige; they were not a luxury in the community; they performed essential functions. About one-quarter of all performances in Midwest were by children. Even infants penetrated a few settings to the performance level, and younger school children were joint leaders of some settings. The settings children entered to the performance zones were not primarily those which were created especially for children; in fact, more than half of them were "adult" settings. The meaning of this for the children of Midwest was that their achievements were not relegated to unimportant settings; children had the opportunity to achieve power and status in behavior settings which were generally prestigious.

The freedom, power, and status of Midwest children increased with their age. The territorial range of infants covered 60 per cent of the town's settings; this expanded regularly to 79 per cent in adolescence. The increase in the territorial range of children was a slow, regular process. It usually involved a number of tentative entrances or apprenticeship experiences in each new setting. Furthermore, there was a regular increase with age in the maximal depth of penetration into behavior settings. Growing up in Midwest had advantages in the way of greater freedom, status, and privileges, and these were achieved with infrequent matriculative traumas. Children were, however, subordinate to adults or aged persons in all community settings. Despite their positions of power and prestige, the children of Midwest were subject to the control of adults.

The public behavior areas of Midwest were safe and secure places for the children of the town. Because almost all of the town was familiar, because almost all people (with their idiosyncrasies) were known, because there were few sudden transitions to new positions, because children were not without power in many settings, and because responsible adults were present in all settings, children (and their parents) saw Midwest as a generally safe place.

Children were alert in Midwest. On a usual day, a Midwest school child entered only about 8 per cent of the town's available behavior settings. At any moment, the town contained parts which were unknown to him, and each new behavior setting he entered was likely to contain conditions and forces which he did not anticipate. Midwest was, therefore, not without the surprising and the unforeseen. It required of its children some degree of alertness and some readiness for quick adjustment.

On the other hand, as we have noted above, almost all of Midwest's community behavior settings were generally familiar to most inhabitants of the town. For most school children, the scope of the daily habitat was related to the area of familiarity and to the totality of behavior settings in approximately the ratio 1:10:12. This relationship of the directly apprehended, the familiar, and the total community scope appeared to provide most children of Midwest with both stimulation and security.

Midwest provided its children with a general behavioral context in which sociability, play, work, and education dominated the behavioral landscape. Government, religious, artistic, and nutritional activities were less prominent, but still clearly perceptible. Actions concerned with physical health, orientation, personal appearance, and philanthropy were minor, but by no means imperceptible features of the behavior landscape of Midwest. This was the general behavioral context which Midwest provided for its children. The action patterns most prominent in the territorial range of infants were sociability, play, eating and drinking, religion, and art. The emphasis changed slowly and consistently throughout childhood, adolescence, and adulthood to old age where behavior concerned with sociability, work, play, and government were most prominent. This change can be characterized as a movement from less reality-bound behavior patterns in early childhood to more reality-bound behavior patterns in old age.

Midwest provided its children with a general context of behavior mechanisms in which thinking, gross motor activities, and manipulation were dominant over looking, listening, and affective behavior. Active coping with the real world was dominant over passive viewing and feeling. The behavior mechanisms most prominent in the territorial range of infants were talking, affective behavior, and thinking. The emphasis slowly and consistently changed throughout childhood and adolescence to adulthood and old age where thinking, gross motor activity, and manipulation were most prominent. As with action patterns, this may be characterized as a shift from behavior relatively little concerned with reality to behavior primarily involved in coping with the real world.

The community behavior settings of Midwest presented children with a picture of males and females in positions of power with about equal frequency; but with males more often in the highest positions; of social group members about equally powerful in toto, but with a greater *proportion* of Group I members in the highest positions; and of Negroes in peripheral positions.

Data from the Lawton School for physically disabled children reveal a number of differences between this institution and Midwest in behavior settings: (*a*) Behavioral variety was greatly restricted both for Lawton as a whole and for the individual pupils. Lawton's 57 behavior settings were too meager to provide much potential variety, and the Pa/Pe ratio of 2.4 indicates that the responsible participation of Lawton children in the available behavior patterns was, in fact, low. (*b*) Lawton provided great security, but little need for alertness; the new and the unexpected were infrequent at Lawton. (*c*) Children had lower status in Lawton; there were no settings where children penetrated to Zones 5 or 6 (joint or single leaders); they achieved the position of performers only in children's settings. (*d*) Growing up in Lawton had few advantages so far as increased freedom was concerned. All ages from younger school children to adolescents had essentially the same territorial range, and the same depth of penetration. (*e*) At Lawton, action pattern characteristics differed markedly from those of Midwest. Except for sociability and recreation, which were of highest prominence in both places, Lawton was characterized by a reversal of the prominence of action patterns. Those concerned with nutrition, physical health, and personal appearance were the dominant behavioral figures, and business, earning a living, government, and religion were of very low visibility.

Behavior Objects

Behavior objects constitute a transition between behavior settings and behavior episodes. They are conceptually allied to behavior settings but, in this investigation, are identified and enumerated in terms of their occurrence in the behavior episodes of specimen records. Behavior objects are the counterparts with respect to things, of behavior settings with respect to regions.

Behavior objects in three specimen day records, each on a different child, were studied. The three children were roughly comparable in age and general cultural background; they differed in sex (Mary vs. Raymond and Bobby), physical normality (Bobby vs. Mary and Raymond), rural-urban residence (Bobby vs. Mary and Raymond), and season of the year the observations were made (Bobby vs. Mary and Raymond). It will be noted that Bobby differed from the other two subjects on three of these four physical-cultural variables, Mary differed from the others on one of them and Raymond was the deviant member on none of them.

The three children transacted behavior with many objects. Mary, Raymond, and Bobby, in the course of a day used, respectively, 571, 671, and 749 different objects, involving 1,882, 2,282, and 2,490 separate behavior transactions. A different object entered the habitats of the subjects every 1.5, 1.2, and 1.0 minutes; and transactions occurred, on the average, every 28, 21, and 18 seconds. The rate of object transactions per unit of time declined cyclically throughout the day for each of the three subjects, with the peak rate occurring in the middle of the day in each record.

Transactions were not equally distributed among the behavior objects. About 2 per cent of the objects were involved in 30 per cent of the transactions. The most common behavior objects in the lives of all three subjects were nonsocial; these were four times as frequent as social behavior objects (individuals). However, object transactions with social behavior objects were about four times as frequent as with nonsocial objects, so that the number of transactions with social and nonsocial objects was approximately equal. Nonfamily social behavior objects were more frequent than family members, but the number of transactions with family members was much the greater. Transactions with the mother numbered 137, 110, and 150, and with the father numbered 20, 80, and 20. Among the nonsocial objects, man-made things were three to six times more frequent than natural ones; about half of the objects were the personal property of the subject or his family; objects having an educational or recreational significance within the culture were frequent, those having a religious significance were low, and those having a nutritional, aesthetic, or personal appearance significance were intermediate in frequency.

The differences between the children in their transactions with behavior objects follow the order of the differences between them on the physical-cultural variables.

The Structure of Individual Behavior

The findings regarding the structure of individual behavior in terms of behavior-situation episodes and their interrelations are based on data for 12

Midwest children from 2 to 10 years old and 4 disabled children within this age range. We shall begin with the children of Midwest.

Each of these children was seen to engage in a great many behavior episodes; the number of things a child did in a day, according to our criteria of episodes, varied approximately from 500 to 1,300. Duration of the episodes ranged from a few seconds to 121 minutes, with more than 70 per cent of them being shorter than 2 minutes.

Most of the episodes did not occur in isolation. Behavior was more often like the interwoven strands of a cord than like a row of blocks in that the molar behavior units often overlapped. In one-half to three-quarters of all episodes in the different records more than one behavior strand occurred at one time. When the behavior was cord-like in this way its strands were limited in number. Only about 10 per cent of all overlapping episodes involved more than two strands. Most of the overlapping was a matter of the intersection of the whole of a short episode and a relatively small part of a longer one. The behavior continuum was cord-like, too, in the sense that overlapping episodes often did not terminate at the same time but formed an interwoven merging continuum. On the average, the transitions of more than half of the episodes were of this kind. Sequences of structurally interrelated episodes, called linkages, averaged about 400 per day. They included up to 81 episodes each, with the median number, 2.3.

Episodes were not always continuous from beginning to end. Two per cent or less of all in each day were interrupted at some point and later resumed after the interpolation of one or more episodes. Not more than 10 per cent of the episodes in any record were interpolated between segments of discontinuous units.

Episodes seen to be spontaneously initiated by the child were about as frequent as those in which some external instigation or pressure was observed. For all of the children spontaneous terminations of episodes were more frequent than instigated and pressured terminations.

The children completed more than 70 per cent of their episodes. Some release of tension was judged to occur in every such case. Episodes with definitely "good" endings (attainment, gratification, or success) occurred in 5 to 19 per cent of the episodes of every record, and episodes with "bad" endings (nonattainment, frustration, or failure) occurred in from 0 to 9 per cent.

With increasing age the structure of behavior changed. The younger children tended to shift from one action to another, to do things sequentially, one at a time, and to abandon episodes before completing them more frequently than the older children, and the latter tended to engage more often in episodes of longer duration, to carry on more than one action at a given time, and to complete a higher proportion of their episodes. We have found it surprising that the frequency of success, failure, and frustration was not related in any way to age among the children, and to find also that age and the spontaneity of episode initiation and termination were not positively age related.

A surprising and significant result is the absence of clear-cut evidence that the physically disabled children differed appreciably from the normal children of Midwest in behavior structure. There are only suggestions that more interpolated episodes and more instigated initiations and terminations may have occurred in the days of the disabled children. The second of these indications may be attributable to the more adult-permeated living conditions under which most of the disabled children lived.

Some general comments may be made regarding these results. Many structural characteristics of behavior varied widely from subject to subject; here is an area of great individual differences. In some characteristics, however, the differences are small despite a wide range of age and physical status. The predominance of completed episodes and "good" outcomes over incompleted episodes and "bad" outcomes is in accord with data from the behavior setting survey which indicate that life was in general, satisfying for Midwest children. The absence of clear structural differences between the normal and disabled children, particularly the lack of differences with respect to completion of episodes and with respect to success, failure, frustration, and gratification seems to carry two important implications: (a) the structure of behavior in terms of episodes is centrally, not peripherally determined; (b) the outcome of behavior episodes in so far as it is related to release of tension, success, failure, frustration, etc., is in children virtually unrelated to motor and intellectual abilities. The fact that the 2-year-olds and the 10-year-olds, the physically disabled and the normal children were perceived to experience the same episode outcomes would seem to indicate that some governing apparatus is functioning to protect the weak and disabled from too great psychological consequences of their limitations.

Social Action and Interaction

Analysis of the social components in some 10,000 episodes of eight Midwest children, divided equally as to sex and social group, and distributed in age from 2 years through 10, has revealed a number of facts and relationships in the area of social action and interaction. A day of episodes in the life of each child was studied.

The psychological habitats of the children were predominantly social in that well over half of the episodes in every day involved the child in relations with an associate. Also, the social parts of these episodes generally outranked the nonsocial in potency and, where social and nonsocial episodes overlapped, the former were almost always of greater relative weight. So the days of the children were both extensively and intensively social. In about one-fifth of all social episodes, action by the child in relation to an associate met with no reaction. In all remaining social episodes, however, behavior

occurred in response to what the child did. Thus, a complete social interaction took place in approximately four-fifths of the social episodes. Associates of the children were usually single individuals rather than groupings of
two or more individuals. All of the findings now to be reviewed, with the
exception of those at hand on associate identity, are based upon analysis of
4,661 episodes with superior potency of social parts and high relative weight,
in which a single individual and the child did interact.

Associates of the children were adults much more often than children.
They were mothers most often. Episodes with mothers as associates
exceeded those with fathers on the order of three to one. Among adults,
teachers participated in the second largest number of episodes. These statements exclude observers who will be left out of account here by reason of
their chiefly methodological significance.

Greater rated power of associates was a generally prevailing rule of the
children's social situations. Frequent exceptions occurred only when the
associate was a child of an age equal to or under that of the subjects; the rule
held firm for interactions with adults, who consistently far outweighed the
children in power. Yet the children did not characteristically wait for
associates of any class to "take the lead." All of them initiated about half
of their behavior transactions with others of every associate class. Interaction between associate and child, however started, continued beyond a
single act and response much more often than not; involvement of the
children with others was cyclical in this sense in about two of every three
interaction episodes.

Data on eight modes of action in behavior of the children and their associates are summarized in Tables 13.1 and 13.2, both of which list prototypic
verbalizations of these different action modes. Table 13.1 represents the

TABLE 13.1

MODES OF ACTION BY MIDWEST CHILDREN AND THEIR ADULT ASSOCIATES

Mode of Action		Associate Side	Child Side
Dominance:	Quiet! Quiet!	*****************	****
Nurturance:	Let me help you	*************	****
Resistance:	No	******	********
Appeal:	Please	*****	***************
Compliance:	I will	*****	******
Aggression:	Take that!	***	***
Submission:	I give in	**	***********
Avoidance:	You repel me		*

NOTE.—Each row of symbols represents the number of occurrences of a mode in every 50 episodes. For
example, the row of symbols on the child side and opposite dominance shows that in 4 episodes of every 50,
dominance occurred in behavior of the children with adult associates. The data are based on analysis of
4,661 episodes of eight specimen day records.

frequency of each mode of action by, and of the children toward, adult
associates, while Table 13.2 does the same with reference to child associates.

The asterisks show the number of occurrences of each mode on the average in every 50 episodes. These schematic approximations tell their own story. Several generalizations emerge from facts which they express.

It appears that the children lived their days with adults in a benevolent autocracy. Evidence for this lies in salient complementary relationships between adult behavior and child behavior. Adults were often dominative, while the children often submitted to adults. Grownups, then, frequently controlled the children in an authoritarian way. The children often appealed to adults, while adults were often nurturant. Thus, grownups frequently acted to benefit the children who, at the same time, showed dependence by their frequent solicitation of benefit. The regimen of the children with adults had also the common authoritarian feature of centralization, most of all in mothers, and next in teachers, of power used in dominance and nurturance; the autocracy was matriarchal.

This benevolent autocracy was not characteristically subjugative or bridling, for the children resisted adults only a little less often than they submitted to them, even in interactions with mothers, who dominated them most. Furthermore, in some episodes, the children did attack or act to dominate grownups; resistance, dominance, and aggression occurred either singly or together in 30 per cent of the children's interactions with adults. Also, by initiating roughly every other interaction with a grownup, as with all others, the children exhibited freedom to approach and call upon their elders, to lead off, speak up, and have a say with them. Grownups did not cow the children.

This autocracy was not characteristically indulgent, for adult resistance ranked just below adult action to benefit. Nor was it hostile, as the high frequency of nurturance and the rarity of aggression by adults imply, to say nothing of independent evidence that the children got from grownups much more approval and plus affection than disapproval and minus affection. Neither was the adult-over-child situation characteristically rejective, to judge from the virtual absence of avoidance by adults. Nor was it conflictive in the particular sense that the children frequently met dominance with counterdominance. Also, there was little outright aggression on either side.

Turning now in Table 13.2 to the action pattern of the children with children, we note first that it is not featured by an authoritarian control relation. Child associates were quite often dominative. But the children were by no means commensurately submissive. On the other hand, they were frequently resisting. And they showed even somewhat more dominance than their friends and siblings. Thus, instead of submitting to contemporaries, the children held out against them or countered their dominative behavior. The children were given much more to contention in general with other children than with adults, who were more powerful; dominance, aggression, and resistance occurred in 52 per cent of the episodes with other children. This could mean that impulses to contend against strong authority were transferred to weaker associates. Something of a dependency relation does appear in the pattern of action involving the children with children; for frequent appeal by the children complements frequent nurturance by child associates. Differences in age between child and child associates may account for this relationship, but episode by episode data on these differences are not now available.

We have seen that the mode-of-action picture, while it does show adult control and child dependence, also reveals beneficence in the social situation of the children with adults. Rounding out this picture, data on affection, mood, and evaluation as attributes of all social behavior disclose a characteristically friendly, pleasant, and approving situation with grownups, and

TABLE 13.2

MODES OF ACTION BY MIDWEST CHILDREN AND THEIR CHILD ASSOCIATES

Mode of Action		Associate Side	Child Side
Dominance:	Quiet! Quiet!	*******	************
Nurturance:	Let me help you	**********	*********
Resistance:	No	************	********
Appeal:	Please	******	*********
Compliance:	I will	***	***
Aggression:	Take that!	****	******
Submission:	I give in	******	***
Avoidance:	You repel me	**	*

NOTE.—See legend under Table 13.1.

others as well. These data show also that the children generally gave what they got from all others in affection, mood, and evaluation. Although much more often approving than disapproving, evaluation of the children by their associates, and vice versa, varied a great deal more than affection and mood on the part of both associate and child. Social pressure, as a fourth basic attribute of social action, was exerted on the children by their associates in nearly half of all interaction episodes, but on associates by the children in only about one-third of these episodes. This, one might easily expect from the findings on relative power. Also, in line with the power findings, adults outdid child associates, while mothers and teachers surpassed associates of every other class, in bringing pressure to bear upon the children.

So much for action by the children and action by their associates. This leaves interaction per se as a social process. Harmonious types of interaction (conjunction, coöperation, and friendly rivalry) outnumbered disharmonious types (disjunction, conflict, and unfriendly rivalry) about two to one. The most frequent single kind of social interplay was conjunction, defined as friendly interaction short of coöperation, which occurred in 60 of 100 interaction episodes; and the type next in frequency was disjunction, or discord short of conflict, which occurred in 25 interaction episodes of every

100.   In only 5 interactions per 100 did the children get into outright conflict with associates.   But, on the other hand, full fledged coöperation occurred in but 3 interactions per 100.   Friendly and unfriendly rivalry together account for just 1 interaction per 100.   On the whole, these Midwest children got along quite impressively well with others.   This fact is summed up by the finding that, on a scale (for accord) of 11 points, which extends from extremely disharmonious to extremely harmonious social relations, the mean rating on every child falls between 8 and 9.

Some of the ways in which the pyschosocial habitat and behavior of the children differed according to class of associate have been mentioned. But several other such differences remain.

Adults surpassed all child associates, mothers exceeded both child friends and siblings, while teachers surpassed child friends in power over the children as well as in frequency of measurable pressure exerted upon them.   Further, teachers exerted pressure at a higher rate than mothers.   Pressure from associates en masse, from adults, from mothers in particular, and from fathers was more frequent than pressure by the children upon each of these.

As for modes of action, adult associates exceeded child associates, and mothers exceeded child friends, in frequency of dominance.   At the same time, the children submitted more often to adult than to child associates, and to mothers more often than to child friends.   Also, the children understandably gave in to mothers more frequently than to siblings.   Child friends avoided the children more often than did mothers.   The children complied with adults more frequently than with other children, and yet resisted adults more often than child friends.

Direct comparison of associate behavior with behavior of the children in terms of action modes shows *dominance* by the children less frequent than by adults en masse, mothers, and fathers; *submission* by the children more frequent than by all adults, mothers, fathers, and teachers; *appeal* by the children more frequent than by all adults, mothers, and fathers; *nurturance* by the children less frequent than by mothers and fathers; *resistance* by the children more frequent than by their child associates.

Child friends of the children displayed greater and more stable affection for them than did their mothers while, as if to reciprocate, the children showed greater affection for child friends than for their mothers.   Yet they got into conflict with child associates more frequently than with adults in general.   Also, they got into conflict with mothers and child friends more often than with teachers.   They were happier, too, with child friends than with adults in general.   They were happier with fathers than with mothers; and their social interplay was more often harmonious with fathers than with mothers.

Some of the variables in this analysis of social action were related to the age of the child.   With increase in age of the children there occurred: a gain in the complexity of social partners as shown by an increase in groupings of two or more individuals as associates; a decrease in the frequency of adults and especially of parents as associates; an increase in child associates among whom, moreover, the proportion of children younger than the subjects rose; an increase in amount of power and in fluctuation of power from episode to episode in relations with associates en masse; a definite power gain in interactions with other children; a decline in the frequency of cyclical interplay with adults; a decline in resistance against the children by grownups in general and mothers in particular; a partial change in the relation of dependency upon adults, marked by a decline in appeal to grownups without loss, however, in nurturance of the children by grownups; a gain in action to benefit adults and also a gain in appeal by adults to the children; an increase in action by the children to benefit child associates; an increase in compliance with associates en masse and with adults in particular; a decrease in avoidance of adults and especially of mothers; a gain in momentary liking for other children; an increase in harmonious relations and a decrease in conflict with other children, and a decrease in conflict with adults. Psychologists have known that development brings change in social situation and behavior. Here are intelligible measurements of such change under naturally occurring conditions.

Findings from three day-records on disabled children were compared with the findings from the eight records on Midwest children. A number of differences emerge from the comparisons.

Relatively great dependency of the disabled children appeared in more frequent nurturance by their mothers and more frequent appeal to these mothers and to the generality of adults. Mothers of the disabled children displayed greater affection and better mood than mothers of the Midwest children.

Child friends of the disabled subjects were more often aggressive, while the disabled subjects themselves also were more often aggressive and resisting, yet also more frequently submissive as well, with all child associates. Child friends of the disabled were less approving and less steadfastly affectionate. The disabled children, in their relations with child associates, showed greater variability in affection, mood, and evaluation and, like their child friends, lesser approval of action by the other person. Conflict with child friends occurred more often, and interaction with these friends was generally less harmonious in the episodes of the disabled children. In general, child associates were stress centers for the disabled children, while their mothers were centers of relief from stress. Our data do not indicate that the serious physical disabilities of these children had consequences for the other psychosocial variables of the study.

Postscript

As we come to the conclusion of this study, two lines of thought are uppermost in our minds. One is concerned with *methods* of psychological ecology.

Early in the research we had to choose whether to concentrate our resources on methods or on problems. We chose to do the latter. We adopted the policy of dealing with methodological issues, and especially with techniques to the smallest extent necessary for the ecological problems before us. We did this in the belief that the perfection of scientific methods more profitably follows than precedes their initial application to a problem. The reader will know that even with this limitation we have had to give much attention to methodology. However, we have had to leave many problems of method unsolved and many untouched. If psychological ecology, as we have defined it, expands as an area of investigation, much research directed at methods and techniques will be required.

The other line of thought pertains to the *problems* of psychological ecology. At each turning of the trail of exploration we have followed, we were confronted with alternative problems. Some of them we investigated, and we have reported what we found; but most of them we have had to pass by or explore only partially because science is long and time and energy are short. We will resist the temptation to tell what we might have done, what we started to do but did not complete, and what we see to do in the future. Some of this is reported elsewhere (**6, 7, 8, 9, 10, 30, 44, 50, 51, 53, 61, 62, 63, 64**). Every reader will have his own ideas on the last point.

When we look back over what has been said here about Midwest children and their circumstances and behavior, much of it sounds like American children almost anywhere, as far as one can tell by living in some different parts of the country, by reading *Tom Sawyer* or even Herman Wouk's *The City Boy*, by going to some movies, by visiting schools, by having an American family. But some of it is unique to Midwest. How much, we do not know. We have found little direct aggression by and against Midwest children. Is there more in Brooklyn? Perhaps children of English villages do not start as many as half of their social episodes. Do mothers of Park Avenue in New York spend as much time with their children as do mothers of Midwest? No kind of casual observing can answer such questions. But systematic ecological methods of one kind or another can. We hope, of course, that these and other uses of psychological ecology mentioned in the first chapter and at other places in the volume will eventuate from this and other beginnings. We like to think that the day will come when the psychological situations will be as well mapped as the physical areas of the world, when the regions of psychological underprivilege and advantage will be as well charted as economic levels, when we will know much more of the things men do in their daily lives, and when changes in psychological living conditions and behavior will be as carefully plotted and scanned as changes in birthrate. The data of psychological ecology should be of both theoretical and practical value if these things are accomplished.

References

1. Adams, D. K. A restatement of the problem of learning. *British Journal of Psychology*, 1931–32, **22**, 150–78.
2. Baldwin, A. L. *Psychological development in childhood*. New York: Dryden, in press.
3. Baldwin, A. L., Kalhorn, Joan, & Breese, F. H. Variables of parent behavior. *Journal of Abnormal and Social Psychology*, 1941, **30**, 525–42.
4. Baldwin, A. L., Kalhorn, Joan, & Breese, F. H. The appraisal of parent behavior. *Psychological Monographs*, 1949, **63**, No. 4.
5. Barker, R. G., Dembo, Tamara, & Lewin, K. Frustration and regression: A study of young children. *University of Iowa Studies in Child Welfare*, 1941, **18**, No. 1.
6. Barker, R. G., & Wright, H. F. Psychological ecology and the problem of psychosocial development. *Child Development*, 1949, **20**, 131–43.
7. Barker, R. G., Wright, H. F., Nall, J., & Schoggen, P. H. There is no class bias in our school. *Progressive Education*, 1950, **27**, 106–10.
8. Barker, R. G., & Wright, H. F. *One boy's day*. New York: Harper & Bros., 1951.
9. Barker, R. G., Wright, H. F., & Koppe, W. A. The psychological ecology of a small town. In Wayne Dennis (Ed.), *Readings in Child Psychology*. New York: Prentice Hall, 1951. Pp. 552–66.
10. Barker, R. G., & Wright, H. F. The psychological habitat of Raymond Birch. In J. H. Rohrer & Muzafer Sherif (Eds.), *Social psychology at the crossroads*. New York: Harper & Bros., 1951. Pp. 196–212.
11. Barker, R. G., *et al.* *Adjustment to physical handicap and illness: a survey of the social psychology of physique and disability*. Bulletin No. 55, Revised 1953; New York: Social Science Research Council.
12. Bates, M. *The nature of natural history*. New York: Scribner, 1950.
13. Bingham, H. C. Selective transportation by chimpanzees. *Psychological Monographs*, 1929, **5**, No. 26.
14. Brunswik, E. *Systematic and representative design of psychological experiments*. Berkeley: Univ. of California Press, 1947.
15. Champney, H. Measurement of parent behavior. *Child Development*, 1941, **12**, 131–66.
16. Dollard, J., Doob, L. W., Miller, N. E., Mowrer, O. H., & Sears, R. R. *Frustration and aggression*. New Haven: Yale Univ. Press, 1939.
17. Dootson, Lily Lee. *A riddle book*. Chicago: Rand McNally & Co., 1927.
18. Festinger, Leon. The significance of difference between means without reference to the frequency distribution function. *Psychometrics*, 1946, **11**, 97–105.
19. Frank, L. K. Time perspectives. *Journal of Social Philosophy*, 1939, **4**, 293–312.
20. Gingerilli, J. A. The principle of maxima and minima in animal learning. *Journal of Comparative Psychology*, 1930, **11**, 193–236.

21. Goldstein, K. *The organism: a holistic approach to biology derived from pathological data on man.* Vol. II of series. New York: American Book Co., 1939.

22. Guetzkow, H. Unitizing and categorizing problems in coding qualitative data. *Journal of Clinical Psychology*, 1950, **6**, 47–58.

23. Guthrie, E. R. *The psychology of learning.* New York: Harper & Bros., 1935.

24. Halverson, H. M. The development of prehension in infants. In R. G. Barker, J. S. Kounin, & H. F. Wright (Eds.), *Child behavior and development.* New York: McGraw-Hill, 1943. Pp. 49–65.

25. Heider, F. Ding und medium. *Symposion*, 1927, **1**, 109–57.

26. Heider, F. Social perception and phenomenal causality. *Psychological Review*, 1944, **51**, 358–74.

27. Heider, F. The psychology of interpersonal relations. In preparation.

28. Kendall, M. *Rank correlation methods.* London: Charles Griffin & Co., 1948.

29. Koehler, W. *Mentality of apes.* Translated by E. Winter. New York: Harcourt Brace, 1925.

30. Koppe, W. A. A study in psychological ecology: a survey of the behavior settings of Midwest. Unpublished Doctoral dissertation, Univ. of Kansas, 1954.

31. Kounin, J. S. Intellectual development and rigidity. In R. G. Barker, J. S. Kounin, and H. F. Wright (Eds.), *Child behavior and development.* New York: McGraw-Hill, 1943.

32. Lewin, K. *Dynamic theory of personality.* Translated by D. K. Adams, & K. E. Zener. New York & London: McGraw-Hill, 1935.

33. Lewin, K. *Principles of topological psychology.* New York: McGraw-Hill, 1936.

34. Lewin, K. *The conceptual representation and the measurement of psychological forces.* Durham, N.C.: Duke Univ. Press, Contributions to psychological theory, 1938, **1**, No. 4.

35. Lewin, K. *Field theory in social science.* New York: Harper & Bros., 1951.

36. Lewin, K., Dembo, Tamara, Festinger, L., & Sears, Pauline. Level of aspiration. In J. McV. Hunt (Ed.), *Handbook of personality and the behavior disorders.* New York: The Ronald Press, 1944.

37. Lippitt, R. An experimental study of the effect of democratic and authoritarian group atmospheres. Studies in topological and vector psychology. *University of Iowa Studies in Child Welfare*, 1940, **16**, No. 3.

38. Littman, R. A., & Rosen, E. Molar and molecular. *Psychological Review*, 1950, **57**, 58-65.

39. Luck, J. M. Food prices in Palo Alto. *Science*, 1953, **118**, 362–63.

40. McDougall, W. *Outline of psychology.* New York: Scribner, 1923.

41. Mead, Margaret. *And keep your powder dry.* New York: W. Morrow & Co., 1943.

42. Muenzinger, K. F. *Psychology: the science of behavior.* New York: Harper & Bros., 1942.

43. Murray, H. A. *Explorations in personality.* New York: Oxford Univ. Press, 1938.

44. Newton, M. R. A study in psychological ecology: the behavior settings in an institution for handicapped children. Unpublished Master's thesis, Univ. of Kansas, 1953.

45. Novikoff, A. B. The concept of integrative levels and biology. *Science,* 1945, **101,** 209–15.

46. Piaget, J. *The language and thought of the child.* London: K. Paul, Trench, Trubner, & Co., Ltd., New York: Harcourt Brace, 1926.

47. Preyer, W. *The mind of the child, Part I, the senses and the will.* New York: Appleton, 1888.

48. Rickers-Ovsiankina, Marika. Die Wiederaufnahme Unterbrochener Handlungen. *Psychologische Forschung,* 1928, **11,** 302-79.

49. Ruesch, J., Jacobson, Annemarie, & Loeb, M. B. Aculturation and illness. *Psychological Monographs,* 1948, **62,** No. 5.

50. Schoggen, P. H. A study in psychological ecology: a description of the behavior objects which entered the psychological habitat of an eight-year-old girl during the course of one day. Unpublished Master's thesis, Univ. of Kansas, 1951.

51. Schoggen, P. H. A study in psychological ecology: structural properties of children's behavior based on sixteen day-long specimen records. Unpublished Doctoral dissertation, Univ. of Kansas, 1954.

52. Sherman, M. The differentiation of emotional responses. *Journal of Comparative Psychology,* 1927, **7,** 265–84.

53. Simpson, J. E. A study in psychological ecology: the social weather of Midwest behavior settings based on sixteen day-long specimen records. Unpublished Doctoral dissertation, Univ. of Kansas. In preparation.

54. Stern, W. *Psychology of early childhood.* New York: Henry Holt & Co., 1930.

55. Terman, L. M., & Merrill, Maud. *Measuring intelligence.* Boston: Houghton Mifflin Co., 1937.

56. Tiedemann, D. *Beobachtungen uber die Entwickelung der Seelenfahigkeiten bei Kindern.* Altenburg: Oscar Bonde, 1897. First published in 1787. (From Tiedemann's observations on the development of the mental faculties of children. Translated by C. Murchison, & S. Langer. *The Pedagogical Seminary and Journal of Genetic Psychology,* 1927, **34,** 205–30.)

57. Tolman, E. C. *Purposive behavior in animals and men.* New York: Appleton-Century, 1932.

57a. Walker, H. M., & Lev, J. *Statistical Inference.* New York: Henry Holt & Co., 1953.

58. Warner, W. L., Meeker, Marchia, & Eells, K. *Social class in America.* Chicago: Science Research Associates, 1949.

59. Watson, J. B. *Behaviorism.* New York: The Peoples Institute Publishing Co., 1924.

60. Wheeler, R., & Perkins, T. *Principles of mental development.* New York: Crowell, 1932.

61. Wright, H. F., & Barker, R. G. *Methods in psychological ecology.* Lawrence, Kansas: Department of Psychology, Univ. of Kansas, 1950.

62. Wright, H. F., & Barker, R. G. The elementary school does not stand alone. *Progressive Education,* 1950, **27,** 133–37.

63. Wright, H. F., Barker, R. G., Koppe, W. A., Meyerson, Beverly, & Nall, J. Children at home in Midwest. *Progressive Education*, 1951, **28**, 137–43.

64. Wright, H. F., Barker, R. G., Nall, J., & Schoggen, P. H. Toward a psychological ecology of the classroom. *Journal of Educational Research*, 1951, **45**, 187–200.

65. Zeigarnik, B. Uber das Behalten von erledigten und unerledigten Handlungen, *Psychologische Forschung*, 1927, **9**, 1–85.

66. *Dictionary of Occupational Titles. Definitions of the Titles.* Vol. **1**. 2nd Ed.; U.S. Dept. of Labor. Washington, D.C.: Government Printing Office, 1949.

67. Kansas State Board of Agriculture. *37th Biennial Report.* Roy Freeland, Sec., Topeka, Kansas, 1950.

68. Soil Conservation Service and Agriculture Conservation Program. Joint report on Existing Conditions in Midwest County. Unpublished, 1953.

69. *Statistical Abstract of the U.S.: 1950.* U.S. Dept. of Commerce, Bureau of the Census. Washington, D.C.: Government Printing Office, 1952.

70. Traffic Flow Map No. 46, 1950. Midwest County, Kansas. Prepared by State Highway Commission of Kansas, Highway Planning Dept.

71. *U.S. Census of Housing: 1950 I.* U.S. Dept. of Commerce, Bureau of the Census. Washington, D.C.: Government Printing Office, 1952.

72. *United States Census of Population: 1950 II. Characteristics of the Population.* U.S. Dept. of Commerce, Bureau of the Census. Washington, D.C.: Government Printing Office, 1952.

Appendix 1

Twelve Representative Midwest Children

In addition to defining more precisely the children selected for special study, the following sketches will provide a more concrete account of typical family situations than the general, statistical data have been able to provide.

The sketches are given in order of the ages of the children, from younger to older. The following identifying data are given at the beginning of each sketch in this form:

> Code Name (Sex, Social Group, Age)
> Date of Specimen Record; Time of Specimen Record

> Subject: Mary Chaco (F, 2, 1-10)
> Time: October 10, 1950; 7:00 a.m.–9:45 p.m.

Mary Chaco, almost two years old, was pert, small-boned, blond, and brown-eyed. It was possible to understand much of her ready chatter.

Mary's first year of life had been precarious. A severe case of thrush mouth when she was only two weeks old sent her to the hospital and here she was severely burned in a steam tent. There was great anxiety, first for her life, and then for possible deformity. After several weeks in the hospital it appeared that there would be no lasting damage, though her complete recovery was a matter of months.

Mary's father, Gary Chaco, came to Midwest after serving in the Army. He owned and operated his own service station and car repair business. Mr. Chaco was active in the American Legion and was one of the youngest members of the Rotary Club.

Mary's mother, Odessa Chaco, was attractive and efficient. She was an excellent housekeeper, active in the Homemaker's Club, and president of the American Legion Auxiliary. The Norfolks, her father and mother, younger brother and two sisters, lived in Midwest. The Chaco children were often cared for by their grandmother and aunts.

Otto, Mary's brother, was a lively four-year-old.

The Chacos rented a small, frame house close to Mr. Chaco's station. The single bedroom held Mary's crib, Otto's roll-away-bed, and the parent's bed. The kitchen and bathroom were modern and well equipped. Gas stoves heated the house. The living room was attractively furnished; the dining room served as a sewing-play room most of the time. The back yard was about 40 × 50 feet but it blended imperceptibly with the yards of the two neighbors with both of whom Mary was on visiting terms.

Subject: James Sexton (M, 2, 1-11)
Time: February 8, 1951; 7:20 a.m.–8:10 p.m.

At 23 months, Jimmy Sexton was a rosy-cheeked, blond boy with sparkling, brown eyes. He was an only child. Jimmy talked a lot, often in understandable sentences. He was skillful at manipulating such things as door knobs or toy wind-up trucks.

James Sexton, Jimmy's father, was a tall, rangy man in his late twenties. After attending high school in Midwest, James Sexton had gone to State College for a short time until called into the Army. On leaving the Army, he had contracted asthma; this led him to spend a couple of years in Arizona, after which he returned to the old home farm near Midwest and purchased an additional acreage. He married in 1946, and in 1948 rented a house in Midwest from which he operated his two farms. He and his wife sponsored the Methodist Youth Fellowship and he was active in other church groups, the American Legion, and the Masonic Lodge.

Jimmy's mother, Amy Sexton, was a slight, vivacious, blond young woman in her late twenties. She expressed herself forcefully and well. Before her marriage, she finished Midwest High School and attended a radio school in Capitol City. She returned to Midwest to take a position with the Home State Power and Light Company, which she kept until just before Jimmy's birth. She was active in Methodist Church groups, Eastern Star, Homemaker's Club, American Legion Auxiliary, and was a leader of the Brownie Scout Troop.

Jimmy's paternal grandfather and an aunt lived in Midwest. His maternal grandparents lived a few miles east of town on a farm.

The Sextons had a docile, Scottie dog.

The house which the Sextons rented was a white, frame bungalow set in a large yard. A living room, dining room, kitchen, two bedrooms, and a bathroom made up the house. The dining room served as a sewing room for Mrs. Sexton and a play room for Jimmy.

Subject: Lewis Hope (M, 2, 2-11)
Time: November 21, 1950; 7:00 a.m.–9:15 p.m.

Lewis, better known as "Chuck," was almost three years old. He was the third in a family of four children. Chuck was a robust, sturdy child with an unusually friendly, winning manner. He spoke clearly and expressed himself well.

Chuck's father, Lewis Hope, Sr., was in his middle thirties. He was slender, of average height, and had a friendly, confident manner. Mr. Hope was graduated from the State Agricultural College and taught agriculture in a high school before his appointment as instructor in the Veterans Administration Vocational Farm Training Program in Midwest. His teaching career had been interrupted by service in the Navy which included time in the South Pacific. He was a member of the American Legion, the Farm Bureau, and the Presbyterian Church Choir.

The mother, Corrine, also in her middle thirties, was friendly, calm, and gentle. She was graduated from the State University and taught English in a high school for several years before her children were born, and again while her husband was in the service. She was an active member of the Homemaker's Club, American Legion Auxiliary, Home Demonstration Unit, Eastern Star, P.T.A., and the Presbyterian Church.

Stanton, the eldest son, was 10 years old and in the fourth grade. Alma, the only girl in the family, was 8 years old and in the second grade. Ben, the baby of the family, was 11 months old.

The Hope family had a large, yellow cat and a dog as household pets. They also had three calves and one milk cow which were housed in a small barn on their lot and pastured in a neighboring five-acre pasture. Chuck proudly claimed one calf as his own.

The Hopes had lived in Midwest just one year. They owned their five-room, one-story, white frame house. This was the same house in which the Reid's lived at the time of the day study of Margaret. (See p. 370.)

Subject: Dutton Thurston (M, 3, 3-10)
Time: November 3, 1950; 7:06 a.m.–9:16 p.m.

Dutton Thurston, nicknamed Chuck, was 3 years and 10 months old at the time of the day study. He was the youngest in a family of three children. Dutton was a sturdy, active, well-coördinated child. His babyhood had been marred by attacks of asthma which he seemed to have out-grown.

Dutton's most constant playmates were his big dog, Spot, and a kitten, called Inky, which belonged to his sister. No families with children lived near the Thurstons.

William Thurston, Dutton's father, was a slender, medium-tall, man. He had been brought up on a farm in the county and had farmed for most of his life. The Thurstons rented a place just at the edge of Midwest, with something under 60 acres of pasture land. They had several dairy cows as well as a number of pigs, chickens, and horses. Mr. Thurston worked at the Midwest Hardware and Implement Store as a mechanic.

Mrs. Thurston had also been brought up on a farm in the county and had completed high school in a neighboring town. She was president of the P.T.A. and a member of the Homemaker's Club. Mrs. Thurston raised chickens. She worked on Friday mornings and all day Saturday in Cabell's Department Store.

The oldest child in the family was Alfred Thurston, who was graduated from Midwest High School in 1950 where he had starred in football and basketball. He lived at home and was employed as a mechanic at the Midwest Hardware and Implement Store where his father worked. Shirley, 14 years old, was a sophomore in high school.

The maternal grandparents lived in Midwest. Dutton's grandfather worked in Hopkins Feed Store. The paternal grandparents still lived about six miles from Midwest.

The Thurstons rented a big farm house supplied with electricity, but without running water. Heat was provided by kerosene-, wood-, and oil-burning stoves. Dutton shared a downstairs bedroom with his parents, and Alfred and Shirley each had a room upstairs.

Subject: Margaret Reid (F, 3, 4-6)
Time: June 2, 1949; 8:00 a.m.–10:17 p.m.

On June 2, 1949, Margaret Reid was four years and six months old. She was a daintily-built child of average height for her age, had a pleasant disposition and was animated and alert.

Margaret's family was composed of her father, mother, and 18-month-old brother, Bradley. Both maternal and paternal grandparents lived in Midwest and were frequent visitors at the Reid home.

Milton Reid, Margaret's father, was a large-framed, blond young man about 26 years of age. He worked in Kerr's Grocery. Milton Reid's chief hobbies were raising hunting dogs, and hunting with them. He owned 14 dogs which were penned in the Reids' back yard.

Milton and Frances were married soon after their graduation from Midwest High School. He was not in the armed services because of the residual effects of rheumatic fever. Frances Reid, Margaret's mother, was a pretty, vivacious brunette, about 24 years of age. She possessed a beautiful voice, and her singing was often in demand at church and community affairs. She was active in Methodist Church groups and attended the Methodist Sunday School with Margaret and Bradley.

Tiny, a fox terrier puppy, was the children's pet.

The Reids owned their home, which was a one-story, white, frame building consisting of a living room, dining room, kitchen, bathroom, a bedroom for the parents, and a bedroom for the two children. Its location offered plenty of shade and play space. The house was heated with gas stoves.

Subject: Maud Pintner (F, 1, 5-0)
Time: December 5, 1950; 8:26 a.m.–7:44 p.m.

Maud was just a few days over five years old on the day of the study. She had not yet entered school. She was a blond, blue-eyed girl of small, wiry build with more than average agility and pertness.

Maud learned to talk early and, before she was two, knew by heart many nursery rhymes. She often enlivened Sunday-School programs and Ladies' Aid meetings with a recitation or song.

Maud's family consisted of her father and mother, her 20-month-old brother, Frederick, and her maternal grandmother, who was disabled by arthritis.

Charles Pintner, Maud's father, was a dark-haired, slight, easy-going man in his late twenties. He was graduated from the local high school, had a year of college work and some specialized bookkeeping training. After service in the Army, Charles joined his brother-in-law in the abstract business and later took over completely the operation of that office. Charles Pintner belonged to the American Legion and sang in the Presbyterian Church Choir.

Della Pintner, Maud's mother, was in her late twenties. She married Charles a year or two after she was graduated from high school. She was a petite woman with a quick, emphatic manner, and an attractive smile. She was born and reared in Midwest and had worked as a stenographer before she and Charles were married. Della belonged to the Eastern Star, the Presbyterian Church Choir, American Legion Auxiliary, and Women's Club I.

Kemo, the large, long-haired dog, was the children's long-suffering playmate. The Pintners lived in a modern, white, frame house which belonged to Maud's maternal grandmother. It consisted of a living room, music room, dining room, kitchen, dinette, four bedrooms, and a bathroom, all on one floor. The house furnishings, many of them antiques, were attractive and arranged tastefully. Many full book shelves, a record player, and a grand piano indicated some of the family interests. The yard surrounding the house was well landscaped.

Subject: Roy Eddy (M, 3, 6-2)
Time: February 22, 1949; 7:00 a.m.–8:31 p.m.

On February 22, 1949, Roy Eddy was just over six years of age. He was about average height and weight for his age. Roy was quite robust, in spite of having had pneumonia the previous winter. He was in the first grade in school.

Roy lived with his father, mother, two older sisters, and one older brother. He attended the Presbyterian Sunday School regularly, with his older sisters and brother and had won a perfect attendance award in 1948/49.

Martin Eddy, the father, farmed until about 1945 when he moved to town because of his health. He worked on the county road crew. Martin Eddy was one of the advisors for the 4-H group.

Claudia Eddy, the mother, was a brisk, busy woman. She worked as cook in a local cafe, helping to plan and manage as well as cook. Besides this, she managed to encourage and work with her children, especially in their 4-H projects. Mrs. Eddy belonged to the Presbyterian Church and P.T.A.

The entire family, Roy excepted, contributed to the family economy. The oldest sister, Lola, a junior in high school, worked at Poole's Grocery after school. Mollie, a freshman in high school, took the responsibility of housekeeping at home. Vernon, a 12-year-old, was raising two calves besides milking the family cow. He delivered the weekly advertising sheet for Kane's Grocery. A cocker spaniel was an accepted part of the family group.

Mr. and Mrs. Eddy were natives of Midwest State and had both come from farm-home backgrounds. At this time, Mrs. Eddy's parents lived in a neighboring town while Mr. Eddy's parents were on a nearby farm.

The Eddys rented a one-story, white, frame house with two bedrooms, a dining room, kitchen, bathroom, and living room. All meals were eaten in the large kitchen, leaving the dining room for Roy and Vernon as a sleeping room. The furnishings throughout the house were sturdy and worn. The floors were covered with linoleum rugs and the house was heated by gas stoves.

Subject: Raymond Birch (M, 2, 7-4)
Time: April 26, 1949; 7:00 a.m.–8:33 p.m.

Raymond Birch was a sturdy boy, slightly shorter and heavier than the average boy of his age. At seven years and four months, he was the youngest among the second graders in the Midwest school

Raymond was an only child. He had no relatives in Midwest, but both his maternal and paternal grandparents lived on nearby farms and he was a frequent visitor in their homes.

Jack Birch, Raymond's father, was in his early thirties. Raymond's mother,

Joan Birch, was in her late twenties. After graduating from the same high school in a small town near Midwest, both Jack and Joan Birch had been employed in a government agricultural office in Midwest. They were married in 1941, and Mr. Birch took a position in a nearby war plant where the government classified him as essential for the war's duration. The family had lived in a housing unit near the plant. When the plant closed after the war, Mr. Birch returned to Midwest to accept a position with the Midwest Hardware and Implement Company. Mrs. Birch did not work outside the home until Raymond entered school, when she took a position in the office of the County Clerk.

Honey, a fat old fox terrier, was considered almost a member of the family.

The Birch family rented an apartment in a white, frame house, which, though more than 60 years old, was well preserved and modernized. Their apartment had a living room, dining room, kitchen, two bedrooms, and a bathroom. There were two adjacent apartments. The Birches were responsible for the care of the premises. There were also a tall barn, a double garage, a place for a vegetable garden, and a well kept lawn. The whole place looked neat and comfortable.

Subject: Benjamin Hutchings (M, 1, 7-4)
Time: November 23, 1948; 7:33 a.m.–8:00 p.m.

Benjamin Hutchings at seven years and four months of age was a slender, dark-haired, sober-faced second grader. He appeared quiet and seemingly preoccupied a good deal of the time but this was offset by his alertness and sparkle when entertained or aroused. Ben was taller than the average for his age group.

James Hutchings, Ben's father, had a law office over the bank in Midwest. He had a law degree from the State University and had been established in Midwest about five years. Verna Hutchings, Ben's mother, worked part-time as secretary in her husband's office. She had worked as a newspaper woman after completing college and before her marriage. Both Mr. and Mrs. Hutchings were active in the Methodist Church. She was president of the Methodist Ladies Aid and he, chairman of the Church governing board. The Hutchings were active also in community and social circles, with membership in bridge clubs, Women's Club I, the Rotary Club, and the Parent-Teachers' Association.

Ben's sister, Sarah, was 10 years old and in the fifth grade. Ben shared two pet dogs and one pet cat with his sister.

The Hutchings lived in their own home, a roomy, two-story, white, frame house on a spacious corner lot. The house had a living room, dining room, and kitchen downstairs, and three bedrooms and a bathroom upstairs. It was heated by a gas furnace. Music and books were easily available to the children.

Subject: Mary Ennis (F, 2, 8-7)
Time: May 12, 1949; 7:00 a.m.–9:25 p.m.

Mary Ennis was a blond, blue-eyed, eight-year-old; she was small-boned and dainty. She was in the third grade, took piano lessons, sang in the Junior Choir, belonged to the Brownie Scouts, and attended the Methodist Sunday School.

The family dog, Chico, a large, white shepherd, was much beloved by her.

Arthur Ennis, Mary's father, a civil engineer employed by the Federal Government, was in charge of a county-wide project. He had taken specialized college training for his work. Mr. Ennis had remained an active reserve officer following extended service in the Army. He was active in the community, belonged to the Rotary Club, taught an adult Sunday-School Class, and sang in the Methodist Church Choir and a male quartet.

Mary's mother, Penelope Ennis, besides being a good housekeeper was also a mainstay of a number of community activities. She directed the church choir, was president of the Methodist Women's Evening Guild, belonged to Women's Club I, the Rotary Anns, and the American Legion Auxiliary. She was in demand as an accompanist or soloist at musical functions and before her marriage had taught rural school.

Timothy, the second child, was a happy, healthy, seven-month-old boy.

The Ennis family had lived in Midwest three years. They bought their home and had done much to make it efficient and attractive. The house, all on one floor, had a living room, a dining room, two bedrooms, bath, a modern kitchen, a large, screened back porch, and a basement laundry and utility room. A spinet piano added to the charm of the living room, and a new gas furnace added to the comfort of the house.

The Ennis home was catercorner from the Hutchings'. It had a relatively small yard (40 × 100 feet), with a magnificent tree, and a swing, shading an attractive play place.

Subject: Douglas Crawford (M, 2, 9-2)
Time: April 18, 1949; 7:28 a.m.–9:45 p.m.

Douglas Crawford, on April 18, 1949, was nine years and two months old. He was in the third grade. Douglas, larger than any other child in the third- and fourth-grade room, was well-built, weighed about 90 pounds and had an enviable reputation for strength, toughness, and physical prowess. He was dependent on his glasses for adequate vision and was greatly bothered by them in his playing. Douglas had a lively interest in hunting and fishing and was also interested in rocks, fossils, flowers, and animals.

Douglas' immediate family consisted of his father, mother, 13-year-old brother, Thomas, and 6-year-old sister, Norah. Also, very important to the whole family were the maternal grandparents, the Tiltons, who lived on a farm about a mile south of town. Thomas lived with his grandparents much of the time to help his grandfather with the chores. Douglas sometimes helped his grandfather by driving a tractor.

James Crawford, Douglas' father, was a well-proportioned, six footer in his middle thirties. James was graduated from the local high school. He kept some cows to milk, raised some pigs, and owned 40 acres of land adjoining the maternal grandfather's farm. He did farm labor and sawed timber with a motor driven saw.

Polly, Douglas' mother, belonged to an old Midwest County family. Her father's family had been in the banking business, and her mother's father ran a book store. Polly married upon completing high school.

Thomas was a husky, six-foot, eighth grader. Norah was a sociable, independent child.

All the family attended the Presbyterian Sunday School. Douglas was well on toward his seventh year of perfect attendance, and the other children were equally regular. Mrs. Crawford was secretary of the Ladies' Aid and a member of the Missionary Society.

The Crawfords lived in a large, old, white, frame house with about an acre of land around it. The house was equipped with electricity, heated by gas stoves, and had running water but no bathroom. On the first floor were the kitchen, dining room, living room, the parents' bedroom, and a utility room. Norah and the boys had bedrooms upstairs.

Between their house and that next door was a large lawn. West of the house were a number of miscellaneous sheds and chicken yards. The Crawfords always planted a large vegetable garden, and Douglas helped to care for the animals and the garden.

Subject: Claire Graves (F, 3, 10-9)
Time: January 28, 1949; 7:20 a.m.–9:40 p.m.

Claire Graves, 10 years and 9 months old, was a slight child with dark eyes and curly, black hair. When animated she was vividly pretty. She was about medium height for her age but looked less mature than many of her classmates. Claire belonged to the Girl Scouts and attended the Methodist Church where she sang in the Junior Choir. She had definite duties at home and sometimes helped the older brothers with their paper route, as well.

Claire's parents, James and Betsy Graves, were married when they were graduated from high school. They were in their middle thirties and had both come from Midwest County families. They had moved to Midwest about five years before, because they thought it better for their large family than the city where Mr. Graves worked.

Mr. Graves worked in a neighboring city at the railroad yards doing construction work. He was, however, subject to transfer to other yards in the general area. He was often away and at best, got home twice a week.

Mrs. Graves had been critically ill before and after the birth of Charles, her youngest child. At the time of the study, however, she was in fair health. Mrs. Graves was president of a club of young married women, the Homemaker's Club, which she had helped to organize. She was a member of the Parent-Teachers' Association and the Methodist Church.

The children in the family were Wendell, a high-school junior; Ruth, a sophmore; Stanley, an eighth grader; Claire, a fifth grader; Frances, a fourth grader; and Charles, who was four years old and not yet in school.

Included in the family were a big dog and several cats.

The large living room and kitchen of the Graves' one-story frame house were the center of the family activities, particularly in winter when the coal stove kept these rooms warm. There was a bedroom for the girls, one for the older boys, and one for Charles and his parents. The kitchen had running cold water and a gas cooking stove. There was no bathroom in the house.

The large yard provided plenty of play space, room for a big vegetable garden, and a chicken yard.

Appendix 2

Four Disabled Children

Subject: Sue Dewall (F, 4, 7-1)
Time: June 6, 1951; 6:30 a.m.–8:08 p.m.

Sue Dewall was almost a month over seven years old and was in the first- and second-grade group at the Lawton School.

She was a slight, small-boned, fair-skinned girl with straight, taffy-blond hair, who usually wore a short, clean, cotton school dress, orthopedic shoes, and anklets; she also wore plastic framed glasses to help correct a severe myopia. Sue's manner was intent, childishly serious, and vigorous. The impression of serious intensity was derived, in part at least, from the way she bent her head close to whatever she was doing.

Sue was diagnosed as cerebral palsied, spastic type. Although her general health on entering the Lawton School was poor, she was in fair health at the time of the day study.

Sue was 45 inches tall and weighed just under 50 pounds. She had less strength than a nonhandicapped child, yet she stood out in the group at the school as one of the more active children. Sue could do almost anything expected of a normal child, although she would be perceived to be a handicapped child. She walked on the balls of her feet, and as she hurried along, held her arms akimbo. When she ran, it was with an unsteady, tripping flurry, not as fast as a normal child, but with as much energy.

Sue was born three months prematurely. Her mother died soon after Sue's birth, and she was raised by an older, married sister until her admittance to Lawton at five years of age.

Sue was described at the time of her entrance into the school as having few social graces. The staff members mentioned such things as disorderliness and destructiveness in connection with her own clothes and toys. During her two years at the Lawton School she had learned to keep herself and her things neat and clean.

Sue was the youngest of seven children, all of whom lived with the father except the oldest sister and Sue. The father worked intermittently as a day laborer.

Subject: Verne Trennell (M, 3, 7-5)
Time: June 21, 1951; 7:00 a.m.–9:32 p.m.

Verne Trennell, seven years and five months old, was a day student at Lawton School. He was a pleasant-featured boy with unusually rosy cheeks. Verne wore plastic framed glasses to correct his crossed eyes. He walked with Canadian-type crutches; his gait on these crutches was fascinating. Rather than placing the two crutches on the ground and swinging his body between them, Verne used

484

the crutches as extensions to his arms and walked with a four-legged gait. He chopped along thus when he was in a hurry, with surprising speed.

Verne had been a day student at the school for almost two years, and had made such progress in school that he expected to start as a second grader in a parochial school the next year.

Verne was born on January 30, 1944, and was recognized immediately as not a normal child. The diagnosis taken from the report of a general physical examination of Verne, in September, 1949, was as follows: "Neurogenic bladder, probably of hypotonic type, resulting from the congenital anomoly *spina bifida.*" Verne's physical condition at the time of entrance to the school was complicated by several features. He was slightly hydrocephalic. His eyesight was impaired by an internal strabismus. A grade-two systolic murmur was noticed in the heart examination. A slightly enlarged abdomen was noted, as well as undescended testicles.

Due to neural damage, Verne's legs were partially paralyzed and he had no bladder control. He was forced, therefore, to wear a rubber urinal strapped to his right leg. A rubber tube fitted rather tightly over the end of his penis and drained into the rubber bladder. The family and the school staff worked hard to teach Verne to empty this urinal every two hours.

His general health had been good, aside from the usual childhood diseases: measles, chickenpox, and scarlet fever.

On weekdays, Verne was at the Lawton School from 8:30 a.m. to 3:30 p.m. On Sundays he went to the Lutheran Church and Sunday School with his parents. Verne had won a perfect attendance pin the previous year. The Trennell family said grace at meals and had daily devotions. Verne seemed to get along well with the neighborhood children.

Verne's family consisted of two older sisters, one younger sister, and his father and mother.

Mr. Trennell, a quiet, gentle-appearing man in his middle thirties, worked at an industrial plant in Capitol City as an inspector. He was a member of his union's Executive Council, and was chief steward of the union at the plant. Working in an essential industry prevented Mr. Trennell from being called into military service. He was a member of the school board of the Lutheran School Association, and Superintendent of the Lutheran Sunday School. He encouraged Verne to help him repair the car, to fix things about the house, and to be as independent as possible.

Verne's mother was a slender woman in her middle thirties. She did her own housework, sewed for the girls, and canned fruits and vegetables from the garden. She was active in the church where she was a member of the choir and taught a Sunday-School class. Mrs. Trennell and her husband had worked closely together in their effort to give Verne the care his handicap demanded; necessarily, however, the main responsibility of his care was hers.

Verne's oldest sister, Sarah, worked as a carhop at a drive-in café in the afternoons and evenings. Verne played more with Saralee, the youngest sister, than with Sherlyne, aged nine. Cuddles, a fox terrier, belonged to Verne and was his close companion.

The Trennells owned their house which was located on a dirt road in a section where the houses were spaced rather far apart. It was of white, frame construction, with a kitchen, living room, bedroom, and bathroom.   An additional room was being repaired as the girls' bedroom; meanwhile, the girls' bed was in the living room.   Almost every house in the neighborhood had a vegetable garden, as did the Trennell's.   There was a large area of play space in the yard.

Subject: Wally Wolfson (M, 3, 4-3)
Time: July 9, 1951; 8:00 a.m.–7:35 p.m.

Wally Wolfson, four years and three months old, was an attractive, blond child of a little more than average height and of about average build. He lived with his mother, father, and younger sister in the town of Manchester in Midwest County.   Wally was unable to walk due to the residual effects of poliomyelitis. He could stand with support and could pull himself up readily with his strong arms and shoulders.   He had full leg braces which he used when he walked with crutches.   Ordinarily, though, around the house Wally either crawled very adeptly on his hands and knees, or was carried.   Outdoors he rode his express wagon and could put one knee in the wagon and push with the other leg.

Wally's health was excellent except for his disability.   He was a little past two when he contracted polio and, since leaving the hospital, had received physical therapy treatments in a nearby city.   In addition, Mrs. Wolfson gave Wally infrared heat treatments and massage twice a day.

Wally's immediate family consisted of his father, his mother, and a younger sister, Maud, not quite two years younger than he.   Almost within the family circle were Wally's aunt, uncle, and his four cousins, who lived in the next house. His cousins were Dorothy, 13; Jimmy, 8; Ben, 6; and Betty, 2.   These children were Wally's and Maud's constant playmates.   Two younger brothers of the father, Phil and Rex, were often in Wally's home.   Wally's paternal grandparents lived on a nearby farm.   The Wolfson family were Midwest County people and a good many branches of the family lived in the vicinity.

Mr. Douglas Wolfson, the father, in his middle thirties, was a veteran of World War II.   At the time of the study, Mr. Wolfson was doing carpenter work on an independent basis, but had recently been employed by a contractor over a period of months in Capitol City.

Mrs. Wolfson's family lived in southern California, but had come from Manchester.   Mrs. Wolfson went to high school in Manchester where she met Doug.

The Wolfson's owned their white, frame, two-story house, and had done much to improve it.   The rooms consisted of a living room and kitchen on the first floor, and two bedrooms upstairs.   Manchester had no city water, so the Wolfsons had a pump and an outdoor toilet.

Wally had a number of playthings including a wagon, a tricycle, and a number of toy trucks.   At the time of the study, the Wolfson's dog, a hunting dog, had a litter of very young puppies.

Subject: Bobby Bryant (M, 2, 7-4)
Time: March 26, 1949; 8:35 a.m.–9:42 p.m.

At seven years and four months of age, Bobby Bryant was living a restricted but, for him, busy and interesting life.   He suffered from a congenital heart defect diagnosed as Eisenmengers Complex.   Because of the opening in the interventricular septum, much of his blood, after returning to the heart, entered the peripheral circulation without first going through his lungs. At seven years of age, Bobby was small, unable to engage in any strenuous activities, was required to rest several hours each day, and was unable to attend school.

Bobby's family consisted of his father, mother, two brothers, and his father's older sister. Bobby's father, Mr. Bryant, was a professional man whose work kept him away from home a good deal. Bobby's mother was an attractive woman in her thirties. Although her main interest was to make a comfortable home for her family, she also was active socially in the group made up of her husband's colleagues 'and their wives.

Bobby's brother, Kenny, an 11-year-old "All American boy," and Jack, an active 3-year-old, spent much of their time with other children.

An important member of Bobby's family was Aunt Alice, who had come to live with them when Bobby had first shown a desire to learn. She was the widow of a missionary and had been a public school teacher, so that she had the required background for tutoring Bobby, as well as the understanding and love required to deal with Bobby's particular situation. She had accepted Bobby as her particular charge.

The Bryant's house, a white, two-story frame structure in Lawton was located on a much traveled street. It had an elusive sort of charm in both its outside and indoor appointments. Set on a large lot, it was surrounded by trees and shrubs which softened its severe lines.

Appendix 3

Instructions for Unitizing Midwest Behavior Settings

Four staff members of the Field Station were given a random sample of 100 items from the initial behavior setting inventory. Cards (size $3'' \times 5''$) bearing the names of the sample items were arranged in the same random order for all four judges. On the table where each judge worked were papers of the following sizes and colors: white ($5\frac{1}{4}'' \times 8\frac{1}{2}''$); yellow ($11'' \times 17''$); brown ($24'' \times 36''$). The following instructions were given to each judge privately; judges worked independently:

1. On these cards are the names of some probable Midwest behavior settings that have appeared in the *Midwest Weekly* and the Telephone Directory. You are to sort them by placing together those which are parts of the same larger setting. Some of these stand alone; they are not parts of any other setting. In other cases, two or more group together as parts of a more inclusive setting, and it may be that in some cases two or more of these groups of settings combine to make a still larger all-embracing setting.

2. In sorting, be sure to remember your criterion that parts of the same larger whole go together, *not* that similar things go together. The two drug stores are similar, but they are not parts of any larger setting, so they would not be placed together. On the other hand, the Fire House is not very similar to Spring Clean Up, but they are both parts of City Government, and would be placed together.

3. Place individually on the table, settings that are separate from every other setting in the pack. Place two or more settings that belong together on white sheets. Place two or more of these white groups that go together on yellow sheets. Place yellow groups or yellow and white groups that go together on brown sheets.

Instructions for Eliminating Nonsettings from the Initial Settings Inventory

The instructions presented below were given to the judges who had unitized the Midwest behavior setting inventory. These judges were given a typed list of probable behavior settings as they had been unitized (see Appendix 3). They were instructed to draw a line through every item which did not meet the criteria of a behavior setting. Judges were instructed regarding these criteria as follows:

1. Eliminate those items which lack well defined milieu characteristics. A setting has a well defined milieu if:

   a) it involves an arrangement of milieu parts which are associated with the behavior pattern of the setting, e.g., the arrangement of stands, gridiron, football, refreshment stand at a Football Game; the arrangement of flag pole, benches, retaining wall of the Courthouse Lawn;

   b) it involves a person or group of persons with uniforms, badges, or paraphernalia of relevance to the behavior, e.g. Bakery Route;

   c) it involves a predetermined, delimited time span. Examples of settings with an observably limited time span are Boy Scout Meetings, Fourth of July, Church Worship Service.

2. Eliminate those items from the inventory which lack the quality of enterability, i.e., in which the milieu is not circumjacent to the behavior. A setting is enterable if:

   a) a person can pass physically within its boundaries, e.g., people enter the Kane's Grocery by going through the door, the Old Settlers' Midway by passing the barricades, the High-School Basketball Games by entering the gymnasium;

   b) the milieu parts are geographically dispersed and the behavior pattern occurs in the interstices, e.g., paper route, game of tag;

   c) a definite, predetermined time interval surrounds the behavior, e.g., Fourth of July, dinner time.

3. Eliminate those items which involve no clearly discriminated behavior pattern, e.g., abandoned structure on West Side of Square.

4. Eliminate items which involve no clear synomorphy (congruence, fittingness) of behavior and milieu, e.g., the street on the south side of the Square has associated with it no pattern of behavior which is congruent with it as a separate part of the trafficways of the town.

5. Eliminate those items which fall beyond the limits of the survey. A setting falls within the limits of the survey when:

a) it occurred within the one year time span designated for the survey;

b) it occurred within the town or originated within a town behavior setting and continued outside the limits of the town, e.g., Boy Scout, Patrol Cookout.

6. Eliminate those items which have a visibility that is near zero; this may arise from very infrequent occurrence and/or limited awareness by the population of Midwest, e.g., storage room in basement of Midwest Hardware.

Appendix 5

The Interdependence Scale for Judging Value of K

SCALE for judging the degree of interdependence of any pair of behavior settings A and B. On all criteria, a low rating indicates interdependence, and a high rating indicates independence of setting A and setting B.

1. Rating of population interdependence, i.e., of the degree to which the people who enter setting A (P_A) are the same as those who enter setting B (P_B). The per cent overlap is judged by the following formula:

$$\frac{\text{Per Cent}}{\text{Overlap}} = \frac{2\,P_{AB}}{P_A + P_B},$$

where P_A = Number of people who enter setting A,

P_B = Number of people who enter setting B,

P_{AB} = Number of people who enter both setting A and setting B.

This per cent overlap is converted to an interdependency rating by the following scale:

Rating	Per Cent Overlap
1	95–100
2	67–94
3	33–66
4	6–32
5	2–5
6	trace–1
7	none

2. Rating of leadership interdependence, i.e., of the degree to which the leaders of setting A are also the leaders of setting B.

This is judged in the same way as population interdependence for persons who penetrate to Zones 4, 5, or 6 of settings A and B.

3. Rating of spatial interdependence, i.e., the degree to which settings A and B use the same or proximate spatial areas.

Rate on the following scale. In the case of scale points with two definitions, the most appropriate one applies; if more than one applies give the lowest scale rating.

Rating	Per Cent of Space Common to A and B		
1	95 to 100		
2	50 to 94		
3	10 to 49	or	A and B use different parts of same room or small area.
4	5 to 9	or	A and B use different parts of same building or lot.
5	2 to 4	or	A and B use areas in same part of town.*
6	trace to 1	or	A and B use areas in same town but different parts of the town.*
7	none	or	A in town, B out of town.

* Three parts of Midwest were identified: (a) South of the square (approximately 15 square blocks); (b) area of town square (approximately 5 blocks); (c) north of the square (approximately 15 blocks).

4. Rating of interdependence based on behavior objects, i.e., the extent to which behavior setting A and behavior setting B use identical or similar behavior objects.

Rate on the following scale. In the case of scale points with two definitions, the most appropriate one applies; if more than one applies, give the lowest rating.

Rating			
1	Identical objects used in setting A and setting B; i.e., all behavior objects shared.		
2	More than half of the objects shared by A and B	or	Virtually all objects in A and B of same kind.*
3	Half of the objects shared by A and B	or	More than half of the objects in A and B of same kind.*
4	Less than half the objects shared by A and B	or	Half the objects in A and B of same kind.*
5	Few behavior objects in A and B identical	or	Less than half the objects of A and B of same kind.*

Rating

| 6 | Almost no objects shared by A and B | or | Few behavior objects of same kind* in A and B. |
| 7 | No objects shared | or | Almost no similarity between objects in A and B. |

* Objects of the same kind are different instances of objects that have the same dictionary definition ; e.g., spoons are used in the behavior setting School Lunch Room and the setting Clifford's Drug Store Fountain, but they are different spoons.

5. Rating of interdependence based on molar action units, i.e., degree to which molar behavior units are continuous between setting A and setting B.

The molar behavior in behavior settings A and B may be integrated in two ways. The inhabitants of setting A may interact across the boundary with the inhabitants of B, e.g., the person in the cytosetting Preacher interacts directly with the members of the cytosetting Congregation in the Church Service. On the other hand, behavior begun in one behavior setting may be completed in the other, e.g., delivering lumber for a construction project starts at the setting Lumber Yard and is completed at the setting House Construction. Scales are provided for both kinds of behavior integration. For each kind of behavior integration, use the highest per cent which applies. The average of the two ratings is the final rating.

Rating	Per Cent of Behavior in A Having Direct Effects in B, or Vice Versa. (Highest Per Cent Counts)	Per Cent of Behavior Actions Beginning in A Which are Completed in B, or Vice Versa. (Highest Per Cent Counts)
1	95–100	95–100
2	67–94	67–94
3	34–66	34–66
4	5–33	5–33
5	2–4	2–4
6	trace–1	trace–1
7	none	none

6. Rating of interdependence based on temporal contiguity, i.e., the degree to which settings A and B occur at the same time, or at proximate times.

Most behavior settings recur at intervals. Any pair of settings, therefore, may occur close together on some occasions and be temporally separated at other times. For example, the American Legion meets monthly, while the Boy Scout Troop meets weekly; once a month their meetings occur during the same week. The closest temporal proximity of setting A and setting B determine the column to enter in the table below. The per cent of contact at the point of closest proximity determines the interdependence rating in the column at the right. The per cent of contact is computed as the ratio between the number of occurrences of both settings at this closest point of contact divided by the total number of occurrences of both behavior settings.

TABLE A.1

SCALES FOR RATING TEMPORAL INTERDEPENDENCE

INTERDEPEND- ENCE RATING	CLOSEST TEMPORAL PROXIMITY (PER CENT OF CONTACT)					
	Simultaneous	Same Part of Day	Same Day	Same Week	Same Month	Same Year
1	.75–1.00					
2	.50–0.74	.75–1.00				
3	.25–0.49	.50–0.74	.75–1.00			
4	.05–0.24	.25–0.49	.50–0.74	.75–1.00		
5	0–0.04	.05–0.24	.25–0.49	.50–0.74	.75–1.00	
6		0–0.04	.05–0.24	.25–0.49	.50–0.74	.50–1.00
7			0–0.04	0–0.24	0–0.49	0–0.49

Example: The Boy Scout Troop met every Monday night during the survey year. The American Legion met the first Wednesday of every month. The closest temporal proximity of these settings was "Same Week." Enter column headed "Same Week." The 12 Scout and the 12 Legion meetings which occurred in this close contact were added and the sum divided by the sum of the 12 Legion meetings and the 52 Scout meetings, as follows:

$$\frac{12 \text{ Scout Meetings} + 12 \text{ Legion Meetings}}{52 \text{ Scout Meetings} + 12 \text{ Legion Meetings}} = \frac{24}{64} = .37$$

In column "Same Week," .37 falls at scale point 6. The temporal interdependence score then, is 6.

7. Interdependence based on similarity of behavior mechanisms, i.e., the degree to which behavior mechanisms are similar in setting A and setting B. Ratings are based on the following 12 behavior mechanisms:

Gross Motor	Writing	Eating
Manipulation	Observing	Reading
Verbalization	Listening	Emoting
Singing	Thinking	Tactual Feeling

The interdependence score is determined by the number of behavior mechanisms present in one setting and absent in the other as indicated in the following table.

Interdependence Rating	Number of Mechanisms Present in One Setting and Absent in the Other
1	0–1
2	2–3
3	4–5–6
4	7–8
5	9–10
6	11
7	12

The interdependence score K

The total interdependence score K is the sum of the separate interdependency ratings; the value of K can vary between 7 and 49.

Occupancy Time Grouping Intervals, Assumed Interval Score, Interval Score Code, and Frequencies

In order to manipulate occupancy times for settings, it was necessary to group the actual occupancy indexes into intervals. These intervals had to be broad enough to limit their absolute number but narrow enough to make reasonable discriminations among settings. Two factors blocked the use of a simple arithmetic grouping. First, the distribution of settings on a scale of occupancy time was badly skewed toward a small number of person-hours. Hence, the interval score of an arithmetic scale would consistently over-estimate the number of person-hours represented in that interval. Secondly, due to the nature of the formula for estimating occupancy time, errors were magnified for settings where more time was spent. For example, at the Old Settler's Horse Shoe, the number of persons present could not be estimated within 10 to 25 individuals. Since it lasted almost six hours, errors of 60 to 150 person-hours are not unreasonable. Fourteen persons spent about an hour at the Presbyterian Youth Fellowship Devotion at Pleasant Nursing Home, an event which lasted an hour. The possible error here was probably within one person-hour. For these reasons, a geometric scale of intervals was favored over an arithmetric scale of intervals.

Intervals were numbered consecutively from 1 through 63. These numbers were called the *interval code*. The intervals designated by the interval code were made equal to the square of the code. Thus, the interval with the code number *6* had a width of 36 person-hours on the occupancy index scale. This meant that the lower limit of any interval was fixed as the sum of the squared codes *not* including the interval in question. Thus, the lower limit for the interval with the code *6* was $(1)^2 + (2)^2 + (3)^2 + (4)^2 + (5)^2$ and was equal to an occupancy index of 55. In practice, we established 55 as the upper limit of interval *5*, and $55 + 1$ or 56 as the lower limit of interval 6.

There remained then the problem of establishing the interval midpoint. We arrived at this in the same way as we established the lower limits of the interval. We conceived of the coded intervals as having a width of one unit and the midpoint of that interval as being .5 units from the lower limit. Thus, the *coded* midpoint for interval 6 was $6 - .5$ or 5.5. The temporal index corresponding to this coded midpoint was then computed in the same way as for the lower limit. For interval 6 it was equal to $(5.5)^2 + (4.5)^2 + (3.5)^2 + (2.5)^2 + (1.5)^2 + (.5)^2$ or 71.50 person-hours. We called this the *assumed interval score*. The general formula for finding the assumed interval score is $(n - .5)^2 + (n - 1.5)^2 + (n - 2.5)^2 + \ldots (.5)^2$ where n equals the interval

496

code number. Empirical checks indicated that when random samples of occupancy indexes were summed in terms of assumed interval scores, the total closely approximated the sum of ungrouped occupancy indexes. Following are listed the characteristics of occupancy time intervals.

Occupancy Time Grouping Intervals, Assumed Interval Score, Interval Score Code, and Frequencies

Grouping Interval	Assumed Interval Score	Code	Frequency
0–1	.25	1	0
2–5	2.50	2	11
6–14	8.75	3	32
15–30	21.00	4	43
31–55	41.25	5	43
56–91	71.50	6	41
92–140	113.75	7	32
141–204	170.00	8	47
205–285	242.25	9	40
286–385	332.50	10	35
386–506	442.75	11	23
507–650	575.00	12	28
651–819	731.25	13	18
820–1015	913.50	14	30
1016–1240	1123.75	15	17
1241–1496	1364.00	16	18
1497–1785	1636.25	17	10
1786–2109	1942.50	18	8
2110–2470	2284.78	19	7
2471–2870	2665.00	20	11
2871–3311	3085	21	11
3312–3795	3548	22	7
3796–4324	4054	23	5
4325–4900	4606	24	7
4901–5525	5206	25	7
5526–6201	5857	26	6
6202–6930	6559	27	6
6931–7714	7315	28	5
7715–8555	8127	29	5
8556–9455	8998	30	5
9456–10416	9928	31	2
10417–11440	10920	32	4
11441–12529	11976	33	3
12530–13685	13099	34	4

Grouping Interval	Assumed Interval Score	Code	Frequency
13686–14910	14289	35	4
14911–16206	15549	36	2
16207–17575	16881	37	2
17576–19019	18288	38	3
19020–20150	19749	39	1
20151–21750	21330	40	0
21751–23431	22970	41	0
23432–25195	24693	42	0
25196–27044	26499	43	0
27045–28980	28391	44	0
28981–31005	30371	45	1
31006–33121	32441	46	0
33122–35330	34604	47	0
35331–37154	36860	48	0
37155–39555	39212	49	0
39556–42055	41662	50	0
42056–44656	44213	51	0
44657–47360	46865	52	0
47361–50169	49621	53	0
50170–53085	52484	54	0
53086–56110	55454	55	0
56111–59246	58534	56	0
59247–62495	61726	57	0
62496–65859	65033	58	0
65860–69340	68455	59	0
69341–72940	71995	60	0
72941–76661	75655	61	0
76662–80505	79438	62	1
80506–84474	83344	63	0

Some Conventions Followed in Judging Action Patterns and Behavior Mechanisms

Action Patterns

As described in Chapter III, the Action Patterns are divided into four sub-scales: participation, supply, appreciation, and learning. A rating is made for each subscale in terms of the per cent of the total person-hours of the setting which is involved in the behavior described by the subscale. While Occupancy Time ratings include only persons who are residents of Midwest, Action Pattern ratings include the entire population of the setting regardless of where they live. To establish the proportion of the person-hours for each subscale, the total estimated person-hours spent in the setting is used as a denominator, and the total estimated person-hours devoted to behavior described by the subscale is used as a numerator. The proportion is translated into a rating in terms of the scales given in Chapter III. For example, at each meeting of the Home Demonstration Unit which has a total of 60 person-hours per meeting, 21 person-hours are devoted to formal education. This proportion is 35 per cent of the total person-hours of the setting and would therefore receive a rating of *3* for participation.

In some instances, the same action can have significance both for participation and for supply. This is the case, for example, in selling feed in Hopkins' Feed Store. Here, the act of selling is both participation in Business and supplying objects for Business in other settings. In such cases no limit is set on the total rating which can be given on the subscales for participation and supply. In other instances participation and supply are judged to be mutually exclusive. In Clifford's Drug Store, the action pattern Nutrition is either participation (eating ice cream), or supply (providing ice cream for eating is another setting). In such cases we have established the rule that the combined ratings on participation and supply cannot exceed *6*. This applies also to Aesthetics, Earning a Living, Government, Personal Appearance, Physical Health, Recreation, and Religion. The combined ratings on participation and supply for Business, Education, Philanthropy, Orientation and Social Contact can exceed *6*.

Where we have found difficulty in judging certain action patterns, we have used additional cues to enable more consistent judging. It did not seem necessary to provide further cues for all subscales for all Action Patterns. Those which seemed most helpful are included in the following paragraphs.

Aesthetics

Participation. A purely functional setting such as a machine shop is rated zero. A setting such as a cafe where there is a minimal effort to make it attractive is rated *1*.

Supply. Does the behavior of the inhabitants provide materials for beautifying another setting? Artisans (paperhangers) provide beautification for settings other than settings within which they function.

Evaluation and Appreciation. Is the behavior of the inhabitants explicit recognition of the orderliness or beauty of a setting? Wherever persons have occasion to comment on decorations or musical program, appreciation is rated *1*.

Learning. Is art (music, home decoration, dressmaking, etc.) formally taught here? Incidental learning about art is not rated as learning.

Business

Participation. Is payment obligatory for goods, services, or privileges? Payment can be the price of merchandise or service, organization dues, or taxes. There is an obligation to pay for merchandise at a church food sale, therefore a church food sale receives a rating on participation in the action pattern Business. There is no obligation to put money in the collection plate at a worship service, therefore a church worship service is not rated for participation. Settings in which salaried persons perform their duties but nothing is bought, sold, or paid for as in school classrooms are not rated for business.

Earning a Living

Participation. Children operating a lemonade stand are not Earning a Living; adolescents working part time are Earning a Living.

Supply. Paying salaries within the setting in which the employee works is not included. Establishing the annual budget at the Presbyterian Church Annual Meeting is included as supply as it provides money for the minister to earn in other settings.

Education

Participation. Does anyone take the role of teacher with the intent to educate others in this setting? Teachers only maintaining order are not rated as teaching. The behavior of both teacher and learners is included in computing the person-hours. Giving information about coming events is Orientation, giving help with tax forms is Business, Government, and Earning a Living.

Government

Participation. Is there behavior in this setting due to governmental influence? All settings requiring licences are rated at least *1*. All settings where there are legal restrictions such as that which prohibits the presence of dogs in a cafe are rated at least *1*. All the time at work for government employees such as those in county or federal offices is counted as participation for that setting.

Nutrition

Participation. Does anyone in the setting eat or drink? Any setting that has coke- or other food- or drink-vending machines is rated at least *1*.

Orientation

Participation. Does anyone in this setting formally inform others in the setting by word or deed about the present locations of people or things, schedules of contemporary events, or newly acquired status of persons? Status is formally defined at weddings and commencement exercises. Casting a play orients persons in relation to their responsibilities. Announcement at meetings of special events to be held in the future is orientation. Orientation within a setting, for example, announcing the order of business at a meeting is not rated. Medical information such as that given by a physician is rated as Physical Health, financial information such as that given at a bank is rated Business, spiritual information given at a worship service is rated as Religion.

Supply. Are bulletins, maps, notices of sales written or printed for distribution in other settings, or are bulletins distributed which announce forthcoming events?

Philanthropy

Participation. Obligatory dues or gifts given to friends, for example, at Baby Showers are not considered philanthropic. Voting money for public welfare is philanthropy; voting money for civic improvement is not.

Physical Health

Participation. Athletic activities conceived as improving physical health are included. Social conversation about health is not rated as participation.

Supply. Are materials, instruction booklets and books, money, or medical supplies provided in this setting for promoting physical health elsewhere? Sale of sporting equipment is included. Does not include sale of food for ordinary nutrition but would include special foods such as vitamins.

Recreation

Participation. Is the behavior intended to be recreational? Movies strictly for instruction, meetings strictly for business may be incidentally enjoyable but this is not intentional, therefore is not rated as recreation.

Supply. Are materials supplied in this setting that promote enjoyment in other settings? Selling gasoline to persons using their cars for recreation is rated supply for Recreation. Decorating for a party is considered supply for Recreation.

Religion

Participation. Does anyone in the setting pray, sing hymns, listen to sermons, or read Scripture?

Evaluation and Appreciation. Sermons always include some evaluation and appreciation of religion.

Social Contact

Participation. Do individuals enjoy face-to-face or voice-to-voice (telephone) interaction? This does not include social contact mediated by letters, motion pictures, or other nonpersonal intermediaries. The actual amount of social contact rather than intended amount is rated, for example, in setting First-Grade Academic Activities, (3), the actual proportion of social contact probably exceeds the intended amount.

Behavior Mechanisms

Five of the seven Behavior Mechanisms are described in Chapter IV in terms of three subscales, participation, tempo, and intensity. Participation indicates the proportion of the person-hours of the setting in which the population engage in the mechanism. Tempo and intensity are measures of different aspects of the mechanism when it occurs. It is possible, therefore, for a setting to receive the maximum rating on all three subscales.

APPENDIX 8

Scales for Rating the Behavior Mechanisms
Looking and *Listening*

To rate the occurrence of Looking and Listening in a behavior setting the degree to which blindness and deafness would interfere with participation in the action patterns of the setting was estimated as follows.

The ratings assigned a setting on the 13 action patterns were noted and the amounts they would have been reduced if the inhabitants had been blind (or deaf) were estimated. The sum of these differences represent the extent to which sight (or hearing) was judged to be involved in the behavior setting. The final score was the ratio between the sum of the reductions and the sum of the original action pattern ratings. Here is an example for the setting, School, Fourth-Grade Academic Activities.

Action Pattern	Original Action Pattern Rating	Reduction in Rating Because of Blindness
Aesthetics	3	3
Business	1	0
Earning a Living	1	1
Education	7	3
Government	2	2
Nutrition	1	0
Orientation	2	0
Personal Appearance	1	0
Philanthropy	1	0
Physical Health	2	1
Recreation	0	0
Religion	0	0
Social Contact	6	1
Totals	27	11

The Looking mechanism score for this setting is 11 divided by 27, or .41, i.e., it was judged that lack of vision would, on the average, reduce involvement in the action patterns of the setting by 41 per cent. Ratings of Listening were done in the same way. The per cent scores were converted into a rating by multiplying the dividend (.41) by 10 and rounding to the nearest whole number (4).

Appendix 9

Technical Problems in Grouping Behavior Settings into Varieties

Two problems were encountered in grouping settings by varieties. The first was the very large number of computations necessary to compare every pair of settings, an impossible task from the standpoint of time available. This problem was handled by relying upon direct judgments of similarity except in questionable cases, and by checking direct judgments against the computed S-index in every twentieth case.

The second problem arose from the different degrees of similarity between the members of the same variety. Setting A might be similar to setting B and to setting C, but setting B might be judged dissimilar to setting C. This is the case with 4-H Food Sale, Murray's Grocery (where the sale was held), and 4-H Club Meeting mentioned above. This problem was solved by the following procedure:

Step 1. S-indexes were computed between all the members of a random sample of 25 settings. These formed a small number of varieties.

Step 2. The setting in each of these varieties that had the highest general richness index was chosen as the *core setting* of that variety.

Step 3. The other 560 settings were compared with the core settings of the varieties with which they were likely to be most similar, either by direct judgment or by computing S-indexes where the relationship was uncertain. New varieties were formed for those settings that were not similar to any of the existing varieties. When a setting with a higher richness index than the core was added to a variety, it then replaced the original core setting.

Step 4. The setting varieties formed were rechecked perceptually by independent judges, and settings which seemed inconsistent with the other members of the variety were again checked by the S-index.

Appendix 10

Behavior Settings Preferred by Members of Each Age, Sex, Social Group, and Race Subgroup in Midwest

THE following occupancy indexes are based upon the occupancy times *of the subgroups*, i.e., upon the total number of hours members of each subgroup spent in community behavior settings.

Infant

	Occupancy Index (Per Cent of 10,822)
Mrs. Lawrence, Baby Care (148)	27.7
Trafficways (26)	11.2
Mrs. Deland, Baby Care (153)	9.2
Mrs. Denham, Baby Care (152)	2.3
Clifford's Drug Store (46)	2.1
Pearl Cafe (85)	1.7
Methodist Church; Infant's Sunday-School Class (215)	1.4
Presbyterian Church; Kindergarten Sunday-School Class (222)	1.4
Homemaker Club Regular Meeting (255)	1.4
Saturday Night Dance (235)	1.4

Preschool

	Occupancy Index (Per Cent of 22,420)
Trafficways (26)	21.4
Culver Shoe Repair (273)	6.7
Midwest Theater (49)	6.2
Mrs. Deland, Baby Care (153)	4.5
Methodist Church; Kindergarten Sunday-School Class (216)	3.3
Mrs. Denham, Baby Care (152)	3.3
Presbyterian Church Kindergarten Sunday-School Class (222)	2.0
Clifford's Drug Store (46)	1.7
Pearl Cafe (85)	1.6
Saturday Night Dance (235)	1.3

Younger School

	Occupancy Index (Per Cent of 60,546)
Second-Grade Academic Activities (4)	12.5
Third-Grade Academic Activities (5)	12.0
First-Grade Academic Activities (3)	11.4
County Jail and Sheriff's Residence (202)	5.6
Trafficways (26)	5.0
Midwest Theater (49)	4.6
Primary-School Playground (204)	3.3
Culver Shoe Repair (273)	3.0
Primary School, Coatroom (164)	2.2
Second-Grade Classroom (328)	1.8

Older School

	Occupancy Index (Per Cent of 81,549)
Fifth- and Sixth-Grade Academic Activities (7)	18.9
Fourth-Grade Academic Activities (6)	9.9
Fifth- and Sixth-Grade Science and Mathematics (8)	7.9
Trafficways (26)	4.4
High-School Building, Halls (166)	4.4
Midwest Theater (49)	4.3
County Jail and Sheriff's Residence (202)	4.2
High-School Playground (205)	3.7
Culver Shoe Repair (273)	2.2
Grade-School Music Classes (286)	1.5

Adolescent

	Occupancy Index (Per Cent of 167,094)
Seventh- and Eighth-Grade Academic Activities (10)	11.8
High School, Social Sciences (21)	8.2
High School, Study Hall and Library (22)	6.5
High-School Assemblies (66)	5.9
Seventh- and Eighth-Grade Math and Science (11)	5.4
Trafficways (26)	3.2
Midwest Theater (49)	2.9
High-School Building, Halls (166)	2.7
High School, English (16)	2.6
High School, Algebra and Geometry (13)	2.2

Adults

	Occupancy Index (Per Cent of 593,994)
Trafficways (26)	8.1
Telephone Co. Office (156)	2.9
Garnett's Grocery (34)	2.6
Kane's Grocery and Feed Store (29)	2.6
Gwynn Cafe (89)	2.5
Bank of Midwest (179)	2.5
Wherry Window and Door Co. (180)	2.4
Midwest Theater (49)	2.4
Clifford's Drug Store (46)	2.4
Midwest Hardware and Implement Co. (110)	2.1

Aged

	Occupancy Index (Per Cent of 92,430)
Trafficways (26)	13.0
Berth Nursing Home (150)	7.8
The *Midwest Weekly* (274)	4.7
Midwest Theater (49)	3.8
Tills' Watch Repair Shop (359)	2.8
Sherwin Furniture Store (107)	2.7
Cabell Department Store (45)	2.7
Dixon's Barber Shop (161)	2.7
U.S. Post Office (234)	2.4
Everging Variety Store (48)	2.4

Male

	Occupancy Index (Per Cent of 563,531)
Trafficways (26)	8.3
Midwest Theatre (49)	2.7
Eastman Garage and Automobile Sales (42)	2.1
Gwynn Cafe (89)	2.0
Midwest Hardware and Implement Co. (110)	1.8
Wherry Window and Door Co. (180)	1.8
Fifth- and Sixth-Grade Academic Activities (7)	1.6
Clifford's Drug Store (46)	1.6
Bank of Midwest (179)	1.4
Seventh-and Eighth-Grade Academic Activities (10)	1.4

Female

	Occupancy Index (Per Cent of 468,599)
Trafficways (26)	6.6
Midwest Theater (49)	3.2
Telephone Co. (156)	2.8
Seventh- and Eighth-Grade Academic Activities (10)	2.5
Garnett's Grocery (34)	2.3
Kane's Grocery and Feed Store (29)	2.3
Fifth- and Sixth-Grade Academic Activities (7)	2.0
Clifford's Drug Store (46)	2.0
High School, Social Sciences (21)	1.7
Bank of Midwest (179)	1.6

Group I

	Occupancy Index (Per Cent of 147,980)
Trafficways (26)	5.4
Clifford's Drug Store (46)	5.4
Bank of Midwest (179)	3.7
The *Midwest Weekly* (274)	3.0
French, French, French Attorneys; Midwest County Abstract Co. (122)	2.7
Midwest Hardware and Implement Co. (110)	2.4
Cabell Department Store (45)	2.0
Hutchings, Attorney and Publishing Co. (112)	2.0
Midwest Theater (49)	2.0
Sherwin Furniture Store (107)	2.0

Group II

	Occupancy Index (Per Cent of 358,072)
Trafficways (26)	7.5
County Jail and Sheriff's Residence (202)	3.1
Midwest Theater (49)	2.8
Wherry's Window and Door Co. (180)	2.0
Seventh- and Eighth-Grade Academic Activities (10)	1.7
Clifford's Drug Store (46)	1.7
Gwynn Cafe (89)	1.7
Garnett's Grocery (34)	1.6
Kane's Grocery and Feed Store (29)	1.6
Denton's Drug Store (47)	1.4

Group III

Occupancy Index
(*Per Cent of 493,537*)

Trafficways (26)	7.9
Midwest Theater (49)	3.2
Seventh- and Eighth-Grade Academic Activities (10)	2.2
Kane's Grocery and Feed Store (29)	2.0
Garnett's Grocery (34)	2.0
Culver Shoe Repair (273)	1.8
Gwynn Cafe (89)	1.8
Fifth- and Sixth-Grade Academic Activities (7)	1.7
Pearl Cafe (85)	1.5
High School, Social Sciences (21)	1.4

Negro

Occupancy Index
(*Per Cent of 32,789*)

Trafficways (26)	12.2
High School, Social Sciences (21)	4.6
Midwest Theater (49)	3.4
Kane's Grocery and Feed Store (29)	3.0
Garnett's Grocery (34)	3.0
Fifth- and Sixth-Grade Academic Activities (7)	2.4
Fourth-Grade Academic Activities (6)	2.3
High-School Building, Halls (166)	2.2
High School, Study Hall and Library (22)	2.2
Seventh- and Eighth-Grade Academic Activities (10)	1.9

APPENDIX 11

Behavior Objects Occurring in Three Day-Records

THE following lists contain all the behavior object varieties identified in the day records of Mary, Raymond, and Bobby. They are divided into broad categories, or kinds, of behavior objects. The varieties marked with an asterisk are the relatively prominent ones in the record of the child, constituting 1 per cent or more of the individual objects used by the child and/or 1 per cent or more of the child's total number of object transactions. The total number of different behavior objects of each kind and the object transactions with each kind are given at the end of each list.

Kind of Behavior Object : Food

Mary: bacon, beans, bread, butter, chewing gum, hot chocolate, cookie, dessert, dog food, egg, lettuce, milk, popsicle, pudding, radish, salad, sandwich, scraps, soup, steak, toast, tomato juice, vegetables. Total individual objects, 33; total object transactions, 46.

Raymond: apricot sauce, cake, candy*, coffee, cookie, egg, flour, food, fruit mix, hamburger, lettuce, milk, oatmeal, peanuts, pickle, pill, popcorn, pork, potatoes, radish, salt, sandwich, tea, toast, tomato, vegetables. Total individual objects, 41; total object transactions, 54.

Bobby: animal cracker, applesauce, banana, beer, bread, cake, candy*, cereal, carrot, chewing gum, cookie*, cracker, dough, egg, flour, food, gravy, groceries, hamburger, ice cream, jam and jelly, milk, pepper, pickle, pudding, salmon loaf, salt, sandwich, sauce, soft drink, strawberry, vitamin, glass of water. Total individual objects, 93; total object transactions, 176.

Kind of Behavior Object : Animal

Mary: bee, bird, bug, dog*, worm. Total individual objects, 7; total object transactions, 42.

Raymond: bear, bird, bug, cat, cow, dog*, fish, frog, gorilla, horse, monkey, mule. Total individual objects, 22; total object transactions, 58.

Bobby: beaver, bird, bug, chicken, cow, dog, elephant, fish, fox, frog, goat, horse, lion, monkey, pig, rabbit, wolf. Total individual objects, 40; total object transactions, 49.

Kind of Behavior Object : Plant

Mary: bush*, flower*, grass, leaf*, mushroom, tree*, vegetable. Total individual objects, 60; total object transactions, 116.

Raymond: bush, flower*, grass, leaf, tree*, vegetable. Total individual objects, 49; total object transactions, 75.

Bobby: flower, grass, tree. Total individual objects, 5; total object transactions, 5.

Kind of Behavior Object : Clothing and Articles of Adornment

Mary: apron, barrette, bathrobe, button, diaper, dress*, fingernail polish, hairbrush, handkerchief, jewelry, pyjamas, perfume, ribbon, shoes*, socks, tooth brush, tooth paste, underclothing. Total individual objects, 46; total object transactions, 102.

Raymond: belt, charm, coat*, hair oil, handkerchief, hat, pyjamas, pants, purse, raincoat, safety pin, shirt, shoes, socks, tooth brush, tooth paste, underclothing. Total individual objects, 27; total object transactions, 95.

Bobby: belt, button, clothes, coat, dress, fingernail scissors, gloves, hairpin, handkerchief, hat*, pyjamas, pants, purse, shirt, shoes*, socks, underclothing. Total individual objects, 60; total object transactions, 122.

Kind of Behavior Object : Furniture, Household and Office Equipment, and Parts of Buildings

Mary: bannister, basket, bed, bed linen, blinds, box*, can, can opener, chair*, chest of drawers, cleansing powder, clock, cup, desk (home, school, office)*, door (cupboard, room)*, drinking fountain, faucet, floor, fork, furnace, furniture (unspecified), hammer, key, knife, lamp, meter (housing of gas meter), nail, pan, piano, piano bench, pitcher, porch, radiator, refrigerator, screen, sewing machine, sink (bathroom, kitchen), sink stopper, sofa, spoon, steps, stove, table, tablecloth, toilet, towel (cloth, paper), typewriter, wall plug, washcloth, washing machine, wastebasket, water glass, window, wires (electric). Total individual objects, 96; total object transactions, 196.

Raymond: bannister, basket, bathtub, bed, bed linen, blinds, bottle, carpet beater, chair*, chest of drawers, clock, coffee pot, counter of office, cradle, desk (home, school, office)*, door (cupboard, room)*, frying pan, hook (coat), jar, lamp, pail, piano, pillar of porch, refrigerator, rug, salt shaker, sink (bathroom, kitchen), soap, soap rack, spoon, steps, stove, sugar bowl, table, tape measure, tea kettle, toilet, towel (cloth, paper), vase, washcloth, wastebasket, water glass, window, wall. Total individual objects, 85; total object transactions, 175.

Bobby: basket, bed, bed linen, box, booth in cafe, breadboard, can (empty), chair*, chest of drawers, clock, comb, cup, cupboard, curtains, cutter (cookie), dish, display case (meat, groceries), door (cupboard, room), doorbell, faucet, fork, hook (coat), ironing board, knife, lamp, mailbox, needle and thread, pail, pan, plate, pushcart (grocery), radio-phonograph*, records (phonograph)*, refrigerator, rolling pin, rug, seat of bus, silverware, sofa*, soft-drink machine, spoon, stool, stove, table*, tea kettle, telephone, television, towel (cloth, paper), wall plug, water glass. Total individual objects, 150; total object transactions, 355.

Kind of Behavior Object : Playthings

Mary: blocks, bicycle, designs in dirt or sand, dolls, doll dress, May basket, merry-go-round, paints, paint brush, playing cards, rules of game, slide, swing*, toy animals, wagon, whirlagig. Total individual objects, 23; total object transactions, 88.

Raymond: ball, ball bat, ball glove, bicycle*, bicycle parts and accessories*, cars (miniature), designs in dirt or sand, fishing rod, gun, gun caps, May basket, paints, tire (miniature), tractor (miniature), wagon. Total individual objects, 38; total object transactions, 143.

Bobby: "atomic" ring, bicycle, dominoes*, gun*, gun caps*, jungle-gym, merry-go-round, playground equipment, "peg" (game of), radio program*, roller skate, swing, teeter-totter, toy animals. Total individual objects, 59; total object transactions, 237

Kind of Behavior Object : Outdoor Equipment

Mary: barrel, board, clothes line, pump (water), sidewalk, trash pile, wall (retaining). Total individual objects, 19; total object transactions, 34.

Raymond: bench (outdoor)*, board (sticks, poles)*, brick, clothes line, crate (large box)*, curb, fence, lawn mower, pipe, post, rake, shingle, spike, tile, trash pile, wall (retaining). Total individual objects, 40; total object transactions, 113.

Bobby: bench (outdoor), clipper, hedge, crate (large box), hoe, post. Total individual objects, 6; total object transactions, 8.

Kind of Behavior Object : Earth Materials

Mary: earth (dirt, ground, mud), rock (small, gravel, pebbles), rock (large), sand (sandpile). Total individual objects, 15; total object transactions, 34.

Raymond: earth (dirt, ground, mud), rock (small, gravel, pebbles), rock (large), sand (sandpile, quicksand). Total individual objects, 16; total object transactions, 31.

Bobby: sand (sandpile). Total individual objects, 2; total object transactions, 2.

Kind of Behavior Object : Vehicles

Mary: automobile, truck, wagon. Total individual objects, 4; total object transactions, 5.

Raymond: automobile*, automobile horn, truck, truck fender, tractor (including bulldozer), vehicle (unidentified). Total individual objects, 21; total object transactions, 22.

Bobby: automobile, automobile horn, automobile tire, bus, plane, taxi, train, tractor (including bulldozer). Total individual objects, 19; total object transactions, 42.

Kind of Behavior Object : Money

Mary: half-dollar, money. Total individual objects, 3; total object transactions, 5.

Raymond: dime, money, quarter. Total individual objects, 5; total object transactions, 8.

Bobby: dime, dollar, money, nickel, penny, quarter. Total individual objects, 14; total object transactions, 16.

Kind of Behavior Object : People

Mary: boys*, girls*, children (unspecified)*, men, women*, adults (unspecified), persons (unspecified), observers (male)*, observers (female)*, observers (unspecified). Total individual objects, 107; total object transactions, 870.

Raymond: boys*, girls*, children (unspecified)*, men*, women*, persons (unspecified), observers (male)*, observers (female)*. Total individual objects, 121; total object transactions, 1026.

Bobby: boys*, girls*, children (unspecified), men*, women*, adults (unspecified), persons (unspecified)*, observers (male)*, observers (female)*. Total individual objects, 98; total object transactions, 1087.

Kind of Behavior Object : Physique

Mary: arm, eye, face, foot, finger, fingernail, hair, hand, knee, leg, lip, mouth, nose, teeth, thumb. Total individual objects, 18; total object transactions, 49.

Raymond: arm, blood, body, cheek, chest, ear, eye, face, foot, finger, fingernail, hair, hand*, head, knee, leg, mouth, nose, stomach, sore, teeth, thumb, tongue. Total individual objects, 30; total object transactions, 104.

Bobby: arm, back, ear, eye, face, foot, finger, fingernail, hair, hand*, head, heel, hip, knee, leg, mouth, neck, nose, saliva, stomach, teeth, throat, thumb, tongue. Total individual objects, 50; total object transactions, 123.

Kind of Behavior Object : Reading, Writing, School Supplies, and Equipment

Mary: blackboard, book (general)*, book (text)*, book (school workbooks) book (music), book (comic or comic strips), book cover, chalk (pieces), chalk (crushed), crayons and box, eraser (blackboard), inkwell, letter (correspondence), magazine, newspaper, paper (lesson)*, paper (writing, construction)*, pen, pencil, pencil sharpener, picture (own and ready-made), poem, problems (arithmetic)*, ruler, scissors, seating chart, song. Total individual objects, 103; total object transactions, 203.

Raymond: blackboard, book (general)*, book (text)*, book (school workbooks), book (music), book (comic or comic strips)*, bookcase, bulletin board, chalk (pieces), chalk box, chalk rail, crayons and box, eraser (blackboard), magazine, music (piano piece), newspaper, paper (lesson), paper (writing, construction)*, pen, pencil*, pencil box, pencil sharpener, picture (own and ready-made)*, problems (arithmetic), rubber stamp, school supplies (unidentified), scissors, song*. Total individual objects, 116; total object transactions, 238.

Bobby: book (general)*, book (text), book (school workbooks), book (music), book (comic or comic strips)*, clipping (newspaper), crayons and box, envelope, eraser (pencil), ink, letter (correspondence), map, newspaper, paper (lesson), paper (writing, construction)*, paste, pencil, picture (own and ready-made), poem, problems (arithmetic)*, song, story*. Total individual objects, 86; total object transactions, 156.

Kind of Behavior Object: Miscellaneous

Mary: bag for blocks, bank (coin), baton, bell (school), belongings (unspecified), birds' eggs, blessing, camera, cane, castle, cobwebs, fish skeleton, paper (wrapping, Kleenex, cellophane), pasteboard, pencil shavings, rope, spectacle case, string, sun, ticket (bus token), violin, water, writing board. Total individual objects, 26; total object transactions, 80.

Raymond: bell (school), bird-feeding station, bolt, bow (ribbon), camera, cartridge, cement (powdered form), cement (solid form), dog house, drain, flagpole, flashlight, horsetails, manhole and cover, moving picture film, package, paper (wrapping, Kleenex, cellophane), paper punch, road sign, rope, rubber (piece), sign (advertisement), spray, sprayer, stapler, straps, string, tent, thumbtack, tin-can lid, whistle, window (store display), water, whistle (noon), writing board. Total individual objects, 49; total object transactions, 99.

Bobby: ash (piece from gun cap), bar (iron), bell pull (bus), bill (for food at cafe), bullet, cigarette, compass, cross (Christian symbol), disk (aluminium with name), dust, falling star, fire, garbage, gasoline, ghost, hook, iron filings, manhole and cover, match, moon, nest, note of song, nut, paper (wrapping Kleenex, cellophane), prayers, rags, raindrops, reflection in window, rope, rubber band, sign (advertisement), smoke, spark, stamp, sun, target to shoot at, tent, ticket (bus token), trombone, wheel, window (store display), water, writing board, unidentified object. Total individual objects, 64; total object transactions, 91.

Index